The Media

The Media: An Introduction

Edited by
Adam Briggs & Paul Cobley

An imprint of **Pearson Education**

Harlow, England • London • New York • Reading, Massachusetts • San Francisco • Toronto • Don Mills
Ontario • Sydney • Tokyo • Singapore • Hong Kong • Seoul • Taipei • Cape Town • Madrid • Mexico City
Amsterdam • Munich • Paris • Milan

Pearson Education Limited
Edinburgh Gate
Harlow
Essex CM20 2JE
United Kingdom
and Associated Companies throughout the world

Visit us on the World Wide Web at:
http://www.pearsoneduc.com

First published 1998
10 9 8 7 6 5
05 04 03 02 01

ISBN 0 582 27798 1

British Library Cataloguing-in-Publication Data

A catalogue record for this book is available from the British Library

Library of Congress Cataloging-in-Publication Data

Set by 35 in 10/12pt New Baskerville
Printed in China
NPCC/05

Contents

Contributors

Professor Patrick Barwise
London Business School

Neil Blain
Glasgow Caledonian University

Oliver Boyd-Barrett
University of Leicester

Raymond Boyle
University of Stirling

Brian Braithwaite
Freelance Magazine Consultant

Sean Brierley
Marketing Week

Adam Briggs
London Guildhall University

Paul Cobley
London Guildhall University

Professor John Corner
University of Liverpool

Andrew Crisell
University of Sunderland

Guy Cumberbatch
Aston University

Professor James Curran
Goldsmiths College,
University of London

Jessica Evans
University of Westminster

Professor Ivor Gaber
Goldsmiths College,
University of London

Professor Nicholas Garnham
University of Westminster

David Gordon
Royal Academy of Arts

Andrew Higson
University of East Anglia

Patricia Holland
Goldsmiths College,
University of London

Anne Jäckel
University of the West of England

Brian McNair
University of Stirling

Sarita Malik
British Film Institute

Andrew Medhurst
University of Sussex

Irene Costera Meijer
University of Amsterdam

David Miller
University of Stirling

Ralph Negrine
University of Leicester

William Osgerby
Southampton Institute of Higher
Education

Jerry Palmer
London Guildhall University

Richard Paterson
British Film Institute & Birkbeck College

Terhi Rantanen
University of Helsinki

Roger Sabin
Freelance Journalist

David Saunders
Griffith University

Roy Shuker
Massey University

Sue Stoessl
Head of Broadcasting Research, BBC

Linda Ruth Williams
University of Southampton

Liesbet van Zoonen
University of Amsterdam

Acknowledgements

The editors would like to give a big thanks to Sarah Caro who commissioned this book and whose energy, commitment and cheerfulness were indispensable in carrying the project through. We would also like to acknowledge the good humour and diligence of Christian Turner and Christine Firth in bringing about the final product that is now in your hands.

Clearly, this book could not go ahead without the cooperation of the contributors to this volume, a distinguished body of experts who have generously provided samples of their own leading work in the field of media studies. We owe a debt to their professionalism and accomplishment.

Finally, we must acknowledge those who suffered the perspiration (as opposed to the inspiration) required to produce this book: Philippa, Emily and Alison.

Chapter 1

What you need to know before you start to use this book

ADAM BRIGGS AND PAUL COBLEY

As editors, we expect that this book will be invaluable to students of media, communications and cultural studies in learning what the media actually are.

This introduction seeks to do two things. First, it aims to help you use this book as an effective study tool. The introduction gives information on how this volume is structured and how it can be most fruitfully read.

Second, it aims to focus attention on the difficulty of arriving at an understanding of what this thing 'the media' is. What is often forgotten is that the term 'media' is the plural of 'medium'. What is generally referred to as 'the media' (implying singular) is actually a diverse collection of industries and practices, each with their own methods of communication, specific business interests, constraints and audiences.

The enormity and complexity of the public arena known as 'the media' has meant that the study of media has entailed constant reiteration of questions of definition. Is 'the media' a collection of industries? Is it a collection of practices? Is it a collection of representations? Is it a collection of the products of economic and statutary regulations? Is it a collection of audience's understandings? Is it a means of delivering audiences to advertisers or is it a public service?

The answer to all these questions is 'yes'.

Of course, the media are *also* in a state of perpetual flux. As consumers of media we know very well that the media's content changes from day to day. Also media outlets are continually being bought, sold and created. Regulations change; so do technologies and audiences.

Undoubtedly, when we are in the thick of media study, these facts are crucial. Before this study can begin, however, we need some means of grasping the broader picture. Our first task is to acquire an initial overview of the general scope of media.

One way of achieving this is to consider the media in terms of a communications process. What all media entail is a process that involves senders, messages and receivers as well as a specific social context in which they operate.

Senders

'Senders' of media messages can usefully be understood as institutions. These institutions

- are economic entities which have to maintain a sufficient cash flow to continue/expand their activities
- work within legal and governmental frameworks of regulation
- are peopled by professionals implementing specialized practices
- facilitate the transmission of certain messages embodying certain worldviews (and not others).

Messages

Media 'messages'

- differ from medium to medium
- are not simple reflections of the world
- are thoroughly constructed entities
- emanate from 'senders' operating within the parameters noted above
- are often aimed at target audiences
- are often rich and open to interpretation
- are subject to political, cultural and legal constraints.

Receivers

The 'receivers' of media messages

- are commodities sold to advertising agencies
- have demographic characteristics
- are not passive consumers or 'cultural dupes'
- make meaning of messages according to pre-existing values, attitudes and experiences
- sometimes apprehend depictions of themselves in messages and assess the nature of these depictions, sometimes fail to apprehend depictions of themselves and sometimes notice their absence from messages.

Specific social context

The 'specific social context' of the media discussed in this book is Europe. Europe has

- its own models of media operation and regulation
- diverse national traditions, languages and audiences
- diverse traditions of representation
- an ambiguous relationship to American media.

The book is divided into three parts, each of which, in different ways, is concerned with European media.

What are the media?, as the part title suggests, describes the media as a series of *separate* and *distinct* industries and practices rather than as a monolithic entity.

Part II, **'Outside' the Media**, deals with those issues that directly impinge (from without) on the different media: audience feedback and beliefs about 'effects', broadcast policy and differing traditions of organizing, studying and funding media. These issues may seem like a 'backdrop' to media but they are more than this; in fact, they *determine* the kinds of media that we get. The discussion of such determinants also serves to demonstrate that there is some accuracy in the common sense understanding of a monolithic 'media' in that it draws attention to the way in which separate media are increasingly being linked by common owners and technologies.

Part III, **In the Media**, examines some of the things that actually appear (and *do not* appear) in the media. This part deals with the manner in which different media represent different facets of the 'real' world.

This book is not designed to be read sequentially, all at once, like a novel. Use this volume as a sourcebook: each chapter is self-contained and can be consulted

- as an introduction to the particular medium in question (**What are the Media?**),
- as an introduction to relevant external influences upon the media we consume (**'Outside' the Media**),
- as an introduction to the kinds of representations and agendas that occur across the media (**In the Media**).

However, you should *not* simply use this book to gain a little information on one specific topic which has an appeal to you. You will learn more from reading about other topics covered in this volume, over and above those in which you are especially interested. Such a reading strategy will enable you to

- compare, contrast and thereby recognize the distinctiveness of a given topic
- identify consistencies across topics.

As well as providing introductions, each chapter in the volume will enable you to pursue further study by offering subjects for discussion (in the form of three questions) and by suggesting further reading. In many cases you will find references to published works in the main body of the chapter; this can serve two purposes: for the author of the chapter the reference supplies details of the evidence being used; for the reader, it supplies a source for further study in whatever facet of the area is under discussion.

Are we already experts?

There can be no doubt that the study of media is rapidly expanding. One reason is that as we move into the new millennium the media are increasingly a central part of our lives, our cultures and global economies. Another reason, not unconnected to this, is that the study of media is very exciting.

What makes the study of contemporary media special is that the ubiquity of media, and the human engagement that it allows, means that we are all already, in a sense, experts. This book seeks to go beyond the knowledge that accrues as a consequence of our daily media consumption into a realm much different from our *experience* of radio, film, books, TV, newspapers, magazines, and so on. The consuming of various media products is a different activity from the *understanding* of what those products consist of and how they have come about. The *study* of media, like the media themselves, is not a singular practice but is made up of a range of different approaches.

The study of the media and media studies

The study of contemporary media – as opposed to the study of media throughout human history (oral cultures, cave painting, theatre, illuminated manuscripts, town criers, and so on) – emerged alongside the contemporary mass media, and predates the establishment of the discipline known as 'media studies'. Various disciplines cast their gaze over the developing media in a way similar to the current moment where media are still the object of study in a range of disciplines such as sociology, politics, economics, psychology, cultural studies, anthropology, electronics, communications, cybernetics, geography and history, to name but a few.

Leaving technical considerations aside, two broad strands of media study can be identified in the early decades of the twentieth century. The first was made up of North American sociologists and psychologists who sought to *measure* the content and the 'effects' of mass media. The crux of their research involved a use of 'scientific' method to establish the power of the mass media in individuals' lives. The second evolved in Europe and can be closely identified with the Frankfurt School of Social Research in Germany (Adorno and Horkheimer 1973 [originally 1944]) and the work of literary critics such as F.R. Leavis in Britain (Leavis 1930; Leavis and Thompson 1933) who, in spite of their different academic and political perspectives, claimed to recognize the detrimental effect of the media on their audiences. Leavis and the Frankfurt School feared what they believed to be a

'mass culture' which, in a crude outline of their view, was vulgar and homogenized, created a community of uncritical and passive consumers (apart
from elites such as themselves, of course), excluded engagement with 'higher
things', and rendered the 'masses' acquiescent to the owners/controllers
of the mass media (which sometimes included the state). For Leavis, these
features of 'mass culture' – a newly developed phenomenon characteristic of what is now known as 'modernity' – threatened the values which he
believed to underpin a 'great tradition' in Britain; for the Frankfurt School
they acted as a narcotic distracting from mass social organization against
the ruling order (see Swingewood 1977).

As can be seen from a cursory glance at these broad strands, much theorizing about the media has been concerned less with the internal workings
of the media themselves than with identifying data to inform speculations
about their social and political consequences. On the other hand, particularly in the American tradition (but elsewhere as well), much research into
media has been carried out for commercial purposes rather than strictly
academic ones. Paul Lazarsfeld, one of the founding fathers of this tradition,
described such work as 'administrative' (as opposed to 'critical') research
(Lazarsfeld 1941). Frequently, data which might be incorporated into media
study were (and remain) less concerned with 'understanding' audiences,
for example, than with conceptualizing audiences as traceable commodities
and transforming audience's media consumption into statistical entities which
could serve as the basis for financial transactions between media executives
and advertisers.

Like all areas of knowledge, then, the study of media is bound up with interests, biases, influences, arguments, motives and instrumental applications.

Pluralism and perspectives

Clearly, all serious writing and investigative work takes place within its own
perspective. Work funded by media industries, for example, will have its
own agenda and uses; work carried out from a political standpoint will also
have its own characteristic slant; work using different theoretical tools will
produce different data; work focusing on different aspects of a subject will,
again, produce different forms of understanding (an emphasis on media
institutions will produce accounts of media differing from those that emphasize audiences or output). Different perspectives act to frame information and lead to different varieties of knowledge.

Not only is it necessary, therefore, to identify perspectives, but also it is
useful to be able to identify

- that which is absent from any account of a subject
- the way in which one perspective challenges, or is in conversation
  with, the premises of another perspective.

Taking this as a cue, then, we should offer some comments on the partiality of the volume in your hands.

What this book does not contain is a 'toolkit' or systematic introduction to approaches for the study of media. Such a toolkit would consist of expositions of 'narrative', 'genre', 'realism', 'semiology/semiotics', 'psychoanalytic theories', 'identity', 'deconstruction', 'discourse analysis', 'feminisms', 'post-colonialism', 'queer theory' and accounts of their usage as concepts in the understanding of media representations; plus expositions of 'hegemony', 'public sphere', 'political economy', 'globalization/localization', 'postindustrialism', 'postmodernism', 'culture', 'community' and accounts of their usage as concepts in the understanding of media institutions (these lists are by no means exhaustive; see Boyd-Barrett and Newbold 1995; Branston and Stafford 1996; Dines and Humez 1995; Strinati 1995).

There are, however, numerous perspectives which you will find in this book although they will not necessarily appear in isolation with strict definitions attached. As a reader, you will need to be active in identifying the perspective that informs each discussion. You may even find that not only does this volume as a whole contain many different perspectives but also individual articles fruitfully utilize arguments from different traditions and viewpoints. In this respect, this book can be described as 'pluralist', containing multiple perspectives without giving overt privilege to one and recognizing the equal validity of seemingly contradictory ideas.

Moving on from *this* collection of media studies, we now examine 'media studies' as a distinct discipline. Media studies emerged in the 1970s, evolving from sociology, 'mass culture' theory and the study of 'mass communications'. While often attempting to be 'pluralist' and open, in general media studies tended to incorporate the agendas that were already embedded in its ancestors. Nevertheless, it might be argued that, at present, a different tension bifurcates the field. Throughout the 1980s and 1990s media studies has found that its scholastic aspirations have been continually called into question by students, the media industries, selected academics and educational policy-makers, all of whom have argued the need for a more practical/vocational emphasis within the field. Put simply, such arguments have criticized an exclusive devotion to hostile analyses of the media and demanded a practical education in the skills necessary for working in the media industries.

It is worth considering the way in which this distinction between 'vocational' and a more 'critical' approach to media may be a false dichotomy on a number of levels. Exclusive hostility toward the media implies a position of distance from both the media industries and the consumers or – as the 'mass culture' theorists would have it – 'dupes' of the media. Unsurprisingly, this attitude encourages elitism and a withdrawal from anything other than a purely intellectual engagement with media. However, a singular emphasis on the supposed 'vocational' aspects of media – 'learning on the job', using a camera or sound equipment, for example, without prior planning, thought or supervision – can only ever equip students with a competence to deal with some technical, plugs 'n' sockets aspects of the media.

In short, an effective and credible vocational emphasis in the study of media cannot exist without a 'critical' component. It is important to realize that 'critical' here does not necessarily entail an endless catalogue of media sins against humanity; instead, it points to the acquisition of a thorough-going insight into the media, their uses, their significance in contemporary life and their modes of operating. As potential future media employees you will benefit from a knowledge and understanding of media institutions as economic and professional entities; you will also gain much from a prior knowledge of the diversity of media audiences and what brings audience members together as possible constituencies; you will also be well-placed if you are equipped with an understanding of the social realities of audiences and how this impacts on media consumption (Who likes football? What makes who change channel, switch off, cancel a subscription, switch news-paper, fail to buy a CD? What kind of things do people want to hear, see, read, subscribe to?).

Even if you do not aspire to be a future media employee the study of media is central to any understanding of the culture in which we live and yields its own competencies and transferable skills. In the same way that students of English literature are not necessarily motivated by the desire to be a novelist, poet or playwright – (in fact, very few English graduates *do* go on to publish novels, poems or plays) – students of media do not have to be motivated by pre-established career plans.

Whatever your motivation, nobody could deny that the study of media offers access to a cultural literacy befitting the start of the new millennium.

Questions

1 Compare media studies to any other discipline studied in higher education. How does it differ from other disciplines and how is it similar?

2 List all the things that the creator of any media representation may need to know before embarking upon the creative process. Leave your list for a while and then reread it, adding components where necessary. Will the list need to be substantially changed for different kinds of representation (e.g. news as opposed to 'fiction')?

3 Using knowledge gained from this book and elsewhere try to construct a list of possible
   (a) media 'senders'
   (b) media 'messages'
   (c) media 'receivers'
   (d) media 'contexts'.
   Do not worry if your lists become very long.

References

Adorno, T.W. and Horkheimer, M. (1973 [1944]) *Dialectic of Enlightenment,* London: Allen Lane.

Boyd-Barrett, O. and Newbold, C. (1995) *Approaches to Media,* London: Arnold.

Branston, G. and Stafford, R. (1996) *The Media Student's Book,* London: Routledge.

Dines, G. and Humez, J.M. (1995) *Gender, Race and Class in Media: A Text-Reader,* London and Beverly Hills, CA: Sage.

Lazarsfeld, P.F. (1941) 'Remarks on critical and administrative communication', *Research Studies in Philosophy and Social Science* IX: 2–16.

Leavis, F.R. (1930) *Mass Civilization and Minority Culture,* London: Heffer.

Leavis, F.R. and Thompson, D. (1933) *Culture and Environment,* London: Chatto & Windus.

Strinati, D. (1995) *An Introduction to Theories of Popular Culture,* London: Routledge.

Swingewood, A. (1977) *The Myth of Mass Culture,* London: Macmillan.

Part I

What are the media?

Introduction to 'What are the Media?'

ADAM BRIGGS AND PAUL COBLEY

As we have been at pains to stress, the media are diverse. Part I addresses this diversity in detail by providing definitions and descriptions of various important media.

It may seem strange to start off with a chapter on comics. Often we think of the media as dominated by the high profile products of electronic communication. Yet, as Roger Sabin demonstrates in Chapter 2, much of our media consumption is specialized, private and motivated by specific enthusiasms and prejudices. Our choice not to consume certain media forms – for example tabloid newspapers or comics – may be informed by prejudices about form and cultural value. However, a medium such as the comic – which has been a victim of such value judgements – is as much a part of 'the media' as newspapers or cinema are.

David Saunders similarly deals with 'a neglected topic' in Chapter 3. The publishing industry in Europe is huge but has singularly failed to become a repeated focus of media studies in the way that, say, television has. This is curious because it has many different points of interest for media students. One such issue is that of intellectual property: who owns the copyright of the 'content' of media texts? Another is the relation of print publishing to the new electronic media: why has the book failed to die out? Yet another is the diversification of formats within this medium: the book has proved to be very flexible.

One traditional area of media study is advertising. More often than not, however, there has been an emphasis on the texts of advertising – the advertisements – at the expense of an attention to their production. Sean Brierley's Chapter 4 rectifies this and examines the current crisis in the advertising industry by relating it to changing media, marketing and consumer environments. This crisis is a serious matter for the media as advertising is not only very much a part of the media but also one of the primary means of funding many other, different media (see Barwise and Gordon, Chapter 14 in this volume).

Unlike advertising, which is popularly recognized as being in the business of selling products/services and changing behaviour, news is often thought to consist of 'information'. Granted, it is widely believed that news is often presented by newspapers, radio and television within certain *perspectives* (party political or otherwise); but this still presupposes that there is some 'objective' entity out there called 'news'. Even before it is collected, news is subject to sifting, selection, evaluation, structuring and classification (see Palmer, Chapter 27 in this volume). One of the first links in the chain of collecting news, as Oliver Boyd-Barrett and Terhi Rantanen discuss in Chapter 5, is the news agency. But, news is not just a matter of collection. As David Miller shows in Chapter 6 on journalism and promotional strategies, news is often *delivered* with an in-built perspective and thoroughly managed by interested parties. In this sense it is often difficult to judge what is news and what is public relations 'spin'.

In addressing the press, therefore, James Curran shows in Chapter 7 that it is difficult to utilize only one simple perspective. He explores the current state of British newspapers by comparing and synthesizing two very different approaches to understanding this medium. The first he characterizes in general as 'liberal' and presenting, for many, an 'optimistic' view about the workings of the press. The second he characterizes as 'radical'; this approach, he suggests, offers a far more critical and 'pessimistic' understanding. Neither approach, he suggests, can offer an adequate account of the role of the press in society.

Much different from those media involved in conveying news are those that are (usually erroneously) considered as exclusively 'entertainments' media: magazines, radio, cinema, television, pop music. There is clearly a problem with the notion of 'entertainment' as a distinct entity which imputes a singular character to certain media. For instance, supposedly non-entertainments media such as newspapers are themselves often responsible for entertainment: features, lifestyle coverage, reviews, and so on. Moreover, what has traditionally been understood as news has been increasingly *packaged* as entertainment. Conversely, for many, television is the main source of *news and current affairs* (McNair 1995) which also constitutes large parts of much of radio and many magazines. Although it must be conceded that the pop music industry and cinema *are* devoted to entertainment, pop groups and film stars are an increasingly frequent staple of news output.

Magazines, as Brian Braithwaite demonstrates in Chapter 8, are currently the subject of rapid expansion. Two main reasons for this concern niche markets and technological advances. Technology has enabled more cost efficiency in producing media that reach more accurately the readers who are also target markets for advertisers (see also McNair, Chapter 13 in this volume). This avoids what is known as 'wastage', that is buying advertising space in publications which reach a broad set of readers, many of whom may not belong to the desired target market.

The development of the 'invisible medium', radio, has had a similar trajectory in its recent profusion of services. Radio appears to have been used as a kind of policy testbase for the process of 'deregulation'. As Andrew Crisell shows in Chapter 9, many different markets for radio have existed for some time; but has diversity truly been delivered by the move from a small number of radio stations to a larger number of stations catering for what are often niche markets? The limits of radio's ability to satisfy the diverse musical tastes of the British public are clearly demonstrated by the health of the many 'pirate' radio stations.

In the case of the television industry, Richard Paterson (Chapter 10) adopts the concept of the value/supply chain to analyse the recent dispersal of the medium's functions. Rather than conceiving of television as a group of companies which control every stage of the supply of television services to audiences, he shows that it is now more accurate to consider the television industry as comprising a number of contributors to a 'supply chain'. *Radio*, given current uncertainties about the introduction of digital audio broadcasting, continues to operate, despite considerable recent expansion, within the limits of spectrum scarcity. Television in Europe, on the other hand, is on the eve of a new multi-channel digital future.

The indigenous cinema in Europe, by virtue of its eclipse by Hollywood, has received a woeful lack of attention. As Anne Jäckel illustrates in Chapter 11, this may be because of the European cinema's size (relatively small) and its profitability (again relatively small). Much focus on film has taken the film text – narrative, photography, genre – as its primary interest. Jäckel discusses the way in which film texts come to be produced in the European context. A similar lack of attention to the industry has characterized previous studies of pop music which have usually been concerned with the subcultural influences on the production and consumption of music. Roy Shuker shows in Chapter 12 that there is actually an elaborate network of practices responsible for the production and marketing of pop music. Between the producers and consumers there lies a number of important mediating factors: radio, clubs, concert tours and festivals, videos, the music press and the charts. Pop music is not just spontaneous expression; it is a highly complex multimillion dollar (or yen) global business.

'What are the media?' concludes with a topic that impinges on all media and is rapidly producing new ones. In one sense, as Brian McNair discusses in Chapter 13, the new technology produces new kinds of media and new audiences. An example of this is the new media texts and the immediate feedback which the Internet makes possible. But the new technologies also provide different (and sometimes quicker) ways of producing the 'old' media such as newspapers or pornography. Moreover, there are new digital technologies which have and will continue to have a radical influence on the distribution of media.

This has thrown up new issues of media policy and regulation, which are addressed in Part II.

Reference

McNair, B. (1995) *News and Journalism in the UK: A Textbook*, 2nd edn, London: Routledge.

Chapter 2

Comics

EUROCOMICS: '9TH ART' OR MISFIT LIT?

ROGER SABIN

This chapter is about comic books. Why, you may ask, should such a subject be relevant to a book about media studies? The answer is simple, but commonly not expected: that comics constitute 'a medium' just like film, television, novels, virtual reality, and any other medium you care to mention, and are therefore equally worthy of consideration within the parameters of media studies. They have their own properties, and generate their own 'kick': they are not 'movies on paper', nor are they some half-way house between 'literature' and 'art'. Rather, they involve a co-mingling of words and pictures that can be breathtaking in its sophistication (as well as, on occasion, sigh-making in its banality), and which rivals any other medium for depth of expression. (On the mechanics of how comics work, see McCloud 1994.) In other words, comics matter.

In Europe, comics matter more than in most parts of the world, and in keeping with the focus of the rest of this book, our attention will be turned to here. There are, of course, noble comics traditions elsewhere (especially in North America and Japan), but in Europe, the form has become culturally respectable in a way that is unmatched. To be more specific than this, we can say that although there are as many comics traditions in Europe as there are countries, it is fair to talk of a unified comics market. This is because comics in Europe share properties that are distinct from any other region in the world: these include not only cultural status, but also kinds of formats, and, above all, underlying economics. One European country, however, does not fit into this template: namely, the UK. In comics, as in politics and so much else, the UK remains separate. A secondary theme of this chapter, therefore, is what makes British comics so different, and why the country has never become part of the 'European Comics Community'.

The most immediate way to obtain a sense of the place of comics in European life is to make a few basic observations. First and foremost, European comics culture is essentially an 'album' culture. This is to say that comics are produced as hardback books, usually of about forty-eight pages in length, containing a single self-contained story, with high quality production values and full colour throughout. The artwork is often superb, and they have an aesthetic value that until recently was virtually unknown in Britain and the USA. This is duly reflected in the price (between roughly £7 and £20), and the fact that they are sold not from newsagents, but from bookshops. These comics are not intended to be read and thrown away after one sitting, but to be kept on bookshelves and returned to.

There are some exceptions to this rule. There exist, for example, monthly comics magazines that consist of anthologies of serialized stories. However, they are, again, usually of a much higher quality than their British and North American counterparts, and the publishers' aim is typically to 'pre-publish' stories so that they can then be collected into album form at a later date. This system has a long history in Europe, and originally had the advantage of 'testing the waters' in the sense that if a story did not prove popular in the magazine, it would not make it into hardback. Today, however, stories are almost always guaranteed to be released as albums, and the magazines play a less significant role. Moreover, the trend since the mid-1980s has been for first publication to be in album form, thus circumventing the magazines altogether.

In terms of content, we can also observe that the subject matter covered by the comics includes 'something for everybody'. A quick scan of the shelves in a typical Parisian bookshop, for example, reveals an astonishing range, from 'funny animal' stories for young children, to hard porn for adults. In between, the storytelling styles can encompass the dumbest-of-dumb pulp fiction to hyper-literate meditations on philosophy and art. The point is better made by considering a random handful of hit albums from the 1980s and 1990s:

- *The Town That Didn't Exist* (in translation through Titan). Written by acclaimed French novelist Pierre Christin (also a Professor of Journalism at Bordeaux University), with artwork by Enki Bilal (born in former Yugoslavia), the story revolves around the impossibility of building a utopia. In an (unspecified) age of industrial decline, a mysterious wheelchair-bound woman inherits a fortune and proceeds to spend it on constructing a city where no one need work ever again. This is a downbeat, often very weird, allegory for the contradictions of Marxist theory.
- *The Towers of Bois Maury: Babette* (in translation through Titan). Written and illustrated by Belgian 'Hermann' (Hermann Huppen), this historical drama, set in the early medieval period, concerns the rape of a peasant girl by a noble, and the murderous events this sets in train. Plenty of action – swordfights, jousting and hideous torture – all rendered in exquisite photo-referenced linework, and held together by a meticulously researched script. What it lacks in wit, it makes up for in pace and atmosphere.
- *Pixy* (in translation through Fantagraphics). Written and drawn by Dane Max Andersson, the frankly indescribable story involves a

procession of bizarre characters and inventions, including buildings that eat people, and gun-toting foetuses. There is a satirical theme underpinning the strangeness, but this is basically an ultra-violent surrealist nightmare: alternately compelling and repulsive.

- *Little Ego* (in translation through Catalan). Written and illustrated by Italian Vittorio Giardino, a slice of soft porn about a beautiful brunette ingenue (Ego) who cannot help losing her clothes. The storytelling and artistic style is a nod to the classic American newspaper strip 'Little Nemo', about a little boy's dreams, and Ego's deeply un-politically correct erotic fantasies are always set in the world of the surreal (the publisher's blurb asks, a little disingenuously: 'Who could object to Ego's frolics – with men, women, the occasional reptile or household implement – when it's all just a dream?').
- *Lea* (in translation through Fantagraphics). French writer Serge Le Tendre and artist Christian Rossi collaborated on this gripping thriller, which owes as much to Hitchcock and Truffaut as any comics tradition. An innocent man is branded a child-killer, and descends into mental breakdown. At once an effective psychodrama and a meditation on scapegoating, it is filmic, fast-moving and terrifying.
- *Blueberry: Chihuahua Pearl* (in translation through Epic Comics). Written by French novelist Jean-Michel Charlier and illustrated by fellow countryman Jean Giraud, one of the most acclaimed artists in the industry, this gritty Western has the feel of a Sergio Leone movie. Long coats, cigar-chewing, and stubble are *de rigueur* for both goodies and baddies, as US cavalryman Lieutenant Blueberry investigates misdeeds across the Tex–Mex border. It is a pretty basic shoot-'em-up, redeemed by evocative artwork.
- *The Incal: Volume 1* (in translation through Titan). Written by Chilean film-maker Alexandro Jodorowsky and illustrated by 'Moebius' (a pen-name for Jean Giraud, as above), this first part of a science fiction 'cosmic epic' features the adventures of private detective John Difool on a faraway planet. New Age and Tarot card references add colour to this Philip K. Dick-influenced story, packed with violence, grotesque monsters, and vast spaceships. Narratively drivesome in places, but a feast for the eyes.

You might notice that this selection of titles is essentially aimed at a teenage and adult audience. This is a fair reflection of the bulk of European comics publishing at the moment, at least in terms of numbers (for reasons we shall explore in a moment). However, it is important to add that the really big hitters in regard to sales rely on more traditional formulas, and are orientated towards a juvenile and family readership. In particular, two characters dominate: Tintin and Asterix. Both have been around for decades (Tintin since the 1930s, Asterix since the 1950s), and such is their fame, both in the UK and the USA, that we need not detail their history here (on Tintin, see Thompson 1991; Peeters 1992; on Asterix, see Kessler 1995). Suffice to say that between them, the be-quiffed boy-reporter and the diminutive ancient Gaul have sold more comics than any other characters put together (sales of Tintin albums alone are estimated to be in the hundreds of millions). Today, although the creator of Tintin (Georges 'Herge' Remi) and the writer of Asterix (Rene Goscinny) are dead, the back-catalogues for both characters continue to sell extraordinarily well, and they are also stars of stage, screen, television, computer game, and – in the case of Asterix – theme park.

Other big sellers after Tintin and Asterix also tend to be marketed towards a juvenile/family audience, and are worth mentioning in passing. For example, translations of Disney comics do very well throughout Europe (famously, Disneyland Paris is in bitter competition for punters with the Asterix park), while other successful European-originated titles include The Smurfs (from the Netherlands), about cute blue elves; Lucky Luke (from France), about a gormless cowboy; and Blake and Mortimer (from Belgium), about a pair of time-travelling English detectives. Most of these comics have also developed huge adult followings on top of their intended young readership.

Continuing our survey, we can tell one more thing simply by looking at the titles available in the shops: that some countries are more important than others in terms of who publishes what. It soon becomes clear, for example, that France is the centre of the Eurocomics world. More titles are published in France than anywhere else, while there is a long tradition of cartoonists from all over Europe being published by French houses. Companies like Dargaud (who publish Asterix) and Glenat are prolific and powerful. Similarly, the Benelux countries have strong industries (it is point of pride among Belgians that statistically more comics are sold per head here than in any other part of Europe. (At time of writing, the best-selling book in Belgium happens to be a Blake and Mortimer album.) Casterman (who publish Tintin) is another major European publisher. It is difficult to say which countries come next in ranking order. The north of Europe, including Scandinavia and Germany, is served by the giant corporation Carlsen, based in Germany, which often publishes translations of titles originated elsewhere in Europe. Meanwhile, Italy and Spain are certainly big comics consumers, and have thriving indigenous titles.

Moving away from the specific comics in the shops, we can also observe that in Europe, due to such a wide-ranging industry, there has developed a culture surrounding the form that is unique. For example, people commonly learn to read using comics, and continue to buy them throughout their lives. There is no 'cut off' point as there is in Britain and the USA. Thus, many comics characters become household names, and their exploits permeate everyday parlance. Perhaps the most visible expression of this love of comics are the comics festivals, which take place every year in most European nations. These tend to be large-scale events, not just for committed fans, but for all members of the family. The biggest, in Angoulême in south-western France, takes over the whole of the town for a period of several days, with exhibitions, talks, film shows, stalls, and, of course, artists' signing sessions (if you are lucky you get a sketch too). Angoulême markets itself very much as 'pour la famille', and regularly attracts over 100,000 visitors: in other words, roughly a hundred times as many as the comparable (fan-orientated) event in the UK, and twenty times that in the USA. Other no less lively festivals are held in Lucca (Italy), Brussels (Belgium), Grenoble (France) and Hamburg (Germany).

That is probably as far as we can go in analysing the European scene just by looking. To dig a little deeper, we need to explore two areas that are not immediately obvious: the comics' history and their underlying economics. Both themes are very closely linked, of course, and both are essential elements of any media studies investigation. Let us begin with the extraordinary level of intellectual respect that comics command in Europe, something that has influenced their history quite considerably. It is true to say that they are written about and deconstructed in the same way as any other artform. To give the most prominent example of a scholar with an interest: whenever the Italian Umberto Eco (author of *The Name of the Rose*) holds forth about contemporary culture, in books, TV and radio documentaries, and newpaper columns, he invariably includes comics. (Eco's best known book (in translation) to deal with comics is *The Role of the Reader* (1981), which includes a classic essay on Superman.) He is not the only one: academics all over Europe have made comics an integral part of degree courses. There are serious critical magazines about the subject, and specialist archives and study centres (such as those in Angoulême and Brussels).

This embracing of comics by Europe's 'intellectual class' (as it is still often referred to there) itself has a history. The trend dates back to the 1960s (although before this it is possible to find erudite discussions of titles like Tintin), and in particular to the French 'rediscovery' of early American comic strips. Comics study groups started to emerge, which focused primarily on strips like 'Little Nemo', 'Krazy Kat', 'Flash Gordon' and 'Dick Tracy'. A similar process had started in the late 1950s, when French intellectuals started to take American movies seriously – at the time, a very unusual concept. Now comics were being given the same treatment, and it was not long before critical and theoretical magazines were founded, and exhibitions organized. Undoubtedly an important moment in the growth of the movement was an exhibition of (largely American) comics at no less prestigious a venue than the Louvre in 1968 (the catalogue for the exhibition was published as a book: Couperie *et al.* 1968).

The co-option of comics into serious cultural debate continued into the 1970s. More and more, European intellectuals concentrated on European rather than American comics, and the new decade saw the form being referred to as 'the ninth art' (film and television had been added to the list a few years earlier). More than this, and partly as a result, the whole notion of what constituted 'culture' *per se* was being reconfigured. Old notions dating fom the Victorian era that culture essentially meant 'high culture' – for instance, fine art, classical music, opera, and literature drawn from a 'respected' canon of authors (Shakespeare, Goethe, and others) – were being challenged as (mainly) French intellectuals progressively elevated 'low culture' (movies, television, jazz and rock music, and, of course, comics) to the status of bona fide artforms. It was an exciting period in intellectual history, and perhaps had its ultimate flowering in the works of French philosopher Roland Barthes, who argued that culture should include everything, and that the distinctions between 'high' and 'low' were outdated (see in particular Barthes 1977). Barthes, too, frequently included comics in his analyses.

A corollary of this shifting of cultural priorities was that there developed close links between European comics and other artforms – especially with movies. It is possible to argue that the same kind of thing happened in the UK and the USA: but in these countries, comics, because of their low cultural status, were primarily seen as 'raw materials' to be stolen from at will by movie-makers. In Europe, a far more respectful tradition took shape whereby comics creators and film-makers collaborated and shared ideas. The career of great Italian movie director Federico Fellini is very instructive in this respect. He was a founder member of an important comics study group in the early 1960s (Centre d'Etudes des Literatures d'Expression Graphiques, or CELEG for short), and frequently paid homage to comics in his films. Later in his career, he would collaborate with comics artists to produce comics albums, notably *Trip to Tulum* (1989), drawn by Milo Manara, which was based on a once-discarded film script. Other European movie-makers closely associated with, and influenced by, comics include the Frenchmen Alain Resnais and Jean-Luc Godard. Equally, comics creators often worked in the movies: Enki Bilal, for instance, directed his own film, a science fiction yarn entitled *Bunker Palace Hotel* (1990).

A similar process was evident with regard to novelistic fiction. Writers of comics would also pen novels, while novelists would try their hand at comics. For example, in our list of hit comics albums above, two of the writers happen also to be internationally recognized novelists: Pierre Christin and Jean-Michel Charlier. There are many more such examples, notably Jerome Charyn, a Europhile American author, whose collaborations with French artist François Boucq (*The Magician's Wife*, *Billy Budd: KGB*) have produced some of the best comics thrillers in recent years.

Because of this relative parity among the artforms, comics creators command a level of respect in Europe that is comparable to film directors or novelists – again, a concept that would be totally alien to the comics scene in the UK or the USA. Sometimes, it is even true that star creators assume the status of '*auteurs*' (a French word denoting a creative artist who has a controlling influence over their work). Such is the case with the aforementioned Jean ('Moebius') Giraud, and to a lesser extent with Enki Bilal and Milo Manara. In the case of these creators, comics can be marketed on the basis of their names, just in the same way as novels are sold as 'the new William Gibson' or films as 'the new Francis Coppola'.

These factors have greatly influenced, and been influenced by, the economics of comics production in Europe. Because of the cultural respect that comics command, creators have never been exploited in the same way that they have in the UK and the USA. Rather, comics have traditionally been a natural place for upcoming creative talents to ply their trade – as natural as working in movies, novels, advertising, illustration and so on. The crucial issue has always been rates of pay: whereas in the USA and the UK creators have traditionally been paid a flat fee calculated by the page, in Europe, creators receive royalties as well; in other words, they earn a split of any profits their work may make.

The development of the album system was a major step forward in this respect. It was the Tintin albums that established the form, in the 1930s. What was unusual about them was that they were published by a Catholic publisher, Casterman, whose code of practice entailed a 'moral obligation' to pay creators a decent royalty. Thus, Tintin's creators received not only a royalty when strips appeared first in magazine form, but also a second royalty when they were collected together as albums. This system has endured through the ensuing decades throughout the European comics industry, and has ensured not only a reasonable living for creators, but also a higher standard of work. It stands to reason that if creators are paid well, then they take more pride in what they are doing: this in turn means that it is easier to take comics seriously as an artform.

Most creators also retain copyright over their creations, which means that they rather than the publishers determine what happens to them. For example, if a creator decides to stop producing stories starring a particular character, then there is no way a publisher can step in and hire another creator to continue the strip without the originator's permission (which would additionally require financial remuneration). More than this, control of copyright means that it is the creator who benefits from any film or TV adaptations – always very important in the world of comics, as we have seen.

Other historical factors have also combined to bolster the economics of the comics industry. For example, there has been a more successful history of unionization and collective bargaining among comics creators in parts of Europe than in North America and the UK. This has meant that when disputes arise, they are settled in a manner which at least takes the views of creators into account (very rare in the latter countries). Also, the intervention of governments in some European countries has meant certain advantages for the industry. For instance, after the Second World War, the French government introduced a law which limited the importation of comics from abroad: the French industry was thus protected against foreign competition, and allowed to develop at its own pace. More recently, governments in some countries have actually subsidized the comics industry. The most famous example of this was the construction of the museum and study centre in France (Centre nationale de la bande dessinée et l'image, or CNBDI), part funded by the government to the tune of millions of francs. Once again, the fact that comics have cultural kudos was a major factor in the government's decision: the centre was opened by the then minister for culture, Jack Lang.

So we can see that economics and cultural acceptance have combined in Europe to create a unique comics culture. But the question remains, what about the UK? Of course, the UK is a part of Europe in many respects; but in terms of comics, there is different sensibility at work. Certainly, the British industry has produced its own classic titles in the past – *The Beano*, *The Eagle*, *2000AD* and *Viz* to name just a few. But it can be argued that these have been successful despite the production system rather than because of it. For in the UK, comics have traditionally been culturally despised as either lowest-common-denominator trash, or as literature for children, or both. Underlying this prejudice, as we have seen, there has existed an iniquitous economic situation that has meant that comics have usually been the last place anybody would want to work.

Thus, the British comics tradition has been dominated by titles aimed at an 8-to-12 age-range, produced on cheap, poor-quality paper, and designed to be binned after one read. As for the contents, despite some notable exceptions, the norm has been mediocre storylines, produced to string the reader along for week after week, and unexceptional artwork. In other words, the work-for-hire, fee-per-page system that has prevailed in the UK has ensured that comics remain the preserve of hacks, and thus have never acquired any kind of cultural respectability. Many of the beneficial aspects of comics production that we have discussed with regard to European comics, and which are largely taken for granted there – the collecting of stories into albums, the way in which royalties are split among creators, how they retain copyright, and so on – have (historically) barely made an impact on the British scene. Arguably this is one reason why the British industry has shrunk from its heyday in the 1960s to its present level, consisting of merely a handful of publishers of weekly and monthly product (notably Gutenberghus/Fleetway, publishers of *2000AD*; John Brown, publishers of *Viz*; and DC Thomson, publishers of *The Beano*), plus a few book publishers who put out a limited range of 'graphic novels' – more about which in a moment.

Yet recently, things have been changing. With the growth of a network of specialist shops orientated towards hardcore comics fans (usually, it should be said, fans of American superhero titles), there has developed a more European approach to the economics of comics production. In the 1990s, many publishers now offer creators royalty splits, plus control over copyright – concessions that were extremely rare even in the 1980s. Part of this evolution has been due to the particular economics of the specialist shop system (see Sabin 1992: ch. 5), but partly it has been down to the influence of the European industry itself. For example, people involved in the British scene have become more aware of working conditions in Europe since the mid-1970s, when fan shops began to import European albums aimed at an adult and teenage audience. This was followed by a spate of translations of top albums by small British and American publishers, and the emergence of a British fan following for Eurocomics (albeit a very limited one). This gradual rise in awareness prompted some publishers to question previous employment practices, and some creators to press for change.

The rise of the 'graphic novel' in the UK and North America in the 1980s was part of this process. Graphic novels are basically lengthy comics in book form – in other words, an indigenous version of the European album. Although other factors were involved in their origination, the European paradigm was certainly influential: anglophone creators had long sought the opportunity to experiment with longer stories and more sophisticated artwork in tune with their European counterparts. So, too, the European idea of selling comics from bookshops was exploited more fully: graphic novel shelves were erected, and efforts were made to ensure that they were reviewed in the literary pages of the newspapers. In this way, a readership was solicited which might not otherwise have come across comics – the kind of readership that publishers in Europe had been serving for decades. Progress, as ever, is slow.

Thus, the question of whether the UK can ever join the European Comics Community is not entirely closed. Graphic novels and European albums are pretty much the same in terms of format, quality, and price, and this does mean that the comics are more easily sellable across the markets. Yet, when it comes to content, it is still true that the UK has a lot of catching up to do before publishers can offer the same range of subject matter as exists in Europe. Things are improving, and there have been a few British hits across the Channel, just as there have been a few Euro-hits in the UK. But any realistic appraisal of the situation would have to conclude that in the mid-1990s, British readers still prefer British and American comics, while European readers prefer European comics. In the end, each finds the other 'a bit too foreign'.

Questions

1   Is it possible to talk of a 'European Comics Community'?

2   Why is the British comics industry distinct from the rest of Europe?

3   How far have economic factors influenced the history of Eurocomics?

References

Barthes, R. (1977) *Mythologies*, Harmondsworth: Penguin.

Couperie, P. *et al.* (1968) *The History of the Comic Strip*, trans. E.B. Hennessy, New York: Crown.

Eco, U. (1981) *The Role of the Reader*, London: Hutchinson.

Kessler, P. (1995) *Asterix Complete Guide*, London: Hodder.

McCloud, S. (1994) *Understanding Comics*, London: HarperCollins.

Peeters, B. (1992) *Tintin and the World of Hergé*, Boston, MA: Little, Brown.

Sabin, R. (1992) *Adult Comics: An Introduction*, London: Routledge.

Thompson, H. (1991) *Hergé and his Creation*, London: Hodder & Stoughton.

Further reading

Unfortunately, there is not very much in English about European comics. My own books (Sabin 1992; 1996) contain chapters on the subject. The other volumes listed below also usefully cover European territory, but are out of print, and therefore available only from libraries. The best up-to-date information is available in fanzines (fan magazines), which can be purchased from specialist comics shops. Those with a particular interest in European comics include *Comics Forum* and *The Comics Journal*.

Clark, A. and Clark, L. (1991) *Comics: An Illustrated History*, London: Greenwood.

Horn, M. (1976) *World Encyclopaedia of Comics*, 6 vols, New York: Chelsea House.

Kurtzman, H. (1991) *From Aargh! to Zap!*, New York: Prentice Hall.

Reitberger, R. and Fuchs, W. (1972) *Comics: Anatomy of a Mass Medium*, London: Studio Vista.

Sabin, R. (1992) *Adult Comics: An Introduction*, London: Routledge.

Sabin, R. (1996) *Comics, Comix and Graphic Novels*, London: Phaidon.

Chapter 3

Publishing

EUROPEAN PUBLISHING: A NEGLECTED TOPIC

DAVID SAUNDERS

This chapter explores a commercial and cultural institution with a five hundred year history: the European print publishing industry. This industry has contributed to building and destroying religious, moral and political values. Its principal product, the book, has entertained millions of people, once they acquired interest and competence in reading for pleasure. Book publishing has been as much a vehicle for the commercial writer of the best-selling work of popular fiction as for the publicly funded academic writer of hyper-specialized critiques of late capitalism, unsaleable if not pre-scribed in university curricula yet themselves dependent on their niche in the book market.

For all its history (or because of it), print publishing is said to face an uncertain future. The factors cited are several. Some are commercial. In the 1980s mergers and acquisitions broke the book trade's traditional patterns of ownership, transforming equally antique patterns of work and labour relations to gain competitive advantage in local, national and international markets. Other factors are political. Within its delegated powers, the European Union trade bloc presents nationally based publishing industries with novel political, legal and administrative circumstances. There is the factor of communications technology. The first technological revolution in publishing is converging with the second in the confluence of printing and computing. In the emerging multimedia environment – professional and domestic – publishers turn from print to off-line optical publishing such as CD-ROMs and on-line services such as are now routinely available via the telephone system to the legal and medical professions. There are cultural factors too. Discursive literacy levels are falling, it is said, and young people are not habituated to the cultural regimen of readers of print.

Given such a catalogue, talk of uncertainty is no surprise. In the mid-1960s the cultural prophet Marshall McLuhan (1962) foretold that the book would disappear in an epochal shift from print to electronic communica-tion. He was wrong. Print publishing is not in the museum. European publishers now produce some 300,000 book titles annually in 300 million copies, to say nothing of the newspaper, magazine and catalogue sectors. By the century's end some million titles each year will be published worldwide. A hundred years ago English publishers produced 6000 titles annually.

As for retailing, in 1980–90 bookselling came second only to fast food as the fastest growing retail sector in the USA. Book promotions are stronger than ever, from international trade shows such as the Frankfurt Buchmesse and the London International Book Fair to national events such as la Fureur de lire in France and Belgium, the Bologna children's book fair and Now Read On in the UK. Unlike in film, television and recorded music, in book publishing Europe is not in deficit, outperforming North America by a ratio of three titles to one.

Notwithstanding its history and scale, the book publishing industry has not been taken up as a subject of university study on the same scale as journalism, media and communications (although there are courses at Loughborough, Napier, Oxford Brookes, Robert Gordon, Stirling and Thames Valley Universities). The media studies industry produces innumerable works about 'text'; however, published studies of the actual book trade are few. Talk of 'text' allows meanings to be endlessly deepened and invites theory; talk of the book concerns an industrial, commercial and intellectual product and requires descriptive work. The excitement of media technology might also explain the relative neglect of publishing. The printed book might be an analogue product with half a millennium of history, but today's publishing process is anything but pre-technological.

To grasp something of European book publishing in its commercial, legal, technological and cultural circumstances, this chapter will be descriptive rather than critical or socially transformative (in the manner of literary and cultural studies). Nor will it be claimed that a theoretical breakthrough or a critical reflection reveals some hidden process behind these empirical circumstances. It is not clear that we would understand the empirical commerce of the book trade any better by referring it to some higher theory or deeper structure. In this chapter, then, book publishing will not be made an occasion for critique or a platform for counter-politics. However, we assume that readers have some idea of the division of labour between publishers, printers and booksellers, and some sense of the publishing process itself – identifying markets, investing capital, commissioning authors, obtaining readers' reports, editing, design and graphics, legal arrangements, manufacturing, promotion and publicity, sales to distributors and booksellers, stockholding, payments and accounting.

The scale of European book publishing

First things first: some basic definitions. These turn out to be less self-evident than might be expected. To count how many books are published, it has to be decided what should count as a book rather than, say, a leaflet. Is there a minimum number of words, sentences or pages? Is a printed musical score a book? Or government documents? In 1964 UNESCO defined a 'book' as 'a non-periodical printed publication of at least 49 pages excluding covers'. To count how many publishers there are, a decision is needed on what to count as a publisher. The Fédération des éditeurs européens (FEE) set the limit at firms that published at least five titles per year and achieved a turnover of at least 100,000 ECU (£80,000). All such boundaries are arbitrary and could be different. Their adoption as standards is the achievement.

Here are the 1994 figures for the number of book titles published in major national markets and a percentage comparison with 1993:

France	41,560 titles (+1.6 per cent)
Germany	70,643 titles (+5.1 per cent)
Italy	46,676 titles (+6.7 per cent)
Spain	51,048 titles (+3.5 per cent)
UK	89,738 titles (+6.6 per cent)

Average print run – the total number of titles divided by the total number of copies – is a useful indicator of activity in these book markets. In 1994 in France, for instance, according to the Syndicat national de l'édition, the average print run across the 41,560 titles rose by 5.8 per cent to 9069 (it had been 9180 in 1992 but dropped to 8753 in 1993). In paperbacks (*livres de poche*) there were fewer titles but larger printings, the average print run being 12,727 across 9674 titles, a rise of 4.6 per cent (it had been 13,409 in 1992 and 12,170 in 1993). In this instance, the 1994 figures suggest modest confidence in a small increase of demand. But in France as elsewhere, publishing remains a risk business. Roughly 20 per cent of titles generate 80 per cent of revenue, but that 20 per cent cannot be identified with absolute certainty in advance, even with market research and promotion. The ratio of copies unsold and returned to copies sold can be very high.

Categories of books

European publishing is segmented by language differences and cultural variations. For all the talk of media globalization, major print publishers still do most of their business in their national home market, particularly for newspapers and magazines. Each national territory has a developed print publishing industry, hence the calls for cultural protection of specific language-area publishing to preserve a local heritage. National industries have differentiated their product according to multiple subsectors and local circumstances, developing different kinds of book for different kinds of reader.

Against this enduring backdrop of cultural and economic processes operating at the national (or subnational) level, the adoption of international standards remains a fragile, if not utopian prospect. In particular, given the social gravity of national linguistic cultures and lifestyles, the development of a global set of book categories by subject marks a fascinating mutation in commercial and administrative practice.

It is not simply a matter of trade and academic, consumer and professional (to cite categories of publisher as well as of publications). In the UK, the Publishers' Association *Book Trade Year Book* employs the following subject categories for titles published in paperback and in hardcover in 1994 (the total figure being 89,738 as indicated for the UK in the list above):

fiction	5392 paperback, 3312 hardcover
non-fiction	15,469 paperback, 8505 hardcover
children's books	3589 paperback, 3483 hardcover
school texts	2165 paperback, 597 hardcover
STM (scientific, technical, medical)	8706 paperbacks, 8792 hardcover
academic/professional	16,728 paperbacks, 13,461 hardcover

To an extent, the categories used by the French Syndicat national de l'édition correspond to those of the Publishers' Association, but they also include *sciences humaines, histoire et géographie, littérature générale, encyclopédies et dictionnaires,* and *livres d'art.* The point is not that the one classification is truer than the other. The value of the system of categories depends on how appropriate the system is to its circumstances and purpose.

The UNESCO *Statistical Yearbook* uses twenty-three subject categories derived from the Universal Decimal Classification. A publication such as the *European Specialist Publishers Directory,* as we might expect, deploys yet more categories. No fewer, in fact, than the following fifty-five: agriculture and farming; animals; antiques and collecting; archaeology and anthropology; architecture and design; atlases and maps; aviation and transport; bibliographies and library science; biography and autobiography; building and construction; business and industry; careers and vocational training; children's; computing and computer software; crafts and hobbies; directories and yearbooks; DIY (do-it-yourself); earth sciences; educational and textbooks; ethnology; fashion and costume; film; financial; fine and limited editions; fine art and art history; food and drink; gardening; gay and lesbian; genealogy and local history; health and beauty; history; humour; languages and linguistics; law; life sciences; literature and criticism; marketing and advertising; military and war; music; new age, magic and the occult; periodicals, magazines and newsletters; photography; physical sciences; poetry; politics and current affairs; printing and publishing; psychology and sociology; reference; religion and philosophy; science fiction and fantasy; sports and games; STM (scientific, technical and medical); theatre and drama; travel and travel guides; women's studies.

In trade practice, these categories are themselves subdivided. For instance, children's books are further segmented according to age-group norms:

0–5, 6–8, 9–12, and teenage. The trend towards special interest publications generates finer categorizations. We can take these as signs of movement away from mass communication towards a segmented market.

A particular circumstance may bring a certain category into favour. For instance, when governments legislate on national curricula, the category of 'school textbooks' can grow in importance. This was the case in the UK following the Education Reform Act 1988. After three years' growth in school texts associated with the new National Curriculum, the Publishers' Association *Year Book* for 1995 records a decline of 4.8 per cent. In France in 1993, school texts could record an 11 per cent increase while sales of children's books were declining by 5.3 per cent.

Prices

Publishing is a wonderfully impure activity that combines but does not synthesize commerce and culture, business profit and civilizing mission. At least in the former aspect its worth is calculable. By comparison with 1993, in 1994 the value of book publishing in France rose 2.6 per cent (on a 1.6 per cent increase in titles and a 7.5 per cent increase in copies). In the same period, German production rose in value by 3.7 per cent (on a 5.1 per cent increase in titles). The British figure shows a growth of 3.5 per cent to £2.8 billion sterling. British publishers enjoy something of a natural monopoly in selling to a worldwide market of English readers. Indeed, in 1994, one-third of the total book production was exported (although the Overseas Trade Statistics show nearly half of these exports were to the European Union market).

How is the price of a book decided? This can be a gritty question, given that the fortune of each title is different. Is price decided by material weight or length? By conceptual genre, such that philosophy should be priced above (or below) agriculture? Should anticipated sales decide the price? Should a reprint be priced at the same level as a new title? Given that most new titles achieve their maximum sale within one year from publication and rarely remain in print for longer, should the price of a book unsold after a year be adjusted upwards in step with inflation, remain the same, or be reduced to encourage a sale? Perhaps the Goldilocks principle fails us here.

The book is thus an object of commerce. On the other hand, it is also a subject or bearer of culture. To be completely committed to the latter view would be to believe that books are immune to the price factor. This high-minded view – that the book has its special status as a bearer of culture and thus its singularity as a public good – has constituted the publishers' defence of a British practice since the mid-1950s: price fixing or, more flatteringly, retail price maintenance. This practice, known as the Net Book Agreement (NBA), came into force in 1957. It codified an existing practice whereby the Publishers' Association enforced a minimum price for books by making admission to the register of booksellers dependent on the bookseller agreeing to adopt the price fixed for those titles that the publishers deemed 'net books'. Only marginal flexibility was allowed, such as temporary price cutting during the annual National Book Sale and the 1994 provision that allowed a publisher to remove a title from the list of net books six months after publication. The stated purpose of the NBA was to maintain an orderly market in books.

In 1962 the NBA was challenged in the Restrictive Practices Court. Highmindedly, the publishers argued the special nature of the book as something more than a mere commodity. As such, the book deserved public support in the form of legal recognition of publishers' entitlement to fix a minimum price. Without the NBA, they claimed, book prices would rise, the number of titles would fall, and fewer bookshops would hold widely based stocks. However, when someone says 'It's not the money, it's the principle' . . . it's the money! Commentators remained ambivalent on the economic argument, seeing the NBA as 'rigidifying' the book market by preventing open competition but conceding that a 'cultural' case might be made (Curwen 1986: 213). In the event, the Court found in favour of the publishers and the NBA was not curtailed.

However, in September 1995 the NBA collapsed under pressure from retail bookselling chains such as Dillons and Waterstones, which have come to hold one-third of the book market. The major booksellers are now calling the tune on the prices charged to the public, marketing books like any other commodity. A regulated market has given way to a deregulated environment in which booksellers will pursue the North American mode of retail exposure: direct selling, price promotions on certain titles or imprints, telemarketing. In fact in the USA, given continental scale and the variety of local jurisdictions and trading practices, price fixing Britishstyle never took hold. With the ending of the NBA, the price factor – selective discounting – can be used to generate sales. However, the first indications are that the immediate post-NBA period has seen most book prices rise faster than the inflation rate, despite discounting on bestsellers.

Elsewhere in Europe the picture is less clear. Price fixing is in force in the Netherlands and Germany – the practice was in fact established in Germany in the late nineteenth century and taken up by British publishers early in the twentieth. It has been dropped in Italy. The European Commission and the European Court have ruled against net book pricing as a restraint of trade when applied across national boundaries. The Federation of European Publishers, however, has held to the 'absolutely imperative maintenance of the fixed book price'. This is the view of Joost Kist (1992: 201) on a pricing policy to protect publishing in the Dutch language area, a regional policy for which he seeks legal buttressing in the form of a general regulation. Publishing thus lays claim to protection, the polar opposite of free trade in the Single Market. Alongside this regionalist logic must be set transnational publishing initiatives such as co-production: contributors from different nations collaborate on a book too costly for any one national company but viable if published in multiple language versions.

The French case on price fixing is interesting, given the statutory buttress provided by the Law of 10 August 1981. Driven by Jack Lang, Minister of Culture in the Socialist Government, this legislation responded to the 1979 abolition of the *prix conseillé* or recommended price and its consequences: publishers had cut slow selling titles from their lists, large booksellers had lowered prices but small booksellers had raised them, and books had generally risen in price. The 1981 law required the fixed price to appear on the book, and limited discounting to no more than 5 per cent of that price for two years from publication. This provision was contested by FNAC, the French bookselling chain that offers a general 20 per cent discount (after opening branches in Belgium – including Brussels – but closing in Berlin, FNAC is now establishing outlets in Spain, where retail price maintenance remains in force).

The relation of author and publisher is also price-dependent. Authors' royalties are calculated as a percentage – typically between 2 per cent and 10 per cent – of the published price on copies sold, although this is very variable by contractual agreement, as when massive advance payments go to best-selling authors. The typical royalty rate seems minuscule when set against the fact that publishers may pass the retailer as much as 50 per cent of the published price. Around 15 per cent is allocated to manufacturing costs, the publisher's own costs and profit being met from the balance that remains.

State interventions and taxes

By comparison with those cultural sectors that have operated in public service mode, directly subsidized by government as a welfare provision, the European publishing industries have depended on a paying public of readers. The rule of the game has been commercial. Even in France, in the late 1980s direct state aid made up less than 2 per cent of total publishing revenues. Other fiscal and administrative measures played a role, such as the 0.02 per cent tax on book sales and the 3 per cent tax levied on the sale price of reprographic equipment. This revenue passes to the Centre National Littéraire, an agency that 'enables the state to intervene in the life of books and authors', is 'administered with the participation of authors and professionals of the book' and 'has as its purpose to encourage writing, publishing, circulation and reading of high-quality works' (Vessilier-Ressi 1993: 82).

Other fiscal arrangements impact on the publishing industry, such as postal rates for printed materials. The major taxation issue on which European publishers have campaigned is that of Value Added Tax (VAT). As things now stand, for cultural goods that aid the free flow of ideas and information, states may introduce rates below the standard 15 per cent VAT but not less than 5 per cent. The publishers' organizations, however, call for a zero rate for books, magazines and newspapers. In the UK, the zero rate was maintained well into 1997.

Laws

Different facets of book publishing are regulated by different areas of law: property by copyright, publishing markets by trade practices and competition law, published content by laws against defamation. It is therefore best not to generalize.

Copyright has been an element of the English book trade from before the 1710 Statute of Anne, an Act 'for the Encouragement of Learning, by vesting of the copies of printed books in authors or purchasers of such copies during the times therein mentioned'. Today it is a matter of European Commission directives on the duration of copyright, photocopying, the protection of databases, and other issues that respond to a commercial reality: for publishers, domestic and international intellectual property rights – created and traded with other publishers and media companies – now represent significant financial assets.

Movement towards uniform copyright legislation in Europe faces historically divergent legal traditions. In the common law systems of England and the USA, copyright was, and is, an exclusive economic right created by the legislator. By statute the copyright holder can exclude other persons from making copies of the work and take certain actions against them if they do. A different conception, more coloured by natural law thinking, emerged in the civil law systems of France and Germany in the nineteenth century: that of author's right (*droit d'auteur* or *Urheberrecht*). Here the rationale was to protect the personality of the individual creator.

We can distinguish between copyright as a property right attaching to the work and authors' right as a personality right attaching to the individual author of the work. The author's right system expands the sphere of personal rights in order to protect the non-economic 'moral right' (*droit moral*) of individual authors. The moral right has two principal components: the right of attribution (the author can require that uses of the work identify its authorship) and the right of integrity (the author can exercise control over uses of the work, in particular to prevent unauthorized alterations that interfere with the work's 'integrity'). The right of integrity embodies a natural law notion of the individual's ideal inviolability, our intellectual creations being seen as an inviolable (and inalienable) part of our very person.

These conceptual distinctions between copyright and author's right have their importance, but at a practical level they are often blurred. The UK Copyright, Designs and Patents Act 1988 thus provides a qualified protection for moral rights. The overarching international law on copyright, the Berne Convention for the Protection of Literary and Artistic Property 1886, requires all signatory states to extend to authors of other member states protection of creators' moral rights. In late December 1996, the Diplomatic Conference of the World Intellectual Property Organisation (WIPO) adopted two treaties, the WIPO Copyright Treaty and the WIPO Performances and Phonograms Treaty. These treaties, now awaiting signature and legislation by member states of the Berne Convention, advanced the work of international legal regulation of digital communication.

Within its own procedures and categories, the law responds to changes in the commercial, technological and cultural environments. In relation to newspapers, magazines and databases, publishers are now demanding that copyright should belong to them, not to the authors they employ. What is more, they claim that publishing companies should be treated as creators of intellectual property. If this was granted, companies would acquire moral rights on a par with individual authors, traditionally the sole bearers within the author's right system. Once upon a time a company could no more have a moral right than it could fall in love. Yet now this might come to pass. In the multimedia environment, corporate publishers have every interest in being able to control and trade rights quickly, freely and internationally, without interference from individual authors seeking to safeguard their moral rights of attribution and integrity. In this environment, it seems, European copyright law is slipping away from the individualism of the French and German tradition.

As with tax regimes, the Single Market pursues legal standardization in place of historically divergent national policies. Thus in 1993 the European Commission 'harmonized' the period (or term) of copyright protection after the author's death. To have terms that vary from nation to nation, it was said, impedes fair competition by maintaining an anomaly: a work is protected in one national territory but not in another. A norm of seventy years' *post mortem* protection was adopted in a directive to member states. This raised copyright protection to the highest (German) standard, but created problems for a reprint industry that operated on the basis of a life plus fifty-year copyright.

The advent of the Single Market and the free movement of goods within it has also raised the issue of territorial copyright and parallel importation: the exclusive right to publish a given title in a given national territory. For British publishers, the Single Market offers an opportunity even as it poses a threat. The opportunity is that of obtaining exclusive English-language rights to publish a work in the whole of Europe. The threat is that European booksellers will import editions of English-language titles that are legally and more cheaply published in the USA and re-export them to British booksellers, undercutting British publishers. Before we sympathize 'h them, the traditional practice of British publishers has been to control 'isive rights for the English-speaking territories of the Commonwealth 's Australia, restricting the market to themselves by excluding the 'st US editions as piracies.

'er protectionist devices, territorial copyright is defended by its 'commercial and cultural grounds but attacked by advocates of 'pyright and competition law clash over parallel importation.

We begin to appreciate why we cannot yet say to what extent the European book trade is a protected industry or to what extent the interests of the book-buying public are denied.

Bureaucratic regulations

Law alone, unsupported by governmental and industry bureaucracy, does not do too much. This is so with copyright. In Europe today much of the legal-cultural action is driven through two of the European Commission's twenty-six Directorates-General, DG XIII and DG XV. The former has responsibility for telecommunications, information market and exploitation of research, and thus has carriage of policy-making for the Information Society under Martin Bangemann's Forum. DG XV has responsibility for the internal European market and financial services. Here too, it seems, there is a tension. The January 1996 *Newsletter* of the European Magazine Publishers' Federation records 'one of the great tussles of our age being conducted between DG XIII, widely seen to be on the side of "the producers" of new media, and DG XV, taking the side of "the creators"'. We are not told who is on the side of book purchasers.

Europe-wide copyright norms are being constructed in the European Commission's 1988 Green Paper on *Authors' Rights and the Technological Challenge* and the 1993 White Paper on *Growth, Competitiveness and Employment* (although these documents focus on the electronic media). New norms for the protection of intellectual property are on the agenda of agencies such as the Information Society Forum. This work of construction responds to novel issues: how to ensure remuneration for electronically transmitted information? How to remunerate percentage value adding (where ease and speed of access to the information might be more valuable than the originality of its expression, the traditional object of copyright protection)?

Publishers have for the most part criticized the European Commission for giving too little attention to the printed media. Certainly the 1988 Green Paper neglects the industry of the written word. While noting the *Community Plan on Books and Reading* approved by the European Council of Ministers in 1989, Ruipérez (1992: 224) none the less judges that 'in practice few resolutions of lasting importance have been passed', that is, resolutions dealing with book pricing, taxation and international trade. However, this relative neglect of print publishing is in keeping with an important administrative fact that distinguishes contemporary publishing from other media institutions: the book trade is much less the object of governmental regulation than the telecommunications industries.

For its part, the publishing industry has its own bureaucratic agencies, including the Federation of European Publishers, the European Magazine Publishers' Federation, and the European Booksellers' Federation. The common aim of these organizations is to promote the publishing industry. Bureaucracy is not a feature of the state sector alone.

Firms, futures and formats

The 1980s have seen general economic recession, deregulation of markets, reduction of governmental provision and public spending, extraordinary corporate mergers and acquisitions. The publishing industry has been anything but immune. Indeed, change in the industry has been intensified by the generalized adoption of electronic means for creating, storing and distributing information.

In the later 1980s, traditional patterns of ownership in the British book trade were transformed by significant concentrations of ownership. Formerly independent family-based publishers became parts of larger publishing groups. These larger combinations were in turn incorporated – with varying degrees of autonomy – into sprawling industrial conglomerates with interests beyond publishing and, sometimes, beyond communications. In the UK, the US company Random House amalgamated with the Anglo-American Century Hutchinson to form Random Century, an organization housing Bodley Head, Chatto & Windus and Jonathan Cape. International Thomson embraced Routledge (now independent) and Nelson. Pearson incorporates Addison Wesley Longman, Penguin, Viking, Michael Joseph and Hamish Hamilton; it also owns the *Financial Times* in the UK, Les Echos in France and the Recoletos group in Spain. Reed International (now Reed-Elsevier) includes Butterworths, the leader in law texts. The jury is still out on the results of such concentrations. But there is no call to romanticize independence. Having remained independent does not guarantee that Cambridge University Press and Oxford University Press will publish only sweet-scented 'progressive' works. It is interesting to note that not all movements lead to concentration of ownership. Independence from Thomson came when Routledge was purchased by Cinven, a major venture capital company. Routledge is now largely a self-managing publisher of books and journals, with Thomson providing such services as international distribution and payment of authors' royalties.

In France, 60 per cent of the market is held by two major publishing corporations, Hachette and the Groupe de la Cité, the former much the larger, the latter much more focused on publishing. To concentrate its book publishing capacities, the Groupe de la Cité acquired Bordas, Larousse, Laffont and, through Havas, France-Loisirs, the principal French book club. By contrast, Hachette has major interests not only in publishing but also in distribution and retail sales, as well as in film and television. Hachette's Book Distribution Centre can handle half of France's published materials while its Nouvelles Messageries monopolizes deliveries to news-stands and magazine kiosks. Alongside this duopoly are famous medium-scale publishers such as Albin-Michel, Flammarion, Gallimard and Le Seuil. Their reputation for quality and their potential for expansion make them targets for takeover, as occurred – unsuccessfully – at Gallimard in 1990.

In Germany there has been the same trend to concentration of ownership. 3 per cent of the 2000 recognized publishers hold 65 per cent of sales, by far the largest turnover being that of the Verlagsgruppe

Bertelsmann. In fact, like Hachette, the Bertelsmann corporation is a multi-national media conglomerate, having entered the English-language print market with its purchase of the British Corgi and US publishers Double-day, Bantam Books and Dell. In 1994, Bertelsmann became the fifth largest US consumer magazine publisher with its purchase of the New York Times Company's women's magazines.

No less striking an international creation is Reed-Elsevier, formed by the 1993 merger of the British Reed Group and the historic Dutch publisher Elsevier (the founder of the house, Louis Elzevir, published his first book in 1583 in Leyden). Elsevier is world leader in scientific journals and the second largest newspaper publisher in the Netherlands. This giant publishing corporation with annual turnover of £2.7 billion has since purchased Mead Data Central, a US company specializing in electronic distribution. With this purchase, Reed-Elsevier has become the major European-owned on-line publisher.

Printed books now compete with electronic distribution for capitalization and with CDs for our disposable income. CD-ROM is an established publishing market. From 1994 to 1995 Frankfurt Book Fair – whose 1992 slogan was 'Frankfurt goes electronic' – saw a doubling of the number of exhibitors in the electronic publishing section and a 50 per cent rise in visitors. The major German publishing interests are active in the new field, Bertelsmann, Suhrkamp and Burda, and a catalogue of 17,000 CD titles with an average edition of 4000 now sells around 5 million copies annually. Various growth forecasts are given. The German publishers and booksellers' association – the Börsenverein des Deutschen Buchhandels – estimates that some 3 per cent of German publishing is now in electronic mode, rising to 20 per cent by 2000.

The impact of CDs on books will be variable: reference works, for instance, will be more generally affected by electronic alternatives to print than works of literature. Policy on pricing, marketing and retailing will be rethought in relation to the new medium. Legal issues will have to be settled, given the multiple rights involved in multimedia products and the present uncertainty as to conditions of access by third parties. As with licensing on-line uses of copyright materials, these problems of development and distribution will be resolved as issues are tested in the courts and workable systems of remuneration and control are legislated.

Meanwhile, print is anything but dead. It is not a matter of an absolute alternative. In France, Arborescence – a branch of Havas Edition Electronique – is marketing a collection that packages a printed book together with a *cédérom*. Paperbacks, *livres de poche*, *Taschenbuchen* or *tascabili* have become a key part of the European book publishing scene since Penguin's appearance in the post-Depression 1930s (although the Venetian printer Aldus Manutius invented the 'pocket book' format in 1501). In Italy in 1992, Marcello Baraghini of *Stampa Alternativa* (Alternative Press) launched the *libro a millelire* or 1000 lira book, the 'book that costs less than a cup of coffee'. The launch title – well out of copyright – was Epicurus' *Lettera sulla felicità* (Letter on Happiness). The miniature format and minimal pric have certainly made Baraghini happy. The new format has achieved generic status as a *millelire* and generated a category of books now known as *supereconomici* from other Italian publishers, among them smaller competitors such as Newton Compton – founded by Vittorio Avanzini – and older established major publishers such as Rizzoli and Mondadori.

Penguin followed suit, responding also to the launch of Wordsworth Editions' Classics (at £1), and in July 1995 announced their own 'super-economic' format: the Penguin 60s (60 titles at 60 pence each to mark the company's sixtieth anniversary). This series is now augmented by Penguin 60s Classics. Also in the UK, Orion's Phoenix 60s further imitate the Italian initiative, with Epicurus' *Guide to Happiness* among the titles. The Bloomsbury Quids are a subsequent manifestation on the minibook scene. In France the *livres d'un soir* have made their appearance.

It is not yet clear how profitable these minibooks are, even when their authors have been dead well beyond the European Commission's seventy-year *post mortem* copyright term. The promotion of dead and famous authors is less costly than that of the living and new, and the same is true for new titles. Nor is it clear that these books are effective as loss leaders. Although it is too soon to say that the *millelire* has reorientated publishing policy even in the Italian market, the factors of format novelty, low price and mass distribution – less through bookshops or book clubs than through news stands where they sell alongside other media merchandise – are well recognized.

In November 1995 a seminar on *Il libro tascabile: mercato finito o mercato infinito?* ('The paperback: finite market or infinite market?') was held in Venice under the Italian–German auspices of the Scuola per librai U.E. Mauri and the Akademie des Deutschen Buchhandels in collaboration with the Bertelsmann Foundation. The seminar showed that differences remain between publishers in different national markets. The Italians were mostly enthusiastic that the *supereconomici* could open new channels of distribution, draw in new readers and enlarge the total book market. On the other hand, the Germans mostly foresaw that if low price became the key factor in publishing policy, a downward spiral away from quality would serve only to set future limits to the market, not least in prices.

In fact, in Italy, things have already moved on. Disregarding UNESCO definitions, in April 1996 Baraghini launched the *libro a centolire* or 100 lira book, the 'book' that 'costs less than a cigarette'. The first title is *Come si fa un libro a centolire*. The format is a single A4 page photocopied with thirty-two miniature pages. Had there been forty-nine, would it have been a book? Four folds and a cut produce a microbook of 5.4 × 4 cm. The sheet will be ˙stributed directly to readers, bypassing booksellers altogether. The *centolire* ˙ not be the perfect icon of a future 'Europe of the book'. However, its ˙ion signals an enduring energy in print. On the basis of the precept ˙ impossible to be chivalrous without a horse, perhaps we should not ˙mplate being knowledgeable without a book.

˙'s gesture also has a concrete lesson for those studying today's ˙costs and capitalization for print publishing are far lower than ˙nications, as is the level of government regulation. In fact the book publishing industry and the new media – networked or CD-based – reveal a similar structure where alongside a few very large firms many small to medium enterprises specialize in niche marketing to particular audiences. There may be more to learn about the future of communications from studying the book trade than from deconstructing the ostensible meanings of television programmes.

Acknowledgements

Much of the information in this chapter is synthesized from the Italian language periodical literature, the *Giornale della libreria* being a particularly useful source on the European publishing scene. My thanks also to Jeanette Gilfedder, for her invaluable help, and to Ian Hunter and Julian Thomas for their comments on the draft version.

Questions

1   What features specific to the European book publishing industry might justify making it a focus for contemporary media studies?

2   Given commercial facts and legal realities, are books really different from other products of the cultural industries, as the advocates of the Net Book Agreement claimed?

3   What commercial, legal and cultural questions are raised for publishing policy by the minibook format that the Penguin 60s, the Orion 60s and the Bloomsbury Quids borrowed from the Italian *millelire*?

References

Curwen, P. (1986) *The World Book Industry*, London: Euromonitor.

Kist, J. (1992) 'The Netherlands in the European Community: a cultural area of modest proportions with a few large publishing companies with international interests', in F. Kobrak and B. Luey (eds) *The Structure of International Publishing in the 1990s*, New Brunswick, NJ, and London: Transaction.

McLuhan, M. (1962) *The Gutenberg Galaxy: The Making of Typographic Man*, Toronto: University of Toronto Press.

Ruipérez, G.S. (1992) 'The publishing industry and the Single European Market', in F. Kobrak and B. Luey (eds) *The Structure of International Publishing in the 1990s*, New Brunswick, NJ, and London: Transaction.

Vessilier-Ressi, M. (1993) *The Author's Trade: How Do Authors Make a Living?*, New York: Center for Law and the Arts, Columbia University School of Law.

Further reading

Journals

Book Research Quarterly
The Bookseller
European Bookseller
ISBN Review
Logos
Publishers' Weekly
Publishing History
Publishing News

Directories and yearbooks

The Book Trade Year Book, London: Publishers' Association.
Multilingual Directory of Publishing, Printing and Bookselling, London: Cassell and
   the Publishers' Association.
UNESCO Statistical Yearbooks.

Books and articles

Altbach, P.G. and Hoshino, E.S. (eds) (1995) *International Book Publishing: An
   Encyclopedia*, New York and London: Garland.
Briggs, A. (ed.) (1974) *Essays in the History of Publishing*, London: Longman.
Clark, G. (1994) *Inside Book Publishing*, London: Blueprint.
Curwen, P. (1986) *The World Book Industry*, London: Euromonitor.
Feather, J. (1988) *A History of British Publishing*, London: Routledge.
Feather, J. (1993) 'Book publishing in Britain: an overview', *Media, Culture and
   Society* 15(2): 167–81.
Graham, G. (1993) *As I was Saying: Essays on the International Book Business*,
   London: Hans Zell.
Katz, B. (1995) *Dahl's History of the Book*, Metuchen, NJ, and London: Scarecrow
   Press.
Kobrak, F. and Luey, B. (eds) (1992) *The Structure of International Publishing in the
   1990s*, New Brunswick, NJ, and London: Transaction.
Lanham, R.A. (1993) *The Electronic Word: Democracy, Technology and the Arts*,
   Chicago: University of Chicago Press.
Owen, P. (1993) *Publishing Now*, London: Peter Owen.
Saunders, D. (1992) *Authorship and Copyright*, London: Routledge.
Unseld, S. (1980) *The Author and his Publisher*, Chicago: University of Chicago
   Press.

Internet

SHARP Web: http://www.indiana.edu:80/~sharp (Society for the History of
   Authorship, Reading and Publishing)

Chapter 4

Advertising and marketing

ADVERTISING AND THE NEW MEDIA ENVIRONMENT

SEAN BRIERLEY

Advertising is possibly the most prevalent cultural form of the twentieth century and will probably have the greatest longevity. Though the power of media advertising appears to be at its zenith – $200 billion was spent world-wide on advertising in 1995 – the industry which was entwined with the growth of mass media has for a number of years been in a state of crisis.

The rise of modern advertising

Advertising arose out of the industrial revolution. Overproduction of mass market goods through new manufacturing techniques and low consumption meant that consumer goods companies needed to stimulate demand. New channels of distribution such as transportation and mass retailing opened up the possibility of reaching new markets.

After the removal of taxation and regulations on advertising and the media by the Prime Minister, William Gladstone, in the 1850s, manufacturers were able to turn to the mass media to appeal to consumers over the heads of retailers in an attempt to control prices and distribution.

By the turn of the century global advertisers such as Heinz, Procter & Gamble and Ford were opening factories across the globe and used market research to identify prospective consumers. They developed consumer classification systems such as demographics which measured the population in terms of occupational class, age, sex and region to read off certain values and assumptions about spending. The advertisers would match this profile to an appropriate medium which offered the highest number of the target market.

Research in this context was generally used to recruit new customers. Consumers were constructed and classified as sets of statistical data, tendencies and frequencies that are mapped in order to find out who are the 'most likely' and 'predisposed' groups to buy and use the brand. While consumer markets were still expanding market research would segment markets to identify 'predisposed' groups to recruit. In the 1970s advertisers started to add lifestyle and attitudinal categories to demographics. Now advertisers would target campaigns at certain 'types' such as 'nest builders' and 'forward thinkers'.

The new mass media environment also gave rise to the modern advertising industry structure. Advertising agents had sold space for regional newspapers to national advertisers in the early nineteenth century for a percentage of the sale in commission. Advertisers are those companies and organizations that pay for media advertising. They are the advertising agency's clients. The advertising agency began to create and plan advertising campaigns and buy media time and space on behalf of the advertiser/client. In return for this, the agency received a percentage in commission from the media owner.

As consumer markets and the national media grew the agents switched to representing the advertisers. This was a significant shift, entailing as it did a different source of revenue for the agencies. Whereas in the past there were many small regional newspapers searching a limited number of national advertisers, now there were many national advertisers and more concentrated national media groups. Agencies therefore became media brokers for advertisers in the late nineteenth century. By having a portfolio of large clients, agents could use the combined strength of their advertising spend to gain cheaper deals from media owners. The agencies began to produce creative work for advertisers and by the 1920s advertising agencies became more clearly defined as an intermediary which manages, creates and buys media space for advertising campaigns on behalf of clients.

Agencies were now 'full service', offering sales support, creative work, research and product development in addition to the basic job of media broking. They even managed to strike a deal with the Newspaper Proprietors' Association (the national newspaper trade association) to set up a recognition system in 1932 that was to dominate advertising for most of the twentieth century. It effectively squeezed out any other forms of advertising business relationship in favour of the full-service advertising agency (Brierley 1995: 64–8). It included a no-rebating clause, which means that the commission could not be rebated to the client and must stay in the agency; this effectively prevents price competition among agencies who may wish to offer only media buying.

When commercial television came in 1955 the advertiser–agency relationship fundamentally changed. Previously agencies had made ads for all commission-based media – that is all media that remunerate agencies on the basis of commission, e.g. TV, radio, magazines, and posters. This is termed 'above the line' advertising. Public relations, sales promotion and direct marketing services and sponsorhip – all media that do not remunerate on the basis of commission – are defined as 'below the line'. Advertisers and agencies were gripped by the belief in the power of the new medium and most of the advertising spend was channelled into producing commercials. Agencies became more clearly defined as 'above the line' agencies; most of the 'below the line' activity, if there was any, was farmed out.

The commission system also supported the emergence of new agencies. There is an optimum level at which a large agency can reach because of the problem of client conflict. For instance, if an agency such as Grey Advertising in London has Mars on its roster it is forbidden from pitching for any other confectionery or pet-food business which would seem to compete. Since the Second World War, there have been a great many mergers and acquisitions of agencies resulting in concentration and the growth of a handful of global agency networks. These mergers often produce client conflict from which new agencies emerge.

Up to the 1980s most full service advertising agencies were structured in the same way. They all had account handlers who liaised with the client and coordinated the development of campaigns, a creative department where ads are devised, a media department where the media schedules were planned and time and space bought for the campaigns, a control department where the whole process is coordinated. And a new business department, because of the relatively short period of time that accounts stay with agencies.

The bigger advertising agencies also had research departments, and in response to client concerns that advertising was becoming less effective many in the 1970s started to develop planning departments which identified the target audience and ran advertisement research.

Advertising in crisis

Since the mid-1980s, the industry which manufactures advertising has been in a state of crisis. It is unable to deliver what it has previously promised, unsure about its effectiveness and desperately trying to redefine its role with companies and organizations. The reasons are partly to do to with widespread structural shifts in western economies away from industrial production towards the service sector; a long-term crisis in consumer demand; and a shift towards deregulation which has accompanied the communications revolution.

Advertising took much of the credit after the war for being able to stimulate demand, but the biggest help for consumer goods manufacturers came in the form of the welfare state. Working-class people were provided with safety nets of social security, free education, health and pensions and were able for the first time to afford cookers, fridges, washing machines, TV sets, cars and foreign holidays.

By the late 1960s, western economies began overproducing again and markets became saturated. Companies tried to encourage consumption with interest-free loans, credit cards and cash-back schemes.

In the 1980s the decline in the manufacturing base of most western eco-nomies and the wilful destruction of the welfare state in the UK contributed to the crisis in demand. Markets became more saturated. Many of the con-sumer goods companies had to contend with static or declining markets, rather than expanding them.

Rather than attempt to recruit new customers, one of the most import-ant functions in the marketing department became retaining existing ones. Market research started to focus on researching those who purchase and use their brands, separating existing users of brands into light, medium and heavy; encouraging medium users to become heavy users and heavy users to become even heavier, for instance.

New products also found difficulties. By the 1990s around 80 per cent of all new brands on the market had to be withdrawn within a few years because of market saturation. The service sector, rather than the manufac-turing sector, had become the most significant area of growth. As a conse-quence, some of the biggest advertisers came from fast food restaurants, lotteries, utilities, travel and leisure companies, hospital trusts and charities, political parties and government departments. But the most significant shift of all since the mid-1970s has been the shift from manufacturer to retail advertising.

One of the reasons for the growth in manufacturer advertising at the turn of the century was due to the growth of retailer power. Manufacturers developed brands to appeal to consumers over the heads of retailers. They were able to control prices and charge a premium for adding values. Most branded groceries were able to charge over 20 per cent more than non-branded ones. Brands added value to products and apparently created 'brand loyalty'.

From 1950 when the first supermarket appeared in Croydon to 1995 when supermarkets accounted for over 80 per cent of the total grocery market (compared to 44 per cent in 1971) the supermarkets began to advertise themselves as brands in their own right, transforming the con-sumer's question of what to buy, to where to buy. Sainsbury's, Safeway and Tesco managed to establish high quality own-label brands to compete dir-ectly with established brands such as Kellogg and Lever Brothers' Persil. The result is that traditional branded goods' sales have been hammered by own-label products, which now account for around 40 per cent of total sales in supermarkets. The fundamental ability of manufacturers to control prices and sales has been undermined by the more powerful retailers.

Before the Second World War most product markets had a small number of brands and limited amount of mass media to provide messages. Adver-tisers perceived consumers to be 'loyal' towards their brands, rather than just buying them out of habit, lack of interest, or lack of choice. One of the main reasons why 'brand loyalty' has eroded has been because the satur-ated markets have provided more choice for consumers. The 'power' of the brand was eroded by the increase in the number of brands and greater choice. Technological advances have limited the ability of manufacturers to make products different to their competitors. As soon as an innovation is made competitors can copy it almost immediately. Rather than buying a single brand, consumers can buy a variety. With some of the biggest brands, in some cases over 60 per cent of a brand's customers buy the product just once a year.

The erosion of such brand loyalty has provided problems with the idea that advertising could create and sustain brand loyalty. 'Advertising is a weak force (which is why we need so much of it), and mostly reinforcing rather than strongly persuasive' (Ehrenberg and Barnard 1994: 13). Advertising tries, and on the whole fails, to stop the long-term slide in sales of individual brands.

Since the 1970s most consumer goods markets have experienced intense concentration with mergers and acquisitions causing the rise of oligopolies, that is markets where only three or four firms control the market; for example in confectionery just three, Mars, Cadbury and Nestlé, predominate.

Furthermore, in the 1980s, the basis of ownership of many UK companies had changed considerably, from many private firms run by boards, towards companies being run by financial institutions. Between 1970 and 1991 pension funds and insurance companies increased ownership of UK companies from 20 per cent to over 50 per cent (Briggs 1993: 20). These changes affected the expenditure decisions of big firms. They often had huge acquisition debts to finance and wanted more return for their costs. The marketing people in firms were responsible to boards run by financial institutions and investors who wanted dividends.

Improving sales performance became more important. Advertising was seen as an integral net cost rather than an investment in the brand. In corporate culture, costs are perceived as essentially bad things that need to be reduced to have a healthy, profitable company. If advertising is seen as an investment, supporting the long-term future of the company's brands, advertising budgets would not be one of the first to be slashed when recession hit. Because company finance directors view advertising as a net cost, because they cannot quantify the benefits of advertising, it is always one of the first budgets to be cut in a company. As one executive from Smith-Kline Beecham remarked in 1993, the company spent more on media advertising that it did on blackcurrants for its Ribena brand (Cook and Waldman 1993: 24). One consequence of this reassessment of advertising's role is the effect on the organizations and companies which serviced advertisers needs.

When consumer markets were expanding, advertising agencies in particular grew successful and powerful, claiming the credit for sales success. They claimed that success could be attributed to mass media advertising's ability to stimulate, control and shape consumer demand. However, the saturation of markets, increased cost of media (Barwise and Gordon, Chapter 14 in this volume) and the inability of agencies to deliver what they promised has led companies to seek alternative ways to target customers.

Deregulation and the media explosion

The 1980s can be characterized as a period of intense deregulation. Much as Gladstone's reforming ministries of the nineteenth century contributed to an explosion in advertising, the Thatcher government also provided the advertising industry with new opportunities. The financial services and pharmaceuticals industries produced some of the biggest advertisers following deregulation and the government's privatization programme of telecommunications, gas, electricity and water also boosted advertising industry fortunes. Additionally, advertising restrictions on charities, religious organizations and professions such as solicitors were lifted.

But the most significant deregulations of the period was in the media industry. Advertisers had successfully lobbied to increase the availability of advertising airtime. The introduction of cable and satellite and the deregulation of television and radio with the Broadcasting Bill 1990 allowed TV sponsorship for the first time and created more TV channels and radio stations. It therefore increased competition in all media markets (see Paterson, Chapter 10 in this volume).

But the explosion in media has caused fragmentation. Whereas in the 1970s there was just one commercial TV channel – ITV – in the 1990s there are over thirty cable, satellite and terrestrial TV channels. Such an explosion has caused audiences to fragment.

The increase in availability of the media has provided problems for advertisers. Whereas in the past an advertiser such as Lever Brothers could 'hit' 70 per cent of all UK 'housewives' by placing an ad for Persil in the break in *Coronation Street*, the fragmentation of audiences means they could expect to get only half that amount in 1995. To get the same coverage as the 1970s Lever Brothers now needs to spend more money, buying more spots and using more media.

The changes in audience share show that in twelve years the main commercial TV channel – ITV – has declined considerably (see Table 4.1). Channel Four, launched in 1982, doubled its share of audience in this period; cable and satellite increased from nothing to 9.1 per cent. TV, newspapers and magazines had to respond to the increased competition from more media by tailoring their editorial to advertiser requirements to deliver the right kinds of consumers with consumption-orientated programmes and features. To gain extra revenue some sold editorial space in the form of 'advertorials', an editorial feature that is paid for or sponsored by an advertiser and often includes the product name and company logo (it usually includes the words 'advertisement feature' at the top).

Quality newspapers moved into classified advertising, and brought in colour to attract food, fashion and drink advertisers. They also developed travel, motoring, TV listings, and lifestyle sections to gain extra revenue.

Television also began to segment. Channels on satellite aimed specifically at children, women and men segmented audiences further. ITV has responded to the decline in audience share for *Coronation Street* by increasing

Table 4.1 Audience share in January 1984 and January 1996

	1984 (%)	1996 (%)	Change (%)
BBC1	36	32.4	−3.6
BBC2	10	11.2	+1.2
ITV	49	36.6	−12.4
Channel Four	5	10.7	+5.7
Others	0	9.1	+9.1

Source: BARB

the number of times it is shown a week. From 1979 when it was shown just one night a week to 1996 *Coronation Street* increased to four times with episodes repeated at other times during the week, and is now sponsored by Cadburys. This helps to bump up ratings and pull in more advertisers in the face of increased competition from satellite.

In the nineteenth century, mass media advertising was a cheap means to appeal over retailer's heads to consumers. By the 1990s it had become extremely expensive, favouring those companies with deeper pockets. However, an even greater concern for advertisers was not so much the size of audiences for programmes, as the fact that technological advances had meant that TV viewers could now avoid watching programmes. Remote control viewing allowed people to zap to other channels when ad breaks were on, and where there are multi-channel sets in satellite households the remote control allows viewers to 'cruise' stations, rather than watch ads. The rise of video recording also allowed viewers to zip through ad breaks with the fast-forward button, dampening the impact of commercials.

Though the explosion of media has made them almost ubiquitous, and audiences have become more fragmented and specialized, the use of zapping (switching channels on a short-term basis by remote control) and zipping (fast-forwarding through material on video recordings) meant that fewer commercials are actually being watched. In addition to increases in production costs and media airtime, this made advertisers increasingly sceptical about the use of TV advertising, and some stopped using TV altogether.

Advertisers perceive that the inflated media costs and fragmented audiences have been exacerbated by weakened commercial messages.

This has added to the perception that advertising's ability to affect consumer behaviour has also declined. The effectiveness of advertising became an issue only when markets became saturated and advertisers wanted to know why sales did not increase.

The new advertising environment

Advertisers have sought to respond to the problem of effectiveness by trying new creative treatments. In the past they would use more persuasive messages to try and encourage consumers, such as providing a reason for purchase or providing an emotional reason for buying the goods.

But from the 1970s on the crisis in effectiveness meant that new treatments were needed. Advertisers developed psychological theories to unlock the motivations of the consumers.

It focused on an activity engaged in by the target 'type' such as playing sport or drinking in wine bars. People do not have to be using the product, just doing the kinds of things that people who use this product do such as driving fast cars, or ice skating. Advertisers also used the new lifestyle analysis to segment their brands. This became particularly prevalent in the 1980s where brands were launched to target specific personality and lifestyle 'types'. The personality of the consumer had to be matched by a personality for the brand. Consumers were meant to self-identify with brand personalities, 'she is me'.

But the biggest problem for creating effective advertising was the media explosion. According to research from the USA the average US child will have seen around 350,000 commercials by the age of 18 (Law 1994: 28).

Research has also suggested that of the fifteen hundred opportunities to see advertisements that people have each day, only between seven and ten are remembered by a consumer.

This was combined with advertisers' frustrations that they were less able to reach consumers – in 1993 Persil had only a quarter of the TV exposure it had eight years earlier (Heller 1993: 8) – media costs were increasing and sales declining.

The combination of increased choice of brands and the 'clutter' of more media messages meant that advertisers needed to do more than simply make a 'rational' appeal to customers to buy its brand rather than others. Media clutter is where there are too many advertising and media messages vying for the attention of the consumer. Because of the cluttered media environment, consumers are perceived to be less susceptible to single advertising messages.

The biggest problem became grabbing attention. The rise of humorous ads in the 1970s had been one way of doing this. It had partly developed as a way to prevent people switching channels to the commercial-free BBC. But the main principle was to get people to warm to the advertising, rather than the brands. By the 1990s the use of comedians, comic sketches and puns in TV commercials became widespread, indicating that advertisers need to cut through the clutter.

Advertising also tried to co-opt other media to cut through the clutter, for example Levi's jeans commercials, which use popular songs targeting the youth market, from 'Heard it through the Grapevine' in the 1980s, to Shaggy's 'Boombastic', and Babylon Zoo's 'Spaceman' in the 1990s. Advertisers have also tried to tie campaigns in to current films, TV shows and sporting events by using stars or mimicry to try and stand out.

Another PR tactic of this kind was to make ads that are controversial in order to get maximum press coverage. Wonderbra in 1994 embarked on advertising poster campaigns which showed half-naked women, guaranteed to gain more publicity. The agency which created the Wonderbra ads claimed to have gained £50 million worth of extra publicity from a poster campaign that cost the client only £500,000.

Unusual, amazing and entertaining advertising is used to attract the reader and fight against the advertising clutter. Advertisers perceive that because of the media explosion and the rise of a generation who are exposed to thousands more advertising messages, consumers are more advertising literate and discriminating than in the past. Because of this, grabbing attention is more difficult.

Though advertising has always sought to try to break down the resistance of consumers, agency planners claimed that a new breed of 'savvy' consumers would make communications more difficult. Agencies have developed advertising that parodies existing advertising genres and developed interactive ads to appeal to these consumers (Brierley 1995: 233–7).

Advertisers have invested a great deal of money to find new ways of getting consumers to interact with their companies, from direct response telephone numbers at the end of ads to developing interactive sites on the Internet. Advertisers have also changed their approach to brands in response to the crisis, by finding additional locations for them. One straightforward way to respond to saturated consumer markets in the west is to move into new ones. Global advertisers have either moved into new geographical markets such as eastern Europe and China, or tried to move their brands into other product markets, such as alcoholic drinks moving into the soft drinks market in 1995 to launch alcoholic lemonades and colas, or Unilever extending its Persil clothes soap brand into a washing-up liquid in the early 1990s.

Another way is to try and get those people who are frequent users of the brand to use it more. Kellogg has launched advertising aimed at getting people to eat Corn Flakes in the evening and Mars tried to get people to put the bars in the fridge in summer to try and increase summer consumption. This led to other ways of exploiting the brand through the development of new products such as the Mars ice cream bar. Because of the saturation of consumer markets in western countries, and the decline in brand loyalty, the focus of many advertisers has been therefore to try to increase the weight of buying of existing users, or encourage brand switching from rival brands.

In response to declining sales, manufacturers have launched new versions of the same product and brands targeted at specific consumers. Such segmentation strategies are aimed at protecting the main brand. For instance, in the toothpaste market, whereas in the 1950s there were fifteen toothpaste brands, all with virtually the same formula, in the mid-1990s there are four main brands with over a hundred different product sizes and variants including smokers', different mint flavours, milk teeth, tartar control, whitener, baking soda, gel and gum protection.

The biggest problem for these, however, remains the retailers who have their own versions of these brands. The resultant squeeze on profit margins

for manufacturers' branded goods has meant that many, such as US household goods company Procter & Gamble, which makes Ariel and Daz, have
had to sharply reduce global costs.

Manufacturers switched to alternative forms of promotion to try to stimulate sales such as direct marketing – direct mailing and phoning customers
– and running sales promotions such as competitions and money-off coupons to keep sales up. Advertisers are returning to a pre-mass media definition of 'the media' which covers all forms of promotional material which a
company or organization relays to the public. With the help of deregulated
telecommunications, manufacturers try to build up databases of consumers
and deal with them *directly* via telephone, mail, fax or computer. Instead of
communication on a 'one to many' basis, the emphasis is increasingly on
'one to one' (or, at least, 'one to not very many'). The aim of this is mainly
to keep existing customers and reward their 'loyalty', rather than woo new
ones.

The supermarkets too have entered this arena, launching their own loyalty card schemes, such as Tesco Clubcard and Sainsbury's Reward Card.
The aim is to encourage customers to shop with them and reward them
with a discount of goods if they stay loyal to that store. At the end of 1995
Tesco switched a substantial amount of its advertising spend into 'below the
line' promotion to support its Clubcard scheme. Its advertising agency,
Lowe Howard-Spink (LH-S) effectively lost a substantial amount of agency
business to direct marketing. LH-S's response was to launch its own direct
marketing agency, Lowe Direct, in April 1996, in an effort to rest back some
of the money that clients were shifting from advertising to direct marketing.

The full service agency system – where advertising agencies provided all
the services for 'above the line' advertising – began to break down in the
1970s when the Restrictive Practices Act 1976 and the Office of Fair Trading ruling in November 1978 that fixed commission was anti-competitive
and monopolistic, killed the recognition system that had been set up in
1932. This opened up the possibility of fees, payment by results, and for the
first time since the interwar years, it also meant that agencies could compete for client business on price. In 1965, media commissions accounted
for 76 per cent of agency income (Cowan and Jones 1968: 17). By 1993,
only 36 per cent of agencies in a survey classified commission as the biggest
element of income (Willott 1993: 22).

The changing income base for agencies meant that many of the services such as research, TV commercial and print production could now be
out-sourced (entrusted to diverse companies rather than, as in the past,
from one full service agency) by the client who would increasingly simply pay a fee for the creative ideas. By the 1990s it became established
practice for big advertisers to have a number of creative agencies working
on separate brands, separate agencies to run direct marketing and sales
promotion (often the subsidiaries of rival advertising agencies), and a
separate (often rival) agency to plan and buy media for its entire portfolio
of brands.

It would continue to use a number of agencies for its creative work, but the media buying for its entire portfolio of brands would be channelled through just one agency. By centralizing their media buying in a single buying point, advertisers could get extra discounts from media owners. Companies have sought to use the benefit of size to drive down media costs. As the corporate world has merged and concentrated in the 1980s, companies have built bigger portfolio of brands, for example Unilever buying up Brooke Bond, Birds Eye, Walls, Elida Gibbs, Fabergé and Helene Curtis.

Multi-brand clients could now centralize their media buying into a single buying point to force better deals from media owners. Nearly 80 per cent of the top 100 advertisers in Britain had centralized their media buying in this way by 1993.

The clout that advertisers can get through centralizing their media through one big agency or buying point can be demonstrated by the fact that in 1995 the top five non-government advertisers – Unilever, Procter & Gamble, Vauxhall Motors, Mars and BT – spent £639 million in 1995 accounting for 13 per cent of the total ad revenue. But the five main buying points – i.e. the media buying agencies – spent £1.4 billion accounting for almost 30 per cent of the total market. The clout of the big advertisers is doubled by the volume concentration of the big buying points. Because of the growth of centralized media buying most large and medium sized agencies now have separate media buying agencies who devise media strategies and buy advertising space and time. In 1995 just three media buying agencies, Zenith Media, Initiative Media and TMD Carat, were responsible for buying 25 per cent of all TV advertising.

Sales contractors amalgamated and concentrated in response to the collapse of full service agency. In the past the fifteen ITV sales companies sold advertising individually. Different sales houses amalgamated and realigned their sales to form large buying points. By 1994 there were just three ITV selling points for agencies to deal with. Some advertisers such as Kellogg were known to be demanding discounts from ITV companies of up to 75 per cent in 1992 for children's TV, not only because of the erosion of children's TV from satellite, videos and computer games, but also because of the recession and the company's buying clout. The big clients tend to make deals around a year in advance with the sales houses, guaranteeing volume.

If a single buying point controls all of the business of a major mid-market retailer, it would be more sensible for a newspaper group (with some weak titles) to make one deal across all titles, than to try to secure separate deals, than to try and haggle over price on an individual basis. As a result, to keep advertising income up and costs down, the media have merged their sales forces.

Because of competition for advertising revenue, TV programming has been structured by what people consume rather than the demographic group; travel programmes, motoring programmes, consumer affairs programmes, food and drink programmes.

Conclusion

Traditional big brand advertisers have had to radically change their approach to communications because of the explosion in new media. Consumers are perceived to be more remote and difficult to reach at the same time that advertising costs have soared. New methods and techniques have been adopted with the aim of retaining loyal customers and trying to encourage them to consume more, rather than woo new ones. Mass media have fragmented audiences and ad agencies have had to search for new roles as manufacturers switched to new forms of promotion.

This has combined with a structural shift from manufacturers towards the service sector, with retailers, banks and leisure industries now featuring as some of the biggest advertisers.

Though manufacturer's fundamental ability to control prices had been undermined by the more powerful retailers, deregulation has resulted in greater economic power resting with a handful of advertisers, media buying agencies and media owners.

Questions

1   Why can traditional advertising relationships be considered to be in a state of crisis? How effective is advertising in the new media environment?

2   What can advertisers do to make advertising more effective? What alternative methods can businesses and organizations use to communicate with consumers?

3   Discuss the methods and techniques used by companies to stimulate demand. How might new media such as the Internet affect the way advertising is constructed and consumed?

References

Brierley, S. (1995) *The Advertising Handbook*, London: Routledge.

Briggs, M. (1993) 'Why Ad agencies must change', *Admap* 28(1): 325.

Cook, R. and Waldman, S. (1993) 'Altogether now', *Media Week* 13 August: 24.

Cowan, D.S. and Jones, R.W. (1968) *Advertising in the 21st Century*, London: Hutchinson.

Ehrenberg, A. and Barnard, N. (1994) 'Justifying advertising budgets', *Admap* 29(1): 336.

Heller, R. (1993) *Observer* Business Section, 26 September.

Law, A. (1994) 'How to ride the wave of change', *Admap* 29(1): 336.

Willott, R. (1993) 'The latest state of pay', *Campaign* 13 August: 22–3.

Further reading

Brierley, S. (1995) *The Advertising Handbook*, London: Routledge.

Evans, R.B. (1988) *Production and Creativity in Advertising*, Southport: Pitman.

Goldman, R. (1992) *Reading Ads Socially*, London: Routledge.

Leiss, W., Kline, S. and Jhally, S. (1990) *Social Communication in Advertising*, 2nd edn, London: Routledge.

Nevett, T.R. (1982) *Advertising in Britain: A History*, London: Heinemann.

O'Sullivan, T. (1996) 'Agencies put faith in revival strategy', *Marketing Week* 22–3.

Schudson, M. (1993) *Advertising: The Uneasy Persuasion*, London: Routledge.

Wernick, A. (1991) *Promotional Culture*, London: Sage.

Chapter 5

News agencies

NEWS AGENCIES IN EUROPE

OLIVER BOYD-BARRETT AND TERHI RANTANEN

What are news agencies and why are they important?

News agencies have been classically defined as 'wholesale' media, gathering news for the purpose of distributing it to other media, mainly newspapers and broadcasters, who package news agency news for their own distinctive readers and audiences. For newspaper and broadcast customers, the main advantage is that news agencies reduce the cost to them of 'mining' raw information. The main disadvantage is a competitive one, namely that the same information is available to all those who wish to subscribe to the news agency service. For clients who operate in competitive markets this could potentially make it difficult to present an image of independence and exclusivity. But many clients operate in markets where there is little direct competition; in any case clients do not generally deal only in 'spot' news (i.e. news of events that have occurred within the past 24 hours or are actually occurring), and they have their own staff writers who may draw on news agency news as one of a variety of sources in their coverage of any given news story.

News agencies link with many of the key issues that concern scholars of media and society. They represent the archetype of 'syndication' and in this way they raise questions about whether the apparent diversity of 'retail' media is much less than it seems if those same diverse media are in fact drawing from the same sources of supply. The argument applies not only to the number of supply sources (currently there are three major global players in print agency journalism), but also to their representativeness (two are European, one is American); if we look at the major international television news suppliers, whether wholesale or retail, most are American. Concern can be extended to content: the agencies reflect the usual 'western' news values (e.g. priority to elite nations, elite sources, recency, negativity), values which today probably influence the news selection practices of most mainstream media in most parts of the world; they are primarily in business to provide news of major 'national' stories of economic, political and military affairs, and sport – the stories thought most likely to interest international audiences – as well as news of international relations and conflict; they are interested in events more than processes.

Where major national media may deploy a couple of dozen foreign correspondents, at most, and typically rather fewer than that, the main international agencies (see pp. 55–7) between them have several thousand full-time staffers and more stringers in most major cities of the world. Given the strength of these 'public' intelligence networks these services are of interest not only to news media, but also to governments, intelligence services, and financial institutions. They are frequently the first sources of 'breaking' stories. In times of protracted conflict they may be the only organizations which maintain correspondents on a permanent basis in or near to war zones. Their news services can be important influences in the construction of a nation's image in the eyes of political and economic elites, and may therefore have profound political and economic consequences.

Origins of global news system

News agencies can be said to have been among the first highly visible manifestations of 'globalization' in the nineteenth century, a process of the interlinking of different national economies through the activities of transnational economic and financial trade. However, the agencies (especially at national level) have also been important symbols of national identity as well as contributing to the development of the nation-state by rationalizing the national organization of news collection and dissemination.

In postulating five stages of globalization, Robertson (1992) argues that a second phase began in Europe in 1750–1870. While he places international communication only in his third, 'take-off' phase (1875–1925), news agencies had already started their global operations earlier. If we define globalization, as Waters (1995) does, as a social process in which the constraints of geography on social and cultural arrangements recede and in which people become increasingly aware that they are receding, it is of considerable significance that news agencies operated as the first electronic media playing a major role in the process of transmitting news instantaneously from different parts of the world and thus overcoming the constraints of geography.

The French Havas agency, founded in 1832, is considered to be the world's first news agency. It started by translating items from domestic and foreign newspapers. In the beginning it was a private firm owned by an ex-banker, Charles Havas. The second agency in Europe, the German Wolff, was founded in 1849. Its owner, newspaper proprietor Bernhard Wolff, first delivered economic news to his own newspaper *National-Zeitung* and extended it to other newspapers and enterprises. Contemporaneous with Wolff, Julius Reuter (originally Isaac Beer Josaphat) founded a news agency in Paris. Both Reuter and Wolff had once worked for Havas in Paris. The new Reuters agency soon had to move, first to Aachen and then to London, where it started operations in 1851. (The Associated Press was founded in New York in 1848 as a press cooperative.) Establishment of these agencies was subsequently followed by a national agency in almost every European country. By the end of the century most European countries had their own news agencies, and the trend has continued worldwide during the course of the twentieth century.

By its very nature, news transmission has always been international, crossing the boundaries of nation-states. That is why, even in the early years of the first news agencies, foreign news transmission played a major role. The three pre-eminent European agencies – Havas in France, Wolff in Germany and Reuters in Britain – transmitted foreign news in the first years of their operation, while other agencies continued to operate mainly within a national framework. Reuters was the only agency that began its operations as an international agency, with a special agency (the Press Association) being established in 1868 to provide domestic news to national newspapers in the UK and Ireland. These major agencies specialized in political and financial news, above all else, and their clients were mainly news media, financial institutions and governments. Political and financial affairs have always had a strong international component, and transnational links of this kind had grown much stronger, more intense, and more numerous in the wake of industrialization.

Before the first news agencies were founded, newspapers received their foreign news mainly by quoting foreign newspapers or, if they could afford it, used reports from their own correspondents. When the news agencies started operations, foreign news-gathering then became their responsibility, primarily. Reuters, Havas and Wolff soon established their own foreign correspondent networks and started to deliver news to foreign countries as well.

Simultaneously news was commercialized and monopolized. The news agencies established exchange arrangements between themselves in order to further reduce costs and rationalize operations as well as in the interests of controlling competition and protecting markets. The first extant and verifiable agreement among the three big agencies was signed in 1859. These agreements were revised periodically and constituted the foundation of a powerful news cartel that lasted for more than seventy years. Although the cartel itself was dismembered in the 1930s, its long period of operation established an institutional hierarchy or global news system which bequeathed very significant advantages to some of its leading members, notably Associated Press, Reuters, and to Havas and its successor Agence France Presse.

Through the cartel agreements, the global agencies allocated themselves control over given territories on an exclusive or shared basis. For example, according to the 1909 agreement, Reuters controlled outside its home territory Canada, India, most of the Far East, Australia, New Zealand, and its dominions in Africa, while it shared certain other territories with Havas. Each global agency was to negotiate appropriate agreements with a national agency in its domain. The national agencies obtained through these agreements exclusive rights to the news from the global agencies. News from the cartel agencies would be funnelled through to the national agency by the particular global agency with which a national agency had to deal. Inevitably, this inspired great concern on the part of some national agencies and their respective governments about the ways in which news of the world was represented by the global agency, and about how the global agency represented news of their country to the rest of the world through the cartel. In signing these agreements, national agencies relinquished their right to transmit news abroad, either directly or through any other agency. They could send this news only through the global agency with which they had concluded the agreement. In addition, the national agencies paid commissions to the global agencies, not vice versa.

There were several attempts to break the cartel by national agencies, but it was only the partnerships established by the two rival US agencies, the United Press (founded by W. Scripps in 1907, and later to become United Press International) and the Associated Press (AP) with other national agencies that finally crushed the system. The German Wolff had already lost its position as a global agency after the German defeat in the First World War, and its former territories were taken over by Reuters and Havas. The United Press, which had operated outside the cartel, had already started to serve South America, previously Havas territory, and the AP followed it. The AP managed to extract a major concession with the cartel in 1918, when it concluded a separate agreement with Havas that gave the AP a free hand in South America.

Both US agencies were interested in the Asian market as well. While the United Press operated outside the cartel and successfully competed with it, the AP became more and more anxious to operate freely without the restrictions set by the cartel (AP finally became a member of the cartel in 1927). United Press was free to start operations in Asia, therefore, but the AP faced the problem that the Far East belonged to Reuters, which was much stronger there than Havas had been in South America. The cartel finally collapsed in 1934 with the US agencies playing the decisive role. If the Second World War had not broken out when it did, the US agencies would have become completely global by the late 1930s. The USA became the only country to have two global agencies in the world's news market (indeed, for several decades there were three, including Hearst's International News Service). The other two western agencies that now dominate the global print news market are the French Agence France Presse (AFP, founded in 1944 as direct successor of Havas) and Reuters.

The 'global' news agencies

News agencies operate at a number of geographical levels. Most celebrated of all are the major global print news agencies, including AFP, AP and

Reuters. While these do operate globally, gathering news from most countries of the world, and selling it to clients in most countries of the world, each of these also has a long-established national identity, and two of the 'Big Three' have a strong European identity. AFP is a public entity constituted according to French law, with headquarters in Paris and controlled by a governing council on which is represented the French newspaper press, the agency's journalists, and its major state clients. State clients still account for over half of the agency's revenue, and the bulk of this derives from French media and other clients. Once a private limited liability company owned by the national and provincial daily newspaper press of the UK and Ireland, Reuters is today a commercial company quoted on the London stock exchange. Its total earnings are far greater than those of any other news agency; it is listed as one of the leading UK companies, and is one of the world's largest media enterprises. Most (94 per cent) of its revenue is generated through the sale of financial and commodity information and services, including electronic dealing, to traders throughout the world. AFP and AP are also involved in financial news services (AFP in partnership with Bloomberg – which is American; and AP in partnership with Dow Jones/ Telerate), but not to the same extent. Of the major geographical regions of the world, Europe is Reuters' most lucrative market. Associated Press has its headquarters in New York and is cooperatively owned by the daily newspapers of the USA, which accounts for the major part of its revenues through subscriptions. It sells its news services throughout Europe and other parts of the world. Unlike Reuters but like Agence France Press (for France), AP operates as both a domestic national news agency (for the USA) and as an international agency.

In recent years, the major transnational news agencies have become wealthy corporations. This is most spectacularly true of Reuters, whose revenue multiplied some forty times from 1977 to a 1995 total of £2703 million. Revenues from media services grew approximately sixteen times. In 1977 Reuters and AP were on a level but by 1993 Reuters had ten times the turnover of AP. Revenue for Reuters' media service alone was equal to AP's total revenues. In the 1960s, Reuters' economic services accounted for 30–50 per cent of total revenue. This increased to 85 per cent in 1980 and 94 per cent in 1995. In 1980 there were 13,000 clients; in 1995 there were 327,000 customer screens across 154 countries. In 1977 there were 350 editorial staff out of 2377 personnel operating from 60 bureaux worldwide; by 1995 this had grown to 1863 journalistic staff out 14,348 personnel operating from 143 editorial bureaux and a total of 207 offices in 90 countries. (AP in 1995 had 143 domestic US bureaux and 93 international bureaux; Dow Jones had 10,000 employees). Reuters' top executives each earned between £340,000 and £650,000 in salary and benefits in 1995.

The success of Reuters has occasioned a significant shift in discourses about news agencies, away from general political news towards financial news and television and multimedia news provision, because these markets may hold the key to future growth or survival. One of Reuters' principal competitors is the Dow Jones corporation, which generated $2091 million (approx. £1394 million) revenue in 1994, in contrast with Reuters' earnings that year of £2309 million. Its information services, the closest standard of comparison with Reuters' activities (but including major newspapers) stood at $977 million (£651 million), or a little more than a quarter the size of Reuters. One of its fastest-growing divisions was Dow Jones/Telerate which operates worldwide. Dow Jones also owns the Dow Jones News Service (North America) and operates a joint venture with Associated Press, AP–Dow Jones, delivering economic, business and financial news to subscribers around the world. There has been substantial increase in AP–Dow Jones reporting strength in the 1990s, especially in Asia. Dow Jones News/Retrieval service gives on-line access to the same-day text of the *New York Times* News Service, the *Wall Street Journal* and the *Financial Times*. Other ventures include: *Wall Street Journal* versions which now go to Asia, and also to South America (Spanish language); the *Far Eastern Economic Review, Barron's magazine,* Dow Jones business television network, including a 30 per cent holding of Asia Business News and 70 per cent of European Business News; Business Information Services; and Multimedia, which runs the Dow Jones Investor Network – the company's video business news and information services delivered to North American desktop computers in the business and financial communities.

Multimedia services

Attention to the supply of news in 'wholesale' mode cannot be limited only to print news services. First, most 'print' services are today on-screen. Second, the leading agencies also supply still-image (news photo), audio (for radio channels) and moving image for television news services. Reuters Television and Associated Press Television are two of the three leading global 'wholesale' providers of television news to broadcasters. Reuters Television (1995) distributes to over 200 broadcasters and affiliates. APTV (1995) sells to 100 major news organizations, and will soon provide video content to the organization Multimedia Services, a packaged on-line news service of AP words, pictures, graphics, sound and video. The third major wholesale player in television news is WorldWide Television News (WTN) owned mainly by the US broadcast network, ABC (acquired by Disney Corporation) and the UK commercial network news channel, Independent Television News (ITN), selling to over 200 broadcasters. WTN evolved out of an earlier organization, UPITN, which had been a partnership between ITN and what at that time was the world's fourth major commercial news agency, United Press International. UPI has since declined, and is now owned by the Saudi-associated Middle East Broadcasting Centre.

All the world's major television news agencies have headquarters in London. A major client and a major source for these agencies is Eurovision, which is a system of television news exchange organized under the auspices of the European Broadcasting Unit on behalf of Europe's leading public service broadcasters. The global wholesale television agencies also provide news services to international television broadcasters including Ted Turner's CNN, now part of Time-Warner, and services that are wholly or partly owned by Rupert Murdoch, including BSkyB (Europe), Fox Television (USA) and Star Television (Asia). Like its competitors Dow Jones/Telerate and Bloomberg, Reuters also operates a financial television service. This is fed on-screen alongside text-based general and financial news services. It is not continuous, and no effort is made to package it for a non-specialist market; it aims to provide footage of breaking financial news stories which are likely to influence traders and other financial players: it is said that even the facial expression of a spokesperson coming out of a meeting and walking to the microphones may be sufficient to influence major trading decisions.

The agencies are increasingly interested in the Internet and in private electronic networks ('intranets'). Reuters is part owner of some Internet gateways, and provides news services to other service providers: it can earn revenue from the number of 'hits', from payments for service provision, and from payments by advertisers for space on Reuters news pages.

National news agencies

The global news agencies are the most significant players of a global news system made up of global, national and city media. Global agencies monitor local media, pick up information from local media for elaboration, customization and distribution to world markets; their local clients include national news agencies with whom they often maintain close ties. Some local media were established directly or with the aid of the global agencies; Korrespondenz-Bureau of the Austrian–Hungarian empire and Associated Press of the United States formed junior members of the international cartel, governed up to 1934 by the dominant agencies (Reuters, Havas, Wolff); international agencies typically supply international services to national agencies and as part-payment they receive the services of the national agencies. Directly, or indirectly through national agencies, local media take international news from the global agencies (which are often the sole first-hand source for such news), and their prioritization of international news is generally influenced by the agencies' own rankings of news stories. Local media will have access to other international news sources, including the international press (much of it North American and European, including publications such as *Time, Newsweek*, the *Asian Wall Street Journal* and the *International Herald Tribune*). These are not first hand, nor are they instantly available – though some content is accessible through on-line services – and their own international coverage will have been influenced by and to a varying extent drawn from the global news agencies, while also adding valuable and sometimes more in-depth coverage of leading news events and issues. This is not a system without conflict, however. Some national and regional news agencies have been established with a view to reducing dependence on the global agencies, generally in vain. In a few markets, the global agencies provide national news services in competition with national or other local news agencies, as is the case, for example, in Germany and France, and is increasingly the case of Reuters in eastern Europe. In addition to national agencies there are city or local-regional agencies, and specialist agencies dealing with particular categories of news, for example parliamentary, sport, finance, crime or, royalty.

The Press Association of the UK and the Irish Republic is one of the oldest of the European national agencies (and for many years, until 1984, it owned Reuters in partnership with the Newspapers Publishers' Association). It supplies news and pictures, including ready-to-print and screen-ready pages of sports results, stock exchange prices, race-cards, TV listings and weather information. Each day it transmits 400,000 words, 1000 camera-ready pages and 100 pictures, graphics and maps. Its main services are PA News, PA Sport and PA Data Design. It has three other companies which specialize in investor relations and public relations industries in the UK and Canada. It maintains foreign correspondents based in Brussels for coverage of the European Parliament. Its PACE service provides a comprehensive editorial and picture service for evening newspapers; this includes 500-word leads covering all major angles of breaking stories, collections of 'Brights, Funny Old World items, People Pars [i.e. single paragraph stories] and celebrity birthdays, columns of Britain Tonight briefs, and election results, etc.'. A PACE Overnight file, distributed at noon to help editors plan for the following day, provides advance features, embargoed material, critical guide to broadcast programmes and the news agenda. News pages can be created in virtually any style and to any deadline. PA also has a photo library and a teletext service.

This agency is a good example of a privately owned company (owned primarily by provincial newspapers of the UK) operating without benefit of state subsidy (which was the case of many of the European agencies, although far less so now), maintaining a strong profile in the news business, but experimenting with new ways of packaging news and for different client groups. In the early 1990s the PA survived an attempt to weaken its national monopoly by a coalition of newspapers who planned to set up a rival and cheaper service. The planned competition tried without success to persuade the Associated Press (which with Reuters supplies international news to the PA) to change allegiance. This kind of threat to the role of a national news agency has been experienced in other countries, including France, especially where the monopoly status of a national agency is not sanctioned by a special government–agency relationship. Where media markets are wealthy enough to make competition feasible, such a threat can exert a constant downward pressure on the price of general news services and inspires diversification tactics, that is national agencies are under ever increasing pressure to explore ways of making money from different (but related) domains or by delivering news in different packages.

Although Europe has two of the biggest global agencies and some major national agencies such as the German DPA, the Spanish EFE and the Russian ITAR-TASS – which traditionally have also exercised a transnational role, though not on the same scale as the giants – most European agencies are relatively modest and strictly national concerns which were founded in the wake of nationalism in the latter half of the nineteenth century. In principle, there have been three models for the constitutional arrangements for such news agencies: private, cooperative and state-owned, or a mixture of any of these.

Most of the early agencies were of private nature. Some of them still carry the name of their founder, such as Reuters, or Ritzau (Denmark), although these have since become shareholding companies.

The world's first cooperative agency was the US Associated Press, founded in 1848, and this model of cooperative ownership became popular among news agencies after the First World War. Some of these agencies, however, take the form of media-controlled commercial companies, as indeed, were the Press Association and Reuters for many years of their respective histories. The Scandinavian agencies – the Finnish STT, Danish Ritzau, Norwegian NTB, Swedish TT – are all examples of cooperative agencies. Most of them (except TT) were already founded in the wake of nationalism in the latter part of the nineteenth century. Although they enjoy either a monopoly or a leading position on their home market, they also reflect the difficulties which cooperative agencies in general face in the present situation. While most of the successful agencies receive more than 50 per cent of their revenues from their non-media clients (including financial clients for economic news services and government subscribers), cooperative agencies are over 85 per cent dependent on their media clients.

The agencies that appear to have the most pressing financial difficulties, currently, are the so-called cooperative agencies owned by media. As the retired president of the French AFP (which manifests a mixture of cooperative and state control) complained, the agency's statutes do not allow that its tariffs should be negotiated on an individual basis with each client, but are agreed at board level (*Le Figaro*, 26 January 1993). Media representatives on the board, not surprisingly, are interested in protecting their own enterprises from rising costs. Further, they are reluctant to allow the agency to move into new areas or operations that they themselves are interested in. This makes it exceedingly difficult for such news agencies to generate alternative sources of revenues.

The third category, the state-owned or supported agencies, has been common from the beginning and has been increasing since the reawakening of east European nationalism, although now they may compete with privately owned agencies on their home market. Most of the agencies in eastern Europe are either state-owned or receive state subsidy. The percentage of the agencies' annual budget which is accounted for by government subsidy varies between 11 per cent and 75 per cent. Simultaneously, the disentanglement of the agencies from the state is in process in some east European countries. For example, the Czech CTK has been changed into a public organization with no financial support from the state. Similar attempts are planned in Poland and Hungary. Not only do agencies in eastern Europe receive state-support, but also the French AFP does: the French government is represented by three members of the agency's administrative council, and although these are outnumbered by media and journalist representatives, they do exercise considerable influence because of the importance of the state as a source of subscription revenue for the agency's services. The agency's director-general is elected from among the members of the administrative council.

The Soviet TASS was once considered to be one of the big five with the AP, UPI, Reuters and AFP. During perestroika, TASS lost its former domestic monopoly when the first private agencies were founded in 1989. After the break-up of the USSR, TASS was replaced by a new state agency, ITAR-TASS. Numbers of staff have dropped from 5000 to about 3500, of whom 900 are journalists. The privately owned Interfax now successfully competes with the ITAR-TASS and the other state-owned agency RIA (former APN) on its home market. Interfax has 600 employees and several branch offices both at home and abroad. ITAR-TASS, RIA and Interfax are now the big three agencies in the CIS.

State-supported agencies do not necessarily have to be state-owned. For example, the Italian ANSA is a cooperative agency owned by 62 newspaper publishers, but one-third of its customers consist of the government and different ministries. The agency can afford a staff of 1150, of whom 600 are journalists, while an average western European agency usually has a staff of 100–150 journalists. The biggest agencies in eastern Europe still hire staff of over 500 people (PAP, MTI, Tanjug) even after reductions in the early 1990s.

Although national news agencies have traditionally been dependent on the global agencies for their foreign news coverage, some have also had their own foreign correspondents, mainly for covering events of direct relevance to their own domestic interests but which occur overseas. But this practice is in decline. Most of the national agencies in Europe have very few foreign correspondents. The Scandinavian agencies share a correspondent pool, to which each of them provides one correspondent. By contrast, some east European agencies still have a correspondent network of more than ten correspondents. The overall trend, however, is a reduction in numbers of foreign correspondents, because of their expensive maintenance costs. This has made national agencies more and more dependent on the foreign news coverage of global agencies.

Traditionally, foreigners have been excluded from ownership of national agencies. Baltic News Service is an example of a new kind of agency, however, that operates in three different countries, in Estonia, Latvia and Lithuania. It is owned by media companies together with private individuals in several countries. It competes simultaneously with the national agencies in three Baltic countries. In the future, the number of regional or specialized agencies may increase and even threaten the position of national agencies.

National news agencies sometimes find themselves in competition with global news agencies, especially with Reuters. The competition does not take place in general news transmission, so much as in economic news in which national agencies would like to expand their activities. However, Reuters is so strong in economic news transmission in almost every country that national agencies find it almost impossible to compete with it.

Issues

A principal issue of concern is diversity of supply. In the field of major transnational news agencies offering text services in Europe, there has been a decline. In the field of transnational television news services there has been an increase in both 'wholesale' and 'retail' modes, although much of the increase has come from the USA with the establishment of APTV in the wholesale market, and of transnational operations of CNNI, CBS, MSNBC, etc. It could be said that between all of these there is not much variation in terms of the commodified news values to which they all appear to subscribe. Within the existing range there is some doubt about how long the global market can support so much competition. There is a growing range of print and television financial news services, but these are for select markets. Significant alternative players, concentrating, for example, on 'process' news rather than on events, are still fairly weak: these include Inter Press Service which, although based in Rome and subsidized to an extent by the Dutch government, does not have a strong presence in Europe; there is also the London-based Gemini News Service which disseminates twelve to fourteen feature articles a week for use in many newspapers in the developing world but also does not have a very strong European presence. Some of the middle-ranking news agencies of Europe, such as DPA or EFE, have a significant presence beyond the frontiers of their natural domestic markets, but this mainly reflects linguistic or diplomatic affiliation.

A second major concern is revenue generation. Even the privileged members of the elite global club are not free of anxiety on this score. It is open to question whether the global market is big enough to support more than three major television news 'wholesalers', for example. Associated Press is constrained by its cooperative structure in the extent to which it can test the goodwill of its members by relying heavily on their subscription income, and must argue its case with the membership in exploring new areas of activity that might impinge on their own domains, such as provision of news services through the Internet. National agencies which have depended heavily on government subsidy commonly find that governments are less inclined to want to spend money on media activities which can be run equally or more effectively as private businesses; yet without government subsidy it is not always clear that there is sufficient revenue from other sources to be earned, particularly in general news. It may be self-evident that there is a role for a national news agency in developing countries where the few media that exist are likely to be concentrated in urban areas, and where there are strong needs for a vehicle that can be harnessed to development campaigns of agriculture or education, for example, and where the national agency can provide a national news service that is also a help to the government's own bureaucratic channels of information. But in media-saturated, developed countries, the clarity of role may be less obvious, and this may indicate a need for a fundamental reclarification of purpose and potential about the very nature of the news agency business at national and subnational levels.

Questions

1 What is the distinction between 'wholesale' and 'retail' media? Why is it important, and what might be the relevance to this issue of the new electronic media such as the Internet?

2 What are the contributions of news agencies to the gathering, distribution and social construction of news?

3 In what ways might the operations of news agencies be said to facilitate or to impede plurality of news sources for print and broadcast media?

Further reading

Boyd-Barrett, O. (1980) *The International News Agencies*, London: Constable.

Boyd-Barrett, O. and Palmer, M. (1981) *Le Traffic des nouvelles*, Paris: Alain Moreau.

Boyd-Barrett, O. and Rantanen, T. (forthcoming in 1998) *The Globalization of News*, London: Sage.

Boyd-Barrett, O. and Thussu, D.K. (1992) *Contra-Flow in Global News*, London: John Libbey.

Cohen, A.A., Levy, M.R., Roeh, I. and Gurevitch, M. (1996) *Global Newsrooms, Local Audiences*, London: John Libbey.

Fenby, J. (1986) *The International News Services*, New York: Shocken Brooks.

Ingmar, G. (1973) *Monopol pa nyheter: Ekonomiska och politiska aspekter pa svenska och internationella nyhetsbyraers verksamhet 1870–1914*, Uppsala: Esselte Studim.

Johnston, C.B. (1995) *Winning the Global TV News Game*, Boston, MA: Focal Press.

Rantanen, T. (1990) *Foreign News in Imperial Russia: The Relationship between Russian and International News Agencies, 1856–1914,* Helsinki: Suomalainen Tiedeakatemia.

Rantanen, T. (1994) *Howard Interviews Stalin: How the AP, UP and TASS Smashed the International News Cartel,* Roy W. Howard Monographs, no. 3, Bloomington, IN: Indiana University.

Rantanen, T. and Vartanova, E. (1995) 'News agencies in post-Communist Russia: from state monopoly to state dominance', *European Journal of Communication* 10 (2): 207–20.

Read, D. (1991) *The Power of News,* Oxford: Oxford University Press.

Robertson, R. (1992) *Globalization, Social Theory and Global Culture,* London: Sage.

Tunstall, J. and Palmer, M. (1991) *Media Moguls,* London: Routledge.

Waters, M. (1995) *Globalization,* London: Routledge.

Wilke, J. (1991a) *Die Nachrichten-Macher,* Cologne: Bohlau Verlag.

Wilke, J. (1991b) *Telegraphenburos und Nachrichtenagenturen in Deutschland,* Munich: K.G. Saur.

Chapter 6

Public relations and journalism

PROMOTIONAL STRATEGIES AND MEDIA POWER

DAVID MILLER

Contemporary society has become more promotional. Public relations (PR) and promotional strategies are now central concerns of government, business, trade unions, popular movements and even the smallest single-issue protest group. The rise of promotion parallels, and is intimately intertwined with, the expansion of the role of the media in societal decision-making and development. In the UK and many other countries, the sheer amount of media space which needs to be filled has markedly expanded since the end of the 1970s. The need to plan promotional strategies has brought with it the rise of promotional professionals in advertising, marketing and especially public relations. As Robert Jackall has remarked: 'Few areas of our social lives are untouched by the visual images, narratives, jingles, rhetorics, slogans, and interpretations continuously produced by these experts with symbols' (Jackall 1994: 7).

With the rise of public relations has come a periodic debate about the impact of 'promotional culture' (Wernick 1991) on the democratic process. In recent times the routine reporting of matters of politics and policy has increasingly discussed the role of public relations and information management in public life. Barely a week goes by without some new revelation about the 'spin doctors' of the political parties or the role of lobbying companies in influencing parliamentary procedures (see Gaber, Chapter 28 in this volume). Pressure group tactics have joined the debate as the activities of environmental organizations, road protesters or animal rights activists are queried in the media. So how should we understand the relationship between promotional strategies and the media?

News and media strategies

In liberal pluralist theory the media provide a public space in which information is shared and the public informed. By this means the free media function as watchdogs on the actions of government. Free competition for media space and political power ensures that a variety of voices are heard in the media (Blumler and Gurevitch 1995; Gans 1980; Sigal 1986). In contrast much Marxist theory sees the media as an agency of class control in which official messages are reproduced by journalists and functions to indoctrinate the masses and perpetuate capitalism (see Curran 1991; Curran and Seaton 1995: ch. 16).

It has been widely noted however, that the identification of these two positions as self-contained opposites can rather overstate the difference between them (Curran *et al.* 1982). While some differences between the approaches remain, until recently both have been highly 'media-centric' (Schlesinger 1990: 64) in their analyses and explanations of promotional strategies. They have tended to assess the activities of sources by either examining media content or interviewing journalists and have therefore failed to examine 'source–media relations from the perspectives of the sources themselves' (Schlesinger 1990: 61; see also Ericson *et al.* 1989: 24).

The use of media-centric methods of research has affected the kinds of analysis of source power available. In one variant of Marxist theorizing about the media, often referred to as 'structuralist', it is argued that the opinions of the powerful receive a 'structured preference' in the media and become 'primary definers' of media coverage (Hall *et al.* 1978). This approach has tended to overemphasize the power of official sources and to underestimate the extent to which pressure groups and others can manage the news (Miller 1993).

By contrast pluralist approaches tend to underemphasize the crucial importance of official sources of information and overplay the fluidity of competition. An approach which moves beyond 'media-centrism' and directly examines the promotional strategies of government, business and interest or pressure groups has been advocated and a number of studies are now in existence (e.g. Anderson 1991, 1993; Cook 1989; Deacon and Golding 1994; Ericson *et al.* 1989; Miller 1994; Miller and Williams 1993; Schlesinger and Tumber 1994; Tilson 1993). This chapter reviews some of the important features of promotional strategies and their relationships with the media. First, we briefly examine the rise of public relations and promotional culture.

The rise of 'promotional culture'

The rise of public relations as a specific profession occurred around the turn of the century in the USA and slightly later in the UK. The development of propaganda and public relations suggests that reaching public opinion became more important in this period. We might ask why public opinion suddenly became so important that it needed to be managed? According to Robert Bernays (in 1923) twentieth-century capitalism brought with it an increased readiness of the public, due to the spread of literacy and democratic forms of government, to feel that it is entitled to its voice in the conduct of large aggregations, political, capitalist or labour.

(cited in McNair 1994: 112)

Thus universal suffrage and other democratic reforms were a key factor in increasing the influence which could be exerted by the people on decision making. In other words, the rise of public relations as a specialism was a *response* to the modest democratic reforms of this period. These followed increased social unrest and the rise of organized labour.

At the same time new communication technologies were being developed and it became possible to reach a new mass market. Some writers suggest that it was advancing communications technology which pushed the powerful into propaganda techniques. However, it should be remembered that one of the key reasons for the development of the new communications technologies was the use to which they could be put in wartime propaganda.

PR posts have tended to be established at moments of crisis for the powerful, whether at war, under attack from colonial possessions or organized labour. For example, the Foreign Office and the armed forces first appointed press officers during the First World War and in 1919 Prime Minister Lloyd George's aide set up a covert propaganda agency to incite hostility against trade unionism, funded by employers' federations (Tulloch 1993). Business PR became important after the end of the Second World War. An organization called Aims of Industry was founded by business leaders in 1942–43 and it soon saw action assisting the medical profession in resisting the introduction of the National Health Service and campaigning against the nationalization of the sugar and iron and steel industries (Kisch 1964). The PR industry has expanded markedly in the 1990s and there is a wide variety of consultancies to choose from (Nelson 1989; Stauber and Rampton 1995). Since 1945 we have witnessed a mushrooming of information posts in government (Tulloch 1993), both in civil ministries (Crofts 1989) and in colonial counter-insurgency (Carruthers 1995), leading latterly to the rise of the 'public relations state' (Deacon and Golding 1994: 4) and in the political parties the emergence of the 'spin doctor' (Jones 1995). Business PR and PR consultancies have also mushroomed. In 1963 one estimate put the total number of public relations professionals in Britain at 3000 (Tunstall 1973: 158). By 1995 the top 150 consultancies alone (i.e. excluding companies' in-house departments and government) employed a total of 4854 staff (*PR Week* 1996). With the growth has come a myriad of specialisms such as media relations, public affairs, issues management and lobbying (Moloney 1996). The activities of lobbyists have themselves become a major public issue following the exposure by the media of the cash-for-questions controversy when some MPs were revealed to be secretly working for undeclared lobbying interests (Leigh and Vulliamy 1997).

It was only in the 1970s that organizations such as trade unions started to appoint PR officials and prioritize media relations (Jones 1986). As the media have become increasingly important or as other avenues for influence or change are closed off, so pressure groups and other campaigners have been forced to try to attract the attention of the media in order to pursue their aims. Since the 1970s there has been a change in the character of protest. Mass marches and demonstrations have become less popular and are increasingly seen as ineffective (Engel 1996; Porter 1995). Instead radical or counter-cultural movements increasingly understand the value of smaller and more focused actions which are more likely to have televisual appeal (Grant 1995; Vidal and Bellos 1996). For example the lesbian and gay rights organization Outrage deliberately courts the media by staging colourful and unusual 'actions' with a small number of people rather than attempting to get large numbers of activists on to the streets (Glasgow University Media Group 1997).

The focus of much lobbying and public relations activity has also shifted from the centres of power in the nation state to transnational bodies. In Europe, Brussels has become a much more important target for both pressure groups (Mazey and Richardson 1993) and the PR industry (Andersen and Eliassen 1995).

Promotional resources

The contemporary experience is that government, business and pressure groups actively compete for media space and definitional advantage. However, in the competition for access there are very marked resource inequalities between organizations. One obvious way in which this is the case is in financial and personnel budgets. Government promotion is carried out by the Government Information Service, which employs around 1200 information officers, plus support staff, and has a budget running into hundreds of millions. The top 150 PR consultancies earned £292 million in fee income in 1995 (*PR Week* 1996). It is only government, corporations and the bigger interest groups who can afford long-term support from PR consultancies. In other words, the central institutions of the state and big business enjoy structured advantages in the competition. By resources, however, we also mean the extent to which an organization is institutionally secure. For example the central institutions of the state are plainly among the most institutionalized, whereas government-created statutory bodies are less institutionally secure. Outside the ambit of the state are major pressure groups such as Greenpeace or professional associations such as the British Medical Association. These are long-term bodies, which may not always be fully secure. The least institutionalised organizations are those with little formal organization, arising out of specific campaigns or circumstances, whether as a result of particular campaigns such as attempts to block new motorways or bypasses or to stop the closure of a local school. A third type of resource is cultural. Respectability, authoritativeness and legitimacy are all key elements here. These are largely decided by and dependent on the perceptions of others and can decisively influence the credibility of an organization. Cultural capital resides even in the smallest feature of personal presentation such as the accent of the speakers and how they dress. On the basis of the unequal distribution of resources we can identify some groups as 'resource-poor' (Goldenberg 1975) or resource-rich. However, the resources available to the institutions of the state also exist in the context of broader structures of power and authority. Both the state and business have more power to police disclosure and enclosure than other groupings.

Policing enclosure and disclosure

The state is a key site for the policing of information. It controls a huge bureaucratic machinery for the production of research, official statistics and public information. The backbone of the machinery of media management in the UK is the system of mass unattributable briefings, known as the lobby system, by which journalists receive the latest 'off-the-record' comment and political spin on the stories of the day. These appear in news reporting with the source of the information disguised in phrases such as 'the government believes' or 'sources close to the Prime Minister suggest'. The advantage for the government is that since it is not attributed it is, as one minister put it, 'no skin off anyone's nose if [the information] turns out to be wrong' (Cockerell *et al.* 1985: 33; see also Cockerell 1988; Franklin 1994; Harris 1990; Ingham 1991).

The production of government information can itself be influenced by the party political interests and there have been a number of controversies in Britain about the accuracy of official statistics. Furthermore, the accuracy of government information in general has been increasingly questioned. From the massaging of the figures for unemployment to disinformation in times of war, state personnel regularly involve themselves in misinformation.

Successive Cabinet secretaries have provoked opprobrium for their slippery definitions of the concept of truth. Sir Robert Armstrong famously acknowledged in an Australian court that he had been 'economical with the truth' in the British government's attempt to suppress the book *Spycatcher.* In the Scott inquiry into the Arms to Iraq affair, his successor Sir Robin Butler maintained that Parliament had not been misled even though it had been given only partial information. 'Half the picture can be true', he stated (see Norton-Taylor 1995: 91).

However, such evasions can be complemented by wholesale falsehoods when governments face conflict. In Northern Ireland, before the IRA cease-fire, both the police and the army engaged in disinformation. In the case of the 1988 Gibraltar shootings, quite false information was given to the media (about a non-existent bomb, and a gun battle which did not happen) to suggest that the killing of three unarmed members of an IRA Active Service Unit was legitimate (Bolton 1990; Miller 1991). During the Gulf War in 1991, western governments built up a picture of Saddam Hussein as a Hitler figure, threatening western civilization (Philo and McLaughlin 1995). Atrocity stories similar to those of the First World War, involving Iraqi troops looting incubators and leaving the babies occupying them to die, were circulated by PR company Hill and Knowlton for the Kuwaiti government. These stories were false, but had their effect in influencing sceptics in the US Congress to vote for war (Kellner 1992; MacArthur 1993: 37–77). Furthermore, the war was presented as a high-tech operation in which the western forces were able to attack targets with 'surgical precision' using 'smart' weapons. However, such weaponry accounted for only 7 per cent of weapons used in the Gulf and 40 per cent of those apparently missed their targets (Kellner 1992: 163). The key result, was that, in this 'clean' war, an estimated 30,000 to 40,000 Iraqis (around 20–25 per cent of them civilians) died (MacArthur 1993: 255–7) and as the BBC's correspondent John Simpson concluded after the war, 'We didn't see much of that' (cited in Philo and McLaughlin 1995: 155).

The state also defines the laws that govern the disclosure of official information (the Official Secrets Act among others) and the suppression of other categories of information (Leigh 1980). For example, there are powers in the Prevention of Terrorism Act, the Emergency Provisions Act, the Police and Criminal Evidence Act and the Criminal Justice Act to seize journalistic materials. Furthermore the use of such legislation has increased markedly since the 1970s (Miller 1994: ch. 1).

Of course, the existence of such laws is not a strict limitation on the ability to communicate particular information. In fact official sanction on the disclosure of information exists so as to allow state personnel the ability of selective communication (Downing 1986). As Margaret Thatcher's former Press Secretary Bernard Ingham acknowledged:

> I must tell you that I . . . have never regarded the Official Secrets Act as a constraint on my operations. Indeed, I regard myself as licensed to break the law as and when I judge necessary; and I suppose it is necessary to break it every other minute of every working day.
>
> (Ingham 1991: 348)

However, the concept of public service and the limited public accountability of government does mean that they have a greater openness than large corporations whose activities are not required to be publicly scrutinized (Gandy 1992; Rowell 1996, Chapter 4; Stauber and Rampton 1995). PR and lobbying companies also operate secretively since PR practitioners acknowledge that the best PR leaves no trace.

Promotional strategies: lobbying vs media relations

Resources determine the strategies that organizations are able to employ. But resource-rich organizations do not always devote the main part of their efforts to managing the media. It may be that low-profile and discreet lobbying in Whitehall or Brussels is seen as a more effective way of pursuing interests. Indeed it has been suggested that the groups most able to implement this type of 'insider' strategy (W. Grant 1995) are by definition resource-rich since they have superior contacts and are perceived as more respectable, credible and authoritative or representative.

Furthermore, given that British society is characterized by marked inequalities of power and status, the defenders of the current order are likely to need to engage in media management only in so far as change is threatened or desired. This is one explanation of the observation that business tends not to be as visible as its critics in the media (Tumber 1993).

Both of these factors influence the strategies of resource-poor groups. An absence of contacts with government and the aim of political or cultural change can condemn resource-poor groups to strategies and tactics which resource-rich organizations would rarely even consider. Moreover, resource-poor groups may not wish to become entangled in consultative procedures with government for ideological or strategic reasons (W. Grant 1995).

The tactic of outing allegedly gay bishops or MPs is an example of such a strategy, as is the use of demonstrations, anti-road protests and even that of armed struggle. As Gerry Adams of Sinn Fein has put it:

> The tactic of armed struggle is of primary importance because it provides a vital cutting edge. Without it the issue of Ireland would not even be an issue. So, in effect, the armed struggle becomes armed propaganda.
>
> (Adams 1986: 64)

More prosperous groups tend to concentrate on more orthodox media relations. Nevertheless resource-poor groups are sometimes able to gain coverage in the media and can on occasion influence public debate. This is particularly the case with issue-based campaigning groups which appear to gain a higher profile than those that simply attempt to raise resources or their own profile (Deacon 1996). For example Peter Tatchell of the lesbian and gay activist group Outrage has commented:

> We produce very good quality press releases that back up what we say with hard facts and statistics. It makes it much easier for people to take us seriously.
>
> (cited in Miller and Williams 1993: 132)

The imaginative and highly controversial tactics of Outrage have allowed them to capture the media spotlight for lesbian and gay issues at an unprecedented level. It is this kind of skill and innovation in campaigning strategy which can help the resource-poor group. But however sophisticated their public relations skills, small alternative groups are unlikely to be able to gain sustained positive media coverage in the face of strong competition from resource-rich organizations.

Problems of coherence and division

Conversely, resource-rich organizations are not always able to plan and execute coherent and unified promotional strategies. All organizations, whatever their resources, are likely to contain a variety of competing agendas, political perspectives and professional rivalries. In government departments, for example, there is a history of rivalry between promotional professionals and administrative civil servants (Miller 1993). Furthermore; the involvement of a variety of official bodies in a particular issue can lead to, or be symptomatic of, serious disputes over strategy and tactics. The rivalry between different government agencies in Northern Ireland such as the police, the army, the various intelligence bodies and the Northern Ireland Office are well known and in 1974 the divisions were so serious that a strike by Protestant workers succeeded in bringing down a power-sharing assembly in the face of the government's inability to speak with one voice (Miller 1993). In recent years the food scares over salmonella (in 1988–9) and BSE (Mad Cow Disease in 1990 and 1996) have revealed significant divisions between the Department of Health with its brief for public health and the Ministry of Agriculture with its concern for the farming industry, which have resulted in the two ministries issuing contradictory advice to the public and even attacking each other in off-the-record briefings to the media (Miller and Reilly 1995).

When powerful and resource-rich organizations suffer serious internal problems, are caught in indefensible positions, are attacked by seeming allies or try to maintain a low media profile, resource-poor groups are often able to step into the media spotlight to provide answers to the apparent crisis or fill the news vacuum. Thus in relation to salmonella, radical pressure groups such as the London Food Commission or, in relation to BSE, alternative 'experts' such as Professor Richard Lacey or Stephen Dealler were able to some extent to take the PR initiative (Miller and Reilly 1995).

Yet, too much publicity can be dangerous for radical organizations. Success in gaining media coverage may lead to internal dissent as spokespersons become media friendly. The suspicion within the organization that newly visible spokespersons might become infatuated with their own celebrity and have 'sold out' is never far from the surface (see Anderson 1993; Gitlin 1980; Glasgow University Media Group 1997). Furthermore divisions over strategy and tactics are commonplace, especially of radical or countercultural movements or groups. Divisions within environmental and animal rights groups have increasingly appeared as some become more mainstream. The divisions between organizations campaigning for rights for people with disabilities are absolutely typical. Here the old style of incremental campaigning now competes with the more radical direct action approach of organizations such as the Disabled People's Direct Action Network (DAN), which eschews the gradualist approach and agitates for civil rights rather than 'charity' and sympathy (see Evans, Chapter 24 in this volume). One campaign slogan, fusing radical politics with newsworthy punchiness, reads 'piss on pity'. For the old-style campaigners such tactics are more likely to alienate policy-makers. According to one: 'if you go up to an MP with that on I don't think he or she's likely to warm to you – if they're not already interested' (Parker 1995: 6). For the radicals such an approach smacks of tried and failed reformism. Such differences of emphasis on strategy, tactics and goals are of course partly genuine political differences, but can also indicate strategies of 'product differentiation' and a means of generating extra pressure on decision-makers.

Of course there are occasions on which it is seen as better to cooperate on particular issues. Resource-poor groups can enter tactical or long-term alliances with their resource-rich competitors or even with their apparent enemies. But more commonly pressure groups will join other statutory and non-statutory bodies to create a common strategy, perhaps at European level (Mazey and Richardson 1993).

Media factors

The media operate within a complex set of pressures of ownership, editorial control and economic interest. Journalists do have some measure of autonomy in their daily work routines. But this varies greatly between radio, television and the press, between different channels or newspapers and even between different formats, be they news, current affairs or discussion programmes in the broadcast media or news, features, columns and editorials in the press. These variations are in part a result of variations in news values (see Palmer, Chapter 27 in this volume), but they also reflect the promotional networks which form around varying journalistic beats. At the pinnacle of the news values of broadcasting, the broadsheet press and some elements of the tabloid press is hard news. This typically revolves around the news beats of central government that are covered by political correspondents or lobby journalists. Down a notch in terms of news value are more peripheral government departments such as Defence, Education, Agriculture or Health, which typically have their own corps of specialist journalists. As a result of this form of organization the bulk of political news originates with the central bureaucracies of Whitehall and the political party's news-management apparatus. However, the specialist correspondents are also engaged in attempting to cover the major policy debates or new developments in their field. Furthermore they may have a special page devoted to their output in broadsheet papers such as the health, science or education pages. Such factors do mean that specialists can be more interested in the intricacies of policy debates or in the activities of resource-poor groups than their non-specialist colleagues on the news desk. As a result resource-poor groups who target specialist journalists can often build up a valuable relationship with them and will tend to gain more access to the inside specialist pages than to other sections of the paper. The relationship also has advantages for the specialist journalist in that pressure groups can be used as a research resource. On the other hand, specialists do tend to gravitate towards official sources in their area and may be less likely to view pressure group stunts as newsworthy than their news desk.

Deacon and Golding (1994) suggest that journalists tend to see news sources as either *advocates* of a point of view or constituency who can be used to give a 'balancing' comment, or as *arbiters*, as 'expert witnesses' who can judge the significance or import of events. Both rich and poor groups can move between these designations, though achieving arbiter status is harder than advocate status. Groups at the poorer end of the resource spectrum may be designated arbiters only by specialists. When an issue leaves the specialist pages to move higher up the news agenda to the front pages, most likely when official pronouncements or action are involved, an organization may have to contend with reverting to advocate status. Such differences are also inflected by varying news values across the media. For example, 'cuddly charities', the ones which deal with animals, children or health, are more heavily featured in tabloid and television coverage (Deacon 1996).

The impact and success of promotional strategies

The success and impact of promotional strategies are hard to measure, first, because they have a myriad of aims which are not always clearly conceptualized. Second, they work at different levels. That is, some target international opinion or government, while others simply want to raise funds. Clearly success in raising money at a jumble sale is not the same thing as a successful revolution.

The self-denying status of propaganda, the behind-the-scenes nature of lobbying and the endemic secrecy surrounding the policy process in the UK are further reasons why evaluations of success or impact are difficult. Finally, we should beware of judging success in terms simply of the amount or quality of media coverage, since media coverage does not necessarily or straightforwardly translate into influence (cf. Cracknell 1993). Nevertheless, it is sometimes possible to identify some elements of the process by which decisions come to be made.

Governments, business and interest groups try to manage the media because of a widespread recognition that media reporting can impose limits on organizational action and provide opportunities for extending or moderating public perceptions, and the distribution of power and resources in society (Linsky 1986; Walsh-Childers 1994: 827).

Media strategies can also help to sell government policies such as the privatization of the public utilities in the 1980s (Franklin 1994; Philo 1995). Conversely, even flagship policies of strong governments such as the 'Poll Tax' can fail despite concerted marketing campaigns (Deacon and Golding

1994). In the longer term the strategies of social movements and associated struggles can lead to marked changes in the status and power of social constituencies such as women, Black people and lesbians and gay men. The emergence of issues like racism, violence against women, child sexual abuse, homophobia and even the environment were preceded by long and, on many occasions apparently unsuccessful campaigns to raise awareness and change society (cf. Tiffen 1989: 197–8).

Changing trends?

In contemporary Britain as in many other advanced societies there is an ever increasing spiral of expertise and sophistication in promotional strategies. One indication is the recent use by pressure groups such as Greenpeace of video news releases which are supplied to newsrooms complete with commentary and newsworthy footage. In an increasingly competitive and deregulated international media market strongly influenced by commercial pressure, the ability of rich sources to supply 'information subsidies' is likely to become more not less important.

In addition, the public relations and journalism industries are increasingly converging. One symptom of this is the practice of journalists giving training in public relations technique to politicians or business people, such as the media training venture set up by HTV in 1995. In March 1996 BBC journalists were warned about the potential conflict of interest in giving media training to people whom they are subsequently required to interview, although media training activities were not outlawed (Methven 1996).

It was revealed in 1995 that Independent Television News (ITN) owned a half share of Corporate Television Network (CTN). CTN makes video news releases for corporate clients, some of which had been shown on ITN bulletins (Brooks 1995). This highlights the potential for increased conflict of interest as media companies grow larger and diversify into other parts of the industry. The fact that PR multinational Burson Marstellar owned the other half of the agency also indicates that there is a potential for media companies to become more closely linked with the public relations industry. Such trends will tend to place limits on journalistic integrity and to erode distinctions between the news media and the PR industry as increasingly multinational media conglomerates move into both promoting and reporting news.

And finally . . .

This brings us back to debates about the effects of 'promotional culture' on the democratic process. On the one hand, it can be argued that there has been an increasing sophistication in news management on the part of the powerful, especially in government and business. On the other, that some countervailing pressure has been exerted and that particular social constituencies have to some extent advanced their position in our culture. This seems to speak of an increasing sophistication of promotional strategies on the part of the powerless too. Yet, before we embrace the comforting pluralist notion of relatively open competition for power and resources we should examine both the extent of inequality, the relative prominence of official sources in the media and the results of promotional strategies on the distribution of rewards and resources in society. While winners and losers vary and the type and extent of inequality in contemporary society does change, it is clear that western countries remain radically inegalitarian societies. Indeed in some cases (such as Britain), whatever the victories of the resource-poor in the media, inequalities of wealth and power have actually become dramatically wider since the beginning of the 1980s.

Public relations and promotional politics can be viewed as positive or negative for democracy, but it is difficult to see the promotional dynamic in wholly negative terms when it provides some of the very few opportunities for the powerless to answer back. Furthermore, there is no intrinsic reason why the inequalities of promotional politics should not be diminished by political intervention. This would of itself secure a greater and wider public participation in the public sphere. Whether or not such developments come to pass, the promotional dynamic is here to stay.

Questions

1 Is the government always more credible for the news media than a pressure group?

2 Are pressure groups condemned to rely on publicity stunts to promote their aims?

3 Using an example selected from contemporary news coverage, analyse the promotional strategy of one or more of the following: a government department, a corporate organization, a pressure group, and attempt to assess the relative success or failure of the strategy.

References

Adams, G. (1986) *The Politics of Irish Freedom*, Dingle, Co. Kerry: Brandon.

Andersen, S. and Eliassen, K. (1995) 'EU lobbying: the new research agenda', *European Journal of Political Research*, 27: 427–41.

Anderson, A. (1991) 'Source strategies and the communication of environmental affairs', *Media, Culture and Society* 13(4): 459–76.

Anderson, A. (1993) 'Source–media relations: the production of the environmental agenda', in A. Hansen (ed.) *The Mass Media and Environmental Issues*, Leicester: Leicester University Press.

Blumler, J. and Gurevitch, M. (1995) *The Crisis of Public Communication*, London: Routledge.

Bolton, R. (1990) *Death on the Rock and Other Stories*, London: Optomen/W.H. Allen.

Brooks, R. (1995) 'ITN "has fingers in both pies" on video news', *Observer* 10 September: 4.

Carruthers, S. (1995) *Winning Hearts and Minds: British Governments, the Media and Colonial Counter-Insurgency, 1944–1960*, Leicester: Leicester University Press.

Cockerell, M. (1988) *Live from Number 10*, London: Faber.

Cockerell, M., Hennessy, P. and Walker, D. (1985) *Sources Close to the Prime Minister*, London: Macmillan.

Cook, T. (1989) *Making Laws and Making News*, Washington, DC: Brookings.

Cracknell, J. (1993) 'Issue arenas, pressure groups and environmental agenda', in A. Hansen (ed.) *The Mass Media and Environmental Issues*, Leicester: Leicester University Press.

Crofts, W. (1989) *Coercion or Persuasion: Propaganda in Britain after 1945*, London: Routledge.

Curran, J. (1991) 'Rethinking the media as a public sphere', in P. Dahlgren and C. Sparks (eds) *Communication and Citizenship*, London: Routledge.

Curran, J. and Seaton, J. (1995) *Power without Responsibility: The Press and Broadcasting in Britain*, 4th edn, London: Routledge.

Curran, J., Gurevitch, M. and Woollacott, J. (1982) 'The study of the media: theoretical approaches', in M. Gurevitch, T. Bennett, J. Curran and J. Woollacott (eds) *Culture, Society and the Media*, London: Methuen.

Deacon, D. (1996) 'The voluntary sector in a changing communication environment: a case study of non-official news sources', *European Journal of Communication* 11(2): 173–99.

Deacon, D. and Golding, P. (1994) *Taxation and Representation*, London: John Libbey.

Downing, J. (1986) 'Government secrecy and the media in the United States and Britain', in P. Golding, G. Murdock and P. Schlesinger (eds) *Communicating Politics: Mass Communications and the Political Process*, Leicester: Leicester University Press.

Engel, M. (1996) 'Protest locale that can't square the circle', *Guardian* 25 March: 2.

Ericson, R., Baranek, P. and Chan, J. (1989) *Negotiating Control: A Study of News Sources*, Buckingham: Open University Press.

Franklin, B. (1994) *Packaging Politics*, London: Edward Arnold.

Gandy, O. (1980) 'Information in health: subsidised news', *Media, Culture and Society* 2: 103–15.

Gandy, O. (1992) 'Public relations and public policy: the structuration of dominance in the information age', in E. Toth and R. Heath (eds) *Rhetorical and Critical Approaches to Public Relations*, Hillsdale, NJ: Lawrence Erlbaum.

Gans, H. (1980) *Deciding What's News*, London: Constable.

Gitlin, T. (1980) *The Whole World is Watching*, Berkeley, CA: University of California Press.

Glasgow University Media Group (1997) *Dying of Ignorance: AIDS, the Media and Public Belief*, London: Sage.

Goldenberg, E.N. (1975) *Making the Papers: The Access of Resource-Poor Groups to the Metropolitan Press*, Lexington, MA: D.C. Heath.

Grant, L. (1995) 'Just say no', *Guardian Weekend* 3 June: 12–22.

Grant, W. (1995) *Pressure Groups, Politics and Democracy in Britain*, 2nd edn, Hemel Hempstead: Harvester Wheatsheaf.

Hall, S., Critcher, C., Jefferson, T., Clarke, J. and Roberts, B. (1978) *Policing the Crisis: Mugging, the State and Law and Order*, London: Macmillan.

Harris, R. (1990) *Good and Faithful Servant*, London: Faber.

Ingham, B. (1991) *Kill the Messenger*, London: HarperCollins.

Jackall, R. (ed.) (1994) *Propaganda*, London: Macmillan.

Jones, N. (1986) *Strikes and the Media*, Oxford: Blackwell.

Jones, N. (1995) *Soundbites and Spin Doctors*, London: Cassell.

Kellner, D. (1992) *The Persian Gulf TV War*, Boulder, CO: Westview.

Kisch, R. (1964) *The Private Life of Public Relations*, London: MacGibbon & Kee.

Leigh, D. (1980) *The Frontiers of Secrecy*, London: Junction.

Leigh, D. and Vulliamy, E. (1997) *Sleaze: the Corruption of Parliament*, London: Fourth Estate.

Linsky, M. (1986) *Inpact: How the Press Affects Federal Policymaking*, New York: W. W. Norton.

MacArthur, J. (1993) *Second Front: Censorship and Propaganda in the Gulf War*, Berkeley, CA: University of California Press.

McNair, B. (1994) *Political Communication: An Introduction*, London: Routledge.

Mazey, S. and Richardson, J. (1993) 'Pressure groups and the EC', *Politics Review*, 3(1): 20–4.

Methven, N. (1996) 'BBC restates ban on outside work by freelances', *UK Press Gazette* 22 March.

Miller, D. (1991) 'The media on the rock: The media and the Gibraltar killings', in B. Rolston (ed.) *The Media and Northern Ireland: Covering the Troubles*, London: Macmillan.

Miller, D. (1993) 'Official sources and primary definition: the case of Northern Ireland', *Media, Culture and Society* 15(3): 385–406.

Miller, D. (1994) *Don't Mention the War: Northern Ireland, Propaganda and the Media*, London: Pluto.

Miller, D. and Reilly, J. (1995) 'Making an issue of food safety: the media, pressure groups and the public sphere', in D. Maurer and J. Sobal (eds) *Eating Agendas: Food, Eating and Nutrition as Social Problems*, New York: Aldine de Gruyter.

Miller, D. and Williams, K. (1993) 'Negotiating HIV/AIDS information: agendas, media strategies and the news', in Glasgow University Media Group, *Getting the Message*, London: Routledge.

Moloney, K. (1996) *Lobbyists for Hire*, Aldershot: Dartmouth.

Nelson, J. (1989) *Sultans of Sleaze: Public Relations and the Media*, Toronto: Between the Lines.

Norton-Taylor, R. (1995) *Truth is a Difficult Concept: Inside the Scott Inquiry*, London: Guardian Books.

Parker, I. (1995) 'Spitting on charity', *Independent on Sunday Review* 9 April: 4–6.

Philo, G. (1995) 'Television, politics and the rise of the new right', in G. Philo (ed.) *The Glasgow Media Group Reader, vol. II*, London: Routledge.

Philo, G. and McLaughlin, G. (1995) 'The British media and the Gulf War', in G. Philo (ed.) *The Glasgow Media Group Reader, vol. II*, London: Routledge.

Porter, H. (1995) 'Crowd control', *Guardian G2* 12 October: 2–3.

PR Week (1996) 'Boom time', 26 April: 15.

Rowell, A. (1996) *Green Backlash: Global Subversion of the Environment Movement*, London: Routledge.

Schlesinger, P. (1990) 'Rethinking the sociology of journalism: source strategies and the limits of media-centrism', in M. Ferguson (ed.) *Public Communication: The New Imperatives*, London: Sage.

Schlesinger, P. and Tumber, H. (1994) *Reporting Crime*, Oxford: Clarendon.

Sigal, L. (1986) 'Who? Sources make the news', in R.K. Manoff and M. Schudson (eds) *Reading the News*, New York: Pantheon.

Stauber, J.C. and Rampton, S. (1995) *Toxic Sludge is Good for You: Lies, Damn Lies and the Public Relations Industry*, Monroe, ME: Common Courage.

Tiffen, R. (1989) *News and Power*, Sydney: Allen & Unwin.

Tilson, D. (1993) 'The shaping of "eco-nuclear" publicity: the use of visitors centres in public relations', *Media, Culture and Society* 15(3): 419–36.

Tulloch, J. (1993) 'Policing the public sphere: the British machinery of news management', *Media, Culture and Society* 15(3): 363–84.

Tumber, H. (1993) '"Selling scandal": business and the media', *Media, Culture and Society* 15(3): 345–62.

Tunstall, J. (1973) *The Advertising Man*, London: Chapman & Hall.

Vidal, J. and Bellos, A. (1996) 'Protest lobbies unite to guard rights', *Guardian* 27 August: 5.

Walsh-Childers, K. (1994) '"A death in the family": a case study of newspaper influence on health policy development', *Journalism Quarterly* 71(4): 820–9.

Wernick, A. (1991) *Promotional Culture*, London: Sage.

Further reading

The best general reading advice is to read the papers and watch television!

Cockerell, M., Hennessy, P. and Walker, D. (1985) *Sources Close to the Prime Minister*, London: Macmillan.

Deacon, D. and Golding, P. (1994) *Taxation and Representation*, London: John Libbey.

Franklin, B. (1994) *Packaging Politics*, London: Edward Arnold.

Harris, R. (1990) *Good and Faithful Servant,* London: Faber.

Ingham, B. (1991) *Kill the Messenger,* London: Harper Collins.

Jones, N. (1995) *Soundbites and Spin Doctors,* London: Cassell.

Kellner, D. (1992) *The Persian Gulf TV War,* Boulder, CO: Westview.

MacArthur, J. (1993) *Second Front: Censorship and Propaganda in the Gulf War,* Berkeley, CA: University of California Press.

McNair, B. (1994) *Political Communication: An Introduction,* London: Routledge.

Miller, D. (1994) *Don't Mention the War: Northern Ireland, Propaganda and the Media,* London: Pluto.

Scammell, M. (1995) *Designer Politics: How Elections are Won,* London: Macmillan.

Schlesinger, P. and Tumber, H. (1994) *Reporting Crime,* Oxford: Clarendon.

Stauber, C. and Rampton, S. (1995) ' "Democracy for hire": public relations and environmental movements', *The Ecologist* 25(5): 173–80.

Stauber, C. and Rampton, S. (1995) *Toxic Sludge is Good for You: Lies, Damn Lies and the Public Relations Industry,* Monroe, ME: Common Courage.

Tulloch, J. (1993) 'Policing the public sphere: the British machinery of news management', *Media, Culture and Society* 15(3): 363–84.

Chapter 7

Newspapers and the press

NEWSPAPERS: BEYOND POLITICAL ECONOMY

JAMES CURRAN

This chapter looks at the various influences that shape the media and in particular the press. However, there is a tendency for any summary of the relevant literature to become confusing due to the diametrically opposed viewpoints of many of the leading analysts. This chapter suggests that in order to find a way through this maze of contradictory opinion and analysis, some form of critical synthesis needs to be achieved; towards this end a brief case study of the British newspaper industry is included.

Liberal optimism

The press in liberal democracies is, according to liberal orthodoxy, an independent institution that empowers the people. This upbeat view is at the very heart of traditional liberal press history (e.g. Alexander 1981; Emery 1972). Thus, according to this theory, the press evolved from being an agency of the state to becoming the adjunct of political parties, before its final liberation through commercialization (Koss 1981, 1984). This resulted, it is argued, in the press being controlled by market-led pragmatists who follow public demand. The dominating influence over the press in this final 'free' phase is said to be the sovereign consumer (Koss 1984).

This celebratory historical tradition is implicitly qualified by liberal ethnographic studies of news organizations. These tend to play down the influence of consumers, and stress instead the central role of media professionals who are sometimes uninformed about what their audiences want but have strong views about what they need. The best known of these ethnographies, a study of US news media by Herbert Gans (1980), advances the key argument that the division of labour within media organizations leads to a dispersal of control. For example, the separation of advertising and editorial departments results in story selection and advertisement placements taking place separately, and coming together only at the last moment, in a way that limits the power of advertisers. Similarly the power of owners, Gans claims, is limited by the delegation and subdivision of authority within news organizations. While big business corporations are 'nominal managers', 'news organisations and journalists are the actual ones' (Gans 1980: 229).

Gans's second key argument is that 'delegation of power also takes place because the news organisation consists of professionals who insist on individual autonomy' (Gans 1980: 101). Pressures on journalists to follow a line or suppress information are rare, and are strongly resisted. They conflict with the professional values of journalists who derive their self-respect from their professionalism, and who receive strong support from their peers in doing so. This professional orientation includes a strong commitment to detachment and objectivity, and a belief in the importance of ensuring that the public is adequately informed.

Gans's (1980) conclusions find support in Tunstall's (1970) pioneering study of British specialist correspondents and Hetherington's (1985) later study of British news organizations. However, all three studies contain 'small print' statements or evidence that qualify their portrayal of professional autonomy. These suggest that reporters have less personal decision-making power than they think they have because they are part of a production process. They have no control over whether their copy is published or how it is subedited. They also tend to feel free because they are inclined to internalize the norms of their employing organization, or regard its routine requirements as legitimate. Research since Gans's landmark work also suggests that North American news media have become more subject to consumer/market influence (Hallin 1996; McManus 1994). Tunstall's (1996) later study also argues that editors in the British national press have become more assertive, and that the bottom end of the journalism profession has become more economically insecure in way that is likely to weaken their professional independence.

If liberal history celebrates the consumer, and liberal ethnography salutes more guardedly the media professional, there is a third liberal tradition that focuses on the news source. According to this third tradition, it is the suppliers of news, not its purveyors or consumers, who are the real figures of power. Allegedly, only an excessive 'media-centrism', an undue preoccupation with internal organizational processes, has masked the extent to which control lies outside news media (Schlesinger 1990). Liberal versions of this argument, such as that advanced by Hansen (1991), emphasize competition between these sources, reflecting the plurality of different groups vying for media attention and influence (see Miller, Chapter 6 of this volume).

A fourth strand of liberal interpretation sees the media as reflecting the cultural values of a socially harmonious society. The news judgements employed by journalists, the premises and assumptions on which their reports are grounded, are said to be framed by the common culture of society. Good examples of this general approach are provided by two studies of the Swedish press which demonstrate that newspaper editorials and advertising came to express more egalitarian values (Block 1981; Nowak 1984). This is attributed to a shift in the core values of Swedish society, also registered in a movement towards a more egalitarian distribution of incomes.

Clearly, these different arguments can be woven together into a coherent liberal synthesis (of which the most persuasive is a maverick version advanced by Schudson 1996). News media can be seen as being shaped by consumer demand, the professional concerns of media workers, pluralistic source networks, and the collective values of society. While the liberal tradition is not agreed about the relative weight that should be accorded different influences, it has in common a general tendency to see the media as serving the public.

There is also beginning to develop a distinctive postmodernist version of this approach. Essentially, it rehearses traditional liberal themes but in a context of society characterized by rapid change, fluid identities and increasing pluralism. An eloquent example of postmodernism is the work of Angela McRobbie (1994, 1996) on women's magazines. In contrast to traditional radical feminists who have been inclined to view the women's press as vehicles of patriarchal culture, McRobbie argues that the women's magazine press is changing, and that some successful magazines now offer relatively liberated definitions of what it is to be a contemporary woman. This is, she suggests, a direct consequence of the way in which these magazines operate. They conduct market research into what their readers want; they respond to circulation shifts in a competitive market overflowing with titles; they recruit young journalists, some exposed to feminism through media studies courses, many of whom have developed a strong rapport with their readers; and as organizations they are subject to 'complex and contested social processes'. It is because these publications are exposed to a multiplicity of influences that they are responsive to the flux and change around them, and in particular to changing gender values.

Radical pessimism

Such accounts are shrugged off by radical critics as naïve. According to this alternative viewpoint, both liberal and postmodernist approaches overstate the power of human agency because they fail to grasp the way in which personal choices are structured by standard formats, conventions and the play of power. What is meant by this rather intimidating line of argument?

One standard radical theme is that media enterprises have grown from relatively small, independent organizations, their characteristic form in the nineteenth century, into units within large business corporations that are strongly oriented towards maximizing profits rather than promoting good journalism. These corporations have extensive holdings in industry and finance (Bagdikian 1992; Murdock 1990), and consequently a strong interest in the tax, interest rate, labour relations, industrial and contractor policies of the government. This influences both their orientation towards government and the politics of the media under their control (Herman and Chomsky 1988). Furthermore, a corporate culture and web of interlocking director-ships have evolved in a form that has encouraged the development of a shared outlook between commercial media and other business leaders (Murdock 1982a, 1982b). Rather than functioning as an independent fourth estate, media businesses are thus increasingly commercial mercenaries. As Douglas Kellner (1990: 172–3) writes, 'it is because of the control of media institutions by multinational capital (big business) that the media have been biased towards conservatism, thus furthering what they see as their own economic interests'.

Media owners, and those to whom they delegate power, shape the ethos of media organizations. They determine overall policy, set budgets, make senior appointments and establish a reward structure that encourages staff conformity. Dissident staff tend not to be given good assignments, and are liable to be shunted sideways or simply sacked. However, controls usu-ally operate unobtrusively through initial staff selection, and through self-censorship, rather than through overt coercion (Chomsky 1989; Parenti 1993).

The power of owners is supplemented by that of advertisers and the capitalist state. Advertisers provide the main source of revenue of most newspapers and free-to-air TV channels. They sometimes use this economic power, it is argued, to promote their ideological commitments, as well as to silence radical critics (Bagdikian 1992; Baker 1994). The state also features in radical accounts, particularly of broadcasting organizations, as a source of direct and indirect censorship exercised through control over appoint-ments, funding and broadcast regulation (Miliband 1973).

The general thrust of this analysis is to see the media as being subject to multiple controls exercised by a dominant class or group in a deliberate and intentional way. However, there is another strand of radical argument that owes more to neo-Keynesianism than to Marxism. This argues that the media are subject to constraints rather than controls, and that these arise out of impersonal processes that are largely unsought and undesired (Curran 1986; Golding and Murdock 1996; Gustafsson 1993). Yet, their effect is to skew profoundly the way in which the media relate to society.

The start-up costs of new enterprises in the mass media market have also risen to such an extent that all but the rich are excluded. This is, according to critics, a key form of invisible censorship. Second, there is a recurring tendency for media concentration to develop, leading to reduced choice and less consumer control. Third, advertising is drawn disproportionately to media used by affluent audiences, which encourages media producers to privilege their concerns. Finally, the economic benefits of size create a magnetic pull, it is argued, towards the terrain of maximum sales and, con-sequently, the ideological middle ground.

This approach is paralleled by radical social organizational studies. These argue that the media are bureaucracies guided by procedures directed to-wards serving their own welfare rather than that of the public (Fishman 1980,

1982; Sigal 1987; Tuchman 1978). News media organize news-gathering around a network of powerful institutions and groups because these seem to be at the centre of things, and employ public relations executives who make the work of journalists easier. Journalists also write up their stories within formats that are designed to make it easy to write quickly, in relation to topics that they know nothing about, with limited time and resources at their disposal, in a form that is liable to minimize offence. The result is twofold: news organizations typically rely on a narrow range of elite sources, and they use self-effacing formulae (such as quoting opposed statements, the truth of which is not evaluated) that result in delegating considerable editorial control to these sources. The implications of this argument can be wrenched, as we have seen, into a pluralist groove by stressing source competition. However, the way this argument is usually presented in traditional radical research is to maintain that the media reflect the elite consensus (Fishman 1982; Hall 1986).

A further way in which informal control is exercised over the media is through the dominant discourses of society patterned over time by the superior symbolic and material resources available to powerful groups. An eloquent illustration of this argument is provided by Graham Murdock in a study of news reporting of urban disturbances in the early 1980s (1984). He shows how reporting drew upon a conservative 'common-sense' view of the sources of civic disorder, partly prompted by news informants but also cued by a readily available repertoire of imagery and explanation. This not only derived from recent reporting of muggers, football hooligans and Irish terrorism but also drew upon time-worn themes from the past developed around alien agitators, Black hordes and 'King Mob'. News media absorbed and reproduced right-wing interpetations that were carried, like pollen, in the air that journalists breathed.

These different radical descriptions of the media have been synthesized in a number of accounts. The most influential of these is that offered by Herman and Chomsky (1988) who see the media as being controlled through a combination of private ownership, advertising power, elite sources, state pressure and cultural dominance. These are likened to 'filters' that siphon out radical meanings, leaving only a residue of largely conservative interpetation. Some debate takes place within the media but only within defined limits consonant with the interests of established privilege.

Context and difference

We are thus presented with diametrically opposed accounts of the media. In the traditional liberal approach, the media are bottom-up channels of popular power; in the traditional radical one, they are strictly top-down agencies of control.

One response to this head-to-head confrontation is to consider whether discrepancies of interpretation are the result of differences between countries. After all media systems vary, as do the wider societal contexts in which the media operate. The extent to which this is the case tends to be concealed by the available English-language literature on the media which tends to concentrate on relatively few countries.

However, some contradictory interpetations can relate to the same country at the same time. Others are presented as generalized models, in Chomsky's (1989) case for example as a revelation of how thought control operates in liberal democracies and in Alexander's (1981) case as an ideal-typical account of how free media contribute to the welfare of liberal democracies. They cannot all be valid.

This means that either we have to come down on one side or the other, or we have to consider whether it is not preferable to arrive at a synthesis of these conflicting approaches. The case study that follows suggests that this third option has much to recommend it. The British press, as we shall see, is subject to both top-down and bottom-up 'countervailing' influences. Elements of both liberal and radical interpretation can be combined in a way that seems to illuminate the influences that shape British newspapers.

British newspapers: economic regulation

In contrast to most other countries, the UK has a dominant national newspaper press which accounts for about two-thirds of total daily circulation. In 1997 the national press comprises ten daily and nine Sunday titles operating in a highly competitive market. This is in marked contrast to the local press which consists largely of local monopoly daily papers, and local weekly (paid and freesheet) papers which are often part of a regionally dominant newspaper chain.

The national press is more right-wing than its readers. In three general elections (1983, 1987, 1992), the Conservative vote never rose above 42 per cent. Yet the Conservative press accounted for between 64 and 78 per cent of national newspaper circulation (Seymour-Ure 1996: 218–19). In other words, it exceeded by at least half the Conservative party's share of the vote.

One key to understanding why there should be such a profound difference between editorial and electoral opinion is the closed shop nature of publishing. It costs over £20 million to establish a new national daily newspaper. This high cost excludes talent with limited resources. Over half the national paper titles in the UK were launched before 1920. All the remainder were launched, or acquired, by a leading newspaper group.

This pattern of market exclusion results in a national press owned not by a plurality of social groups but overwhelmingly by big business. Some groups like News International and the Telegraph Group are part of global media empires: others like the Mail Group (Associated Newspapers) are centred in Britain. Some like the United Media-MAI Group still have extensive interests outside the leisure industries: most others have focused their core activities around communications. Yet common to them all is a shared vested interest in having a government and policies favourable to large-scale, corporate enterprise.

However, what differentiates the press from other large commercial organizations is that most newspaper groups are still dominated by a single shareholder. These dominant shareholders have been more inclined to use their economic power to promote right-wing positions in their newspapers. Typical of this more interventionist generation of publishers is Rupert Murdoch. 'Murdoch, the paper spread out before him', recalls one of his editors, 'would jab his fingers at some article or contribution and snarl, "What do you want to print rubbish like that for?" or pointing to the by-line of a correspondent, assert that "That man's a Commie"' (Giles 1986; cf. Evans 1983). His successor, Andrew Neil, handpicked by Murdoch as an editor with similar views to his own, describes how his proprietor dominated his thoughts even when he was absent.

> Rupert has an uncanny knack of being there even when he is not. When I did not hear from him and I knew his attention was elsewhere, he was still uppermost in my mind. . . . Rupert expects his papers to stand broadly for what he believes: a combination of right-wing Republicanism from America mixed with undiluted Thatcherism from Britain.
>
> (Neil 1996: 165)

The second way in which economics influences the national press is more indirect but no less important. Advertisers pay more to reach high-income than low-income readers; this affects the structure of the national press and its orientation to the public. Five out of ten national daily papers are prestige papers aimed at the top end of the market, and account for a mere 20 per cent of circulation. They cater for, and articulate, the interests of Britain's political class. They also help to sustain elite domination of British politics since they are now the only national newspapers that provide detailed coverage of public affairs. There have been other newspapers offering full accounts of public affairs, written from a different class perspective and some with far larger circulations, but they all closed because they reached less affluent readers and failed to attract adequate advertising. Thus, what keeps alive a prestige press, and amplifies elite perspectives, and denies an equivalent voice to others, is an unequal advertising subsidy rooted in disparities of income and wealth in society.

Political regulation

The American scholar Michael Schudson (1996) complains that political economists tend to focus on the economic to the exclusion of the political. The implication is that restrictive political controls tend to be underplayed.

Certainly, the British press is subject to more restrictive laws than those in the USA. In particular, the Official Secrets Act and defamation law in the UK are more limiting than their equivalent across the Atlantic (Robertson and Nicol 1992). The British press also lacks any constitutional protection upholding freedom of expression, or a right of access to public records, of the sort established in the USA.

There are various other ways in which state regulation or policy impinge on the press. Since 1965, the press has been subject to special anti-monopoly rules designed to restrict the growth of press concentration. Broadcasting regulation has limited the expansion of the press into terrestrial television and radio. In addition, the press receives a very large subsidy in the form of zero VAT rating on newspaper sales. The Press Complaints Commission, the heir to the Press Council, with a remit to investigate public complaints against the press, also exists only because of external political pressure.

In principle, therefore, there are a number of levers that could be manipulated by public officials in order to secure a favourable press. But in practice, this has not happened. The Press Complaints Commission has no powers, and its strictures can be – and are – ignored at will. Anti-monopoly controls limiting the growth of press concentration have been consistently bypassed over a thirty-year period, while limits on cross-media ownership were substantially eased by the Broadcasting Act 1996. No government has threatened to withdraw the press's VAT concession. Indeed, rather than the press being intimidated by government, it would be truer to argue that successive governments have been intimidated by the press. In reality, the press largely defines the regulatory environment in which it operates (Tunstall 1996).

Press and politics

Yet although the press is 'deregulated', it has been at times intensely loyal to the government. During the run-up to the 1987 general election, for example, the national press consisted mainly of passionately pro-government newspapers. During the same period, the broadcasting system offered much more space to critical and anti-government perspectives despite being subject to extensive content and structural regulation by the state.

What this seeming paradox highlights is the limitations of conventional liberal analysis. This portrays the press as an independent institution forever locked into an adversarial relationship with government which it oversees on behalf of the people. Only the extension of state powers over the press, according to this view, can 'chill' the press's zeal in critically scrutinizing the actions of government. What this conventional analysis fails to acknowledge is that the press is not fully independent. It can be loyal to the government of the day because those who own and control it are government supporters. What it also fails to grasp is that it is possible for a media organ-ization like the BBC to be an institution of the state, yet owe its allegiance to the public.

The key to explaining the politics of the press during the 1980s was the Thatcherite mobilization of a social bloc including large-scale business. Under Thatcher's leadership, the Conservative government promised economic regeneration on the basis of low taxes, a slimmed down state, anti-union legislation and privatization, and for a time seemed to be delivering on its prospectus. Much of the national press were the government's principal cheer-leaders.

Yet this relationship was more fragile than it appeared at the time. It was not rooted in party funding of the press, as in the early twentieth century. Nor was it anchored to secure partisan loyalties, as in the 1950s. Powerful publishers like Murdoch and Black (owning between them six Conservative newspapers) were global business tycoons with right-wing views but with no special attachment to the Conservative Party as an institution. During 1994–5 much of the Conservative press attacked the Conservative Prime Minister, John Major, with a vehemence usually reserved for the left. This was fuelled by right-wing factional opposition, a loss of confidence in Major as leader, and divisions within the business community over Europe. However, this is only part of the explanation: the press was also responding to professional journalistic concerns and public disaffection.

The press is not simply the product of those who own and control it, and of the hinterland they occupy; it is also powerfully influenced by counter-vailing influences both inside and outside newspaper organizations.

Some countervailing influences

The power of owners is constrained by the professional culture of journal-ists. This professional culture has a craft element based on pride in a tech-nical job well done, which is essentially conformist. But it has also a normative element rooted in beliefs about how journalists should serve society. It is this public interest component, transcending newspaper organizations, which provides a potential counter-balance to press control.

Thus, journalists at the *Sunday Times* put up a determined rearguard action during the early 1980s against what they saw as a management-inspired, right-wing shift in the paper's news agenda. Their colleagues at the *Observer* went even further, and were considerably more successful, in resisting changes during the same period also inspired by a new owner, Tiny Rowland. Thus, Rowland backed down in 1984 after ordering his editor, Donald Trelford, to suppress a report of atrocities in Zimbabwe, which jeopardized the parent company's extensive business activities in that country. The rea-son for Rowland's humiliating reversal was that he was opposed not only by his editor but also by the paper's entire journalistic staff.

Professional norms are not confined to journalists but penetrate deep into the culture of newspaper management, a significant number of whom are former news reporters. It also transcends political differences. One significant reason why the Conservative press turned on the Conservative government after 1992 was because it became associated with political 'sleaze'. Politicians' sale of influence in return for money, symbolized by the asking of Commons questions for cash payments, was exposed and attacked as much by newspapers on the right as on the left. It violated journalists' own professional norms, and what they thought should be the norms of democracy.

The professional culture of journalists has also contributed to the evolution of news conventions and formats. These are currently in a process of transition. Traditional distinctions between fact and opinion are weakening with the gradual blurring of news and features; so-called 'straight' reports are giving way to more transparently angled ones; former standards of accuracy are declining, at any rate in the eyes of the public. But it is still the case that contending opinion is routinely quoted in news reports of contentious issues in the national press. This convention significantly limits the partisanship of national newspapers.

One of its consequences is that the press routinely responds to shifts in the balance of power in society because this leads to changes in the composition and status of 'accredited' news sources. The relationship between societal change and source change is imperfect because the press is skewed towards elite sources (an issue discussed further by Miller, Chapter 6 in this volume). But the very fact that the news convention of 'balance' exists at all means that the press responds, however inadequately, at the level of interpretation and signification, to changes in the political environment. Thus, Stuart Hall and his colleagues (1978) show how in the early 1970s the press responded to a closed loop of news sources – the police, judiciary and politicians – who fostered a moral panic about muggers, and promoted a repressive law and order agenda. Yet, Schlesinger and Tumber (1994) show how law and order had become almost two decades later a highly contested terrain in which effective pressure groups, with significant political and other allies, gained access to the press (especially broadsheets) and opened up a fusillade of criticism concerned with prison reform, police violence and miscarriages of justice. The contrast seemingly reflected the intensification of pressure group and campaigning activity. Similarly, Deacon and Golding (1994) offer a classic exposition of how popular, political, local state and specialist professional opposition profoundly influenced press representations of the poll tax, including coverage in papers supporting the Thatcher government which introduced the new tax.

If professional and source influences are potentially a countervailing force limiting economic control of the British press, so too is the culture of society. The political culture of Britain is ambivalent. It contains profoundly conservative elements sustained by a state that has never been fully modernized. But it contains tenacious social democratic elements, that not only are strongly embedded in the culture of the working class but also penetrate all sections of society. This generates an opposed stream of images and explanations that can spring unsummoned into the minds of journalists. When a right-wing tabloid newspaper, for example, calls a highly paid head of a privatized utilty company a 'fat cat', it is giving visceral expression to an underlying egalitarianism that exists beneath the surface of British society to a much greater extent than in the USA.

The balance and admixture of conservative and social democratic elements in the UK's political culture changes over time, and this can influence the press in another profound but more indirect way. It can affect the way in which different journalistic conventions are applied. There are some topics and times (e.g. Remembrance Day) when journalists are unqualifiedly affirmative because they feel that they are giving expression to the shared values of society. There are other topics which are the subject of legitimized controversy (e.g. the government's autumn Budget) where journalists adopt a more 'balanced' approach by quoting or paraphrasing opposed views. And, lastly, there are topics where journalists assume again the collective voice of society, but this time to condemn and stigmatize (as in relation to paedophiles). There are of course gradations between these three modes of address. But the key point is that the boundaries between them shift over time, in response to wider changes.

This is borne out by press coverage of the royal family. In the late 1970s and early 1980s, immediately following the Queen's Silver Jubilee celebrations in 1977 and the marriage between Prince Charles and Lady Diana Spencer in 1981, the royal family were reported in a largely celebratory way: they were projected as symbols of national unity and moral consensus. But in response to their own domestic upheavals, and the accelerated erosion of social deference during the Thatcher years, they came to be profiled in the national press (and also TV) in a more critical way. They featured more often as a form of royal soap opera and the purpose and future of the monarchy were discussed more frequently within the conventions of neutrality, with loyal support balanced by criticism. The royals (with the partial exception of the Queen) lost their sacral status: they ceased to belong to the domain where journalists suspend their critical judgement and act as priests in rites of national communion. Indeed, one former member of the royal family – 'Fergie', Duchess of York – even acquired for a time the status of 'moral deviant', and came to be denigrated in a journalistic voice usually reserved for social outcasts.

One key dynamo in this process, and in the wider connection between press and society, is consumer power. This power is qualified by the oligopolistic structure of the national press. Just five, relatively centralized groups control 96 per cent of national newspaper circulation in the UK so that the large number of national newspaper titles in fact exaggerates the real range of choice available (Department of National Heritage 1995). Consumer power is also limited, in political terms, by the increasing dominance of entertainment content in the tabloid press with the result that growing numbers of people select newspapers without reference to their political allegiance. But even so, the freedom of press controllers to preach right-wing politics is constrained by the freedom of readers, with different views and perhaps more importantly different social experiences, to buy only those papers that they find pleasurable. This sets up a field of tension between the ideological commitments of press controllers and the different perspectives of large numbers of readers.

This conflict has been negotiated or resolved in different ways. Historically, one way has been for political coverage to shrink in relative terms in favour of content (such as human interest stories, entertainment features and sport) that the generality of readers find more interesting. By 1976 no popular newspaper devoted more than 20 per cent of its editorial content to coverage of public affairs (Curran and Seaton 1997).

Another has been for publishers to be overridden, at times, by the market. An example of this was when the *Daily Express* secured an exclusive story about Princess Diana making nuisance calls to her former friend, Oliver Hoare, which was spiked on the instructions of the paper's proprietor, Lord Stevens, on the grounds that the story would damage the royal family. The *News of the World* then obtained the story, forcing the *Sunday Express* to run it as a 'spoiler'. Audience demand for soap opera stories about the royal family overpowered the protective conservatism of a traditionalist proprietor.

Sometimes, however, publishers have imposed their views in opposition to those of many of their readers. This is borne out by the gulf between editorial and electoral opinion. At other times, the conflicting demands of propaganda and profit are left unresolved resulting in tensions, contradictions or a 'lack of fit' between different elements of the same paper. For example, most right-wing tabloids published leaders during the mid-1980s extolling the need to regenerate Britain through the cultivation of a free enterprise culture. But this recommendation was not reflected in their entertainment pages by articles glamorizing business leaders and holding them up as models for admiration and emulation (in the way that model workers were celebrated in the Soviet press in support of an opposed value system). Press controllers, operating in a market environment, knew that this would have invited derision and boredom – and falling circulations.

Finally, market pressures give rise to different kinds of newspapers catering for different sorts of readers. As indicated earlier, these pressures are distorted by advertising, market entry barriers and the advantages of size. But they are still a pertinent form of influence. Perhaps their most important consequence has been to sustain two national newspaper groups (out of seven in the UK) that publish centre-left newspapers. One of these, the Mirror Group, is effectively owned by banks and financial corporations, and includes among its senior executives people who are strongly anti-socialist. But its national papers are committed to Labour, and the causes of social democracy, because this is thought to be commercially advantageous.

In short, a number of influences propel the British national press towards the orbit of established privilege. But national newspapers are also exposed to countervailing pressures, pulling in a contrary direction. This gives rise to an ambiguous press system that is linked to the power structure of contemporary Britain, without being wholly integrated into it.

Questions

1 What are the main strengths and weaknesses of the radical and liberal approaches to understanding the media?

2 In what ways – if at all – can they be usefully combined in a single analysis?

3 Take a newspaper, and see if you can infer from its content some of the influences – cultural values, professional norms, its ownership, sources, market pressure, etc. – that shape it.

References

Alexander, J. (1981) 'The mass media in systemic, historical and comparative perspective', in E. Katz and T. Szescho (eds) *Mass Media and Social Change*, Beverly Hills, CA: Sage.

Bagdikian, B. (1992) *Media Monopoly*, 4th edn, Boston, MA: Beacon.

Baker, C.E. (1994) *Advertising and a Democratic Press*, Princeton, NJ: Princeton University Press.

Block, E. (1981) 'Freedom and equality: indicators of political change in Sweden, 1945–1975', in K. Rosengren (ed.) *Advances in Content Analysis*, London: Sage.

Chomsky, N. (1989) *Necessary Illusions*, Boston, MA: South End Press.

Curran, (1986) 'The impact of advertising on the British mass media', in R. Collins, J. Curran, R. Garnham, P. Scannell, P. Schlesinger and C. Sparks (eds) *Media, Culture and Society*, London: Sage.

Curran, J. and Seaton, J. (1997) *Power without Responsibility: The Press and Broadcasting in Britain*, 5th edn, London: Routledge.

Deacon, D. and Golding, P. (1994) *Taxation and Representation*, London: John Libbey.

Department of National Heritage (1995) *Media Ownership*, London: HMSO.

Emery, E. (1972) *The Press in America*, 3rd edn, Englewood Cliffs, NJ: Prentice Hall.

Evans, H. (1983) *Good Times, Bad Times*, London: Weidenfeld & Nicolson.

Fishman, M. (1980) *Manufacturing the News*, Austin, TE: University of Texas Press.

Fishman, M. (1982) 'News and non-events: making the visible invisible', in J. Ettema and D.C. Whitney (eds) *Individuals in Mass Media Organizations*, Beverly Hills, CA: Sage.

Gans, H. (1980) *Deciding What's News*, London: Constable.

Giles, F. (1986) *Sundry Times*, London: Murray.

Golding, P. and Murdock, G. (1996) 'Culture, communications, and political economy', in J. Curran and M. Gurevitch (eds) *Mass Media and Society*, 2nd edn, London: Arnold.

Gustafsson, K. (1993) 'Government policies to reduce newspaper entry barriers', *Journal of Media Economics* 6(1).

Hall, S. (1986) 'Media power and class power', in J. Curran, J. Ecclestone, G. Oakley and A. Richardson (eds) *Bending Reality*, London: Pluto.

Hall, S., Critcher, C., Jefferson, T., Clarke, J. and Roberts, B. (1978) *Policing the Crisis: Mugging, the State and Law and Order*, London: Macmillan.

Hallin, D. (1996) 'Commercialism and professionalism in the American news media', in J. Curran and M. Gurevitch (eds) *Mass Media and Society*, 2nd edn, London: Arnold.

Hansen, A. (1991) 'The media and social construction of the environment', *Media, Culture and Society* 13(4).

Herman, E. and Chomsky, N. (1988) *Manufacturing Consent*, New York: Pantheon.

Hetherington, A. (1985) *News, Newspapers and Television*, London: Macmillan.

Kellner, D. (1990) *Television and the Crisis of Democracy*, Boulder, CO: Westview.

Koss, S. (1981, 1984) *The Rise and Fall of the Political Press in Britain*, 2 vols, London: Hamish Hamilton.

McManus, J. (1994) *Market-Driven Journalism*, Thousand Oaks, CA: Sage.

McNair, B. (1996) *News and Journalism*, 2nd edn, London: Routledge.

McRobbie, A. (1994) *Postmodernism and Popular Culture*, London: Routledge.

McRobbie, A. (1996) 'More! New sexualities in girls' and women's magazines', in J. Curran, D. Morley and V. Walkerdine (eds) *Cultural Studies and Communications*, London: Arnold.

Miliband, R. (1973) *The State in Capitalist Society*, London: Quartet.

Murdock, G. (1982a) 'Class, power and the press: problems of conceptualisation and evidence', in H. Christian (ed.) *The Sociology of Journalism and the Press* (Sociological Review Monograph 29), Keele: University of Keele Press.

Murdock, G. (1982b) 'Large corporations and the control of the communications industry', in M. Gurevitch, T. Bennett, J. Curran and J. Woollacott (eds) *Culture, Society and the Media*, London: Methuen.

Murdock, G. (1984) 'Reporting the riots: images and impact', in J. Benyon (ed.) *Scarman and After*, Oxford: Pergamon.

Murdock, G. (1990) 'Redrawing the map of the communications industries: concentration and ownership in the era of privatization', in M. Ferguson (ed.) *Public Communication: the New Imperatives*, London: Sage.

Neil, A. (1996) *Full Disclosure*, London: Macmillan.

Nowak, K. (1984) 'Cultural indicators in Swedish advertising 1950–1975', in G. Melischek, K. Rosengren and J. Stappers (eds) *Cultural Indicators:*

An International Symposium, Vienna: Verlag der Osterriechischen Akademie der Wissenschaften.

Parenti, M. (1993) *Inventing Reality,* 2nd edn, New York: St Martin's Press.

Robertson, G. and Nicol, A. (1992) *Media Law,* 3rd edn, Harmondsworth: Penguin.

Schlesinger, P. (1990) 'Rethinking the sociology of journalism: source strategies and the limits of media-centrism', in M. Ferguson (ed.) *Public Communication: the New Imperatives,* London: Sage.

Schlesinger, P. and Tumber, H. (1994) *Reporting Crime,* Oxford: Clarendon.

Schudson, M. (1996) 'The sociology of news production revisited', in J. Curran and M. Gurevitch (eds) *Mass Media and Society,* 2nd edn, London: Arnold.

Seymour-Ure, C. (1996) *The British Press and Broadcasting since 1945,* 2nd edn, Oxford: Blackwell.

Sigal, L. (1987) 'Sources make the news', in R. Manoff and M. Schudson (eds) *Reading the News,* New York: Pantheon.

Tuchman, G. (1978) *Making News,* New York: Free Press.

Tunstall, J. (1970) *Journalists at Work,* London: Constable.

Tunstall, J. (1996) *Newspaper Power,* Oxford: Clarendon.

Further reading

Curran, (1986) 'The impact of advertising on the British mass media', in R. Collins, J. Curran, R. Garnham, P. Scannell, P. Schlesinger and C. Sparks (eds) *Media, Culture and Society,* London: Sage.

Curran, J. (1987) 'The boomerang effect: the press and the battle for London, 1981–6', in J. Curran, A. Smith and P. Wingate (eds) *Impacts and Influences,* London: Methuen.

Curran, J. (1996) 'Rethinking mass communications', in J. Curran, D. Morley and V. Walkerdine (eds) *Cultural Studies and Communications,* London: Arnold.

Curran, J. and Seaton, J. (1997) *Power without Responsibility: The Press and Broadcasting in Britain,* 5th edn, London: Routledge.

Deacon, D. and Golding, P. (1994) *Taxation and Representation,* London: John Libbey.

Franklin, B. and Murphy, D. (1991) *What News?,* London: Routledge.

Gans, H. (1980) *Deciding What's News,* London: Constable.

Gitlin, T. (1994) *Inside Prime Time,* revised edn, London: Routledge.

Golding, P. and Middleton, S. (1982) *Images of Welfare,* Oxford: Martin Robertson.

Golding, P. and Murdock, G. (1996) 'Culture, communications, and political economy', in J. Curran and M. Gurevitch (eds) *Mass Media and Society,* 2nd edn, London: Arnold.

Hall, S., Critcher, C., Jefferson, T., Clarke, J. and Roberts, B. (1978) *Policing the Crisis: Mugging, the State and Law and Order,* London: Macmillan.

Herman, E. (1995) 'Media in the US political economy', in J. Downing, A. Mohammadi and A. Sreberny-Mohammadi (eds) *Questioning the Media*, 2nd edn, London: Sage.

McNair, B. (1996) *News and Journalism*, 2nd edn, London: Routledge.

Negrine, R. (1994) *Politics and the Mass Media in Britain*, 2nd edn, London: Routledge.

Schlesinger, P. and Tumber, H. (1994) *Reporting Crime*, Oxford: Clarendon.

Schudson, M. (1996) 'The sociology of news production revisited', in J. Curran and M. Gurevitch (eds) *Mass Media and Society*, 2nd edn, London: Arnold.

Seymour-Ure, C. (1996) *The British Press and Broadcasting since 1945*, 2nd edn, Oxford: Blackwell.

Sparks, C. (1986) 'The media and the state', in J. Curran, J. Ecclestone, G. Oakley and A. Richardson (eds) *Bending Reality*, London: Pluto.

Sparks, C. (1995) 'Concentration and market entry in the UK national daily press', *European Journal of Communication* 10(2).

Tunstall, J. (1996) *Newspaper Power*, Oxford: Clarendon.

Chapter 8

Magazines

MAGAZINES: THE BULGING BOOKSTALLS

BRIAN BRAITHWAITE

The medium

The final years of the twentieth century witnessed the thrusting and ever-expanding activity of electronic media – terrestrial, satellite and cable television, the explosion of new radio stations, the domestic revolution of video recorders and the resurgence of the cinema, attributed to the expansion of multi-screen complexes as well as 'blockbuster' films. But against this exciting explosion of feverish growth the magazine industry across Europe is not only alive and kicking but ever innovative and expansive with new products. In the UK there are over 2400 consumer magazines and 3000 specialized, professional and 'business to business' journals. In the rest of Europe there are over 9300 consumer magazines and 22,000 professional trade titles. Even in the former Eastern bloc magazines are thriving – Poland has 300 consumer titles and nearly as many trade titles, while the Czech Republic can boast 2900 consumer and specialized magazines.

(In general magazines are defined as 'consumer' providing readers with leisure-time information and entertainment, or 'business and professional', providing information relevant to readers' working lives. There are also 'specialist' titles, aimed at readers with particular interests such as cars, boats, hobbies, and so on.)

This is an industry which is intensely competitive within itself, constantly evolving and (the secret of its success?) able to split itself into myriad niches to attract and retain audience segments that will appeal to advertisers. This is the factor that makes magazines so singularly unique among the media. Not for magazines the broad sweep of the general audience with the attendant dissipation (or 'wastage') of advertisers' money. (The US magazine business received the message in the 1950s when it endeavoured to compete with television, with the resultant crash of the dinosaurs *Life*, *Look* and the *Saturday Evening Post*.) Magazines have niche markets of women, men, motorists, slimmers, parents, gardeners, teenagers, retired people, 'telly addicts', computer freaks, train spotters, farmers, golfers, holidaymakers, photographers and other specialized reading groups. The range of women's magazines, for instance, is so wide and diverse that advertisers can select their potential audience by age, social class, hobby or leisure interest (see Stoessl, Chapter 18 in this volume). Industry research has always shown intense and discrete loyalty of readers to their magazines – a 'one-to-one' dialogue between editor and reader that is symptomatic of the strength of the medium. Publishers, of course, are never slow to exploit this selling ingredient.

And we are still looking at a growth industry. In the decade 1984–94 the number of consumer titles in the UK alone grew by 45 per cent and business and professional titles by nearly 90 per cent.

The players

The UK

The magazine industry in the UK has experienced considerable ownership changes since the 1950s, particularly in the consumer sector. The formation of the International Publishing Corporation (IPC) in 1968 mopped up, through various take-overs, the distinguished prewar companies of Fleetway, Newnes, Odhams and Hulton Press. So under one roof (in the high-rise offices on London's South Bank, originally dubbed by the trade the Ministry of Magazines) came a complex near-monopoly of women's weekly and monthly titles and specialized magazines. Previous 'eyeball to eyeball' rivals such as *Woman* and *Woman's Own*, *Amateur Gardening* and *Popular Gardening*, *Ideal Home* and *Homes and Gardens*, were suddenly working cheek by jowl and subsequently were to be marketed together. But there were other contenders in the women's market. Two American-owned companies have operated in the UK since 1910 and 1916 respectively: the National Magazine Company and Condé Nast, both specializing in British versions of their successful USA titles including *Vogue*, *Good Housekeeping*, *House and Garden*, *Cosmopolitan*, *Country Living*, *Brides* and *Harpers & Queen*.

The German 'invasion'

The 1980s saw the emergence of two significant magazine publishing companies. From Germany came Gruhner & Jahr (G & J of the UK) with its new monthly *Prima*, already successful in mainland Europe. The magazine, after a successful launch, is still the highest selling women's monthly in the UK. After *Prima* G & J launched the weekly *Best*. G & J was followed into the UK by H. Bauer, publishing the weekly *Bella*. Bauer also publishes the weeklies *Take a Break* (the UK's biggest selling weekly for women) and *That's Life*. These German-owned titles are printed in Germany by their publishers with considerable cost savings. The UK-based publishing company which has made important strides since the 1970s has been EMAP (East Midland Allied Press). Originally a local newspaper company, based in Peterborough, EMAP expanded into specialized newsprint titles in the fishing and motorcycle areas. It moved in the 1980s into teenage titles (*Just 17* and *More*) and made an important move later in the decade by acquisition, notably buying the Murdoch magazines when that giant media company decided to concentrate on newspapers and television. EMAP owns a portfolio of important women's magazines, including *Elle, New Woman* and *Just 17*. It also has considerable trade publishing interests.

The publishing giants

Although there are still many other publishers, often with single publications, the consumer publishing business is dominated by these giants. The continental influence is also evident, apart from the Germans, with *Hello!* from Spain and *Marie Claire* from France. The Dutch company VNU publish a string of puzzle magazines as well as many computer titles. D.C. Thomson in Scotland still publish *People's Friend* (began 1869) as well as their famous children's comics, *The Beano* and *The Dandy*.

Reed, the owners of IPC, merged with the Dutch Elsevier company in 1994. Reed-Elsevier have wide-ranging trade and professional titles in the UK (see Saunders, Chapter 3 in this volume). Other trade players are Haymarket and Miller Freeman.

The pages of *British Rate & Data* (BRAD) illustrate the massive scope of all magazine titles in the UK – not only in the number of titles but also in the width of ownership. There are similar publications for all other European countries.

Europe

Magazines are big business right across Europe. France, for instance, has 2000 consumer titles (1200 business/professional), Denmark 600 (50), Finland 258 (1959), Germany 1800 (3700), Italy 1128 (9119), Switzerland 867 (990), Norway 347 (269), the Netherlands 1200 (4000) and Spain 155 (150). Giant players include Germany's Bertelsman, Axel Springer, Burda and H. Bauer, Italy's Mondadori, France's Bayard Presse and Fillipacchi and Hachette, the Netherlands' VNU and Sweden's Bonnier Group, to name just a few. Many publishing companies also own newspaper and/or television interests.

Some titles have successfully crossed national frontiers including *Vogue, Cosmopolitan, Essentials, Hello!, Reader's Digest, House and Garden, Prima, Marie Claire, Elle, GQ* and *Esquire*. This cross-fertilization of suitable titles is a trend that is likely to develop right across the world. Usually, but not always, the editorial is entirely indigenous – only the titles and the editorial ethos are the same.

Cost structures

The medium has witnessed monumental changes in the past decades. This was a medium dominated by photogravure and litho-printing for the big circulation magazines and by letterpress printing (hot metal) for the thousands of titles with circulations under 100,000 copies. The advent of new technology with computer typesetting and desktop computers, giving editorial staff the ability to interpret their words and designs, has created a publishing revolution that is not only creative but also financial. Design work stations enable the designer to create layouts, including colour originals, tinted lettering and panels as well as incorporating text. Pages of text and mono originals can be made-up on screen and output via a laser printer, with the cost of software being within the resources of even small publishers. Although colour scanning is still in the domain of the professional repro house, the whole effect of the giant strides in printing technology in the pre-press area has meant significant savings in the editorial and advertising departments.

Publishers have seen dramatic rises in the price and even availability of paper – particularly the coated papers used by the quality magazines. This has presented publishers with the sort of dilemma often not experienced since wartime publishing – to cut the number of pages or to reduce the format. Sometimes the remedy has been to do both, but the choice of smaller and more compact sizes has generally been the more popular solution for the publisher. Cutting pages also means rationing advertising (at least in theory) – a ploy always to be avoided.

The publisher as a juggler

Magazine publishers have two economic weapons at their disposal to endeavour to counteract the rising costs of production and paper. They can increase cover prices and/or increase the advertising rates. These options can offer an esoteric balancing act. Cover price rises tend (but it is not a cast-iron rule) to depress circulations, even if sometimes only temporarily. In the case of falling circulations (if not readership) the advertiser will resist rate-card increases. It is a delicate balance to preserve and one that constantly occupies the minds of publishers.

Publishers' rate cards are notoriously unscientific. A newly launched magazine, for instance, will assess the competition and base the page rates on a comparable, if competitive, rate structure. Advertising rates have increased significantly over the years – generally above the rate of inflation – and in the cutting edge of media competition, coinciding with the explosive development of media-buying shops and media specialists, the rate card has become at best elastic and at worst obsolescent (in extreme cases, obsolete). The advertiser buys not only on circulation but also on readership, and the six-monthly National Readership Survey (NRS) figures are keenly picked over for falls and rises and other more subtle nuances. So publishers who allow the cover price rise to outstrip reader demand, and who see readers leaving for a competitor because of price (quality is another matter), could easily see their circulation counteracted by a fall in the advertising revenue.

Quality of readership is the key

But advertisers also buy on 'quality' of circulation: breakdowns of sex, age and class. The NRS is keenly reflective of the quality of the reader so a powerful magazine like *Vogue*, with its wealthy and aspirational readership, has an influence for the advertiser far beyond the mathematics of its circulation or even readership figures. But publishers who are able to charge their customers a premium on their pages have to continue to justify that premium or join the slippery slopes of falling revenues.

The whole history of the magazine business is attended by continual deaths of titles as they run out of editorial steam or fail to deliver the right audience at the right price to their advertisers. Competitors, already exisiting or those waiting in the wings, are eager to take advantage of a magazine 'on the skids', sometimes as a result of editorial obsolescence but sometimes because a publisher has failed to balance the important cost factors which will keep the magazine economically attractive to both readers and advertisers.

It is relevant to note that across Europe the big weekly is still popular and a successful formula. Germany's *Stern* and *Neue Revue*, Spain's *Ola!* and France's *Paris Match* are examples of the genre still up and running. Perhaps the UK could in theory resurrect a popular title like *Picture Post* but in practice the dominance of the dozen 'free' newspaper colour magazines and the enormous popularity of television in the UK (backed by the 80 per cent ownership of video recorders) must be a deterrent to would-be big circulation magazine enterprises.

Distribution

Distribution is the basic engine of the magazine industry – the function of getting the magazine into the hands of the reader at the right time at the right place. Good distribution builds circulations with the minimum of wastage at a reasonable price to the publisher. This simple-sounding operation is, however, beset with difficulties, problems, politics, recriminations and sometimes (but not often) chaos.

There was a time when distribution was a basic function of the publisher who delivered the copies to the wholesaler who, in turn, delivered them to the retailer. Sometimes the copies were 'firm sale' (at a subsequent loss to retailers if they were left with unsold copies at the end of the magazine's on-sale period) or more recently 'sale or return' (SOR), which tends to

encourage retailers to be bolder in their ordering but opens up the possibility of waste in the system. But this is simplifying what has become a
highly complex set of possibilities for the magazine publisher.

Changing times

The whole distribution chain has been subject to a great deal of change,
basically engendered by the newspaper industry which has cut the number
of wholesalers throughout the UK in order to reduce costs and make the
business more efficient. Many small private and family businesses have gone
to the wall as the bigger wholesalers have been appointed on exclusive
geographical contracts. The 'big three' wholesalers in the UK are still WH
Smith, John Menzies and Surridge Dawson; the first two are also retailers
but because of the system of allocation they often supply magazines and
newspapers to each other's shops. The magazine industry has had to go
along with all the changes which broadly have not affected the sales of titles
adversely.

The third force in the distribution chain has emerged since the early
1970s. This is the distributor – the link between the publisher and the
wholesaler – and ultimately the retailer. The distributor is appointed by the
publisher on a brokerage basis to handle the circulation sales – responsible
for the contact with the wholesalers and the bigger retailers. Many of the
biggest publishers tend to own and run their own distribution companies,
which also take on third-party contracts for other publishers. For instance,
Britain's leading distributor is COMAG, jointly owned by Condé Nast and
the National Magazine Company. Not only does COMAG distribute all the
titles published by both companies but it also holds contracts to circulate
a large number of other magazines for outside companies. Even without
these client publishers COMAG finds itself, when distributing the house
titles, selling into the trade such hugely competitive titles as *Vogue, Harpers
& Queen* and *Tatler*. The dominant financial partner in COMAG is the
National Magazine Company but it means that Condé Nast (a confrontational company in selling advertising against the National Magazine titles)
enjoys revenue from every copy of such successful magazines as *Cosmopolitan*
and *Good Housekeeping*.

The whole concept of third-party contracts has become popular in the
business in the UK. IPC, in addition to distributing its own eighty or so
titles, actively encourages outside business. The BBC and EMAP own a joint
distribution company called Frontline to handle house titles (including *Radio
Times*) and third-party magazines.

So the publishing director of a magazine has quite a few people to hold
responsible when explaining a downturn in circulation, but could, of course,
personally take the full credit for an upturn! The director can blame the
distributor, the wholesaler or the retailer, and will probably also have an
in-house circulation department to liaise with the distributor.

Distribution is a difficult game, particularly when the going gets tough. A fall in circulation can be attributed to many areas – poor editorial, a weak front cover, lively competition, inadequate publicity, lack of advertising funding, late delivery from the printers, and so on. A look at the bookstalls on railway stations, or the so-called 'news runs' in the local WH Smith, is immediate evidence of the problem: a bewildering mass of magazines all calling for attention. And the shelf life is all too ephemeral, particularly for the weeklies.

So let us examine the three methods of distribution open to the publisher.

The news trade

The news trade is broadly divided into the CTN multiples (CTN is the trade abbreviation for Confectioner, Tobacco, Newsagent, the three prongs of existence for the retail shop) such as WH Smith, Menzies, Martins and Forbuoys, with many smaller provincial chains, and the 'corner shop', which still survives in the UK. With each type of store there is a diversity of product: books and stationery in the multiples and anything from drinks to groceries, or even film processing, in the corner shops. Each outlet will have costed the priority to selling magazines as against, say, dog food in the corner shop or books in the multiples. Distributors can play a useful role in advising the retailer on display and setting up better news-runs to be able to carry more titles, preferably 'full face' to the potential customer.

The news trade in the UK still boasts over 30,000 shops nationally, despite falling numbers over the years. Many shops are opening as 'convenience stores' (such as '7 to 11') which stay open long hours and sell magazines as part of their general mix of products. But the conventional news trade, which often offers home delivery, is still the important backbone of the magazine distribution process. Across Europe there is a dominance of kerbside kiosks, selling newspapers, tobacco and magazines, rather than the newsagent shops. Other vital sales points are at railway stations and airports.

Supermarkets

The ever-expanding supermarkets are now an important factor in selling more magazines. At first in the UK supermarkets were confined to the sale of just two titles, *Family Circle* and *Living*. These two magazines, which were not on sale through the news trade, were owned by the late Canadian newspaper tycoon Roy Thomson, who negotiated with supermarkets for the exclusive availability of his two titles. Not only were they the only magazines in the supermarkets but also, equally importantly, they were situated at the check-outs: the supreme position for last-minute impulse purchases. The success of the magazines was phenomenal, with *Family Circle* gaining an unheard-of circulation of 1 million copies at the height of its success. Distributors and wholesalers were not involved – Thomson's circulation staff looked after the supply and distribution of the magazines. (Not popular with the news trade!) The ubiquitous IPC purchased the titles from Thomson in the late 1980s and by doing so opened the floodgates for other magazines, both at the check-outs and in news runs in the stores. Tesco was quick to see the advantages of magazine sales (quite effective against many grocery products) but Sainsbury's was slower off the mark. Both groups of stores, and many other supermarkets throughout the UK and mainland Europe, are now fully converted to the big profits to be made from selling magazines, particularly those of interest to women. Sainsbury's now publishes its own title *Sainsbury's, the Magazine*, which is exclusive to the stores and has become a best-seller.

The supermarkets are supplied by the wholesalers, although there are fears in the trade that the big stores are now so powerful that they could move into a position of negotiating directly with the publishers. This could be to the fundamental detriment of both the publishers and, of course, the wholesalers. A trade criticism of supermarkets, convenience stores and garage forecourts has been that they 'cherry pick' the best titles, in other words they select only the biggest and fastest selling magazines and are not interested in handling a wide range of titles outside the top 200. The corner newsagent feels umbrage at this, being expected to handle many more titles which are not such attractive fast movers.

Subscriptions

Subscriptions in the UK are a newer phenomenon. At one time the concept of receiving a copy of a consumer magazine by post was simply not considered practicable or viable. The reader had to be charged the cost of the magazine plus hefty postage. Before the days of polythene wrappers, which deliver the product flat and pristine, a magazine would arrive in the letter box rolled up with a tear strip that often damaged the edges of the magazine. (Professional journals, not available through the news trade were, of course, totally reliant on postal subscription.) So the potential reader of, say, *Good Housekeeping* or *Vogue* would find it easier and less expensive simply to call in to the local WH Smith and buy a copy, which would probably have been in the shop some days before the postal copy.

But the business has changed and moved on. The British Post Office came up with sensible and viable postal rates for printed matter and the polythene wraps were a revolution. Publishers began to advertise their subscription services persistently, either by direct mail or through the magazines themselves. In order to make subscriptions attractive to the reader they have to offer inducements: straight price cuts or tempting presents or extras. British customers have taken to postal subscriptions in a big way – there are national titles with as much as 20 per cent of their circulations obtained this way. It is expensive to maintain subscription departments with their attendant computer systems and mailing devices but the publishers obtain the full cover price with no discounts to the trade. (The normal trade discount is about 45 per cent, with 25 per cent to the retailer while the distributor takes about 10 per cent brokerage: figures vary.) All in all, a subscription nets about the same to the publisher as a trade copy when the various costs are weighed up.

Subscriptions also have one advantage. A subscription copy is a sold copy, with no returns. So publishers can set their print orders with more confidence when they know that a particular percentage of the print run is spoken for.

The news trade – retailer, wholesaler and distributor – are unenthusiastic about the growing move to subscriptions. Retailers feel aggrieved because every postal copy is, in theory but not necessarily in fact, a lost sale to the shops. Retailers' indignation grows more intense when they realize that many of the magazines on their shelves are carrying subscription advertisements or pull-out leaflets offering the magazine to the potential subscriber at less than the cover price in the shops. Much dialogue has taken place between publishers and the trade but subscription selling is so effective in increasing circulations that protestations of unfair practice fall on deaf publishing ears.

The system works!

The distribution of magazines is a sort of internecine war but the whole system does work and millions of copies of magazines are sold over the counters of retail shops, the railway station units and the CTNs, or bought in the supermarkets or received in the post.

Do not be left with the impression that the distribution of the hundreds of consumer titles is a mess. The distributors and the wholesalers have spent millions of pounds since the mid-1980s in setting up complex computer systems to analyse the sales patterns of each title – where they would be most likely to sell and in what quantity. Their systems will allocate the number of copies a retailer should receive and the possibilities of reordering when supplies are sold out. Magazine fulfilment has become almost an art – an inexact science full of imperfections maybe, but rationalization and technology are constantly striving to make the complicated business work better.

Europe

The divide between subscriptions and retail sales differs widely across Europe. In Finland, for instance, 91 per cent of magazine sales are by subscription with 60 per cent in Sweden and the Netherlands. In France 70 per cent of sales are retail and 56 per cent in Germany. Italy sells 81 per cent through the shops, Norway 65 per cent and Ireland 90 per cent. Greece eschews the subscription route entirely with all copies sold through retail. And in the UK, despite the immense strides made by the publishers, still 90 per cent of titles are sold through the trade.

Lifestyle

'Lifestyle' is a buzz word much bandied about in the world of magazine publishing. Although the word may have sprung into more general usage in the 1960s and the 1970s, the concept is as old as magazines themselves. The very nature of magazine editorial is to associate itself with lifestyle, or the mode of living of the sort of reader it seeks to attract.

Women's magazines have always been positive in this approach to the cultural subdivisions of their audience. The first woman's magazine, *The Ladies Mercury*, was published in 1693. It was publicized as aiming to answer all 'the most nice and curious questions concerning love, marriage, behaviour, dress and humour of the female sex, whether virgins, wives or widows', so we may assume that the editor was seeking to attract a positive lifestyle; not only women, but also women with a positive attitude to their lives. Down through the ages women's magazines have classified their potential readerships into such broad categories as domestic, the working woman, the sportswoman, the socialite, the fashion conscious, the political, the flighty, the serious or the light-hearted. The very nature of magazine publishing is to exploit those cultural differences.

If you had the time or the inclination to spend a couple of hours at the news runs of WH Smith or any other magazine store, you could peruse the acres of glossy pages to ascertain that although many titles seem to be not unidentical (every successful new title speedily acquires a like-minded competitor), all those editors of all those magazines are out to find a particular lifestyle to make the magazine a 'must' purchase every week or every month. One lifestyle may well be repelled by another – the magazine for ferret fanciers will not necessarily appeal to the readers of *Majesty* or *Vogue*.

The general magazine – RIP

The day of the general magazine is long dead, when *Picture Post* and *Illustrated* were the big-selling photo-story titles, with *John Bull* and *Everybody's* supplying general interest, light-hearted cartoons and fiction. The norm circulation for these titles was about 1 million, an easily acquired figure in those days before television. In the USA, the big picture magazines reached mega-millions – eventually to die because the television audience found moving pictures more enthralling than still ones and the magazines were unable to compete against the television ratings. Cheaper and cheaper subscriptions, in order to emulate the television millions, helped the magazines along the road to ruin. The same pattern occurred in the UK thus necessitating the search for the lifestyle of readerships to deliver to advertisers segments of the sort of people they specifically wanted to reach. They could purchase the mere bulk of millions of consumers either in the newspapers or else on TV. In publishing jargon, magazines were offering the rifle sharp-shooting approach against the mass readership blunderbuss.

Another factor came into the lives of magazine publishers. Electronic media have one outstanding virtue: they move very fast. A major piece of news flashes around the country and the world minutes after the event, whether by radio, television, teletext or on the Internet. The newspapers can pick up the story next day and shade in the picture, fleshing it out with comment and analysis. So we no longer rely on our newspaper to give us the hot news – we have heard it or seen it hours before. The tabloid newspapers became only too aware of this failing and increasingly have turned to 'features' to keep their readers' attention. These features are frequently of particular interest to their women readers: fashion, beauty, diets, and so on. A study of the pages of the *Daily Mail, Express, Mirror* and other tabloids (and to some extent the broadsheets) compared to the same papers in the mid-1970s will emphasize this. It cannot therefore be a coincidence that during this period the circulations of the big women's weeklies (*Woman, Woman's Own*, etc.) have considerably declined. In the 1950s the circulation of *Woman* was 3 million copies a week and *Woman's Own* 2.5 million. In the mid-1990s those circulations are down to about 800,000 each; much of their natural editorial ground has been occupied by the popular press. Many magazines over the same period with lower circulations and weaker editorial personalities have sunk without trace.

Magazines are a lifestyle

A magazine has to be certain that it is projecting a positive lifestyle. By necessity this lifestyle will not attract vast quantities of readers – the days of the 3 million weekly have gone for ever. The woman's weekly is not yet dead, however; there are currently thirteen in this crowded market. The top seller is the German *Take a Break*, topping the market at 1.5 million. But if this appears a bit contradictory it should be noted that a new ingredient is part of this weekly mix. Puzzles and competitions, led by *Take a Break*, occupy many pages with attractive prizes for many of the competitions, while others are just coffee-break time-fillers.

The monthly magazines pursue the lifestyle image with particular vigour. They are very clearly divided into the living styles and aspirations of their readers – the extensive range of home interest titles from *House and Garden* to *House Beautiful*, or fashion (*Vogue*), or society (*Tatler, Harpers*), or slimming, beauty, parenthood, teenagers, brides, crafts and the young women's titles such as *Cosmopolitan, Company, New Woman* and others which have taken an increasing and almost obsessional interest in sex since the mid-1980s.

Enter the men's magazines

Men are not to be left out of the equation. The male sex has always, if rather sporadically, been a lifestyle target for the magazine publisher. The first men's magazine, *The Gentleman's Magazine*, was published as early as 1731, and actually coined the description 'magazine'. There were several examples of male magazines in Victorian days and the genre was particularly lively in the 1930s to the late 1950s, when the accent was on pocket magazines with a strong humour content. By the early 1960s they had all ceased publishing, more the victims of the publishing mergers of the period rather than the lack of audience.

The re-emergence of magazines which deliberately emphasized 'lifestyle' came with the launches in the 1980s of *Arena* and *The Face*. Their coverage of fashion, films, music and travel was bisexual but with a slight bias towards men. The male magazine sluice gates really opened with the appearance of *GQ* from Condé Nast, a British version of the old-established American title. This was swiftly followed by National Magazine's *Esquire, FHM, Men's Health, XL, Loaded* and *Maxim*. Publishers are always swift to leap on a bandwagon and the sudden surge of men's magazines is as much publishing rivalry as a hungry demand from the male sex for their own magazine capacity. The fact is that the circulations of all the men's titles combined only just pass the circulation of *Prima* and there are no signs of a weekly title for men or a monthly with the circulation performance of *Marie Claire* or *Cosmopolitan*.

Nevertheless, the explosion of so many titles for men illustrates both the division of magazines into lifestyle categories and the continuing energy of the industry to discover new niches and to respond to contemporary demand.

So is the general magazine a lost dinosaur? Such a question seems to be confounded by the phenomenal success of *Reader's Digest*, the monthly title which is the epitome of general interest and sells 1.6 million copies a month. The magazine sells a paltry number on the bookstalls – the secret of its success is its cunning and brilliant employment of direct mail techniques, including its occasional sweepstakes. (The jest that it is impossible to get off the subscription list once on it, because of the direct debit system and the publisher's persistence, bears the hallmark of some truth.) Otherwise it is difficult for an objective commentator to assess the widespread reader appeal of comparatively banal editorial to such an historically high audience. The magazine must be the exception that proves the rule.

General or specialized?

Other magazines with a more general appeal are harder to find. The *Spectator*, originally published in 1828, is doing better than ever with a circulation of 50,000 copies weekly. Although the kernel of the editorial content is political, the magazine carries many features on books, the arts and general comment. It does considerably better than the *New Statesman*, which has declined from its former glory of a 100,000 sale to one-fifth of that figure. *The Economist* is an impressive international success but the content is entirely financial and business comment. *Time* and *Newsweek* (the leading US news magazines) both have British and European editions but have never achieved the prestige or circulations they would like. Their editorial slant is perhaps too transatlantic.

Europe still publishes its big general magazines in several countries (*Paris Match, Stern,* etc.) but it might be worth noting that television advertising does not have such full rein as it does in the UK or the USA.

Mention has to be made of the television listings magazines, which received a shock when British television programme copyright was 'decontrolled' in the mid-1980s. This meant that all newspapers could carry programme details, which were no longer the exclusive publishing property of either the BBC's *Radio Times* or ITV's *TV Times.* Two more weeklies quickly appeared – *TV Quick* from the German Bauer and *What's On TV* from IPC (who also own *TV Times*). Together they sell over 5 million copies every week, an interesting circulation considering the free and extensive publication of programme details in all the newspapers. But the television magazines run plenty of features about personalities and 'behind the scenes' so one might consider that, in some way, they are lifestyle papers – if you consider television addicts a market segment and watching television a lifestyle.

The future

The future of the magazine industry is bright. The state of the art shows a higher degree of professionalism than ever before, in editorial, business and technology. The rationalization in publishing companies, and the methods of distribution, together with the high standards of the magazines themselves, point the way to an industry which knows where it is going and which has the ability to compete with the 'mega bucks' poured into the newspaper and electronic media.

Magazines have strategic benefits. We have seen their unique quality of the classification of audiences for the assistance of advertisers and the advantage of their long life when compared to the ephemeral flash of the television or radio commercial or the necessarily limited on-sale period of the daily or Sunday newspaper. Magazines have staying power, quality of presentation, honed editorial talents and the ability to talk to their vertical audiences with authority, energy and a unique one-to-one quality.

The magazine industry is so diverse and so brilliant at finding audiences for the hundreds of categories of literate readers, from the glittering array of the women's market, to sports and hobbies, professional titles, the explosion of computer magazines and the thousands of business-to-business titles covering every trade activity. Perhaps it is the *Hello!* society gossip or the sexual exploits of the *Cosmopolitan* editorial which make the headlines but bear in mind the importance of the trade and professional journals which are required, essential reading in their respective fields. Magazines like *New Scientist, Farmers' Weekly, The Economist,* the *Lancet,* the *Builder, Nursing Mirror,* the *Grocer* and *Caterer and Hotelkeeper,* to take some random examples, uphold the traditions of their own spheres of influence and are paradigms of the unique power and prestige of the magazine business. Right across

Europe publishers are providing highly respected professional journals to their industries.

Plenty more to come

There will be plenty of new titles over the years, occasionally replacing more obsolescent ones and sometimes brilliant new ideas to catch the moods of new audiences or new mores. The fact is that people love magazines. The Internet may represent the flashier future but magazines will continue reaching out to their specialized audiences who still enjoy the power of words and pictures. Magazines enjoy a universal marketplace: in 1995 there were 54,000 sales outlets in the UK and the trade expected these to grow by at least another thousand during 1996. The efficacy of magazines as a contact advertisement medium is confirmed by the quality and quantity of response rates obtained by offers and coupons. Magazines have been most creative in exploiting this response factor with imaginative advertising promotional pages, 'widgets', perfume sachets, stick-on reply cards and other aids to easy response.

Note also another new element – the 'contract' magazine. These are titles produced by specialized publishing companies on behalf of clients, either to be sold or given away to their particular audiences. Encouraged by the success of in-flight magazines there is a raft of exclusive titles such as those for InterCity, Marks & Spencer, Sainsbury's, Tesco, banks and other financial institutions, estate agents, hotel groups, and others. This is a booming, fast-growing sector that will become even more visible over the next few years.

Sales of magazines will continue to grow, as will the number and variety of titles, despite the millions of 'free' colour magazines given away by the weekend newspapers, often with high editorial quality. But newspapers with their characteristically generalized readerships cannot take the place of magazines with their targeted audiences any more than the electronic media will destroy the printed word.

Appendix: some 'snapshot' figures

Numbers of titles

Sports titles	284
Computer titles	260
Motoring magazines	123
Medical magazines	401
Social science titles	200
Business management	277
Women's magazines	55
Home interest titles	43

Sources of revenue

Consumer magazines:
  advertising revenue   39%
  circulation revenue   61%
Business and professional:
  advertising revenue   78%
  circulation revenue   22%

Circulation growth

Since 1989 UK magazine circulation has grown by 18%.
Largest circulation growth (1993 over 1985):
  TV and video and film   96%
  Children's   46%
  Sport   25%
Biggest circulation weekly: *What's On TV* 1.4 million
Biggest circulation monthly: *Reader's Digest* 1.7 million
Value of consumer magazine sales in UK: £1 billion plus.
Consumer magazine publishing receives *c.* £645 million net cover price
revenue per year.

Estimated net advertising revenues in UK (1995)

All magazines   £1494 million
Consumer   £584 million
Business and professional   £910 million

Readership

50% of women in UK read women's weeklies
50% of women in UK read women's monthlies

Estimated net advertising revenues in millions of ECU (1993)

Austria   132
Belgium   190
Denmark   99
Finland   63
France   1515
Germany   2219
Greece   76
Ireland   13
Italy   861
Netherlands   402
Norway   88

Portugal	38
Spain	690
Sweden	110
Switzerland	234
UK	1176

Magazines' share of total advertising (over all other media) (1993)

Austria	16%
Belgium	27%
Denmark	15%
France	27%
Germany	21%
Greece	17%
Ireland	4%
Italy	19%
Netherlands	22%
Norway	18%
Portugal	11%
Spain	12%
Sweden	11%
Switzerland	18%
UK	17%

Questions

1 As the publisher of a specialist magazine will you take the subscription option or rely on news-stand sales? Discuss the pros and cons. Which will be more important: income from readers or advertisers? How can you balance the equation?

2 Magazines are becoming increasingly international, even in the polyglot European market. How will national publishers cross the European borders in the future, taking into consideration the developments of the past few years?

3 Will the electronic media win the day? Will magazines become obsolete? If not, why not?

References

Braithwaite, B. and Barrell, J. (1988) *Business of Women's Magazines*, London: Kogan Page.

British Rate & Data, EMAP Media Group, 33–9 Bowling Green Lane, London, EC 1.

Federation of International Publishers, *World Magazine Trends*, London: FIP.

Periodical Publishers' Association, *Magazine Handbook*, London: PPA.

Further reading

Braithwaite, B. (1996) *Women's Magazines: The First 300 Years*, London: Peter Owen.

Periodical Publishers' Association (1989) *Inside Magazines: A Career Builders Guide*, London: PPA.

Periodical Publishers' Association (1996) *A Career in Magazines*, London: PPA.

Periodical Publishers' Association (1997) *The Magazine Handbook*, London: PPA.

Periodicals Training Council (1994) *The PTC Magazine Training Directory*, London: PTC.

Wharton, J. (1992) *Managing Magazine Publishing*, London: Periodicals Training Council.

NB: The address of the PPA, PTC and FIPP is Queen's House, Kingsway, London WC2 6JR.

Chapter 9

Radio

PUBLIC SERVICE, COMMERCIALISM AND THE PARADOX OF CHOICE

ANDREW CRISELL

Radio in the 1990s: sound in health?

On the face of it, radio in the UK is thriving as never before. The publicly funded BBC, which tradition places at the heart of the broadcasting system, had switched its four networks to FM by the beginning of the 1990s and used two of the AM wavelengths these had vacated to launch another, Radio Five. Though this suffered teething troubles it relaunched as a news and sport channel, Five Live, in 1994 and is now gaining popularity. A year later the Corporation inaugurated the UK's first digital radio service, a technology which in quality of signal and number of channels offers the same vast opportunities for sound as for vision (Williams 1995: 61).

But thanks to the Broadcasting Act 1990, the most remarkable expansion of radio has been in the 'independent' or commercial sector. ('Independent' was a sly term devised for commercial television at its inception in the 1950s: the aim was to disguise its money-making intentions and at the same time to imply that its rival was feebly dependent on government largesse!) Whereas in 1984 the public could tune to a mere 48 independent stations, there were 130 in 1993, outnumbering the BBC's by almost three to one.

Yet what was significant was not just the quantity but the levels of provision: for the first time in the history of British broadcasting there were legal, home-based, *national* commercial stations: Classic FM from 1992, Virgin 1215 from 1993, and Talk Radio UK from 1995. Also for the first time, *regional* commercial stations could be heard, as well as vastly more stations at *local* level. Early in 1995 commercial radio's total audience share at last overtook that of the BBC.

The expansion of the former has brought with it a long-awaited boom in radio advertising (Horsman 1996: 17) and, mercifully, some rise in the production standards of radio commercials. Advertising revenue rose from £141 million in 1992 to £270 million in 1995. Though advertisers tend naturally to exaggerate, their promotional slogan for the medium itself seemed no more than the strict truth: 'Commercial radio. Its time has come'. Between

1993 and 1996 the annual increase of revenue was 23 per cent, and radio became a particularly attractive prospect for companies which already had substantial holdings in other media and were seeking to expand into new sectors. With the government about to relax its rules on cross-media owner-ship, the national newspapers are expected to lead the stampede.

To sum up: in the 1990s there has been an absolute increase in the num-ber of radio stations, and for the first time competition between the BBC and the commercial sector at all three geographical levels. But has the numerical increase brought with it a commensurate increase in choice? The answer would appear to be no. Commercial radio has enriched output in one or two areas, notably pop and rock music, but not in many others such as documentary, features, drama, comedy and light entertainment, where the BBC's near-monopoly has been left largely unchallenged.

The apostles of consumer sovereignty, such as Professor Sir Alan Peacock, would be unfazed by this. In 1985 Professor Peacock was appointed by the government to chair a committee to consider new ways of financing the BBC. Though the committee recommended the short-term retention of the Cor-poration's licence fee it proposed the adoption of subscription funding when more TV and radio channels became available, thus introducing a closer connection between supply and demand (McDonnell 1991: 95–103).

The essence of Peacock's view was that types of programming should stand or fall entirely on the strength of consumer demand for them. How-ever, it could be claimed that demand and choice are a more complex and elusive matter than free market economists might assume – a claim which Peacock half acknowledges when he concedes that consumers are some-times willing to pay as taxpayers and voters for what they are not prepared to buy as consumers (McDonnell 1991: 99). What we choose and what we esteem are not always the same thing: choice is often made on the basis of ignorance and timidity, of pleasure rather than benefit. We might greatly enjoy or gain from what we would not freely have chosen to listen to, and few would agree with the proposition that the best programme is defined by what is preferred by the greatest number.

However, if we look back at the history of broadcasting we can see how a purely quantitative approach to audience choice has led not only to a lack of it with respect to certain types of programme, but also to an overall reduction in the number of those programmes. As we noted earlier, only BBC radio continues to broadcast features, plays and comedy, but whereas these could once be found on each of the three networks it operated, they are now largely confined to one: Radio Four.

Early radio and the 'brute force' of monopoly

Although they have been explored in detail elsewhere (Crisell 1994), we begin with a brief description of the characteristics of radio. It is an entirely non-visual or 'blind' medium in the sense that it lacks not only the pictures of television or cinema but also the visible symbols of print. This means that its messages lack the 'stability' of literary and to some extent television texts since they exist in time rather than space. However, one important and invincible advantage of radio is that it is a 'secondary' medium: its messages can easily be absorbed while the person who is receiving them is engaged in some other activity such as driving, cooking or even dozing.

Before the mid-1960s there was a little regional but almost no local radio in Britain: sound broadcasting was mostly conducted on a network or national scale and was the virtual monopoly of the non-commercial British Broadcasting Corporation. However the BBC had originally been a quasi-commercial organization, the British Broadcasting Company, which was itself a consortium of wireless manufacturers such as Marconi, British Thomson Houston, General Electric and Metropolitan Vickers.

With the beginnings of 'wireless' (the older name for radio) in the early 1920s, many of these manufacturers had individually sought broadcasting permits from the Post Office, at that time the government body overseeing public communications, and several were licensed on a temporary and local basis. They wished to broadcast in order to stimulate the sale of their wireless receivers, but the Post Office, fearing the kind of aerial mêlée that was developing in the USA, where scores of stations were trying to drown one another out of scarce spectrum space, invited the manufacturers to form a single consortium to which it would grant a *de facto* though not a *de jure* monopoly.

The British Broadcasting Company therefore went to air in 1922, but without any government prescription as to what its programmes should consist of. Within the laws of the land, it might be as trivial or populist as the need to sell wireless sets dictated. Nevertheless, the company's first general manager, John Reith, took a rather more elevated and moralistic view of broadcasting's capabilities. He believed that so scarce and precious a form of communication should offer the best of everything to everyone who cared to receive it and quickly evolved a philosophy of what came to be known as 'public service broadcasting'. It had four main tenets (Briggs 1961: 235–8):

1 The British Broadcasting Company, which was largely funded by a licence fee levied on the listeners, did not exist solely to make money. Unlike its constituent companies it did not depend on the profit motive.
2 It aimed to serve everyone in the community who wished to listen.
3 It maintained unified control as a monopoly which would resist sectional pressures, whether commercial or political.
4 It pursued high programming standards, setting out to provide the best of everything.

These tenets, which on 1 January 1927 resulted in the BBC becoming a public corporation, a status it has maintained ever since, were embodied in the principle of *mixed programming*. At first the BBC operated a single network, but soon added a second (known respectively as the National Programme and the Regional Programme); in 1945–6 it established three: the highbrow Third Programme, the middlebrow Home Service, and the populist Light Programme. But each of these networks contained a variety of output – news, drama, sport, talks, light and classical music, religion, features, light entertainment, specialized programmes for women, children, farmers and so on – in which, during the early years at least, routine scheduling was largely avoided.

The aim of mixed programming was not simply to provide 'something for everyone' but, at whatever level, 'everything for someone': that is, to cater for the particular interests that individuals already had, but also to introduce them to areas of experience they had not previously encountered – to enlarge knowledge and foster new enthusiasms. Though radio was a scarce medium, there was certainly room for more than one broadcaster on the spectrum. But Reith insisted on what he called the brute force of monopoly. If the BBC were allowed a rival, each would be under pressure to maximize its audience by abandoning minority and quality programming and offering merely that which was preferred by the greatest number: or, put the other way round, if listeners were allowed a choice they would be likely to avoid the challenge of new experiences inherent in mixed programming and opt for the less demanding fare that a competitor of the BBC would almost certainly provide. Indeed despite Reith's demands that the monopoly be defended, the BBC was embarrassed before the war by competition from two commercial stations, Radios Normandie and Luxembourg, which were able to circumvent Post Office restrictions by transmitting into Britain from the European mainland.

Telly versus tranny

The public service notion of mixed programming made good sense as long as radio remained the primary broadcasting medium. But when television overtook it during the 1950s, its audience did not merely decline – it plummeted. By 1959 the average number of the BBC's evening listeners had fallen by 5.5 million in ten years (Paulu 1961: 155). If television was both far more popular than radio and had the advantage of vision along with sound, it was a much more appropriate medium for mixed programming. It is true that from 1955 BBC television was exposed to competition from ITV, but since the latter had its own very different source of income the competition was not cut-throat; in any case ITV was also in some measure bound by the Reithian principles of public service. The question, then, was what role would be left to radio. Would it even disappear altogether?

Fortunately a new technology was at hand which would guarantee the medium's survival yet also help to confirm its secondary role – ensure that it would seldom be the primary object of attention it had often been in the days before television. This new technology was a tiny semiconductor device called a transistor. Previously radio receivers were objects whose size, weight and attachment to aerials and the mains electricity supply made them difficult to move about. They contained valves (known as 'tubes' in North America) which looked rather like light bulbs; when the set was switched on these took time to heat up before anything could be heard. Valves were also fragile and expensive to replace.

The transistor, which was developed in 1947 at Bell Laboratories in the USA, performed all the functions of the valve without any of its disadvantages. It was much smaller, lighter and stronger. It consumed less power, produced less heat, cost less money – and the result was a new generation of radio receivers which could be economically powered by small batteries. They were cheap, light, small, reliable and very easily carried about. The first transistor radio to appear in the UK was made by Pye in 1956 and called 'Pam'; transistor sets soon became so popular that for many years 'tranny' was the main name by which a radio set was known, especially among young people.

The major consequence of the transistor was that it changed the way in which the sound medium was used. In the old days of the immovable mains receiver, wireless was often treated as a background or secondary medium, but also, during leisure periods and in the absence of television, not infrequently used as a focus. In the evenings or at weekends people might choose to do nothing but sit and listen to the radio, or at any rate to do only those things that could accompany the primary business of listening, instead of listening as a merely incidental accompaniment to the primary business of work.

In its leisure role as the main focus of attention radio was, as we have seen, rapidly superseded by television; the transistor meant that radio was used in an almost entirely secondary way. But it could be so used in many more places and situations than ever before – not only in the kitchen, sitting room or workplace but also in the garage, the garden, the countryside, at the beach or in the car. One kind of output that was well suited to secondary listening was of course music; for the intermittent attentiveness of so many modern listeners the short and simple tunes of pop music were positively ideal. How convenient, then, that the arrival of rock music should coincide with that of the transistor: the craze for Elvis Presley and Bill Haley also developed in 1956. By the early 1960s radio's largely musical destiny was becoming steadily clearer.

Nevertheless the BBC was in a difficult position. Despite its rapidly dwindling radio audience, its *raison d'être* as a public service broadcaster was to provide a range of programming, not just popular music; in any event the number of records it could play was restricted by Phonographic Performance Limited (PPL), the organization that acted on behalf of the record companies and in league with the Musicians' Union. Radio Luxembourg, on the other hand, was bound neither by PPL nor by public service dogma and was much more in touch than the BBC was with contemporary developments in popular music (Briggs 1979: 759).

Yet Radio Luxembourg was also limited. Its programmes in English were broadcast only during the evenings and its signal in many parts of the UK was weak. Those of us who are of a certain age will have vivid memories of being huddled under the bedclothes with a 'tranny', and – we hoped – out of earshot of our parents as we struggled to retune the fading sounds of the Everly Brothers, Jerry Lee Lewis, Little Richard and Buddy Holly.

As is well known, it was the arrival of the offshore pirate stations in 1964 which most clearly signposted the future of radio. Their growth and impact has already been much chronicled (Baron 1975; Chapman 1992; Harris 1970). Here it must suffice to say that as typified by the two most successful, Radio Caroline and Radio London, they were professional and highly commercial operations; most not only were dedicated to pop music but also based their playlists on the current Top Forty chart. Presented at last with a choice between two clearly audible kinds of sound broadcasting, millions of listeners rallied to the Jolly Roger, putting the conservative programming policy of the BBC under ever severer strain.

The Labour government of Harold Wilson swept the pirates off the air with the Marine Broadcasting (Offences) Act 1967, but only on the understanding that the BBC would satisfy the huge demand they had created, or at least identified. Its response was to launch a streamed pop music network, Radio One, on one of the Light Programme's old frequencies. The other three networks were renamed Radios Two, Three and Four, but for a further two and a half years continued to offer mixed programming. Hence public service broadcasting was there if you wanted it, and not if you didn't: but since, as we have seen, this kind of choice was inimical to public service in its original Reithian form, there was a sense in which it had disappeared altogether.

One, two, three – format!

In April 1970 Radios Two and Three also moved into streamed, specialized programming, the former offering mostly middle-of-the-road, the latter mostly classical, music. BBC local radio, which had begun in Leicester in 1967, was already confined mainly to sequences of information and light music, so Radio Four remained the only repository of mixed programming – news and current affairs, talks and discussions, drama, documentaries and features, special interest programmes, comedy shows, quiz games – though it broadcast very little music. Thus although programme variety was lost at highbrow and populist levels it persisted on Radio Four: but if the networks were taken as a whole, there was clearly much less of it than before.

The streaming or specialization of output became known during the 1970s as 'format radio'. As has already been hinted, the ideal material for formats is music, but certain kinds of speech content, notably rolling news or current affairs, also suit the routinized, background use to which radio is often put. In essence 'rolling news' consists of a sequence of segments, some updated and some simply repeated – headlines, weather forecasts, traffic and travel information, stock market bulletins, interviews, correspondents' reports – these catering for the intermittent listener in the way that pop songs do.

In fact the trend towards formats has been all but unstoppable. When independent local radio (ILR) began in 1973, its regulator, the Independent Broadcasting Authority (IBA), was expected by the government to impose public service requirements on the stations in the form of some programming variety. Such variety was, however, completely at odds with commercial radio's need to target consumers, and in order to stay afloat most of the stations soon moved to mainly pop and Top Forty formats, with the reluctant consent of the IBA. BBC Radio Five tried to buck the trend in 1990 by launching as a mixed programme channel, but it failed to win a coherent audience and was obliged to relaunch four years later as a news and sport format.

Within the huge majority of stations that are now formatted, a further large majority are devoted to mainstream pop, whether chart (Radio One, now known as One FM, and most ILR stations); adult rock (Virgin 1215 and the Irish-based Atlantic 252); or golden oldies (the 'Gold' stations on AM, most of them ILR operations). Some stations offer specialist or ethnic music (Classic FM, Jazz FM, Melody Radio, Choice FM) and yet others offer speech formats (London News Radio, recently relaunched under its predecessor's name of LBC, and Talk Radio UK) – though few of them are thriving.

Although in the provision of pop music there is a greater diversity than before (yet not, perhaps, quite the diversity that is implied by the proliferation of names: indie, reggae, ragga, acid house, garage, hip-hop, jazz-funk, punk, thrash metal, new wave, and so on), it is hard to see how formats have increased or even matched the overall range of output which was once provided by three BBC networks; even if they have, they are individually uniform and predictable in what they provide. This is, of course, their whole point: it is always open to individuals to introduce their own element of relief or variety by tuning to another channel. But what is largely lost is, as we shall see, the exposure to new radio experiences *by chance*.

The polarities of modern radio

We might plot the position of the various radio stations along two axes. The first axis is *national*, or network, and *local* (regional is a third category, though one which makes little difference to the discussion that follows); the second axis is *format* and *mixed programme*.

In the UK, home-based commercial radio began at local level: there was no national station until 1992. Why? Part of the reason was to parallel the already regional nature of commercial television, which had itself been something of a reaction to what was seen in the 1950s as the excessively centralized, metropolitan nature of the BBC. But the main reason was to exploit the modern technology of VHF/FM, which would allow a large number of stations on to the spectrum and give advertisers the opportunity to target local as well as national markets. There was also the hope that the system would yield locally originated programming and even afford broadcasting access to local listeners.

Virtually all the stations do carry local elements: news, sport, phone-ins, advertising; but as the preponderance of pop music formats implies, the pull of cosmopolitan culture is almost irresistible. Whether in Cornwall or Durham, ILR is, like McDonald's hamburgers, a reassuringly uniform experience, its music originating in neither and mediated by mostly 'accentless' presenters whose pleasantries and platitudes seldom assume a knowledge of the locality or its culture.

This relative absence of local flavour has largely been matched by a lack of local ownership. Colin Seymour-Ure (1991: 81) points out that there was at first a fair spread of local investors in ILR, including the press, but that as the stations became quoted on the stock exchange their ownership dispersed and with it their local character. Later, as market competition and economies of scale began to take effect, ownership became concentrated among a few large groups: Crown Communications and Capital Radio during the 1980s, then East Midlands Allied Press (EMAP), the Metro Group and Great Western Radio (GWR) in the 1990s. Broadcasting technology itself conspires with concentration of ownership to work against localism and individuality in programme origination, for the output of a local station which is part of a group can in theory originate from another station in the group which may be on the far side of the country.

Until recently, an ILR station not far from where I live provided a relatively modest instance of this phenomenon: Sun City FM, 'Sunderland's own music station'. Sun City was, in fact, part of the Minster Radio Group which owned two other stations: Minster Radio in York and Yorkshire Coast Radio (YCR) in Scarborough. Though their music was programmed by computer the disc jockey spinning records at a console is now pretty much a thing of the past – each of the stations originated almost all of its own output.

However, between 10 p.m. and 4 a.m. the output of all three stations originated in York, a lack of localness for YCR and Sun City listeners which was disguised by the insertion of local commercials, and by an '0800' number which they could use to phone requests to their 'local' presenter situated some forty or eighty miles away. We might describe this as networking by stealth or as a kind of syndication, the process by which whole programme packages are centrally produced and pre-recorded and then delivered to a spread of local stations. Syndication has long been a feature of local broadcasting in the United States (Fornatale and Mills 1980: 143–5; Tunstall 1986: 153).

It seems fair to say that BBC local radio, with its news and chat programmes, phone-ins and reports on neighbourhood issues, has focused to a much greater extent on the communities it serves than ILR has. Nevertheless it has been dogged by difficulties. In an organization which has always been highly centralized on London and whose great achievements have been on a national or even international scale, it seems all but a contradiction in terms.

Not surprisingly, local radio has never been able to claim a high priority within the BBC. It has been poorly funded and has generally drawn small audiences. Moreover there is a common impression both outside and inside the Corporation that it became involved in local radio not through any ideological commitment but in order to exploit VHF/FM technology and pre-empt the influence of ILR, and that it maintains its involvement only because local radio feeds the networks with news stories, programme ideas and promising young journalists and production staff. The problems of BBC local radio were summarized by Lewis and Booth (1989: 95).

If from the standpoint of the listener 'national' has largely overshadowed 'local', whether institutionally, as in the case of the BBC, or in the sense that the content of ILR is largely indistinguishable from that of the networks, we might also say that 'format' has almost totally extinguished 'mixed programming'. Except on one network . . .

What is this Radio Four?

The only network that offers anything like the old Reithian programme diet is Radio Four; even here there is a virtual absence of music. There is also some output, notably *Today* in the early morning, which does not so much resemble programmes in the traditional sense as the kinds of rolling sequences that we expect from stations broadcasting an all-news format.

Nevertheless Radio Four swims against the current of modern radio in a highly distinctive and significant way, and it is worrying that in the structural changes being made at the BBC, with radio and television to be combined within a single administration, this fact does not seem to be adequately recognized by the Corporation's own management.

The network is distinctive first of all because in the variety and nature of its output it presupposes a *listener*, not someone for whom radio is merely a noise in the background. Certainly there are aspects of both its form and content which acknowledge the likely secondariness of its consumption (traffic information for motorists is only one obvious example); but it is one of the few surviving stations which would not dissatisfy anyone who chose to treat its output as primary.

Certain of its programme genres paradoxically demonstrate radio's strengths by pushing against its limitations. Drama, which is normally a spectacle, something to be watched, thrives here by stretching the listener's imagination. Comedy, another genre which normally depends on the visual, must on radio literally live by its wits – survive on its more cerebral ability to create laughter through words alone. What Radio Four does above all is to reclaim for its audiences, situated as they are at the end of several centuries of a predominantly 'literate' culture, something of the archaic value and pleasure of listening to 'talk' or speech.

Because we inhabit a culture of writing and print many of us feel that there is something trivial and self-indulgent about talk. In much broadcasting it is often apologetically referred to as 'chat'. But the value of orality is something quite distinct from, if equivalent to, that of literacy (Ong 1982: 31–77): it is language which is *dynamic* – inflected by the human voice and personality and often under pressure from thought or emotion rather than lying disembodied on the page. This dynamism is an important element in any kind of spoken language – interviews, discussion, argument, persuasion, explanation, anecdotes, jokes, sustained narratives – whether it is language which has never been anything other than speech or language which originated as writing.

Radio Four's *From Our Own Correspondent*, a collection of reports by its foreign news staff, is a type of programme that might seem to be better suited to the print medium, but few who hear it would agree. It is a classic instance of the peculiar power of the spoken word. Its reports, perhaps of a certain situation in Africa or eastern Europe, typically comprise a vivid physical description – the sights, sounds and smells of the situation – together with certain more abstract observations of a social or political nature.

Yet because the report is spoken, everything seems to be transfigured by the correspondent's own consciousness and personality in a way which is much less obvious in the 'objective' medium of print. As well as accent and voice tone, we are acutely aware of the correspondent's choice of language, intellectual cast of mind, and the peculiar impression which the situation has made upon him or her.

Of course television also offers the benefits and pleasures of 'talk', providing its own correspondents' reports, discussion programmes and much else besides, but not in an equivalent way. Radio talk is often 'secondary' in the sense that the listener hears it while doing something else, but paramount on its own terms because the medium is blind: with the possible exception of some accompanying noises which must in any case be verbally identified, words are all there is. Unlike television's they are not drowned in an often superfluous visuality.

But Radio Four is distinctive and significant not only because so many of its individual programmes are substantial enough to be listened to and not merely heard, but also because of the overall *range* or variety of its programmes. It seems fair to say that no independent radio station could deliver such range because the lifeblood of commercialism is format: by typifying content you can typify the listener and deliver her to the advertiser. As Fornatale and Mills (1980) argue, differing formats are devised not to provide diversity for its own sake, nor in response to any government regulator's requirement, nor – in essence – to satisfy listeners' demands. They exist simply in order 'to deliver to advertisers a measured and defined group of consumers, known as a segment' (1980: 61), and it is not surprising that the history of radio formats is closely linked to the history of market research.

In complete contrast, Radio Four is built round the essentially Reithian principle of serendipity, the faculty of discovering pleasing or valuable things by chance. In a curious way the listener who chooses Radio Four *resigns* the principle of choice in order to gain a less predictable, more varied and ultimately richer experience. From this it is apparent that although public service broadcasting is so often discussed in terms of television, it has a special relevance to radio. Although TV formats are on the increase, mixed programming remains more widespread on television than on radio; but from a modern public service point of view it makes rather less sense, since viewers are much more attentive and active in the use of their medium and can obtain as much variety as they feel they need by switching channels.

However, few take the trouble to switch channels on the radio because listening is generally secondary to some other activity. They are thus more likely to be exposed to fresh things by chance and to persevere with them – which makes mixed programming on the sound medium an especially valuable asset.

We recall from its origins that what is of real importance about the mixed programming of Radio Four is not its variety *per se* but the social and psychological values that underlie it. In fact the social context of radio is worth special study, not simply at the demographic level – which socio-economic groups listen to what stations? – but at the philosophical level. What do the different stations posit about human psychology and about what used to be called, in more generalizing times, human nature?

The commercial strategy of format, by ostensibly elevating individual autonomy and the principle of consumer choice, actually seems to take a reductive, deterministic view of human behaviour. It assumes that the individual is significant or definable only in terms of one particular interest or preoccupation, and that free choice is usually timid and conservative. Choice resists plenitude, settles for what is easy and familiar, declines to acknowledge the value of new experience or the possibility that benefit and pleasure may sometimes be different. Consequently, given a certain type of content, you can confidently predict that so many thousands or millions will listen to it.

Mixed programming, on the other hand, requires the listener's passive, old-fashioned submission to a selection of material which is made by others who presumably 'know better', the acceptance of a hierarchy of expertise and values which neatly complements the patrician approach of the early

BBC. But its ultimate consequence is intellectual enlargement, the expo-sure to a much wider range of knowledge and experience, and thus the basis for autonomy of another kind. Mixed programming exalts the indi-vidual because it assumes that in the potentially infinite nature of their interests, listeners transcend the simple categories of market research: they are human beings even more than they are 'types of consumers'.

Radio may now be the Cinderella medium. Despite the proliferation of networks and stations there seems to have been an overall shrinkage of its content. Yet it still affords much food for thought, its inherent character-istics placing it at the heart of the public service debate.

Questions

1   Most television commercials make great use of the varied visual resources of the medium. Select a radio commercial which in your opinion effectively compensates for, or even exploits, sound broadcasting's lack of vision, explaining how you think it does so.

2   Listen over a period of time to the output of Classic FM and then attempt some detailed analysis of it. In its presentation and promotion of classical music how far does the station resemble, how far differ from, a conventional pop music station, and what can you infer about the identity of its target audience?

3   From your own listening do you think the difficulties which 'talk' radio is presently undergoing stem from the individual station's approach to it, or, given radio's function in the modern world, from the nature of the medium itself?

References

Baron, M. (1975) *Independent Radio*, Lavenham: Dalton.

Briggs, A. (1961) *The History of Broadcasting in the United Kingdom, vol. 1, The Birth of Broadcasting*, London: Oxford University Press.

Briggs, A. (1979) *The History of Broadcasting in the United Kingdom, vol. 4, Sound and Vision*, Oxford: Oxford University Press.

Chapman, R. (1992) *Selling the Sixties: The Pirates and Pop Music Radio*, London: Routledge.

Crisell, A. (1994) *Understanding Radio*, 2nd edn, London: Routledge.

Fornatale, P. and Mills, J. (1980) *Radio in the Television Age*, Woodstock, NY: Overlook Press.

Harris, P. (1970) *When Pirates Ruled the Waves*, 4th edn, London and Aberdeen: Impulse Books.

Horsman, M. (1996) 'On radio advertising's boom', *The Independent Section Two* 16 April: 17.

Lewis, P.M. and Booth, J. (1989) *The Invisible Medium: Public, Commercial and Community Radio*, London: Macmillan.

McDonnell, J. (1991) *Public Service Broadcasting: A Reader*, London: Routledge.

Ong, W. (1982) *Orality and Literacy*, London: Methuen.

Paulu, B. (1961) *British Broadcasting in Transition*, Minneapolis, MN: University of Minnesota Press.

Seymour-Ure, C. (1991) *The British Press and Broadcasting since 1945*, Oxford: Basil Blackwell.

Tunstall, J. (1986) *Communications Deregulation*, Oxford: Basil Blackwell.

Williams, R. (1995) 'BBC switches on CD-quality radio', *The Independent* 28 September: 6.

Further reading

Barnard, S. (1989) *On the Radio: Music Radio in Britain*, Milton Keynes: Open University Press.

Barnett, S. and Morrison, D. (1989) *The Listener Speaks: The Radio Audience and the Future of Radio*, London: HMSO.

Briggs, A. (1995) *The History of Broadcasting in the United Kingdom, vol. 5, Competition 1955–1974*, Oxford: Oxford University Press.

BBC (1969) *Broadcasting in the Seventies*, London: British Broadcasting Corporation.

Donovan, P. (1992) *The Radio Companion*, London: Grafton.

Home Office (1986) *Report of the Committee on Financing the BBC* (Peacock Report), Cmnd 9824, London: HMSO.

Montgomery, M. (1986) 'DJ talk', *Media, Culture and Society* 8: 421–40.

Moss, P. and Higgins, C. (1984) 'Radio voices', *Media, Culture and Society* 4: 353–75.

O'Sullivan, T., Dutton, B. and Rayner, P. (1994) *Studying the Media*, London: Edward Arnold.

Reith, J. (1924) *Broadcast Over Britain*, London: Hodder & Stoughton.

Scannell, P. (ed.) (1991) *Broadcast Talk*, London: Sage.

Scannell, P. and Cardiff, D. (1982) 'Serving the nation: public service broadcasting before the war', in B. Waites, T. Bennett and G. Martin (eds) *Popular Culture: Past and Present*, London: Croom Helm.

Chapter 10

Television

CONTEMPORARY TELEVISION: A FRAMEWORK FOR ANALYSIS

RICHARD PATERSON

Television is in transition throughout the world. The structures and organizational patterns of the days of spectrum scarcity, when television channels were allocated only a small part of the radio spectrum for broadcasting their signals, are fast being overturned. The future is digital and the days of dominance of public service broadcasters in Europe are coming to an end. So the rhetoric would have us believe – but what analytical framework can we bring to bear on change in the television industry?

The television industry has been marked by constant revolution since the mid-1980s; previously in the UK and mainland Europe, there had been a relatively settled regulatory and organizational structure based on a perceived scarcity of spectrum. The advent of first satellite transmission and later digital transmission has increased the number of channels which can be delivered to viewers at an economic cost and has led to a rapid proliferation of services. In the UK, after an initial period of high risk investment, BSkyB has emerged as the financially strongest TV company. This position is based on its dominance of the satellite market through providing the leading film and sports channels, with an increasing number of long-term exclusive deals with many of the leading sports and a virtual monopoly on licensing deals with the Hollywood studios. To date the satellite channels have produced little original programming (with the exception of news and sports programming) and have relied heavily on imports of fiction and entertainment programmes from the USA. In addition, News Datacom, a subsidiary of News Corp (the largest shareholder in BSkyB), currently holds the monopoly in the UK on conditional access and subscription management services for satellite channels.

The terrestrial broadcasting companies in both the public and private sectors have had to respond to these developments. There has been concentration in commercial television with a series of take-overs of the ITV franchises by the larger companies; a re-examination of the range of businesses has also been undertaken. The ITV companies' important competitive advantage has been based on their dominant position in advertising sales which has given them the ability to produce high quality and high cost programmes that mirror British society and are attractive to viewers. A review of future strategy has also taken place inside the BBC, which retains the proceeds of the licence fee and continues to operate under a royal charter that empowers and obliges it to produce a diverse range of programming. However, all of the recent changes at the BBC have been based on the need to reduce costs in order to be able to compete and maintain audiences in the ever more competitive marketplace for viewers' attention.

This chapter sets out to map an economic model of contemporary television in Europe, especially the UK, and then briefly to describe its changing impact in the cultural field on the areas of programming and audience response. Television is both culture and commerce and it is important to consider the cultural effects of policies and practices in the industry.

What has been lacking heretofore in much media studies is an analytical framework that identifies the 'business' (or more accurately the 'businesses') of television. The basic analytical tool which I propose to introduce here is the 'value chain'. A common enough concept in any study of industry, it has great power in explaining significant relationships and changes within the audiovisual industry. In particular, it enables an examination of the changing nature of television, and of the income streams for software, in the digital domain.

Value chain: an overview

The value chain model analyses the media industries as a series of interrelated but discrete activities, like most other industries. This value chain can be broken down in many ways but for the sake of this argument it can be understood as follows:

> contributors and rights holders → content creation/programme-making →
> → broadcasting/distribution → gateway → audience

The components of the value chain model may be defined as follows:

1 *Contributors and rights holders* The key to any television programme is the ideas and those who realize them through their creative endeavour. With 'ideas' come rights – intellectual property rights – which are protected by copyright and related laws for the rights holders.

2 *Content creation/programme-making* The makers of a programme – a production company – will take ideas and invest to create a programme. The source of the investment will vary; usually in the UK programmes are commissioned by one of the channels for their own schedule and they will retain the right to distribute the resulting production.

3 *Distribution* In television the act of distribution has normally been called transmission and in the UK was dependent on scarce radio

spectrum until satellite technologies allowed new services to be provided directly to the home or via a cable network.

4 *Gateway* Advances in technology have resulted in a direct relationship between the broadcaster and the consumer using subscriber management and conditional access systems which enable only those who have paid a subscription to view the transmitted television signal. This is called a gateway.

5 *Vertical integration* Companies which have activities in different parts of the value chain are vertically integrated. So, for example, the BBC or Granada Television not only have production activities but also run television channels – they are vertically integrated companies.

Until recent changes affected the place of the integrated 'broadcaster' in the value chain, there had been a relatively settled situation – spectrum space was allocated because of its deemed 'scarcity'. In the UK, which introduced commercial television in 1955, there was a division of the sources of income between the BBC and ITV – respectively the licence fee and advertising revenue. For commercial broadcasters, which were invariably vertically integrated organizations, profit margins were adequate, indeed substantial. Individual companies were able to sustain their businesses; in particular, the larger television companies (like Granada Television) produced, broadcast and distributed their programmes within the regulated and protected broadcasting economy. However these monopolies, or cartels, came under increasing economic pressure from the mid-1980s onwards from various quarters. (A cartel is formed when a group of companies combine to exclude competition and maintain an agreed level of price of a good, while a monopsony exists when there is one buyer and many sellers – a condition which pertained in British commercial television until the early 1980s.)

In the UK this economic pressure had started with the legislation setting up Channel Four in 1981. Its remit included a requirement that the channel should give access to new voices and, in particular, that programmes should mostly be sourced from independent producers. When the Peacock Committee (ostensibly set up to report on the future financing of the BBC) suggested in 1987 a minimum 40 per cent quota of independent productions on ITV and the BBC, the place of the independent producers in the UK television industry, or at least those that could survive the difficulties of uncertain commissions and low capitalization, was confirmed (Home Office 1986).

The independent sector grew rapidly in the 1980s until it was estimated there were more than a thousand independent production companies in existence by the early 1990s, most being very small operations run by people who would find freelance work in between occasional commissions. Channel Four continued to be the main source of commissions for smaller independents after 1990 with both the BBC and ITV (effectively forced to take 25 per cent of independent productions by the Broadcasting Act 1990) commissioning from relatively few, and usually larger, independent production companies.

It was the introduction of a number of new means of broadcast distribution – satellite and cable – and to a lesser extent the impact of video, which disrupted the so-called cosy duopoly of BBC and ITV and then the value chain in British television. The new subscription gateway, requiring the provision of decoders, subscriber management and billing, underpinned the increasing financial strength of BSkyB as satellite penetration increased. The value to be extracted and the distribution of power and profit across the chain have been radically altered as control of the gateway and the associated technology have become a new high profit business. Furthermore, it is expected to become an increasingly important one as it gives access to invaluable market information about consumer tastes.

Uncertainty about which future strategy to follow has become a dominant concern for companies in the media market. It affects both existing media companies and potential new entrants as they seek competitive advantage and a good rate of return on capital invested. The competition authorities are beginning to take alarm at the possibility that larger and more powerful conglomerates might gain a stranglehold on the market, with heightened sensitivity because of the 'propaganda' fears associated with media ownership. In both national parliaments and in the European Commission and European Parliament this has led to proposals for new regulations.

Such situations of increased market power of media companies have emerged before, particularly in the USA, and have led to action by competition authorities: the forced divestment of cinema theatres by Paramount in the late 1940s resulted from earlier fears of market domination, and the introduction in the 1970s of the finance and syndication rule to prevent the networks dominating programme production. In Europe, however, there has never, until recently, been the potential for such domination beyond national borders across the European audiovisual market, in part because of the previous dominance of a public service orientation in most European broadcasters. The size and power of a Bertlesmann or Canal Plus has not previously worried politicians. Indeed, in the UK in recent years there has been a constant lament that British companies seem to lack sufficient size to compete in global markets and the subsequent phase of mergers encouraged. The same thinking about UK Television plc has also affected the BBC, leading to the establishment, with government encouragement, of BBC Worldwide, to exploit the brand name on a global basis.

We shall now consider some key analytical issues.

What is the business?

The uncertainties in organizations within the television industry about their future strategies and positioning in the economy has led to defensive (or aggressive) position-taking and a series of alliances. These are based on assumptions about the economic drivers of future markets and the optimum company strategy for maximizing profitability in the future information society. It is interesting in this respect to look at how different European companies have positioned themselves, and the economic logic of the strategy. The most significant political and cultural consequence of these new market realities is their effect and lasting influence on public sector broadcasters as they engage with these competitive forces. It will almost certainly have a fundamental effect on programming – generalist channels like BBC1 and ITV will survive but their ability to provide first-run high cost drama may reduce over time as premium services emerge for which subscribers are willing to pay extra. As the number of channels increases with the huge additional capacity provided by digital broadcasting we can also expect to see ever more niche channels targeted at specialist audience groups.

An interesting precursor to future change in the UK is the strong relationship that has emerged between the BBC and BSkyB. In the mid-1990s the BBC purchased new American series in Los Angeles in partnership with BSkyB and participated (with the rights to match highlights) in the Premier League football rights deal negotiated with BSkyB. But such situations are subject to change and influenced by political calculations as much as commercial considerations.

In any examination of restructuring of businesses in the UK television industry perhaps the most significant has been that undertaken by the BBC. After the introduction of an internal market (as Producer Choice) in the early 1990s, the BBC announced in 1996 a fundamental restructuring into five Divisions (Broadcast, Production, News, Resources and Worldwide). In so doing the BBC has given itself greater flexibility than was possible in an integrated public service orientated company. It has attempted to redefine its core operations into areas in the broadcasting value chain where it can maximize revenues in high profit areas. At the same time it has entered various partnerships to develop the use of BBC resources outside the UK – to act as a global media company.

All media businesses have begun to recognize that the key activities within the audiovisual sector are now on the one hand the control of rights in material, and on the other control of the gateway to services and to the information available from this servicing. Programme production does not, in itself, add significant economic value but it remains important in terms of the need to sustain creativity and innovation – the addition of cultural value.

The development of the gateway (or subscription management) induces new players to begin to invest in a range of areas, however tentatively, because of the uncertain future disposition of technologies and networks, and hence of profit and influence. The involvement of the telecommunications companies, each of which has enormous potential economic power but little current knowledge of the value added markets, of which the media are clearly one, is highly significant. The change in relationships between companies is understood as convergence between formerly separate industries because of technological and organizational change, but in fact it is a convergence where the main interest of companies is where value will be added (and high profits can be made) in the future. Convergence has both economic and significant cultural consequences. So, for example, News International, a US-based conglomerate with interests in 20th Century Fox, the Fox network, satellite broadcasting in different regions of the world (with subscriber management facilities), newspapers and publishing (including the *Sun* and *The Times* in the UK), is linked with MCI and BT (Concert), the merged telecommunications company. It has an interest in offering new services and maintaining a competitive edge in future distribution networks. The longer-term consequences of this kind of activity are unknown and one way to account for such strategies is that they are cases of defensive investment across a number of potential future developments. What is clear is that the end result will almost certainly be a need for regulation to prevent dominance by a small number of powerful conglomerates in the distribution market which would otherwise have an overwhelming influence on production.

In this respect the inability of the EU, despite much comment to the contrary, to establish a common set top box standard for subscription television through legislation is a worrying precedent. And no matter what the outcome of these strategic shifts, in the longer term the important factor will be the skills of the workforce to create images and representations of the cultures of Europe which audiences want to watch, as much as the brand you have available to sell.

Old models in Europe: public service and private

European television was distinctive in its public service orientation until the 1980s. Even in the UK, which had pioneered commercial television in the 1950s, this was undertaken within a definitive public service mode.

The economic model was based on a vertical integration which allowed programme-making to develop within the broadcasting institution. That a TV service was many businesses (production, facilities, broadcasting and transmission) was masked by the priority given to the cultural or public service mission of television in Europe and the lack of competition and protection of the different parts of the business.

When an independent production sector re-emerged in the UK in the 1980s (it had been effectively extinguished during the 1960s) it created first uncertainty and then led to the gradual erosion of the duopoly's control. The certainties for the commercial ITV companies were swept away. A system based on monopsony and cartelization, in 'competition' with the BBC, had been justified culturally into the mid-1980s but in fact had become extremely inefficient.

The justification for limited channel availability was technological and based on the limited radio spectrum available. Rationing broadcasting licences was necessary because of the need to plan frequency use and achieve near universal service across the UK (the fundamental access principle of public service broadcasting). But the elite position of television had led to an increasing range of interests – both commercial and cultural – calling for change. The recommendations of the Annan Committee on the Future of Broadcasting (Home Office 1977) for an Open Broadcasting Authority led to the decisions in 1981 by the first Thatcher administration to create Channel Four with a remit to encourage a range of different voices on television. This model cleverly blended enough certainty for the ITV companies (who funded the Channel's inception but sold and retained advertising revenue until 1992) with an opening for a new and vibrant 'independent' production sector.

New possibilities for additional channels were opened up in Britain first by satellite technology then by the huge increase in channel capacity offered by the digital revolution. The other mode of delivery, cable, had had varying success across Europe in the 1960s and 1970s but despite several attempts in the UK to achieve widespread uptake in cable (particularly in the early 1980s) it took direct-to-home satellite broadcasts by BSky B finally to break the BBC/ITV duopoly. Cable companies finally achieved a more significant market impact when allowed to sell voice telephony as well as entertainment services and thus broke the BT monopoly in the local loop with a competitive pricing strategy. The large investments by the American telecommunications and cable companies led to the UK being seen as a laboratory for the cable–telephony interface.

New model

Changes across the value chain in the television industry, alongside altered expectations of the role of small and medium size enterprises in the market, have had a profound effect on all sectors. Another way of thinking about the value chain is as a supply chain – with an upstream (where programmes are produced) and a downstream (where they are transmitted and viewed).

As noted above, if we conceive of the television industry as a supply chain then the major companies, which previously operated as vertically integrated organizations, have had to identify where the most efficient deployment of their capital can be achieved. No longer is there an assured situation of super profits for commercial broadcasters based on an effective monopoly on advertising sales, nor a sufficiency of income for the public service broadcaster to undertake every activity. (At one point in the 1980s the BBC was seen to want to be a part of every innovation in the industry – be it breakfast television or satellite broadcasting; only financial realism and competition changed this attitude.) All organizations have to address the problem of identifying their core business and which parts of their operational needs might be as well or better supplied by others.

This raises the key question of where value is added, and the future income streams of the business. It is not always simple to determine the answers when an industry is in flux. However, what is clear is that content will always be primary (to attract customers or the advertisers attracted by the customers), and that owning intellectual property rights on programming will ensure a continuing future income. Television once was seen as a single business. Now it is seen as a series of related activities. Furthermore new businesses are emerging including the 'navigation' and tracking customer or viewer preferences – effectively gathering intelligence from services offered in order to supply yet other services.

In the new European television system commerce does not just meet culture, it is feared that it might overwhelm it. At a political level in some European countries, television is still seen as above all else culture – albeit aware of the American pre-eminence in the audiovisual industries – which has led to a series of measures from the European Commission to protect the diversity of European culture and create a strong European audiovisual industry.

Political concerns

In Europe (and in the USA) there has been a concern to maintain a diversity of voices and opinions on the airwaves. In the new commercial era in European television, the need to control cross-media ownership has replaced previous concerns about press dominance. In some countries this can be achieved through regulation of ownership of media in different sectors (press, television, radio) and insisting on transparency of shareholdings. In others, political conditions notwithstanding, some market positions have been treated with caution by politicians due to the powerful influence that key owners (for example, Rupert Murdoch) may have in supporting or opposing particular political parties, and the lack of action justified by the need for them to reap the reward from speculative investments.

A second political concern has been the US dominance in the balance of trade in audiovisual products. This is seen as a threat not only economically, but also in terms of loss of identity – the idea that television and film produced in a country reflect and mirror society and sustain its self-image. The French government has been particularly keen to restrict American influence (or increase European influence) by imposing quotas on air-time for American products. An unsuccessful attempt in 1995/6 by the French government to strengthen the quota clause in the EU's Television Without Frontiers directive followed a successful disruption of the final stages of the Uruguay Round of the GATT (General Agreement on Tariffs and Trade) negotiations in relation to the trade in audiovisual services.

The major fear of European governments, bred on insecurity and with memories of war and deprivation, is the loss of the 'social glue' which public television represented. Social democracy and the welfare system are integral to European political life and their standing reinforced by media which convey and reassure through these messages of identity and unity within a diverse set of cultures.

The other political concerns have focused on areas of moral regulation. The influence of television is seen as potentially harmful and in an era when social cohesion is undermined television has often been labelled as the scapegoat. In the UK this has resulted in agreed practices like the 9 p.m. 'watershed' and family viewing policy (since the early 1960s), the drawing up of editorial guidelines within broadcasting organizations, and since the late 1980s the creation of the Broadcasting Standards Council to offer guidance on questions of taste and decency. These issues have acquired a new airing in the age of the Internet (as they did with the advent of video) with governments unsure whether to allow the market to decide or whether they should regulate.

New market considerations

In the new audiovisual market 'content is king' and ownership of intellectual property is seen as crucial to future prosperity by many companies on both sides of the Atlantic. The supply chain is seen to require a constant input of new programming as well as enabling the further exploitation of existing programming by rights' owners. For those with large libraries of material (whether produced and owned, or acquired) the key to profitability is to sell into secondary markets while continuing to produce or acquire new material.

New rules have begun to be applied in the new audiovisual marketplace under the influence of competition law and the public sector is facing increasing difficulties now that its protected position has disappeared. Where previously there was a guaranteed role for public broadcasters in all European countries this position has changed at a rapid rate. No longer possessing the largest guaranteed income (even when bidding together with public broadcasters from other countries) the public broadcasters are slowly losing their pre-eminent position within the national cultures. The consequences of the Single European Market legislation are benefiting large conglomerates able to take a controlling position, while the European public sector broadcasters, when they have tried to achieve the same end (through for example their pan-European sports channel, Eurosport) have been found guilty of unfair competition. Indeed sport is an area where the new satellite broadcasters with large revenues available from subscription channels have been able to outbid the public broadcasters for rights to many events.

In analysing these changes the centrality of distribution – which for television means the control of broadcasting and commissioning – as the controlling function in the audiovisual industry becomes clear. Not for nothing did the European Commission's Think Tank identify the need for Europe's film distribution system to be rationalized to improve its commerciality. But this rationalization is happening first in television with new gateways to subscription channels and the control of these gateways owned at present by monopoly suppliers. Global and local markets are being redefined. It is the market which is forcing these changes rather than a political settlement.

Production consequences: skills and structures

The European Commission, in its Green Paper on the future competitiveness of Europe's industry, stressed the potential of the information industries (1993). It focused attention on employment. The key factor for commercial prosperity in television is the availability of a skilled workforce, deployed effectively in a well-functioning industry able to harness and sell on its creativity.

A new functional map of the skills required in the television industry is emerging following the changes in the technical infrastructure associated with digitization. The changes are partly evolution, partly innovation, and require responses by firms acting in the market and by governments seeking competitive advantage or to retain culturally specific programmes. If Europe is to compete in the audiovisual sector it needs a viable supply chain, supported at each stage by a sufficiently skilled workforce. In the UK television industry the previous certainties of employment in the BBC or one of the ITV companies have been replaced in the 1990s by increasing casualization of employment (estimated by 1996 to be about 60 per cent of the workforce) with potentially disastrous consequences for creative endeavour.

Outputs

Television output evolves gradually. The standard television genres are well known – fiction (single plays and TV movies, series and serials – crime, medicine, melodrama), factual (documentaries, current affairs), news, entertainment (including situation comedy), sport and features. Public service broadcasting on generalist channels has been characterized by the balance of tastes it has catered for – an attempt to please all of the audience some of the time across the whole output: to inform, to educate and to entertain. TV fiction has been seen as both a mirror and a window to the society it represents in all its diversity. The news is seen to play a key role in offering impartial information to citizens and to secure the functioning of the democratic processes.

There is continuity and innovation across the genre in programme output by television channels in Europe and an appropriate mix, cleverly scheduled, can lead to ratings success. However, the greatest competition has recently come from niche channels (whether film, sport, children or documentary) and this trend seems likely to continue. It is a truism that in most countries the locally produced fiction tends to attract the largest audiences but why American programmes should achieve great success in Europe when few European programmes are successful outside their country of origin is difficult to explain. If the US studios can offer a universal language attractive to most of Europe then, it is often argued, European producers should be able to identify a winning solution to achieve the same end. However, analysis has failed to identify the range of cultural indicators attaching to successful programming.

The audience

All endeavours to alter television output are dependent on consumer uptake. Without an audience, public service broadcasters lose their legitimacy, commercial television cannot sell advertising air-time and subscription channels go out of business. Most academic work and industry research on audiences in the UK has been ill suited to achieving an understanding of what uses audiences make of television. The notion of television as the glue for the nation's democratic future is untestable; the various quasi-anthropological approaches to audience study have been based on minimal evidence. Equally, the industry's determination to use the currency of the ratings, demographically interpreted, to conduct its business – whether the BBC in debates about its future or the commercial channels in negotiations with the advertisers – conceals much about the ways television is used in different types of households.

Recent research has shown the complexities of the individual's use of television. The industry now faces an uncertain future, with little knowledge of how or why its audiences have engaged with its products in the past. The one certainty that seems to shape many current investment decisions is that while the future of the industry is uncertain, it will be highly profitable for those players able to secure high quality programming and ensure the continuing attention of their audiences.

Conclusion

Television in the future will be different from the past and the changes in structure will have an impact on the programmes made. Whether it will be better or worse only time will tell. That the different sectors which constitute the television industry remain ultimately dependent on the willingness of the viewer to watch remains unaltered. However, using the value chain as an analytical tool allows a clarity of approach for both the researcher and student, the investor and the policy-maker, as these fundamental changes unwind in response to the market's whim.

Questions

1   Review how the different television channels in the UK – BBC, Channels Four and Five, ITV and the cable and satellite channels – gain their supply of programmes. Comment on the various proportions of US and independently produced programming on each channel.

2   What is an appropriate framework for regulating the ownership of television channels in the UK in order to ensure a diversity of views on the airwaves?

3   If the three UK television channels in the 1970s were the 'glue' for the democratic order, what function do the forty-plus available channels play in the 1990s?

References

EC Green Paper (1993) *Growth, Competitiveness, Employment – The Challenges and Ways Forward into the 21st Century*, Com (93) 700, December.

Home Office (1977) *Report of the Committee on the Future of Broadcasting* (Annan Report), Cmnd 6753, London: HMSO.

Home Office (1986) *Report of the Committee on Financing the BBC* (Peacock Report), Cmnd 9824, London: HMSO.

Further reading

BBC (1996) *Extending Choice in the Digital Age*, London: BBC.

Hood, S. (ed.) (1994) *Behind the Screen*, London: Lawrence & Wishart.

KPMG (1996) *Public Policy Issues Arising from Telecommunications and Audiovisual Convergence*, London: KPMG and European Commission.

Mulgan, G. and Paterson, R. (eds) (1993) *Reinventing the Organisation*, BBC Charter Review no. 4, London: British Film Institute.

Petrie, D. and Willis, J. (eds) (1994) *Television and the Household,* London: British Film Institute.

Pettigrew, N., Paterson, R. and Willis, J. (1995) *Industry Tracking Study: Interim Report,* London: British Film Institute.

Porter, M. (1985) *Competitive Advantage,* New York: Free Press.

Silverstone, R. (1995) *Television and Everyday Life,* London: Routledge.

Smith, A. (ed.) (1995) *Television: An International History,* Oxford: Oxford University Press.

Stevenson, W. (ed.) (1993) *All Our Futures: The Changing Role and Purpose of the BBC,* London: British Film Institute.

Chapter 11

European cinema

CINEMA IN EUROPE

ANNE JÄCKEL

In 1995, Europe celebrated the centenary of cinema by honouring its pioneers, the Lumière brothers (whose Cinematograph allowed them to project moving pictures on to a screen to an audience for the first time on 28 December 1895 in Paris), Max Sladanowsky (with his Bioscope in Berlin) and many others. However successful European inventors, film-makers and business people were before 1914, the First World War put an end to their global commercial ambitions. (Before the war broke out, the French entrepreneurs Léon Gaumont and Charles Pathé had started to build a world empire. Pathé had established studios in several European countries and in the USA. They were also able to distribute their own films in North America by forming a virtual cartel with Edison and others.)

The First World War also ruined Europe's film industries, leaving the Hollywood studios unhindered to pursue their strategic vertical integration and fully exploit technological innovations (sound and colour). ('Vertical integration' is a form of concentration often associated with the Hollywood Studio System whereby a film studio owns or controls the production company (with exclusive staff and development funds) as well as the distribution and exhibition circuits.)

Cinema an art but also an industry

Many young people's first experience of cinema may be American but it is in Europe that cinema was first elevated to an artform (the French call it 'the seventh art'). It is in Europe that a strong tradition of film culture has developed and flourished through specific art movements whether international (avant-garde, surrealism) or national (Soviet cinema, German expressionism, the British documentary movement, Italian neo-realism, the French and Czech new waves, and so on), gaining critical recognition from film journals, theoreticians and intellectuals.

Europe has a long-standing tradition of 'Auteur Cinema'. In film theory, 'la politique des auteurs' (an expression first used by the French film magazine *Les Cahiers du Cinéma* in the 1950s) is based on the proposition that the film director, like a literary author or any other artist, is the prime author of a film. In the 1970s, the theory became a critical method for evaluating films. According to this theory, a film became identified with its director, an 'auteur' with a recognizable style. The theory has led to numerous debates over the years.

As Ginette Vincendeau noted:

> The subjective vision of individual auteurs has been part of national identity formation, providing a guarantee of authenticity and belonging and a personal 'refraction of dominant national concerns'. . . . Some are synonymous with their whole country (Bergman, Oliveira), some have acted as its 'humanitarian conscience' (Wajda), or raised its international profile, either in a repudiation of previous generations (the French New Wave film-makers) or after a period of oblivion (the New German auteurs); others have played the 'enfant terrible' or 'artiste maudit' (Polanski, Akerman, Godard) or militated in favour of a particular group (Brückner for women directors) or the whole of Europe (Beineix, Bertolucci and Tavernier during the GATT negotiations). Directors like Kieslowski and Wenders have almost ceased to be Polish or German, and become 'European': recently Wenders declared that working in the USA made him realise that it was 'a much nicer profession to be a European film-maker.'
>
> (Vincendeau 1995: xiv)

This tradition may have served Europeans well at crucial moments in film history (transition from silent to sound, competition from television) and cinema may still be 'the artform of the twentieth century' but Europe's screens are now dominated by Hollywood films and European films are more often seen at film festivals and relegated to the 'art-house ghettos' than shown in mainstream cinemas, even in their country of origin. Since the mid-1980s, the more popular tradition of film-making (comedies and thrillers) has often been produced by and for television. In the 1990s, self-indulgence on the part of European directors, the reluctance of European actors and actresses to 'play the star game', along with the protective schemes that some governments continue to operate to support their domestic film industries, are usually blamed for the poor commercial performance of European films.

The complex debates about high and low culture, national and global films are only two of the issues affecting the future of cinema. At a time when the new technologies are threatening to flood the audiovisual market with an increasing flow of pervasive entertainment, the strengths of 'Hollywood' lie as much in the current box-office performance of a few blockbusters as in its libraries and worldwide delivery systems. (When discussing US cinema, it is necessary to distinguish between 'the majors' (in Hollywood) and 'the independents'; the latter have the same problems as European film-makers and would not really want to be associated with the majors.) The 'American studios' being now a cartel of multinational companies operating on a global scale, 'Hollywood' may be an obsolete term but the stakes have now become enormous and the US industry is better placed than any other to take advantage of the economic and cultural potential of the audiovisual industries. During the 1993 GATT negotiations, the campaign for 'cultural exception' led by the French revealed that US film exports to Europe generated US annual revenues of over $3.7 billion (£2.5 billion) while Europeans had to content themselves with less than 2 per cent of the US market. No one doubted the supremacy of US popular culture in the audiovisual sphere (Americans command between 80 and 85 per cent of the world's film market) but to non-Americans, the position of Americans in the long battle over the right of European countries to support their own film and television productions seemed greedy and 'imperialistic'. In the name of free trade, liberal USA called 'protectionism' what the French considered keeping a stake in their own culture and encouraging local talent and creativity.

In December 1993, Europe obtained 'cultural exception', the (temporary) exclusion of audiovisual works from the General Agreement on Tariffs and Trade but within Europe, the GATT negotiations exposed the uneven playing field in which film industries continue to operate. Benefiting from a whole array of subsidies and tax incentives, France remains the only European country with both a prolific film industry and a strong film culture. Lacking government support, some national industries are struggling to survive. Between 1988 and 1993 the share of national films in their domestic market has also fallen considerably.

At European level, recent attempts have been made to improve the situation. With the construction of multiplexes and the proliferation of distribution outlets (television channels, video, CD-ROM) the cinema experience is also changing.

On the eve of the twenty-first century, what are the chances of Europe's national film industries? Can European cinema offer a viable alternative to the Hollywood-style pictures made for the international market?

Funding

Most European countries operate support schemes for their national film industries. Subsidies take essentially two forms. One is an automatic aid in the form of a tax on cinema tickets which goes to a support fund to help producers raise finance for their next film; the other is a selective aid whereby projects are assessed by committees which give 'soft loans' for production (known as 'advance on receipts'). Several nations also have cultural and regional film funds (France, Germany, Scotland).

However, it is not local subsidies but television which is now one of the most important sources of financing in the larger European territories –

France, Germany, Spain and Italy. In France, the five terrestrial television broadcasters have to invest 3 per cent of their turnover in film production while the pay-TV channel, Canal Plus, invests around 20 per cent. In Germany, government's subsidies usually go to films which already have television backing. In the UK, broadcasters are under no obligation to invest in film production, but Channel Four has a long tradition of commissioning films and the BBC recently started to follow suit.

The combination of government and television financing has made film-making in Europe an attractive proposition for financial institutions; in France, Italy and Spain, state-owned banks have long invested in film production.

It has been argued that the network of conglomerates and powerful financial institutions willing to invest in films, along with local subsidies and television funding, has led to the creation of 'a three-tier European industry':

> All the territories have producers who make low-budget films, supposedly 'art-house' films. A second tier of producers, mainly in the larger territories, also make medium-budget archetypal European films with international reputations such as TOTO LE HEROS, HIGH HEELS, EUROPA EUROPA and MEDITERRANEO. The third tier of producers, best represented in France, provides the European blockbusters – CYRANO DE BERGERAC, ATLANTIS and LES AMANTS DU PONT NEUF.
>
> (Shepherd and McCartney 1992: 17)

While the failure of Besson's and Carax's films at the box-office illustrates the famous maxim of Hollywood novelist and screenwriter William Goldman, 'in the film business, nobody knows anything', least of all what a 'potential' blockbuster is, the concept of 'a three-tier industry' is particularly appropriate to describe and assess the state of the European film industry.

Investments

In Europe, only France, the UK and Ireland appear to be able to raise finance for large-scale productions, although average film budgets are low (around $5 million in 1994) in comparison with the average cost of an American picture ($34 million plus $14 million of prints and advertising in the USA) (BFI 1996: 27; see also Table 11.1).

In 1994, investments in the UK and Ireland accounted for 31 per cent of all investments in the European Union, France for 32 per cent.

Before the French authorities introduced legislation to curb the production of films with a French majority share in a language other than French, 'French films' made in the English language under the official co-production agreement with the UK ranked among the most expensive films ever produced in Europe: Milos Forman's *Valmont* (1988), Jean Jacques Annaud's *The Lover* (1992), Roland Joffé's *City of Joy* (1992), all had budgets between $20 million and $30 million while Ridley Scott's *1492, Conquest of Paradise,*

Table 11.1 Average investment per film 1989–94 ($m)

	1989	1990	1991	1992	1993	1994
Belgium	1.54	1.76	3.04	2.98	1.99	2.50
Denmark	1.16	1.53	1.83	3.05	3.96	1.46
France	3.62	4.39	4.43	4.75	3.62	4.68
Germany	1.86	2.79	1.99	2.24	3.20	3.52
Greece					0.43	
Ireland	2.52	8.15	3.66	—	4.28	5.86
Italy	2.13	2.49	2.87	2.71	2.15	2.76
Luxembourg			1.24	0.31	0.47	0
Netherlands	0.78					
Portugal	0.81	0.42	0.5	0.75	0.44	0.25
Spain	1.26	1.62	1.84	1.51	1.30	1.17
UK	4.98	5.94	6.05	6.27	3.34	5.72

Source: Idate/*Screen Digest*

a British–French–Spanish co-production (released in October 1992 to com-
memorate the anniversary of Columbus's discovery of America) cost $44
million (over £20 million). With the exception of *The Lover*, these large-
budget European films made before 1993 entailed some North American
involvement, whether artistic (Annette Bening and Meg Tilly in *Valmont*),
financial (the US major Paramount committed 20 per cent of *1492*'s budget
in exchange for North American rights), or both (Patrick Swayze starred in
City of Joy and the film was partly financed by Warner Bros and Tristar). If
the introduction of new language regulations in France seemed to jeopard-
ize the production of such large-scale films with French partners after 1992,
it has not prevented French conglomerates like Chargeurs, Canal Plus or
Gaumont from investing in English-language productions made in the USA.
Gaumont backed *Leon*, Luc Besson's thriller – released with 250 copies in
France and 1000 copies in the USA in the autumn of 1994 – while Le
Studio Canal Plus and Ciby 2000 have also produced American/global
pictures using the facilities they have acquired in Hollywood.

Higher investments in the UK (despite the lack of tax advantages) and
Ireland (where the combination of recent financial incentives and the re-
establishment of the Irish Film Board have helped raise the country's output from a mere three films in 1990 to seventeen in 1994) are mainly due
to the increased activities of US companies there.

In Britain, twenty-one US films (with an average budget of £13.3 million)
were made in 1994 compared to ten in 1993 and seven in 1992. While
British studios have welcomed this exceptional influx of US productions,
industry observers have remained cautious: 'if there is one thing we have
learned from the British film history,' wrote Terry Ilott (BFI 1996: 26) in
a recent report on the British film industry, 'it is that Americans cannot be
relied upon to be consistent investors: the level of their activity rises and
falls according to a host of factors, notably the exchange rate'.

Large-scale European productions and their reception in Europe

European producers with global ambitions have little difficulty in raising finance and Europe has now developed a thriving industry in works rooted in a 'genuine' national culture by rediscovering its literary heritage and reconstructing its imaginary colonial past. The Merchant-Ivory films, Régis Wargnier's *Indochine*, Bille August's *The House of Spirits*, Claude Berri's *Germinal*, Jean Paul Rappeneau's *The Horseman on the Roof* are only a few in a long list of large-scale productions drawing on Europe's history and high culture and made to appeal to audiences worldwide.

However, there is a feeling in Europe that these super-productions may be doing more harm than good to a European film culture which is still defined in terms of 'Auteur Cinema'. Large-budget historical film-events such as *The King's Whore* or *1492, Conquest of Paradise* often have a bad press. (*The King's Whore*, a French–Italian–British film which flew the European banner at the 1990 Cannes Film Festival, was quoted as 'the classic Euro-pudding of all time', a label also bestowed upon *1492*, the Columbus epic with Gérard Depardieu heading a multinational cast.)

Critics have not been kinder to the big-budget films of the new *enfants terribles* of French cinema, Besson (*The Big Blue, Leon*), Beineix (*IP5*), Carax (*Les Amants du Pont Neuf*) or Jeunet and Caro (*The City of the Lost Children*).

In Europe, critical acclaim rarely concurs with box-office performance. Also, audiences are far less homogeneous than in the USA. Audience surveys show that these big-budget films of the *enfants terribles* cater almost exclusively for young audiences' tastes while historical epics and melodramas are more popular with older and female audiences (*CNC Info* 1993).

Overall, the public reception of these film-events made in Europe has been mixed, ranging from overwhelming enthusiasm (*Delicatessen, Nikita, Indochine, The Fifth Element*) to mild approval (*The Horseman on the Roof*) or total indifference (*IP5*), but there is some evidence that large-budget productions – particularly those shot in English and/or with American stars – are easier to sell to agents and distributors and therefore more capable of reaching global audiences.

The second tier of films produced in Europe consists of medium- to low-budget pictures, usually financed by producers from more than one country and with the support of the European programmes.

European coproductions

Co-productions are nothing new in Europe. Many countries have a long and successful tradition of cooperation. (Not only did *Pelle the Conqueror* win the Cannes Palme d'Or (1988) but also Nordic consensus declared Bille August's film Best Swedish film in Sweden and Best Danish film in Denmark!)

In the 1990s, co-productions represent an activity without which small countries would not have a national film industry. With a minute home market (6 million and 6.4 million admissions in 1994 respectively), a Greek or Portuguese film industry almost seems a contradiction in terms. In a country like Belgium which is divided into two cultural parts, the likelihood of an indigenous film making a profit in its country of origin is small.

It is not only for Greek, Portuguese, Belgian, Danish or Dutch film-makers that co-production has become a way of life. With production and post-production costs rising and investments declining throughout Europe, in recent years, all countries have felt the need to spread the financial burden of film production and the search for more co-production partners has become a necessity. Production surveys conducted over the last few years led the authors of the *Screen Digest*'s reports to conclude in 1994:

> Regardless of whether creativity is stifled within the cultural generalisations of coproduction, such films are becoming more and more entrenched within the European industry. Indeed, it may be the case that the future ability of Europe to sustain current levels of production will depend largely upon the viability of coproduction.
>
> (*Screen Digest*, July 1994: 158)

Multilateral arrangements have been encouraged by both the European Community Programme, MEDIA, and the Council of Europe Fund, EURIMAGES.

European initiatives

MEDIA (Measures to Encourage the Development of the Audiovisual Industry) was instigated in 1987 to provide aid and encourage initiatives designed to fulfil the needs of the entire audiovisual sector. It includes programmes for research and development, finance, training, production, distribution and the encouragement of minority languages. EURIMAGES was set up in 1989 by the Council of Europe to create a pan-European fund supporting film and documentary coproductions and their distribution.

MEDIA

From a pilot scheme of ten projects in 1988 (ranging from script-writing to a European Film Academy), MEDIA grew into fully fledged Community programmes under the names of MEDIA 1992 and MEDIA 1995. (In 1990, the Council of Ministers granted MEDIA a budget of Ecu200 million (£140 million) to be spread over five years. For a summary of the various projects supported by MEDIA, see Hill *et al.* 1994: 29–31.) The aim was to create 'cross-border synergies' by establishing networks of cooperation among professionals.

Considering that MEDIA is a fairly modest programme – in financial terms – suffering from various ailments such as underfunding, lack of mechanisms for the recoupment of loans and the occasional duplication of resources, its achievements in its first five years of existence have been remarkable. Whether one looks at the several hundreds of projects and networks it has helped set up, at the number of producers and distributors it has encouraged or the range of ventures it has supported (fiction and documentary films, dubbing and subtitling, etc.), the results are extremely valuable.

Yet, the development of those cross-border synergies has not brought about the arrival of a European audiovisual industrial structure strong enough to face the future. In a larger (but recession-hit) European Union, MEDIA has been allowed to continue but the nineteen initiatives of MEDIA 95 have been trimmed down. Given a Ecu310 million budget (over five years), MEDIA II has, from 1996 onwards, concentrated its efforts on three action lines: training, development and distribution.

EURIMAGES

Initially, the Council of Europe Fund supported only low- and medium-budget films. Between 1989 and 1992, it helped produce 144 feature films. In its first four years, EURIMAGES also supported the co-production of eighteen documentaries (total budget Ecu 52 million). Total production costs of both fiction and documentary films was Ecu 469 million (of which 11 per cent was financed by the Fund: figures supplied by EURIMAGES). They include Xavier Koller's *Journey of Hope*, Lars von Trier's *Europa* (1989), Jaco van Dormael's *Toto le Heros*, Gianni Amelio's *Il Ladro di Bambini* (1990), Fernando Trueba's *Belle Epoque* (1991), Kieslowski's *Blue* (1992) and Nikita Mikhalkov's *Urga* (aid for distribution).

From its inception, EURIMAGES has granted its support to 'works which uphold the values that are part and parcel of the European identity'. While there is no attempt to define such identity beyond general references to diversity and common cultural heritage, many of the EURIMAGES-supported films speak for themselves, inclined as they are to tackle contemporary issues (e.g. of belonging, or not belonging) and explore cross-cultural exchanges.

The success of EURIMAGES can also be measured by the ever-increasing number of applications to the Fund. It has been estimated that of all films made in Europe in 1994, over a quarter of them had applied to EURIMAGES (*Eurimages News* 1994).

Table 11.2 Film production figures 1989–95[a]

	1989	1990	1991	1992	1993	1994	1995
Austria	10 —	14 (5)[b]	11 (0)	10 (0)	11 —	10 —	
Belgium	10	12 (9)	3 (3)	9 (8)	5 (4)	8 (6)	
Denmark	18 (2)	13 (1)	11 (6)	9 (5)	11 (3)	14 (3)	
Finland	10 —	13 (3)	12 (6)	11 (8)	13 (2)	11 (4)	
France	136 (70)	146 (65)	156 (83)	155 (83)	152 (85)	115 (50)	141 (78)
Germany	68 (15)	48 (10)	72 (19)	63 (10)	67 (17)	57 (11)	66[c]
Greece	8 —	13 —	15 —	14 (3)	18 (3)	11 —	
Ireland	3 —	3 —	1 —	4 —	17 —	17	
Italy	117	119 (21)	129 (18)	127 (13)	106 (20)	95 (24)	75 (15)
Luxembourg	3 —	1 —	2 (1)	3 (2)	4 (4)	0 —	
Netherlands	13 —	13 —	14 —	13 (0)	16 —	16 (4)	
Portugal	7 —	9 (7)	9 (3)	8 (7)	12 (8)	9· (9)	
Spain	47 (8)	42 (10)	64 (18)	52 (14)	56 (15)	44 (8)	70[c]
Sweden	26 —	25 (5)	27 (17)	20 (11)	19 (8)	19 (8)	
UK	27 —	47 (8)	46 (22)	42 (13)	60 (29)	70 (32)	73 (56)

Source: Screen Digest, ICAA
Notes: [a] Figures are for feature film production by country
[b] 14 (5) indicates produced films (of which co-productions)
[c] estimated

There are signs that a Europe-wide audiovisual policy can play a significant part in the state of the European film industry. The growth in co-productions involving European partners (from 144 in 1990 to 198 in 1993) is largely responsible for the upward path taken by European production in the early 1990s. The number of films produced in the European Union went from 518 in 1990 to 567 in 1993 (see Table 11.2).

However, by then, the popularity of the European Funds with European producers had not been matched with a greater cross-border appeal of European films. Bearing this in mind, in 1993, the EURIMAGES Board decided to pay special attention to 'high-quality coproductions capable of pleasing large audiences' and put more emphasis on the Fund's recoupment of its interest-free loans. Recently, the European Union's programme MEDIA has also been pledging to support 'more commercially orientated projects'.

The introduction of market-orientated criteria has now initiated a downward trend in film production in Europe. In 1994, production figures fell below 500 films for the first time since the 1940s with an increasing concentration of investments in a smaller number of films.

The risk to low-budget locally made productions must not be underestimated. Few European countries operate, like France, a system which supports first-time film-makers and secures films' theatrical distribution.

Unreleased European films

In France, only films which have a statutory theatrical release are allowed to qualify for cinema funding. Without such regulations, other European films often fail to secure a theatrical distribution deal even in their domestic country. In 1994, only 60 per cent of the feature films made in Germany and Italy were screened at a cinema; the others went straight to television or video. In the UK in 1993, 52.5 per cent of British films were still unreleased theatrically within a year of completion; worse still, of the UK films released that year, 25 per cent had a wide release (opening on thirty or more screens around the country) and 22.4 per cent had limited distribution (mainly in art-house cinemas or a short London West End release: see British film Institute 1996: 32).

Britain was the first European country to welcome the multiplex revolution. The conclusion of a 1994 report on the supply and exhibition of films, stating that independent producers faced 'enormous hurdles in securing effective theatrical distribution in their home market', seemed to offer little hope for European films (Bridge Media 1994). According to the report, British films were 'disadvantaged' by the system. Ken Loach's *Riff Raff* (winner of the European Film Award for best film in 1991) and Louis Malle's *Damage* were cited as examples of films being pulled out to make way for pre-booked American films.

Table 11.3 Market share of domestic films 1989–93 (%, including co-productions)

	1989	**1990**	**1991**	**1992**	**1993**
Belgium*	2.6	3.8	3.1	4.2	5.5
Denmark	15.0	14.7	10.8	15.3	16.0
Finland	5.8	7.6	6.7	10.0	8.0
France	34.2	37.6	30.6	34.9	34.6
Germany	16.7	9.7	13.6	9.5	7.2
Greece	9.0	8.0	7.0	2.0	—
Ireland	2.0	5.0	2.0	—	—
Italy	21.7	21.0	26.8	24.4	18.0
Luxembourg	2.0	2.0	2.0	—	—
Netherlands	4.6	3.0	2.3	13.0	4.1
Portugal	1.0	1.0	1.0	—	4.0
Spain	7.3	10.4	10.0	9.4	8.5
Sweden	20.4	8.9	25.5	28.0	14.7
UK	10.0	7.0	13.8	—	—

Source: Chiffres clefs du cinéma européen, Media Salles, 1995
Note: *Brussels only

Film distribution and multiplexes

With the development of multiplexes, the fall in cinema attendances has now been checked or reversed. Admissions in the European Union have risen from 553 million in 1992 to a record high of 675.5 million in 1994. The major cinema operators have been actively involved in the construction of multiplexes. Offering better and cheaper facilities, multiplexes were not only deemed to have a profound influence on the exhibition sector but to 'significantly affect the relationship between exhibitor and distributor, providing an opportunity for the retailing of independent films' (London Economics 1993: 20).

So far, the greater chances for independent films to find exhibition space alongside mainstream films have not materialized. US films continue to account for a major share of Europe's national markets (see Tables 11.3 and 11.4).

Massive advertising and promotional support (including a high number of copies) ensure that a small number of (mainly American) blockbusters are successful at the box-office. In the year of the GATT negotiations, France was the only country with a domestic film at the top of its box-office chart. (The popular comedy of Jean Marie Poiré, *Les Visiteurs*, sold more than 13 million tickets in France.) Everywhere else, *Jurassic Park* was the 'uncontested top earner of the year'. Made with high production values (special effects, stars) to appeal to young,cinemagoers, who represent a majority of the audience today, and launched with a huge publicity campaign and massive press coverage, Spielberg's film secured the best distribution and exhibition opportunities.

Table 11.4 Market share of US films 1989–93 (%)

	1989	1990	1991	1992	1993
Belgium*	69.5	73.4	79.6	72.9	71.8
Denmark	63.7	77.0	83.3	77.7	74.0
Finland	70.0	80.0	80.0	63.0	63.0
France	55.5	55.9	58.0	58.2	57.1
Germany	65.7	83.8	80.2	82.8	87.8
Greece	86.0	87.0	88.0	92.0	—
Ireland	75.0	87.0	91.5	—	—
Italy	63.1	70.0	58.6	59.4	68.1
Luxembourg	87.0	80.0	85.0	78.0	80.0
Netherlands	75.6	85.8	92.5	78.8	89.3
Portugal	81.0	85.0	85.0	—	61.2
Spain	73.0	72.0	69.0	77.1	75.5
Sweden	69.3	82.3	70.5	65.5	72.7
UK	84.0	89.0	84.0	—	—

Source: Chiffres clefs du cinéma européen, Media Salles, 1995
Note: *Brussels only

In the 1990s few films find success without a significant promotion budget. At a time when the theatrical life of a film is made shorter by the development of ancillary markets, a film is expected to make more and more admissions in a smaller and smaller number of weeks and its promotion budget has become a sign of its commercial potential. (Just over one-third of all films directly cover the cost of their cinema release: 13 per cent make a profit and 24 per cent recoup the cost of prints and advertising.) Even bad publicity can help sell a film (e.g. *Waterworld*).

The ways a film can recoup its costs have greatly increased with the proliferation of distribution outlets via the growth of video retail, cable, satellite, pay-TV, pay-per-view and CD-ROM but the commercial value of a film is still determined by the number of cinema tickets sold.

Limited medium-term growth potential of the US market has led European and US conglomerates to seek to strengthen their positions in European distribution markets in order to maximize revenues and be ideally placed to exploit the latest technological advances in distribution. This has often led to mergers between European and US distributors (Gaumont with Buena Vista and UGC with Fox in France).

Up to now, concentration in the distribution field has done little to improve the situation of European films. Examining the French results of 1994, Michel Ciment inferred that such mergers increased the potential success of American films.

> Of the 146 American pictures that were released in 1994 (126 in 1993), 58 per cent opened in more than 20 Paris theatres (51 per cent in 1993). Out of the 387 films distributed, 138 were French, 146 American and 103 from other countries though 74 per cent of this last category opened in fewer than five Paris theatres, thus having little chance to reach a wide audience.
>
> (Cowie 1996: 151)

Popular European cinema

Soaring production and marketing costs are now threatening to destabilize the Hollywood studio system.

Large-budget films are not necessarily profitable. In 1994–5, the world-wide commercial performance (estimated at over $250 million) of the $4.5 million-budget film (£3 million), *Four Weddings and a Funeral*, was hailed as a watershed. Yet, the most successful 'British film' of the first half of the decade probably owes its success as much to Polygram's take-over of Working Title – the small independent British company which had developed the project – as to the film's creative team. (The take-over came at the time the giant international record conglomerate had decided to launch a rapid expansion into the audiovisual business. Hoping to become 'the only European-based studio', Polygram put all its weight behind the film.) Recalling the many tests, previews and the huge promotion efforts of the (Dutch-owned) international conglomerate, Duncan Kenworthy (1995), the producer of *Four Weddings and a Funeral*, declared: 'They were terrific. . . . Polygram needed a hit – they were hurting for a hit – and we were happy to supply it'. Although also widely considered 'British', *The Full Monty* (1997) – the highest grossing film to date in the UK with a reported cost of £1.6M (BFI, 1998) – was backed by an American studio.

Comedies

Foreign-language comedies do not travel so well but, on their domestic market, they are still the most popular genre. *Les Visiteurs*, France's hit in 1993, was not a unique success story in Europe. In the Netherlands, drawing an audience of 1.2 million, Dick Maas's comedy, *Flodder does Manhattan* (*Flodder in America*) drove *Basic Instinct* into second place at the Dutch box-office in 1992. The following year, *Der Bewegte Mann* (*The Most Desired Man*) registered over 6 million admissions in Germany, Roberto Benigni's *Il Mostro* took $21.2 million at the Italian box-office and in Spain, the top two domestic releases were also comedies.

By relying on local audiences' knowledge of the national history and socio-political system as well as viewers' familiarity with comedians, language and other specific cultural icons, locally made comedies are often inaccessible to audiences coming from a different cultural background (Dyer and Vincendeau 1992: 3) However, the inexportability of local comedies should not be exaggerated. *Les Visiteurs* was a considerable hit in the French-speaking regions of Belgium and Switzerland and did well in Spain. If the German hit *Schtonk*, a comedy based on the forged Hitler's diaries scandal, was a flop on the international scene in 1992, two years later *Der Bewegte Mann* was an enormous success in Austria, Switzerland and Finland; its dubbed version also performed well in Spain. Spanish theatrical quotas for European productions may well be responsible for the greater popularity of between countries (i.e. Nordic versus Latin) no doubt also play a part in the shared fortunes of many European titles.

Films exploring European issues

In the mid-1980s, Vincent Porter asked:

> Can we look forward to a film culture which offers something more imaginative, which brings together the experiences and feelings that men and women of the different European cultures have in common and which plays down, or better still resolves, the nationalistic differences that can divide them?

> (Porter 1985: 6)

Many of the films supported by MEDIA and/or EURIMAGES correspond perfectly to Porter's longing for images of cultural collaboration, dealing as they do with love and friendship between people of different cultures (*Urga, Prague, Orlando, Before the Rain, The Extraordinary Adventures of Private Ivan Chonkin, Someone Else's America*); immigration (*Journey of Hope, Lamerica*) or the search for a new identity in an indifferent or hostile modern environment (Theo Angelopoulos' *Ulysses' Gaze*, Kieslowski's trilogy, *Blue, White* and *Red*).

Interestingly, among the film-makers most engaged in works that manage to reconcile the somewhat contradictory aims of the Council of Europe 'to work for European unity by protecting and strengthening pluralist democracy and human rights as well as seeking solutions to the problems facing European society', there are many directors originating from the former central and eastern European countries (Nikita Mikhalkov, Jiri Menzel, Milcho Manchevski, Goran Paskaljevic and Krysztof Kieslowski). All of them have had the support of the French Centre National de la Cinématographie. Far from bearing the stigma attached to French/European cinema (narcissist and elitist), their films offer a form of cinematic expression which is essentially concerned with social and moral questions (Jäckel 1997).

So far, those (medium- and low-budget) European co-productions commenting on socio-political issues in contemporary Europe have won critical acclaim and prizes at film festivals but have not fared well with audiences.

However, several low-budget films directed by a new generation of film-makers, sharing the same thematic concerns as the co-productions of the Russian, Czech, Macedonian or Polish directors, have not only been covered with awards but have also achieved critical and public success and been sold outside their national territory (Isaac Julien's *Young Soul Rebels*, Cyril Collard's *Savage Nights*, Mathieu Kassovitz's *La Haine/Hate*). *La Haine*, a black-and-white film by the young French director about a day in the life of three young men in a deprived suburb outside Paris, has even secured a distribution deal in the USA.

The year 1995 was marked by a stabilization of audiences. This was mainly due to the disappointing performance of US blockbusters and lack of choice. (It was reported that not a single US studio (American-owned or otherwise) had made a profit on the theatrical business in 1995: *Screen International* 22 March 1996: 12.) While Dolby stereo, large-screen facilities and a user-friendly and comfortable environment can bring audiences back to the cinema, too much of the same can turn them away just as quickly.

Hollywood's losses may be Europe's gains. Multiplexes are starting to show foreign-language films (usually in their dubbed versions). With 'art-house films' slowly moving into the mainstream, European productions are finding greater acceptance with distributors.

A changing marketplace

The rapidly changing audiovisual environment requires a new look at the marketplace. When films rely on ancillary outlets to recoup their cost and revenues from export overtake those from domestic takings, an agenda for the future which includes making films for the global market and establishing a better distribution and marketing system becomes a necessity.

Europe is currently repositioning itself. The Spanish subsidy system is to include box-office results in its allocation of grants and the French automatic aid may take into account export revenues. European and pan-European programmes are also committed to support projects with 'commercial potential'. However, the idea of 'making movies that make commercial sense' has been taken to task by European cinéphiles. Many argue that the auteur tradition, with its preference for works of personal expression, social commentary and aesthetic exploration, remains both an easily identifiable and valuable cultural practice and a well-established market niche. Besides, as the film critic Alexander Walker pointed out in his defence of a strong British national cinema, it is unlikely that anyone ever

> set out deliberately to make a film for small audiences. . . . Mike Leigh, Kenneth Loach, Peter Greenaway, all hope their 'elitist Art-house' productions reach as wide an audience as possible.
> (quoted in *London Evening Standard*, 18 March 1994)

Paradoxically, it is outside their native country that the reputations of Loach and Greenaway have blossomed (France, Italy and Spain for the former, Germany, the Netherlands and France for the latter). Rivette and Rohmer, the most 'elitist' masters of the 'old' French new wave, now have little difficulty in exporting their 'unquestionably Art films'. Thomas Elsaesser (1992) explained the success of *La Belle Noiseuse* by the fact that audiences saw in it 'a qualified but nonetheless comforting reaffirmation of the values not only of Art, but also of European art cinema'.

The audience for Loach, Rivette and Rohmer's films may not be a vast one, but culturally it is a vital one. The same goes for the production of low-budget pictures from first-time film-makers.

Nobody would deny that to survive the multimedia explosion a strong European film industry needs a preponderance of commercially viable products. It also needs to apply corrective mechanisms to monopolies that have emerged (or may emerge) and to adopt a system whereby success can be used to help local talent. Over the years in Europe, France has offered a unique example of a cinema capable of retaining its identity and of renewing it. Sharing a common language with the North American continent, British cinema has been better able to survive than most, with much help from Channel Four in the 1980s, financing from Europe and the USA in the early 1990s and new sources of funding (National Lottery) and renewed interest from the Labour Government (introduction of tax breaks) in the late 1990s – not to mention British talent.

Colin McArthur concludes his study of film-making in Scotland by saying: 'the lesson has to be learned that national cinemas or film movements do not simply happen, they are in great measure constructed' (Hill *et al.* 1994: 125). It applies to Scotland as much as to England, France, Greece or the whole of Europe. Ian Christie (1995) describes Europe's needs in terms of Europe's 'capacity to produce and exhibit its own films if it is to survive as a cultural force in a world where visual literacy is fast outstripping verbal literacy', adding, 'a continent that has no self-image on its own screen, and none to represent it elsewhere, has become invisible.'

Regional and national institutions as well as European organizations have a role to play in the construction of these images. In a fragmented plurilingual market, only a healthy level of public subsidy at European and local levels can guarantee that cultural plurality and artistic integrity be safeguarded.

The acknowledgement by the editor of the *Encyclopedia of European Cinema* that MEDIA- and EURIMAGES-aided film-makers such as Wim Wenders, Theo Angelopoulos and the late Krysztof Kieslowski (also supported by the French CNC) have 'become European' serves to testify that the combined efforts of the national policies of (some) EU member states and the European and pan-European initiatives can bring about distinctive works which offer Europeans a common vision of hope for the future.

Ultimately, it is on the production, distribution and marketing of these films (whatever the size nf their budget) and on the existing possibilities for new talent to emerge that rests the future of European cinema.

Questions

1   To what extent can it be said that the economics of the European film industry determines the cinematic content of European films?

Do modes of production, distribution and exhibition affect the characteristics of films?

2 Why might the survival of national film industries in Europe be important?

3 Can films be defined in terms of their origins (financial, technical and artistic input)?

References

Bridge Media (1994) *Factors Influencing the Production, Supply and Exhibition of Independent Films in the UK Market*, Bridge Media Report for Pact.

British Film Institute (1996) *BFI Film and Television Handbook 1996*, London: BFI.

Christie, I. (1995) *Independent on Sunday*, 26 February: 23.

CNC Info (1993) 245 (January).

Cowie, P. (ed.) (1996) *Variety International Film Guide*, London.

Dyer, R. and Vincendeau, G. (eds) (1992) *Popular European Cinema*, London: Routledge.

Elsaesser, T. (1992) 'Rivette and the end of cinema', *Sight and Sound* 1(12): 12.

Eurimages News (1994) 7 (September): 1.

Hill, J., McLoone, M. and Hainsworth, P. (eds) (1994) *Border Crossing: Film in Ireland, Britain and Europe*, London: British Film Institute.

Kenworthy, D. (1995) Interview by Sheila Johnston, *The Independent*, 26 January: 24.

Jäckel, A. (1997) 'Cultural cooperation in Europe', *Media, Culture and Society*.

London Economics (1993) *Retailing European Films*, London: Media Business School.

Porter, V. (1985) 'European co-productions: aesthetic and cultural *implications*', *Journal of Area Studies* 12: 6.

Shepherd, L. and McCartney, N. (1992) 'Europe by numbers', *Impact* 4 (May): 17.

Vincendeau, G. (ed.) (1995) *Encyclopedia of European Cinema*, London: British Film Institute.

Further reading

British Screen Advisory Council (1992) *The Challenge of Language in European Film*, London: BSAC/Media Business School Seminar.

Cahiers du Cinéma (1992) 'Il était une fois l'Europe', special issue.

Coopers & Lybrand (1991) *European Film Industry or Art?*, London: Coopers & Lybrand.

Dale, M. (1992) *Europa, Europa, Developing the European Film Industry*, London: Media Business School.

Drummond, P., Paterson, R. and Willis, J. (eds) (1993) *National Identity and Europe: The Television Revolution*, London: British Film Institute.

Durie, J. (1993) *The Film Marketing Handbook*, London: Media Business School.

Dyer, R. and Vincendeau, G. (eds) (1992) *Popular European Cinema*, London: Routledge.

European Cinema Yearbook: A Statistical Analysis (1996) European Audiovisual Observatory.

Finney, A. (1993) *A Dose of Reality: The State of European Cinema*, London: Screen International.

Hancock, D. (1996) *Mirrors of our Own*, Eurimages.

Hill, J., McLoone, M. and Hainsworth, P. (eds) (1994) *Border Crossing: Film in Ireland, Britain and Europe*, London: British Film Institute.

London Economics (1992) *The Competitive Position of the European and US Film Industries*, London: London Economics.

London Economics (1993) *Retailing European Films: The Case of the European Exhibition Industry.*

Petrie, D. (ed.) (1992) *Screening Europe*, London: British Film Institute.

Pirelli, P. (1991) *A Level Playing Field?*, London: British Film Institute.

Sorlin, P. (1992) *European Cinemas, European Societies 1939–1990*, London: Routledge.

Vincendeau, G. (ed.) (1995) *Encyclopedia of European Cinema*, London: British Film Institute.

Chapter 12

Pop music

MARKETING AND MEDIATING POPULAR MUSIC: THE EUROPEAN
POPULAR MUSIC INDUSTRY

ROY SHUKER

During 1995, the Beatles Anthology album made its début at number one
in the USA to become the fastest selling double album of all time; Sony
Music Publishing confirmed a $500 million deal to merge with Michael
Jackson's ATV Music Publishing to create SONY/ATV Music Publishing;
and European music retailers reported record Christmas sales. In the UK,
Oasis, Blur, and Robson & Jerome vied for top sales and awards; British
Phonographic Industry (BPI) trade figures showed record sales for 1994, with
the market up 16.8 per cent on 1993; HMV launched HMV Direct, a home
shopping service offering over 20,000 titles; the twenty-fifth Glastonbury
Festival was a huge success, with the audience for Channel Four's coverage
peaking at 900,000; and Sony and George Michael reached a settlement to
their long-running music industry dispute, with the artist leaving the label
in return for two new songs and a greatest hits package.

Such events and statistics indicate the international commercial and cultural significance of popular music. Defined here as commercially produced
music for a mass market, and including the variety of genres variously
subsumed by terms such as rock 'n' roll or rock and pop, popular music is
ubiquitous. We are exposed to popular music through 'muzak' in shopping
malls; on the streets and in the parks with 'ghetto blasters' and Walkman
personal stereos; on film soundtracks; on music video through MTV Europe and television shows like *Top of the Pops*; on radio in the home and
workplace; 'live' in a variety of settings, from the stadium concert to pub
gigs; in clubs; and in the music press.

In cultural terms, the significance of this consumption is clearly of enormous importance in people's daily lives, and for some consumers is central
to the construction of their social identities. While there are problems with
obtaining reliable figures (see Negus 1993: Appendix 1), in economic terms
the products of the music industry far outweigh those of any other cultural industry, with income including the sales of recorded music, copyright
revenue, tour profits, sales of the music press, musical instruments and
sound systems. For example, the importance of music to the British economy

was revealed by a recent report in *The Observer* on invisible exports (in this case primarily income from royalties), which showed they grossed $2.25 billion in overseas receipts.

This chapter examines some aspects of the production, marketing and consumption of popular music in Europe, particularly the UK. A central concern is the relationship between the power of the music industry to shape and even construct audience tastes, and the autonomy of market choice exercised by those who consume the music (see Garofalo 1987; Shuker 1994). The topics considered are the nature of the music industry, especially the relationship between the majors and the independent record companies; the various mediators of the music, operating between production and consumption – live performance (the club scene; concerts; festivals), radio, music video, and the music press; and the role of the charts. The chapter ends with a brief look at three key trends: the changing nature of the audience for popular music, especially the decline of the traditional youth market; the promise and threats of new technology, including popular music on the Internet; and the increased importance to the music industry of income generated from the sale of rights.

The emphasis is on the political economy of popular music: the industry and its relationship to its audience. The brushstrokes are broad, and readers must look elsewhere for detailed consideration of how the music industry operates on an everyday basis (Fink 1989; Negus 1993). I have also not had space to consider several important aspects: the important role of government, both local and central, in promoting and regulating popular music (see Bennett *et al.* 1994; Cohen 1991); the nature of youth's creative engagement with popular music, through subcultures and practices such as home taping (Hebdige 1979; Savage 1992; Willis *et al.* 1990) and the shifting popularity of various formats, especially the rise of the CD (*Business Week*, 16 October 1995: 150, 'LPs Are Back'; International Federation of the Phonographic Industry – IFPI 1990). Given the constantly shifting nature of popular tastes, I have chosen to say little about trends and performers; these can be better followed though readers' own eyes and ears.

The music industry

The music industry is an international multibillion dollar business. Historically, the music industry has been centred in the USA, with the UK making a significant artistic contribution to an Anglo-American popular music hegemony. This Anglo-American dominance has waned in recent years, with the reassertion of the European Union market and the emergence of Japanese media conglomerates as major players in the music industry.

> In terms of record sales, the European Community has recently overtaken the USA. In 1990, the retail value of discs and tapes sold in the twelve member states of the EC was $8.4 billion, equivalent to 35 per cent of the

global total and one-quarter higher than the 1989 total. US sales represented 31 per cent.

(Laing 1992: 128)

While reliable data are difficult to obtain, various sources indicate the economic significance of the products of the music industry. At the global level, after a decline in the early 1980s, world sales reached a retail value of $US 21 billion–22 billion in 1989, boosted by the increasing popularity of CDs (IFPI 1990). Worldwide music industry sales have continued to increase steadily, but at a slower pace. Aside from the sales of recorded music in its various formats, there is also the considerable revenue to be gained from associated activities and products.

In the mid-1990s, the international record industry was dominated by six major companies: Thorn-EMI (UK based); Bertelsmann Music Group (Germany); Sony/CBS or Sony Music Entertainment (Japan); Time/Warner (USA); MCA (Japan); and Philips-Polygram (Netherlands). 'Middle-range' companies (Virgin, Motown, Island) have increasingly been absorbed by the majors, while the smaller record companies, the independents, important as the main developers of new talent, are often closely linked to the majors through distribution deals. Thorn EMI's chairman, Sir Colin Southgate, confirmed he was splitting up the company, leading to speculation that its music arm would be sold off to foreign hands, with a consequent loss of vitality in the British music scene. (EMI has a 14 per cent share of the world market.)

Each of the majors has branches throughout the Americas and Europe and, in most cases, in parts of Asia, Africa and Australasia. Further, each embraces a number of labels: the Philips labels include Polydor, Deutsche Grammaphon, Phonogram and Decca; the Sony music stable includes CBS, Epic and Def Jam. The Bertelsmann Music Group operates in twenty-seven countries under many labels, including RCA and Arista, and its artists include Whitney Houston, the Grateful Dead, Cowboy Junkies and Lisa Stansfield.

Estimates of the degree of market control exercised by the majors, and the relative share of the market enjoyed by each, are difficult to determine. Various authorities place the majors' market share of the global production, manufacture and distribution of recorded popular music at between 80 and 90 per cent (Burnett 1993; Negus 1993; Wallis and Malm 1992). In Europe, the dominance of the multinationals is clear and increasing. IFPI figures for 1990 placed it around 90 per cent in most countries, ranging from Austria 94 per cent, to Portugal 89 per cent, France 83 per cent and the Netherlands 75 per cent (Laing 1992: 129). Laing shows how, since 1988, several of the majors have embarked on 'a concerted effort to absorb locally owned record companies'. For example, EMI absorbed Chrysalis in the UK (in 1991), Medley in Denmark (1991), Minos Matsas in Greece (1991) and Hispavox in Spain (1988). The major companies also take major shareholdings in independent labels with promising artists, an investment which can pay off: Oasis's label Creation is 49 per cent owned by Sony.

These music companies are part of transnational corporations with interests encompassing a range of leisure and entertainment media, and providing industry and domestic hardware and software. For example, Bertelsmann's primary interests are in print media, but also include major radio stations, film companies, pay-TV channels, and production facilities for the various electronic media (see Barnet and Cavanagh 1994: ch. 3). This situation reflects the battle for global dominance of media markets, with companies attempting to control both hardware and software markets, and distribute their efforts across a range of media products – a process labelled 'synergy' – which enables maximization of product tie-ins and marketing campaigns and, consequently, profits. For example, Sony purchased CBS Records (for $2 billion) in 1988 and Columbia Pictures (for $3.4 billion) in 1989, while Matsushita acquired MCA, the sixth largest music company by sales at that time, for $6.1 billion in 1990. In the UK, in March 1995 HMV took over the management of the Dillons bookstore chain after it was bought by Thorn EMI.

The crucial issue is whether such concentration affects the range of opportunities available to musicians and others involved in the production of popular music, and the nature and range of products available to the consumers of popular music. Initial analyses of the relationship between concentration, innovation and diversity in popular music suggested a negative relationship between concentration and diversity in the recording industry, relating this to a cyclical pattern of market cycles (Peterson and Berger 1975; Rothenbuhler and Dimmick 1982). The basis for this analysis was the proportion of top-selling chart records sold by the majors. During periods of greatest market concentration, there were fewer top-selling records. Conversely, during periods of greater market competition, with noticeable competition from the independents, there were a greater number of top selling records in the charts.

This view was challenged by Burnett (1993) and Lopes (1992), who both argued that a very high level of concentration was accompanied by a high level of diversity. Similarly, in a sophisticated analysis of the Dutch music industry, Christianen (1995) 'found a cyclical movement where, at present, we seem to witness an increase in competition together with an increase in diversity and innovation'. These analysts argue that innovation and diversity in popular music in a period of high market concentration depends on the system of development and production used by major record companies. Major record companies develop an open system of development and production, based on 'a multidivisional corporate form linked with a large number of independent producers' (Lopes 1992: 70). Negus (1993) points out the importance of the number of decision-makers within a firm, as a variable in explaining the diversity and innovation generated by a major record company. Examining this situation necessitates paying more attention to the gatekeeping process, the filtering processes at work before a particular piece of music reaches the charts.

An important aspect of the role of the majors in national popular music markets is the question of the possible conflict between the local and the global, in relation to national musical vitality. The basic concern is that the transnationals will promote their international artists at the expense of local artists, and international preferences and genres at the expense of more 'authentic' local popular music, and developing only local talents and genres with global sales potential. At a more general level, it is noteworthy that English is the language of popular music, arguably a form of linguistic imperialism. Do the policies and activities of the multinationals inhibit the development of indigenous music in the European popular music market? The response is complex, and varies from country to country (for examples, see on Sweden, Burnett 1992; on Austria, Larkey 1993; the case studies in Wallis and Malm 1992 and Robinson *et al.* 1991).

Marketing and mediating the music

There are a number of important media forms, institutions and practices which serve to articulate the industy and the consumers of popular music, by not only standing between but also connecting the two: the club scene; concerts and concert tours; rock festivals; radio; music video; the music press, and the charts. All of these forms mediate the music, creating an inextricable link between performer, text and consumer. Their significance in determining meaning in popular music lies in the interrelationship of ritual, pleasure and economics in the music. In various ways, each form operates to create audiences, to fuel individual fantasy and pleasure, and to create rock icons and cultural myths.

The club scene

Clubs (and some pubs) are the main venues for live music on a regular and continuing basis. They serve as training grounds for aspiring performers operating at the local level, and provide a 'bread and butter' living for more established artists, often through being part of an organized circuit of venues. The equation of live performance with musical authenticity and 'paying your dues' as a performer remains a widely held ideology among fans, musicians and record company executives. Clubs have historically assumed mythic importance for breaking new acts, as with the Who at the Marquee in London. They can also establish and popularize trends, as in English punk at London's 100 Club and the Roxy (Savage 1992). A community network of clubs or pub venues can create a 'local' sound, such as the 'Merseybeat' sound associated with the Beatles, Gerry and the Pacemakers, and the Searchers in the early 1960s; and the Manchester sound (the Happy Mondays, James, and the Stone Roses) of the early 1990s. While the cohesion of their 'common' musical signatures is frequently exaggerated, such localized developments provide marketing possibilities by providing a 'brand name' with which consumers can identify.

Despite the importance of music video as a marketing tool, club venues remain important for establishing new trends and their associated groups, such as the various forms of techno. The UK music press in the mid-1990s documents the resurgence of the club and disco scene, partly through a new popularization of dance (see *MUZIK* magazine). The cult of the DJ (disk jockey) is a central part of the current club scene, a star figure whose skill is to judge the mood on the dance floor, both reflecting and leading it, all the while blending tracks into a seamless whole.

Concerts and concert tours: on the road again

One-off performances (gigs) and concert tours expose performers and their music to potential fans and purchasers, building an image and a following. Through the 1980s and into the 1990s, live perfomances have remained the best way to maintain audience interest in a successful act and a key factor in breaking a new one. Concerts are complex cultural phenomena, involving a mix of music and economics, ritual and pleasure, for both performers and their audience (for a detailed discussion, see Eliot 1989; Fink 1989; Weinstein 1991: ch. 6). Concert tours are about promotion as much as performance; artists appear on radio and TV shows, make personal appearances at record stores, and generally do anything that will help promote sales. In June 1996, BBC Radio relaunched its Music Live festival as a three-week travelling roadshow of concerts and events around the UK, broadcasting live events, including Blur's only UK concert for the year (*Music Week*, 18 March 1996) and the return of the Sex Pistols.

Rock festivals: from the Isle of Wight to WOMAD

Rock festivals play a central role in popular music mythology. A number of festivals at the end of the 1960s helped create the notion of a youth-orientated rock culture while confirming its commercial potential: Monterey, Woodstock, and the Isle of Wight. The 1980s saw the reassertion of the music festival, with the success – both financially and as ideological touchstones – of the politically motivated 'conscience concerts': the concert for Bangladesh, Live Aid, and the Amnesty International concerts. The Knebworth and WOMAD (World Music and Dance) concerts have become an established feature of the UK popular music scene. Other festivals in Europe include Roskilde in Denmark, Torhout-Werchter in Belgium and Paleo in Switzerland.

As do concerts, festivals work at both the economic and ideological levels. They reinforce popular music personas, creating icons or myths. At the same time, the performers are made 'accessible' to those attending the concert, and, increasingly via satellite television, to a worldwide audience. This audience is created as a commodity. The event itself, if it attracts the projected audience, is a major commercial enterprise, with on-site sales of food and souvenirs, the income from the associated TV broadcasts via satellite to a global audience/market, and the subsequent 'live' recordings.

Radio

Until the advent of MTV (Music TV) in the mid-1980s, radio was indisputably the most important medium for determining the form and content of popular music. The organization of radio broadcasting and its music formatting practices have been crucial in shaping the nature of what constitutes the main 'public face' of popular music. As listeners, we can all conjure up vivid memories of the sheer physical and emotional impact of first hearing a song which, associated with a particular period, event or person in our everyday lives, became part of our personal rock history. These songs were usually first heard on the radio, and radio air-play continues to play a crucial role in determining and reflecting chart success.

Radio stations are distinguishable by the type of music they play, the style of their disk jockeys, and their mix of news, contests, commercials and other programme features. The music is central to this mix, with station and programme directors responsible for ensuring a prescribed and identifiable sound or format. This is based on what the management of the station believes will generate the largest audience – and ratings – and consequent advertising revenue. Quarterly rating figures are crucial in the competition for audiences and advertising revenue, witness the bidding wars for new licences issued by the Radio Authority in the UK. Historically, radio formats were fairly straightforward, and included 'Top Forty', 'soul' and 'easy listening'. Recent formats are more complex, and include 'adult orientated rock', 'golden oldies' and 'contemporary hits radio'.

High rotation radio air-play clearly remains vital in exposing artists and building a following for their work. Radio exposure is also necessary to underpin activities like touring, helping to promote concerts and the accompanying sales of records. The very ubiquity of radio is a factor here; it can be listened to in a variety of situations, and with widely varying levels of engagement, from the Walkman to background accompaniment to activities such as study, domestic chores, and reading (see Crisell, Chapter 9 in this volume).

Music video

The term 'music video' has several distinct yet overlapping meanings: MTV and similar cable/satellite music channels; individual programmes within general broadcast television channel schedules; and the long form music video cassette, available for hire or purchase. Taken together, these exert enormous influence in the marketing of popular music (Goodwin 1992). The common component of the three formats is individual music video clips, which follow the conventions of the traditional single. They are usually approximately three minutes long, and function, in the industry's own terms, as 'promotional devices', encouraging record sales and chart action.

The value of the video retail market continues to grow, with a 13 per cent increase in 1995 to £789 million. Boosted by the success of *Riverdance* and Robson & Jerome, the two biggest selling music videos of the year, the music genre in 1995 had a 10.6 per cent share of this. The rental market also grew, reaching its highest level since 1989 (*Music Week*, 18 March 1996).

The role of television popular music programmes is illustrated by *Top of the Pops* (TOTP), which is currently enjoying a revival and increased audiences – 8.4 million viewers by 1995. 'In the past twelve months, the programme has been transformed from an insipid showcase for mainstream single releases and unwatchable dance bands to a varied and bold show featuring album tracks, more live performances, new acts and celebrity presenters' (*The Times* 22 February 1995: 23, 'Top of the Pops back on track'). The potential of the programme to create industry interest was exemplified by the response to Glasgow's Bis's appearance as the first unsigned band on TOTP in March 1996, with its management company subsequently being inundated with calls about the band.

Launched in 1987, MTV Europe broadcasts to over 60 million households across the continent. The language is largely English, but the veejays (video jockeys) come from all parts of Europe and the channel aims to create programming that reflects tastes, styles and issues distinctly 'European', collapsing national distinctions in the process (Sturmer 1993).

The music press

The music press plays a major part in the process of selling music as an economic commodity, while at the same time investing it with cultural significance. Popular music and culture magazines do not simply deal with music; through both their features and advertising they are also purveyors of style. At the same time, these magazines continue to fulfil their more traditional function of contributing to the construction of audiences as consumers. The majority of popular music magazines, however, focus on performers and their music, and the relationship of consumers (fans) to these.

These magazines fall into a number of fairly clearly identifiable categories, based on their differing musical aesthetics or emphases, their sociocultural functions, and their target audiences. For example, 'Teen glossies' emphasize vicarious identification with performers whose music and image are aimed at this youth market (e.g. *Smash Hits*); *Melody Maker* and *New Musical Express* (the 'inkies') have historically emphasized a tradition of critical rock journalism, with their reviewers acting as the gatekeepers for that tradition; and the 'style bibles' (*The Face*) emphasize popular music as part of visual pop culture, especially fashion. Several relatively newer magazines offer a combination of the 'inkies' focus on an extensive and critical coverage of the music scene and related popular culture, packaged in a glossier product with obvious debts to the style bibles (*MOJO*, *VOX*). Musicians' magazines (*Guitar Player*) inform their readers about new music technologies and techniques (see Theberge 1991).

The European music press is differentiated in a similar fashion to its UK counterparts. It includes *Ruta 66* (Spanish rock monthly), *Puls Furore* (Norwegian weekly, covers mainly rock, also jazz, techno, roots etc.), *Rockerilla* (Italian music and film monthly oriented towards alternative rock and older readers) and *Pop* (Swedish bi-monthly mainstream magazine, aimed at younger readers, covering mainly rock and pop).

This is a volatile and highly competitive market: *RAW*, the 'Britpop fortnightly' launched in 1995 to fill the gap between *Smash Hits* and the monthly *Select*, ceased publication after five months, despite selling around 40,000 copies per issue. An ICP survey of the readers of twenty-seven music magazines showed *Smash Hits* to be the most read title (3.3 million readers across an entire year, reaching 7.1 per cent of the group surveyed), followed by *NME* with 2.4 million readers (5.3 per cent) and *Q* with 2.3 million (5.1 per cent). The survey showed that 57 per cent of those who read music magazines buy an album every month and a further 30 per cent do so every two to three months (*Music Week*, 18 March 1996).

Music press reviews form an important adjunct to the record company's marketing of their products, providing the record companies (and artists) with critical feedback on their releases. In the process, they also become promotional devices, providing supportive quotes for advertising and forming part of press kits sent to radio stations and other press outlets. Both the press and critics also play an important ideological function, distancing consumers from the fact that they are essentially purchasing an economic commodity, by stressing the product's cultural significance. This is reinforced by the important point that the music press and critics are not, at least directly, vertically integrated into the music industry (i.e. not owned by the record companies). A sense of distance is thereby maintained, while at the same time the need of the industry constantly to sell new images, styles and product is met.

Popular music is mediated through its performance in clubs concerts and festivals via radio airplay, music video and coverage in the music press. These forums merge consumer ritual and pleasure with economics, and in the process imbue a commercial product with ideological significance. The various media reinforce each other, in a cross-fertilization process; e.g. BBC Radio's first Music Live festival, in Birmingham over five days in May 1995, attracted more than 40,000 people and broadcast sixty hours of live music to a radio audience of around 11 million (*Music Week* 18 March 1996: 'BBC takes to the road'). It all coalesces around the charts.

The charts

The record charts play a major role: 'to the fan of popular music, the charts are not merely quantifications of commodities but rather a major reference point around which their music displays itself in distinction and in relation to other forms' (Parker 1991: 205). The charts both reflect and shape popular music, especially through their influence on radio playlists, and controversies abound over perceived attempts to manipulate them. RCA's Robson & Jerome album rebounded up the chart following a WH Smith promotion which offered the cassette format for £1 (to those spending £20 in the store). Angry rival firms saw the promotion as 'like giving away free records for the chart' and 'not good for the business because it devalues the product' (*Music Week* 18 March 1996). In 1996 the BPI (British Phonographic Industry) brought legal action against Rock Box Promotions, the company it identified as a buying team in a chart-hyping probe, in an attempt 'to protect the integrity of the chart' (ibid.).

Trends and issues

We turn finally to three major trends evident in the marketing and consumption of popular music.

The changing audience for popular music

As Goodwin (in Frith and Goodwin 1990: 259) observed at the end of the 1980s: ' "older" music has become contemporary for audiences of *all* ages'. Throughout 1994 and 1995 'nostalgia rock' has continued to be to the fore in popular music, with the release of 'new' Beatles material ('Live at the BBC', etc.); the launch of *MOJO* magazine, placing rock's past firmly at its core and with 35 per cent of its readers aged 35-plus; and successful tours by the Rolling Stones, Pink Floyd, the Eagles and Sex Pistols, among other ageing stars. This continued high level of interest in popular music's past was evident among both greying consumers and younger people, with the latter being constructed by the popular and academic media, and the advertising industry, as 'Generation X': a very media self-conscious group of youth, primarily associated with 'grunge' as a style.

This repackaging/marketing of our collective memories is hardly new, of course, but the scale is different, and it raises questions about the vitality of popular music in the 1990s. As an age cohort, seen usually as around 13 to 24 years of age, youth have historically been popular music's major consumers, and young people remain a major consumer group with considerable discretionary income for the leisure industries to tap (see Osgerby, Chapter 23 in this volume). The straightforward association of popular music with youth, however, now needs qualifying. The absolute numbers of young people entering the labour market in the UK and Europe for the first time declined during the 1980s, and will continue to fall until the end of the century. 'In material terms, the traditional rock consumer – the "rebellious" teenager – is no longer the central market figure' (Frith 1988: 127). The market for popular music has extended to those who grew up with the music in the 1950s and 1960s, and who have continued to follow it. Ageing along with their favoured surviving performers of the 1960s, these older consumers largely account for the present predominance of 'golden oldies' radio formats and occupy an increasing market share of record sales, especially 'back catalogue' releases.

Copyright

Copyright is central to the music industry. The basic principle of copyright law is the exclusive right to copy and publish one's own work; copyright owners have the right to duplicate or authorize the duplication of their property, and to distribute it. The full legal nature of copyright is beyond our scope here (see Fink 1989: 36–47; also Saunders, Chapter 3 in this volume); its significance lies in its cultural importance. The role of new technologies of sound recording and reproduction have been associated with issues of intellectual property rights, copyright and the control of sounds. For the music industry, the 'bogey man' of the 1990s is posed by threats to copyright.

In addition to deriving income from unit sales of records, record companies, performers, songwriters and music publishers derive income from the sale of rights. Ownership of rights is determined by copyright in the master tape, the original tape embodying the recorded performance from which subsequent records are manufactured. The global music industry is now less concerned with the production and management of commodities, and more with the management of rights. As Frith (1993) observes, the advent of new technologies of sound recording and reproduction have coincided with the globalization of culture, and the desire of media/entertainment conglomerates to maximize their revenues from 'rights' as well as maintaining income from the actual sale of records. What counts as 'music' is changing from a fixed, authored 'thing' which existed as property, to something more difficult to identify.

The Rome Convention and the Berne Convention are the major international agreements on copyright (see Frith 1993). The International Federation of the Phonographic Industries (IFPI) globally regulates the application and enforcement of copyright, supported by various local and regional agencies (in the UK, the British Phonographic Industry). According to the IFPI, the UK music industry leads the developed world in the battle against piracy, which was slashed by 40 per cent there during 1995, after several high profile raids and prosecutions (*Music Week* 13 May 1996). However, attempts to ensure international uniformity in copyright laws have met with only partial success; even within the European Union conventions and practices vary considerably. Attitudes towards copyright diverge depending on whose interests are involved. There is an emerging hostility towards copyright among many music consumers and even some musicians, due to its regulatory use by international corporations to protect their interests. On the other hand, the companies themselves are actively seeking to harmonize arrangements and curb piracy, while the record industry associations (especially the IFPI), which are almost exclusively concerned with copyright issues, largely support the industry line. Ultimately, it is market control which is at stake. As case studies of the legal and moral arguments in the cases associated with records by the JAMS, M/A/R/R/S, De La Soul, and others show, there are extremely complex issues involved. These centre around questions of what is actually copyrightable in music. Who has the right to control the use of a song, a record, or a sound? And what is the nature of the public domain?

Popular music on the Internet

The Internet has added a major new dimension to the marketing and reception of popular music, while creating new problems for the enforcement of copyright. It includes on-line music shops; Web sites for record companies and performers; on-line music journals; on-line concerts and interviews; and bulletin boards. In sum, these represent new ways of inter-linking the audience/consumers of popular music, the performers, and the music industry (Hayward 1995). Most discussions of the significance of such electronic commerce emphasize the business/economic aspects: the bene-fits to firms and consumers; the barriers and difficulties associated with doing business via the Net; the demographics of Net users; and the oppor-tunities for companies on the Net. But there are also significant cultural issues associated with popular music on the Net, which link up with several of the ongoing debates in the study of popular music, discussed earlier.

The Net may create greater consumer sovereignty and choice by bypass-ing the traditional intermediaries operating in the music industry (prima-rily the record companies). Any new medium or technological form changes the way in which we experience music, and this has implications for how we relate to and consume music. In the case of the Net, the question is what happens to traditional notions of the 'distance' between consumer and product, and its technological mediation? Finally, the nature of intellectual property rights, and the regulation of these, has been brought into even sharper focus with the electronic retrieval possibilities implicit in the Net, and the ongoing debates over sampling in popular music texts.

Questions

1 Consider the implications, both economic and social, of the ageing of the market for popular music.

2 If possible, check out some music sites on the Internet (see p. 172). What cultural and economic changes do they indicate for the future of popular music?

3 Investigate the music industry of one European country. Do the policies and activities of the multinationals inhibit the development of indigenous music in that popular music market?

References

Barnet, R. and Cavanagh, J. (1994) *Global Dreams: Imperial Corporations and the New World Order*, New York: Simon & Schuster.

Bennett, T., Frith, S., Grossberg, L., Shepherd, J. and Turner, G. (1994) *Rock and Popular Music: Politics, Policies, Institutions*, London: Routledge.

Burnett, R. (1993) 'The popular music industry in transition', *Popular Music and Society* 17(1): 87–114.

Christianen, M. (1995) 'Cycles of symbolic production? A new model to explain concentration, diversity and innovation in the music industry', *Popular Music* 14(1): 55–93.

Cohen, S. (1991) *Rock Culture in Liverpool: Popular Music in the Making*, Oxford: Clarendon.

Eliot, M. (1989) *Rockonomics: The Money Behind the Music*, New York/Toronto: Franklin Watts.

Fink, M. (1989) *Inside the Music Business*, New York: Schirmer/Macmillan.

Frith, S. (1988) *Music for Pleasure: Essays in the Sociology of Pop*, Cambridge: Polity.

Frith, S. (1993) *Music and Copyright*, Edinburgh: Edinburgh University Press.

Frith, S. and Goodwin, A. (eds) (1990) *On Record: Rock, Pop, and the Written Word*, New York: Pantheon.

Garofalo, R. (1987) 'How autonomous is relative: popular music, the social formation and cultural struggle', *Popular Music* 6(1): 77–92.

Goodwin, A. (1992) *Dancing in the Distraction Factory: Music Television and Popular Culture*, Oxford, Minneapolis: University of Minnesota Press.

Hayward, P. (1995) 'Enterprise on the new frontier: music, industry and the Internet', *Convergence* 1(2): 29–44.

Hebdige, D. (1979) *Subculture: The Meaning of Style*, London: Methuen.

Hill, D. (1986) *Designer Boys and Material Girls: Manufacturing the 80's Pop Dream*, Dorset: Blandford Press.

International Federation of the Phonographic Industry (1990) Hung, M. and Morencos, E.G. (compilers and editors) *World Record Sales 1969–1990: A Statistical History of the Recording Industry*, London: IFPI.

Kaplan, E.A. (1987) *Rocking Around the Clock: Music Television, Postmodernism, and Consumer Culture*, New York: Methuen.

Laing, D. (1992) ' "Sadeness", Scorpions and single markets: national and transnational trends in European popular music', *Popular Music* 11(2): 127–40.

Larkey, E. (1993) *Pungent Sounds: Constructing Identity with Popular Music in Austria*, New York: Peter Lang.

Lopes, Paul (1992) 'Aspects of production and consumption in the music industry, 1967–1990', *American Sociological Review* 57(1): 46–71.

Negus, K. (1993) *Producing Pop: Culture and Conflict in the Popular Music Industry*, London: Edward Arnold.

Parker, M. (1991) 'Reading the charts: making sense with the hit parade', *Popular Music* 10(2): 205–17.

Peterson, R. and Berger, D. (1975) 'Cycles in symbolic production: the case of popular music', *American Sociological Review* 40: 158–73.

Robinson, D., Buck, E., Cuthbert M. *et al.* (1991) *Music at the Margins: Popular Music and Global Diversity*, Newbury Park, CA: Sage.

Rothenbuhler, E. and Dimmick, J. (1982) 'Popular music: concentration and diversity in the industry, 1974–1980', *Journal of Communication* 32: 143–9.

Savage, J. (1992) *England's Dreaming: Sex Pistols and Punk Rock*, London: Faber & Faber.

Shuker, R. (1994) *Understanding Popular Music*, London: Routledge.

Sturmer, C. (1993) 'MTV's EUROPE. An imaginary continent?', *Channels of Resistance: Global Television and Local Empowerment*, London: British Film Institute.

Theberge, P. (1991) 'Musicians' magazines in the 1980s: the creation of a commodity and a consumer market', *Cultural Studies* 5(3): 270ff.

Wallis, R. and Malm, K. (1992) *Media Policy and Music Activity*, London: Routledge.

Weinstein, D. (1991) *Heavy Metal: A Cultural Sociology*, New York: Lexington.

Willis, P. *et al.* (1990) *Common Culture: Symbolic Work at Play in the Everyday Cultures of the Young*, Milton Keynes: Open University Press.

York, N. ed. (1991) *The Rock File: Making it in the Music Business*, Oxford: Oxford University Press.

Further reading

Bennett, T., Firth, S., Grossberg, L., Shepherd, J. and Turner, G. (1994) *Rock and Popular Music: Politics, Policies, Institutions*, London: Routledge.

Blake, A. (1992) *The Music Business*, London: Batsford.

Burnett, R. (1992) 'Dressed for success: Sweden from Abba to Roxette', *Popular Music* 11(2): 141–50.

Burnett, R. (1996) *The Global Jukebox: The International Music Industry*, London: Routledge.

Cohen, S. (1991) *Rock Culture in Liverpool: Popular Music in the Making*, Oxford: Clarendon.

Eisenberg, E. (1988) *The Recording Angel: Music, Records and Culture from Aristotle to Zappa*, London: Pan.

Finnegan, R. (1989) *The Hidden Musicians: Music-Making in an English Town*, Cambridge: Cambridge University Press.

Frith, S. (1983) *Sound Effects: Youth, Leisure and the Politics of Rock 'n' Roll*, London: Constable.

Frith, S. (ed.) (1993) *Music and Copyright*, Edinburgh: Edinburgh University Press.

Middleton, R. (1990) *Studying Popular Music*, Milton Keynes: Open University Press.

Negus, K. (1993) *Producing Pop: Culture and Conflict in the Popular Music Industry*, London: Edward Arnold.

O'Sullivan, Tim *et al.* (1994) *Key Concepts in Communication and Cultural Studies,* London: Routledge.

Qualen, J. (1985) *The Music Industry: The End of Vinyl?,* London: Comedia.

Savage, J. (1992) *England's Dreaming: Sex Pistols and Punk Rock,* London: Faber & Faber.

Shepherd, J. (1991) *Music as Social Text,* Cambridge: Polity.

Shuker, R. (1994) *Understanding Popular Music,* London: Routledge.

Wallis, R. and Malm, K. (1992) *Media Policy and Music Activity,* London: Routledge.

Weinstein, D. (1991) *Heavy Metal: A Cultural Sociology,* New York: Lexington.

The daily operation of the music industry is best followed by trade publications, particularly *Music Week* (UK) and *Billboard* (US). The British Phonographic Industry (BPI) publishes an *Annual Yearbook,* which includes very comprehensive statistics.

Trends and performers can be followed through the music press, and on music video channels and programmes such as *Top of the Pops.*

Internet popular music sites include:

BPI: <http://www.bpi.co.uk/>
Music Week: <http://www.dotmusic.com/MWhome.htm>
Internet Music Resource Guide: <http://www.teleport.com/~celinec/ mus_gnrl.htm>

This last gives access to numerous other music sites.

Chapter 13

Technology

NEW TECHNOLOGIES AND THE MEDIA

BRIAN McNAIR

One of the greatest challenges to the media in recent years – and one that will intensify further as we enter the new millennium – is the potential impact of new information and communication technologies (NICTs) on the form and content of media output, the processes through which media messages are produced and consumed, and on the role of the media in society. Such challenges are not new, of course, and the history of the mass media is a history of technological development with profound social consequences and implications at every stage. But there are strong grounds for believing that contemporary media are undergoing particularly dramatic technologically driven change, heralding a qualitatively new phase in the cultures of advanced capitalism. This will be an era characterized by media interactivity, accessibility and diversity, with new freedoms for the audience (or the 'consumer', as we may prefer to call him or her). It will also be the era of 'cyberporn', information overload, and the decline or disappearance of some traditional media.

This chapter examines these developments and attempts to assess their implications, positive and negative, for the media culture of the twenty-first century. It considers both print and broadcast media, and media which are neither print nor broadcast, such as the proliferating Internet services. The discussion will focus on news and journalistic media, around which public debate on the impact of NICTs is the most lively, but issues relating to entertainment and recreational media, such as the emergence of 'cyberporn' on the Internet, will also be included.

'Cyberporn' is one issue which has prompted some academics, politicians and other interested parties to be pessimistic about the impact of new media technologies on the quality of cultural life. Others have expressed optimism about the potentially democratizing, decentralizing effects of NICTs as they spread. This chapter will aim to make some contribution to that debate, while providing the reader with a fair summary of the issues and the evidence cited by those who participate in it.

New technologies and the media industry: changing structures and practices

Before examining those debates, we must acknowledge the huge and continuing impact which the introduction of NICTs has had on structures of ownership and control, patterns of employment, and processes of production within the media industry. For four decades or so following the Second World War, media organizations enjoyed relative stability, and their employees relative security. British newspapers, for example, in the early 1980s still used printing methods first introduced in the nineteenth century. Journalists and technical staff were secure in their positions within the production process, enjoying high wages and status (members of the Fleet Street print unions were 'labour aristocrats' in the classic sense). Newspapers were not particularly profitable institutions, often being used by rich men as what Robert Maxwell once called 'megaphones' for the wielding of political influence. Then, in January 1986, Rupert Murdoch imposed new technology and associated working practices on a shocked staff, leading to mass sackings, resignations, and picketline violence of exceptional ferocity and bitterness.

When the Wapping dispute was over (won by Murdoch with the political support of the Thatcher government) the way was clear for a technologically driven 'revolution' in the British newspaper industry. The print unions were all but banished from the production process, and journalists forced to learn new computer-based methods such as direct-inputting. Both groups saw their wages driven down and their working conditions drastically altered. Newspaper profits increased sharply, allowing Rupert Murdoch to fund his Sky operation (McNair 1996b) and unleashing the highly competitive pricing, promotional giveaways and design innovation that have characterized the British press environment since 1986.

These same pressures were at work in other countries (often initiated by the same companies and individuals, notably Murdoch, who were establishing themselves as truly global media barons) although not always as rapidly and ruthlessly as in the UK. In the USA, for example, Murdoch's News Corporation met with more effective resistance from the unions than was the case in the UK.

As James Curran predicted (Curran and Seaton 1991), the introduction of new technologies to the print media did not fundamentally change the long-established structures of ownership and control, which remained predominantly the preserve of a small number of proprietors. New technologies produced huge cost savings, certainly, but these were reinvested in the launching of competitive strategies such as the introduction of Saturday supplements and multiple sections by newspapers, or the price cutting which has been a key feature of the British newspaper market since 1993 or so. As a consequence, and with the obvious exception of Robert Maxwell's empire, those who dominated the press before the introduction of new printing technologies in the 1980s still do so now. Their employees, on the other hand, are rather less well-paid and secure, expected to do more, and more varied work for less money than in the days of 'hot metal'.

NICTs have had this impact on many other spheres of work – changing the nature of tasks, undermining professionalism, encouraging casualization and short-term contracts – but media workers have experienced the effects more severely than most.

For the newspaper and periodical industry the drive for change has been made more urgent by the development of electronic 'on-line' data services, distributed on the Internet (see pp. 181–4). In the early years of the information revolution, these took the form of highly specialized services providing, for example, up-to-date information about share prices to computer users in the finance industries, or abstracts of printed articles for researchers in academia. By their nature they were of little or no interest to the wider population, and quality journalism was not their priority. Now, however, the Internet is awash with electronic publications and news services of increasing journalistic quality which, in the view of some observers, threaten the long-term viability of print as a media form. Cultural futurologists have long speculated about the decline of print, but the debate has taken on a distinctly more apocalyptic tone as the Internet expands and penetrates into mainstream consumer markets across the globe.

Reports of the death of print are probably exaggerated since, as the American analyst Jon Katz (1995) has put it, 'newspapers are silent, highly portable, require neither power source nor arcane commands and don't crash or get infected. They can be stored for days at no cost and consumed over time in small, digestible quantities'. Newspapers and magazines (and printed books, also perceived to be at risk in the new era of electronic publishing) will always enjoy the unique selling point of their user-friendliness. Computer terminals are not suitable for a quiet read on the bus or in the pub. Reading from the printed page is a different and, in many respects, superior experience to that of scrolling through text on a computer screen. But the advent of electronic publishing on a commercial scale can nevertheless be expected to have some impact on the readerships and revenues of the traditional print media, and prudence dictates a response.

Most UK newspapers now publish on-line versions, eager to be seen as part of the information revolution rather than standing outside of it. New computer-aided design, layout and printing techniques are being used to make the look and content of print media attractive, and more contemporaneous in a world where the immediacy of information is highly valued. In these and other ways – most of which require radical change in working practices and conditions – newspapers and periodicals will strive to protect their market share in the twenty-first century.

NICTs and broadcasting

In broadcasting, the changes have been somewhat slower and (by comparison with the Wapping experience) more sympathetically managed, but no less profound in their consequences for those who work in the industry.

Digitalization and 'bi-media' (in which material is produced for transmission on both radio and television) has forced broadcasting professionals to become more flexible and adaptive in a context of ever-increasing competition from NICT-based media such as on-line data services (see p. 175). As with workers in the print media, deskilling, casualization and permanent job insecurity are the consequences. Regardless of how we assess the impact of NICTs on media content (see pp. 178–81) they have made the lives of media workers more difficult and complex. In early June 1996 (as the final draft of this chapter was being prepared), the BBC's director-general John Birt announced a further major restructuring of the corporation's management and production apparatus designed, as he put it, to prepare the BBC for the coming digital era of multi-channel broadcasting. The restructuring would include further merging of the BBC's television and radio news production in the name of 'bi-media' – a process that began in the early 1990s (McNair 1996b) – leading, some critics argued, to a downgrading of the status of radio in the BBC's overall scheme of things (Tusa 1996).

Unpopular with employees though these changes understandably are, they are viewed by BBC management as a necessary response to a changing media environment which could otherwise threaten the corporation – in its present form – with extinction. Digitalized television and radio services, disseminated through cable and satellite to audiences at home and abroad, promise hundreds of channels available to the average household in the near future. Since the mid-1980s there has already been a proliferation of channels in the UK, but within a framework recognizable as 'broadcasting'. The future will be one of 'narrowcasting', as increasingly specialized services are targeted, with the help of digital technologies, on evermore distinctive niche markets. These will, in the main, be pay-per-view subscription services, allowing 24-hour news junkies to have their daily fix of journalism, and sports fans to watch their activity round the clock. Consumers will use these services to make purchasing decisions, and to handle financial transactions. Electronic media will become like print in their form and function – distinctive packages of information and entertainment bought, as newspapers and periodicals are currently bought, by audiences willing to pay the premium.

Such services already exist in embryonic form, and the first British payperview sporting event – the Frank Bruno vs Mike Tyson heavyweight boxing match – was transmitted by Skysport in early 1996, and few doubted that this was but a taste of things to come in the digitalized, multi-channel era ahead.

The BBC (and other broadcasting organizations) are compelled to enter this developing market, even while striving to maintain a public service broadcasting operation of sufficient quality and popularity to maintain the case for the licence fee. In John Birt's view his proposals for change are intended to allow the reconciliation of the two goals, supporting a 'free at the point of delivery' public service comprising the existing BBC TV and radio channels, with an expanding commercial element targeted on consumers who are willing to pay extra. Although it has survived the bitter anti-public service campaigns of the Thatcher years (not least due to the management's skilful negotiation of those troubled waters) the BBC cannot stand still while the digital revolution proceeds all around. On the contrary, as its managers see it, the BBC should use its immense stocks of resources, experience and reputation to become a leading player in the twenty-first-century media business. This, more than anything, will permit it to maintain its public service role in the domestic British market.

This approach is being applied to the global market as much as to the domestic. NICTs have allowed national organizations like the BBC to become *global* broadcasters, transmitting their programmes to countries around the world. Both BBC and ITN supply news and current affairs material to the Russian market, for example, while the BBC World Service provides a vast range of radio (and increasingly television) services in a multitude of languages. In the twenty-first century the potentially huge global market for quality journalism and entertainment will be dominated by a small number of transglobal corporations, such as Ted Turner's Cable Network News and News Corporation. The BBC, of all British companies, is the best placed to compete in this market, having not only the experience and infrastructure developed for international operations, but also a reputation for quality unequalled by any other organization. With some justification the BBC is perceived around the world as the best provider of information, education and entertainment programming, a reputation persuasively reinforced by Mikhail Gorbachev when under house arrest in the attempted coup of 1991. At the most life-threatening moment of crisis, he testified later, he turned to the World Service for a reliable account of what was happening back in Moscow.

Having established its reputation in an earlier, less competitive time, the BBC aims to consolidate and strengthen its position in the expanding television market created by the introduction of NICTs, often in cooperation with commercial companies like Pearson, with whom it is cooperating in the establishment of new satellite channels.

Opponents of this approach are numerous, however. Dennis Potter's valedictory *Cold Lazarus* might be read (among other things) as an allegory of what happens when the values of public service and civic responsibility (represented by Frances De La Tour and her team of scientists exploring the brain of Daniel Feeld) are 'sold out' to those of commerce – in particular, to the global media industry. The playwright, as a leading practitioner of quality public service broadcasting in his lifetime, was clearly warning us off the superficial attractions of virtual reality and cultural globalization.

Similar views are held, if in less aesthetically refined form, by many concerned observers. As the BBC and others go digital, argue the pessimists, the needs of commerce will come to outweigh those of public service; quality (however we may define it) will be diluted; and electronic media will become a cultural desert filled with home shopping and cheap entertainment.

On the other hand, as is argued by the proponents of change, and especially by representatives of the organizations like Sky which are in the vanguard, the end result will be *more* television, *more* radio, *more* choice. In the past, for example, the British football fan had *Match of the Day* once a week, showing edited highlights of one or two games. Now, even before the digital revolution has taken hold, there are three dedicated sports channels on Sky, showing more football than anyone could have time to watch, and a host of other minority sports previously excluded from television. The service is not free, but if British sports fans are willing to pay the price, why the concern? Especially when, as a result of the competition from Sky, the traditional terrestrial broadcasters are forced to be more responsive to audience demands in their own sports programming, and the sporting bodies themselves are sharing in the new revenues?

Similar arguments can be made in other spheres of programming. Not everyone, for example, wants access to 24-hour news, but for those who do, Sky provides it. The BBC has used savings from the introduction of NICTs and 'bi-media' to set up Radio Five Live, and promises 24-hour news on television as part of its development into digital TV. There may be a cost to the viewer for this service, but why not, given that readers of a daily newspaper will spend nearly £200 a year on one title?

The key issue here is not whether digitalization and the other technology-driven processes associated with it are good or bad – they are unstoppable and irreversible – but the extent to which *existing* TV and radio services, on established BBC and commercial channels, can be protected, allowing a core of socially responsible, public service broadcasting to coexist with the new, market-driven products.

NICTs and content

If the current phase in the development of NICTs is forcing major changes in the structure and practice of the media industries, it is also shaping the content of what they produce. This process has been most apparent in the sphere of television news and journalism, where it has also generated the most controversy (because of the perceived importance of this particular category of media output).

NICTs have (as was noted above) greatly increased the quantity of news and current affairs available to television audiences, by creating more transmission outlets. Cable and satellite technologies began the process, and Cable Network News (CNN) led the way in the 1980s, before being joined by other organizations. The digital revolution will accelerate it, and there will soon be more than enough news on the air for the most dedicated journalism junkie. But NICTs have also fundamentally altered the process by which news is gathered and made ready for audiences.

The development of technology has greatly improved the efficiency and immediacy of TV news. Until the 1960s TV news was filmed on 35 mm stock, meaning a two- or three-day delay in transmission. Telecommunications satellites increased the immediacy of news in the late 1960s, as did the coming of electronic news-gathering in the 1970s. More recently, portable VCRs (video cassette recorders) and edit suites, combined with satellite transmission of video and telephone reports, have gradually cut out the need for the processing of material, and enhanced the role of journalists in the field. For one observer, this is a 'fundamental development with lasting significance for the way in which events are reported on the television screens of the world' (McGregor 1994). We now live in the era of 'real-time news', where events are reported to us, in the comfort of our living-rooms, as they happen. Cruise missiles make their way through the streets of downtown Baghdad; rioters in Los Angeles loot shops and beat up truck drivers; a politician is assassinated – we are intimate witnesses to these events in a way that was never possible before the advent of electronic news-gathering.

From one perspective these are positive developments. More news, and more immediate news, is generally viewed as a good thing, strengthening the democratic rights of populations. Brent McGregor cites as an example the case of the 1992 pro-democracy riots in Bangkok, Thailand. Thanks to the speed of news-gathering and transmission, video-taped news footage of the events was circulating among participants within twenty minutes of their taking place, thus spreading awareness about the unfolding crisis. During the 1991 coup in Moscow (in which NICTs such as e-mail and fax also played an important anti-coup role) Russian TV audiences were able to see with their own eyes (mediated by the journalists) that opposition to the plotters was widespread, including among the military. Resistance was strengthened, and the coup failed. In these cases and others, the immediacy of news was a positive influence on the development of the events being reported.

Some observers have, however, cautioned against the trend towards ever-more immediate and 'live' news coverage of events, particularly in the international arena. For leading British television journalist Nik Gowing (1994), the development of real-time news has major and unwelcome implications for governmental crisis management, especially in the sphere of foreign affairs. Because of the immediacy and all-pervasive nature of media coverage, politicians can no longer respond to conflicts and crises with what he characterizes as the desirable restraints of *control, confidentiality* and *coolness.* Instead, they must deal with a situation in which mass publics are gaining access to information as quickly as the politicians and their advisers themselves. Moreover, that information is undigested and raw – frightening, emotionally charged images of destruction and atrocities which may obscure the underlying complexities of an event or conflict and generate ill-informed, if well-intentioned and understandable shifts in the public's mood. In a conflict situation where real-time news is present, in short, politicians *lack* control and confidentiality. Rather than maintaining coolness, they are under pressure to act in the heat of the moment. Real-time news may force a policy response geared to public opinion rather than the needs of the situation. As Gowing puts it, 'governments frequently go out of their way to appear to modify policy when little or nothing of substance has changed' (1994: 11). Politicians increasingly 'fear that emotive pictures provided by real-time TV coverage forces them into an impulsive policy response when the reality on the ground is different [from that portrayed in the news]'.

Of course, the impact of real-time news in this sense will be moderated by other factors. In Rwanda and Burundi, real-time images of massacre and genocide did not influence western policy. In Somalia (images of a dead US serviceman being dragged through the streets), Srebrenica (concentration camps) and Kurdish Iraq (refugees), they did. In this sense, TV coverage may be 'a powerful influence in problem recognition, which in turn helps to *shape* the foreign policy agenda. But television does not necessarily *dictate* foreign policy responses' (Gowing 1994: 18).

The American journalist and writer James Fallows argues that the immediacy of news, combined with its relentless focus on drama, violence, and negativity, generates citizen apathy and a 'huge collective demoralisation for the people masochistic enough to watch [it]' (1996: 200). Contemporary news depicts a world out of control, a conclusion which applies as much to domestic as to international events. In the context of real-time coverage of the LA riots, or O.J. Simpson's failed attempts to flee after becoming a suspect in the murder of his wife, Fallows' observations are a useful qualifier to the general enthusiasm with which developments in news-gathering technology are greeted, not least by professional journalists:

> There is increasing evidence that [the news media's] cynical handling of issues and their contextless presentation of violent events make society's problems harder to solve than they would otherwise be.
>
> (Fallows 1996: 202)

The term 'compassion-fatigue' has been used in the context of this discussion, with reference to the perception that television audiences are growing tired of hearing about (and watching) the tragedies of less fortunate societies unfold on their screens. Since the news coverage which accompanied the 1984 Ethiopian famine, it is argued, one crisis after another has generated a similar pattern of journalistic response. Armed with the latest in electronic news-gathering technologies, journalists are dropped into a crisis zone (Tien an Mien square, former Yugoslavia, Rwanda), from where they produce horrific images of human brutality and suffering for as long as editorial offices back home dictate that the event is a 'story'. After a certain period of time, determined by such factors as the presence of oil or some other strategic reason for western interest in the situation, newsworthiness declines and the journalists move on to another 'hot spot' where, again, horrific, decontextualized violence and cruelty is served up as news. Compassion fatigue signifies the gradual loss of interest (and compassion) on the part of audiences, as they grow tired of the feelings of guilt and powerlessness that often accompany exposure to such scenes. Just as some sociologists argue that watching fictional violence on television desensitizes the viewer to real-life violence, so too, it is argued, we become blasé and complacent about the never-ending succession of human tragedies presented to us as news.

While NICTs have made such news possible for the first time in human history, it is the pressure of competition which has encouraged its growth. Since CNN pioneered the concept of live 24-hour news in the 1980s, other broadcast news organizations have felt themselves obliged to participate. In the Gulf War, for example, news organizations accepted the restrictive demands made upon them by the military (such as the requirement that journalists work in 'pools', with military minders making sure that access to controversial or contentious material was denied) not least because they could not (or so they believed) afford to be left out. In the TV ratings battle which was a by-product of the conflict, every news organization wanted access to the war zone, and the images which it generated. For this, they were prepared to have their coverage sanitized and managed in such a way as to censor out images that might have presented their audiences with a messier, less technologically clean war (MacArthur 1992).

Commercial competition dictates that where one leading news organization goes – be it Burundi or Bosnia – others must follow, all with the objective of supplying what they genuinely perceive to be informative real-time news. Consequently, only audience dissatisfaction as measured in ratings, or direct efforts to manage and control coverage by political and military authorities, can be expected to moderate the tendency.

NICTs and democracy: the Internet

Of all the developments in NICTs currently impacting on the production and consumption of media, the most significant is probably that of the Internet – the growing global network of linked computers – also known as the information superhighway – through which information can be passed at an unprecedented rate.

The Internet links some 40,000 computer networks (as of 1995, although the number is constantly growing) by satellite and cable, offering access to the WorldWideWeb – mainly used by commercial organizations – and Usenet, a network for private individuals organized into thousands of 'newsgroups'. These facilities can be used for advertising and promotion (including that of university departments, many of which now have a Web page profiling their activities); for on-line publishing of the type discussed earlier in the discussion of print media; and for communication between individuals by e-mail. The latter may be used for the circulation of data by researchers (for example, I subscribe to Moscow-based services supplying up-to-date information about the Russian media) or for two-way communication between geographically disparate users with a common interest. As the Internet develops and the infrastructure becomes more sophisticated it has become routine for 'virtual conversations' to take place in 'cyberspace', involving many individuals sending and receiving messages almost as quickly as if they were in the same room.

The power of the Internet was first demonstrated during the San Francisco earthquake of January 1994, when it was used to send out the first information about the disaster, beating CNN and other news organizations to the 'scoop'.

But the significance of the Internet for media culture goes beyond that of another leap in the speed of information dissemination. It constitutes an entirely new medium, harnessing the vast information-handling potential of modern computers, now easily accessible to the mass consumer market as well as the traditional scientific and industrial users, and the distributive power of cable and satellite delivery systems. For the first time, Marshall McLuhan's concept of the global village takes on real shape, as people in California 'talk' to people in the UK, Japan, Russia and Australia. The Internet presents a further, and to date the most radical dissolution of the barriers of time and space which have constrained human communication since we left the savannas and learnt to use language.

Speculation about what the Internet will do for and to human society abounds. From one perspective – which we might describe as utopian – the Internet does indeed herald the emergence of a true global village, a benign virtual community accessible to anyone with a computer terminal and a knowledge of how to use it. This perspective stresses the accessibility and interactivity of the new medium – the fact that it allows ordinary people to communicate across continents at the pressing of a 'Return' key, at relatively low cost (by comparison with telephone and fax), on all manner of topics and specialisms. The Internet is not owned by any state or multinational company, and no state or company can control its use. The Internet's relative freedom from the commercial and political constraints which have accompanied all previous communicative media, combined with its accessibility and interactivity, make it a uniquely democratizing technological innovation: a medium which evades censorship, regulation, and commercialization like no other.

An opposing, 'dystopian' view sees the Internet as the latest in a long line of dehumanizing technological developments, producing a population of 'computer-nerds' who, if they are not watching TV or fiddling with their playstations, are addictively 'surfing the Net'. The Internet, it is argued, encourages not communication but isolation, in which one talks not to real people, but disembodied screens.

Concerns about the implications of the Internet are often based on a fear of its anarchic, uncontrollable character – precisely the qualities welcomed by its most enthusiastic advocates. The Internet, it is argued, provides an uncensorable platform for the dissemination of all kinds of antisocial messages. Many US newsgroups are devoted to the rantings of extreme right-wing, pro-gun 'militias', for example. 'Cyberporn' is also cited in this connection, particularly in relation to children and young people. *Time* magazine in July 1995 devoted the bulk of an issue, and its cover, to the problem of cyberporn (Elmer-Dewitt 1995). The cover depicted a young boy, face reflecting the green light of a computer terminal, his eyes wide open with amazement. The article inside warned (and also pointed would-be users in the right direction) that the Usenet and WorldWideWeb networks were being used to distribute pornography all over the world, including – as the cover illustration made clear – to children and young adults. The material being distributed, moreover, was of the most extreme kind. An American academic's analysis of the cyberporn phenomenon concluded that 'computers and modems are profoundly redefining the pornographic landscape by saturating the market with an endless variety of what only a decade ago mainstream America defined as "perverse" or "deviant" ' (Rimm 1995).

Cyberporn nicely illustrates the threat posed by the Internet, as seen by some. To a greater extent than is true with traditional forms of disseminating pornography (and this applies to all forms of morally or legally sanctioned information) the Internet permits a private mode of consumption (no need for guilty browsing among the top shelves); it is user-friendly, allowing a high degree of selection and choice for anyone familiar with the system; and it is free of censorship, respecting no 'community standards' (the usual test of obscenity) or national boundaries. Traditional means of regulating and restricting pornography are useless on the Net (McNair 1996a). And as children and young people are known to be among the most frequent and adept users of the Internet, cyberporn thus emerges as a serious threat to new generations.

This dystopian view, which views the Internet as the harbinger of not only technological slobbery and information overload, but also moral chaos and anarchy, without the control of legislators, acknowledges the inherent difficulty in imposing traditional constraints on the medium. As the *Time* article puts it, 'the key issue is whether the Internet is a print medium, which enjoys strong protection against government interference, or a broadcast medium, which may be subject to all sorts of government control' (Elmer-Dewitt 1995). In fact, the Internet is neither print nor broadcasting, but a qualitatively new medium, to which conventional means of exerting control are extremely difficult, if not impossible, to apply. It remains to be seen if the global community (and it would have to be a genuinely global effort) can agree on standards of taste and decency for the Internet which are both enforceable and acceptable to the growing population of users.

For this writer, neither the optimistic nor pessimistic views described above represent a realistic appraisal of the Internet's significance for media culture. Certainly, as the utopian perspective asserts, the Internet permits a qualitatively new level of communication between human beings, and hitherto unimagined access to all kinds of information. But the resulting 'global village' can be no more benign than the individuals who use it, and the materials sent down its superhighways and byways. The Internet, like all previous developments in communication technology, is destined to reflect the best and the worst that humanity has to offer. It will continue to evade state censorship and arbitrary moral regulation – undeniably a good thing – but it will certainly be subject to a creeping commercialization, as its economic potential becomes clear. This process has already begun, and will accelerate in the twenty-first century.

But if the optimists are perhaps a little too optimistic, so the dystopian perspective may be viewed as a familiar blend of moral panic, social conservatism and cultural elitism. Children and young people will not become drooling slaves to the computer terminals in their bedrooms. Some children will find and watch cyberporn on the Net, as earlier generations watched 'video nasties', but there is no reason why the majority cannot be taught by parents, teachers, siblings and peers to use the technology fruitfully, gaining access to vast areas of knowledge denied previous generations.

Conclusion

The new information and communication technologies discussed in this chapter have raised issues and generated debates which are not in themselves new. Successive waves of 'information revolution', from the invention of the printing press to film and television, and now 'cyberspace', have each presented problems of control and regulation for our legislators; problems of adaptation and restructuring for the media industries; new challenges and temptations for audiences. We have, as human societies, dealt with these problems and challenges in the past, and we will surely do so with the latest wave. It is, as always, up to us.

Questions

1   Evaluate the impact on either (i) the press, or (ii) broadcasting of the technological developments discussed in this chapter.

2   Is it possible, or desirable, to censor or otherwise restrict the dissemination of information on the Internet?

3   In your view, does 'real-time news' have a negative or a positive impact on public opinion and political decision-making? Illustrate your answer with examples.

References

Curran, J. and Seaton, J. (1991) *Power without Responsibility: The Press and Broadcasting in Britain*, 4th edn, London: Routledge.

Elmer-Dewitt, P. (1995) 'On a screen near you: cyberporn', *Time*, 3 July.

Fallows, J. (1996) *Breaking the News*, New York: Pantheon.

Gowing, N. (1994) 'Real-time television coverage of armed conflicts and diplomatic crises', Harvard University, Cambridge, MA.

Katz, J. (1995) 'Tomorrow's word', *Guardian*, 24 April.

MacArthur, J. (1992) *Second Front*, New York: Hill & Wang.

McGregor, B. (1994) 'Crisis reporting in the satellite age', paper given to the European Film and Television Studies Conference, London, July.

McNair, B. (1996a) *Mediated Sex*, London: Arnold.

McNair, B. (1996b) *News and Journalism in the UK*, 2nd edn, London: Routledge.

Rimm, M. (1995) 'Marketing pornography on the information superhighway' (on-line version), first published in *Georgetown Law Journal* Spring 1995.

Tusa, J. (1996) 'A mission to destroy', *Guardian*, 10 June.

Further reading

McNair, B. (1996) *News and Journalism in the UK*, 2nd edn, London: Routledge.

Yorke, I. (1995) *Television News*, Oxford: Focal Press.

Part II

'Outside' the media

Introduction to ' "Outside" the Media'

ADAM BRIGGS AND PAUL COBLEY

The chapters in Part II all deal with factors that might be considered 'outside' the media; however, this is not an entirely accurate formulation. Each factor is 'outside' only in so far as it can be conceived of as having some kind of independent existence apart from the media. In fact, each is so thoroughly a part of the fabric of the media that they can be understood to be 'inside'.

Economics, for instance, has a wider frame than just the media; yet media economics determines the production of representations as well as their consumption. *Policy* is made by governments and sets the parameters for models of media institutions' ownership and distribution and in this sense is also 'outside' the media; but like economics, it determines the kinds of media that are offered to us. Audiences are clearly made up of people, large parts of whose lives are separate from media; nevertheless, audiences also consist of consumers whose viewing/reading/listening activity is registered as feedback, whose engagement differs according to different 'forms' of media text, and whose behaviour is often attributed to the 'effects' of media.

In Chapter 14 on 'Economics', Patrick Barwise and David Gordon discuss the way in which representations found in the media are totally dependent on budgets. In short, no budget equals no media. Every media institution needs to raise cash in order that it may not only produce representations, but also reproduce itself (i.e. maintain its existence and even expand). Advertising, for example, has become crucial for many commercial media institutions as the primary source of revenue. Moreover, advertisers target consumers whose 'quality' and 'quantity' are measured by audience researchers (see Stoessl, Chapter 18 in this volume). Such ratings research establishes who consumes what media and in what numbers, and therefore the likelihood of these audiences apprehending the advertising associated with these media. But media economics has numerous different guises so Barwise and Gordon go on to outline systematically the different funding issues relevant to specific media.

As Barwise and Gordon note, Lord Thomson described the setting up of commercial television as a 'licence to print money'. The making of large sums of cash out of the media has increasingly become a subject of government regulation. Those who have the most revenue to invest can, potentially, invest further and control large portions of output from different media within any one national market. With this, it is argued, comes a limitation on the diversity of media output. This criticism has frequently been lodged against the (once) Australian media mogul Rupert Murdoch by those who are hostile to his cross-media empire. The important question posed by Lord Thomson's statement is 'How can the activities of media owners be regulated in the public interest?'

Media activity is regulated by broadcast policy, which is the subject of Nicholas Garnham's Chapter 15 and also frames Ralph Negrine's discussion in Chapter 16 of models of European media institutions. In general, for broadcast media, policy is applied to two traditions of operation: commercial and public service. Put simply, commercial media (as exemplified by ITV, Channel Four and Channel Five) in the UK is funded primarily from advertising revenue; in spite of this it is not completely independent because it is subject to regulative bodies set up by government. Public service (such as the BBC in the UK) is set up by government but is relatively autonomous; although public service is subject to government-appointed regulative bodies, many of its operations take place independently of government. The government does, however, set the licence fee which provides a major source of revenue and allows programming for many interests rather than simply those of ratings maximization. The government is also ultimately responsible for the renewal every ten years of the BBC's charter to broadcast.

There can be no doubt that study of broadcast policy is essential to understanding media. However, it cannot account for everything. While policy study reveals the legal, economic and regulative underpinnings of the media that we consume, it can tell us very little about the kinds of texts that the models of media institutions facilitate. What are the 'forms' of representation with which audiences engage? How do they act to *present* a specific 'content'? John Corner in Chapter 17 shows that this can never be a simple issue. A content such as 'violence' can never be conceived as a straightforward category independent of the form in which it is presented. To say that certain texts are 'violent' is to say too little.

Frequently, all that we can say with certainty about an *audience's engagement* with media texts is that it took place. There is little that can be said definitively about the 'quality' of that engagement. Sue Stoessl's Chapter 18 looks at media research on audiences from what we have called, after Lazarsfeld (see Chapter 1, 'What you need to know before you start to use this book'), an 'administrative' standpoint. 'Administrative' research on audiences measures ratings, and this is as important for public service broadcasters as it is for commercial broadcasters, as the former have to seek to provide justification for their licence fees in an increasingly competitive environment. What such measurement cannot address are the complexities of actual audience members' 'reception' of media material. How do audiences make sense of media texts? With what 'effect' do they do this (if any)? These questions have come to the forefront of much media study, especially since the early 1980s (see, for example, Ang 1996; Hermes 1995; Morley 1992).

The question of media 'effects' is the subject of Guy Cumberbatch's Chapter 19. You will have noticed that throughout this volume we have referred to 'effects' in inverted commas. The reason for this is that, although in everyday discourse it is often assumed that the media have powerful effects upon their audiences, there is little conclusive evidence that this is the case. As a social psychologist, Cumberbatch is sceptical about the evidence that has been used to support the media-effects thesis. As he shows, this thesis has a very powerful grip on the popular imagination, so much so that it does not escape the attention of policy-makers. Yet it is unsubstantiated.

One possible reason for the popularity of the effects thesis may be the way media representations, for many people, *do* seem to permeate our lives. Without proposing direct 'effects', this theme is picked up by the contributors to Part III, In the Media.

References

Ang, I. (1996) *Living Room Wars: Rethinking Audiences for a Postmodern World*, London: Routledge.

Hermes, J. (1995) *Reading Women's Magazines: An Analysis of Everyday Media Use*, Oxford: Polity.

Morley, D. (1992) *Television, Audiences and Cultural Studies*, London: Routledge.

Chapter 14

Economics

THE ECONOMICS OF THE MEDIA

PATRICK BARWISE AND DAVID GORDON

This chapter looks at the economic forces that shape the media. It is essential to have a good understanding of these forces because they help to determine what we read and what we see in the media.

The chapter begins with an analysis of the key economic characteristics of the media in general and describes the particular characteristics of the main print and broadcast media today. It then discusses the impact of new digital media such as the Internet, and concludes by briefly outlining three scenarios for the evolution of the media in the next decade.

Once you have read this chapter, you might become more questioning about the media that you, as a reader and viewer, 'consume'. What made you watch this or that programme on this or that channel? What determines the scheduling of programmes on television? Why do newspapers have so many sections on Saturdays and Sundays? Since television and radio news is so up-to-date, how can tomorrow's newspapers compete with them? How can the thousands of magazines that line the news-stands all stay in business? How much is it costing you per hour to read a book compared with watching a video compared with watching ITV compared with subscribing to Sky – and were you dimly aware of the relative costs before doing the exercise? Are you sensitive to the price of different media?

Of course there is much more to the media than economics, money and business. The media inform, influence, entertain and educate. Newspapers, magazines, television, radio, and other media are powerful forces in society shaping the way that we know about things, look at things, think about things. As other influences affecting the political and moral climate of the UK have receded, 'the media' have taken on an ever more prominent position as chief culprit for the ills of society. But apart from the BBC and Channel Four, the media are owned by companies that are seeking to make money.

Judging by the size of the media industries, it would seem that all tastes and all shades of opinion are catered for. Is this true? Do we get the media that we want, or do we get the media that others decide we want? Rupert

Murdoch fashioned the *Sun*, which led the other tabloids downmarket in a search for circulation via sensation. If Murdoch had not done so, would someone else have spotted this gap in the market and filled it?

Are all the varied gaps and niches in the market being filled? Certainly, looked at as an industry, nearly every indicator shows an upward trend: there are increasing numbers of radio stations, television channels, new magazines, books, CD-ROMs, cinema admissions, accesses to on-line services and the Internet – and students enrolled on media studies courses. Some indicators show decline, such as newspaper circulations, but new entrepreneurs with new ideas are buying up regional newspapers, so it is possible that this trend might be reversed.

But overall within media, growth is the story. Why? What are the factors underlying this trend?

- As consumers get richer, they spend an increasing proportion of their expenditure on leisure, pleasure, entertainment and information. So media get a bigger slice of the pie.
- As economies get richer, the pie gets bigger.
- Despite the increased working hours experienced by some sections of the workforce, the amount of time that people spend on media consumption seems to be growing. This is partly due to the fact that many people have more leisure time as a result of the impact of automation and new technologies, and partly due to higher levels of unemployment – though inevitably the types of media that can be enjoyed by unemployed people are more limited due to financial constraints. Of course, some media can be consumed while doing other chores – listening to the radio while ironing, listening to a CD while driving, having a Walkman blaring out while on the bus, even watching a miniature TV set while at a football match.
- Technology has had a dramatic effect on most aspects of existing media and has ushered in new media. More channels, enticing gizmos, lower costs, the ease of getting entertainment and information, all have empowered and excited consumers.
- The coming together of the telecommunications, computer and media industries has attracted investment from large companies and entrepreneurs who seek to build up competitive advantage on a worldwide scale by having a dominant brand, or great distribution power, or powerful content, or ideally all three. Many of these companies have expanded from one medium, such as newspapers, into another, such as television, so that it is accurate, though grammatically inelegant, to refer to the media (plural) industry (singular).
- Governments have been deregulating and privatizing, and allowing private capital into areas that once were state monopolies, such as broadcasting and telecommunications.

Money, time, technology and deregulation are the economic and industrial factors which, combined with the cultural and sociological factors dealt with elsewhere in this book, explain why media are likely to remain a growth industry for the foreseeable future.

Who pays the piper?

Most media are paid for by the consumer direct and/or advertisers wishing to reach the consumer. In some countries, some media are subsidized by the government either directly out of taxes or indirectly by giving certain media certain privileges. For example the BBC is given the right to collect the licence fee from anyone with a television whether or not they ever watch or listen to the BBC. (This works better than it sounds. In practice, everyone does watch or listen to the BBC, at an average cost of a few pence per hour. But it would be harder to justify if most people stopped using BBC services.)

An example of getting money direct from the consumer is that 600,000 households each paid between £9 and £14 (depending how early they signed up) to watch the 1996 Bruno vs Tyson fight on Sky television. A more common example is the purchase of a book.

An example of advertisers paying for the privilege of getting their messages to consumers is ITV. To the viewer this is 'free', or at least, painless and invisible, to the extent that some of the cost is paid by buying the advertised products (Ehrenberg and Barwise 1983). It is the job of the ITV companies to put on good enough programmes to get a large enough audience to charge advertisers enough money to pay for the programmes, the overheads and a profit to shareholders.

An example of both streams of revenue is a newspaper, which charges its readers the cover price and also takes advertising. Newspapers are a 'joint product' like a sheep, which is both in the market for wool and in the market for lamb. A newspaper has to appeal in the market for readers. And it then has to sell those readers in the market for advertising.

All commercial media fall somewhere on a spectrum with charging consumers the full cost of the product at one end and all-advertising at the other end.

Advertising

The main reason that organizations advertise is to sell more of their particular brand – Coca Cola or London Guildhall University – than they would have sold without the advertising. This does not necessarily mean selling more than before the advertising; a campaign for a long-established brand like Heinz baked beans could be cost justified if it helped to maintain sales in the face of cut-price supermarket brands. You may remember a TV commercial a few years ago with dancing milk bottles. This was aimed at *slowing down the decline* in doorstep delivery. It succeeded in doing this, more than covering its costs, but did not cause doorstep delivery to start growing again.

Usually, increasing the sales of a brand means capturing a higher share of the market rather than increasing the total size of the market (Barwise 1994; Barwise and Ehrenberg 1988: Appendix A). An advertisement for London Guildhall University is unlikely to persuade many people to go to university – the aim is to increase the proportion of people applying to that particular university. Some campaigns are directly aimed at taking sales from the competition. One well-known example was Pepsi-Cola's 'Pepsi Challenge', which showed many consumers that under 'blind' conditions they preferred the taste of Pepsi to Coke.

In some cases, advertising for a particular brand does increase the size of the total market. The main aim of BT's campaign with Bob Hoskins was to encourage us all to use the telephone more – partly because it costs less than most of us think. As an unwanted side-effect, this campaign has probably increased the revenues of BT's competitors, Mercury and the cable companies. Advertising can also accelerate the growth of a new market like the Internet, although if a product or service is really new it also benefits from a lot of free media coverage.

Advertising can help a brand sell at a higher price than competing brands. Coca-Cola, Absolut vodka, Levi's jeans, Nike trainers, Benson and Hedges cigarettes, and Andrex toilet tissue all sell at a higher price than their 'no-name' competitors and most consumers know this. Stella Artois has even been advertised as 'reassuringly expensive'.

For the economy as a whole, however, the effects of advertising on prices are complex. Advertising in some form is a necessary part of a competitive market economy. It does cost firms money, but without it, competition is reduced and prices can be higher. For instance, when opticians in the USA were allowed to advertise, the price of spectacles sharply decreased (see Brierley, Chapter 4 in this volume).

How much money do advertisers put into the media?

Total UK advertising expenditure in 1995 was about £11 billion. This includes direct mail advertising, posters, directories such as Yellow Pages, and business and professional magazines. Excluding these, almost £8 billion was spent on advertising in the mass consumer media this book is about. This is about 1.6 per cent of total consumer expenditure on goods and services. Most of this was spent on press and TV advertising, 4 per cent (and growing) went into radio and just under 1 per cent into cinema advertising (see Table 14.1).

Table 14.1 UK mass media advertising expenditure 1995

	£ billion	%
National newspapers	1.57	20
Regional newspapers	2.15	28
Consumer magazines	0.58	7
All newspapers/consumer magazines	4.30	55
Television	3.10	40
Radio	0.30	4
Cinema	0.07	1
Total	7.77	100

Authors' estimate based on Advertising Association (1996). These figures include production costs but exclude advertising agency fees/commissions.

It is not only big companies that advertise. If you place a small ad for someone to share your flat or your life, the money you spend will be included in the advertising statistics. Classified advertising – job vacancies, houses, cars, and so on – accounts for a substantial part of total advertising expenditure among print media – as much as 60 per cent in the case of regional newspapers.

Virtually all the money spent on classified advertising goes to the media themselves. For display advertising, about three-quarters of what companies spend goes to the media. The other quarter goes to the advertising agencies who develop the advertising and buy the time or space, and to the printers, photographers, actors, producers and technicans who produce the advertisements themselves. When Coca-Cola hires Michael Jackson for a commercial, or British Airways hires the director Ridley Scott and a large number of extras, the result can cost more on a per second basis than even the most expensive Hollywood feature film. For the audience, great advertisements are an important genre in their own right (see Brierley, Chapter 4 in this volume).

What advertisers want: numbers and demographics

In choosing which media to use, advertisers' main aim is to reach as many people as possible within their target market. Other things being equal, a media vehicle with a large readership or audience can charge more for the space or time it sells to advertisers.

For instance, in 1995 the price of a full page in the *Daily Mirror* for a black-and-white advertisement was £25,900. The *Daily Mirror* had a circulation of about 2.4 million copies. That is, it sold about 2.4 million copies of each issue. Each copy was read by an average of 2.7 adults, giving a total adult readership of 6.5 million. This is the number of people who would have had an 'opportunity-to-see' your advertisement. Dividing the cost of the space (£25,900) by the number of readers (6.5 million) gives a cost per thousand (CPT) of about £4.00. This is equivalent to 0.4 pence for each adult reader.

As an advertiser, you could instead have bought a full page in the *Daily Star* for only £9,400. But in this case you would have reached only 2.2 million readers, not 6.5 million. The cost per thousand would have been slightly higher than for the *Daily Mirror*, about £4.30. The *Daily Mirror* can charge more than twice as much as the *Daily Star* because it has more than twice as many readers. (Official 'list prices' from Advertising Association (1996). The actual prices paid are usually lower and depend on many factors but these do not affect the main argument here.)

Size is not everything, however. The advertisements in the *Daily Mirror* are for things like records, car and home insurance, disposable razors, cold sore cream, made-to-measure furniture covers, personal loans, and car parts – products and services aimed at the mass market. Most advertisers, however, want to reach a specific 'target segment' of people. In some cases this is extremely difficult. For instance, firms advertising dog food or dishwasher liquid have no major media for reaching customers efficiently. Instead they have to use mass media with a lot of wastage, or develop costly direct marketing channels such as direct mail.

Often, however, there are media whose readership/audience closely matches the advertiser's target market. The most general way of categorizing consumers is by 'demographics' – age, sex and household income. Consumer magazines are highly targeted in terms of the age, sex or special interests of their readers. This is reflected in the types of products and services advertised in them and in the style of the advertisements. Radio stations can also have highly segmented audiences, especially in the big cities with many local stations including those for specific ethnic audiences. Nationally, Virgin Radio and Classic FM reach quite different audiences.

The most valuable consumers to advertisers tend to be those with the most spending power. For some media, notably the *Financial Times* (*FT*) and the business sections of the other quality national newspapers, this includes their influence on purchases by organizations as well as readers' own personal purchases. Advertisements in a typical day's *FT* are for commercial property, trade shows in Singapore, Financial Information Services, business courses, cheap flights to Amsterdam ('finance director's dream ticket'), various personal financial services, and a lot of corporate publicity announcements such as one listing all the banks that have arranged a $75 million loan for an Hungarian investment fund. A half-page black-and-white advertisement in the *FT* in 1995 (the same size as a full page in the tabloid *Mirror* or *Star*, but with arguably less visual impact) would have cost £16,800, to reach a readership of just 700,000 adults. This works out at a cost per thousand of about £24 – six times the CPT of the *Daily Mirror* and *Daily Star* (see Curran, Chapter 7, and Stoessl, Chapter 18 in this volume).

Television audiences are largely unsegmented (Barwise and Ehrenberg 1988). Most people watch all four of the main channels and spread their viewing across most programme types. There are some differences: the average programme on ITV has somewhat more viewers who are down-scale, older and watch a lot of television than for the average programme on the other three channels; soap operas tend to be watched by women, soccer by men, news by older viewers and 'action' (i.e. violent) programmes by young males. But there is nothing like the strong segmentation of print media and radio. For instance there is no TV audience with the same profile as the *FT* readership, which can therefore be sold to advertisers at a high cost per thousand viewers.

This is important as we move towards multi-channel television. Many of the new channels are 'narrowcasting' rather than broadcasting, in the sense that they show only one type of programme (movies, sport, news, etc.) In some cases like MTV, which has a very young audience, the audience is strongly skewed towards the target segment, as you would expect. But this does not mean that advertisers will pay a premium price for this audience, even on a cost per thousand basis. This is partly because few of these audiences are from especially valuable segments; partly because they are available only in homes with satellite/cable (still less than one home in four) which limits their reach; and partly because their viewers are also heavy viewers of network television. They do not enable advertisers to reach viewers that other channels do not reach. Broadly similar arguments apply in the USA and other countries with high cable penetration. The overall effect is that air-time on so-called narrowcast channels sells at a lower price, even on a cost per thousand basis, than for the main commercial channels. For somewhat similar reasons, the CPT on daytime television is less than for prime time in the evening.

As well as efficiently reaching their target customers, advertisers also look for high impact. Television is usually the highest impact mass medium for advertising although it is, as just discussed, not efficient at reaching narrow segments, especially high income segments. It is also unsuited to campaigns which need to communicate a lot of detailed information such as a list of 100 shops across the UK which stock the product. Advertisers are well able to compare the cost efficiency of different media of the same broad type – different television programmes, different mass market daily newspapers – but comparisons between different types of media – print versus television versus radio – involve more art than science.

Issues to do with advertising

Advertising – like media in general – has had its fair share of criticism. In the past it has been seen as wasteful, as making people buy things they did not really want or need, and as anti-competitive. The view today is more balanced. Economists now recognize that advertising is a necessary part of competition. Few people today believe that advertising has a very powerful effect on how much we spend on broad categories such as cars, holidays, and fast food. But the extent of advertising's influence is still controversial.

If advertising is a big source of revenue for a media business this will strongly influence the content of the medium. Consumer media funded by advertising have to provide content which will attract a large readership/ audience of high value to advertisers. In the case of print media and (with enough spectrum) radio, the result is to produce a wide range of vehicles suiting many different tastes and interests. In the case of television funded by advertising, this process works less well. Minority programmes which are relatively demanding to watch tend to be unable to generate enough advertising revenue to cover their costs. For those consumers willing and able to pay more for more, subscription TV can fill this gap. A cheaper and arguably more equitable alternative is the traditional policy in Britain which combined licence fee funding for the BBC with advertising funding for ITV and Channel Four and with all four main channels required to show a wider range of programmes than is found on deregulated advertising-funded networks as in the USA or Italy.

Advertisers may also seek to influence programming policy directly. This especially applies to media in a small community where everyone knows everyone. This is why the news stories in local newspapers and in trade magazines tend to be bland: the local newspaper may be afraid to criticize an important local businessman in case he and his friends stop advertising in it. Even national mass media can be subject to pressure. In the USA, the Moral Majority, a pressure group for so-called 'family values', has successfully driven off air several programmes of which it disapproved (e.g. *Soap*) by organizing a consumer boycott of the brands advertised on the programme.

Regulation and deregulation

As each medium comes in, and is at first scarce, those in power try to exercise control. Knowledge is power. Before the days of printing, the Church kept a tight control of manuscripts and copying them was a specialist occupation of monks. Then came the printing press and governments tried hard to keep control of what was printed.

In the UK, radio was made a monopoly and handed to the government-owned, if not government-controlled, BBC.

We take it for granted that the government should regulate parts of the media. The news media have a huge impact on views, the entertainment media on social attitudes. Ministers are asked in Parliament to do something about the level of violence on television. What has given governments the standing to exercise control has usually been the technical need to allocate scarce capacity. For many years that was the excuse given for the tiny number of radio stations in the UK compared with the USA. As became gradually clear, the truth of the matter was that the Home Office did not think it good for people to have a lot more radio. The retreat of the Nanny State together with technological developments has led to the sudden discovery of more radio bandwidth, and a fifth television channel.

But there are also good reasons why governments think that media are different from sausages and that some care ought to be exercised in passing control over to the owners of bandwidth that has been in the past limited. Rupert Murdoch had to become a naturalized American before he could be entrusted with the ownership of television stations.

As the number of channels of television are increased through cable and satellite, the degree of regulation will decrease. Many regimes control media for political reasons. The Soviet government tried to control all access to photocopiers and did not give telephone directories to ordinary citizens. The Chinese government is trying to control access to the Internet. Various British politicians have accused the BBC of political bias.

The characteristics of particular media

Television: broadcast, cable and satellite

The most famous quotation about the economics of television in Britain was made by the Canadian television and newspaper proprietor, Lord Thomson, ten years into his ownership of the main ITV franchise for Scotland: 'It is just like having a licence to print your own money.'

Until 1955 the BBC, owned by the state, had a monopoly of broadcasting, and put out one rather staid national television service and three radio services. The Conservative government of the day, after much lobbying, agreed to a new channel to be financed entirely by advertising, as in the US model.

Those hostile to 'commercial' television feared that the need to attract large audiences would lead to endless game shows, cheap sitcoms and American imports, and would sap national morals and morale. The concerned government obliged the new service, which its supporters termed ITV, for Independent (rather than 'commercial') Television, to satisfy a new authority, the Independent Television Authority (now the Independent Television Commission), that it was keeping up standards of production in drama and entertainment, producing enough documentaries and current affairs programmes, and so on. The licence conditions also laid down that ITV had to have its own high-quality news service, ITN, which, in the event, showed a clean pair of heels to the stodgy, complacent and over-respectful BBC news.

In a worthy attempt to spread the benefits of producing for this new channel around the country, and to foster some regionalism in the new television culture, the franchises were awarded on a regional basis. Hence Lord Thomson, who owned regional newspapers, became a major shareholder in Scottish Television.

What he and the other owners of the channel found was that viewers' appetite for popular programmes, and advertisers' appetite to reach this receptive mass audience, led to viewing and revenues much higher than anyone had anticipated. The regional companies did not in practice spend much on less remunerative local programming and spent most of their production budgets on programmes that were networked, i.e. shown nationwide. ITV rapidly established dominance and by 1962 had a 70 per cent share of television viewing, leaving the BBC in the shade.

The BBC fought back. BBC2 was introduced to cater for the more highbrow tastes and have a showcase for the BBC's more public service endeavours, freeing BBC1 to respond to ITV with programmes that aimed to be not only distinctive – justifying its non-commercial stance – but also popular, on the grounds that licence-fee payers should be given something they enjoyed watching. The BBC has always been on the horns of this dilemma. In the event, by the late 1960s, the BBC (with two channels) and ITV were each attracting about 50 per cent of viewing. The British system was widely admired as showing a wide range of programmes which were good of their kind ('making good programmes watchable and watchable programmes good') as well as for its political independence.

The slow release of television frequencies led in 1982 to the fourth nationally available broadcast network, Channel Four. It was a real innovation. Channel Four was solely a broadcaster: it owned the airwaves but commissioned its programmes from newly formed independent production companies who were paid a fee on commission and the balance on delivery, in the same way as a book publisher commissions and pays authors. It had a charter from the regulator requiring it to meet the needs of specialist and minority audiences. It was financed by the sale of advertising – until 1993 sold by the ITV companies but since then by Channel Four itself.

The effect of having the BBC and two advertising-financed channels which have to meet quality terms laid down in charters and franchise agreements has been that the range and variety of television programmes has been greater than on the main networks in the USA which (despite having massive resources) all chase the same audiences with the same formulas and the same mix of programmes. In an uncontrolled mass market like television or selling petrol there is a tendency towards sameness. There is an old joke in the USA that American television is like the movie *Battleship Potemkin* – it shows what happens when the ratings take over.

The expansion of the television market has been brought about so far by an increase in the amount of choice and by an increase in the amount of time to enjoy the greater choice. The latter may be coming to an end, and yet the number of channels available on cable and satellite is mushrooming, and with digital satellite TV the number of channels available will soon be in the hundreds. This means that the market will fragment; given a now-fixed quantity of eyeball-hours, the audience for any one channel is likely to decline.

First, existing broadcasters have cut their operating costs. The controversial reorganization of the BBC by its director-general, John Birt, has been designed to reduce the costs of programme-making, and to generate more income by selling programmes more aggressively abroad as television follows other industries into becoming more global. The ITV companies, now freed (within limits) to buy each other up, have done so and been able to reduce the overheads of the old regional set-up. In many cities, the headquarters of the ITV company was the second most imposing building after the town hall.

Second, the cost of making some programmes, especially factual programmes, is coming down, aided by new technology (smaller cameras, digital editing), higher productivity and lower salaries. In the days of the television duopoly the television unions were able to push salaries up to levels achieved by old Fleet Street print workers. On the other hand, the sums paid to 'the talent' – the on-screen faces and some of the writers – is going up fast as broadcasters try to attract audiences in a more competitive environment. Similarly, the cost of television rights for movies, sport, and shows like *The Three Tenors* has escalated.

Third, viewers are prepared to pay much more money for the programme of their choice. With the TV licence fee at £90 (1996), and an average viewing in each home of 1500 hours a year, BBC television is incredibly good value at 6p an hour (with radio thrown in free). BSkyB has now signed up over 5 million cable/satellite subscribers paying some £240 a year, who on average watch about 10 hours of cable/satellite-only programmes per week, or 45p an hour. This compares with a cinema visit for two people costing, say, £10 just for tickets, leaving aside transport, popcorn and baby-sitter.

Looking ahead, technology is making it easier and cheaper for television programmes to be delivered to consumers, at a time of their choosing instead of in a linear stream that obliges them to sit and watch or to remember to set the video recorder. The indications are that viewers are prepared to pay a great deal more per hour to get what they want when they want it. This is particularly true of sports fans. Thus BSkyB began the process of bidding up the rights to sports (part of 'the talent') to win viewers for its specialist sports channels. These sports channels have the advantage that there is little wastage of viewers – no anti-sport viewers who are being put off. And also of generating some revenue, from advertising targeted at an audience with more homogeneous characteristics than a general audience.

It seems likely that the same viewers who are sometimes in search of specialist channels will most of the time want to relapse into couch-potato mode, with choices being made for them by channel controllers, and at a much lower price per hour, for much of their viewing. Stream-viewing does allow a skilful scheduler to some extent to build audiences although this 'audience inheritance' or 'lead-in' effect is only shortlived (Barwise and

Ehrenberg 1988). In the mid-1990s, Channel Four made Friday nights comedy night and in 1996 entertained an upmarket end-of-working-week audience with *Cybill* at 9 p.m., *Friends* at 9.30, *Frasier* at 10 p.m. and *Whose Line Is It Anyway?* or *Rory Bremner* at 10.30.

All this implies that the existing mass-market broadcasters will continue to enjoy a substantial audience, retain the bulk of the advertising revenue, benefit from substantial economies of scale and coexist with specialist subscription channels and programmes delivered on a pay-per-view basis.

Radio

Radio is the oldest electronic mass medium. The BBC began in 1922. For decades travellers would return from the USA telling of the plethora of radio stations in all large American cities, while in the UK there were a handful of national stations, all BBC. Those with powerful radio sets listened to Radio Luxembourg to get the popular music they craved. In the 1960s pirate radio stations on ships within transmission distance of big cities founded the careers of many disk jockeys (DJs). The first reaction of the then government was to make illegal the selling of advertising on these pirates. It was only in 1973 that the first licensed commercial radio station, LBC, got on the air.

In the privatizing, deregulating world of the 1990s it is hard to believe that only thirty years ago the attitude of the regulators was to restrict the amount of radio and television. The arguments were based on a supposed technical shortage of frequencies, but underlying them was the Reithian belief that more would mean worse and have a corrupting effect on the nation's mental and spiritual well-being. Radio shows the braking effect of regulation on a media industry. In the mid-1990s there are 160 local radio stations in the UK and 3 national networks. Advertising revenue in 1995 was £300 million and growing. Much of this could have happened earlier (see Crisell, Chapter 9 in this volume).

Radio remains regulated; the Radio Authority issues a licence for a particular kind of station and the staff monitor the station to check that the owners are broadcasting what they promised, although with, say, Jazz FM it is debatable whether this has really worked.

The radio industry illustrates in simple form one general characteristic of media, especially broadcast media: all the costs of radio are incurred before there is a single listener; each extra listener adds nothing to costs; therefore the aim is to get as many listeners as possible (while staying within the bounds of the licence promise), to generate the maximum amount of advertising revenue. Given the number of radio stations, most of which are music-based, each station has to carve out a loyalty based on a definite personality, expressed in its music policy, the kinds of presenters and DJs it uses, its jingles, and the predictability of its output at various times of day. Since the advent of television, radio has become a secondary medium. People are usually doing something else at the same time as they listen:

getting dressed to Radio Four or driving to Atlantic 252 or working to Classic FM or listening to those independent local radio (ILR) stations that have in general established stronger local credentials than the BBC ever did.

A change in the Broadcasting Act 1990 allowed greater freedom in the ownership of stations. Once a licence is awarded, the station can be sold, and there are now a few large groups eager to buy up the minnows, which can dramatically reduce the operating costs of the acquired stations while still meeting the requirements of the licence. This illustrates another characteristic of media industries: media owners can often extract considerable value from 'horizontal integration', that is, buying other similar businesses.

Newspapers

The national newspapers are the mirror of the nation. In Britain there are an unusually large number of national daily and Sunday newspapers, reflecting a nation that is serious and balanced about matters affecting commerce and industry (*Financial Times – FT*), critical of the government from the right (*Daily Telegraph, The Times, Daily Mail, Daily Express, Sun, Daily Star*) and from the centre and left (*The Independent, Daily Mirror* and *Guardian*), transfixed by the royals (most of them), obsessed by sex scandals relating to minor TV personalities and footballers (the tabloids). It is interesting to note, however, that although traditionally party allegiances have been seen as fixed, the *Sun*, which was always perceived as a Tory paper, very publicly announced its support for the Labour leader, Tony Blair, in the run up to the 1997 General Election.

The economic fundamentals of newspapers are that, unlike for radio and television, each extra copy sold does cost money for paper and distribution. The mass-market newspapers get about three-quarters of their revenue from the cover price and only one-quarter from advertising, whereas the quality newspapers, which have smaller circulations, get at least half of their revenue from advertising – up to three-quarters in the case of the *FT* – despite their higher cover price.

As already discussed, advertising is sold on the basis not only of the number of readers but also of their spending power: having 1000 rich readers will justify a higher advertising rate than 1000 poorer ones. Since advertising is crucial to the quality newspapers, the need to appeal to the more affluent readers partly explains why traditionally there have been more newspapers on the right of the political divide than on the left. The other reason is that there are more right-wing than left-wing newspaper owners.

Still, there are a large number of titles, with a fair range of opinion, competing in an overcrowded and mature market. A variety of survival strategies have been deployed in this competitive market:

- merger
- price
- adding sections
- promotions.

Merger

Rupert Murdoch was allowed to side-step newspaper monopoly regulations (on the grounds that he was coming to the rescue of titles that would otherwise die) and assemble a large stable of titles (1970s). He took on the overweening print unions of his day and brought production costs down dramatically (early 1980s), from which all proprietors and newspaper readers benefited, and was also able to reap the benefits of having printing economies from one huge plant at Wapping. The *Guardian* bought the ailing *Observer* (1994). The Mirror Group took over management control of *The Independent* (which had itself been launched as a result of the lowering of entry costs brought about by Mr Murdoch).

Mergers allow overhead, production and distribution cost economies, and also cross-promotion of other titles – or BSkyB, in the newspapers owned by Rupert Murdoch.

Price

In a mature market, each manufacturer is tempted to increase market share by cutting prices. Other manufacturers are obliged to lower their prices to retain their market. The weakest are forced out of the market and once excess capacity has been removed, the remaining companies can then put prices back up again.

In newspapers this tactic has been attempted off and on by tabloids in periodic circulation wars, but until Mr Murdoch slashed the price of *The Times* from 45p to 30p in September 1993, the conventional wisdom was that the strong loyalties of the readers of the quality newspapers would overcome a cut of a few pennies in a product that does not in any case cost much. In the event, the circulation of *The Times* rose 85 per cent from 354,000 in August 1993 to a peak of 656,000 in July 1995 when the price war abated. Even so, once a week on a Monday *The Times* is still available at the nominal price of 10p. The idea was to build up such a commanding circulation and readership lead that what was lost in circulation revenue would be more than made up in advertising revenue. It was also widely believed that the aim was to drive *The Independent* out of business. Other newspapers had to follow suit – except for the *Guardian*, which stayed resolutely at its old price of 45p, and did not lose readers.

Recent price wars have been limited mostly to the quality newspapers because circulation revenue is far less important to them than it is to the tabloids, whose circulations are in the millions and for whom therefore a cut of 10p would be even more costly.

Adding sections 'which, sometimes, improve the product'

The *Sunday Times* was the pioneer in the UK in copying the *New York Times* in making a newspaper so voluminous with endless sections appealing to many different interest groups that it would drive out the competition by sheer volume of newsprint (its advertising slogan in 1996 was 'The Sunday Times *is* the Sunday newspapers'). Each newspaper used the savings from cheaper production to add new sections and magazines, hoping to make itself the only game in town; to broaden it to cover topics that had usually been left to magazines like health, food and lifestyle; and to sell advertising in each section aimed at those most likely to read it.

Promotions

Cheap videos, games, competitions – all designed to retain fickle readers whose traditional loyalties to an editorial position or style have weakened. No national newspaper – except *Today* – has recently disappeared and the overall effect of these various competitive stratagems has been to reduce the profits of all. The owners have deep pockets or deep pride. History shows that national newspapers rarely go out of business. Someone, usually a would-be newcomer to the establishment, comes to the rescue, hoping for the kudos and influence that come from being a newspaper tycoon and the invitation to take tea at Number Ten.

Regional newspapers

The regional and local newspaper segment of newspapers is large (over £2 billion in annual revenue), but unglamorous. Each local newspaper tries to become a local monopolist, and there are few areas of the country where two local newspapers survive. Where this does occur one is typically a 'free' (wholly advertising-supported) title. Local newspapers rely heavily on classified advertising which accounts for over 60 per cent of their advertising revenue. In the long term this makes them vulnerable to the migration of classified advertising to new electronic media such as the Internet. Some local newspapers are getting together to provide an electronic service themselves.

The big media groups have been selling off their regional titles, but the builders of new regional newspaper empires might find a way of rejuvenating the industry.

Magazines

There are some 14,000 consumer magazines in Britain, covering every imaginable subject and special interest under the sun. Magazines are versatile and flexible. Barriers to entry are low: it costs far less to start a magazine than to start a newspaper or television channel. Hundreds of new magazines are launched each year. Readers tend to have a strong loyalty to their magazine; this can be buttressed by turning casual readers into subscribers – who then pay a year's subscription in advance, reducing the need for outside funding. There is a wide range of formats, sizes, paper types, designs – all of which allow great distinctiveness to an original magazine idea.

Of all traditional old media, magazines allow the greatest ability to form a community of the like-minded. Although there are large magazine companies, the magazine industry is more fragmented than for other media. This is because although there are economies in owning a stable of magazines – shared overheads, skill in print buying, a 'feel' for starting new magazines based on an understanding of markets, the capital for launches – each magazine needs to have its own dedicated editorial, advertising and marketing staff in order to portray its distinctive character to readers and advertisers. There is always room for one more magazine (see Braithwaite, Chapter 8 in this volume).

The Internet

The Internet is a fast-growing medium formed by linking personal computers to each other around the world. The main part of the Internet is known as the WorldWideWeb, or just 'the Web'. Web revolutionaries would argue that the Web is not just a new medium – it will eventually be the medium that encompasses all the others. What most web users experience in the mid-to-late 1990s is the freedom to trade text from one point on the globe to another fairly quickly, cheaply and easily, and simple graphics slowly and with more effort and cost. The Internet's capacity will increase. But it already has extraordinary characteristics:

- point-to-point communication, rather than one-to-many broadcast communication, for the one rather than for the many
- 'hyperlinking' from one server to another: by clicking on a highlighted word, the user is directly switched to another database, perhaps on the other side of the world
- ability to search vast amounts of data
- increasingly intelligent software agents that sift what they have learnt the user wants to get hold of
- instant and interactive community creation, on a global basis.

The Internet provides a model for the way we may receive television, telephony, magazines and newspapers in the not-too-distant future. The capacity in the form of wires, cables and satellite dishes, and the decoding boxes to turn the digital stream into text, sound and pictures – the digital superhighway – is gradually being laid.

At present the highway layers in Britain are the cable companies, BSkyB and British Telecom. Because of deficiencies in the current payment system, bottlenecks are appearing where capacity is running out. (Americans are not charged for local calls, so local telephone companies get no more revenue from the average 20-minute Internet connection than for the average 4-minute telephone connection.) By the end of the 1990s, new pricing regimes or the development of a higher-capacity 'Internet II' will channel money to those who need to invest.

Once the digital highway is laid, the economics of all the media industries will change: the content suppliers will be able to choose the cheapest and best path into the home or office, and pay carriage to the highwaymen, and the competitive battle will be about (in order of importance) content (who has the best material to see or read), marketing (how to tell viewers about the needles in the haystacks) and customer service. But in the years before the highway is completed, the battles will include distribution – who owns which pipe to the consumer.

Three scenarios

The media industry is very dynamic, ever freer of regulation, and with the prospect of more and more creative competitors. But there are strong pressures for concentration within and among media.

With growing competition, there are three broad scenarios:

- more means worse as competition leads to lurid sensationalism and sex
- more optimistically, more means more diversity as each shade of taste and opinion is catered for by an appropriate medium able to target an interest group economically
- a hybrid with policies to ensure access by everyone to a basic tier of communication, but with an additional huge variety of services available to those who can pay.

With growing concentration, the issue is whether diversity is increased or whether there will be a tendency towards bland, inoffensive entertainment.

Questions

1   Do the owners of media owe a duty of care for the state of society – or only one of profit to their shareholders? Is there a conflict between the two? Do they have to behave 'responsibly', and what does that mean?

2   Analyse a media company. Look at not only which media it is in but also which activities within those media it carries out, and why.

3   Has the desperate race for readers improved or reduced the quality of the editorial in newspapers? Has there been a different effect on the qualities, mid-market newspapers, tabloids? What economic

factors explain why one newspaper is different from another? Give specific examples.

References

Advertising Association (1996) *The Media Pocket Book 1996*, Henley-on-Thames: NTC Publications.

Barwise, P. (1994) *Children, Advertising, and Nutrition*, London: Advertising Association.

Barwise, P. and Ehrenberg, A. (1988) *Television and its Audience*, London and Beverly Hills: Sage (2nd edn 1998).

Ehrenberg, A.S.C. and Barwise, T.P. (1983) 'How much does UK television cost?', *International Journal of Advertising* 2(1): 17–32.

Further reading

Advertising Association (1996) *The Media Pocket Book 1996*, Henley-on-Thames: NTC Publications.

Barwise, P. (1994) *Children, Advertising, and Nutrition*, London: Advertising Association.

Barwise, P. and Ehrenberg, A. (1988) *Television and its Audience*, London and Beverly Hills: Sage (2nd edn 1998).

Davis, M.P. and Zerdin, D. (1996) *The Effective Use of Advertising Media: A Practical Handbook*, 5th edn, London: Century.

Economist (1996) *Going Digital*, London: Economist Books.

Ehrenberg, A.S.C. and Barwise, T.P. (1983) 'How much does UK television cost?', *International Journal of Advertising* 2(1): 17–32.

Hirsch, F. and Gordon, D. (1975) *Newspaper Money*, London: Hutchinson.

Negroponte, N. (1995) *Being Digital*, New York: Alfred A. Knopf.

Chapter 15

Policy

MEDIA POLICY

NICHOLAS GARNHAM

What is media policy?

First, the study of media policy is the study of the ways in which public authorities shape, or try to shape, the structures and practices of the media. These authorities may be national – the UK government; regional – the European Union; international – the ITU (International Telecommunication Union of the UN) or WTO (World Tourism Organization). This chapter will focus on the national level, but the UK media are affected by policies made and enforced at all three levels, especially and increasingly at the European level (see Negrine, Chapter 16 in this volume).

Second, it is the study of the reasons for these policies, both in the sense of the reasons given by policy-makers for their policies, for instance in a White Paper, and also in the sense of the economic, social, political and cultural forces to which the explicit policy is a response. Thus we always need to ask the question why this policy in this form now and in whose interest is it designed? Neither policies nor their presentation should ever be taken at their face value.

Third, it is the study of the impact of these policies. Here crucially it is important to stress that policy may have unintended and unanticipated consequences. These may in their turn require a further policy response. Thus we are analysing a continuous and historically situated process within which policy-makers are operating within the constraints, institutional forms and vested interests created by previous policies and with a high degree of uncertainty about the future. Policy-making is not and can never be the tidy creation of ideal situations. Compromises and trade-offs are endemic. In particular over the period we are examining a major problem has been judging the pace and direction of technological development.

Finally, media policy may be positive or negative. Positive policy is the active intervention of government through laws or other regulatory instruments. Negative policy is the refusal to intervene in the face of public pressure for intervention, for instance by allowing the press and advertising industries to remain self-regulating or by refusing to create tax breaks for UK film production. The most celebrated negative policy is the First Amendment to the US Constitution, which forbids the government to pass laws abridging the freedom of the press.

The reasons for media policy

In modern societies it is recognized that governments may legitimately regulate the activities of their citizens for a number of reasons. So far as the media are concerned we can identify three classes of reason: economic, political and socio-cultural.

Economic

In spite of the pervasive myth of *laissez-faire* and the 'free' market, in fact private economic activity rests everywhere upon a necessary foundation of regulation, legal property rights, contract, company law, competition law, tax and subsidy policies and upon the public funding of infrastructure. The media as economic activities are subject to these general provisions. But because of their special economic characteristics they have also, to date, been subject to specific economic regulation. In particular the use of radio frequencies and the operation of telecommunications networks have been subject to regulation because of their scarcity or natural monopoly characteristics. As we shall see, a major media policy debate at present is whether technological development has made such special regulation redundant so that problems of media monopoly power can be dealt with, like any other products or service, under general competition legislation.

Political

The media, as the vehicles for the exercise of the rights of free speech, play (it is generally agreed) a special role within democracies that justifies special regulatory attention. Thus media monopolies are subject to special control, for instance newspaper mergers are subject to special and more stringent controls under UK competition law and the Broadcasting Act 1990 places specific and complex limits on cross-media ownership. In addition it is for political reasons that special controls are laid upon the broadcasting of politics, especially at times of election. Thus the UK system, unlike the US, forbids the sale of political advertising on radio and TV. In some countries, e.g. Sweden, schemes to subsidize loss-making newspapers have been justified on the grounds of political pluralism and a similar case can be made for licence-financed public service broadcasting.

Socio-cultural

No society runs, or has ever run, on completely libertarian principles. It is recognized, in different ways in different societies and cultures, that certain forms of public expression are outside the society's moral norms. It is also recognized that certain forms of reporting or portrayal may expose individuals to unjustified harm. Thus there may be controls on the media for reasons of taste and decency, for libel, for invasion of privacy. The nature of these controls is a matter of media policy and the lines to be drawn at any time are a matter of public debate. For instance, as we shall see, whether the UK press should be covered by legislation to protect privacy has been and remains a matter of controversy and raises the central media policy question of the balance to be struck between the value of free speech and a free press on the one hand and the rights of individuals to privacy or groups to the protection of their cultural values on the other.

In addition media policy is concerned with the protection and enhancement of cultural values, for instance by subsidizing certain forms of cultural production, by imposing film or broadcasting quotas or, until recently, by protecting the production and distribution of books through the Net Book Agreement (NBA).

The challenge of convergence

From the vantage of 1997 we can see that a new period in UK media policy started in 1979 with the coming to power of the first Thatcher government with its commitment to free market policies and the rolling back of the state and its determination to break with what it saw as a failed social democratic past. However, with hindsight we can also see that the changes were far less radical than might have been expected.

In order to understand the key trends in UK policy over this period it is useful to start with the position in 1997. The buzz words in media policy circles are convergence, multimedia and the digital revolution. These terms point to a series of linked technological developments bringing together computing and telecommunications which make it possible to convert all forms of expression, from a telephone conversation to a television programme, into the digital language of computers and in this form transmit them all down the same communication channel, whether cable or radio based, and whether it will eventually be received in the form of print, sound or pictures.

Why do these technological developments pose a potential problem for media policy? Because to date media policy everywhere has been based upon a series of technological distinctions between different media. Indeed the everyday words we use to describe these media, print, film, broadcasting and telecommunications describe their underlying technologies of production and distribution. Around each of these distinct technologies has grown up a set of distinct regulatory regimes and policies. Print has been largely unregulated on the basis of free press doctrine. In broadcasting access to scarce frequencies has been licenced by the state and used as a basis for strict content regulation by specialized regulatory agencies, in the UK the BBC governors, the Independent Television Commission (ITC) and the Radio Authority. In telecommunications the operation of the network has been tightly regulated, and frequently organized as a monopoly, while the content, private conversations has been protected from control as free speech. In the UK these different media sectors have been the political responsibility of different ministries: the Home Office and later the Department of National Heritage (DNH) for broadcasting, and the Department of Trade and Industry (DTI) for telecommunications and the press. Clearly if, as some now claim, we are in the future to receive all our information and entertainment in digital form down one fibre-optic cable, this whole structure and its underlying philosophics is thrown into question. In this new, digital world do the media need regulating and if so why and how? For instance, do restrictions on cross-media ownership make any sense when what we now call a newspaper, a TV programme, a radio programme, a musical recording, a film or a telephone conversation all arrive down the same wire and are 'read' via the same personal computer (PC) or terminal. Is a multimedia Internet the model of the future?

Whatever we may think of the reality or speed of this technological and market prognosis UK media policy since 1979 can be read as a series of tentative, often confused and abortive, approachs to that set of questions.

UK media policy since 1979

At the start of this period broadcasting policy was still dominated by a tradition of 'public service' going back to the foundation of the BBC in the 1920s. According to this tradition, reasserted by a succession of postwar public inquiries – Beveridge (Home Office 1951), Pilkington (Home Office 1962), and Annan (Home Office 1977) – broadcasters, whether the non-commercial BBC or the commercial ITV and independent local radio (ILR), received their licences to broadcast as a public trust. The state granted them access to a scarce national resource – the radio frequency spectrum – and in return imposed strict conditions to ensure this resource was used 'responsibly' and in the public interest. The BBC was granted a privileged source of revenue through a quasi-tax – the licence fee – and its charter and licence was designed to ensure that, under the supervision of government-appointed governors, it provided to the whole country a balanced, high quality range of information, education and entertainment. The ITV companies were granted a monopoly of TV advertising revenue in their regions and in return their commercial and programming actions were strictly controlled, in outline by the Broadcasting Act 1990 and in detail by the licence granted and supervised by the Independent Broadcasting Authority (IBA). How much and what type of advertising they could carry, the shape and content of their schedules, who was allowed to own them, were all subject to legislative and IBA control.

The last fling of this tradition was the creation of Channel Four. Set up by the incoming Conservative government on the advice of the Annan Committee, it was financed by a levy on the ITV companies – and thus not subject to commercial pressures – and had a specific legal remit to provide alternative programming.

In telecommunications, in spite of long-term concerns about the efficiency of the Post Office, (HMSO 1977) it was assumed that the telephone network was a natural monopoly (a term used by economists to describe a market where one supplier can, for technical reasons, always supply a product or service more efficiently than several competitive suppliers) and, as in most other countries, should be provided by a nationalized monopoly.

The challenge to traditional policy

In the 1980s these governing policy assumptions came under severe challenge for three reasons. First, there was a widespread shift in the thinking of economists and policy-makers in favour of the market and against the state – a movement that started in the USA (Tunstall and Palmer 1990) and has been called deregulation. Second, because the communications sector was seen as occupying an ever more central and strategic economic role (the so-called Information Society thesis: Webster 1995) and thus its efficiency began to concern economic policy-makers. In the UK this was represented by the increasing involvement of the Treasury and the DTI in media policy-making at the expense of the Home Office and later the Department of National Heritage, which remained retreating guardians of the old public service tradition. Third, and a major component of the second shift, rapid and dramatic developments in information and communication technologies (ICTs) grabbed the imagination of politicians, policy-makers and business leaders. Increasingly a key component of media policy was the attempt to ensure not only that the UK had an advanced communications infrastructure but also that the UK manufacturing industry benefited from these developments. Thus media policy became a subordinate aspect of industrial and economic policy (see Department of Trade and Industry 1988; Home Office and Department of Trade and Industry 1983; House of Commons 1994; ITAP 1982).

Cable and satellite

The first sign of this new thinking in broadcasting was the process leading up to the Cable Act 1984 and the attempt to launch a UK DBS (direct broadcasting by satellite) service. The Cable Act introduced cable as a private sector activity with a 'light' regulatory touch from the newly constituted Cable Authority. The main concern of the Act was not, as in the past, the maintenance of programme quality – that was to be left to the market – but to ensure that the cable network was designed to carry state-of-the-art business services in addition to cable TV. In the event this attempt to accelerate the 'wiring' of the UK financed by cable TV revenues failed because the financial returns were not attractive enough to UK investors. It was not until the ban on foreign ownership was lifted that US and Canadian telecommunications and cable companies began the slow, uncertain (and as yet far from finished) business of cabling the UK (in January 1996 1,326,842 homes were connected – 5.91 per cent of homes).

There was a similar failure to use the launch of UK DBS services as a platform for the UK satellite construction industry. The UK government was not alone in the early 1980s in arguing that there was a large potential market for satellites in the developing world (in theory they could be used to avoid the cost of building an expensive terrestrial transmitter network to serve scattered populations) and that the early launch of a domestic national service could be used as a shop window for this market. Unfortunately UK satellites were too expensive. After failed attempts first to interest the BBC and then, by the IBA, to construct a BBC/ITV consortium, the requirement to use a UK satellite was lifted and BSB won an IBA franchise competition. But by now it was too late. The delay allowed Murdoch opportunistically to relaunch his failing European Sky service as a UK domestic service, but using ASTRA, a Luxembourg-based telecommunications satellite outside UK regulatory jurisdiction. In a market where only one operator could survive, Sky's earlier start meant that BSB was doomed and eventually merged with Sky to create BSkyB. The result was to create one of the major issues now facing UK media policy-makers: Murdoch's combined domination of the satellite, cable-programming and newspaper markets.

Broadcasting policy

But these industrial policy-driven developments were at the margins of mainstream broadcasting. Here, with hindsight, policy was much more confused and tentative than might have been expected. In spite of the rhetoric of the free market, competition and deregulation, after seventeen years of Tory rule UK broadcasting is still dominated by a BBC with its charter renewed, its mission reconfirmed and financed by a licence fee, competing with two ITC-regulated channels, an advertising financed, regionally based Channel Three system and Channel Four with its 'public service' remit intact. On the surface the landscape is familiar. None the less, beneath this surface important changes have taken place. Whether they are seismic and represent an irreversible shift in UK broadcasting policy is a matter of debate.

Throughout Europe public service broadcasting came under attack in the 1980s (see Negrine, Chapter 16 in this volume). The UK was no exception. Pressure came from a number of trends. First, technological developments – cable and satellite – were beginning to undermine the spectrum-scarcity argument. The imminent introduction of digital broadcasting and of video-on-demand via the switched telecommunications network reinforces this trend. Second, growing advertising budgets both fuelled a demand for more commercial channels and provided potential funding for them. Third, pressure on public finances made the licence fee increasingly unpopular with government, if not consumers.

In the UK it was the problem of the licence fee that offered the first opportunity to attack the BBC. In response to a request from the BBC for a licence fee rise to keep pace with inflation the government set up the Peacock Committee in 1986 to inquire into the financing of the BBC (Home Office 1986). It was assumed at the time that this was preparation for the BBC taking advertising and possibly its privatization. Certainly, Thatcher herself made no secret of her enmity towards and impatience with the BBC as a symbol of that social democratic British culture which she despised, associated with the UK's economic decline, and was determined to destroy. In the event things did not turn out as anticipated and this illustrates an important point about media policy generally and in Britain in recent years in particular. It is crucial to analyse in detail the forces in play. In this case Thatcher's handpicked liberal economists, having taken a strongly pro-market, consumerist line and having argued that the British broadcasting's protection from commercial pressures led to inefficiency in production and elitism and self-indulgence in programming, combined with an ever-present danger of state censorship, then went on to argue that advertising finance for the BBC was undesirable on two grounds: first, there was not enough advertising revenue to go round, and second, given the absence of a direct payment link between a consumer and a programme, licence-fee finance provides a better approximation of a consumer market than advertising finance. This conclusion was undoubtedly given policy reinforcement by the opposition of both ITV and the newspaper industry to further com-petition for advertising revenue (Home Office 1986).

Thus repulsed, the enemies of the BBC in government had to content themselves with packing the governors with their supporters, with squeez-ing the BBC's licence fee revenue and demanding that they raise more revenue from commercial sources and of holding over them the constant threat of major reform, including the end of the licence fee, at the time of Charter renewal in 1996. In the event by introducing internal markets and a ruthless regime of cost-cutting dressed up in the rhetoric of Thatcherite management consultancy, allied to a play-safe news and current affairs policy, the BBC won its battle for Charter renewal largely unscathed except for the forced sale of its transmitter network. Whether the policies the BBC has itself adopted to achieve this end are or are not a creeping commercialization and a prelude to privatization is a matter of continuing debate. Certainly there now exists a serious tension between its activities as a licence-financed national UK public service broadcaster and its activities as a commercial player on a global broadcasting market (for the full story see Barnett and Curry 1994; O'Malley 1994).

Meanwhile the main effects of the new thinking represented by the Peacock Report were felt not by the BBC but by ITV. With the aim of making the system more efficient and responsive to market pressures a number of crucial changes were incorporated into the Broadcasting Act 1990. First, a system of franchise auctions was introduced. Second, a mandated proportion of independent production was imposed, both upon Channel Three and Four and upon the BBC. Third, the ITC was forced to privatize its transmitter network. Fourth, a fifth terrestrial channel was to be launched on a national rather than regional basis. Fifth, Channel Four was to sell its own advertising. Sixth, the system for commissioning network programming was to be reformed to break the stranglehold of the Big Five.

The aim of these reforms was

- to make the companies more efficient by making them pay the market rate for their use of the spectrum and by opening them to the pressures of the capital market through the threat of take-over; as we shall see this then rapidly raised the issue of cross-ownership
- to make the supply of programmes competitive and, as a side-effect, create an independent production sector capable of competing on the world market
- to make the market for advertising competitive
- to encourage competition in radio-based telecommunication networks and thus encourage the most efficient use of spectrum.

(Home Office 1988)

In its passage through Parliament the free market doctrine of the Broadcasting Act 1990 was modified in the face of a well-organized counterattack by the forces of 'public service'. The ITC was allowed to take 'quality' criteria into account in awarding franchises. In the event the majority of franchises did not go to the highest bidder. And the new franchise holders were given protection against take-over for a limited period.

A key aspect of these developments, which links broadcasting to telecommunications policy, has been the move to break up the vertical integration of the industry by separating transmission from broadcasting, defined increasingly as the construction and marketing of a programme channel – the so-called publisher broadcaster – and the separation of broadcasting from programme production. We can see this trend further developed in the current proposals to license multiplex providers as wholesalers of digital broadcasting channel capacity. This development allows policy-makers increasingly, within a digital environment, to separate the problem of whether, and if so how, to regulate distribution networks from the problem of whether, and if so how, to regulate content. This is an approach familiar in the field of telecommunications policy with the regulatory separation of carriage and content and it is to developments in this sector that we now turn.

UK telecommunications policy since 1979

One way of understanding telecommunications policy and its relationship to media policy more widely since the late 1970s is as an attempt to navigate from a world of specialized and separated distribution networks to one of multimedia. At the start of the period we are considering, broadcasters used radio to distribute TV and radio programmes to mass audiences, while the Telecommunications division of the Post Office used wires to provide a simple switched telephone service to businesses and residential subscribers. The key distinction was that in telephony the network operator provided only the means of distribution. The content – telephone conversations – were provided by the users as private transactions. Access to the network was available to everyone who could pay the price on equal terms.

UK telecommunications policy since 1979 has been primarily concerned with two issues. First, the provision and regulation of networks. Second, the relationship between network operators and the services provided over those networks.

For economic policy reasons, in order to develop and sustain the UK's competitive position within the developing global information economy, it was seen as desirable that the UK should have the most advanced and cost-effective network infrastructure possible. The major reason for the policy initiatives leading up to the Telecommunications Act 1984 and the Cable Act 1984, the breaking of the monopoly of BT (British Telecommunications) and its privatization, the creation of Mercury as a network competitor, the licensing of competitive cellular mobile operators, the encouragement of the growth of cable TV as an alternative network provider, was the perception that BT was failing to modernize its network, that its prices were too high and that it was failing to meet the demand for state-of-the-art business services from its major multinational corporate customers. These developments have been accompanied by a persistent policy argument as to whether switched telecommunications networks remain natural monopolies and therefore as to whether competition is or can be effective. The network has certainly been modernized and prices have fallen in real terms for all subscribers, although more for business than residential subscribers. But whether this can be attributed to competition, rather than the general trend of technological development, remains a matter of dispute. BT, after over a decade of competition backed by a regulatory authority, OFTEL, with a specific remit to foster competition and prepared where necessary to rig the market in favour of BT's competitors, for instance in interconnect terms, still retains over 90 per cent of the UK telephone market.

In spite of a 'duopoly policy' from 1984 to 1990, which protected it against excessive competition, Mercury has failed to establish itself as a realistic competitor. Mercury's failure led to a change of policy with the Telecommunications Act 1990. The cable companies, increasingly largely owned by US telecommunications companies, were now seen as the best hope for effective network competition to BT. But again the market had to be rigged in their favour and so a ban was placed on BT carrying broadcast entertainment services over its network until 2001 at the earliest. Thus the development of telecommunications policy brings us back to broadcasting. The current state of the policy debate is, in essence, simple. On the one side are those who argue that it is useless for a government to try to pick winners or predict technological development and that only network competition can ensure an optimum rate of innovation and efficient prices (DTI 1988). Therefore the government's only job is to create the regulatory climate that favours competition. According to this view the major task is reining back BT. On the other side are those who argue that network competition is unsustainable and inefficient, that BT is the only realistic candidate for investing in and building the broadband infrastructure of the future and that the current ban on BT's entry into broadcasting provision is a regulatory barrier to such investment (House of Commons 1994).

But in addition to the question of who should be allowed to own and operate networks and under what regulatory conditions, there is the question of the relationship between the network and the services that run over them. Historically in both broadcasting and telecommunications, control of the network and services was largely combined. Broadcasters owned and operated their own transmitter network and telecommunication network, operators also sold the telephone service (and indeed the handset). As we have seen there has been a trend in broadcasting to separate these functions. A similar trend can be identified in telecommunications. Here there are two crucial policy arguments. On the one hand it is argued that the economics of networks and services are very different and that more innovative and cost-effective services will be developed if the market for services is structured and regulated differently from that for networks. If this argument is accepted two policy problems arise. First, how to regulate access to the network and, if you allow the network operator also to compete in the services market, how to ensure that it does not use its network control, for instance its privileged information about subscribers and costs, to favour its own service offerings? On the other hand, precisely because of its knowledge of subscribers and of the cost and technological characteristics of the network, the network operator may be in the best position to develop and invest in innovative services. Network operators also argue that they will have no incentive to invest in the upgrading of their networks necessary to deliver such services unless they can share in the revenue streams from them. These arguments underlie not only the argument about whether or not BT might be allowed into the cable TV market, and if so on what terms, but also to the regulation of the decoders for subscription TV. At present in the UK BSkyB controls this access technology as well as providing pro-gramming services and, it is argued, uses this control to favour its own services against competitors. Discussions are currently under way at the European level to try to arrive at a common, non-proprietary standard for such decoders, especially for the new generation of digital services. In short as we enter the converged, multimedia age, perhaps the central policy issue is whether policy should favour one multi-functional broadband network for the delivery of the majority of services from telephony to interactive TV to the home and if so whether common carriage, e.g the separation of network and services, should be the basis of regulatory policy.

UK press policy

I have so far focused on broadcasting and telecommunications policy be-cause they have been at the centre of policy concerns, but the print sector is also increasingly implicated, as we shall now see in the policy debates sparked off by digitalization. How then has policy developed in this sector over the same period? UK press policy has been characterized, in a series of Royal Commissions (1949, 1962, 1977) since the Second World War, by a policy of *laissez-faire*, based on concepts of a free press and thus the un-desirability of any government intervention, accompanied by hand-wringing over the trend to ever greater concentration of control and declining standards of journalism (Curran and Seaton 1991). In the period under review, not only has the special provision of competition legislation control-ling press mergers never been invoked to prevent further concentration, but also the growth of Murdoch's control of the UK press appears to have been positively favoured by Thatcher and those around her. As a result, as we shall see, the Murdoch problem now haunts UK media policy.

The major policy debate over the press has concerned privacy and standards. The Thatcher government combined economic liberalism with moral authoritarianism. In broadcasting this resulted in the setting up of the Broadcasting Standards Council. In the press the problem has been tabloidization, and in particular the antics of the *Sun* in invading and ex-ploiting the privacy of individuals for the titillation of their readers. This not only directly and increasingly affected MPs themselves, but also began to produce a reaction from the public to which politicians felt they had to respond. Self-regulation through the Press Council was increasingly seen as inadequate. As a result in 1989 the Calcutt Committee was set up to investigate the issue.

Calcutt recognized that industry self-regulation by the Press Council was not working well. He recommended that self-regulation be given one more chance by inviting the press industry to set up a truly independent Press Complaints Commission. If that failed, he regretfully concluded that a statutory body would be unavoidable. At the same time he rejected calls for privacy legislation on the lines of that existing in Germany or France. There for the present the matter rests, a time-bomb ticking away to await the next scandal of press intrusion. With the increasing electronic capture, storage and manipulation of personal data and the growing penetration of electronic, Internet-type services into homes and businesses the issue of personal privacy and its protection will loom increasingly large on the media regulatory landscape.

Cross-media ownership

But apart from the issue of privacy and the regulation of standards of press conduct in reporting, the key policy issue affecting the press is now cross-ownership. Because plural control of media outlets is seen to be desirable for reasons of free democratic debate, it has been normal in many countries to place controls not only on the amount of any one media anyone can control, e.g. the number of TV licences, but also on cross-ownership between media. The Broadcasting Act 1990, following previous Broadcasting Acts, placed a limit on the number of TV and radio licences any one person could control, and on cross-ownership between radio and TV; it also placed strict limits on press ownership of either. These rules came under attack from two quarters. The TV companies argued that, because they were restricted to a small share of the UK commercial TV market they were vulnerable to take-over from continental European TV companies who suffered from no such restrictions in their home countries. They also argued that, with cable and satellite, the market for TV programmes and advertising was becoming much larger and more competitive, that compared to Murdoch's BSkyB they were minuscule and that it was necessary to be large to compete on global markets with the likes of Time-Warner, Murdoch or CNN. At the same time the newspaper industry argued that in a world of convergence it was anachronistic to erect barriers to cross-ownership on the basis of old technological divisions between media; that it was inhibiting the development of new, multimedia products and services and that, because of a regulatory loophole, Murdoch owned both newspapers and BSkyB and was using the revenues from BSkyB to subsidize his press price war. Therefore, current cross-media ownership restrictions should be lifted and replaced with a threshold based upon a share of the total media market (DNH 1995). This is an issue which is being debated at both UK and pan-European levels. After considerable debate and hesitation in the face of warring media interests the government partially lifted the restrictions to allow a consolidation of Channel Three franchisees and incorporated new rules in the Broadcasting Act 1996. In brief these maintain some restrictions on both single media and cross-media ownership. In particular they place a threshold on the proportion of national newspaper circulation below which newspapers are allowed to own terrestrial TV licences, which cleverly stops Murdoch's News International and the Mirror Group from expanding further but allows everyone else in. Whether this is a stable situation in the face of European and global oligopolization across the media sector and the development of converged media delivery systems is doubtful. It is almost certain that some total media market share measure will have to be used within general competition rules. But whether that share should be based on revenues or audience share (so-called share of voice) and whether the various media should be differentially weighted remain unresolved issues.

Conclusion

But underlying all these debates lies an overarching policy issue. In a converged, digital, multimedia media environment can media-specific regulation with different specialized regulatory bodies such as the ITC and OFTEL, be sustained or on the contrary should we give up trying to regulate media content and regulate the media solely as economic entities through general competition law?

Questions

1 Can media-specific regulation any longer be justified?

2 To what extent has UK media policy since 1979 been driven by technological change?

3 What do you understand by the term 'deregulation' and to what extent can it be used to describe UK media policy since 1979?

References

Barnett, S. and Curry, A. (1994) *The Battle for the BBC: A British Broadcasting Conspiracy?*, London: Aurum.

Curran, J. and Seaton, J. (1991) *Power without Responsibility: The Press and Broadcasting in Britain*, 4th edn, London: Routledge.

Department of National Heritage (DNH) (1995) *Media Ownership: The Government's Proposals*, Cmnd 2872, London: HMSO.

Department of Trade and Industry (DTI) (1988) *Macdonald Committee Report*, London: HMSO.

HMSO (1977) *Report of the Post office Review Committee*, Cmnd 6850, London: HMSO.

Home Office (1951) *Report of the Broadcasting Committee* (Beveridge Report), Cmnd 8116, London: HMSO.

Home Office (1962) *Report of the Committee on Broadcasting* (Pilkington Report), Cmnd 1753, London: HMSO.

Home Office (1977) *Report of the Committee on the Future of Broadcasting* (Annan Report), Cmnd 6753, London: HMSO.

Home Office (1986) *Report of the Committee on Financing the BBC* (Peacock Report), Cmnd 9824, London: HMSO.

Home Office (1988) *Broadcasting in the 90's: Competition, Choice and Quality*, London: HMSO.

Home Office (1990) *Report of the Committee on Privacy and Related Matters*, Cmnd 1102, London: HMSO.

Home Office and Dept of Trade and Industry (1983) *The Development of Cable Systems and Services*, London: HMSO.

House of Commons (Trade and Industry Committee) (1994) *Optical Fibre Networks*, London: HMSO.

ITAP (Cabinet Office Information Advisory Panel) (1982) *Cable Systems*, London: Cabinet Office.

O'Malley, T. (1994) *Closedown: The BBC and Government Policy 1979–92*, London: Pluto.

Royal Commission on the Press 1947–9 (1949) Cmnd 7700, London: HMSO.

Royal Commission on the Press 1961–2 (1962) Cmnd 1811, London: HMSO.

Royal Commission on the Press 1974–7 (1977) Cmnd 6816, London: HMSO.

Tunstall, J. and Palmer, M. (1990) *Media Moguls*, London: Routledge.

Webster, F. (1995) *Theories of the Information Society*, London: Routledge.

Further reading

Beezley, M. and Laidlaw, B. (1989) *The Future of Telecommunications*, London: Institute of Economic Affairs.

Congdon, T. *et al.* (1995) *Cross-Media Revolution: Ownership and Control*, London: John Libbey.

Corry, D. (ed.) (1995) *Regulating in the Public Interest*, London: Institute for Public Policy Research (IPPR).

Curran, J. and Seaton, J. (1991) *Power without Responsibility: The Press and Broadcasting in Britain*, 4th edn, Part IV 'Politics of the Medium' pp. 313–72, London: Routledge.

Department of National Heritage (DNH) (1992) *The Future of the BBC: A Consultation Document*, Cmnd 2098, London: HMSO.

Department of National Heritage (DNH) (1994) *The Future of the BBC: Serving the Nation, Competing World-wide*, Cmnd 2621, London: HMSO.

Department of Trade and Industry (DTI) (1991) *Competition and Choice: Telecommunications Policy for the '90s*, London: HMSO.

Goodwin, P. (1995) 'British media policy takes to the superhighway', *Media, Culture and Society* 17(4).

OFTEL (1995) *Beyond the Telephone, the Television and the PC*, London: OFTEL.

Tunstall, J. and Palmer, M. (1990) *Liberating Communications: Policy-making in France and Britain*, Oxford: Basil Blackwell.

Chapter 16

Models of media institutions

MEDIA INSTITUTIONS IN EUROPE

RALPH NEGRINE

In studying media institutions, it is often unwise to take it for granted that similar forms of communication – television, newspapers, radio, etc. – will have similar characteristics in different settings. For example, though the nature of television as a medium of communication may be (more or less) identical across countries, the organization of that medium for the purposes of delivering a wide menu of content, will vary quite considerably from one socio-political environment to another. In many respects, then, each national broadcasting system (and the same goes for newspapers) will represent a particular – sometimes a unique – arrangement, an arrangement which, in turn, reflects different socio-political traditions, economic forces, geographic features, and so on.

By making comparisons across countries, we can come to appreciate the extent to which there are similarities, and differences, and the possible reasons for either and/or both. Only by addressing the issue of similarities and differences and the significance of both does it become possible to develop a proper understanding of processes of communication in contemporary societies.

The aim of this chapter then is to explore briefly the historical development of broadcasting across Europe, and to identify some of the factors that account for significant differences across institutions. The last section of this chapter will identify technological and political changes in the 1980s which have had a significant impact on broadcasting systems.

The development of broadcasting across Europe

Three brief comments need to be made prior to exploring the various 'models' of broadcasting which have developed historically in some major European countries.

The first is that Europe is made up of different political units (countries), with different dominant languages, different traditions, histories, memories, and so on. Developments in the media to an extent reflect these differences. The economic and cultural repercussions of this are visible today in the light of the European Union's efforts to overcome these differences and so harmonize European media industries in order to meet the challenge from the much larger American media industry (see Collins 1994).

The second factor which played a part in the development of the broadcast media in Europe was the Second World War. This 'interrupted' processes of development; in the case of Germany, the post-1945 media were to a large extent shaped by the Allies on a completely different basis from their previous structures; the Liberation of France in 1944 saw the establishment of many new newspaper titles and a restructuring of many newspaper groups which had been owned by proprietors who had been discredited because of their role in prewar France (Kuhn 1995: 23–4).

The third factor is that governments have regulated broadcasting systems (and the press) in ways which reflected different attitudes towards economic organization, the rights of individuals, political traditions, and so on. Governments committed to non-intervention in economic affairs have been less likely to consider state help for the media, whereas governments keen to sustain a plurality of media have tended to support an element of intervention. This has been the case with the press industry (see McGregor 1977: ch. 12), although there has been a more common approach towards the broadcast media with a strong emphasis on control and regulation given the belief in the power of the media and the limitations of services possible via terrestrial means. Consequently, and unlike the US experience where radio broadcasting developed within a competitive framework with private commercially funded companies running the broadcasting services, European countries mostly favoured some form of state control over broadcasting as a way of avoiding the chaos in the airwaves which was characteristic of an unregulated system and also as a way of ensuring that the 'public interest' was not overlooked.

However, since the idea of the 'public interest' is ambiguous, the methods chosen to ensure that it was not overlooked varied according to the individual political and cultural traditions of European countries (McQuail and Siune 1986; Papathanassopoulos 1990). It is possible, none the less, to identify a number of characteristics which were taken to encapsulate the idea of a broadcasting organization working in 'the public interest' and not simply as commercial, profit-making organizations. These characteristics are often subsumed into a definition of public service broadcasting, a definition which is itself imprecise (see Home Office 1986).

The definition of public service broadcasting usually comprises the following characteristics:

- a universal service available to all irrespective of income or geographical location

- a commitment to a balanced output and to balanced scheduling across different programme genres
- a balanced and impartial political output
- a degree of financial independence from both governmental and commercial bodies.

(Kuhn 1985: 4)

A more elaborate definition would also identify broadcasting's cultural and social missions, including catering for minorities, a concern for 'national identity and community', competition in good programming rather than for audience numbers, and guidelines to liberate programme-makers and not to restrict them (Broadcasting Research Unit 1985: 2). In practice, no public broadcasting organization would claim that it has (always) adhered to all the values which these definitions embrace though they have probably been a guide to broadcasting practices.

The models of broadcasting which eventually developed in European states reflected both individual political, economic and cultural arrangements and attempts to uphold the 'public interest'. Generally speaking, three different European 'models' of public broadcasting can be identified.

The 'integration' model of broadcasting

This model has its roots in the idea that broadcasting could be treated as a natural monopoly and in the belief that this sort of structure could uphold the 'public interest'. The services would be run by councils or committees which comprised representatives of various political, social and cultural groups in society; hence a measure of 'internal pluralism' existed in the organization of the service. In this way, the councils or committees would ensure that a wide variety of perspectives were represented by the broadcasting authorities. In the (then) Federal Republic of Germany, in the postwar period 'there was a common concern to secure broadcasting against capture either by the state or by sectional interests in society'. There was also a concern 'to regulate for pluralism' and to 'assure "balance" and "diversity" in broadcasting'. This would not be done by setting up competing broadcasting bodies but by ensuring that there was 'a balance of opinion and a fair representation of social diversity within each channel' (i.e. internal pluralism) (Humphreys 1988: 113–15).

Like the West German system, the French broadcasting structure was also a monopolistic one but there was less of an effort to ensure 'balance' and 'diversity' within it. Although in theory the broadcasters tried to be impartial in their approach to contemporary issues, partisan political control of broadcasting was the practice with each change of government bringing about changes to the system of control (Kuhn 1995). Both the French and German systems favoured a funding structure which mixed commercial revenue and licence fees (to be paid by radio and television-set owners) within each broadcasting institution. Consequently, there was competition for audiences and advertising revenue within the state monopoly of broadcasting.

The 'duopoly' model of broadcasting

The UK offers a good example of the duopoly model of broadcasting. The duopoly model requires the coexistence of public and private broadcasters who compete for audiences but not for the same sources of revenue: the BBC relies solely on the licence fee, while the commercial companies rely on commercial funding. Initially, the British broadcasting system was organized as a state monopoly with the exclusive rights to broadcasting given to the BBC (British Broadcasting Company 1922–6, later Corporation 1926 onward). After intense lobbying from private interests and advertisers, a Conservative government passed the Independent Television Act 1954, which allowed for the creation of a commercial television service. This became operational in the mid-1950s. The commercial television service (ITV) was overseen by a regulatory body, formerly the Independent Television Authority (ITA) now the Independent Television Commission(ITC). In 1963, a second public service was introduced (BBC2) and in 1982 a second commercial channel (Channel Four) albeit with a very specific remit to cater for minority interests and tastes.

The authorities in charge of broadcasting – the BBC Board of Governors and the ITC – oversee the broadcasters and ensure that they fulfil their obligations as public service broadcasters. Significantly, both private and public authorities pursue broadly similar public service broadcasting obligations. Although the British broadcasting system is considered to be heavily regulated, a great deal of the control exercised over it is indirect, informal and often through private contacts (unlike the more direct mechanisms common across continental Europe: see Negrine 1994).

The 'private sector monopoly' model of broadcasting

One other model is worth taking into account because it has implications for the discussion of the processes of deregulation which swept across European broadcasting systems in the 1980s. This is the 'private sector monopoly' model of broadcasting in the Grand Duchy of Luxembourg. According to Dyson and Humphreys, 'as early as the inter war period, Luxembourg had seen the advantage of creating an appropriately lax regulatory environment so that its national private commercial operator (CLT/RTL) could cream off advertising from its neighbours' (Dyson and

Humphreys 1988: 7). It was a policy which inevitably brought it into conflict with countries which wanted to preserve their cultural dominance and their programming policies (e.g. the UK). Other countries, notably France, which were also likely to lose out financially as funds flowed to Luxembourg, overcame the problem by acquiring stakes in CLT, the broadcasting company.

What problems did these systems encounter? Four stand out:

- Problems of how to organize and control the broadcasting system: these problems were particularly severe in countries which experienced major political dislocations or a readiness on the part of politicians to interfere in all aspects of broadcasting.
- Pressure, roughly from 1950 onwards, to introduce commercial broadcasting services: by the 1970s, and with few exceptions, most European broadcasting systems had embraced some element of competition, adopting commercial practices either in terms of funding and/or in terms of programming. One could in fact argue that in this period – a period before most of the contemporary technological and political changes powerfully challenged the status quo – broadcasting systems had begun to settle into a period of relative calm.
- Recurring funding problems, particularly for the public broadcasters whose funding from the licence fee never quite managed to match the resources of the commercial broadcasters: at the same time, there was often pressure to supplement (or entirely replace) licence funding with advertising revenue.
- Problems arising from the end of the 'scarcity' of frequencies which informed early policies on broadcasting: under conditions of scarcity, monopolies could be justified as 'natural' but once that scarcity was eliminated, other justifications needed to be found, or the monopolies abandoned.

With the challenge from the new technologies of cable and satellite and the advancement of new ideas about how broadcasting systems could be organized in a different technological era, these problems became more acute. For example, could monopolies be justified when there was no longer a scarcity of frequencies? Should the state continue to determine what services should be available to viewers or consumers of broadcasting? How could one continue to justify the licence fee?

Towards broadcasting deregulation

The speed of technological and political change made leisurely discussions about broadcasting immensely difficult. But many of the other issues that had to be confronted were not in themselves new. The threat to established practices and structures from commercial bodies wanting to run broadcasting on commercial lines had always been there. Sometimes the challenges were successful and change came about; at other times, the challenges failed. What is therefore interesting is to begin to identify the points at which such pressures become irresistible.

By the 1980s the pressures for change became very real. On the one hand, governments began to change their attitudes towards the need for regulatory agencies and their activities. Those who advocated 'deregulation' questioned the view that regulatory agencies were in the public interest and saw them as distorting public desires through their regulatory activities. The aim of proponents of these views was to reduce or eliminate regulatory activity and simply let the marketplace dictate the level and the nature of services (see Tunstall 1986; Tunstall and Palmer 1990: ch. 14; Veljanovski 1989). On the other hand, the new technologies of cable and satellite broadcasting, and increasingly sophisticated telecommunications systems, began to challenge the established terrestrial broadcasters by promising or creating the possibility of new broadcasting services. With governments showing interest in these new technologies as part of the development of 'information technologies' for economic and industrial growth, their development was usually encouraged in some way or other. Consequently, new privately funded, commercial cable and satellite television services came into being and began to compete with the established broadcasters. Perhaps the most obvious manifestation of that change took place in countries where public broadcasters had an effective monopoly, e.g. Greece, and where competition was introduced very rapidly and so undermined the monopoly.

Many of these changes – individually or together – have been described as the *deregulation* of broadcasting: this suggests the relaxation of the rules that govern the state-controlled broadcasting monopoly and the emergence of competition. But deregulation is more than the simple removal or relaxation of rules and regulations. According to Dyson and Humphreys (1990), deregulation is central to a neo-liberal strategy for modernizing the economy by privatization and the creation of an 'enterprise culture'. It is also seen as a response to increasing international competition in television by making it easier to create larger broadcasting organizations which are able to compete internationally (Dyson and Humphreys 1990: 231–3).

Such changes were taking place at a time when public broadcasters were facing other difficulties. First, the position of public broadcasters was under attack from within. In 1981, in the then Federal Republic of Germany, the Constitutional Court ruled that 'private broadcasting was constitutional' within a model of 'external pluralism' between competing private channels. In France in 1982, the government abandoned the state monopoly of broadcasting partly as a way of redressing the weaknesses of the traditional system. Second, television penetration had reached saturation point in many countries and consequently funding from the licence fee levelled off. It could not be increased by the sorts of amounts desired by the broadcasters since politicians often feared the electoral consequences of large increases. Commercial broadcasters also suffered the effects of recession and this too highlighted the fact that funding for broadcasting activities would not grow indefinitely. Third, broadcasters were also finding it difficult to adapt to the cultural and moral pluralism which undermined the idea of universal service established in the early years of broadcasting. Fourth, governments were becoming aware of what their neighbours were doing and sometimes benefiting from. Finally, broadcasters now had to contend with the challenge of the new technologies of cable and satellite television. Though they were much slower to develop than initially promised, their high profile forced policy-makers to act and broadcasters to respond to the challenge of having their control over the airwaves put into question.

In these changing circumstances, new commercial broadcasters came into existence. Some took advantage of the new technologies by broadcasting by satellite or cable, others took advantage of a more liberal approach to broadcasting which permitted the development of terrestrial television systems – but all took advantage, one way or another, of the more liberal set of rules which were now in place. Rules, for example, which allowed for commercial broadcasters carrying nothing more than entertainment or merely broadcasting large quantities of imported material. And so what had initially been a fairly closed, state-controlled system characterized by a small number of public broadcasters now became a large competitive environment, with a knock-on effect on the nature of the public broadcasters, on funding systems, on cultures, and so on.

Changes in regulatory policy

What forms did the change in regulatory policy take? Four main types of policy regimes in the deregulation of public monopolies stand out (Scherer 1986). These also contain different phrases or words which are sometimes used interchangeably with 'deregulation' but which, in reality, describe different arrangements and policy consequences. The four types are as follows:

- *Denationalization or privatization*: the transfer of public property from the government-owner to the private-owner. The best example of this is the privatization of TF1 in France under the Chirac government (1986–8). Privatization is usually but not necessarily accompanied by a liberalization or relaxation of the rules which apply to those previously nationalized entities.
- *Privatization of tasks*: one or more (but not all) of the tasks previously protected by a *de jure* monopoly are taken away from the public entity and transferred to private enterprises. An example of this would be the requirements that the BBC and ITV in the UK

adopt a 25 per cent quota of programmes to be made by independent producers.

- *Demonopolization*: abolishing the *de jure* monopoly of the public institution by permitting competition. Thus commercial radio was introduced almost everywhere in western Europe (the UK, France, Greece, Spain, Scandinavia) as a means of breaking the monopoly.
- *Organizational privatization*: some or all of the regulatory constraints under which public, as opposed to private, enterprises have to operate are abolished. This is similar to the process of liberalization since regulatory requirements are removed. The public entity concerned may also be privatized in the process.

If one applies the above typology to European broadcasting systems then it becomes clear that each and every one has adapted to meet different sets of circumstances, but in no case have regulations been completely abandoned. Pressure for new regulations often comes from politicians who fear complete liberalization, and sometimes the new broadcasters themselves seek protection by asking authorities to recognize their fledgling status. The deregulation of broadcasting can often therefore lead to new procedures or bodies, e.g. to the foundation of new regulatory bodies to oversee or license new broadcasters. It may thus be more appropriate to describe certain contemporary changes as bringing about the *re*regulation, rather than the deregulation, of broadcasting. In other words, processes of deregulation have usually been controlled in some way or other; 'savage deregulation', i.e. where no controls are put in place to lessen the 'undesirable' impact of liberalization and commercialization on domestic culture and productions has not taken place (Traquina 1995).

Case study: the UK

The terrestrial broadcasting system remains heavily regulated although the nature of the regulatory regime has changed. This change has involved an alteration in the way that the commercial television regulatory body – the ITC – regulates commercial terrestrial television. In the past it oversaw all aspects of the system; from 1992 onwards, individual programme companies have been made responsible for meeting their licence obligations. Programme companies have thus gained a degree of autonomy. Other examples of change would include the 25 per cent quota of programmes to be made by independent producers which must be carried by the terrestrial broadcasters ('privatization of tasks'), and the removal of the requirement that a certain amount of current affairs programmes has to be carried during peak-time on the commercial channels ('liberalization'). The system for awarding licences to cable and terrestrial broadcasters remains strictly controlled, e.g. strict rules apply with regards to 'erotic' services, and services have to meet guidelines established by the relevant authorities such as the Cable Authority (for cable) and the ITC (for satellite services).

Significantly, while there has been an enormous increase in the number of channels available to households in the UK, these have all come about as a result of the new technologies and of satellite broadcasting in particular. The fifth terrestrial channel began broadcasting in 1997, by which time all broadcasters had to face the prospect of many new services via digital terrestrial and satellite television. Overall, the terrestrial broadcasters continue to dominate the broadcasting scene and their audience share remains large – about 91 per cent of all weekly viewing (Fiddick 1995). Nevertheless, the new competitive environment has had an effect on how the BBC, the public broadcaster, operates now and will operate in the future when its public funding will be reconsidered. As a way of retaining its hold on the audience, and of increasing it, the BBC has entered into a significant alliance with BSkyB over sports coverage and with newspaper interests (Pearson, publishers of the *Financial Times*) to create two satellite services for European distribution. Private commercial broadcasters have also consolidated their position by buying other companies so as to create larger, more competitive, commercial television companies, or by extending their interests into newspapers. The latter is a consequence of current moves to liberalize the existing media cross-ownership rules (Department of National Heritage 1995).

At present, the British media system – like many other systems across Europe – is guided by practices which have attempted to minimize the extent of media concentration within different media sectors as well as across different media sectors. Examples of such practices include the following: newspaper mergers involving large groupings can be referred to the Mergers and Monopolies Commission in order to investigate the potential for abuse of market position; no one organization can own more than two commercial regional (Channel Three) licences (and not both the London licences); newspaper groups are not permitted to control more than 20 per cent of a commercial regional (Channel Three) licences; and so on.

Under pressure from newspaper groups seeking to diversify into television, the British government has moved to liberalize the media ownership rules but, at the same time, to retain an element of control over the system so as to ensure some measure of diversity and plurality across media markets. The Broadcasting Act 1996 should consolidate this trend. Under the proposed new rules, it will become possible for newspaper companies with less than a 20 per cent share of total circulation to control up to 15 per cent of the total television market as defined by audience share. The reverse also applies: a television company which has less than a 15 per cent share of the television audience will be allowed to own a national newspaper. Larger media groups such as News International or Mirror Group Newspapers which have over 20 per cent share of total newspaper circulation will be prevented from controlling Channel Three licences.

The above examples relate only to specific areas. There are numerous other proposals which cover many possibilities across different media sectors.

None the less, the central features of the Act are to make it easier for media groups to move into other media sectors and to allow for the creation of larger groupings of media interests in line with their national and international commercial interests. However, in spite of the moves towards deregulation, there continues to be pressure to maintain a structure which would prevent a concentration of media ownership and which would lead to a loss of diversity, as can be seen in the restrictions imposed on the larger media groups such as News International.

The effects of broadcasting deregulation

The overall change in the thinking surrounding the subject of broadcasting is significant. It replaces an approach to broadcasting which emphasizes social and cultural objectives with an approach which stresses the commercial and economic aspects of broadcasting. A liberalized or deregulated system of broadcasting thus imposes very different requirements on broadcasters to the ones which usually apply in a publicly regulated system.

Some of the effects of broadcasting deregulation are already being felt in diverse countries around western Europe with new commercial players and forces coming into play. But, in the same way that national responses differ, the effects of changes in broadcasting systems (see below) will also differ depending on such factors as the strength of the national culture, the financial strength of existing and new broadcasters, language and cultural differences, political support for public broadcasters, and so on. In sum, then, there are different strategies which can be pursued (see Achille and Miege 1994).

Effects on programmes and scheduling

As new channels develop:

- there is an increase in competition and an increase in demand for programmes
- existing broadcasters (private and state) are forced to meet the challenge of the newcomers in order to retain their audiences
- the content of the broadcasting channels can often become more similar than dissimilar as each competes more vigorously for the attention of the audience.

In terms of scheduling, commercial channels appear to follow a common strategy: initially a reliance on (usually American) imports, a dependence on certain types of entertainment programmes (television games, talk shows, soaps and series) and a move away from informational and educational content. Whether that pattern alters in subsequent years as the new broadcasting systems 'matures' – leading, for example, to new domestic productions – is an issue for future investigation. Nevertheless, the concern over

US imports in the light of the liberalization of broadcasting post-1980 is particularly noteworthy. Europe, as a whole, imports a considerable amount of audiovisual products from the USA but it exports a tiny fraction of that total. This has created an obvious cultural and economic imbalance which the European Union has battled long and hard to counter (see Collins 1992; Lange and Renaud 1989; McAnany and Wilkinson 1992).

Effects on financing

With more competition in television, advertising revenue has to be shared out among even more broadcasters. On the one hand, more competition for programmes increases the costs of programme acquisitions but, on the other hand, it also increases the power of advertisers to negotiate for better prices and a greater range of audiences. The merger between BSB and Sky TV in the UK in 1991 shows how television can be a very profitable medium in a monopolistic environment but less so in a fully competitive one. As a result, new broadcasters are eager to develop new streams of revenue, such as sponsorship and pay-per-view, in order to create profitable enterprises.

As far as the public broadcasters are concerned, their primary source of revenue remains the licence fee. Some, such as the BBC, Norway's NRK and Sweden's SVT, continue to be totally dependent on it. With governments usually unwilling to allow for large increases in the licence fee, these broadcasters have had to engage in radical restructuring so as to adjust (downwards) their costs. Broadcasting organizations which have been in the past partly dependent on advertising revenue have clearly experienced a loss in their advertising revenue share as a consequence of increased competition. In some countries, governments have accordingly granted increases in licence fees or have relaxed rules limiting the amount state broadcasters can raise from advertising. On the whole, though, public broadcasters face a continuing problem as the licence-fee system comes under increasing scrutiny and pressure.

Effects on state broadcasters

Although public broadcasters have faced an erosion of both their viewing share and their revenue, for some that erosion has been more severe than for others. While in Austria, Germany, Ireland, the Netherlands, Norway, Sweden, Spain and the UK, a combination of public broadcasters has managed to retain a large share of the television audience, in some cases, as in Greece, public television's audience has decreased dramatically. The point here is that an erosion in the share of the audience has repercussions on the issue of public funding for public broadcasters.

Effects on media ownership

Media entrepreneurs such as Murdoch, Berlusconi, Kirch and Bertelsmann have taken advantage of the new possibilities that the new television environment has offered. The creation of larger and fewer dominant media groups has been well documented, as have the problems and issues which are associated with it: problems such as a loss of diversity, dangers of monopolization of information and perspectives, and the concentration of power in too few hands (see Mazzolini and Palmer 1992; Tunstall and Palmer 1992). So far, though, the European Commission has not been successful in coping with this issue (CEC 1992). One of the main obstacles to drafting legislation to deal with a concentration of ownership across the audiovisual landscape is determining the market share of any particular media proprietor. Furthermore, with rapid technological change, and media entrepreneurs moving into, and out of, sectors very quickly, the picture is constantly changing.

Conclusion

The changes described above have given rise to very different broadcasting systems to the ones which were in existence at the beginning of the 1980s. New technologies, new policies towards communication sectors and a willingness to question the then existing structures of broadcasting have led to the creation of a more competitive and international broadcasting industry. The old structures have not been dismantled – though they are creaking heavily – but they have been joined by a host of competitors in a more open and more commercial system of broadcasting.

Questions

1 Compare and contrast the media systems of any two countries of your choice and say what factors you think help explain differences and similarities.

2 For many, the commercialization of the broadcast media poses a danger to any notion of the media working in the public interest. Do you accept this view?

3 With the number of television services increasing and viewers more able to act as consumers of television by exercising choices, is there a future for licence-funded public broadcasting?

References

This chapter is based on S. Papathanassopoulos and R. Negrine (1995) 'The Media in Europe' (Unit 17a) and 'The Deregulation of European

Broadcasting Systems' (Unit 35a), Leicester University MA in Distance Learning.

Achille, Y. and Miege, B. (1994) 'The limits to the adaptation strategies of European public service television', *Media, Culture and Society* 16(1): 31–46.

Broadcasting Research Unit (1985) *The Public Service Idea in British Broadcasting: Main Principles*, 2nd edn, London: John Libbey.

CEC (1992) *Pluralism and Media Concentration in the Single Market*, Green Paper by the Commission of the European Communities, Com (92) 480 Final.

Collins, R. (1992) *Satellite Television in Western Europe*, revised edn, London: John Libbey.

Collins, R. (1994) *Broadcasting and Audio-visual Policy in the European Single Market*, London: John Libbey.

Department of National Heritage (DNH) (1995) *Media Ownership: The Government's Proposals*, Cmnd 2872, London: HMSO.

Dyson, K. and Humphreys, P. (eds) (1988) *Broadcasting and New Media Politics in Western Europe*, London: Routledge.

Dyson, K. and Humphreys, P. (eds) (1990) *The Political Economy of Communications: International and European Dimensions*, London: Routledge.

Fiddick, P. (1995) 'TV share', *Guardian G2* 26 June: 10.

Home Office (1986) *Report of the Committee on Financing the BBC* (Peacock Report), Cmnd 9824, London: HMSO.

Humphreys, P. (1988) 'Satellite Broadcasting in West Germany', in R. Negrine (ed.) *Satellite Broadcasting*, London: Croom Helm.

Kuhn, R. (ed.) (1985) *The Politics of Broadcasting*, London: Croom Helm.

Kuhn, R. (1995) *The Media in France*, London: Routledge.

Lange, A. and Renaud, J.L. (1989) *The Future of the European Audiovisual Industry*, Manchester: European Institute for the Media.

McAnany, E.G. and Wilkinson, K.T. (1992) 'From cultural imperialists to takeover victims?', *Communication Research* 19: 724–48.

McGregor, O. (1977) *Royal Commission on the Press: Final Report*, Cmnd 6810, London: HMSO.

McQuail, D. and Siune, K. (1986) (eds) *New Media Politics*, London: Sage.

Mazzolini, G. and Palmer, M. (1992) 'Crossing borders', in K. Siune and W. Truetzscler (eds) *Dynamics of Media Politics*, London: Sage.

Negrine, R. (1994) *Politics and the Mass Media in Britain*, London: Routledge.

Negrine, R. and Papathanassopoulos, S. (1990) *The Internationalisation of Television*, London: Pinter.

Papathanassopoulos, S. (1990) 'Public service broadcasting and deregulatory pressures in Europe', *Journal of Information Science* 19: 113–20.

Scherer, J. (1986) 'Historical analysis of deregulation: the European case', paper presented at the International Symposium, La Dereglementation des Telecommunications et de l' Audiovisuel, Paris: Centre Nationale Researche Scientifique, March.

Traquina, N. (1995) 'Portuguese television: the politics of savage deregulation', *Media, Culture and Society* 17(2): 223–39.

Tunstall, J. (1986) *Communications Deregulation*, Oxford: Basil Blackwell.

Tunstall, J. and Palmer, M. (1990) *Liberating Communications: Policy-Making in France and Britain*, Oxford: Basil Blackwell.

Tunstall, J. and Palmer, M. (1992) *Media Moguls*, London: Routledge.

Veljanovski, C. (ed.) (1989) *Freedom in Broadcasting*, London: Institute of Economic Affairs.

Further reading

Blumler, J. (ed.) (1992) *Television and the Public Interest*, London: Sage.

Burgelman, J.C. (1986) 'The future of public service broadcasting: a case study for "new" communications policy', *European Journal of Communication* 1: 172–201.

Porter, V. (1990) 'Broadcasting re-regulation in Europe – citizenship and consumerism', *EBU Review* 41(6).

Richeri, G. (1985) 'Television from service to business: European tendencies and the Italian case', in P. Drummond and P. Paterson (eds) *Television in Transition*, London: British Film Institute.

Sanchez-Tabernero, A. (1993) *Media Concentration in Europe*, European Institute for the Media Monograph 16, Düsseldorf: European Institute for the Media.

Seymour-Ure, C. (1987) 'Media policy in Britain: now you see it, now you don't', *European Journal of Communication* 2: 269–87.

Seymour-Ure, C. (1991) *The Press and Broadcasting in Britain since 1945*, Oxford: Blackwell.

Siune, K. and Treutzschler, W. (eds) (1992) *Dynamics of Media Politics: Broadcast and Electronic Media in Western Europe*, London: Sage.

Syvertsen, T. (1991) 'Public television in crisis: critiques compared in Norway and Britain', *European Journal of Communication* 6(1): 95–114.

Weymouth, A. and Lamizet, B. (eds) (1996) *Markets and Myths: Forces for Change in the European Media*, Harlow: Addison Wesley Longman.

Chapter 17

Approaches

WHY STUDY MEDIA FORM?

JOHN CORNER

In this chapter I shall look at why the study of form is of key importance in any programme of media studies or, for that matter, of media research. This aim will require some attention to be paid to definitions of 'form' (notoriously, in relation to 'content') and also to ideas about its analysis and to the way in which it is linked with other dimensions or 'moments' in the whole process of mediation. I shall attempt to give the discussion exemplification and grounding by taking one area in which factors of form, for long overlooked, are now being recognized in their full complexity and importance – representations of violence on television.

It is significant for my argument and examples, and for the evaluation and use of them by student readers, that the range of media studies and communication studies available in the UK and mainland Europe shows considerable variation in the scale and kind of attention given to formal analysis. On some courses, particularly those influenced strongly by arts and humanities perspectives, elements drawn from linguistic study are clearly seen as 'core'. On other courses, particularly those generated from a social studies base, such attention may be far less extensive, with few if any opportunities for going beyond a basic awareness. These variations are often a proper reflection of staff specializations but they also indicate a tension within the whole field of media studies, a tension between humanities and social science modes of inquiry and, at bottom, what I have elsewhere (Corner 1995) described as a tension between media studies as a form of 'criticism' (where the primary emphasis may be given to media output) and media studies as a form of 'sociology' (where primary emphasis may be given to history, institutions, production practices and audiences). I do not hold the view that the tension is an irresolvable one or (a different point) that it is necessarily unproductive as a play-off of one kind of approach against another. However, I do think that *one* way in which media studies might develop and progress is by more sustained dialogue between contributing disciplines precisely on issues to do with media form and its interconnection with media production and consumption.

Another good reason for giving formal issues close attention in any course of study is that both in broadcasting and the press there have recently been quite radical changes in form, occasioned by the stronger market need for mediations, as commodities, to appeal to specific viewers and audiences. A key process here has been that of 'hybridization', the mixing of elements from what were previously distinct conventions, thus breaking down some of the older genres, including those dividing off 'higher' from 'lower' forms or demarcating the 'serious' from the 'entertaining'. A quick walk around the magazine racks of a High Street newsagent will show how this has affected the specialist publications sector, with its various and often strident attempts to construct a readership subculture around particular hobbies and interests which have either newly emerged or which have undergone radical change. In broadcasting, one international shift has been towards a new kind of 'reality programme', drawing on documentary formats and dramatic techniques to provide thrilling stories of real-life action (see the overview in Kilborn 1994).

It is perhaps worth noting, as a final preliminary, that from the point of view of many teachers and researchers, media studies has already suffered from an overdose of inquiry into 'form' (the term formal*ism* has quite a long history as a label for distortion and limitation, especially in relation to literary and fine arts scholarship). I have some sympathy with this view, but I would want to argue that the problem, rather than deriving from formal analysis as such, lies with the way in which it has often been done.

My basic claim about the study of form is that only by attending to formal issues can we engage with two things which it is necessary for media studies to tackle. The first of these is the range of ways in which the media industries are engaged in the production of cultural artefacts, 'made things', whether these are 'fictional' or 'factual' by categorization. The second is that any understanding of 'media influence', actual or potential, will come to grief if it is not sensitive to this artefactual character and to the way it is instrumental in cueing those various acts of knowing and feeling – of finding sense and significance and having emotions – which happen in us when we read newspapers, watch television and listen to radio.

Form and content

By 'form' I mean the particular organizations of signification which constitute a given item *as communication,* for instance, an advertising hoarding, an episode of a situation comedy on television, an article in the local evening newspaper. Inevitably, such signification is *conventional,* drawing on what may well be a large and complex range of conventions for doing what it tries to do and for being what it is. These conventions will inform word choice and syntax (as for instance in a popular newspaper's editorial column), and they will be behind the ways in which a particular image is lit and photographed and the items which are depicted in it are composed within a given frame and perspective (as for instance in an advertising hoarding). Even if the communication is designed to read, sound or look highly 'original', conventions of form will be an important constitutive element (perhaps informing decisions about what is omitted or what is done with a significant difference). The basic 'content' of any communication could, in most cases, be articulated by the use of any one of a number of different formal choices. So, for instance, there exists an extremely wide range of English syntactical and lexical variations by which to tell someone in one sentence that you wish them to shut the door through which they have just entered. And there exists a similarly wide range of visual techniques and styles by which to shoot, for the opening of a television programme, the main waterfront buildings of Liverpool. On the other side of the equation, the formal means used in telling people to shut doors and in depicting Liverpool will have a relative independence from their employment in these particular instances. Following the two different lines of possibility thus opened up is, in fact, a key feature of formal analysis – *noting how this instance might have been communicated differently and noting how different instances have been communicated similarly.*

One objection to what I have said so far might come from someone firmly committed to the view that it is impossible to separate 'form' from 'content', with the implication that even to use these terms at all is to slip into self-deception. This seems to me to be an overreaction to those analysts who have gone on about 'form' without any apparent regard at all for 'content' and those who have studied 'content' without paying the slightest attention to 'form'. Certainly, we can agree that any study should connect with *both*, but it is quite legitimate (indeed, absolutely necessary to analytic progress) to see the two as separate, if only the better to understand the way in which they are tightly interconnected. Media analysts have a rather bad track record of claiming the *fusion* of things which, illogically, they also wish to claim are *related* (only separate things can relate!). To make this point about separation clearer, take my own specialism. I have a particular academic interest in documentary film and television, its history and development. In pursuing this, I believe that I can analyse documentaries in a meaningful way while paying primary attention to their particular visual and aural 'shape' and their use of distinctive mediating devices rather than to their content (see, for instance, Corner 1996b). Their content may well be the factor which most directly 'sells' them to an audience (a documentary about drug abuse, for instance, connecting with different expectations, interests and fears from a documentary about the growth of the sport of rock-climbing). However, I am inquiring into the kinds of 'communicational packages' that modern documentaries are, and this is not at all a topic-specific inquiry, even though one of the interesting things in it may well be to see how similar formal systems are modified when they are applied to different substantive themes.

What about the reverse case? Is it possible as a viewer to take the 'content' of a documentary without regard to the form? This question poses the difference between analytic attention to a communication and 'normal' attention. For while it is certainly possible to watch and enjoy a documentary without consciously registering much if anything to do with its communicative design (this is in fact the intended and normative way in which most documentaries *are* watched), the 'content' is made available to meaningful consciousness only *through* the form, so the form is 'at work' even though the viewer (perhaps especially when the viewer) is unaware of it. This complicates the form–content relationship: content, like form, is still a 'separable' element but in any given media artefact it has a high level of form dependency – *it is rendered through the form.* At certain levels of (high) generality, its separability *may* be relatively trouble free for the conduct of an argument (for example, the number of appearances in British television drama of Black police officers in comparison with Black criminals). Elsewhere, abstraction of content may be hazardous (for example, in discussing the frequency of depiction of acts of murder on television – where, as I shall argue later, the matter of the form of depiction is absolutely vital to what is at issue).

So, to summarize, my view is that while content and form indicate elements of communication which cannot usefully be considered in *isolation* from each other – in many instances the interconnections and dependencies are too close for that – they are analytically separable and, indeed, the consequences of their not being so would be extremely dire for media analysis. Certain studies of the media rightly place emphasis on content factors; others are more interested in questions of communicative design and construction. Although there is some truth in the charge that attention to form has sometimes failed to get to grips with the *political and social consequences* of mediation, preferring instead to speculate about the complexities of signification, there is a long history of mass communication research which has rendered itself of limited value by its inattention to the details of language and depiction, to the *means* by which communication gets done. Despite some of the theoretical obscurities it has had a habit of falling into, one of the principal and continuing contributions of 'cultural studies' to international media research has been its refusal to foreclose on what, at the cost of sounding very un-social scientific, we might call the 'mysteries' of signification. It has always tried to remember that mediation is a matter of *symbolic exchange*. In fact, this exchange is, judged from one point of view, very one-sided. The media put out symbols and audiences and readerships 'receive' them. However, this is to miss the point that audiences and readerships invest their own symbolic resources (their ways of attaching meaning and value to, for instance, word, image, narrative and character) in coming to terms with media productions they encounter, enjoying some of them, disliking some and quite possibly not 'getting the sense' of quite a few too. This leads on to the links between form and interpretation.

Form and interpretation

Other chapters in this book refer in more detail to the ways in which study of the variables of interpretation has figured in recent media inquiry. A realization of the extent to which 'meaning' is contingent upon the act of interpretation rather than being a property somehow inherent to media artefacts themselves, simply projected outwards from them, has been the single most important point of development in recent media research. It has given rise to a number of challenging lines of study into the social conditions of interpretability as they vary among different readerships and audiences. It has also broken forever any 'direct' linkage between media items and influence, since it has introduced variables of meaning into the research perspective. Research on influence has always been aware of the importance of variables but it has generally related these to a 'message' whose basic meaning was stable even if the 'use' made of it or its 'trigger' function in prompting behaviour were not. I have written on these issues elsewhere (Corner 1996a) and, indeed, there is continuing debate over just what the implications of interpretation are for *any* theory of influence.

The scope of the debate exceeds this chapter's remit but what I would want to claim here is that an emphasis on the 'role of the reader' in giving meaning to what they see and hear in no way reduces the need for media research to pay attention to questions of signification. Far from it. We shall understand meaning-making 'from' the media as a social process only if we increase our understanding of significatory structures and their operation within the 'spaces and times' of media texts (both written and broadcast forms have spatial and temporal dimensions to their communicative character). Signification also needs to be traced back to specific authorial/editorial/technical production practices too, many of which are self-consciously rhetorical in the sense that they intend to cause certain kinds of response in the viewer or reader (think, for instance, of the 'formal' properties required of photographs which are placed on the cover of outdoor sports magazines, what they are supposed to 'say' about the exhilaration and intensity of skiing, surfing or rock-climbing quite apart from their literal depiction of a sporting act).

The scope of readers/viewers to interpret variably is, in any given case, constrained by the social and biographical factors informing the interpretative framework they mobilize in response to a mediated item. A fanatical surfer will 'read' a shot of a big wave differently from someone who hates the sea, for instance. Someone who has been an unemployed machinist for four years may well understand a television news item on job centres differently from someone who is a successful banker. But interpretative limitations are not the only constraint. The significations themselves carry levels of determination which it would be extremely odd to find varying greatly in their interpretative 'uptake'. At the most obvious level, this is sustained by the social stability of signs themselves. If the news item I mentioned above finished with a shot of individuals shaking their head as they looked at the 'jobs available' board and then leaving the job centre promptly, the visual cues of this little narrativization would be hard not to interpret as indicating a *problem* – an undersupply of jobs – whatever information was carried elsewhere in the story. If the reporter went as far as to run a voice-over across this scene, along the lines 'But disappointment still awaits many who call here', it would be virtually impossible to imagine much inter-pretative latitude among viewers (although there would definitely be differ-ences in social and political response, including the possibility of complaints being made to the broadcasters on grounds of bias). If we take the case of the picture of the big wave, the cultural connotations of waves with 'power' is securely enough established in our culture (reinforced as it is by adver-tising and packaging) to generate that reading for most viewers of the image, whatever their interest in, or experience of, the sea. Of course, the dedicated surfer may be able, at a quick glance, to place the image into a numerical category of power potential!

This general point needs making lest media artefacts end up being seen as kinds of open invitations to create 'individual' meanings. 'Individual' meanings *are* created around media artefacts, and *all* meanings have to be *attributed* to artefacts by those who apprehend them. But meanings are attributed in response to powerful *signifiers*, whose job it is precisely to direct and organize meaning-making, to generate sense and significance and as far as possible to cue feelings too. Is it hardly surprising that, when it comes to dicussing last night's news, film or comedy, we have a lot of meanings to *share* as well as to discuss, debate and perhaps contest?

Elements of formal analysis

Analysis of communicative form has been undertaken in a wide range of disciplines; literary criticism, linguistics and art history have lengthy tradi-tions of inquiry while film studies, cultural sociology, cultural studies and media studies have more recent bodies of work. One of the key factors differentiating the analytic approaches is their level of systematic formula-tion, that is the degree to which they self-consciously follow procedures. Many literary critics analysing a poem, for instance, will do so with extre-mely close attention to its linguistic character, but probably with little by way of procedural explicitness. Linguists, on the other hand, often analyse language with careful regard to their own analytic schemes and its categor-ies, which are made explicit in the analysis. Such a difference is partly a product of the different *aims* of inquiry – in the one case an artistic appre-ciation, in the other a description of language structures – but many types of communicative analyses combine a number of aims, so distinctions of this kind can prove troublesome. Semiotics, the science of signs developed by Ferdinand de Saussure in the early part of the twentieth century, has undoubtedly seemed to many to offer the most general and rigorous system for analysing communication – its emphasis on structural interrelations providing a kind of linguistic framework for use across a whole range of different media forms. Here, the work of Roland Barthes (especially 1972) has been exemplary and highly influential (in media studies, Fiske and Hartley 1978 was a key text). However, the very precision of semiotics has been a problem in so far as it is grounded in too rigid a sense of communicative order (assuming, for instance, a high degree of 'non-changeability' in sign-meanings) and in a frequent ignoring of that process of interpretation, described above, by which meaning is the product of acts of reading and viewing.

Despite some excellent and suggestive work, semiotics has by no means consolidated itself as the dominant perspective on formal analysis it once appeared well on the way to becoming. Another problem here has been that of visual analysis. Clearly, the study of visual depiction, whether in drawing, photography, film, television or whatever, requires different tools from the study of written and spoken language (see Messaris 1994). With language, the signifying units of words and the rules of combination (syntax) may not be immutable but they do have a degree of significatory stability. A dictionary and a grammar primer are (imperfect) indications of this. The units and combinatory rules of, say, photography are far harder to grasp as a formal system. For a start, in a photograph we have no obvious signifying unit to compare with the word. Second, we face the problem that while a sentence is clearly a communicative device capable of generating all sorts of propositional and evaluative information, a photograph of, say, a car in a street may just seem to be 'saying' – 'a car in the street'. In other words, it may appear to have no communicative project apart from presenting a 'likeness'. Barthes's (1977) insightful discussion of the photograph as appearing to be 'a message without a code' takes up this very point. We may recognize that there is *more* communicative work going on than this, and that indeed the 'message' is 'coded', but specifying the visual code system and its particular local application has proved, not surprisingly, to be a formidable and controversial task.

All I will say here on this major question is that any serious project of formal analysis must have reasonably consistent, and preferably explicit, criteria for *identifying* distinctive components of communication. It must have a way of providing a *description* of communicative organization which registers these components in rule-based combination (the rules cannot be 100 per cent tight but they must show good consistency across instances). The project should then be able to offer *explanations* which are able to address the link between particular significatory elements and relative stabilities in socially ascribed meaning. It should, in short, be able to match 'sign' to 'sense'.

Say, for instance, I wanted to look at how elements from 'camcorder culture' had become inscribed within mainstream media output (which they have, in advertising and a range of documentary and magazine programmes). I would need to identify those elements, their combination across a range of instances with other elements, and the kinds of social meaning which they were designed to generate (some clues as to intentions here might be got from contexts of use). Of course, it could turn out that rather different aspects of 'camcorderism' (e.g. authenticity, domesticity, ineptness, expectations of comedy) were being deployed and that analysis needed to move to a *typology* of usage, indicating the range of variants and their associated formal properties. As I noted earlier, ignoring specific 'content' here is likely to lead to elaborate speculation, the subsequent value of which may be very questionable. Alertness to form in relation to specific themes and contexts (and perhaps to production practices and/or the sampled responses of viewers) might make useful headway into charting how the terms of mainstream televisuality are now being modified by non-professional practice.

There is a great deal more to be said about formal analysis at the level of theory and method. However, having drawn attention to at least some of the issues, I want to look at how much of what I have noted so far in this chapter comes to bear on one particular area of concern – screen violence.

The screen violence issue

The issue of 'screen violence' has generated much debate in recent years, both in respect of feature films and of broadcast television. Fears of a negative connection between depictions of violence and real behaviour have been widely expressed, and at the time of writing, the whole issue is being aired again in relation to the availability of the 'V chip', which allows parents electronically to limit the range of material which their children can view. Generally speaking, there have been three kinds of fears. First, there has been fear of depicted violence stimulating real violence. Second, there has been fear of depicted violence reducing sensitivity and proper concern for real violence. Third, there has been fear of depicted violence inducing excessive and unwarranted levels of anxiety among sections of the population about being the victims of violence. However, the first two kinds of fears occur most frequently in the UK, and they have been developed in respect of both fictional and non-fictional material, with particular attention being paid to the vulnerability of young viewers.

Elsewhere (Corner 1995) I have explored some of the broader issues surrounding 'screen violence', including the basic cultural paradox that forms of behaviour which are widely considered to be wrong in reality constitute the basis of quite a wide range of popular culture. It is necessary, I believe, for analysis to come to terms with the widespread *enjoyment* of depicted violence (violence as 'play') across most age-groups and social groups before much progress can be made on the question. In order to do this, in my earlier writing I used the terms 'turn-on' and 'turn-off' violence to indicate two basic ways in which depictions might differ. In 'turn-off' depictions (and the portrayals of most serious TV drama would fit here, as would the majority of violent incidents in soap operas), the aim is to portray the violence within terms of the moral framings of everyday life, so that a degree of unpleasantness, disturbance and even distress will accompany the viewing (directors have to be careful here, *too* much distress might bring a problem for the viewers and then for the broadcasters and the regulating authorities). In 'turn on' depictions by contrast (and a whole range of popular drama formats, including thrillers and many 'cop shows' would fit here) the aim is to portray violence in a way which provides excitement by heightened action, intensified character performance and, perhaps, by spectacular visual effects. Of course, even allowing for the difficulty of applying my categories with consistency and precision, it is quite possible for an item to shift between 'turn-off' and 'turn-on' depictions. In fact, it seems pretty clear that a number of recent films structure this shift into their basic design, often giving rise to a debate about their moral ambivalence.

But it should be immediately obvious how quickly this whole debate turns into a set of questions about *form*, and cannot be properly addressed using items of extracted *content*. So, for instance, it is almost (not entirely) beside the point to note how many murders there are each week on network television. What we need to know is the dramatic context for the incidents and the ways in which the murders were portrayed, since it is clear that a murder done in a certain way on television can leave the viewer relatively unmoved whereas a lower level act of violence, like repeated blows to the body, can be deeply disturbing but can also be exciting or even comic.

On the basis of these general points, we might formulate a rule along the following lines – the more that violence which is judged to be 'turn on' involves sustained, graphic depiction of physical injury, the more worry is likely to be generated around it. We could even go further – the more that this violence lacks obvious action-values (chases, fights, etc.) and therefore depends on the violence itself to generate viewing intensity, the more likely it is that it will be judged controversial.

As I shall indicate, these 'rules' tend to hide some considerable complexities, but they do seem close to the ones which have been applied in recent years, particularly in relation to the newer stylizations of, and preoccupations with, violence to be found in cinema. What specific questions of form do they raise, and how is form related to the particular psychology of viewing, with its broader cultural interconnections, which comes into play when watching violent depictions?

We might initially work with a checklist of factors which, in combination, could be seen to constitute key features of depiction. On it, we would need such items as:

- Strength of prior identification with characters (both those to whom violence is done and those who are violent).
- Links within the narrative to notions of justness and unjustness in relation to specific violent events. The indication of general and local causation would be important here. Clearly, war films tend to have a radically different structure from crime films, which nevertheless vary among themselves.

- The levels of 'realism' (themselves, posing well-attested problems of definition) and of 'entertainment' at work within the surrounding narrative. Themes and characterization would in part reflect these levels.
- The terms in which the violent scene was *acted*; for instance, expressions of pleasure and of pain, the relationships established between act and persons.
- The terms in which the violent scene was *shot* and *edited*; for instance, proximities to action, camera angles, camera mobility and variable viewpoints, duration of shots, explicit indications of physical injury. The presence, and type, of sounds and music on soundtrack.

Such a list might quickly be able to make important differentiations. For instance, scenes designed to have a turn-off effect will not usually be accompanied by an exciting musical score. And that kind of cartoon violence and old-style western violence which (while clearly 'turn-on') appears not to bother many people will have nothing like the degree of explicit indications of injury of more recent productions. We might wonder why 'sanitization' of this kind is thought so culturally acceptable! However, at other points the scheme would be challenged and perhaps even thrown into question. Just *how* subjective in significance are the workings of the various formal factors which are under review? It is certainly possible for someone to find a scene intended as 'turn-off' to work as 'turn-on' (this comes up frequently when directors defend themselves against a 'turn-on' charge) and the reverse is true too, but how varied, for instance, are our thresholds for judging 'comic violence' and what adustments to depiction can make acceptable the previously unacceptable and vice versa?

Here, it would be useful to have the means to produce depictions designed precisely to test depictive factors with sample audiences. A much-cited study (Docherty 1990), although it could not run to this, had respondents do editing and sequence work on scripts containing violent scenes, observing how (simulated) 'producerly' criteria related to the 'consumerly' ones normally used in discussion of responses. In the process, it identified a number of areas of tension and potential conflict in people's relation to the 'violent'.

All these procedures of analysis have limitations on their reliability. But they take us to the heart of this vexed issue, raising questions about culture, imagination and fantasy – as well as about attitudes and behaviour – much more quickly than is achieved by holding up a set of moral norms against statistics showing the frequency of certain depicted acts.

The future of form in media study

This has been no more than a brief opening-up of some questions about media form and its study. Students using this book will probably be doing concurrent work on a range of specific issues involving form and the various questions it poses (for instance, in advertising, television drama, news and current affairs, popular press reporting and feature cinema). I have wanted to stand back a little and address the matter directly at a general level. My fundamental argument is that symbolic exchange is the pivotal moment in mass communication processes, the moment around which both production capacities and intentions and consumer expectations and interpretations gather. If media systems exert power, then it is primarily through the mediations which appear on page and screen (and, by implication, through the absence of those which do not) that this is exercised. To this process, form is central and it is therefore a factor in consideration of media history, media institutions, media policy and media audiences.

The analysis of form poses problems for the analyst, and some work has slipped into obscurity and inconsequentiality, but this is no good reason for displacing attention on to other factors which are thought to present themselves more securely as objects of study. Given its pivotal position in mediation, we need to engage with its complexities as directly as we can.

Questions

1   How do formal factors contribute to the overall meaning of an item? Tape television news of the same lead story from two channels and by examination of their visual and verbal organization (e.g. sequencing of segments, visualization, phrasings, captions) consider the differences produced in the understanding of the event.

2   How varied are the ways in which violence can be depicted? Take six examples of 'violent scenes' (two from written accounts) which you feel to be as different as they could be and examine them in the light of the list of factors outlined in this chapter.

3   How does form relate to variations in interpretation and evaluation? Take a magazine advert which you think works well and one which you think does not and briefly list the reasons for your judgements. Ask a friend to assess the same examples without knowing your opinion and then compare the results.

References

Barthes, R. (1972) *Mythologies*, London: Jonathan Cape.

Barthes, R. (1977) 'The rhetoric of the image', in R. Barthes, *Image-Music-Text*, London: Fontana.

Corner, J. (1995) *Television Form and Public Address*, London: Arnold.

Corner, J. (1996a) 'Reappraising reception: theories, concepts and methods', in J. Curran and M. Gurevitch (eds) *Mass Media and Society*, 2nd edn, London: Arnold.

Corner, J. (1996b) *The Art of Record*, Manchester: Manchester University Press.

Docherty, D. (1990) *Violence in TV Fiction* (BSC Annual Review), London: Broadcasting Standards Council.

Fiske, J. and Hartley, J. (1978) *Reading Television*, London: Methuen.

Kilborn, R. (1994) 'How real can you get: recent developments in "reality television"', *European Journal of Communication* 9(4): 421–39.

Messaris, P.(1994) *Visual Literacy: Image, Mind and Reality*, Boulder, CO: Westview.

Further reading

Bordwell, D. and Thompson, K. (1993) *Film Art: An Introduction*, 4th edn, New York: McGraw-Hill.

Corner, J. (1995) *Television Form and Public Address*, London: Arnold.

Corner, J. and Harvey, S. (eds) (1996) *Television Times*, London: Arnold.

Ellis, J. (1982) *Visible Fictions*, London: Routledge.

Fairclough, N. (1995) *Media Discourse*, London: Arnold.

Keeble, R. (1994) *The Newspapers Handbook*, London: Routledge.

Messaris, P. (1994) *Visual Literacy: Image, Mind and Reality*, Boulder, CO: Westview.

Scannell, P. (cd.) (1991) *Broadcast Talk*, London: Sage.

Chapter 18

Audience feedback

ADMINISTRATIVE RESEARCH OF AUDIENCES

SUE STOESSL

The primary function of research carried out by media organizations is to identify the size and nature of their respective audiences. Though the editorial or creative staff of an organization will be interested in the findings of such research, the main consumers of it are those concerned with targeting that audience through advertising – advertising which in many organizations plays the primary role in funding editorial content.

This has meant that though there are a number of groups with an interest in media research – content-makers, the public, politicians and policy-makers – the type of research and the methods used have been dictated by the demands of those who are prepared to pay for what is an expensive product – the buyers and sellers of advertising.

What is media research?

The majority of media research is carried out through a process of cross-industry cooperation and initiatives. In the UK the press, television and radio industries all carry out contract research which is paid for by all of those who wish to be involved (which usually means the whole sector). The resulting data have been arrived at through mutually agreed practices and are therefore accepted universally as a basis upon which advertising is bought and sold. Some additional studies are conducted by individual titles and stations, but they tend to be viewed with some scepticism and if used to sell advertising criticized by the competition.

This chapter will look at the main industry contracts and how they are carried out, what information they provide and the uses to which it is put.

A short history

The press was the first sector to measure its audience. Magazines were the innovators because they sold advertising in competition with newspapers. Newspapers knew quite quickly the number of copies they sold and they could tell advertisers how many people were likely to be exposed to their messages. Circulation did not take into account the number of readers per copy, but this was not significant in newspapers as an assumption could be made that this was relatively constant between titles.

Magazines have a longer shelf life, varying numbers of readers per copy and the additional complication that readers could pick up the same copy on several occasions. Publishers wanted to tell advertisers about this and therefore set out to ask questions about what the public had read. The purpose was to measure the added value that their magazines could provide to advertisers over the competition. This activity started in the 1930s.

Radio audience measurement started at about the same time. The BBC operated a radio station and were interested in telling the public, who paid a licence fee, that they were getting value for money. They started what became known as the 'Daily Survey', where interviewers asked a sample of people each day what they had listened to on the radio the day before and from this were able to report the audience size of their whole output. This was done to demonstrate accountability to licence payers as no advertising sales element was relevant to the public service broadcaster.

Meanwhile, in the USA a radio measurement system was starting because there advertising-financed broadcasting was first in the marketplace.

In the UK television measurement was initiated by the BBC, which before 1955 was the only broadcaster. Television was added on to the Daily Survey and a method called 'aided recall' was used. This involved showing respondents during street interviews a list of the previous day's programming and asking them which ones they had watched. Up to 4000 people each day were asked these questions and the sample was selected to be representative of the population by region of the country, age, sex and socio-economic group, therefore the results were an accurate measure of what people remembered they had watched, which was perfectly adequate information for editorial purposes and public accountability.

The television industry in the USA had started as a commercial venture. Not only did it carry advertisers' messages, but also a significant proportion of the programmes was either sponsored or even made by advertisers. (Hence the term 'soap opera', because the first programmes of this kind were made by the soap and detergent manufacturers Procter & Gamble.) To continue to get income to pay for shows, some proof had to be provided that the programmes, their advertising and sponsors' messages had audiences of a particular size. The TV audience measurement meter came to fill this demand. A.C. Nielsen, a US market research company, started to measure audiences by a meter attached to the television that recorded the time that the set was switched on, which station it was tuned to, any station-switching and when the set was switched off.

A paper tape recorded all this information and at the end of the week it was taken out of the meter and sent to the research company for analysis. The end result was a measure of the homes switched to each minute of each day for every station but no information as to who was in front of each set. This was collected in diaries that were completed by people all around the USA for four weeks, four times a year. The combination of meters and people diaries produced the data for the multimillion dollar US television and advertising industry until the mid-1980s.

Newspaper and magazine readership research in the 1990s

The National Readership Survey (NRS) is carried out by the Joint Industry Committee for Newspaper Advertising Research (JICNAR). This body is financed by the publishers but all other parties who might use the findings are represented on its management body; it has an independent chairman.

The NRS is put out to tender to market research companies from time to time but the contract has been held by Research Services Ltd for some years. The specification that goes to tender is agreed by all parties involved in the buying and selling of advertising and is a very detailed document. It is recognized as one of the best quality surveys in the UK, because it is based on a random sample, which means that the interviewer has to contact a named person in a particular household. The more normal, cheaper process of a quota sample allows any one in a particular sex, age and socio-economic group to be approached.

To reach the named person, the interviewer will call on the household at varying times of day and different days of the week to try to complete the interview. However persuasive they are, people do refuse or are un-contactable and the final response rate is just over 60 per cent. For this kind of survey, 60 per cent is a high response rate nowadays. A sample size of about 38,500 interviews a year is achieved.

The interviewer uses CAPI (computer assisted personal interview) to put the answers straight into a laptop computer. Respondents sort piles of cards with replicas of publication mastheads into those they have read in the last year. The list of publications that have been read are then taken and more questions are asked about them. These include read yesterday, how acquired, purchased or delivered, frequency of reading, Saturday reader-ship and some readership of sections. Many questions are asked about ownership of various goods and services, other media consumption and demographic details.

The findings of the NRS are published in full twice a year. Information on titles that are read by 1 per cent or more of the population are included in the survey. The estimated total readership is given together with the demographic reach and profile of the readers for over 250 titles. In addition the newspapers, with their regular higher readership, have data available every month based on the average of the last three months measured.

In the past few years the number of supplements to all newspaper titles has increased rapidly. Since the start of the colour supplements in the 1970s the advertisers and their agents have been interested in the readership of supplements separate from that of the main section of the paper. If a million people read the main section, do the same number read the sports, business or magazine sections? It has proved difficult to collect these data as it is recognized that people have difficulties remembering which sections of papers they read the day before. Advertising rates depend on readership, thus the requirement for information will need further work from the industry.

Because the future of sections depends on advertising support, the measurement of readership of sections has a significant interest for editorial staff, who derive satisfaction from knowing that their article has been read; it is also helpful to know who the regular readers are so that the selection of editorial subjects can be geared toward keeping them interested.

Advertisers' use of readership research

Advertising is purchased in schedules. This means that an advertising agency will plan campaigns for a number of insertions for clients, selected by the audience it wants to reach and the amount of money available for the campaign. The first decision is which medium to use. Often a mix of press and broadcast is used but to give examples of how audience measurement affects the decision-making, examples of single media campaigns will be given. Given the selected target audience of women aged under 45 with children, a rank order list can be produced from the NRS of the percentage of the target group that read each publication. After this first step, a list will be needed of the wasted audience, i.e. those not in target audience that will be reached using each of the publications on the list.

> **Example** Publication A is read by 20 per cent of women under 45 with children, but this target audience makes up only 5 per cent of the total number of readers of the publication and therefore 95 per cent of the money spent on buying an advertisement in A is wasted.

The campaign might be aimed at reaching 70 per cent of the target audience, so the next stage is to build up a schedule of publications that when combined will meet this objective. The list might have twenty titles on it before the target is met. A mixture of magazines and newspapers might be needed with the large circulation papers and magazines featuring prominently. The wastage factor will then have to be considered so as to keep within cost-effective budget limits. Another target for the campaign might be that the advertising should be seen a specified average number of times by the target audience. This level of frequency will be determined by the number of times the advertisement needs to be seen to get the message across. To achieve this level the number of publications might have to be extended or the list duplication increased. The NRS data can be used to produce duplication of reading between publications so that the frequency of possible exposure to the advertising can be calculated.

The assumption is made that reading the publication equates to seeing the advertisement. This is clearly not true, but as the publications sell advertising against each other and the same assumption is made for them all, this will not affect the decision-making of those who buy space in publications.

It is in areas such as the amount of the publication read, the time spent reading each title, the attention the reader gives to the publication and even where it is read that are not covered by industry research. Here individual publications do their own research and use the findings to try and give them a competitive selling edge.

Television audience measurement in the 1990s

Television audiences are measured by what are known as 'people meters'. These pieces of electronic gadgetry are wired into television sets, videos and decoders so that they can tell the computer at the research company, daily through the telephone lines, who in the household has been watching what, when and with whom. This is the means by which all countries in the industrialized world now measure television audiences.

Television audience research in the UK is carried out by an industry contract and is paid for jointly by all broadcasters, advertising agencies and some advertisers. The body that awards the contract is BARB (Broadcasters Audience Research Board), which holds the copyright in the data and joint industry ownership of BARB and makes the measurement universally acceptable. A single data source is one of the most important facets of this type of contract.

The audience measurement contract in the UK was awarded to two research companies who started a new contract in August 1991. The contract is split between RSMB and Taylor Nelson AGB.

The process of television audience measurement starts when RSMB carries out a national random sample of households, the 'Establishment Survey'. This is a continuous random survey that carries out interviews with about 38,500 households spread throughout the year. Its purpose is to collect information about the nature of the television-watching universe. It collects demographic details of all the people living in the household, the number of working televisions, the size of each set, which stations it can receive, number of videos, ownership of cable and satellite and estimated weight of viewing to each terrestrial station and, where applicable, cable and satellite.

The Establishment Survey results give the size and nature of the universe for each ITV and BBC area which is the basic geography of local programmes, commercial transmission and therefore the audience measurement. It also determines the proportion of households and each demographic category that will be on the panel in a particular area.

> **Example** 32 per cent of the individuals on the panel in the BBC North West will be living in homes that have non-terrestrial reception; 10.9 per cent of the individuals in panel homes in Northern Ireland will be age 4–9; 31.6 per cent in the South West will be over 55.

The size of the panel in each ITV area is decided by the ITV station so that it can meet its programming and advertising sales needs. The larger the panel, the more the audience data cost the station. Some ITV areas boost the size of their panels to enable them to measure the audiences to different additions of their local programming for use by programme-makers and advertising sales. Others will boost their natural proportional size of the UK population in order to give advertisers information on ratings of small groups such as young housewives or the AB socio-economic men.

After the panel sizes for each area have been decided, the research company will select households from the Establishment Survey interviews to represent the universe. Market research interviewers go out to the selected homes and ask them if they would be prepared to join the BARB panel. They explain what the household will be asked to do.

- A meter will be installed attached to each television set, every video and on cable and satellite decoders.
- All the occupants of the household will have their own handset on which they will have a button to press each time they come into the room when the set is switched on and press it again when they leave the room.

Obviously it is necessary to have the cooperation of all members of the household and as the BARB panels are continuous, people will be required to make a long-term commitment. The households that agree to be on the panel are visited by an engineer who installs all the equipment and gives suitable instruction. After an appropriate length of time the household goes on to the live panel. This does not happen immediately as it takes time for people to get used to pressing the buttons. Starting such a task is likely to make people's habits atypical, at least for a short time.

It all sounds easy, but the proportion of people who agree to join the panel in the first place and those who stay on it for any length of time are a relatively small percentage of those approached. If a first selected home refuses at any stage in the sign-up procedure, then it is necessary to go back to the names and addresses in the Establishment Survey, select a home in the same geographic area, with the same characteristics and start the process all over again. From the engineering stage onwards, the second research company takes over the process and is responsible for the data collection, processing and reporting.

Data collection takes place every night through the telephone lines to which the meter is connected. The times the set is switched on and off, the channels it is tuned to and the people who are present in the room when the set is on are all recorded on the meter and these data are stored throughout the day. The central computer at the research company calls all the homes on the panel every night and downloads the day's viewing. Data are collected from all 4400 homes on the panel and the analysis process is carried out before the start of the next working day.

First thing in the morning, the ratings for the previous day's programming are transmitted to all the television stations and are then disseminated to all the interested parties on both the programming and commercial side. As data are calculated for every minute, it is possible to get actual programme ratings and to have the audience for the minute that a commercial is transmitted by region.

This process produces what is known as the 'overnights', giving accurate audience sizes but only for live viewing. The meter also measures the viewing of recorded material whether it be rented, purchased or recordings off-air. The viewing of 'off-air' recorded material that is watched within a week of transmission is collected to be included in the final ratings published, just over a week after the end of the reporting period.

The overnights are derived from what is known as 'live' viewing and when the recorded viewing is added, the data become 'consolidated'. Here are some examples of the difference between the two sets of data.

Wednesday 13 March 1996

Coronation Street		*How Do They Do That?*	
Live viewing	17.3 million	Live viewing	7.3 million
Recorded viewing	1.4 million	Recorded viewing	0.3 million
Consolidated viewing	18.7 million	Consolidated viewing	7.6 million

Generally, the soaps get the highest level of recorded viewing that is watched in the week immediately after transmission, but drama scheduled against other popular series also has high recorded viewing.

The Top Thirty programmes published each week in the newspapers are based on consolidated viewing. This is taken as the 'Gold Standard' of television audience measurement and is used for trading commercial television air-time. Before looking at how the data are used, it might be helpful to give an explanation of the terms used. Here is a short definition of terms.

TV ratings	This is a percentage. The number of viewers are divided by the number of people in the target audience.
Audience share	If all the people watching any television at a particular time are added together, the share for one programme is its audience divided by all viewers.
Reach	The reach to a series (for example) is the percentage who watched a part of any episode in the

series for at least a predetermined time,
e.g. 15 minutes or half a programme.

The ratings are the standard measure of audience size and can easily be converted into millions. They are an easy method of comparison for audience size but have no more significant meaning.

Audience share tells a more complicated story. It says as much about opposition programming as it does the programme itself. For example, any programme scheduled against *Coronation Street* or *EastEnders* struggles to get high ratings, but the share will say how well it has taken on all the other opposition at the time it goes out.

Series reach is not readily available and needs to be calculated from the raw data. If the reach is high, it could mean that relatively large numbers loyally watched all the programmes or it could indicate that people have tried the series and rejected it, with new audiences coming in for each new programme in the series. The level of reach is also related to the opposition programming so a loyal audience and a low reach could indicate that the programme is successful and could do well in another slot.

How is television audience measurement used?

Within a television transmission company, the areas of interest centre on the relative levels of viewing in particular time slots against other programmes that have been in the same slot and the competitive programming. This information is backed up by an understanding of who the audience is, how loyal it is to the programme and what proportion who start to watch stay with the programme. All this information can be calculated from the raw BARB data. The raw data tapes are made available to subscribers on the ninth day after the end of the transmission week. All the television companies have access to computer systems that allow these analyses to be carried out.

Those buying and selling television advertising look at

- how many ratings have been delivered by the campaign against their target audience
- how many in the target audience have seen at least one transmission of he campaign
- what is the average OTS (Opportunity To See) of the campaign, calculated by taking the ratings points and dividing by the number of people who saw at least one commercial.

Radio audience measurement in the 1990s

Although commercial radio has been in the UK since the early 1970s, it took until the autumn of 1992 for the BBC and independent radio to get together and use the same audience measurement system. This is carried out under the auspices of RAJAR, (Radio Joint Audience Research), owned jointly by the BBC and the Commercial Radio Companies Association (CRCA).

To a specification agreed by all users, including the advertising agencies, RAJAR got tenders for the industry research and awarded the contract to RSL for a period of four years, since extended to the autumn of 1998.

Radio research is carried out by means of weekly diaries which are placed in households the weekend before and collected at the beginning of the week following the one that respondents have been asked to record their listening. An individual diary is left for each household member to complete and where possible the interviewer goes through the instructions as to how to complete the task with everyone in the household. (If the person is not available, the original contact is asked to explain what is required.)

The interviewer is given names and addresses to try as priorities and a back-up list of nearby addresses is provided in case of refusal or non-contact. The sample chosen has to conform to a given quota of age.

The diary consists of a page with the name of stations available in the locality across the top and quarter-hour times down the side. There are pages for every day of the week. The diary asks questions about 'normal' listening behaviour, demographics, and so on. The diary also contains a list of the stations that are printed in the diary and a short description of the kind of output it transmits.

The radio measurement contract recognizes that national and local stations have different data requirements and therefore the contract is split into two different levels of measurement. The first and third quarter, January to March and July to September, consist of about 1000 diaries each week or 12,000 in the twelve-week period. The sample is distributed across the UK in proportion to the population. Because of the relatively low sample measuring a fragmented activity such as radio listening, only national and London stations listening is reported in the first and third quarters each year.

The second and fourth quarters have significantly larger sample sizes as they are designed to measure the listening to BBC and commercial local stations. The sample has to be designed to give each station at least 650 diaries. The UK is split into reception segments, each of which has a separate list of the radio stations that are available. Special diaries are printed for each segment. About 53,000 diaries are completed in each of the large quarters, with slightly more in the spring than the autumn, This is because a few of the very small stations have only one RAJAR measurement each year due to the cost of each wave. The findings from RAJAR are made available only once a quarter, though the data are collected weekly. This means that data can be analysed for shorter periods but for commercial purposes only quarterly information is required.

Radio stations tend to programme by stripping the same output each weekday so it makes sense to show the audiences in this way. This helps the advertiser too as it is easy to know who listens to each strand and buy the appropriate commercials. Radio advertising is purchased in campaigns and it is possible from the RAJAR data to calculate the proportion of people in a target audience that can be reached during a week by a combination of spots on a particular combination of stations.

New commercial radio stations continue to start up and this causes a problem for RAJAR. The diary design used allows for twenty-six station names to be printed on top of the page. Unfortunately in some parts of London the stations that can be listened to already exceeds this number. To cope with this problem (which everyone knew from the start of RAJAR was going to happen) new diary designs were piloted, one chosen for an extensive test and a decision made to change to it in the last quarter of 1996.

The chosen method was a diary with no pre-printed station names. The interviewer asked the respondents to stick all the radio station names that they ever listen to into the diary. This is a relatively complicated operation to explain to respondents, but it is even more difficult for the people in the chosen household that the interviewer did not meet to understand what they were expected to do.

At the end of the first month of the new operation, it was apparent to the research company and the chief executive of RAJAR that there was a steep change in the findings. Much analysis was carried out to try and understand what had caused the differences with the following results.

The average number of stations that people claimed to listen to each week declined when the new diary was used. At the same time the amount of listening increased. Both findings were clearly a result of the changed methodology. The issue that faced the industry was whether the reported steep change in radio listening was acceptable.

Had the changes been equally spread across all stations, the new methodology might have been acceptable. In the event, the decision was made to go back to the original diary for the rest of the existing contract and the already negotiated two-year extension and look for a new technique to deal with the ever-expanding number of radio stations and the arrival of digital radio for the new contract starting in September 1998.

The lesson to be learnt from changing the RAJAR diary is that all alterations to techniques will affect the levels of what is to be measured. The changes are usually unpredictable and therefore things change less in media research than might be expected because a stable currency of measuring audiences, especially for advertising purposes, is thought to be the most important part of an industry media measurement contract.

Qualitative methodologies

Qualitative research looks at what people think of the newspaper/programme/station/presenter and so on. This is done by a number of techniques but the one that is most commonly used at the moment is focus groups. To help explain how these come about an example might be helpful. Let us look at the case of a moderately successful drama series.

The series has about 8 million viewers, is watched more by women than men and appears to have relatively low audience loyalty. Management and the production team would like to have another series and want to know what needs to be done to increase viewing to 10 million.

The decision has been made to conduct some focus groups to find out why viewers watched only one or two programmes and what would encourage more people to watch regularly. The groups must be representative of the whole country as attitudes to programmes vary considerably around the UK. Different age groups need to be covered as well as men and women.

To cover all these variables the decision might be taken to conduct six groups, two in Stirling, two in Sheffield, two in Luton. Three groups would be with men and three with women, split into three age groups, 20–34, 35–49 and 50+. The additional criteria for selection would be if respondents could remember having seen the programme previously or had made a positive decision not to watch it.

The next step is to draw up a discussion guide which lists the issues under investigation. This should take the group leader from some introductory items about television viewing and opinions of drama series in general. The conversation will move to the programme under consideration and clips might be shown as appropriate. The plot, storylines, characters, acting and scheduling will be debated and group members will be asked to give their opinions of what aspects of the programme would need to be changed to make them loyal followers.

The group moderators will take the sound taped material and analyse it to come up with interpretations and recommendations of what they have heard. This will be presented to the client who made the initial inquiry together with anything else that is known about the audience to the series from all other sources such as all analyses available from BARB audience measurement.

One additional source not described yet is the audience-appreciation measurement. This is a BARB service provided by RSL to the broadcasters only. A panel of 3000 people is used to measure television-appreciation scores. Panel members are recruited to complete a weekly diary giving each programme they watch a score out of ten, where ten is high and nil is very low.

The Appreciation Indices (AIs) are provided to all subscribers; where the sample size is large enough, the AIs are produced by age, sex and age within sex.

Together with the viewing diary, a questionnaire is sent to all panel members. This asks specially designed questions about particular programmes, series or issues and the results are private to the broadcaster who asked the questions. The panel members who have access to satellite and cable have an additional task which asks them their appreciation of programming on the largest audience stations and an overall opinion about ones watched less frequently.

Conclusion

This chapter has discussed the various ways in which audiences are measured and how the information is used. Because the users of media are so important to those who own, write, make programmes for and sell advertising in press and broadcasting, an understanding of audiences is crucial to their existence.

Media research supplies those needs and therefore plays an important part in any organization. However, the rating of your programme, the readership of your publication or the reach of your radio station is often the only information to interest senior management.

It is the role of the researcher to explain complicated analyses to their potential users so that there is a wider understanding of subjects like audience flows, why various combinations of publications are read and why radio stations are switched off. As competition for audiences and therefore advertising increases, the role of media research will become ever more important to media organizations.

Questions

1 Why is there a need for research methods to be universally accepted within the media industries? Can you see any drawbacks that arise as a consequence of this need for consensus?

2 In what ways do recent changes in the media have implications for administrative audience research methods?

3 Do media industry research methods 'measure' or 'make' the audience? Make a list of all those factors about the audience that administrative research does not reveal.

Further reading

Ang, I. (1990) *Desperately Seeking the Audience*, London: Routledge.

Blumler, J.G. (1996) 'Recasting the audience in the new television marketplace?', in J. Hay, L. Grossberg and E. Wartella (eds) *The Audience and its Landscape*, Boulder, CO, and Oxford: Westview.

Docherty, D. (1995) 'Cartographies of taste and broadcasting strategies', in J. Palmer and M. Dodson (eds) *Design and Aesthetics: A Reader*, London: Routledge.

Ettema, J.S. and Whitney, D.C. (eds) (1994) *Audiencemaking: How the Media Create the Audience*, London: Sage.

Kent, R. (ed.) (1994) *Measuring Media Audiences*, London: Routledge.

O'Brien, R. and Ford, S. (1988) 'Can we at last say goodbye to social class?', *Journal of the Market Research Society* 30(3): 289–331.

Chapter 19

Effects

MEDIA EFFECTS: THE CONTINUING CONTROVERSY

GUY CUMBERBATCH

One of the most useful volumes yet to be edited in our troubled times would be an encyclopedia of ignorance. What we don't know is probably more important than what we do know – and this is perhaps true in any area of academic enterprise. Perhaps it should be a compulsory final exam paper on every degree course. In mass communications, the tip of the iceberg of knowledge about media effects is probably akin to a pebble on a mountain: the bit underneath is a colossal mass that geologically might turn out to be reasonably representative of the bit above, but might not bear any relationship to it whatsoever. The various possible effects of the enormous diversity of media forms and content have to date been studied only partially with rather clumsy research instruments. The mass media are so deeply embedded in our culture and our lives that disentangling the possible effects on us has proved a frustrating research enterprise.

The most obvious controversies are between various academic disciplines with an additional UK versus USA divide. By and large, media studies tend to reject popular concerns about the harmful effects of the mass media. Psychologists seem inclined to believe that the mass media have harmful effects on society, whereas sociologists tend to the view that the mass media have only served to amplify perceptions of a problem in society. Other disciplines such as criminology and political science tend to ignore the issue, while film, art and literary studies tend to seek out the intrinsic value of media representations and rarely engage in any discussion about media effects.

Misunderstanding media effects

As Geoffrey Pearson (1983, 1984) has pointed out, there has been a long history of moral panics about the possible harmful effects of popular culture, such as penny dreadful comics and amusement houses in the nineteenth century, popular theatre at the turn of the century, followed by cinema, television, comic books again in the 1950s, then video and more recently computer games. However, while each new medium seems to have inherited the legacy of fears and anxieties about earlier media forms, these have not always been eclipsed by new media.

For example the US psychiatrist, Frederic Wertham, was quite generous in his attacks on various mass media. He claimed to have studied adolescents 'who in comic books, movies and TV have seen more than 10,000 homicides' (1954: 20). (See also Sabin on 'Comics', Chapter 2 in this volume.)

The absence of any serious consideration of media effects in much of the literature which might be expected to offer some useful, informed comment is disappointing. After all, popular concern and journalistic interest have probably been vital in the way in which the media have so often taken up the gauntlet and run with a story that the mass media cause harm – an issue that MPs have regularly taken up with some alacrity. The consequence of this is that much legislation surrounding the mass media owes precious little to academic deliberations but to 'intuition' and 'common sense' which have effectively mugged the issues, closing off lines of inquiry and debate which should be at the heart of current concerns. A good example, and an almost perennial one, is the media coverage of violence in society. A particular focus and running story (especially in recent years) has been that film/video violence is an 'obvious' cause of violence in society. Thus controlling film/video violence would, it is often argued, help reduce violence in society. This story gained an unusual momentum in 1993. Early in the year the *Sunday Times* serialized extracts from Michael Medved's book, *Hollywood Versus America* (1993) which is an attack on Hollywood's perceived 'obsession' with violence. Soon after this, various film stars voiced their own concerns about violence in the media. The *Sunday Times* reported these with some satisfaction:

> USA Hollywood Stars Turn their Back on Violence in Films. Clint Eastwood is sickened, Jane Fonda is angry and Richard Dreyfuss has thrown out his television set. Hollywood, accustomed to making a killing out of violence, is experiencing a bout of soul searching which finds expression in Sir Anthony Hopkins' announcement last week that he may not recreate the monstrous role of Dr Hannibal Lecter. Sir Anthony, who won an Oscar for his portrayal of the serial killer in *Silence of the Lambs,* told journalists in Cardiff that he had been alarmed by the success of the horrific film and it might be time to say 'enough is enough'. 'As an actor, I have some responsibility. We have seen some terrible things in Britain recently. It's a terrifying world we live in and I don't want to encourage that through my films'.
>
> (*Sunday Times* 7 March 1993)

Among the 'terrible things' things seen in Britain was the abduction and murder of 2-year-old James Bulger by two 10-year-old boys in February 1993. This abduction had been captured by security cameras in the shopping centre where James disappeared and the child killers were quickly captured. From the outset the whole affair received considerable media attention with clips of the abduction providing the lead story in television and newspaper stories. (See also Palmer on 'News Values', Chapter 27 in this volume.)

The trial was, unusually for such young offenders, a public one providing pages of verbatim copy in all the press. In sentencing the boys to be detained during Her Majesty's pleasure, the judge Mr Justice Moorland commented:

> It is not for me to pass judgement on their upbringing, but I suspect that exposure to violent video films may, in part, be an explanation.
>
> (e.g. *The Independent* 25 November 1993)

It seems clear that many journalists had expected that the trial might produce some 'link' with media violence (a number had contacted me for comment earlier in the year). This link emerged only as a throwaway line at the end of the trial, but it was sufficient to launch major media coverage speculating that violent videos had created two children who were capable of committing an act of 'unparalleled evil and barbarity'. By the following day the witch-hunt for films to blame revealed *Child's Play 3*, which continues the adventures of Chucky, a doll possessed by the evil spirit of a child murderer. In a staged event reminiscent of the execution of witches in medieval times, the popular tabloid the *Sun* organized a public burning of the video, urging readers 'For the sake of ALL our kids, BURN YOUR VIDEO NASTY' (*Sun* 26 November 1993).

Among the 'chilling links' claimed between the film and the murder of James Bulger was the fact that Neil Venables, the father of one of the boys found guilty, had rented the video some weeks before. However, Albert Kirby, who directed the police inquiry, had specifically looked for any possible links and concluded that there were none. Jon Venables was not living with his father at the time and thus the police did not think it possible that he could have seen the film at his father's house. Moreover the boy disliked horror films and was upset by violence in videos – a point confirmed by later psychiatric reports. However, such mundane facts could not be allowed to spoil a good story, or the campaigns calling for a new 'crack down' on video violence.

One of the major players in this was the Liberal MP David Alton, who was convinced that the legislation controlling the supply of videos was ineffective and that children were gaining access to unsuitable and damaging films. With all-party support, he tabled an amendment to the Criminal Justice Bill. This amendment proposed further penalties for trading in uncertificated films and videos, for supplying children with films inappropriate for their age group plus the removal of films which offered 'inappropriate role models' for children or those which could produce 'psychological damage'.

The Home Secretary, Michael Howard, remained unconvinced of the need for such ambiguous and potentially draconian legislation, pointing out that the Video Recordings Act 1984 aready allowed tough fines (such as £20,000 for dealing with uncertificated videos). However, David Alton proved an effective campaigner. He invited a retired professor of child psychology, Elizabeth Newson, to support his case. Her report, *Video Violence and the Protection of Children*, was launched on Good Friday 1 April 1994 via a press release. It became the lead story in almost all newspapers. 'VIDIOTS! At last experts admit: movie nasties DO kill' (*Daily Mirror* 1 April 1994) and ' "Naive" experts admit threat of violent videos' (*Daily Telegraph* 1 April 1994) were typical of the headlines.

Elizabeth Newson's report

Newson's report was a watershed in the long debates about media effects. Speculation that media violence might make people violent was now presented as fact. The Home Secretary reconsidered his position and – in what was widely seen by political commentators as a 'U' turn – essentially adopted David Alton's amendment accepting that psychological harm could be caused by film and video and increasing the penalties laid down by the earlier Video Recordings Act (e.g. 'Howard retreats on "video nasties"' was the lead story in *The Independent* on 12 April 1994).

Newson's report was exceptional in the sympathetic publicity it received. It begins 'Two-year-old James Bulger was brutally and sadistically murdered on 12 February 1993 by two ten-year-old children'. Harrowing details of the murder then set the scene for a different explanation than that the children were simply evil:

> even the most cursory reading of news since then suggests that it is not a 'one-off'. . . . In England, an adolescent girl was tortured by her 'friends' over days using direct quotations from a horror video (*Child's Play 3*) as part of her torment.

The report's success was probably due in no small part to its endorsement by twenty-five 'experts'. However, none of the signatories appear to have published any empirical or indeed clinical findings in the field. Moreover, the report on closer examination mentions only two secondary reviews of media effects and seems largely inspired by Michael Medved's book, *Hollywood Versus America*.

The focus of the report is provided by newspaper clippings (most from the *Nottingham Evening Post*) dealing with the Bulger murder and other cases of violence by young people which, it is argued, show that things have changed and this must be due to the easy availability of videos containing graphic violence. More than one-third of the report seems to be based entirely on press clippings. There would seem little doubt that Newson sincerely believes that film and video can be harmful to children. The issue is simply this: why does she believe so? Apparently it does not come from studying the effects of the media on children. Perhaps the most obvious clue is given in her evidence to the House of Commons Home Affairs Select Committee on Video Violence. In this Newson was asked to explain the links between video violence and real world violence.

Professor Newson: The Suzanne Capper case is another example of very explicit imitation of video and the use of a video and that was *Child's Play 3*.

Sir Ivan Lawrence (chair): We were told this morning that that had been looked into and the Earl Ferries in the House of Lords has denied – I have not got the evidence we heard this morning – that there was a basis in the Capper case of *Child's Play 3*.

Professor Newson: The soundtrack was actually played.

Sir Ivan Lawrence (chair): Can I read from an analysis of this from Mr Ferman of the British Board of Film Classification of course. What was played to her was a rock version of the music from the first *Child's Play* film recorded on Manchester Piccadilly Pop Radio Station. That is all – music not video?

Professor Newson: In that case it depends. That has been widely reported in that case.

Sir Ivan Lawrence (chair): Yes, it has.

Professor Newson: That would depend on whether that particular girl had seen that film and whether she was able to identify the film from the music.

Sir Ivan Lawrence (chair): There were no videos in the houses that this young lady was held in, apparently. That was the evidence. However let us not argue about it.

(Home Affairs Committee, *Fourth Report*, 1994: 12)

This exchange perhaps identifies one important issue in media effects: that even retired professors who should be experienced in evaluating evidential claims may slip into uncritical acceptance of media stories – especially when they are stories that appear to prove their point.

It might well be argued that one of the main goals of academic study is that we should learn to discriminate sources of knowledge in terms of various criteria such as internal validity, logic, reliability of sources and so on. Professor Newson's report provides illusory evidence of expert knowledge. Her description of the Bulger murder as carried out with the 'expectation and satisfaction of deliberate and sustained violence' turns out to be no more than a reading of press coverage of the trial but implies a (false) familiarity with the case as does her (later) use of the name 'Jamie'.

The Newson report raises many issues of concern. Not the least of these is the role of academics in supporting pressure groups, especially when they enter territories outside their own expertise. However, the Newson report was not an original academic study, but a compilation commissioned by the government to advise on policy.

Perspectives on effects

As suggested by the above case history, media coverage of media effects has largely focused on the harmful effects of video/film/television violence. Our analyses of the media violence debate using both manual and electronic searches of press coverage (such as Textline) indicate that well over

80 per cent of stories (and considerably more news space) is devoted to concerns that media violence is bad/harmful. Most are quite vague about the perceived problem but stories which challenge the harm thesis received scant mention – such as a study by Hagell and Newburn (1994) at the Policy Studies Institute which concluded that delinquents have little interest in film and video, despite being released only the week after Newson's report.

Ironically criminology textbooks rarely mention the role of the mass media. In 1989 we examined 159 criminology textbooks in three university libraries searching for references to the mass media/television/film/cinema/video (Cumberbatch and Brown 1989). Surprisingly, only 5 per cent mentioned the mass media as a potential influence on criminal behaviour. On the other hand, nearly one-half (48 per cent) of the social psychology textbooks in these libraries mentioned the mass media and most popularly concluded that they were an important factor in aggression, delinquency or criminality.

It would be interesting to trawl other textbooks to gauge the level of debate in various disciplines but clearly psychology resonates well with media coverage and indeed has contributed much to the public debate on concerns about media effects. How have psychologists contributed to the debate about media effects?

Imitation

In the early 1960s a psychologist, Albert Bandura, at Stanford University, California, demonstrated that children exposed to a film clip of someone (a model) reacting aggressively towards a large plastic Bobo doll were more likely to play in a similarly aggressive manner than a control group of children who had not seen the film (see Bandura 1994). This research has become a classic – one of the most cited in psychology textbook reviews. Bandura became convinced that violence on television would lead to children imitating what they saw and soon became involved in campaigns against violence on television.

Bandura's experiments were certainly impressive in the results obtained. Up to 88 per cent of the children imitated the aggressive acts which they had seen 'on television' (e.g. Bandura 1994). Case established? James Ferman has for more than a quarter of a century been the director of the British Board of Film Censors (now Film Classification). Whenever some crime occurs where claims are made that it is linked to film/video violence he investigates. Does he think that there are cases – as routinely reported in the mass media – of such imitation? (After all Michael Ryan, who murdered sixteen people in Hungerford, apparently imitated Rambo in *First Blood*, in addition to the cases mentioned in the Newson report.) James Ferman was asked this question by the Home Affairs Select Committee in 1994. He replied:

> I do not know of particular cases where somebody has imitated a video and gone out and actually committed a serious crime as a result of what they have seen.
>
> (Home Affairs Committee, *Fourth Report* 1994: 5)

Similar conclusions were reached in 1988 by Kate Adie and her team, who researched six cases where a crime had been 'linked' to the mass media for a special edition of the BBC current affairs flagship programme *Panorama*.

None of the cases, including the massacre in Hungerford, was supported by the evidence. This is perhaps surprising when media audiences are so massive. At their peak, audiences for a James Bond film on television have been around 18 million viewers, while contemporary audiences for a show such as *Cracker* can be 15 million viewers. In the video rental business 1994 statistics reveal that 15 million people saw *Lethal Weapon 3*; nearly 11 million watched *The Hand that Rocks the Cradle* and over 9 million enjoyed *Cape Fear*. There must be little doubt that with the closure of so many psychiatric hospitals and 'care in the community', there must be a fair number of disturbed individuals at large who might be 'influenced' by such films. The absence of convincing evidence for such influence seems remarkable.

Perhaps one of the best known cases where the defence claim was that television had made someone violent was that of 15-year-old Ronnie Zamora, who carried out the apparently pointless murder of his 82-year-old neighbour in Miami, Florida. His attorney, Ellis Rubin, claimed 'subliminal television intoxication' while one expert witness, psychiatrist Albert Jaslow, thought that television had 'blunted his awareness and his capacity to understand his actions' and another expert witness, psychologist Margaret Hanratty Thomas, argued that television violence had 'unbalanced' the boy. The public trial lasting ten days attracted larger television audiences than the popular Johnny Carson show. Central to the argument was Zamora's fascination with Kojak, whom he so admired that he asked his father to shave his head to look like the detective. Perhaps the real flaw in the defence case was that Kojak is a good guy on the side of law and order. The jury were unimpressed by Rubin's defence and found Zamora guilty as charged (see e.g. Fowles 1992).

Despite all of the above, persistent claims have been made for the 'Werther effect', so called after the novel by Goethe (1774) *The Sorrows of Young Werther* which, it was claimed, had led to a number of young people committing suicide in imitation of the hero. The most prolific support for this phenomenon has been Phillips (e.g. 1983). He examined the daily fluctuations in homicide rates in the USA and concluded that these increased (by approximately twelve homicides) following heavyweight boxing championships. Phillips claims a vast range of mediated events produces similar 'contagion' (he does not claim to understand the processes involved). These include publicized suicides, public executions and murder stories.

This research has been controversial. Baron and Reiss (1985) invented (fictitious) dates of prize fights and found similar 'effects'. Thus the effects noted by Phillips may not be reliable and in any case we cannot know whether simply hearing about the fights or even attending them could be a factor (see also Platt 1987 on Angie's drug overdosing on *EastEnders*).

Arousal processes

Perhaps the strongest claims for harmful media effects have come from the experiments conducted from the early 1960s by Leonard Berkowitz in the psychology laboratories at Wisconsin University (Berkowitz 1993). Although the experimental designs evolved over time and his theoretical position became more sophisticated, essentially the studies involved showing either violent or neutral film clips to university students who were then given the opportunity to give electric shocks to someone (who was a confederate of the experimenter and did not actually receive the shocks). Half of the participants were 'anger aroused' by the confederate insulting the participants and half were treated neutrally. Berkowitz concluded that violent film clips produced more aggressive behaviour (i.e. electric shocks) in those who were angry, especially when the violence in the film was justified. While these studies are often cited, Zillman (Bryant and Zillman 1994) has questioned whether the results are due to the violence *per se* in the film clips. He compared responses after a violent film (*The Wild Bunch*) with those to a neutral film (*Marco Polo's Travels*) with a no-film control group. Physiological measures of the participants revealed that the neutral film actually depressed arousal compared with the no-film condition. There were no differences between the no-film and the violent film group in the willingness of participants to deliver electric shocks to a victim.

Rather similar conclusions were reached by Gadow and Sprafkin (1993) in a review of twenty naturalistic field experiments where children were exposed to various film clips or television programmes. They note that while aggressive film clips often produced elevated levels of antisocial behaviour, sometimes the control film produced even more. Even fast paced pro-social/educational programmes produced more aggressive responses in the children.

Although laboratory experiments have featured in many reviews, their popularity has declined in recent years largely due to a concern that they measure only short-term effects, have low ecological validity and may tell us little about how viewers behave in the real world.

Impacts and influences

Social science research has a long history in exploring media effects. Perhaps the most notable of early studies were those by the Payne Fund which was set up in New York in 1928 to study the impact and influences of motion pictures on youth. This produced a series of twelve independent studies published in several volumes with a summary volume written by Charters (1933). The overall conclusions were that despite some public anxiety about the new medium, any influences were fairly modest and superficial in such things as fashion rather than on morals. The researchers were unwilling to attribute criminal delinquency to film-going. UNESCO (1961) noted that in early media research, the cinema provided the focus and European studies predominated, but the emphasis rapidly shifted to North America and to television (UNESCO 1964).

Somewhat similar conclusions were reached in Britain in 1951 by the Departmental Committee on Children and the Cinema (the Wheare Committee) which sponsored a large survey of all juvenile offenders appearing before the courts over a six-month period. This produced an impressive sample of 38,000 young offenders. The committee considered that perhaps in 141 of these (0.4 per cent) cases the offending behaviour might be related to cinema attendance (Home Office 1951).

The most broadly based studies of media effects were carried out as television was being introduced to the UK (Himmelweit *et al.* 1958) and the USA (Schramm *et al.* 1961). Both studies were able to compare areas which had received television with areas which were still waiting for the new medium. They make fascinating reading especially in how people found the time to accommodate television. Himmelweit introduced the concept of 'functional similarity' to explain why some activities declined (like cinema attendance and comic-book reading) but left others untouched (such as teenage social activities and sports). However, the bulk of the time found for television seems to be drawn from time-wasting activities (like watching raindrops run down a window-pane). Essentially similar conclusions have been reached about computer-game playing by young people (Cumberbatch *et al.* 1993).

In terms of harmful effects neither study produced much by way of support for popular concerns but the measures taken of aggression were fairly perfunctory. Schramm *et al.*'s conclusion was a classic in circumspection:

> For some children under some conditions, some television is harmful. For other children under the same conditions, or for the same children under other conditions, it may be beneficial. For most children under most conditions television is probably neither harmful nor particularly beneficial.
>
> (Schramm *et al.* 1961: 13)

Over the decades since these pioneering studies the research picture has not changed much in that any effects reported have been the subject of considerable controversy. Perhaps the most confident claim (e.g. Comstock and Paik 1991; Newson 1994) has always been that media violence aggravates violence in society. However, understanding this one issue has proved illusory and the reasons for this are generic and serve to undermine other claims for media effects.

The most cited of recent research is that by Huesmann and Eron (1986), who orchestrated cross-national comparisons in Australia, Finland, the Netherlands, Israel, Poland and the USA of the long-term effects of exposure to television. These built on earlier research by Eron and Huesmann who had measured aggression and television violence exposure in children aged 8–9 and again ten years later. They claimed a 'Rip Van Winkle' or sleeper effect where early television viewing predicted later aggression. However, while this may be true of one of their measures of aggression in boys, two other measures did not support the hypothesis while none of the measures was significant in the sample of girls. Similar strong claims were made for their more modest cross-national study.

The Dutch researchers, who drew different conclusions from other members of the research team, refused to allow their results to be included in Huesmann and Eron's book and published their findings elsewhere (Wiegman *et al.* 1992). In Australia there were no significant correlations between early television violence viewing and later aggression. In the USA after controlling for initial aggression, the relationship between early violence viewing and later aggression was significant only in girls. In Israel significant effects were found in the city samples but not in the Kibbutz samples. In Poland while the authors recognize the housestyle of the book and concur that 'a greater preference for violence viewing was predictive of greater aggression', they conclude 'nevertheless the effects are not large and must be treated cautiously'.

The Finnish researchers were more confident: 'our study in Finland can be taken to corroborate the previously obtained results that the amount of aggressive behavior in children is related to their viewing of violence on TV'. However, it is apparent from the full report (Viemero 1986) that this relationship is actually negative (−0.324). In other words, the more children watched violent television, the less aggressive they were later!

Understanding media effects

Closer examination of the vast research literature on media effects reveals a consistent tendency to gloss over inconvenient detail to salvage a media harm thesis. For each strong claim there is an abundance of dissenting data. Even the most obvious fact that children are now spending their time watching television and not reading has been hotly disputed. Neuman (1995) for example points out that survey data over decades indicate that children's reading has remained essentially unchanged since before television. It is true that those who watch a lot of television read less than those who watch little but this seems to reflect existing differences between people (such as social class) rather than an effect of television (see Williams 1986). Of course television might have all manner of effects on society and anxieties about these have certainly been fuelled by analyses of media content.

It must be a matter of some concern that there is so much to criticize from the under-representation of minority groups – including women – to the lack of good news. But to argue that media images distort viewers' perceptions is more a good hypothesis than a demonstrated phenomenon. Some findings in the field of media effects point to viewers being singularly attracted to the mass media as a source of entertainment but stubbornly resistant to their influence. Other evidence suggests that audiences are influenced in some areas, but there is no proved causal link between representations of violence on television and violent behaviour.

Questions

1 It would be interesting to know what people remember about media stories where effects have been claimed. This could be usefully done in a focus group discussion with perhaps six people. What stories do they remember, e.g. the Bulger case? What sources do they remember?

2 Some insight into media effects might be obtained from considering how the mass media may have influenced you personally. Again this topic could be a suitable one for group discussion. What about fashions, attitudes, values or fantasies?

3 A popular complaint by some pressure groups is that there is too much violence on television. Go through a week's television programme listings to categorize programmes in terms of whether they are likely to contain 'violence' or not. What kinds of programmes are most likely to contain violence (e.g. UK, Australian, US production; ones where the forces of law and order triumph, and so on)?

References

Bandura, A. (1994) 'Social cognitive theory of mass communication', in J. Bryant and D. Zillman (eds) *Media Effects: Advances in Theory and Research*, Hillsdale, NJ: Lawrence Erlbaum.

Baron, J.M. and Reiss, P.S. (1985) 'Same time next year: aggregate analyses of the mass media and video behavior', *American Sociological Review* 50: 347–63.

Berkowitz, L. (1993) *Aggression: Its Causes, Consequences and Control*, New York: McGraw-Hill.

Bryant, J. and Zillman, D. (eds) (1994) *Media Effects: Advances in Theory and Research*. Hillsdale, NJ: Lawrence Erlbaum.

Charters, W.W. (1933) *Motion Pictures and Youth: A Summary*, New York: Macmillan.

Comstock, G. and Paik, H. (1991) *Television and the American Child*, San Diego, CA: Academic Press.

Cumberbatch, G. and Brown, B. (1989) *Violence to Television*, paper presented at the annual conference of the Social Psychology section of the British Psychological Society, University of Bristol.

Cumberbatch, G., Maguire, A. and Woods, S. (1993) *Children and Video Games: An Exploratory Study*, Worcester, UK: European and Leisure Software Producers Association.

Fowles, J. (1992) *Why Viewers Watch: A Reappraisal of Television's Effects*, Newbury Park, CA: Sage.

Gadow, K.D. and Sprafkin, J. (1993) 'Television violence and children with emotional and behavioral disorders', *Journal of Emotional and Behavioral Disorders* 1(1): 54–63.

Hagell, A. and Newburn, T. (1994) *Young Offenders and the Media*, London: Batsford.

Himmelweit, H.T., Oppenheim, A.N. and Vince, P. (1958) *Television and the Child: An Empirical Study of the Effect of Television on the Young*, London: Oxford University Press.

Huesmann, L.R. and Eron, L.D. (eds) (1986) *Television and the Aggressive Child: A Cross-National Comparison*, Hillsdale, NJ: Lawrence Erlbaum.

Medved, M. (1993) *Hollywood Versus America: Popular Culture and the War on Traditional Values*, London: HarperCollins.

Neuman, S.B. (1995) *Literacy in the Television Age: the Myth of the TV effect*, Norwood, New Jersey: Ablex.

Newson, E. (1994) 'Video violence and the protection of children', *Journal of Mental Health*, 3, 221–6.

Pearson, G. (1983) *Hooligan: A History of Respectable Fears*, London: Macmillan.

Pearson, G. (1984) 'Falling standards: a short sharp history of moral decline', in M. Barker (ed.) *The Video Nasties: Freedom and Censorship in the Media*, London: Pluto.

Phillips, D.P. (1983) 'The impact of mass media violence on US homicides', *American Sociological Review* 48: 560–8.

Platt, S. (1987) 'The aftermath of Angie's overdoses: soap (opera) damaging your health?', *British Medical Journal* 294: 954–7.

Schramm, W., Lyle, L. and Parker, E.B. (1961) *Television in the Lives of our Children*, Stanford, CA: Stanford University Press.

UNESCO (1961) *The Influence of Cinema on Children and Adolescents*, Paris: UNESCO.

UNESCO (1964) *The Effects of Television on Children and Adolescents*, Paris: UNESCO.

Viemero, V. (1986) *Relationship between Filmed Violence and Aggression*, Turkin, Finland: Reports from the Psychology Department at Abo Akademi, Monograph Supplement 4.

Wertham, F. (1954) *The Seduction of the Innocent*, New York: Rinehart.

Wiegman, O., Kuttschreuter, M. and Barda, B. (1992) 'A longitudinal study of the effects of television viewing on aggressive and pro-social behaviours', *British Journal of Social Psychology*, 31, 147–64.

Williams, T.M. (1986) *The Impact of Television: A Natural Experiment in Three Communities*, New York: Academic Press.

Further reading

Cashmore, E. (1994) *And There Was Television*, London: Routledge.

Comstock, G. and Paik, H. (1991) *Television and the American Child*, San Diego, CA: Academic Press.

Cumberbatch, G. and Howitt, D. (1989) *A Measure of Uncertainty: The Effects of the Mass Media*, London and Paris: John Libbey.

Gauntlett, D. (1995) *Moving Experiences: Understanding Television's Influences and Effects*, London and Paris: John Libbey.

Zillmann, D. (1991) 'Television viewing and physiological arousal', in J. Bryant and D. Zillmann (eds) *Responding to the Screen: Reception and Reaction Processes*, Hillsdale, NJ: Lawrence Erlbaum.

Part III

In the media

Introduction to 'In the Media'

ADAM BRIGGS AND PAUL COBLEY

Part III conceives of the media as a set of 'representations'. Whereas Parts I and II ('What are the Media', ' "Outside" the Media') dealt with the media as a collection of institutions, economic entities and determined practices, Part III looks at the media as an ensemble of texts. These texts are import-ant as a result of their ubiquity and because there is widespread belief that they contribute to the production of our 'common sense' understandings of the world. As such, media texts are thought to affect, in a very real sense, the way in which we understand ourselves/others and the way we lead our lives.

This is a different approach to media 'effects' than those 'scientific' stud-ies which create so much controversy and were analysed by Guy Cumberbatch in Chapter 19 in this volume. The 'effects thesis' often serves to swamp more subtle understandings of how media representations contribute to our *shared* systems of belief and are related to the power relations of our cultures. The chapters in Part III all work from the assumption that repres-entations at least partially construct the social fabric of people's lives. The reason that *re*presentations are considered such an important issue is that they do not entail a straightforward *presentation* of the world and the rela-tionships between people in it. As one commentator has noted,

> Representation is a very different notion from that of reflection. It implies the active work of selecting, and presenting, of structuring and shaping: not merely the transmitting of already existing meaning, but the more active labour of *making things mean*.
>
> (Hall 1982)

Moreover, not only are representations thought to be a flawed and limited 'reflection' but also they are considered to be a 'cause' of our social rela-tions. One way in which this is signalled in the chapters is by the recurrent use of the term 'ideology', a term which has been the subject of some debate in numerous fields and, consequently, carries a range of differ-ent (and contested) meanings (Eagleton 1991; Larrain 1979; Strinati 1995;

Thompson 1984). It is worth considering some of the general ways in which ideology has been conceptualized. This will help you to develop a working knowledge of its applications, implications and limitations.

The influential British theorist, Raymond Williams (1977), identifies 'three common versions of the concept':

(i) a system of beliefs characteristic of a particular class or group.
(ii) a system of illusory beliefs – false ideas or false consciousness – which can be contrasted with true or scientific knowledge.
(iii) the general process of the production of meanings or ideas.

(Williams 1977)

Ideology can also be understood as

- Sets of ideas which give some account of the social world, usually a partial and selective one.
- The relationship of these ideas or values to the way power is distributed socially.
- The way that such values are usually posed as 'natural' and 'obvious' rather than socially aligned.

(Branston and Stafford 1996)

As you will notice, all of the above formulations treat ideology as existing in the realm of 'ideas' and 'values'. It is this concept of 'ideology as ideas and values' which highlights the connection with the term 'representation'.

Representation – as the 'active labour of *making things mean*' – necessarily embraces ideas and values. As such, representations are ideological. However, ideology operates beyond the realm of representation; it does so by occupying the space of people's concrete experience, donating a sense of coherence, consistency and 'naturalness' to our lived existence. Ideology, it is argued, functions to 'naturalize' our actual modes of living and working. In so doing, it serves to perpetuate and extend existing power relations which may serve the interests of some at the expense of others (for example, in the classic Marxist version of this formulation, ideology advances the capitalist bourgeoisie at the expense of the proletarian workers – see Marx and Engels 1970).

Ideology, therefore, frequently attempts to make that which is historically and culturally determined not only *appear to be*, but *also be experienced as*, the product of 'human nature'. Yet, it is important to stress, as Terry Eagleton does, that ideology cannot simply be equated with 'falsity' alone:

> Much of what ideologies say is true, and would be ineffectual if it were not; but ideologies also contain a good many propositions which are flagrantly false, and do so less because of some inherent quality than because of the distortions into which they are commonly forced in their attempts to ratify and legitimate unjust, oppressive political systems.
>
> (Eagleton 1991: 222)

The emphasis given to ideology in Part III, however, is less to do with the unjust and oppressive political systems *per se*, than with the manner in which ideology underpins and endows with meaning the constituent components of our identities and what these entail: i.e. what it is to 'belong' to a particular nation, social class, age group; 'race', gender, sexuality, (dis)able(d) group, and so on. As such, ideology precedes media representations but it also charges them with the task of disseminating nutshell versions of the complex configurations of our identities. Media representations reduce, shrink, condense and select/reject aspects of intricate social relations in order to *re*present them as fixed, 'natural', 'obvious' and ready to consume. In brief, media representations as the bearers of ideology (sometimes necessarily) trade in *stereotypes*; thus, ideology, for instance, tells us through representations who should change the baby's nappy.

But it is misleading to talk of just one ideology; there are, in fact, many possible competing ideolog*ies*. Different ideologies of childcare might promote nappy-changing as a practice that is not the responsibility of just one gender. Representations, too, are subject to the same kind of contestation. Because they often offer stereotypes, many representations conflict with our own experiences and ideologies. In fact, representations in general can be considered to be ideological because the very processes of selection and condensation serve not only to stereotype but also to *exclude* many features and ways of understanding the social world. The ideological nature of selection/condensation means that ideology is materialized in all manner of representations where selection/condensation occurs, for example, sport, 'news', pornography, and so on.

As we have noted, ideology has been the focus of heated debate. One reason is that, in its very definition, ideology is opposed to some notion of essential 'truth' or fixed 'reality' (Foucault 1980: 118); it is argued that ideology acts to prevent humans from apprehending the 'real', 'objective', social conditions of life. But *if* there are some that can unmask the workings of ideology and recognize 'objective' conditions, and some that cannot, on what basis do the former claim privileged access to 'truth'? Can ideology be understood as the means of reproducing the conditions by which inequitable distributions of wealth and power in society are maintained? Is it correct to assume that the vast majority of us fail to recognize the ideological nature of representation? Is it, alternatively, the case that we do recognize this even if we may not use the word 'ideology'? Does the recognition of ideology within representations indicate that one has moved beyond ideology (to 'truth') or that one is simply operating from a different ideological position? Is it possible that everything is ideological, through and through?

Given this list of questions (and there are many others), ideology is clearly a very problematic concept. Since the 1980s, the concept of ideology has been complemented (as you will see in this part's contributions), absorbed or replaced by the term 'discourse', a slippery concept with numerous definitions (see Abercrombie *et al.* 1988; Fairclough 1992; Hawthorn 1994: 49–51; MacCabe 1979; Macdonell 1986). The chief reason for this substitution is that the notion of ideology as separate from – and *preceding* – the act of representation while nevertheless still playing an influential role in it, runs into difficulties. It implies that representations disseminate an ideology which, supposedly, has an independent existence. The term 'discourse', on the other hand, suggests that the very act of communicating about the world should be the focus of any investigation into the workings of representation. It suggests that referring to the world is also 'making' the world about which it is possible to refer. 'Discourse', as it is used here, can be defined as 'A way of constructing meanings which influences and organizes both our actions and our conceptions of ourselves' (Hall 1992: 292–3). In this formulation, the very act of communicating actually *produces* the objects about which one can have an ideological understanding.

Many of the contributions in Part III concern representations of specific components of our identities (e.g. age, sexuality, gender). The status of representations as discourse allows us to think of them not just as representing or contributing to pre-existing categories but actually creating the parameters of those categories. Such categories are the shorthand means of labelling deeply felt aspects of our identities – whether we are 'straight', 'gay', 'polysexual', 'perverted', 'middle class', 'English', 'Scottish', 'Jamaican', 'Black British', 'old', 'middle-aged', 'young', 'teenaged', 'male', 'female', 'transsexual', etc. Representations not only promote and circulate an understanding of these and other categories, but also can often generate them. The concept of discourse enables an understanding of representation as creating and giving meaning to the significant differences between people.

It is worth remembering that such classification of identities and differences is invariably the basis of *power relations*. Media representations not only act to tell 'other people' about 'us', but also tell us about other people. And tell us what it means to be ourselves: for instance, what it means to be – what is appropriate behaviour for – the category 'man'. Representations therefore play out the repertoire of some identities extensively (e.g. what it is to be heterosexual or able-bodied or middle-class); conversely, they play out of the repertoire of others in a very limited way (e.g. what it is to be lesbian or disabled or upper-class).

The theory of ideology, then, takes communication or representation as a 'vehicle' for transmitting ideologies in the service of maintaining/extending power relations. 'Discourse', on the other hand, conceives the act of representation *itself* as the very stuff of power relations. Rather than carrying ideology in the content of a representation, 'discourse' indicates that the mere fact of representation shapes our relations to the world, ourselves and others. This argument holds that there is nothing 'outside' a given 'discourse' – no 'reality' as such – except other 'discourses'. Power struggles do not therefore take place between different components of the social world, each of which exist as 'naturally' preconstituted entities. 'Black', defined as a feature of nature such as 'skin colour' or 'natural rhythm', cannot simply be opposed to 'White' as 'Nordic' and lacking rhythm. Something like 'natural rhythm' is a discursively constructed quality.

Power struggles take place, then, in the competition between and within different discourses. These power struggles take place in two ways. First, by challenging the stereotypes that are often a result of certain categories (e.g. race, class, gender) but retaining the idea that these categories are definitive of the person to whom they are applied. Second, power struggles can take place by questioning the validity of categories as being definitive. For example, the statements 'Black is beautiful', 'Welsh is wonderful', 'Gay is great', while challenging pejorative versions of Blackness/Welshness/Gayness, do not abandon the categories themselves, whereas statements such as 'I cannot be defined by my "race"/"nationality"/"sexuality"' do. As such, the latter statements recognize that it is not enough to argue *within* a particular discourse about a category. They imply that *all* categories are discursively constructed and that they compete to define the person.

A person does not exist, for example, as a member of a specific 'racial' identity as if 'race' was a quantifiable biological category inherent in him/her from the moment of birth; there have to be discourses of 'race', operating on many different levels, which 'constitute' him/her as belonging to a 'racial' identity. To begin with, a discourse of 'race' has to identify the following:

- the person's own 'racial' identity (e.g. 'White')
- other 'racial' identities to which that person's 'racial' identity can be opposed in a power relationship (e.g. 'Black' vs 'White')
- a discourse that asserts the centrality of race as a defining feature of a person's identity (e.g. racism)
- other (non-'racial') identities to which that person's 'racial' identity can be opposed/complemented in a power relationship (e.g. 'race' may be outweighed by 'gender').

In addition. 'race' may feature in other prominent discourses which, in turn, contribute to the idea of a 'racial' identity; for example, the discourses of biology, law, media studies, sociology, criminology, demography, sport, music, and so on.

So 'race', in this way of understanding it, is not a simple biological given, nor is it an ideology that precedes the act of communication. Instead it is constructed in and through the working of discourse. Moreover, it is not the only constituent of a person's discursively constituted identity. In this theory a Black Male Liverpudlian Catholic from a working-class background who works in a managerial position and is heterosexual cannot simply be defined in relation to 'race'. He is a participant in the *competing* and, sometimes, *complementary* discourses of 'race', ethnicity, gender, region, religion, social class, occupation and sexuality (at least). Some of these discourses, in different combinations, will be to the fore at some moments and others, in other combinations, will be to the fore at different moments (Hall 1992; Rutherford 1990).

The emphases which we have taken in this introduction will be found reflected especially in those chapters that deal with specific facets of our identities. Equally, in those chapters that are not directly concerned with identities – those on news representations, sport and pornography – there is a focus on the manner in which representation may contribute to a shaping of the many categorizations we use in the world of discourse.

References

Abercrombie, N., Hill, S. and Turner, B. (eds) (1988) *Penguin Dictionary of Sociology*, 2nd edn, Harmondsworth: Penguin.

Branston, G. and Stafford, R. (1996) *The Media Student's Book*, London: Routledge.

Eagleton, T. (1991) *Ideology: An Introduction*, London: Verso.

Fairclough, N. (1992) *Discourse and Social Change*, Oxford: Polity.

Foucault, M. (1980) 'Truth and power', in C. Gordon (ed.) *Power/Knowledge: Selected Interviews and Other Writings, 1972–1977*, New York: Harvester.

Hall, S. (1982) 'The rediscovery of ideology: the return of the repressed in media study', in M. Gurevitch, J. Curran, T. Bennett, and J. Woollacott (eds) *Culture, Society and the Media*, London: Methuen.

Hall, S. (1992) 'The question of cultural identity', in S. Hall, D. Held and T. McGrew (eds) *Modernity and Its Futures*, Milton Keynes, Cambridge and Oxford: Open University Press, Blackwell and Polity.

Hawthorn, J. (1994) *A Concise Glossary of Contemporary Literary Theory*, 2nd edn, London: Edward Arnold.

Larrain, J. (1979) *The Concept of Ideology*, London: Hutchinson.

MacCabe, C. (1979) 'On discourse', *Economy and Society* 8(4): 279–307.

Macdonell, D. (1986) *Theories of Discourse: An Introduction*, Oxford: Blackwell.

Marx, K. and Engels, F. (1970) *The German Ideology*, ed. C.J. Arthur, London: Lawrence & Wishart.

Rutherford, J. (ed.) (1990) *Identity: Community, Culture, Difference*, London: Lawrence & Wishart.

Strinati, D. (1995) *An Introduction to Theories of Popular Culture*, London: Routledge.

Thompson, J.B. (1984) *Studies in the Theory of Ideology*, Cambridge: Polity.

Williams, R. (1977) *Marxism and Literature*, Oxford: Oxford University Press.

Chapter 20

Sexuality

TRACING DESIRES: SEXUALITY AND MEDIA TEXTS

ANDY MEDHURST

How we are seen determines in part how we are treated;
how we treat others is based on how we see them;
such seeing comes from representation.

(Dyer 1993: 1)

An invisible identity

Analysing media representations of sexuality involves many of the same issues, concepts and processes as the analysis of any other form of identity – issues of power and politics, concepts like stereotyping and ideology, processes of production and consumption. There is one crucial difference, however, when sexuality is the focus of study, a difference that complicates Richard Dyer's claim quoted above that the politics of representation is based on the power-relations of 'seeing', and that is the fact that sexuality is one of the most invisible of cultural identities. If (heaven forbid) there was a photograph of me accompanying this chapter, you would see that I am white and male, but you would not be able to know about my sexuality. You might make assumptions, based on whatever preconceptions you carry about how visual codings might be taken as signs of certain sexual identities, but you could not know for sure. The only way to be sure would be for me to declare myself, to say 'I am a homosexual'. Like I just have.

Making that kind of statement might strike you as unnecessarily personal, hardly in keeping with the dispassionate tone often expected in academic writing, but making it has three benefits as far as I am concerned. First, it helps me to establish, concisely and directly, the point that sexuality is not visually evident in the way that other identities like gender and ethnicity almost always are. Second, it lets you know that I have a particular stake in and a particular take on debates around the representation of sexuality, which is important because representation is a battlefield on which none of us can be neutral. Third, it enables me to go on and say that I do not see a statement of my sexuality as a personal issue, since it is my conviction, and the conviction of those theorists and critics who have addressed this topic, that sexuality is not only a matter of personal desires but also a site of political conflicts. Perhaps that sounds odd, since we are culturally encouraged to think of sexuality as something intrinsic, inner, concerned with deeply private emotional investments, but emotions are not devoid of social contexts and desires exist only within ideological frameworks – and one of the most important of those ideological frameworks is the sphere of media representations. Daily, endlessly, media texts and discourses endorse certain sexual options while stigmatizing others.

There is already a contradiction here. If sexuality is invisible, how can it be identified in order for those ideological judgements to proceed? That question is all the more pressing once we realize that not only is sexuality invisible, but also it is multiple, unstable and fluid. Heterosexuality and homosexuality are not the only players in the game, though they tend to receive most of the attention. What about bisexuals, transgendered people, or people who move between sexual identities at different stages in their lives? Even within the category of homosexuality, there are enormous differences between individuals placed in that category – what on earth could a working-class teenage Asian lesbian have in common with a wealthy middle-aged gay Scotsman? Furthermore, there have been many disputes among people who belong to sexual minorities over what label they should choose to identify themselves – homosexual, lesbian, gay, lesbian-and-gay, dyke, queer. These are important questions, which a fully nuanced account of this topic would have to take into account, but this chapter will have to rely on simplifications and generalizations. That is not entirely inappropriate, since the prevailing media representations of sexuality available to us depend precisely on simplified and generalized versions of the multiple complexities of lived experience. After all, simplifying and generalizing are what ideology is all about. (The amount of literature covering the questions raised in this paragraph is intimidatingly vast, but here are some good starting points. On the diversity of lesbian and gay identities and lifestyles, see Ainley (1995), National Lesbian and Gay Survey (1993) and Plummer (1992). For bisexuality see Rose *et al.* (1996). For transgender see Prosser (1997) and Stone (1991). For the controversies surrounding the term 'queer', see Smyth (1992) and Warner (1993).)

Stereotypes, boundaries and power

The prime device through which ideological positions about sexuality are circulated in media texts is the stereotype. That is a word which only ever seems to have negative connotations, as if representations would be better and fairer if all stereotypes vanished. Unfortunately, stereotyping is inevitable in any form of immediate, accessible communication. Since there is never enough time or space to describe people in all the rich complexity that their individuality deserves, short cuts have to be taken, comparisons made, generalizations risked, labels attached. Stereotyping is a process of selection, magnification and reduction: it takes one perceived attribute of a social group, blows that attribute up until it obscures all others, then boils it down until it comes to stand for that group, summarizing that group in a kind of cultural shorthand. To take an example of a sexuality stereotype,

film and television comedies are full of images of gay men as effeminate
screaming queens. Such images are not fabricated out of nothing – some
gay men are just like that some of the time, but what the stereotype does
is to take out those 'somes'. It chooses that one aspect of gay male behaviour (selection), inflates it into the defining characteristic of male homosexuality (magnification), then establishes it as the most easily recognizable
image (reduction).

The ideological implications of stereotyping are obvious, since the groups
most liable to be stereotyped are those with less social and cultural power;
indeed one crucial distinction between powerful and less powerful social
groups is that the former hold the ability to stereotype the latter. Stereotyping becomes ideological the moment it stops being simply a method of
description and becomes a vehicle for values: the image of the screaming
queen does not just mean 'all gay men are like that', it means 'all gay men
are like that and aren't they awful', which in turn means 'and they are awful
because they're not like us'. Here it is important to remember the invisibility and fluidity of sexuality, since if an ideological hierarchy between 'us'
and 'them' is what a stereotype serves to perpetuate, it has to work that
much harder if the boundaries between us-ness and them-ness are so treach-
erously vague and mobile.

This is why stereotypes of sexuality strive so vigorously to create two,
polarized sexualities, hetero and homo, and to insist with such obsessive
reductiveness that people who belong to those poles are easily identifiable
– hence the recurring presence across media texts of the screaming queen
(so *obviously* gay) and his female equivalent the butch dyke (so *obviously*
lesbian). As Richard Dyer has said, such stereotypes exist in order to 'make
visible the invisible, so that there is no danger of it creeping up on us
unawares, and to make fast firm and separate what is in reality and much
closer to the norm than the dominant value system cares to admit' (Dyer
1993: 16). Given the invisibility of homosexuality, homosexuals could be
anyone, could be everywhere, and of course happily we are, but such a
realization seriously challenges heterosexuality's idea of itself as natural and
universal. Traditional stereotypes of lesbians and gays are one way of defus-
ing that challenge, since they construct images that few actual lesbians and
gays would wish to align themselves with, thereby discouraging them from
coming out and affirming their sexual identities. Those sexualities outside the homo–hetero binary are even more troubling for the heterosexual
hierarchy, to the extent that they rarely figure in media representation at
all, except as quite literally murderous – examples of these particularly
extreme and unforgiving stereotypes would include the transsexual serial
killers in films like *Dressed to Kill* (1980) or *The Silence of the Lambs* (1991)
or the bisexuals blamed for 'spreading' AIDS into the heterosexual community in some tabloid accounts of the HIV epidemic.

Lesbians and gays who could not be corralled into one of the polarized
stereotypes of effeminate queen or butch dyke were, until quite recently,
simply not representable in mainstream media texts – not, that is to say, if

their sexuality was to be made unambiguously evident. There are many characters in film and television fiction, however, who while not crudely labelled as queer were sufficiently different from heterosexual norms to offer the possibility of being interpreted in ambiguous ways, and trawling back through media history to uncover and assess these intriguing representations has become one important area of lesbian and gay media scholarship. (Excellent historical surveys detailing lesbian and gay representations in mainstream film and television are Howes (1993), Russo (1987) and Weiss (1992).) There are important questions here about the relationship between representations and audiences, since these less-stereotyped characters may well have been understood in very different ways by mainstream heterosexual audiences, accustomed to seeing homosexuality only in terms of the crassest stereotyping, than by lesbian and gay viewers more attuned to the subtle inflections of subcultural coding.

More recently, as part of a gradual change in social attitudes towards homosexuality, media representations have become more varied; the simplistic stereotypes have not vanished, but they have been supplemented by alternatives which might suggest progression towards more enlightened attitudes. Television talk shows, for example, frequently feature studio debates on matters of sexuality, and these at least give the impression that lesbians, gays and other sexual minorities are free to speak on their own terms rather than being filtered through fictional codes. That is not an impression to be seduced by, however, since shows like *Oprah* and *Ricki Lake* are just as codified, just as bound by genre conventions, as any Hollywood drama or British sitcom. Lesbian or gay guests on talk shows may feel that they can escape stereotyping by speaking directly from their own experience, but that aspiration towards truthfulness runs aground on the gladiatorial organization of the studio space, the role of the host, the audience and the inevitable 'experts' in contextualizing the guests' testimonies in discursive frameworks beyond their control, and the narrative drives of scandal, interrogation and confession that give daily continuity to such series whatever the subject-matter under discussion.

Another response to the problem of stereotyping is to create, with a consciously didactic intention, positive images to counter the negative misrepresentations found elsewhere. Though well intentioned, the call for positive images rests on several shaky foundations. Such a project prides itself on rejecting stereotypes but aims to do so by creating another stereotype, it would do away with 'gay men are effeminate' only to replace it with 'all gay men are masculine': a positive image is really only a stereotype that suits my ideology rather than yours. It also assumes that all members of a social group can agree on what might constitute a positive image of themselves, ignoring differences between lesbians or gay men, some of whom may well feel much more in tune with the characteristics implicitly or explicitly rejected as 'negative'. Connected to this is the suspicion that positive images are primarily concerned with reassuring heterosexual audiences, unable to counter prejudice with anything more than unthreatening blandness.

The Hollywood film *Philadelphia* (1993) would be a typical example of this ploy, encouraging heterosexual spectators to feel sympathy and tolerance for homosexual characters, but lesbian and gay audiences are increasingly impatient with the condescension built in to such approaches, even going so far as to re-examine the old, discredited stereotypes of polarized homosexuality to see whether they may have been unfairly dismissed in the positive-image rush to court heterosexual approval and may, in their unapologetic if ostensibly ridiculed queerness, be ripe for reappropriation. (For a more extensive critique of positive images, see Medhurst 1994.)

The factor which underpins all these debates over stereotyping is the sheer paucity of homosexual representations, the fact that there are simply so few images of sexual variety in media texts. Crude stereotypes might be easier to condone if they were part of a spectrum, and the urge to generate positive images would be superfluous if there were a larger number of lesbian or gay characters through whom the diversity of our experiences could be expressed, but it still remains too often the case that drama series feel able to sum up homosexuality with a single plot line and soap operas congratulate themselves on their liberalism if they feature one lesbian or gay character. Such characters are forced to shoulder the weight of speaking for entire communities, a load that no heterosexual figure would ever be asked to bear. A telling example of that problem was the first gay character in *EastEnders*. Colin was introduced in 1986 and stayed for three years, but he remained a middle-class outsider in a working-class milieu, and was never involved in any of the pivotal storylines. Consequently he stood detached from the soap's centre, all too obviously embodying the well-intentioned positive image, politically praiseworthy but dramatically uninvolving. Colin's mild presence did, however, pave the way for subsequent lesbian and gay characterizations to become textually richer and more emotionally engaging. The early 1990s lesbian couple Della and Binny were less isolated, and though storylines featuring them still centred on sexuality, these were given some interesting twists, such as a heterosexual man's inability to believe that Della could prefer her girlfriend to him. As I write this chapter (Autumn 1996), the most complex gay characters to date have arrived in Albert Square, Tony and Simon, whose varied pasts, variable morals and convoluted familial circumstances mean that they are key players in many plots which do not depend entirely on their sexuality, achieving an integration unattainable to both the marginalized stereotype and the too-good-to-be-true positive image.

In our own voices?

The most effective form of resistance to the hegemonic force of the dominant media is to speak for oneself.

(Gross 1991: 144)

Integration, of course, is not the only option. Many lesbians and gays have felt that expecting equality or accuracy in representations produced by the mainstream media is pointless, favouring instead the setting up of smaller-scale, community-based media projects. In the early 1970s, the Gay Liberation Front (GLF), the UK's first radical gay organization, dismayed by the lack of coverage they had received in the press, decided 'there was only one thing to do and that was to have a newspaper of our own' (Power 1995: 51). Their belief was that in such a forum, lesbian and gay concerns would be unfettered by the constraints encountered when those concerns were represented through heterosexual-dominated media institutions. The GLF path offered one way of minimizing those constraints, setting up a publication that was by, for and about lesbians and gays, creating, at least in principle, a rare unity of production, audience and content. There are inevitable obstacles impeding any such project, not least the dangers, already mentioned above, of homogenizing the multiplicities of lesbian and gay lives into one rather nebulous 'community', the 'oneself' spoken of by Larry Gross in the quote at the beginning of this section. There are some who believe that those dangers are exaggerated, that the solidarity of a shared sexuality overrides other social differences: the gay broadcaster Paul Gambaccini has written of visiting a club and seeing 'a middle-aged white man and a teenage black boy wrapped around each other . . . same-sex passion across age, racial and economic divides. I quickly learned that these gaps simply do not exist for gay people' (Gambaccini 1996: 158), but such a claim is either naïve utopianism on a somewhat heroic scale or a worrying blindness to power-relations of class, age and ethnicity which even if they miraculously evaporate in the heat of the moment will certainly return with the following dawn.

The GLF's magazine *Come Together*, irregularly produced and politically confrontational, collapsed after three years partly under the weight of factional in-fighting and partly because it was eclipsed by *Gay News*, a fortnightly paper which found a much more marketable balance of politics and what would later become known as lifestyle coverage (reviews, interviews, features). The brief dream of *Come Together* was to speak with one radical voice for all lesbians and gays, but the first specialization that *Gay News* undertook, detonating that dream along gender lines, was to become a publication predominantly concerned with gay men rather than lesbians, a direction even more eagerly pursued by its successor *Gay Times*. (Walter (1980) reprints many of the original *Come Together* articles and provides a perceptive overview of the historical and political contexts surrounding the magazine's formation, ambitions and demise.) Now a range of diverse and often contradictory magazines cater for different niches of the varied complexity of contemporary queer lives. Larry Gross's vision of 'speaking for oneself' rests on a degree of unity, a shared common purpose, unsustainable in today's climate, where designer dykes can buy *Diva*, separatist lesbians can subscribe to *Trouble and Strife*, and *Attitude* (an even more lesbian-free zone than *Gay Times*) is aimed at gay men who would rather not buy a magazine with 'gay' on the cover. Whether such a state of affairs reveals a welcome kaleidoscope of representations or a fragmentation that weakens the potential for coherent sexual politics remains an open question.

Television, at least in its pre-digital era, has never been able to match the choice of texts offered by the publishing industry, meaning that the handful of programmes made by and for lesbians and gays have had particular difficulties negotiating the competing demands of representativeness and diversity. If there is only one programme being broadcast that specifically targets a lesbian and gay audience, it runs the risk of turning into a token presence in the schedules, hovering apologetically on the margins like Colin in *EastEnders*. The first nationally broadcast series to take that gamble was Channel Four's *Out on Tuesday*, first aired in 1989 (Channel Four's stated remit to cater for minorities was crucial in allowing the programme to reach the screen). It side-stepped the trap of definitiveness, of saying that this and only this is what homosexual life is like, by adopting a magazine format, featuring items of different length and seriousness, and never shying away from conflicts and debates. *Out* conceptualized its audience as plural, overlapping, not always easily coexisting communities, never reducing it to the impossibly simplified fiction of a single community. Although opinions were sharply divided among its target viewers, *Out*'s greatest strength to me was in taking homosexualities for granted, placing them centre stage but never on display as the object of voyeuristic scrutiny that they would have been in programmes made by and for heterosexuals. (Conflicting evaluations of *Out* can be found in Hamer and Ashbrook (1994), Richardson (1995), and Spry (1991).) With considerable verve and panache, *Out* reversed the standard power-relations of media texts concerned with sexuality, in which heterosexual identities remain unquestioned while homosexual ones go under the microscope.

The two successors to *Out* have learned from its pioneering efforts but have adopted different strategies. *Gaytime TV*, the BBC's first series aimed at lesbian and gay audiences, uses the magazine format but has snipped out all the pages except those concerned with gossip and gloss. Mindful that many had criticized *Out* for its commitment to a politicized representation of sexuality, *Gaytime TV* has emphasized an unashamedly consumerist version of being queer, featuring items on holidays, fitness and interior décor, representing sexuality wholly as a source of individual pleasure and never as a site of social conflict. The ability to represent it as both, and to walk the tightrope between them, seems on that evidence to be a skill that died out with the best editions of *Out*, though it has sometimes been managed by *Dyke TV*, Channel Four's most recent offering for lesbian audiences. *Dyke TV* is not a programme as such, but, in the currently fashionable jargon of television, a zone, where a string of discrete programmes are broadcast under one umbrella title. This has the benefits of range and the dangers of incoherence, but it at least makes possible a more sustained representation of the contradictions of contemporary sexuality than has been achieved on the debilitatingly cheery, complexity-free *Gaytime TV*.

Scrutinizing dominance

Studies of media representation have almost always had as their chief focus the representation of 'minorities', a term used as shorthand for social groups at the less powerful end of the power spectrum. This is not surprising, since the political impetus behind such studies stems from a perception that media representations of less powerful groups play a key role in sustaining the social hierarchies which keep those imbalances of power in place. That focus is now beginning to change, broadening to incorporate studies of how 'majorities', or powerful social groups, are represented (work on the gender construction of masculinity, for example, or the cultural meanings of whiteness), but in general the equation between studying representation and studying 'minorities' still holds. That is one of the reasons why the bulk of this chapter has been about homosexualities, and why neither I as its writer or you as its reader are probably surprised by that emphasis, but I want to suggest now that analysing the codes and conventions through which media texts depict heterosexualities could prove a productive future direction for study and research.

The first barrier that such an investigation runs into is the recurring issue of invisibility and sexuality with which this chapter began. Heterosexuality is not exactly invisible, in fact to my queer eyes it is utterly omnipresent – just look around a High Street shop display of greetings cards to see how heterosexuality is privileged or watch how many television game shows group their contestants in terms of heterosexual domestic units – yet it is not really visible either, in terms of being a category in regular everyday social use. The word 'heterosexual' itself is used incredibly rarely in media texts, a fact that can lead to some pernicious inequalities: if a gay man is involved in committing a sexual crime, for example, news bulletins will routinely refer to his sexuality, but when did you last hear of a 'heterosexual rapist', even though that is what the overwhelming majority of rapists actually are?

The paradox of heterosexual representations is that heterosexuality is both everywhere and nowhere: everywhere, because it is taken for granted as the sexual norm, the centre against which other sexual options are obliged to define themselves, yet nowhere, because it is never required to identify itself, to acknowledge its particularity, to submit to the indignity of a label. Heterosexuality in media texts is flushed into the open only when it does not have the field to itself, when it is placed amid representations of other sexualities: in articles in lesbian and gay magazines, for example, or on Channel Four's parodic game show *Sticky Moments*, where the gay host Julian Clary found much comic mileage in mocking heterosexual lifestyles and dismissively summing up the inadequacies of his stooge by saying 'well, that's heterosexuals for you'. There the straight man truly was the straight man, but with the exception of such isolated examples heterosexuality remains serenely assured of its own centrality, luxuriating in its taken-for-grantedness.

Since heterosexual people almost never have to think of themselves *as* heterosexual, preferring instead to categorize themselves in terms of gender, ethnicity or age, it should come as no surprise that those critics who have begun to analyse the ways in which heterosexuality is culturally constructed are themselves lesbian or gay. (See Dyer 1993: chapter on 'Straight Acting'; Wilkinson and Kitzinger 1993.) Those of us who live outside the mainstream find it much easier to see that although that mainstream may be dominant, it is certainly not universal, and that heterosexuality is not the sum total of human sexual experience. That knowledge enables us to turn some of the standard questions about media representation upside down and gain a usefully fresh perspective by doing so. An analytical model centred on the critique of stereotypes or the hunt for positive images might lament the absence of strong lesbian and gay characters in *Coronation Street*, for example, but if we reset our agenda and ask what that soap has to say about heterosexuality, such a question might yield unexpected answers and help to account for that soap's enduring popularity with non-heterosexual audiences, since the preponderance of happily single women and patently ludicrous married couples could be taken to suggest that *Coronation Street*'s representation of heterosexuality is not a particularly favourable one. It could be argued that my homosexuality inclines me towards making such a reading, and I would not disagree with that accusation, but the point I want to underline here is that a heterosexual viewer's reading would be just as partial, just as slanted, just as rooted in his or her cultural identity, the only difference being that a heterosexual viewer would be far more reluctant to acknowledge this fact than I am. In much the same way that some men think that questions of gender apply only to women, most heterosexuals think that sexuality is something only non-heterosexuals have. Once they shed that misconception, heterosexuals' readings of heterosexual images will certainly prove fascinating.

Trying to put yourself in the film situation in some way

The final issue I want to raise is perhaps the most amorphous of all, the ways in which media consumers belonging to sexual minorities might specifically interpret texts which appear to contain nothing but images of dominant heterosexuality. Lesbian and gay viewers are particularly skilled in reading texts against the grain, for the simple reason that we have only ever had a tiny number of texts offered to us that depicted versions of our own lives and experiences, and even then, as discussed earlier, those versions tend to cause controversy by imposing a false unity on our multiple diversities. Faced with a media world where heterosexuality reigns virtually unchallenged, queer audiences have rapidly learned the survival skills of refashioning heterosexual images to suit our own purposes, reworking them with an adroit subversiveness until they speak to our needs and desires.

(More detailed accounts of such subcultural re-readings are in Medhurst 1991; Weiss 1992: chapter on 'A queer feeling when I look at you'; Whitaker 1985.) Those survival skills were especially invaluable in earlier decades where recognizable lesbian and gay representations were impossible to find in mainstream texts, forcing those in search of such images to resort to the more private realms of fantasy: a survey of Britain's film audiences in the 1940s included the revelation of one schoolboy that 'My film idol is Errol Flynn and I fell madly in love with him after seeing *Dawn Patrol*. I think about him at nights, pretend I am with him and dream about him. I have never felt about a film actress in this way' (Mayer 1948: 49), while an interview with lesbian film fans who grew up having to negotiate their way through the relentlessly heterosexual regime of Hollywood contained this evocative recollection of

> trying to put yourself in the film situation in some way. . . . At times I'd identify with a character. Other times I'd float outside the situation, sort of watching the effect this attractive woman was having on me. I'd imagine Katharine Hepburn and Spencer Tracy together, or sometimes I'd be Katharine Hepburn. And I might be sort of behind Spencer Tracy but I wouldn't *be* Spencer Tracy. I felt a tug of war with that.
>
> (Whitaker 1985: 109)

Those kinds of subversive reappropriations continue even today (plenty of schoolboys dream of Keanu Reeves and many young lesbians want to place themselves somewhere near Jodie Foster), and they are feasible because the sexuality of an image can never be fully secured by those that produce it – the pin-up in *Smash Hits* or the bodies in *Baywatch* may be primarily intended for heterosexual consumption, but there are no stickers on the posters or warnings on the television screen saying 'lesbians and gays keep out'. I began this chapter by stressing the fluidity and instability of sexuality, those factors which can frustratingly make its representation so hard to track and trace, so resistant to definitive summarizing, but those qualities do not just lead to frustration, they can also invite, enable and empower, opening up multitudinous possibilities for text–audience relationships that are subtle, creative and politically dynamic.

Questions

1   Monitor a range of television programmes and note where and how representations of lesbians and/or gay men appear. Are there any characteristics in common across those representations, whatever kind of programme they appeared in, or do different types of television texts treat sexual minorities differently?

2   How would you identify a stereotype of a lesbian or gay man in a film, television programme, newspaper or magazine? What codes,

clues and conventions are used to establish the stereotype? What responses is it supposed to produce in its target audience? What responses does it produce in you?

3   Look at one of the magazines produced for lesbian and gay readers (*Gay Times, Attitude, Diva* and – if you live there – *Gay Scotland* are the most widely available). If you have never seen one before, does it conform to your expectations of what such a magazine might or should include? Would it be feasible to publish a magazine which addressed readers on the basis of their shared *heterosexuality* (possible title: *Het Gazette*), and if so what issues and features should it cover?

References

Ainley, R. (1995) *What Is She Like? Lesbian Identities from the 1950s to the 1990s*, London: Cassell.

Dyer, R. (1993) *The Matter of Images: Essays on Representation*, London: Routledge.

Gambaccini, P. (1996) *Love Letters*, London: Michael O'Mara.

Gross, L. (1991) 'Out of the mainstream: sexual minorities and the mass media', in E. Seiter, H. Borchers, G. Kreutzner and E.M. Warth (eds) *Remote Control: Television, Audiences and Cultural Power*, London: Routledge.

Hamer, D. and Ashbrook, P. (1994) 'OUT: reflections on British television's first lesbian and gay magazine series', in D. Hamer and B. Budge (eds) *The Good, the Bad and the Gorgeous: Popular Culture's Romance with Lesbianism*, London: Pandora.

Howes, K. (1993) *Broadcasting It: An Encyclopaedia of Homosexuality on Film, Radio and TV in the U.K. 1923–1993*, London: Cassell.

Mayer, J.P. (1948) *British Cinemas and their Audiences*, London: Dobson.

Medhurst, A. (1991) 'Batman, Deviance and Camp', in R. Pearson and W. Urricchio (eds) *The Many Lives of the Batman*, London: British Film Institute.

Medhurst, A. (1994) 'One queen and his screen: lesbian and gay television', in E. Healy and A. Mason (eds) *Stonewall 25: The Making of the Lesbian and Gay Community in Britain*, London: Virago.

National Lesbian and Gay Survey (1993) *Proust, Michelangelo, Marc Almond and Me*, London: Routledge.

Plummer, K. (ed.) (1992) *Modern Homosexualities: Fragments of Lesbian and Gay Experience*, London: Routledge.

Power, L. (1995) *No Bath But Plenty of Bubbles: An Oral History of the Gay Liberation Front 1970–73*, London: Cassell.

Prosser, J. (1997) 'Transgender', in A. Medhurst and S. Munt (eds) *Lesbian and Gay Studies: A Critical Introduction*, London: Cassell.

Richardson, C. (1995) 'TVOD: the never-bending story', in P. Burston and C. Richardson (eds) *A Queer Romance: Lesbians, Gay Men and Popular Culture*, London: Routledge.

Rose, S., Stevens, C., *et al.* (eds) (1996) *Bisexual Horizons: Politics, Histories, Lives,* London: Lawrence & Wishart.

Russo, V. (1987) *The Celluloid Closet,* New York: Harper & Row.

Smyth, C. (1992) *Lesbians Talk Queer Notions,* London: Scarlet Press.

Spry, C. (1991) 'Out of the box', in T. Kaufmann and P. Lincoln (eds) *High Risk Lives,* Bridport: Prism.

Stone, S. (1991) 'The empire strikes back: a posttranssexual manifesto', in J. Epstein and K. Straub (eds) *Body Guards: The Cultural Politics of Gender Ambiguity,* London: Routledge.

Walter, A. (ed.) (1980) *Come Together: The Years of Gay Liberation 1970–73,* London: Gay Men's Press.

Warner, M. (ed.) (1993) *Fear of a Queer Planet: Queer Politics and Social Theory,* Minneapolis, MN: University of Minnesota Press.

Weiss, A. (1992) *Vampires and Violets: Lesbians in the Cinema,* London: Cape.

Whitaker, C. (1985) 'Hollywood transformed: interviews with lesbian viewers', in P. Steven (ed.) *Jump Cut: Hollywood, Politics and Counter-Cinema,* Toronto: Between The Lines.

Wilkinson, S. and Kitzinger, C. (eds) (1993) *Heterosexuality,* London: Sage.

Further reading

Bad Object-Choices Collective (eds) (1991) *How Do I Look? Queer Film and Video,* Seattle, WA: Bay Press.

Collis, R. (1994) 'Screened out: lesbians and television', in L. Gibbs (ed.) *Daring to Dissent: Lesbian Culture from Margin to Mainstream,* London: Cassell.

Doty, A. (1993) *Making Things Perfectly Queer: Interpreting Mass Culture,* Minneapolis: University of Minnesota Press.

Dyer, R. (1991) *Now You See It: Studies on Lesbian and Gay Film,* London: Routledge.

Florence, P. (1993) 'Lesbian cinema, women's cinema', in G. Griffin (ed.) *Outwrite: Lesbianism and Popular Culture,* London: Pluto.

Gever, M., Greyson, J. and Parmar, P. (eds) (1993) *Queer Looks: Perspectives on Lesbian and Gay Film and Video,* London: Routledge.

Smyth, C. (1992) *Lesbians Talk Queer Notions,* London: Scarlet Press.

Warner, M. (ed.) (1993) *Fear of a Queer Planet: Queer Politics and Social Theory,* Minneapolis, MN: University of Minnesota Press.

Wilton, T. (ed.) (1995) *Immortal, Invisible: Lesbians and the Moving Image,* London: Routledge.

Chapter 21

Gender

FROM PAMELA ANDERSON TO ERASMUS: WOMEN, MEN AND REPRESENTATION

LIESBET VAN ZOONEN AND IRENE COSTERA MEIJER

It is eight o'clock on a cold winter morning. I am waiting for the bus to the city centre, hardly awake and shivering. The bus stop is lit by a huge billboard just behind me. On it is Pamela Anderson, the star of the popular TV-series Baywatch, *throwing a defiant glance at me and flaunting her big bosom in a very tiny bikini for the Swedish fashion chain H&M. Thanks to H&M's policy of distributing Pamela's posters freely among her fans, the poster is still there, undamaged. Next to me, unaware of Pamela's overwhelming presence, an old man is leaning on the billboard, his head between her voluptuous breasts. A young man comes along and sees the picture of the old man in a paradisal position. He winks at me, as if we both would see a common meaning in this scene. I start to feel uncomfortable. It is a bit much for the early morning: the obtrusive presence of Pamela and her unavoidable breasts, the conspiratorial invitation of the young man to share in the voyeuristic irony created by the picture at the bus stop. Fortunately the bus arrives in time.*

Huge, well-lit billboards protected by thick glass frames have become the latest fashionable advertising outlet in the city of Amsterdam, where we both live and work. They are exploited by a private company which has a contractual obligation to their customers to repair or replace a damaged billboard within 24 hours, thus ensuring Amsterdam citizens of a continuous, perfect and inescapable flow of advertising images. Women, as the ultimate symbols in advertising and other forms of consumer culture, figure prominently on these billboards. In the course of one bus ride to work, we meet not only Pamela Anderson, but also more anonymous but just as stunning and inviting women who put their bodies on display to promote certain kinds of products like bras, underwear, perfumes, candy bars, ice cream, beer, chewing gum, and so on. The intimate parts of women's bodies have thus become inescapably public in the symbolic city landscape of Amsterdam. Men also figure on these billboards, but less frequently. Although we do often see their nude bodies, their private parts are never as obtrusively pushed in our faces as those of Pamela and her clones such as Tyra Banks. The billboard campaigns hardly ever last longer than a week, making it impossible to get used to them and thus become able to ignore them. An incessant stream of continuously but only superficially changing images of women and some men forces itself on the ordinary person with no escape. The ever-increasing ubiquity of visual images in our daily lives, of which these billboards are the latest exponents, keeps the issue of the representation of women and men high on feminist and scholarly agendas (e.g. Geraghty 1996; Van Zoonen 1994). In this chapter we examine the representation of women and men more closely and show the asymmetry of the social relations of looking. We illustrate our arguments with those media and images which we do not consciously seek to use and consume, but which we inevitably run into in the course of an ordinary working day. Before we continue on our way to work, however, let us first consider some aspects of representation in greater detail.

Looking at Pamela Anderson we may only see a picture of a famous actress: an artificially produced reflection of a great, but also artificially produced body. (As has been publicized widely by Anderson she has undergone plastic surgery three times to enlarge her breasts.) In fact, that is how media representations are often looked upon: as a reflection of a certain aspect of reality. Many research projects on women in the media, especially those carried out in the social sciences, claim that their images are not very realistic or 'not representative of women's position in our highly differentiated and complex society' (Cantor 1978: 30). It is indeed easy to see that real women are much different and more diverse than their representations in the media seem to suggest. If media images were indeed a reflection of reality, 'real' women would be relatively rare in most parts of the real world, and Black, older, disabled, lesbian, fat, poor or Third World women would be virtually nonexistent. Men, on the other hand, seem to be hardly present in the imaginary world of advertising, but an abundance of men flood the front pages of newspapers or the screens of sports channels. Representation is not the only issue when looking at the Anderson picture. One may not immediately think of the connection between her voluptuous body, blonde hair and inviting smile and those of earlier sex symbols of western societies like Doris Day, Marilyn Monroe and Brigitte Bardot. The billboard's implicit reference to other images and texts of women, however, is a form of what is usually called 'intertextuality', i.e. a more or less explicit relation between different texts. Thus, following an argument made by Fiske (1987: 108), the billboard's 'intertextuality refers rather to our culture's image bank of the sexy blonde star who plays with men's desire for her and turns it into her advantage'. Thus, how Anderson's real persona is reflected, is not what is primarily at stake in her representation; it is the reflection of a common cultural understanding of western white femininity that produces the *signifying* potential, the range of possible meanings, of her image. Many feminist studies of images of women, especially those from the humanities, have examined how images of women are used to convey meaning to gender and other values. Although these studies differ widely from each other, one inescapable conclusion of this work is that women are usually related to (hetero)sexuality, nature and tradition (Coward 1982).

Also femininity is more closely related to whiteness, whereas masculinity tends to understate differences in colour. White and Black men alike are connected to muscularity. This is apparent in the male sports subculture, where size and strength are valued by men across racial and even class boundaries (Katz 1995: 139). Many advertisers use images of physically rugged or muscular male bodies to masculinize products and services geared to elite male consumers. The powerful male body is at one time a metaphor for the financial security offered by an insurance firm, at others for powerful cars. Violence is another vital part of the construction of masculinity. Katz stresses that violence on-screen, like that in real life, is perpetrated overwhelmingly by males. Males constitute the majority of the audience for violent films, as well as violent sports such as football and hockey. What is being sold, however, is not just 'violence' but rather a glamorized form of violent masculinity (Katz 1995: 140). Race may not be a distinctive pattern in the construction of certain visual constructions of masculinity; it is when it comes to relations of looking. Black men seem to be much more 'on display' than white men. Kobena Mercer and Isaac Julien (1988) compared the aesthetic presentation of black nude bodies in the work of the famous photographer Robert Mapplethorpe with the generic codes that govern the presentation of the conventional subject of the nude: the (white) woman.

> Mapplethorpe appropriates elements of commonplace racial stereotypes to prop-up, regulate, organise and *fix* the aesthetic reduction of the black man's flesh to a visual surface charged and burdened with the task of servicing a white male desire to look – more importantly, assert – mastery and power over the looked-at.
>
> (Mercer and Julien 1988: 145)

The circulation of mass media stereotypes of Black men bears witness to this 'colonial fantasy' in that there is only a rigid and limited set of guises in which Black males become visible: as sexualized and idolized 'others' in sports and pornography.

Both approaches to representation – as referring to a particular reality, or as referring to a culture's values – seem relevant for the analysis of visual images, but pose rather unsolvable issues. The main problem is the question of which or what kind of present is actually *re*presented by media images. What does the Anderson billboard refer to: a particular woman or a general western understanding of white femininity?

In thinking through and debating such issues, we will inevitably end up making assumptions or claims about the way audiences will interpret representations. Meaning, as so many authors have asserted by now, does not reside in images but arises from the interaction between images and audiences, producing a variety of 'texts' – i.e. the various interpretations by audiences – in the process. Fiske (1987: 154) suggests that audiences shift between two different interpretative strategies that can be considered as the far ends of a continuum: a realistic interpretation takes images as reflections of real persons or real situations and enables identification. Discursive interpretations, however, consider images as the 'embodiment of social values . . . and discourage identification'. Which of these interpretative strategies will be activated depends, according to Fiske, on the particular social, cultural and ideological position of audiences. Taking this view to the extreme, representation in fact becomes a non-issue, because the ultimate production of meaning is placed on the side of the audience, regardless of what is represented. In our discussion of the representation of gender we examine to what cultural elements representation may refer, but we also focus on the particular visual and textual strategies by which representations invite audiences to construct their own interpretations and we analyse how particular representations 'speak' to audiences, in other words on their mode of address.

> I get off in the city centre and begin my five-minute walk to work right through the red light district and other more downmarket features of inner city life in Amsterdam. Women of all kinds, sitting barely dressed on pink satin cushions, scan me from behind their well-lit windows. Suddenly I recognize the representational similarity between the Pamela Anderson posters and the prostitutes. This makes me understand a bit more of the uneasiness caused by the scene at the bus stop earlier this morning. Anderson and other advertising models in the billboards are framed just like the prostitutes in the windows I am passing. They all seem to display availability. There is however an important difference in their respective attitudes: the prostitutes actively seek out who to 'address', unlike the Pamelas in their equally well-lit frames who passively interpellate anyone, regardless of their posture or gender. The billboards seem to mean something for both women and men. But what?

In a classic and often quoted work, *Ways of Seeing*, Berger (1972) notes:

> Men act and women appear. Men look at women. Women watch themselves being looked at. This determines not only most relations between men and women but also the relation of women to themselves. The surveyor of woman in herself is male: the surveyed female. Thus she turns herself into an object – and most particularly an object of vision: a sight.
>
> (Berger 1972: 47)

Berger argued that men create a sense of identity by extending out from their body, using its and their evident *power* to control objects and others. This we see clearly in advertisements for cigarettes, alcohol, stereos and, especially, cars. Women, by contrast, work with and within the body. The female body communicates not the woman's power over others, but her *presence*, how she takes herself (Berger 1972: 45–6). Berger positions both women and men as male heterosexual spectators of the female 'sight'. Applying this logic, one writer goes so far as to argue that

> practically all advertising is on behalf of the masculine image, either showing him what kind of status he can hope to attain, or showing a woman what kind of man she can hope to attract.
>
> (Kurtz, 1986)

The Anderson billboards and similar images of women invite us to look at them with a prospective male viewer in mind. The display of women for the pleasure of men has been a long-standing tradition in western patriarchal culture. Pornography is the most obvious and most extreme expression of the use of women's bodies as objects of desire, fantasy and violence. In advertising, cinema and other popular genres, similar textual strategies construct women's bodies as objects to look at and desire. The codes of porn have been easily transferred to mainstream culture: the direct and inviting look at the camera indicates willingness and readiness to submit to the male consumer. The fragmentation of the female body into close-ups of breasts and buttocks reduces women to depersonalized body parts; particular camera angles construct women as powerless and submissive (Coward 1982). Despite the increasing usage of male nudes in a variety of genres there is no such widespread tradition for the male body. Even in gay male pornography, the object of desire displays as much the will to conquer as to be conquered. Richard Dyer (1992) observed that the masculinity of male subjects might be undermined when they are the objects of the gaze, therefore numerous supplementary codes and conventions feature in gay porn and the male pin-up genre – such as the taut rigid and straining body pose; clothing details; narrative plot – in order to stabilize the gendered organization of the look. To be looked at, to be made into a 'thing' for the gaze – to be objectified so to speak – obviously seems the fate of women in western culture, whereas the act of looking and the voyeuristic pleasure produced by it is reserved for men.

According to best-selling American author Naomi Wolff, the results are unpleasant, to say the least. In *The Beauty Myth* (1990) she claims that the cultural construction of femininity as to-be-looked-at has had devastating effects on current generations of American girls who seem obsessed with their bodies and suffer from eating disorders like bulimia and anorexia nervosa. (Chapkis's book (1986) never acquired best-selling status but made similar arguments.)

The cultural construction of femininity as expressed by Pamela Anderson and her look-a-likes is part of an asymmetrical organization of looking in which women are invited to identify whereas men are invited to possess: women can desire to *be* that image while men can desire to *have* the image. The problem is that the invitation to look at other men can threaten men's (hetero)sexual identity: they may *want* the image. To foreclose this possibility, Costera Meijer (1991) noted that in more than half of the Dutch advertisements for perfumes aimed at male consumers, the threat of homosexual associations was countered by including a woman on the photograph.

Femininity is encoded as passive (to be, to appear); masculinity as active (to have, to possess) (Barthel 1988). This system, of course, is not watertight: it 'leaks' so to speak. A series of interviews with Dutch 13 year olds showed that almost all knew Anderson and considered her *the* symbol of female sexiness, but she was despised as well as adored, in particular by the girls (quoted in a Dutch current affairs weekly, *Vrij Nederland* August 1995). We may hypothesize from such data that girls read the Anderson image realistically as well as discursively: some of them may identify with her whereas others will recognize the values of femininity proposed to them and for many of them the realist and discursive interpretation may occur simultaneously. We may even wonder whether a third 'masculine' option, a voyeuristic or desiring interpretation of Anderson-like images, is not available for these girls. Certainly, in contemporary girl culture images of men seem to function as objects of desire (Moore 1988: 1991). The European soccer champions of 1995, FC Ajax from Amsterdam, for instance, deliver a continuous stream of young male sex symbols like Patrick Kluivert and Marc Overmans whose pictures cover many a girl's bedroom. Also, the overwhelming popularity of bands like New Kids on the Block and the former group Take That, which both contained a deliberately constructed variety of male sexualities embodied in the band members, suggest that men can be an object of the gaze and girls are perfectly capable of voyeurism. Apparently the dominant-gendered relations of looking have not succeeded in precluding female voyeurism *vis-à-vis* male bodies. In fact, in a variety of popular genres, the male body is increasingly exploited as an object of female desire. If dominant gender discourse 'leaks' in that direction, there could be other 'leaks' too. Wouldn't there be, for instance, a possibility for a relationship between women and their cultural images that is of a more pleasurable and empowering nature than the self-hate seemingly evoked by identification with women-as-sight? (Evans and Thornton 1989).

> I stop at the news-stand and buy a couple of magazines. Women look at me from the covers of almost all the magazines, regardless of their readership. The cover of *Playboy* hardly seems to differ from the cover of *Cosmopolitan*: yet I don't think of buying *Playboy* whereas I do consider *Cosmo*. The open mouth of the *Playboy* girl puts me off. The *Playboy* girl's apparent expression of pleasure is, unlike that of the *Cosmo*-girl, not for herself but for another (male) person. Also, it would give a very strange impression if I were to walk away with *Playboy* instead of *Cosmo*, given the temporary public identity one takes on by buying a magazine. Most 'cover-boys' I see are well-known politicians or other male public officials, who obviously are on display because their own bodies and their own power matter instead of their representation of more abstract values. Some men's magazines put more anonymous figures on the cover, but their anonymity does not seem to obstruct their radiation of individuality, power, success and control. On closer examination I also discover a couple of body-building magazines in which male bodies do figure as the object of the look, but it doesn't resemble the depiction of women's bodies at all – or does it?

Images of men seem to have a closer link with 'reality' than images of women, but not only for the obvious reason that many images of men occur in the context of genres such as news and current affairs. Goffman (1979) suggests in his classic study on gender advertisements that representations of male models have a certain amount of credibility that is lacking in images of female models. Goffman claims that when we see a man in an advertisement wearing a business suit and carrying a briefcase we believe that he is seriously representing a businessman; if the same man is seen wearing shorts and carrying a racquet we believe, likewise, that he is representing the same man playing tennis. Yet, according to Goffman, when we see a woman wearing business or sports clothes it is as if we are watching a model play-acting at a perpetual costume ball trying on different things, instead of someone whose clothes indicate a real and serious person.

All texts including the representations of gender can be interpreted in a variety of ways: they offer not only dominant cultural interpretations but also possibilities of reading them against the grain. Feminist and Cultural Studies have explored whether and how the dominant representations of gender in mainstream popular culture offer such possibilities to negotiate and oppose the traditional meanings embedded in them (see Medhurst, Chapter 20 in this volume). These studies suggest that the objectification central to the dominant male spectator position is hardly relevant to the oppositional meanings dug up by female audiences. On the contrary, it is the pleasure evoked by the particular subjectivity of both female and male characters on display and the relations between them that distinguish the oppositional but marginal female spectator position. Watching, for instance, a replay of an old movie like *Gentlemen Prefer Blondes* (1953), it is immediately clear how the female stars Marilyn Monroe and Jane Russell are framed as objects of male desire (which for that matter was also their public image) and the narrative is driven by their quest for heterosexual romance. Two feminist authors have pointed out that underneath this dominant patriarchal meaning, there is a story of resistance to male objectification and female love and friendship (Arbuthnot and Seneca 1982). Monroe and Russell never let themselves be looked at passively, they always return the gaze of men defyingly. In their dress and stature they resist objectification which is furthermore prevented by particular camera angles and lighting. We hardly ever see them filmed from the side which would emphasize their body contours. The narrative could also be read as a story of female friendship instead of heterosexual romance: when Monroe and Russell have finally succeeded in finding a husbnd, in the final double wedding scene they look at each other as much as at their husbands suggesting the equal importance of their relationship with each other.

Other authors have found similar alternative reading possibilities in other film and television texts (Brunsdon 1986; Doane 1982; Johnson 1993; Kuhn 1982; Stacey 1987; White 1991; Van Zoonen 1994). The common ground in all these analyses is an attempt to reveal the female pleasures evoked by popular genres and 'to hear the strong feminine resisting voices even within mainstream cultural artefacts' (Byars 1991: 20).

Current trends in the representation of the male body are obviously meant to offer women as well as (young) men sources of pleasure in mainstream culture more directly (Chapman and Rutherford 1988). It has become less rare to see the male body displayed in ways similar to the exhibition of women's bodies. Historically, mainstream culture has always provided possibilities for women to look at men, be it not in a very public way. The music and soccer stars that cover girl's bedrooms are enjoyed in their private space. In melodrama and soap operas that are watched inside the home it has also not been uncommon to see the male body constructed as an object of the female gaze. Their bodies, however, are hardly ever simply objectified and presented as desirable in themselves, but they usually figure in a romantic instead of a sexual narrative. Even the way male bodies are displayed in magazines aimed at women like *Playgirl* supports fantasies of romance rather than of female heterosexual desire (Ang 1983). The models look at us as if we are close friends; the aesthetic photography draws attention to the constructedness of the image rather than suggesting the representation of an available and willing man as in male pornography; finally the accompanying text focuses on personalities rather than on sizes thus preventing objectification. This strategy seems to be following women's wishes. Porn magazines for women such as *For Women* and *Women Only* (founded in 1992 and 1993 respectively) created eroticized images of men specifically for women to consume. Yet, even in the 1990s, their founding editor Isabel Koprowski says that women do want to see

> The Chippendale type, very muscular, oiled bodies. They also want to see men who look as though they've got personality: men who perhaps aren't as well developed: and they want, you know, dark men, fair men, red-headed men – all kinds of men. The thing that really impressed me was that for a men's magazine you could fill it with busty blondes and with very little editorial and men would buy it. You cannot do that with women.
>
> (Evans and Gamman 1995: 31)

Whereas such displays of the male nude as a desirable, be it romantic, subject have long been confined to women's realms and cultural expressions, recently we have come to see images of male bodies in a variety of genres aimed at women and men, or meant for consumption in public space. These displays in no way resemble the way women's bodies are displayed. In advertising, for instance, the typical male nude is muscular which underlines his physical power instead of his submissiveness. Often the model does not look at us directly, but is engaged in some kind of activity in which the audience seems to have caught him. If he looks at us directly it is in a direct and intimidating rather than inviting way. Some years ago, an utterly masculine genre like the police series featured a hero that offered a spectacular physical and romantic sight to female audiences. *Miami Vice*'s Sonny Crockett (Don Johnson) not only exhibited the hard-boiled masculine qualities expected of a tough policeman but also was presented with qualities usually reserved to women on TV: physical attractiveness and a caring and sensitive nature. King (1990) even argues that the visual and narrative codes in *Miami Vice* construct Sonny as predominantly 'feminine' and thinks that much male criticism of the series can be explained as fear of the 'effeminate' man. Women's pleasure in *Miami Vice*, however, had as much to do with Crockett's body as with his romantic and caring image. The latter seems as important for the pleasure that women derive from watching men as their bodily features. The British TV series *Inspector Morse* captured an audience of around 15 million and was arguably the most resounding television success of the late 1980s and early 1990s. Morse is a source of pleasure for many men and women and combines a passionate pursuit of justice and a narrative position of complete control with nurturing and caring qualities. By representing Morse as a hero who is both ideal mother and ideal father the series secures a large (female) audience. Unlike other male detectives, emotion and intuition rather than intellect and deduction are Morse's trademark (Thomas 1995). On top of that, Morse remains, because of his lack of a steady relationship, the ideal lover, 'always more involved than the women in question, and not afraid to admit it'. And we never even get to see his naked body!

Frank Mort (1988) insists that what is going on in the male advertising hype is more subtle than the profit motive.

> Young men are being sold images which rupture traditional icons of masculinity. They are stimulated to look at themselves – and other men – as objects of consumer desire. They are getting pleasures previously branded taboo or feminine.
>
> (Mort 1988: 194)

In the meantime the proportion of cosmetics, a traditional female market, sold to male consumers is rising above 25 per cent. Maybe the issues thrown up here are not only about a politics of gender, but also one of *generation*. The organization of the look in the younger segment of the market seems to cross the traditional gender lines. Advertisements for perfumes, traditionally directed at separate audiences, are focusing on both boys and girls. Fashion statements in magazines like *Arena* and *The Face* transcend gender and cause so-called 'gender trouble' (Butler 1990). Sometimes it is impossible to detect whether the model is male or female. Is it time to distance ourselves from Berger's clichés? Is it time to make space for queer relations of looking?

> One of my students is graduating this afternoon and I have to deliver a speech for her. The Graduation Hall, a former chapel more than three centuries old, is filled with family, friends and fellow-students. On the walls, almost right under the ceiling, there are rows of eighteenth-century paintings of famous academics whose pictures have been painted a long time ago to honour them as benefactors and deans of the university. They look very much alike and I have some difficulty in telling them apart; the classic paintings seem interchangeable. The aura of power, authority and learnedness that is in all of them reminds me in a way of the interchangeable public officials on the cover of the magazines in the news stand. I ask the graduation audience to look up to these men and realize that they are not so much there in their own right but to symbolize the academy and to confer on us the appropriate awe and respect. The family and friends too, I think, have had to pass the red light district to get to the ceremony, but I wonder whether they realize the striking differences and resemblances between male and female symbols. It is not such a long way from Pamela Anderson to Desiderius Erasmus.

Summarizing our analysis, we conclude that the representation of gender in mainstream culture is profoundly asymmetrical. This asymmetry appears in various dimensions of representation. If we think, first, of representations as a reflection of real persons, Goffman (1979) argues that pictures of men have a closer link to reality than pictures of women: they occur more often in non-fictional genres like news and current affairs and – as Goffman claims – their images in advertising have a more direct reference to reality than images of women. Behind the pictures of men audiences will imagine real persons, says Goffman, whereas behind the pictures of women, audiences will see models pretending to be real persons. The 'realistic' qualities of images of men, however, does not preclude a second, symbolic dimension in their representation. As the portrait gallery in our Graduation Hall revealed, pictures of men may also refer to more abstract cultural values such as power, rationality, wisdom and learnedness. Such so-called iconic features are not reserved for old paintings but are part of contemporary images of men as public officials as well; the pictures of world leaders meeting each other in the news or facing us from magazine covers are partly as interchangeable as the paintings on the wall. But the iconic elements of the representation of men are again different from the iconic qualities in the representation of women. Whereas such male icons can be seen to refer to actual social positions of men – for power and its associated values are indeed male preserves in patriarchal societies – female icons mainly refer to social fantasies about women. The Pamela Andersons of this world and her historic, contemporary and future counterparts imply a fantasy of white femininity which is characterized by sexuality and seductiveness. This referential difference between male and female icons has consequences for the mode of address – a third element of representation – too: the public official positions audiences at a distance and invites respect and admiration; the sexy blonde welcomes closeness and invites desire for male audiences (to have) and identification or envy (to be) for female audiences. Although some representations of men and women, especially those currently fashionable in advertising and fashion magazines, try to subvert this pattern by inviting more fluid gender-identifications, asymmetrical gender patterns occur here too. The way that female spectators are positioned by pictures of the male body is characterized by personification and subjectivity, as opposed to the objectification invited by the female body on display; the fantasy evoked by the male pin-up is often one of romance rather than of sex, as with the female pin-up.

Mainstream gender culture as expressed in representation, however, is continuously contested and undermined, by textual characteristics and audience activities alike. It is in the nature of texts to offer multiple meanings and even the ostentatious traditional image of Pamela Anderson is seen to invite oppositional readings, for instance by 13 year olds who recognize and try to withstand the values being sold to them. Whereas gender representation is a powerful and unavoidable part of mainstream sexist culture that we can hardly escape, its effectiveness is contested.

It is running late and I decide to go home. On my way out of the office I pick up my mail hoping to read it on the bus. But it is rush hour and the bus is crowded. I try to find a place to stand comfortably and see space next to the driver. A sign says it is prohibited to stand there. I decide to ignore it and move to the free space . . . nothing happens; the driver doesn't seem to mind. I wonder whether all the gender images and signs we see on a day-to-day basis may function in a similar way. When we decide to ignore them and move into the free space, what would happen? We are approaching the suburbs and the bus empties. I find a seat and check my mail. One interesting letter from England: it is an invitation to write a chapter about representation of gender for an introductory text edited by Paul Cobley and Adam Briggs. I wonder, what angle could I use? The bus arrives at my stop: I get out and step right in front of Pamela Anderson's obtrusive body: I know what to do.

Questions

1 This chapter mentions two approaches to representation. Which two are they and how are they related to realistic and discursive reading strategies?

2 How might it be possible for women to experience media representations of themselves as pleasurable and empowering?

3 What are the different pictorial qualities of the representations of the bodies of women and of men?

References

Ang, I. (1983) Mannen op zicht: Marges van het vrouwelijk voyeurisme, *Tijdschrift voor Vrouwenstudies*, 4(3), 418–35.

Arbuthnot, L. and Seneca, G. (1982) 'Pretext and text in *Gentlemen Prefer Blondes, Film Reader 5*', reprinted in P. Erends (ed.) *Issues in Film Criticism*, Bloomington, IN: Indiana University Press.

Barthel, D. (1988) *Putting on Appearances: Gender and Advertising*, Philadelphia, PA: Temple University Press.

Berger, J. (1972) *Ways of Seeing*, Harmondsworth: Penguin.

Brunsdon, C. (ed.) (1986) *Films for Women*, London: British Film Institute.

Butler, J. (1990) *Gender Trouble*, London: Routledge.

Byars, J. (1991) *All That Hollywood Allows: Re-reading Gender in 1950s Melodrama*, Chapel Hill, NC: University of North Carolina Press.

Cantor, M. (1978) 'Where are the women in public broadcasting?', in G. Tuchman (ed.) *Hearth and Home: Images of Women in the Media*, New York: Oxford University Press.

Chapkis, W. (1986) *Beauty Secrets: Women and the Politics of Appearance*, Dutch translation: Schoonheidsgeheimen, Amsterdam: Sara.

Chapman, R. and Rutherford, J. (eds) (1988) *Male Order: Unwrapping Masculinity*, London: Lawrence & Wishart.

Costera Meijer, I. (1991) 'Seksualiteit in reclame: mannengeur en homo-erotiek', in A. Kaiser and L. van Zoonen (eds) *Blikvanger: Reclame: Het spel van kijken en bekeken worden*, Amsterdam: Uitgeverij In de Knipscheer.

Coward, R. (1982) 'Sexual violence and sexuality', *Feminist Review* 11 (Summer): 9–22.

Doane, M.A. (1982) 'Film and the masquerade: theorizing the female spectator', *Screen* 23(3–4): 74–87.

Dyer, R. (1992) *Only Entertainment*, London: Routledge.

Easthope, A. (1990) *What a Man's Gotta Do: The Masculine Myth in Popular Culture*, London: Routledge.

Evans, C. and Gamman, L. (1995) 'The gaze revisited, or reviewing queer viewing', in P. Burston and C. Richardson (eds) *A Queer Romance: Lesbians, Gay Men and Popular Culture*, London: Routledge.

Evans, C. and Thornton, M. (1989) *Women and Fashion: A New Look*, London: Quartet.

Fiske, J. (1987) *Television Culture*, London: Methuen.

Geraghty, C. (1996) 'Representation and popular culture', in J. Curran and M. Gurevitch, (eds) *Mass Media and Society*, 2nd edn, London: Arnold.

Goffman, E. (1979) *Gender Advertisements*, New York: Harper & Row.

Johnson, B. (1993) 'Lesbian spectacles: Reading *Sula, Passing, Thelma and Louise*, and *The Accused*', in M. Garber, J. Matlock and R.L. Walkowitz (eds) *Media Spectacles*, New York: Routledge.

Katz, J. (1995) 'Advertising and the construction of violent white masculinity', in G. Dines and J. Humez (eds) *Gender, Race and Class in Media*, London: Sage.

King, S.B. (1990) ' "Sonny's virtues": the gender negotiations of *Miami Vice*', *Screen* 31: 281–95.

Kuhn, A. (1982) *Women's Pictures: Feminism and the Cinema*, London: Pandora.

Kurtz, I. (1986) *Malespeak*, London: Cape.

Mercer, K. and Julien, I. (1988) 'Race, sexual politics and Black masculinity: a dossier', in R. Chapman and J. Rutherford (eds) *Male Order: Unwrapping Masculinity*, London: Lawrence & Wishart.

Moore, S. (1988) 'Here's looking at you, kid!', in L. Gamman and M. Marshment (eds) *The Female Gaze*, London: Women's Press.

Mort, F. (1988) 'Boys own? Masculinity, style and popular culture', in R. Chapman and J. Rutherford (eds) *Male Order: Unwrapping Masulinity*, London: Lawrence & Wishart.

Stacey, J. (1987) 'Desperately seeking difference', *Screen* 28(1): 48–61.

Thomas, L. (1995) 'In love with Inspector Morse: feminist subculture and quality television', *Feminist Review* 51 (Autumn): 1–25.

White, P. (1991) 'Female spectator, lesbian specter: *The Haunting*', in D. Fuss (ed.) *Inside/Out: Lesbian Theories, Gay Theories*, London: Routledge.

Wolff, N. (1990) *The Beauty Myth,* London: Chatto & Windus.

Zoonen, L. van (1994) *Feminist Media Studies,* London: Sage.

Further reading

Craig, S. (ed.) (1992) *Men, Masculinity and the Media.* London: Sage.

Dyer, R. (1993) *The Matter of Images: Essays on Representation,* London: Routledge.

Hermes, J. (1995) *Reading Women's Magazines,* Cambridge: Polity.

MacDonald, M. (1995) *Representing Women: Myths of Femininity in the Popular Media,* London: Edward Arnold.

McCracken, E. (1993) *Decoding Women's Magazines: From Mademoiselle to Ms,* London: Macmillan.

Moore, S. (1991) *Looking for Trouble: On Shopping, Gender and the Cinema,* London: Serpent's Tail.

Myers, K. (1987) 'Towards a feminist erotica', in R. Betterton (ed.) *Looking On: Images of Femininity in the Visual Arts and Media,* London: Pandora.

Treacher, A. (1988) 'What is life without my love: desire and romantic fiction', in S. Radstone (ed.) *Sweet Dreams: Sexuality, Gender and Popular Fiction,* London: Lawrence & Wishart.

Zoonen, L. van (1994) *Feminist Media Studies,* London: Sage.

Zoonen, L. van (1995) 'Gender, representation, and the media', in J. Downing, A. Mohammadi and A. Sreberny-Mohammadi (eds) *Questioning the Media: A Critical Introduction,* London: Sage.

Chapter 22

Race and ethnicity

THE CONSTRUCTION OF BLACK AND ASIAN ETHNICITIES
IN BRITISH FILM AND TELEVISION

SARITA MALIK

The British media has had a turbulent relationship with issues of race and ethnicity, particularly when related to Black and Asian diasporas. (I shall use 'Black' as a collective political term to refer to those of African, Caribbean and South Asian descent. I shall also use the term 'Asian' for those specifically from the Indian subcontinent. 'Diaspora' refers to a group of dispersed people, so in this instance it indicates Black and Asian people within the British context.) Indeed, the very word 'race' in the cultural and political terrain has almost universally been aligned with Black and Asian people, as though they are the only racial groups that 'own' an ethnicity. There have been very few occasions when 'Whiteness' itself, and more specifically English people, have been depicted as a racial group with their own distinct culture, ethnicity and identity (see Higson, Chapter 25 in this volume). Whiteness has been naturalized, as though it is an invisible norm in comparison to other ethnicities which are different and distinct. Without wishing to reiterate this 'naturalizing process' enjoyed by White ethnicities, I shall be looking at 'Blackness', to outline some of the key ways in which it has been approached across different media forms and texts.

Different approaches to reading race in the media

Approaches to the reading of race in the context of media representation have generally taken two forms. The first has examined the relationship between audiences of the media and the messages which they transmit about ethnicity. This has involved an exploration of the patterns of media representations of race and the impact of the media on its consumers. Media theorists in the field of race and representation have tended to focus on issues around *textuality* and *content* by analysing how various media forms choose to select and present information on different racial groups. The second strategy has been to investigate possible connections between the consumers of media images and those in control of its output, by considering the dynamics between ownership, control and content. This strand of research has focused on the *process* of media production and considers wider social, political and economic implications of the media. It is connected to issues of authorship and examines whether those in control of output (largely White, middle-class men) affect the types of images which the media produces. It is also related to issues of 'access' and more recently, a consideration of policy and the impact of satellite and 'global television'.

The functionalist vs the Marxist view

Broadly speaking, there are two key attitudes towards depictions of race in the media: one (the functionalist view) argues that programme-makers/ journalists 'cater for what the public wants' and simply reflect attitudes, tastes and opinion on ethnicity; the other (the Marxist view) is that those in control of media output shape how audiences/readers view race. The former, like the 'reflectionist' view, argues that the media are merely a 'window on the world', thus implying that the media are inert industries which simply mirror real life. It overlooks the social construction of images in the cultural field, and the fact that a medium, such as television, constructs a reality and a world of its own.

The latter, the Marxist view, rests on the assumption that the ruling elite deny space and access for competing ideologies and images. Their argument follows that the media merely reproduce the 'dominant ideology' as a means of enabling the ruling class to maintain control over less powerful groups in order to establish a common consensus within society. Thus, certain images of Black people as deviant trouble-makers, for example, are perpetuated by the media in order to encourage the mass audience to view Blacks in that particular way. This, in turn, ensures that Black people are categorized as such and reinforces a dominant ideology that suggests that Black people pose a threat to a civilized status quo. The fundamental distinction between the functionalist and Marxist viewpoints is the differing opinion as to whether the media alter or merely reinforce behaviour and attitudes. Of course, there are many whose views on media portrayals of race rest somewhere between the two or that cannot be said to neatly 'fit' into either category.

The equal opportunity view

Few academics have disputed that the media, in general, have been very selective in their portrayal of Black and Asian people. Many have attributed this to the lack of Black and Asian people in key decision-making positions within media industries. (This was discussed at a Commission for Racial Equality (CRE) Conference on Channels of Diversity in March 1996.) Some of those who advocate 'equal opportunity' in the media industries argue that by employing more Black writers, actors, producers, directors, and others, richer and more diverse portraits of Black people will naturally follow. Although it is difficult to dispute that access to the media is desperately needed in employment terms (particularly in key decision-making positions) this, in itself, is no guarantee that a particular set of images will subsequently be produced. To suggest this would be to assume that all Black people (regardless of age, gender, sexuality) share the same political ground. In addition, it encourages a 'siege mentality which says that anything we do must be good' (Henriques 1988: 18).

Stereotypes: positive and negative images

Much of the debate in the area of race and representation has revolved around the issue of 'stereotyping'. Since the 1960s, the sociological term has been widely used to refer to the process by which a given social experience is simplified so as to produce a reductive image/impression. During the 1970s and 1980s, many who were dissatisfied with representations of Black people in the cultural arena, called for 'positive images' in order to balance out the 'negative images' which were all too often packaged by the media. The mid- to late-1980s, in particular, brought a series of debates in which many argued about the limitations of discussing race and representation in these terms. (For example, at the Black People in British Television event which was held at Cinema City, Norwich (May 1988) and the Black Film British Cinema Conference at the Institute of Contemporary Arts (February 1988).)

As I have argued elsewhere, although it is useful to acknowledge the contexts, processes and interests that stereotypes might serve, leaning too heavily on the 'stereotypes/positive and negative image' rhetoric can be limiting in that there can be no absolute agreement as to what these definitively constitute (Malik 1996: 208–9). The British media may have renewed old myths and actively constructed new ones, but it is limiting to believe that by replacing 'bad/negative' with 'good/positive' or by eliminating what some see as stereotypes, images of Black and Asian people in the media will automatically improve. It does little more than promise that a cosmetic sense of reality will be produced. More recent discussions have focused on how a multiplicity of views, of and from Black people, can be transmitted via the media and on how it can depart from what Stuart Hall has defined as the 'grammar of race'. An example of this type of debate was at the Black and White in Colour Conference at the Institute of Contemporary Arts (November 1992), which was subtitled 'Prospects in Black Intervention in British Film and Television'. This, Hall argues, is the traditional diet for the British media, based on three standard images of 'Blackness' – the native, the entertainer and the social problem (Hall 1981).

Stereotypes are short-hand; they are palatable because they help us to decode people. They appear to simplify the world and its subjects, but they are often complex in that we can associate one aspect of a stereotype with many other things; creating a complex web of beliefs from a seemingly glib categorization. Thus the 'Asian immigrant' or the 'Black mugger' tells us more than just that; our stream of consciousness builds on the basic information (issues of language, cultural values, social background, etc. automatically follow) to create a quite detailed (though not necessarily accurate) profile of what that person constitutes. We often find it easier to blame/focus on the stereotypes which serve to represent ourselves and others, than apportion blame/focus on those who control them. Stereotypes are social constructs designed to socially construct. They do not simply come into being from nothing and they are not 'used' in the same way by everyone. The way in which we use stereotypes in cultural production is as revealing as which stereotypes we choose to represent. Stereotypes, in themselves, are not necessarily offensive or harmful, but the interests they can serve and the context in which they *can* be used have the potential to be precisely that.

> The legacy of several hundred years of western expansion and hegemony, manifested in racism and exoticism, continues to be recycled in western cultures in the form of stereotypical images of non-western cultures.
>
> (Pieterse 1992: 9)

Black British identity and British television: the formation years

Although the BBC first transmitted on 2 November 1936, the 1950s was, in real terms, the decade when the medium was installed on a wide-scale basis. This, together with the mass migration of people from Asia, Africa and the Caribbean was to produce a historically complex relationship between art and life, between the media and Black-British ethnicity. Although there had been many Black people in Britain prior to the 1950s, the hostility towards New Commonwealth Black colonial migrants was to manifest itself in complex ways and the UK soon convinced itself that it had a 'race relations problem'. This was reinforced by incidents of 'racial tension' in Camden (London, 1954), Nottingham and Notting Hill (London, 1958). Immigration was perceived only in terms of Black people and they, in turn, began to be seen as a social problem. (This was despite the fact that 350,000 European nationals came to the UK between 1945 and 1957 to alleviate the chronic shortage of labour which Britain faced during the postwar period.)

Those immigrants from the West Indies, India and Pakistan were brought in to provide postwar semi-skilled and unskilled labour. Their poor employment status, together with biologically essentialist racist notions of what 'Blackness' and 'Asianness' were about, encouraged a specific form of hostility towards Black and Asian immigrants compared to White 'newcomers'. The legacy of imperialism and subjugation faced by colonial migrants, together with the fact that in Britain, 'much more than in countries more accustomed to immigration, an expectation of social conformity and a rejection of claims of distinct ethnic identity' (Donald and Rattansi 1992: 2) existed, prompted the divide between who/what was seen as central, normal and universal versus what was perceived as marginal, alien and specific. Since low-paid immigrant labour (predominantly in textiles, factories and transport industries) was usually obtained in the overcrowded conurbations, immigrants suffered poor housing which resulted in overcrowding and in ghettos which Ceri Peach West (1969) has described as 'the geographical expression of complete social rejection'. So where immigrants were desperately needed to provide labour, they were also seen to be causing problems in terms of 'numbers' particularly in housing and education.

The difficulties in balancing the 'pros and cons' which Black people were perceived to have brought with them, resulted in confusion. This was perfectly embodied in the British media's ambivalent approach to the treatment of Black ethnic communities.

Different 'moral panics' circulated concerning Asians and African-Caribbeans and each were seen to posses their own set of problems. Paul Gilroy has described this racist ideology:

> [West Indians] may not be as different or as foreign as Asians who are, by comparison, handicapped by the strength and resilience of their culture. . . . Where West Indian culture is weak, Asian communities suffer from a surfeit of culture which is too strong.
>
> (Gilroy 1983: 131)

Asians were often seen as overly traditional, unwilling/unable to integrate, having 'language problems' or oppressed by their own communities (often in the form of 'arranged marriages'). African-Caribbeans, by contrast, were often depicted as trouble-makers, as muggers or rioters, or were seen to possess the 'natural attributes' of athletes or entertainers. However they were located, it was always in relation to 'Englishness' which was assumed to be central to 'normal' patterns of behaviour.

Images of Blackness in the 1950s and 1960s

A key feature of postwar programming was the construction of the image of Black people as a social problem. This was particularly perpetuated in news and documentary television programming of the 1950s and 1960s. Early actuality programming revealed not only how Black people were generally viewed in British society, but also how British society viewed itself. British television's 'social eye' had not yet fully developed prior to the 1950s. The BBC aimed to avoid contentious, provocative or 'overtly political' subjects:

> It saw its task as an essentially neutral position of the outside world into the living room, of providing 'a panorama of actualities' that ranged from the rituals of the sporting calendar to those of royalty and the state. In projecting and affirming a corporate national life, the BBC saw itself as

merely reflecting, passing on in an unmediated form to the viewers their
own national heritage.

(Scannell 1979: 7)

It was a turbulent period in home affairs with immigration and decolon-
ization key issues in a postwar welfare-state Britain. In terms of audience
address, early documentaries focused on contemporary problems in British
society from 'our'/the (White) audience's point-of-view. Black people were
not assumed to come within the 'our' category and were regularly located
as troubled social subjects on British television. The first full-length television documentary programme to examine the problems faced by Black immigrants in Britain was *Special Enquiry: Has Britain A Colour Bar?* (31 January
1955). Although the programme implied that the primary reason for discrimination and a colour bar was 'cultural difference' rather than racism,
it provoked emotive responses from many White viewers who felt that it was
a defence of Black people in its acknowledgement that racial discrimination
existed in Britain. Many documentaries at this time such as *Black Marries
White* (1964), *The Negro Next Door* (1965) and *People in Trouble: Mixed Marriage* (1958), by focusing on the social, emptied out the political connotations of racial discrimination. The focus on numbers and statistics in actuality
programming supported Enoch Powell's fears that White British people
would be invaded by their racial Others. (Enoch Powell, a Conservative MP,
supported New Right views in the postwar period and articulated his fear
of Britain being 'swamped by alien cultures' in his notorious 'Rivers of
Blood' speech in April 1968.) The 'numbercentric' approach to analysing
race implied that the presence of Black people in Britain needed to be read
in terms of the problematic:

> You simply have to look at the programme with one set of questions in your
> mind: Here is a problem, defined as 'the problem of immigration'. What is
> it? How is it defined and constructed through the programme? What logic
> governs its definition? And where does that logic derive from? . . . The logic
> of the argument is 'immigrants=blacks=too many of them=send them home'.
> That is a racist logic.
>
> (Hall 1981: 46)

Enoch Powell was regularly called on as an 'expert' in the field on race to
articulate a forecast of trouble caused by Black people's presence. Despite
the British media's self-image of neutrality and balance, it regularly granted
space to those with overtly racist viewpoints, including Ku-Klux-Klan (KKK)
members (e.g. David Duke on an edition of *Tonight*), the British National
Party and the National Front. Although this was done in the name of 'free
speech', it highlighted the risk of providing a public arena for racist dialogue. The popular sitcom *Till Death Us Do Part* (BBC, 1966–74), although
its creator (Johnny Speight) vehemently insisted that it was supposed to
'deal with race' by 'exposing bigotry', allowed its blatantly racist central
character, Alf Garnett, to become a harmless national icon.

Those few programmes which did offer an alternative viewpoint to dominant mainstream representations of race, still tended to be made by White men who attempted to tell Black people's stories (for example, *Fable*, 1965, *A Man from the Sun*, 1956). It was only really in the light entertainment (music and dance) and sport genres that Black people were deemed 'acceptable'. Nearly all representations were done in the voice of somebody else and Black people (particularly in news and documentary programming) were explained to what was assumed to be a White audience. The first programme to recognize that a space should be created for a specific racial audience was *Asian Club* (BBC, 1953–61), but this was basically an integration service where the *difference* of the Asian immigrant was always central to the discourse. *Apna Hi Ghar Samajkiye* (BBC, first transmission 10 October 1965) and *Nai Zindagi Naya Jeevan* (BBC, November 1968–82) had similar objectives but slightly broader repertoires.

One of the most offensive recurrent images of Blackness could be seen in *The Black and White Minstrel Show* (BBC, 1958–78), where entertainers 'blacked up' to re-enact the 'docile, happy Black slave' and 'coy White women' scenario of the American Deep South. The imagery was deeply troubling not only because it caricatured Black people (as gormless singers and dancers), but also because during the two decades in which the Saturday night phenomenon was transmitted, there were very few alternative images of Black and Asian people on British television. Despite (or perhaps because of) its widespread popularity, some such as the Campaign Against Racism in the Media petitioned for its removal from our screens (as early as 1967) and the BBC finally stopped producing the programme in the late 1970s. Bob Woffinden notes that

> the tide had turned, and for the BBC it had developed into a matter of competing embarrassments: the embarrassment of continuing to support the show weighed against the embarrassment of taking it off, which would mean both depriving millions of licence-payers of what appeared to be their favourite programme and also implicitly admitting that if it was wrong at the point that it was taken off, then it must have been wrong all along.
>
> (Woffinden 1988: 11)

Issues of access: 1970s

It was not until the 1970s that Black people began to use the media as a forum to 'answer back' to years of verbal negation and visual absence in the British media.

> The question is ... not whether the media are manipulated, but who manipulates them. A revolutionary plan should not require the manipulators to disappear; on the contrary, it must make everyone a manipulator.
>
> (Hans Magnus Enzensburger in McQuail 1972: 107)

Many different groups in society (women, gays, disabled and elderly people) began to demand better rights and access to institutions such as the media, and became more vocal and cohesive in their criticism of the media's articulation of restricted voices and viewpoints.

Many ITV companies such as London Weekend Television (LWT) began to experiment with schedules by using low-risk off-peak slots to respond to calls to improve minority programming. *Babylon* (LWT, 1979) for example, was a short series specifically targeted at young Black Londoners and the London Minorities Unit was subsequently set up under John Birt (then Head of Factual Programmes at LWT). This was followed by *Skin*, a thirty-minute documentary series aimed at Asian and African-Caribbean communities who were generally seen to be united by discrimination in housing, education and employment. Many criticized the series, however, for explaining the Black minority to a White majority, for being *about* not *for* Black communities and for always discussing Black people in relation to White people.

By the 1970s, analysis of the media (particularly television), its functions and its effects became central to cultural criticism and many Black and Asian people became more vocal and cohesive in their criticism of the media's articulation of restricted voices and viewpoints. Slots such as the BBC's *Open Door* attempted to 'redress the balance' by expressing otherwise underrepresented viewpoints. For example, the Campaign Against Racism in The Media used one such slot to make *It Ain't Half Racist Mum* (1 March 1979), 'a programme *about* the media and racism, *on* the media, *against* the media' (Hall 1981: 47).

'Access' slots formed an integral part of the public sphere, a forum in which the structure of the state could be questioned. At the same time, the concept of 'access' was criticized for being both paternalistic and patronizing by assuming that public service broadcasters such as the BBC should have the power to grant access to those who effectively pay their fee (in the form of the television licence) (Gardner 1979: 19). The paucity of such slots also needed to be noted, since they were not sufficient in themselves to undercut the current of standardized images of Black people in media representation. Such precious slots triggered debates about strategy and about *how* to approach form and content. They also prompted many to voice their concerns about the pressure which limited space brought – not only the pressure to say 'everything' in one slot, but also the pressure to please *all* sectors of Black communities at the same time. This impossible task has been termed 'the burden of representation' (Mercer 1994: 81).

During this time, the treatment of Black people in the representational field was largely uncoordinated and clumsy. There was also an ambivalent response towards the media. On the one hand, it was seen as a site of conflict where dominant power relations in society were perpetuated, but on the other, it was seen as a critical space where voice could be given to otherwise silenced communities. British broadcasting however, was soon to witness one of the most radical moments in the medium's history in relation to the Black British audiences, with the formation of Channel Four.

The emergence of Channel Four and multicultural departments

In response to a growing debate about the role of television in social life, the BBC set up the Independent Programmes Complaints Commission in October 1977 to consider viewer's complaints about particular radio and television broadcasts. In the same year, the Annan Committee promoted the concept of 'liberal pluralism', a free-marketplace in which balance could be achieved through the competition of a multiplicity of diverse and independent voices. This reconceptualization symbolized a shift in terminology and an erosion of the very principle of 'public service broadcasting' on which British television had traditionally been founded. The Committee suggested that 'Good broadcasting would reflect the competing demands of a society which was increasingly multi-racial and pluralist.' Discussions about the fourth channel subsequently began.

Black programming was built into the structure of Channel Four and it was the first time ever that someone had been specifically appointed to commission programmes for a non-White British audience (Farukkh Dhondy replaced Sue Woodford as Commissioning Editor for Multicultural Programming in 1984). Channel Four also signified a new pattern of organized production in that it was to operate as a 'publishing house', commissioning innovative work from different production units. Some commented that Lord Whitelaw's (then Home Secretary) enthusiasm for the channel was only so that a 'safety-valve' could be provided for those who, in the year prior to the channel's launch (1981), had protested on Britain's streets about state racism. Nevertheless, Channel Four had built up a large number of 'black programmes' by the mid-1980s, which formed a significant part of its weekly schedule. These included *Black On Black* and *Eastern Eye* (1982–5), Black magazine programmes which were targeted towards African-Caribbeans and Asians respectively. The regularity with which the programmes were screened was unique in that there was an ongoing weekly presence of Black people on British television. Since then, no terrestrial television channel has matched that consistency in terms of a specifically targeted Black programme, although there have been series such as the BBC's *All Black, East* and *Birthrights* and Channel Four's *Black Bag* and *Bandung File.* Channel Four also screened specifically Black-targeted sitcoms such as *Tandoori Nights* and *No Problem!* which, although they came under criticism for lampooning Black characters and perpetuating stereotypes of Black and Asian people, represented a shift away from the blatantly racist 'name-calling'-style sitcoms of the 1970s such as *Love Thy Neighbour, Mixed Blessings* and *Mind Your Language.* Generally speaking though, Channel Four has been more successful in its actuality programming than in its popular fiction output, in terms of moving beyond racial boundaries which posits one race against another and in escaping stereotypical delineations. The BBC Multicultural Department meanwhile has been severely criticized for reiterating problem-orientated discourses in its documentary series such as *All Black* and *East,* by focusing on issues such as rent boys, prostitution,

Asian pornography and girl-baby killing. Many have argued that Black programmes should do for Black audiences what other programmes fail to do, to use the space to redress the imbalance. As Sivanandan (1983) says in relation to *Eastern Eye* and *Black On Black* in the 1980s,

> What *we* want on 'Black on Black' and 'Eastern Eye' is an unbalanced view. We don't want a balanced view. The whole of society is unbalanced against us, and we take a programme and balance it again.
>
> (Sivanandan 1983: 7)

Indeed the very presence of specialist units and racially targeted programming has sparked off disparate opinion about whether/how they can provide for Black audience needs. The main worry that some have about the existence of multicultural units is that they encourage the 'ghettoization' of Black programmes, experiences and programme-makers by containing them at the margins, and thus always ensuring they remain peripheral to mainstream television developments and portrayals. Furthermore, there is the fear that the existence of minority units allows other commissioners/ departments 'off the hook' since they rely on the specialist units to have a conscience about Black audience needs.

Channel Four and Black British independent film practices

The radical impact of Channel Four, the development of Black British independent film workshops and the centrality of debates around Third Cinema, identity and diasporic experiences are central to any discussions of race, ethnicity and the media. All occurred in the 1980s, a period where contestation over national identity increasingly developed as a central political and social issue and as a preoccupation of emergent forms of representation. In 1978, the soon-to-be-elected Prime Minister, Margaret Thatcher, echoed Enoch Powell's infamous 1968 'Rivers of Blood' speech when she spoke of the threat of being 'swamped by alien cultures'. The jingoistic bandwagon which Thatcher invited the 'authentic' members of the British population to jump on to and her appointment as leader of the Conservative government in 1979, shifted the party increasingly to the Right. Two years later in 1981 there were uprisings in St Paul's (Bristol), Toxteth (Liverpool) and Brixton (London). The politically stifling atmosphere of the 1980s acted as a catalyst, triggering off creativity and a strong desire to express and find a cohesive voice. Echoing the Black Power movement in the 1960s in the USA, many Asian, African and Caribbean people in 1980s Britain began to use the collective term 'Black' as a political term.

One of the most innovative interventions to emerge out of this sociopolitical context was Black British film, mostly in the form of grant-aided regional film collectives. The emergence of independent workshops such as Black Audio Film Collective, Ceddo, Sankofa and Retake Film and Video

Collective in the 1980s, was created within a specific and rapidly changing social, political and, economic framework. Many films made by these Black British cinematic practitioners signified a shift from the dominant linear forms of narrative towards a more experimental, non-linear and eclectic filmic style and, as such, challenged the Hollywood conventions of 'how to tell a story'. In terms of content, documentary films such as *Handsworth Songs* (John Akomfrah, Black Audio Film Collective, 1986) and *The People's Account* (Ceddo, Milton Bryan, 1988) and fictional features such as *The Passion of Remembrance* (Sankofa, Isaac Julien and Maureen Blackwood, 1986) and *Majdhar* (Retake, Ahmed A. Jamal, 1985) tenaciously invested in the notion of identity. *Handsworth Songs*, in particular, with its innovative, unsettling interrogation of the 1980s Brixton 'race riots', prompted a number of debates about how to address Black and White audiences, about the documentary form and about dealing with issues of history and memory.

Many Black British films of the 1980s continued the tradition and extended the framework established by film-makers such as Horace Ove (*Baldwin's Nigger*, 1969; *Reggae*, 1970; *Pressure*, 1975), Lionel Ngakane (*Jemima and Johnny*, 1963) and Lloyd Reckord (*Ten Bob In Winter*, 1963) in the 1960s and 1970s. If one were to identify a key difference between the two sets of films, then it is possible to notice a general drift from a concern with the 'politics of race' in the earlier films (often focusing on notions of belonging and identity for the Black British subject) to an experimentation with form in the films of the 1980s, where the politics of representation was privileged. Black film-makers in the 1980s approached the spaces they struggled for in a creative way – not only as an arena for dismantling given truths about 'Blackness' and 'Asianness' or 'padding out' what people already knew about Black ethnicity, but also as a critical terrain for artistic experimentation where an entire approach to film could be reconstituted. This also involved a reconceptualization of notions of what constituted British film and Britishness. More recent films to emerge from Black British film-makers have tended to echo the 'crossover' (from art-house to mainstream) pattern of earlier films such as *My Beautiful Laundrette* (1985, dir: Stephen Frears). This has partly been because of certain practitioners' desire for commercial and artistic 'independence', but is also a matter of economics where many Black workshops of the 1980s have faced stringent funding cuts and even closure.

The future for Black British audiences

Recent changes in the television infrastructure, as well as affecting on-screen representations of Black people, have altered the nature of Black British independent film and video production since the sector has traditionally been dependent on the television medium. The impact of cable, satellite, Channel Five, deregulation and the Broadcasting Acts 1990 and 1996 have meant that, generally speaking, commercialism, ratings and revenue have been prioritized over 'minority' needs. Channel Four, for example, has been accused of relinquishing its commitment to Black and Asian audiences and programme-makers by relying on guaranteed audience-pullers (such as US sitcoms and films) which have very little to do with the actualities of British multiculturalism. Just as the BBC have been accused of having a narrow conception of the British public it claims to be serving, many have recently criticized Channel Four for failing to satisfy those under-represented groups that it is required, through its remit, to cater for. The central concerns for today's broadcasting institutions are technological developments and the free market. Together these will encourage a trend towards minorities turning to extra-terrestrial channels to get the media they want. With channels such as Identity Television (IDTV – launched in June 1993 as the first Black entertainment channel) and Zee TV (formerly TV Asia), cable and satellite operators have indicated their keenness to attract niche-audiences, of which Britain's Black and Asian people are considered an integral part. Trevor Phillips has said

> The greatest irony in the TV landscape may well be this: the paternalistic, regulated environment of the terrestrial channels may increasingly force minorities off their agenda, whilst the buccaneering free marketeers of the cable and satellite channels could well begin to offer the chance of a presence hitherto unheard of.
>
> (Phillips 1995: 20)

Sadly, as the millennium approaches and pluralism has come to mean 'more choice, more competition, more channels' rather than 'cultural diversity', things have become increasingly geared towards the market rather than towards serving all sectors of British society. As technology advances and audiences become more fragmented and global at the same time, media consumers are finding that they now have the choice to move towards media markets that bother to directly address them. One of the main fears which the prospect of an increasingly global media future prompts, however, is that of a 'downgrading of cultural specificity in themes and settings and a preference for formats and genres which are thought to be universal' (McQuail 1994: 112). Globalization has the potential to replace local and national variations with an homogenized undifferentiated mass in which sameness is favoured over diversity. 'More' does not always mean 'better' and 'global' does not ensure a dilution of western cultural hegemony.

Conclusion

Many feel that Black and Asian audiences are still not sufficiently catered for and that insensitivity towards issues of race and ethnicity still exist. The reality of a lived multiculturalism is not represented on British television and the media in general can by no means be seen as ethnically neutral. Although it is now commonplace to see Black and Asian people on British television who do not necessarily function to solely 'carry' the race theme, the repertoire of imagery still remains limited. We rarely see strong Asian women (Gita in *EastEnders* and Milly in *This Life* are notable exceptions) or Black sporting commentators (although African-Caribbean men play a prominent role in athletic performance) and there are still too few Black people actually controlling the televisual image in terms of directors, scriptwriters and producers. There is, in addition, a lack of cultural authenticity when it comes to detail – thus, mosques are confused with Hindu temples, Black men with dreadlocks are automatically referred to as Rastafarians, Muslim characters are given Sikh names, and so on. Most importantly, however, is the fact that television, by and large, has not relinquished its investment in the slave, entertainer, social problem types, although these may have taken on more modern forms.

It has been said that 'race', although packaged as a reality, is little more than a social construct. If this is true, then the state apparatus, of which the media are an integral part, has played an active and powerful role in the manufacturing of images of Black and Asian ethnicities. It is time that White people in cultural representation, are seen to possess their own distinct race and ethnicity, rather being seen to carry *the* representative human experience (Dyer 1988: 44–65). It is only by problematizing the nature of White spectatorship and imagery that Blacks and Asians will become more than Others to be looked at and framed by western image-makers.

Questions

1   Identify some common stereotypes of Black and Asian people in the British media and discuss how they have been perpetuated or deconstructed in various media texts.

2   Should British television have special 'minority' programmes targeted at specific ethnic minorities?

3   What impact do you think 'global television', satellite, cable and other technological developments will have on terrestrial television's commitment to Black British and British Asian audiences?

References

Donald, J. and Rattansi, A. (eds) (1992) *'Race', Culture and Difference*, London: Sage.

Dyer, R. (1988) 'White', *Screen: The Last 'Special Issue' on Race?*, 29(4): 44–65.

Gardner, C. (1979) 'Limited access', *Time Out* 23 February.

Gilroy, P. (1983) 'C4 – Bridgehead or Bantustan?', *Screen* 24 (4–5): 130–6.

Hall, S. (1981) 'The whites of their eyes: racist ideologies and the media', in G. Bridges and R. Brunt (eds) *Silver Linings: Some Strategies for the Eighties*, London: Lawrence & Wishart.

Henriques, J. (1988) 'Realism and the new language', *Black Film, British Cinema*, ICA Document 7, London: Institute of Contemporary Arts.

McQuail, D. (ed.) (1972) *Sociology of Mass Communications*, Harmondsworth: Penguin.

McQuail, D. (1994) *Mass Communication Theory: An Introduction*, London: Sage.

Malik, S. (1996) 'Beyond "The cinema of duty"? The pleasures of hybridity: Black British films of the 1980s and 1990s', in A. Higson (ed.) *Dissolving Views: Key Writings on British Cinema*, London: Cassell.

Mercer, K. (1994) *Welcome to the Jungle: New Positions in Black Cultural Studies*, London: Routledge.

Phillips, T. (1995) 'UK TV: a place in the sun?', in C. Frachon and M. Vargaftig (eds) *European Television: Immigrants and Ethnic Minorities*, London: John Libbey.

Pieterse, J.N. (1992) *White on Black: Images of Africa and Blacks in Western Popular Culture*, New Haven, CT: Yale University Press.

Scannell, P. (1979) 'The social eye of television', *Media, Culture and Society* 1(1).

Sivanandan, A. (1983) 'Challenging racism: strategies for the '80s', *Race and Class: British Racism: The Road to 1984*, 25(2): 1–11.

West, C.P. (1969) *Indian Migration to Britain: A Social Geography*, London: Oxford University Press for Institute of Race Relations.

Woffinden, B. (1988) 'Blacking up, blacking down', *The Listener* 119(3069).

Further reading

Buscombe, E. (1980–1) 'Broadcasting from above', *Screen Education* 37 (Winter).

Daniels, T. and Gerson, J. (1989) *The Colour Black: Black Images in British Television*, London: British Film Institute.

Donald, J. and Rattansi, A. (eds) (1992) *'Race', Culture and Difference*, London: Sage.

Hall, S. (1981) 'The whites of their eyes: racist ideologies and the media', in G. Bridges and R. Brunt (eds) *Silver Linings: Some Strategies for the Eighties*, London: Lawrence & Wishart.

Mercer, K. (1988) *Black Film, British Cinema*, ICA Document 7, London: Institute of Contemporary Arts.

Perkins, T.E. (1979) 'Rethinking stereotypes', in M. Barrett, P. Corrigan, A. Kuhn and J. Wolff (eds) *Ideology and Cultural Production*, London: Croom Helm.

Pines. J. (1992) *Black and White in Colour*, London: British Film Institute.

Rutherford, J. (ed.) (1990) *Identity: Community, Culture, Difference*, London: Lawrence & Wishart.

Chapter 23

Youth

'THE GOOD, THE BAD AND THE UGLY' POST-WAR MEDIA
REPRESENTATIONS OF YOUTH

BILL OSGERBY

Mixed metaphors: the dual stereotyping of 'youth'

Reading the British press in the late 1950s, it often seemed as though the
nation was teetering on the edge of a moral abyss. Provincial newspapers
warned of a 'new disease' – 'that of the maladjusted young men who
don special clothes and rebel against any form of discipline' (*Brighton and
Hove Herald* 28 February 1959), reporters conjuring with images of a new
brand of vicious hooligan. The perpetrator of a violent street robbery, for
example, was described as wearing 'the uniform of the "Wild Ones", youths
who ape the dress worn by Marlon Brando in the film of the same name'
(*Brighton and Hove Herald* 11 January 1958) and readers' attention was
drawn to the effrontery of a young tearaway who had appeared in court
sporting the racy ensemble of 'black shirt, pink tie and pink-trimmed jacket'
(*Evening Argus* 23 November 1960). Local anxieties reflected a broader sense
of alarm. Subcultural style was seen as a symptom of spiralling juvenile
criminality which, in turn, was taken to exemplify a more wholesale state
of moral debasement and cultural malaise.

There was, of course, nothing new about these images of juvenile deprav-
ity. Geoffrey Pearson (1983) shows that since at least the nineteenth century the UK has witnessed periods in which public opinion has been outraged
by a seemingly unprecedented wave of hooliganism and debauchery among
the nation's youth. At the turn of the century, for example, the 'scuttling'
gangs of Manchester and the 'Peaky Blinders' of Birmingham were subject
to a degree of social disapproval and official opprobrium akin to that which
has attended groups of postwar youngsters. On one level these concerns
have related specifically to the demeanour and behaviour of young people,
but more generally (and perhaps more significantly) they have also condensed a much wider set of apprehensions. An important 'metaphorical'
dimension exists to media representations of young people. A crucial facet
to the 'youth' debate is its capacity to function as a kind of 'ideological
vehicle' that encapsulates more general hopes and fears about shifts in
social relations and the condition of cultural life.

It is, perhaps, inevitable that conceptions of 'youth' and chronological age will figure in attempts to make sense of social change. Nevertheless, many theorists (Clarke *et al.* 1976; Davis 1990; Smith *et al.* 1975) have pointed to the way in which youth's metaphorical capacity becomes powerfully extended at moments of particularly profound transformation. The twilight years of the nineteenth century were one such episode – concerns around hooliganism and delinquency embodying wider qualms about the stability of the social order and the vitality of the British economy. The decades following the Second World War have been another. Since 1945 the themes and imagery of 'youth' have featured within the mass media and impinged upon the public consciousness as never before – the youth 'question' functioning as a medium through which fundamental shifts in social boundaries and cultural relationships have been explored, interpreted and made sense of.

We do not need to search too hard to find negative representations of youth in postwar Britain. Crime, violence and sexual licence have been recurring themes in the media's treatment of youth culture, the degeneracy of the young depicted as indicative of a steady disintegration of the UK's social fabric. Yet representations of young people have never been entirely pessimistic. Media coverage of youth has been characterized by a recurring duality. This Janus-like quality has seen youth culture both celebrated as the exciting precursor to a prosperous future and, almost simultaneously, vilified as the most deplorable evidence of cultural bankruptcy. These contrasting images – which Dick Hebdige (1988: 19) terms 'youth-as-fun' and 'youth-as-trouble' – are obviously distorted and exaggerated stereotypes that bear tenuous relation to social reality. Nevertheless, their connotative power has been potent and throughout the postwar era this dual imagery of youth has been a key motif around which dominant interpretations of social change have been constructed.

'The teenage revolution'

Although Britain was no stranger to crisis and scandal during the 1950s and early 1960s optimism and confidence were never far away. The nation, it seemed, had 'never had it so good'. As David Dutton (1991) contends, Labour and Conservative governments generally shared a set of key social and economic assumptions that embraced a commitment to the welfare state, a mixed economy and the maintenance of high levels of employment. This sense of political consensus arose in a context of economic growth and a sustained rise in real earnings which, taken together, laid the basis for a steady growth in consumer spending. The working class in particular benefited from these changes, enhanced incomes delivering an ever-growing range of consumer products and domestic appliances to working-class homes. The substance and texture of working-class culture was transformed and recast during this period, though the British working class did not, in any sense, decompose or disappear and structured inequality remained pronounced.

Figure 23.1 'Whatever the pleasure...' Player's Cigarettes 1957

Nevertheless, the dominant imagery of the period was of a dawning 'class-lessness'. Political rhetoric held that the pace of economic growth was ushering in a new era of 'post-capitalist' prosperity in which social divisions would be steadily ameliorated and traditional class antagonisms would evaporate. And within this discourse the image of 'youth-as-fun' found a prominent place.

Postwar mythologies of affluent harmony found their purest manifestation in the imagery of youth. Young people seemed to embody all that the consumer dream stood for and throughout the 1950s and early 1960s advertisers habitually used images of young people to associate their products with dynamic modernity and 'with it' enjoyment. Representations of youth were deployed as a shorthand signifier for unbridled pleasure in the new age of hedonistic consumption (see Figure 23.1). Above all, this equation of youth with consumption was exemplified by the addition of the term 'teenager' to everyday vocabulary. A label first coined by North American market researchers during the mid-1940s, the 'teenager' was quickly imported into British popular discourse, 'teenagers' being taken as the quintessence of postwar social transformation. Distinguished not simply by their youth but also by a particular brand of conspicuous, leisure-oriented consumption, teenagers were perceived as being at the sharp end of the new consumer culture. As Peter Laurie contended in his anatomy of *The Teenage Revolution* (1965: 9), 'The distinctive fact about teenagers' behaviour is economic: they spend a lot of money on clothes, records, concerts, make-up, magazines: all things that give immediate pleasure and little lasting use.'

The 'teenager', then, was far more than a simple descriptive term. Rather, the 'teenager' was an ideological terrain upon which a particular interpretation of postwar change was constructed. Central to the concept of the 'teenager' was the idea that traditional class boundaries were being eroded by the fads and fashions of a newly affluent 'gilded youth' (*The Economist* 11 January 1958). 'Teenagers' were presented as a class in themselves, a 'solidly integrated social bloc' (Laurie 1965: 11) whose vibrant, leisure-orientated lifestyle seemed to offer a foretaste of the kind of prosperity that would soon be within everyone's grasp.

The image of the 'affluent teenager' owed a large debt to research conducted by Mark Abrams (1956, 1959, 1961) on young people's spending patterns during the late 1950s. According to Abrams (1959: 9) youth, more than any other social group, had materially prospered since 1945 – with young people's earnings rising by 50 per cent (roughly double that of adults) and youngsters wielding an annual spending power of around £830 million. Abrams' figures were widely publicized and went a long way towards sedimenting notions of a newly affluent group of young consumers patronizing a leisure market of unprecedented scale. Though exaggerated, his figures were not without foundation. Changes in production processes and shifts in employment markets had created a high demand for youngsters' labour and their earning power had been enhanced as a consequence. The range of products geared to this growing market was literally boundless, consumer industries interacting with and reinforcing one another as they sought to cash-in on youth spending.

The prime example, of course, came in 1956 with the arrival of rock 'n' roll, a genre of popular music tied much more closely than its predecessors to processes of mass marketing and youth demand. The film industry also began to orientate itself to the youth market. John Doherty (1988) has documented the postwar rise of the American 'teenpic', exemplified in the films of Roger Corman and Sam Katzman, but the British film industry also began to seek out youth audiences with greater vigour – the 1950s and early 1960s seeing the release of a host of films featuring pop idols such as Cliff Richard, Tommy Steele and the Beatles. Developments in British radio were more faltering. Restricted by limits on 'needle time' (time permitted for the boadcast of recorded music) and official distrust of the 'Americanizing' influences of rock 'n' roll, it was only with the launch of 'pirate' stations in the early 1960s that British radio began broadcasting programmes specifically geared to a 'teen' audience. Television, in contrast, responded swiftly. BBC and ITV both made numerous forays into the field of 'youth' television. However, while the cinema was able to seek out age-specific audiences, John Hill (1991) has shown that early television programmes had to allow for the domestic environment of their viewers, shows like *Six-Five Special* and *Juke Box Jury* having to embrace a heterogeneous, 'family' audience. Nevertheless, by the early 1960s concessions to adult viewers had diminished, programmes like ITV's *Ready, Steady, Go!* revelling in an atmosphere of teen-exclusivity.

'Youth-as-fun' was a central motif within all these texts. Cliff Richard's films of the early 1960s are exemplary. Sprightly musicals *The Young Ones* (dir. Sidney Furie, 1961) and *Summer Holiday* (dir. Peter Yates, 1963) are both tales of ebullient youngsters liberating themselves from the dull conformity of their workaday lives. The young people here are not rebels but responsible and enterprising citizens, the films' unquestioning sense of freedom and optimism epitomizing the notions of prosperity and dawning social harmony that lay at the heart of dominant political ideologies during the early 1960s. Indeed, politicians were well aware of this and were keen to associate themselves with the positive attributes of such imagery. In these terms Harold Wilson's presentation of Variety Club awards to the Beatles in 1964 and his award of MBEs to the Fab Four in 1965 can be seen not as good-natured gestures by a warm-hearted 'man of the people', but as a deliberate attempt to harvest political capital from the 'language' of youth and modernity.

'Teenage rampage'

During the 1950s and early 1960s the media coverage lavished on young people was often up-beat and laudatory. Newspapers and magazines – especially the *Daily Mirror* and *Picture Post* – helped popularize notions of 'youth' as an excitingly new social force, a vibrant contrast to the dull and wearied social order of the past. However, representations of youth have never been unanimously enthusiastic. Even when the cult of the 'affluent teenager' was at its height, images of 'youth-as-fun' coexisted alongside much darker representations in which young people came to epitomize the worst excesses and direst consequences of social change.

As Dick Hebdige (1982) has shown, critical representations of youth have often been a locus for elitist fears of a 'levelling-down' or 'Americanization' of culture – the USA, the home of monopoly capitalism, coming to epitomize processes of cultural debasement. Typical of such an approach was Richard Hoggart's (1958) critique of postwar popular culture, his attack on 'canned entertainment and packeted provision' reaching a climax in his denouncement of the 'juke box boys' with their 'drape suits, picture ties and American slouch' who spent their evenings in 'harshly lighted milk bars' putting 'copper after copper into the mechanical record player' (1958: 248–50).

Related to this critique of youngsters' cultural preferences has been the stereotyping of young people as a uniquely delinquent generation. This line of argument has often taken subcultural style as its target. During the early 1950s, for example, these anxieties cohered around the figure of the Teddy boy. First identified by the media in the working-class neighbourhoods of south London in 1954, the Ted was soon presented as a shockingly new spectre haunting street corners all over the UK, his negative image compounded in the sensational press coverage of cinema 'riots' that followed screenings of the film *Rock Around the Clock* in 1956. By the end of the decade the Ted's drape-suit had been superseded by the chic, Italian-inspired styles of the mods. However, like the Teds before them, the mods' appearance was often presented by the media as not simply a mode of dress but as a symbol of national decline. This approach reached fever-pitch in press responses to the mod 'invasions' of several seaside resorts in 1964, events given front-page prominence by national newspapers who spoke of a 'day of terror' in which whole towns had been overrun by a marauding mob 'hell-bent on destruction'.

Such spectacular reportage is invariably exaggerated and overwrought. In the case of the mod 'invasions', for instance, the initial acts of violence and vandalism were slight and it is likely that press coverage actually engendered and amplified subsequent disturbances. Stanley Cohen has termed such occasions of sensationalized media alarm 'moral panics', a situation in which

A condition, episode, person or group of persons emerges to become defined as a threat to societal values and interests; its nature presented in a stylized and stereotypical fashion by the mass media, the moral barricades are manned by editors, bishops, politicians and other right-thinking people; socially accredited experts pronounce their diagnoses and solutions; ways of coping are evolved or (more often) resorted to; the condition then disappears, submerges or deteriorates and becomes more visible.

(Cohen 1980)

In these terms distorted media coverage plays an active role in shaping events. Media attention fans the sparks of an initially trivial incident, creating a self-perpetuating 'amplification spiral' which generates phenomena of much greater significance and magnitude.

Cohen's case study focused on media representations of the 1960s 'battles' between mods and rockers, charting how media intervention gave shape to these groups and crafted them into threatening 'folk devils'. However, his arguments could easily be applied to media treatment of the procession of subcultural groups that have appeared since. From the skinheads of the late 1960s, through the punks of the 1970s, to the new age travellers and acid house ravers of the late 1980s and early 1990s, youth subcultures have been subject to processes of stigmatization and stereotyping which, paradoxically, have worked to popularize and lend substance to styles that were initially indistinct and ill defined. Media intervention, therefore, gives youth subcultures not only national exposure but also a degree of uniformity and definition. Indeed, without the intercession of media industries it is unlikely that subcultures such as the Teddy boys, punks or ravers would have cohered as recognizable cultural formations, instead remaining vaguely defined and locally confined stylistic innovations.

Young women have been marginal within those moral panics related to public order. Alarm associated with the mods and rockers' lawlessness, the punks' outrageousness or the violence of football hooligans has generally (though not exclusively) focused on the behaviour of young men. In contrast, young women have figured much more visibly in moral panics related to sexual behaviour and 'permissiveness'. The postwar period, for example, has been punctuated by anxieties regarding perceived rises in the number of teenage pregnancies. For example, the *Daily Mirror* (24 November 1991) revealed 'the startling truth about teenage sex', announcing that Britain was 'in the grip of a teenage pregnancy crisis'. Again, however, these representations are hyperbolic. Certainly, the period since 1945 has witnessed major change in young people's sexual attitudes and behaviour. Empirical evidence, however, indicates that 'casual' promiscuity among British youth has been considerably less than suggested in salacious media accounts, sexual activity generally taking place within single, 'serious' relationships (Leonard 1980; Schofield 1965, 1973).

A parallel can be drawn here between the media's stereotyping of youth and its treatment of sexual behaviour. Just as 'youth' has functioned as an 'ideological vehicle' for the discussion and interpretation of more general social issues, Jeffrey Weeks (1985) argues that developments in the field of sexuality have been taken as symbolic of wider patterns of social transformation. Debates around sexuality have been used to condense broader anxieties and to mobilize opinion and energies – increasingly on behalf of the political Right as the postwar political consensus disintegrated and gave way to a more confrontational and abrasive form of political order.

'Where did our love go?'

Media's representations of 'youth', then, tell us little about the realities of life as experienced by young people, yet are revealing about dominant social and political preoccupations. Both lauded as the shape of wonderful things to come *and* reviled as the incarnation of malevolent forces menacing established ways of life, young people serve as a canvas on which debates about more general patterns of social change are elaborated.

During the 1950s and 1960s media representations of young people became a repository for misgivings about the 'state of the nation'. Spectacular subcultures, in particular, were presented as the neurosis of the affluent society – the alienated product of unfettered consumption and cultural decay. At the same time, however, the image of 'the teenager' encapsulated a more positive reading of change – one in which a new era of growth was fast ameliorating inequality and the generation gap was supplanting the class war as the nation's foremost social division. Indeed, while Britain enjoyed a period of sustained economic prosperity it was this positive stereotyping of youth that was most prevalent. Even subcultural 'folk devils' could be embraced in these feelings of optimism. The mod's superficially clean-cut and well-dressed appearance, for example, was easily co-opted within notions of postwar dynamism and mods were fêted as classless consumers *par excellence*, the media eagerly charting changes in the minutiae of mod dress and musical preference.

By the late 1960s, however, the rhetoric of prosperity and optimism was proving difficult to sustain as deep-seated problems within the British economy became evident. Social and political divisions intensified as industrial decline, unemployment and worsening labour relations steadily undercut notions of consensus and affluence. Stuart Hall and his associates (1978, 1983) argue that this period saw a key shift in British political life, the state increasingly dispensing with attempts to rule by consent, embracing instead political strategies that were more visibly repressive and confrontational. In this context the negative stereotyping of youth became more pronounced. The 1960s counter-culture, especially, was cast as part of a more pervasive 'enemy within'. Whereas earlier subcultures such as the Teds or mods had been depicted as *symptoms* of decline, the counter-culture was presented as actively *causing* a collapse of law and order and social stability. Media coverage of episodes such as university sit-ins and demonstrations against the Vietnam War cast student radicals and hippies as a minority of subversive extremists who deliberately sought to undermine the social and moral mainstays of the nation.

The counter-culture, however, was not universally denounced. Its largely middle-class composition worked to temper criticism and media coverage was sometimes ambiguous, occasionally even positive. The hippies' hedonistic lifestyle, even their drug-taking, could be treated with fascination and respect. In 1968, for instance, in its series 'The Restless Generation', *The Times* praised hippy communes such as the Tribe of the Sacred Mushroom for generating

Figure 23.2 'I'll kick your head', *Daily Mirror* 13 July 1988 (courtesy of Mirror Syndication)

'a fresh approach to living' that provided its members with 'livelihood and fulfilment' (*The Times* 18 December 1968). Similarly, when Rolling Stones Mick Jagger and Keith Richards were found guilty of possession of illegal drugs in 1967 *The Times* leapt to their defence in an editorial that attacked their sentences as unreasonably draconian. Indeed, on leaving court Jagger did not face a barrage of media criticism but was whisked by helicopter to appear on Granada Television's *World in Action*, joining church leaders and politicians in a roundtable discussion on the nature of personal liberty.

The fragmentation and decline of the counter-culture during the early 1970s saw the negative stereotyping of youth return to more 'traditional' subjects. Throughout the 1970s and 1980s groups of working-class youngsters were once again paraded as baleful indices of growing lawlessness and social breakdown. Media preoccupation with street crime in the early 1970s, followed by the spectre of the 'inner-city rioter' in the 1980s, saw the addition of a powerful 'racial' dimension to the imagery of 'youth-as-trouble', while a seemingly endless series of moral panics grafted new terrors (lager louts, acid house parties, 'joy-riding') on to older and more established themes of decline – the collapse of the family, moral laxity, crime, and urban disorder (see Figure 23.2).

'Whatever happened to the teenage dream?'

The resurgence of the media's negative stereotyping of young people during the 1970s and 1980s was commensurate with broader political shifts.
Trading on public fears and apprehensions the New Right managed to
enlist support for an 'authoritarian populism' (Hall 1983) which successfully married a 'populist' appeal with the enforcement of a more coercive
brand of authority and order. However, the ensuing 'law 'n' order' bandwagon did not entirely displace images of 'youth-as-fun'.

Governments of the 1980s galvanized popular support not simply through
the promise of 'order'. Also important was the mobilization of people's
concrete aspirations and desires via the promise of consumer empowerment
in a 'property-owning democracy'. In the rhetoric of 'enterprise' and the
'free market' the positive stereotyping of youth found a new lease of life.
In 1988, for example, the popular press acclaimed 'The Young Revolution'
in which 'Britain's youngsters are riding the roller-coaster boom of Mrs
Thatcher's economic recovery. They have seen a new kind of revolution –
giving power to the consumer – and they want to join the action before it
ends' (*Daily Star* 11 May 1988). Advertizers also eulogized a 'new' brand of
youth consumption. In their report *Youth Lifestyle*, market analysts Mintel
claimed to have discovered among young people a 'new consumption and
success ethic' that had been generated by 'the sustained economic growth
of the enterprise culture', while McCann-Erickson's comprehensive survey,
The New Generation, identified a 'New Wave' of 'post-permissive' youngsters
who were committed to a new spirit of possessive individualism and who
exhibited 'the most highly developed form of the new multi-profile consumption in our society' (McCann-Erickson Worldwide 1989: 25).

Nevertheless, representations of youth made only a cameo appearance
within 1980s ideologies of 'consumer empowerment'. Compared to their
ubiquitous presence within discourses of affluence and dynamism during
the 1950s and 1960s images of 'youth as fun' were relatively marginal to the
rhetoric of the 1980s 'boom'. By the 1980s the concept of the 'teenager' as
the embodiment of hedonistic consumption had become untenable. The
commercial market that provided the basis for the 'teenage revolution' had
been undercut by a combination of the demographic contraction of the
youth population and growing levels of youth unemployment. The youth
market became a shadow of its former self, retailers' and manufacturers'
obsession with youth fading as young people's spending power decreased.
In place of the youth market new growth areas emerged – the fashion, film
and music industries all increasingly realigning to the consumer appetites
of 'empty nesters' and the 'thirty-something' generation. Rather than the
'swinging teenager', therefore, it was the image of the more mature and
cosmopolitan 'yuppy' that captured the mood of the 1980s 'good times'.

Indeed, growing levels of youth unemployment may have fundamentally transformed the connotations of the term 'teenager'. Simon Frith has
argued that the term was originally associated primarily with working-class

youngsters and their consumption patterns but has now come mainly to refer to middle-class youth – 'the only young people for whom the problems of consumption remain paramount' (1981: 13). Certainly, there is some truth to this. In both the UK and the USA representations of 'youth-as-fun' now relate almost exclusively to youngsters from green-lawned, well-to-do suburbs. The US television series *Beverly Hills 90210* is archetypal, with its designer-clad adolescents cruising the streets in expensive convertibles and lounging around luxurious swimming pools. Nevertheless, recent years have seen the harsh realities of the contemporary economic environment extend upwards. Falls in student income and the contraction of the graduate job market has meant that even middle-class youngsters have begun to be excluded from the 'teenage' experience.

The concept of the 'teenager', therefore, has not so much been redefined as gradually disappeared from view. Indeed, the term now seems strangely dated, even anachronistic. In place of the 'teenager' images of a 'lost generation' have come to the fore. From Douglas Coupland's (1992) novel of the same name the term 'Generation X' has entered the popular vocabulary. Coupland's quirky, anomic characters were born in the early to mid-1960s, yet Charles Acland (1995: 145–6) argues that 'Generation X' has come to denote a younger cohort of overeducated and underemployed juveniles leading an apathetic and largely aimless existence. Films such as *River's Edge* (dir. Tim Hunter, 1986) and *Kids* (dir. Larry Clark, 1995) have developed the motif, painting a picture of an adolescence that is not necessarily delinquent or depraved but is desolate and alienated. These texts are American, though British films such as *Trainspotting* (dir. Danny Boyle, 1995) and novels such as John King's *The Football Factory* (1996) deal with similar themes of bleak and meaningless young lives.

In the late 1990s, then, it could be that the traditional stereotypes of 'youth-as-trouble' and 'youth-as-fun' are losing their relevance. Instead we are presented with a more ambiguous and open-ended set of images. Moreover, the media's understanding of 'youth' seems, in some respects, to have become increasingly divorced from the lives of young people themselves. The contemporary television, film, music and advertising industries gear themselves less to specific generational categories than to particular 'mind-sets' and attitudes. As Frith observes of recent trends in music television, ' "Youth" no longer describes a particular type of viewer, who is attracted to a particular type of programme but, rather, describes an attitude, a particular type of *viewing behaviour*' (1993: 75). In these terms media representations of 'youth' are now characterized not by generational age but by a particular lifestyle. 'Youth' has become simply a mode of consumption.

Questions

1 How do the dimensions of gender and race influence and mediate representations of 'youth' in the media?

2   How far, and in what ways, do the media exercise an influence over youth subcultures?

3   How are other generational groups represented in the media? Are there particular kinds of social meanings associated with these images?

References

Abrams, M. (1956) 'The younger generation', *Encounter* 6(5): 35–58.

Abrams, M. (1959) *The Teenage Consumer*, London: Press Exchange.

Abrams, M. (1961) *Teenage Consumer Spending in 1959*, London: Press Exchange.

Acland, C. (1995) *Youth, Murder, Spectacle: The Cultural Politics of 'Youth in Crisis'*, Oxford: Westview.

Clarke, J., Hall, S., Jefferson, T. and Roberts, B. (1976) 'Subcultures, cultures and class: a theoretical overview', in S. Hall and T. Jefferson (eds) *Resistance through Rituals: Youth Subcultures in Post-War Britain*, London: Hutchinson.

Cohen, S. (1980) *Folk Devils and Moral Panics: The Creation of the Mods and Rockers*, Oxford: Blackwell.

Coupland, D. (1992) *Generation X: Tales for an Accelerated Culture*, London: Abacus.

Davis, J. (1990) *Youth and the Condition of Britain: Images of Adolescent Conflict*, London: Athlone.

Doherty, J. (1988) *Teenagers and Teenpics: The Juvenilization of American Movies in the 1950s*, London: Unwin Hyman.

Dutton, D. (1991) *British Politics since 1945: The Rise and Fall of Consensus*, Oxford: Blackwell.

Frith, S. (1981) 'Youth in the eighties: a dispossessed generation', *Marxism Today* 25(11): 12–15.

Frith, S. (1993) 'Youth/music/television', in S. Frith, A. Goodwin and L. Grossberg (eds) *Sound and Vision: The Music Video Reader*, London: Routledge.

Hall, S. (1983) 'The great moving rights show', in S. Hall and M. Jacques (eds) *The Politics of Thatcherism*, London: Lawrence & Wishart.

Hall, S., Critcher, C., Jefferson, T., Clarke, J. and Roberts, R. (1978) *Policing the Crisis: Mugging, the State and Law and Order*, London: Macmillan.

Hebdige, D. (1982) 'Towards a cartography of taste, 1935–1962', in B. Waites, T. Bennett and G. Martin (eds) *Popular Culture: Past and Present*, London: Croom Helm.

Hebdige, D. (1988) 'Hiding in the light: youth surveillance and display', in D. Hebdige, *Hiding in the Light: On Images and Things*, London: Routledge.

Hill, J. (1991) 'Television and pop: the case of the 1950s', in J. Corner (ed.) *Popular Television in Britain: Studies in Cultural History*, London: British Film Institute.

Hoggart, R. (1958) *The Uses of Literacy*, Penguin: Harmondsworth.

King, J. (1996) *The Football Factory*, London: Cape.

Laurie, P. (1965) *The Teenage Revolution*, London: Anthony Blond.

Leonard, D. (1980) *Sex and Generation*, London: Tavistock.

McCann-Erickson Worldwide (1989) *The New Generation: The McCann-Erickson European Youth Study, 1977–87*, London: McCann-Erickson.

Pearson, G. (1983) *Hooligan: A History of Respectable Fears*, London: Macmillan.

Schofield, M. (1965) *The Sexual Behaviour of Young People*, London: Longman.

Schofield, M. (1973) *The Sexual Behaviour of Young Adults*, London: Allen Lane.

Smith, A.C.H., Immirizi, E. and Blackwell, T. (1975) *Paper Voices: The Popular Press and Social Change, 1935–1965*, London: Chatto & Windus.

Weeks, J. (1985) *Sexuality and its Discontents: Meanings, Myths and Modern Sexualities*, London: Routledge & Kegan Paul.

Further reading

Fornäs, J. and Bolin, G. (eds) (1995) *Youth Culture in Late Modernity*, London: Sage.

Hebdige, D. (1979) *Subculture: The Meaning of Style*, London: Methuen.

Kellner, D. (1995) 'Social anxiety, class and disaffected youth', in D. Kellner, *Media Culture: Cultural Studies, Identity and Politics between the Modern and the Postmodern*, London: Routledge.

McGuigan, J. (1992) 'Youth culture and consumption', in J. McGuigan, *Cultural Populism*, London: Routledge.

Osgerby, B. (1997) *Youth Culture in Post-war Britain*, Oxford: Blackwell.

Redhead, S. (1990) *The End-of-the-Century Party: Youth and Pop Towards 2000*, Manchester: Manchester University Press.

Redhead, S. (ed.) (1993) *Rave Off: Politics and Deviance in Contemporary Youth Culture*, Aldershot: Avebury.

Springhall, J. (1980) *Coming of Age: Adolescence in Britain, 1860–1960*, Dublin: Gill & Macmillan.

Weeks, J. (1989) *Sex, Politics and Society*, London: Longman.

Chapter 24

Disability

FEEBLE MONSTERS: 'MAKING UP' DISABLED PEOPLE

JESSICA EVANS

The idea of otherness is complicated, but certain themes are common: the treatment of the other as more like an object, something to be managed and possessed, and as dangerous, wild, threatening. At the same time, the other becomes an entity whose very separateness inspires curiosity, invites inquiring knowledge.

(Jordanova 1989: 109)

Representation and the authority of the investigator

Why does representation matter to people who are disabled? Why is the politics of representation now central to the politics of disability? How does representation relate to popular conceptions of disability? How are these categories, these types of personhood, brought to our attention – how do they appear to us? These questions are central to my chapter. It is worth saying at the outset that our answers to them may depend on how we define ourselves; whether you are disabled or not is likely to affect what disability means to you at a personal level. The point of this is to draw your attention to the idea that the debate on cultural representation, on mass media images of disabled people, is not merely a matter of academic interest, but one which touches upon our sense of our 'self' and who we think we are. Images are at one and the same time material objects, placed in certain concrete places (billboards, magazines, books and so forth) and collections of signs that manufacture particular versions of the world to us, which we use to think and feel that world. The word 'representation' is complex and I shall return to its meanings later in the chapter but at this stage it is important to point out that my use of this concept is quite particular. Representation refers to a process in which the world is not just mediated but actively 'made up', assembled in images and in words which do not just reflect the world but transform it in a quite distinctive way.

As such, representation is a potent 'bridge' between what you consider to be your private world and the outside public world. By potent, I mean that representation is powerful in its own right. For example, if you are not disabled, or do not see yourself as such, your image of what 'disability' means might be quite specific. If I showed you a photograph of a wheelchair, it might associate in your mind with ideas and words such as: lack of mobility, physical impairments, needing others, helplessness, dependency, unattractiveness, asexuality. You can see that this is a chain of associated ideas which are also states of feeling, suggesting a particular disposition to the subject matter.

If you are disabled your 'chain of associative concepts' might be very different: 'Wheelchairs are there to enable me to get around; I can't apply for that job because it's not wheelchair accessible', and so on. When referring to representation we draw attention to the aspect of language or image whose function it is to refer to something else (the 'real object'), in its absence. Put quite simply, when we look at a picture of a cat or read the word 'c-a-t' we are looking first and foremost at visual and scriptural forms – we are not looking at cats. So, to talk about representation is to conceive of the image as a set of signs, and signs have two aspects: the forms employed and the ideas they give rise to in the mind of the viewer. I use the word sign because I am concerned with how images signify or *mean* something to somebody. If we consider the wheelchair as a sign we can see that although the form (the wheelchair) is the same in both our imaginary scenarios, the meaning and concepts that get attached to it are different according to who is the interpretant, the viewer of the image. We may also be able to see that this difference could constitute a point of conflict, between people who occupy unequal positions of power and status and who are therefore predisposed to see the world with different interests and motivations in mind.

It can be argued, although for reasons of space I have to make simplifications here, that group membership is a more explicit part of the identity of those in oppressed groups than of those in high status, powerful groups. In fact, one could argue that an indication of how far various peoples have achieved full citizenship rights is whether they are defined *not* primarily as members of a group, but as individuals. For example, we are very used to hearing in the mass media of the generic terms 'Black community' or 'homosexuals' or 'the disabled' but we less often hear of 'White community' 'heterosexuals', or 'the non-disabled'. (A good example of this is the way in which the British press routinely called the violence in South Africa – in the years immediately before the first non-racial election – 'Black-on-Black violence'. In contrast, neither Bosnia nor Northern Ireland has been referred to as constituting 'White-on-White violence'.)

If I show you a picture of a person in a wheelchair it is likely that you will define him or her 'disabled' or 'handicapped'; if I show you a picture of a person who is not visibly impaired, you may be more predisposed to categorize that person in terms of gender or age and be oblivious of his or her apparent status as a non-disabled person. In fact the vast majority of still images, films and television programmes feature people and characters who are not disabled but who are not recognized as such. What does this tell us? It tells us that for people who do not identify as disabled there is at the present time no need for a publicly declared sense of affinity or shared identity with other non-disabled people. Leaving aside their other identities, of age or gender or class, for example, they feel themselves to be an individual, not a non-disabled person. I am not arguing here against the need for a strong sense of collective group identity as an essential plank in the struggle for liberation and equality, for the Disabled People's Movement has made it quite clear that people with impairments form a social group by virtue of their common oppression. What I am interested in is how this process of agenda-setting operates in representation in a way which undermines the possibility of thinking about the political and social creation of disability. And this brings us to the relationship between power, identity and pictorial representation. What I want to draw attention to in this chapter is the way in which the power of non-disabled people lies hidden while the representational spotlight, i.e. what *is* made visible to the viewing audience, is focused on the impaired body. There is a parallel to this in the highly coded way in which White people speak about White society. Think, for example, about the conservative nostalgia for a rural village-orientated society: it is always implicitly pictured before 'foreigners' arrived, as a moment of organic unity, complete in the past. The (White) place *from where* this is spoken is hidden. Whites are not called upon to think about themselves as Whites but only other people as non-White.

One of the most powerful models of disability, which still dominates professional policy and institutional practices as well as existing at a popular level, has been the medical model. Characteristically, as part of a conservative tradition of political thought, this emphasizes individual loss or incapacities, implying that the impairment is what limits and thus defines the whole person. The focus here is on the failure of the individual to adapt to society as it is, and thus the impairment is regarded as the 'cause' of disability. But increasingly the Disabled People's Movement and writers in support of it have countered this with a 'social model' which places emphasis on the power of significant groups to define the identity of the 'other' through the lack of provision of accessible environments, lack of provision of sign language, subtitles on television, braille and so on. So while impairment is just one limited fact about a given individual, an individual becomes disabled because of the failure of the social environment to adjust to the needs and aspirations of citizens with impairments (see Barton 1996). To return to my discussion of representation, we must not forget the important point that interpretation is dependent upon *how* people are represented; it is interesting here that fans of the television series *Ironside*, which starred Raymond Burr as a wheelchair-using detective, report that they were not conscious of his impairment since it was never made significant in the narrative of the series. To refer back to our social model of disability, it seems clear that the character Ironside was not in effect disabled, since no access appeared to be barred.

Essentialism, disability, sexuality

In his book *Mythologies*, Barthes points to the way in which ideology in capitalist society 'continuously transforms the products of history into essential types' so that things lose the 'memory that they were once made' (1973: 155). Essentialism is primarily a philosophy of determinism which holds that within each human individual there is some ultimate essence (biological or moral-behavioural) which does not change and which obliges us to behave, as our lives unfold, within more or less predictable limits. My study constitutes a form of ideology-critique; I am interested in the ways in which the production of meaning and cultural value serves to sustain relations of domination and subordination. Essentialism can be regarded as a common strategy of the ideologist who strives to attribute a natural and thus immutable status to what are socially constituted phenomena. In this manner the prejudicial treatment of people with learning difficulties in particular has been justified by asserting the existence of an incurable and innately useless condition. Photographic realism supplies the evidence for this supposed 'truth' of the impaired person. Disabled people are held to be a homogeneous group of people who are more similar to each other than to anyone else through the unifying factor of a shared nature; and therefore, whose situation, behaviour, actions, thoughts and needs are simply expressions of the truth of a deeper biological pathology.

Studies of the representation of disabled people have shown that disabled people are habitually screened out of television fiction and documentary programmes or else occur in a limited number of roles. (For a 'content' analysis of British TV see Cumberbatch and Negrine 1992; see also Barnes 1992; Longmore 1987.) It is as if having a physical or mental impairment is the defining feature of a person to such an extent that it makes a character less than a whole character: it subtracts from personhood and undercuts one's status as a bearer of culture. Writers over many years have used mental and physical impairment or ugliness to signify badness, evil or moral ambivalence in a character – Shakespeare's *Richard III*, Captain Hook in *Peter Pan*, the *Phantom of the Opera*, the Bond villains, *The Hunchback of Notre-Dame*. Where impairment is used as a cipher in this way, it represents the continuation of Judaeo-Christian archaic, pre-scientific and cosmological systems of thought in which biological wholeness is divine, its opposite cast out as legal impurities (see Parkin 1985). In the medieval period, visibly impaired children were seen as 'changelings' – the devil's substitutes for human children and the product of the mother's involvement with sorcery and witchcraft (see Haffter 1968). The anthropologist Mary Douglas (1966) has important things to say about how traditional societies view anomaly, which may have a parallel in how contemporary culture 'thinks' people with impairments – as neither human nor animal, neither representing life nor death. (For the pre-Enlightenment treatment of 'disability' in western culture in general see Ryan and Thomas 1987.)

Status and authority in images are implicitly associated with an absence of disability. For example, Franklin D. Roosevelt was never seen in a wheelchair although his legs were paralysed. Being President of the USA was felt to be incompatible with being physically damaged – the wheelchair is the ultimate symbol of lack of power. Representations of disability are, however, principally bifurcated by gender. In recent years, for example, the disabled man has been a central character in a number of Hollywood films. The body, its physical aspects and demeanour, are the concrete signifiers which carry associations and concepts of femininity and masculinity. Film-makers rely upon an audience's knowledge of these codes in order to make damage to the body of a character operate as a statement about that character. If masculinity is signified by strength and resolve, independence and will power, then dramatic power can be derived from constructing a narrative around a man who has lost power over his body, for example in the 1990 films *My Left Foot* and *Born on the 4th July*. Judith Williamson, in a review of these films, felt that they were not about disability *per se*. Rather disability was used as a metaphor for the state of mind of the male characters: 'These films are about the hell of dependency for men. And maybe the men have to be in wheelchairs for that dependency to be made vivid' (1990: 26). In the Multiple Sclerosis (MS) Society's campaign 'Tears Lives Apart', posters showed beautiful young bodies being ripped apart by the scourge of MS, a campaign known colloquially by the advertising agency that produced it as 'Beauty and the Beast' (see Hevey 1992: 43). The series of posters is photographed in and out of focus, pictorialist style; bodies intertwine against a black background with the sculptural drama of Rodin's *The Kiss* (see Hevey 1992: plate 3). One shows a 30-year-old man being bathed by a sexualized woman – her sleeves rolled up, their heads bowed together. Here, the implication is that disability for men means a loss of (hetero) sexual virility, for where once the woman might have been his girlfriend, the narrative suggests she is now his mother. The text reads 'How does it feel to have a mental age of thirty and a physical age of one?' as if to anchor the meaning of the poster finally in a sense of childlike dependency. The fear portrayed is that physical impairment inevitably means the final triumph of the body over the mind: to be disabled is to be stripped of fundamental human capacities such as thinking, acting, willing and taking responsibility, and being condemned to endlessly re-enact the 'horror' of one's earliest dependency on a woman – as mother.

Representations of disabled women in film have been significantly different. Since the traditional meaning of femininity is often synonymous with dependency and vulnerability, disability cannot be used to pose a threat to women's autonomy. Disability is more commonly therefore used as a sign of women's excessive vulnerability and so blindness is the central signifier in storylines which create a sense of cumulative foreboding, often ending in physical attack (in films such as *Wait Until Dark* (1967) with Audrey Hepburn, *Blind Terror* (1971) with Mia Farrow, and *Blink* (1994) with Madeleine Stowe).

But it is noticeable that, opposed to this, wheelchair-using fictional women characters have been embittered, aggressive, or assertive of their needs (for example, *What Ever Happened to Baby Jane?* (1962) with Joan Crawford and Bette Davis). In these cases my interpretation is that it represents a cultural fear that a physically damaged woman is incompatible with the requirement to be nurturing and caring (i.e. a good and protective mother), and so her assertiveness is a direct threat, portrayed in revenge scenarios and perhaps even destructive of life. Impairment in representation is seemingly transgressive; pointing to the boundaries of taken-for-granted sexual difference and producing transgressive women who are more masculine and tough and conversely making men dependent and vulnerable.

The charitable mind of state

Michel Foucault, the French historian and philosopher, has argued that from the late eighteenth century the biological traits of a population became relevant factors for economic management and state intervention; the body and its health becomes a key bearer of qualities of fertility, sickness and health, strength and weakness, and moral behaviour. A finer and finer 'grid of observation' is placed over the population, in order to create a whole series of 'functional discriminations' between different types of people, such as the wilfully idle and the involuntary unemployed (Foucault 1980; see also Evans 1988). These categorizations serve as the justificatory framework for the 'career' of a particular individual in the nineteenth-century institutions of the asylum, the medical clinic, workhouse, and prison. The Eugenics Movement, a strong form of applied Social Darwinism, became prominent among the new administrative and professional classes who serviced these institutions; its premise was that the existing social hierarchy resulted from innate differences in the qualities and capacities of individuals (and so it is an essentialist philosophy along the lines I suggested earlier). Culminating in the exterminations in Nazi Germany, ideologues began to apply the term 'degeneration' to people whose mental and physical defects were thought to be the outcome of hereditary factors. Eugenicists linked idiocy, pauperism, criminals and the sick poor with heredity and argued that the sick must be segregated from the healthy, the poor from the weak in order to protect the 'national stock'. In fact, the first charity to deal specifically with people now referred to as 'learning disabled' was called 'The Royal Commission to Control the Feebleminded', and created by the government in 1908. Its specific aim was to curb the evils of idleness and promiscuity which it was felt were wreaking havoc on the stability of society, and to prevent the so-called feeble-minded from reproducing.[1]

Dr Frederick Treves, the surgeon of Mile End Hospital in London, showed John Merrick ('the Elephant Man') to the London Pathological Society just as police were closing down the Victorian freakshows as an indecent spectacle. In the late nineteenth century we can trace an historical shift from the display of disabled freaks as popular exhibits in circuses, museums, fairs and shows, to that of scientific objects for the production of knowledge and for the purposes of human progress. Robert Bogdan's (1988) research shows that the growing opinion in the late nineteenth century was that freaks belong in medical textbooks not sideshows; in their book *Articulating the Elephant Man*, Graham and Oehlsclaeger (1992) examine interpretations (from plays, films and rock videos) of the story of John Merrick, discovered in a freakshow in 1884 and 'rehabilitated' by Dr Treves.)

These are shifts in discursive practice, in the sense that people who have impairments have been the changing objects of thought and investigation. In the nineteenth century, photography had become very important to the formation of new ways of thinking about the relationship between the body, the mind and social relations. The construction of these new kinds of knowledge about the population was executed – within the prison, workhouse, the police force, and psychiatric asylum – through close attention to the visible physiological features by which each individual was measured and compared (see Green 1984, 1996; Tagg 1988). Here the doctrine of physiognomy had pre-eminence as it claimed that a causal relationship existed between the inner pathology of the individual and his or her external, visible characteristics from facial expression to the physical features of the face. Photography, seen as a slave to the visible fact, was perfectly placed to legitimize this 'science' as it promised to show the link between seeing and knowing. However, the postwar charity poster represents the legacy of physiognomic photography but combines it with the mythological narratives of a pre-Enlightenment age of monsters.

Images and publicity published by charitable organizations as part of their fund-raising activities dominate representation in the public sphere. I shall argue that these images undermine disabled people as autonomous human beings with all that that implies – will, purpose and potential. Disabled people become the recipients of others' good will; the charitable ethos *per se* actively structures a mental and social gap between the donor and the disabled recipient. Furthermore, as we shall see, charities invariably reproduce a medical model of disability and undermine the political struggle for citizenship that is being waged by disabled people themselves under the banner of 'rights, not charity'.

During the 1980s the balance between public and private aid for the poor and disadvantaged shifted towards greater reliance on the private charity organizations. Their traditional role of supplementing state provision is being increasingly transformed into one of replacing it, in areas where state support had been withdrawn or decreased. Since the National Lottery was launched (November 1994), on the back of 24-hour television charity 'telethons', the mantra of 'good causes' has helped to drown out any public debate about the privatization of public services and the commercialized regulation of human needs, which are increasingly being cast as private troubles or personal tragedies. It feels like bad faith or just plain cynicism to criticize the whole edifice of a culture increasingly dominated by charity practice and ethos, cast as permeated by unimpeachable motives. As we have seen, there is good reason to be sceptical about the innocence of charities. Jacques Donzolot has written of the way that charitable motivation could 'only be kindled by the fires of extreme misery, by the sight of the spectacular suffering, and then only by the feeling of inflated importance accruing to the giver through the immediate solace his charity brought to the sufferer' (1977: 45). There is a structurally necessary relationship between the portrayal of disability as a disaster or a tragic loss, and the function of raising money.[2] This means that any critique of representation must also link that critique to the institutional practices and ideologies of charity.

The charity sector is a rapaciously competitive big business (Drake 1996: 150). Impairment charities go about the business of constructing publicity campaigns in much the same way that any other business markets its product. But the difference is that unlike other companies, charities are advertising products who happen to be people, whose impairment then becomes the 'unique selling proposition' for the charity product. Only disabled persons, constructed as a particular kind of people, are subject to a process of image specialization and as such their image can be constituted as a transaction in the public sphere: an image of a person who has Down's Syndrome, for example, can be magnified a hundred times on a billboard – just because that person has Down's Syndrome.

But charities play down the fact that they are in the business of marketing their wares as this may not be seen as compatible with voluntary giving. Their byline and logo are often discreetly placed at the bottom of the poster. But more importantly, charities seek to differentiate themselves from the whole world of public commercial advertising by adopting different visual conventions for their posters. One common difference is the use of black-and-white naturalist photography, photographs of 'real' disabled people – although some charities have in the last few years begun to introduce colour and to produce more obviously constructed, graphically based posters. Using monochromatic naturalism allows the charity to associate with the tradition of social documentary, itself embedded in a British tradition of philanthropic paternalism, and to distance itself in a protestant fashion from the commercial world of advertising with its promise of instant gratification and its narratives of the pleasure of acquisitiveness.

The marketing success of each charity depends upon it becoming synonymous with a particular impairment, and it is the impairment which the charity constructs as defining that person. Thus, the adherence to the medical model by charities means that the focus for change lies in the individual, who must be rehabilitated, cured or helped to adapt. This is reflected in the ameliorative and compensatory way in which charities choose to spend their income – for example, on specially adapted minibuses complete with the charity's logo, for the use of designated groups of disabled people: see Drake 1996. The interests of learning-disabled children and adults are assumed to be represented by Mencap, those children who have Down's Syndrome by the Down's Syndrome Association, those of people with cerebral palsy by SCOPE, those with Multiple Sclerosis by the MS Society, blind people by the RNIB (Royal National Institute for the Blind), and so on. In a report on charity advertising commissioned by the King's Fund, Susan Scott-Parker says 'As it stands now, charities tend to commission campaigns as though they owned their particular model of disabled person, in much the same way that Ford owns Fiesta cars. . . . The aim of the campaign is to raise brand awareness for the charity' (1989: 11). The Multiple Sclerosis Society's 'Tears Lives Apart' rip (the corporate logo of ripped paper) has become the sign by which it and multiple sclerosis have become branded, connected together in the public consciousness. (The relationship between branding and stigma is historically an absolutely literal one; Erving Goffman (1963: 19) in his study of social stigmatization borrows the concept of stigma from ancient Greece where it was a sign, cut or burned into the body, and advertising that its bearer was a slave.) As we shall see, it is the body of the disabled person which bears the mark of essential and immutable difference.

A final point to note here is that, in material terms, the entire relationship between charities, ad. agencies and target audiences is an enclosed 'circuit' which does not depend at all upon the participation of disabled people themselves. They are not clients (the charity is), nor the audience/customer (non-disabled people are targeted as the donors of funds or as potential volunteers), nor the product (which is the charity) (see Scott-Parker 1989: 13). From the point of view of the advertising agencies, charity accounts enhance their corporate image, allowing them to offset a hard-nosed corporate image with one which is more for the wider social good. For the charities, the agencies offer discounted rates but in practice this means cheaper advertising with often junior staff working on the account and with less time allocated to it. Furthermore, disability-related charities occupy a special niche within the advertising industry and do not usually join the Advertisers' Association or routinely participate in advertising industry events. A national seminar for the advertising industry in 1987 examined 'The Portrayal of People in Advertising' and the only social group left undiscussed was disabled people (by far the largest 'minority' group in the UK estimated at 10–12 per cent of the population). It is also notable that there has been no major charity conference addressing common issues around the representation of disabled people: see Scott-Parker 1989.

Charity advertisements

An early Mencap poster has a photograph of a young girl ('Nina' in real life) with the words 'Twenty children born on Christmas Day will always have a cross to bear'. A headline on the front cover of *Parents Voice* (the Mencap magazine for its members) in the early 1980s, accompanying a photograph of a smiling baby with Down's Syndrome, read 'Sometimes late is as bad as never'. And on Mencap posters in the late 1980s the following slogans accompanied black-and-white studio portraits of learning-disabled people: 'Joanne can't get better. Her future can'; 'She's different. Her life doesn't have to be'; 'A mental handicap is there for life. So is Mencap' (see

Hevey 1992: plate 5). The charity is bent on informing the public and its own members that the disabled person is inherently damaged goods but that the charity itself is integral to the future of that person. It promises that it can add value to that person's life. 'Mental handicap' is presented as a fixed entity residing in a body from birth, furnishing an individual with predictable limits on life opportunities.

'No Sense, No Feelings?' This headline for a 1985 Mencap poster presents us with the attitude of the prejudiced viewer (indicated by the question mark), which the photograph and the rest of the text are supposed to refute (see Evans 1988: 44). Thus, 'No Sense, No Feelings?' is what the charity is imputing to the prejudiced audience; this is rebutted with 'They may not think as fast but they feel as deeply', representing the authoritative voice of the charity speaking the truth about people with learning disability. But, as we look at the poster, it can only confirm assumptions we might already have about 'mentally handicapped people' as abnormal, inferior, and slaves to their instincts. We are shown a man and a woman with their arms locked together in a heart shape, connoting the wedding or engagement portrait. But although they appear at first to be aspiring to this institution of normal culture, the cumulative effect of the poster is that of a parody of the ideal couple which is apparent when we compare this to the stock conventions of the High Street photographer. The image is a contradictory cohesion of this tradition of honorific portraiture (which continues today in the familial portraits of *Hello* magazine) with the denigratory tradition of nineteenth-century social scientific portraiture. The latter, taken in the prisons and psychiatric institutions, was a form of physiognomic practice, subjecting the individual to the interrogative gaze of the camera in order to establish evidence of innately degenerate types (see Green 1984).

Here we look at two models: joined together but otherwise isolated they emerge as if specimens from a black background; they are photographed with a wide-angle lens which when used in close up projects lips, noses and hands forwards into the viewer's space. The use of top lighting from a small source casts deep shadows into their eyes and under their chins and emphasizes the creases in their clothes. The choice of heavy contrast, small source lighting (which throws deep shadows) and the wide angle lens creates the effect used in expressionist or gothic horror films. Moreover, as if to underline this madhouse, the man has a pocketful of combs, implying an obsessional activity – but this is paradoxically offset by both heads of hair being untidy and uncombed. Such is obviously the innate handicapped character: persons who are perhaps mad, certainly very peculiar, who are masquerading as normal by aspiring to the conventions of the honorific portrait and the institution of marriage. The text is similar to the way in which animal lovers seek to defend animal protection – they may not be intelligent (like humans) but they have feelings none the less. Imagine if the text was to be placed against a picture of another social group: it would be denounced as offensively sexist or racist, for example. That a statement such as this can be publicly endorsed by a major organization (one that purports to act in the very interests of disabled people) is an indication of how little power learning-disabled people have. We can also note the use of the charity's corporate logo, 'Little Stephen' as he was called, on the bottom right. Little Stephen, a forlorn and lonely little boy, was abandoned in 1992 after the charity finally capitulated to years of charges from 'People First' advocacy groups and the disability rights movement that it infantilized disabled people. The impact of the poster, from the point of view of the charity, relies upon it being seen as a truthful portrait of 'real' handicapped people – as if they have just walked in off the street. I have been challenged about this in lectures – how do I know they are models? Of course, I do not know for certain, but from the point of view of the politics of representation and the effectiveness of the image, whether they are technically models is besides the point. The point is that these 'models' have been selected and their 'look' has been constructed by making selections from all the various paradigms of the signifying toolkit – clothing, lighting, camera angle, facial expression, etc. What is interesting is that people never question whether in regular 'commercial' advertising models are 'real people' or models! To believe that the models in this and other charity posters are somehow untampered with and authentically 'real' is to fall into the trap of thinking that we can have a direct experience of the truth and then find evidence for it in a photograph. Oscar Wilde might have been right when he said that 'External nature imitates art. The only effects that she can show us are effects that we have already seen through poetry or in paintings' (Gilman 1982.)

In another advert from the mid-1980s Mencap colludes directly with the institutions of medical science: the text says 'On Friday May 6th 1983 these babies were born mentally handicapped' (see Evans 1988: 46). Below this are laid out geometric and clinical looking rows of medical labels with dates and surnames attached, the kind that newborn babies wear. Then the voice of the charity continues – 'It was an average day'. There is here an ambiguous reference to labelling – the connotations of the medical labels in conjunction with the text which ascribes identity at birth allows the poster to refer at a less conscious level to social labelling and stigmatizing. The advert makes no bones about it – it is a deliberately pessimistic, disparaging attitude to the existence of these babies as if they have absolutely no potential, everything that can be known about them is determined at birth. According to Mencap this is an apparently natural not a social event – 'mental handicap' is established from birth as an entity residing in a body, rather than a matter of social construction and evaluation. This poster invokes fear, implying that there is no protection (except perhaps donating to charity) from the randomness of fate which can deal anyone a dud card – perhaps it could happen to YOU. The dread of bearing monsters is one of the perils of parenthood; the poster demonstrates that the eugenic ideology is alive and well for it is as if certain people already alive should not exist as they threaten our normal existence. It is interesting to note that in western medicine the study of congenital defects is referred to as teratology, a term derived from the Greek word for monster.

Mencap revamped its image dramatically in 1992, although it retained the label 'mental handicap', against the demands of learning-disabled people attending the launch event. The posters it has produced in the 1990s are seemingly different. But as if to show it has learnt from the avalanche of criticisms from both advocacy groups and commentators associated with the Disabled People's Movement, it departed from the documentary naturalism of previous years. Two of these posters were based on a colour graphic. One of the posters showed a blank easel with the caption 'Life with a mental handicap', underneath which is a tin of paints labelled 'Mencap'. The other had the same captions but displayed an empty canoe on a river, below which is a paddle. The implication here is that the meaning and the life of a learning-disabled person is incomplete and empty without the charity to provide it. He or she is a 'tabula rasa' waiting to be filled up with the beneficence of the charity; the 'career' of the disabled person is a shadow of the organization.

The charitable state of mind: psychoanalysis and disability

Why introduce a psychological dimension to my analysis of images of disabled people? It is my contention that the naturalism employed in charity posters is also a project of constructing a belief on the part of viewers in the illusion of objectivity. To believe in something being real is always also a psychical and emotional investment – there is always some trade-off for the viewer and a motivation at stake: why *should* anyone believe in the reality of the image, and what does it do for them? I should point out that there is a body of psychoanalytical work on visual representations which analyses how advertisements act as a catalyst for unconscious desire in their construction of ideal scenarios of pleasure. There is an incitement of idealizing identificatory processes for the viewing subject. But naturalism or documentary genres, whose codes are recognizably the construction of the non-ideal, gritty 'real' world have usually been exempt from a psychoanalytic form of analysis. The debate has focused on how far the realist image distorts 'reality' or generates consensus for ideological views about the world. But to exclude questions of fantasy and identification with the realist image is partly I suspect a result of collusion with the premise of realism, expressed in the mistaken belief that the realist image *is* somehow less constructed and therefore less susceptible to the operations of unconscious process – and therefore less likely to be distorted by the irrational aspects of subjective life.

In the Middle Ages 'indulgences' were bought by church congregations in order to keep their passage to heaven secure. The mental processes engaged by charitable giving are the same – underneath the masquerade of altruism that pervades charity ethos, the psychic reality is that one gives in order to receive. Charitable giving is both a monetary and psychological transaction, one of social insurance against the prospect of damage to the viewer's own body. Presented, as so often is the case, with an aggressive image of pain or debility, the viewer feels relief (that they are not like that), guilt (for feeling relieved), and hatred (for being made to feel guilt). What I want to argue is that pity and altruism, which is the conscious aspect of reacting to disabled posters, are closely linked to hatred and aggression. Giving to charity is at the same time an act of kindness and an act of rejection, making the giver feel whole and separate; these contradictory values are what makes the treatment of disabled people an arena of conflicting values.

The 'separating devices' of charity posters can be understood as defensive strategies, colluded in by both the charity and intended to be colluded in by the audience. We need to examine the way in which fears about dependency, incompetence and debility are projected on to disabled people, who are then denigrated for what people cannot accept in themselves. Freud used the concept of projection to refer to the operation by which the qualities, feelings and wishes which the subject refuses to recognize or rejects in themselves are expelled from the self and located in another person or thing. Projection, then, is a splitting or a denial of 'bad' parts of the self. A psychoanalyst would argue that strong expressions of hate can be a defence against feelings of love or desire which cannot be acknowledged. For example, those who feel so much fear and hatred towards homosexuality that they will beat up gay men on the streets are driven by an excessive need to disown a feeling of desire toward their own sex which they cannot tolerate. In some of the portrait-based posters that have been discussed, it can be seen that the visible differences of people become exaggerated and/or entirely invented – a sign of the unconscious defences at work. Thus these images construct an object of fear which is at the same time a source of fascination. Viewers and disabled people are, in terms of fantasy, deeply bound together and implicated in each others' characteristics, and these exaggerations and distancing devices commonly used in charity posters (such as the 'They' in the 'No Sense, No Feelings?' poster) are a manifestation of this.

What are the fears of – and the desire to look at – the disabled person about? It is my contention that the infantile characteristics of the unconscious are projected on to disabled people who are seen as childish, dependent and underdeveloped and who are then regarded as 'other' and punished by being excluded from ordinary life. Thus popular images and rhetoric of disabled people abound which confront us with people who are imperfect, helpless, disgusting, shitty, dribbling – a threat to rigid ego boundaries. During the socio-developmental processes of early infancy, a range of strict rules of decorum involving standards of privacy, decency and dignity (for example, in potty training) effect a repression of these taboo activities. These codes are enforced to protect us from the disorder, chaos and dependency that, Freud argued, are characteristic of our experiences in the oedipal and pre-oedipal stages of our development. The posters encourage us to expel that which causes unpleasure to the self simply by representing that expelling as *already complete*. We become literally alienated from (and cannot identify with) the object/person we observe.

The paradox that the disabled person as 'other' is seen as *feeble and fearsome at the same time* never becomes clear to the prejudiced person, and the deeply contradictory nature of the beliefs held simultaneously about the 'other' is something that needs to be confronted. Fantasies of disabled people as dangerously threatening (fearsome) and excessively deserving (feeble) – fantasies we see in charity discourse – are products of a psychological splitting and they complement each other. Just as in the archetypal fairy stories, the witchlike qualities that we dread (will they turn us into a toad?) and the helpless, powerless princess/victim, waiting to be rescued, are two sides of the same coin.

Freud and other psychoanalysts have elaborated on the experiences that all small babies have of being in a state of complete dependency on their mothers. The consequent lack of control over their body can be felt as bewildering or even terrifying. In early development anger against the mother and consequent feelings of guilt about the destructive effects of that anger can lead to a bad body image which is carried forward into adult life as a revulsion against dependency and a flight from dependent relationships. This 'badness' can be projected on to others as in the construction of femininity as extreme vulnerability, and particularly on to those who are dependent through disability.

This process is similar to the ways in which old people in our culture are also segregated and treated as people waiting to die. There are very close associations between dependency, illness, dying and death, associations we have already seen operating in the charity adverts which are based on a medical model of disability. It seems that increasingly in our culture there are pressures that encourage a reversion to infantile feelings which have to be madly defended against by the processes of splitting and projection. My point is that defences against dependency can be contained by cultural institutions and social relations or heightened by them, which seems to be the case here.

However, it is important to point out that the disability people's movement can also participate in a manic defence against dependency by not recognizing the limits of the social model.

Conclusion

The relationship between the appearance of the body and the 'state of the mind' is absolutely arbitrary but in the naturalistic media images I have discussed an inevitable relationship is established, so that the whole character of the disabled subject appears to be manifested in the visual appearance of the body. I feel that the charities' obsession with the bodily mark betrays an irrational and even sadistic impulse which goes far beyond their humanist claims to be the defenders of disabled people. I see it as a symbolic violence, but one which is normalized by appearing to be naturally 'of the body'.

The peculiar nature of the 'changing attitudes' charity posters of the 1980s and 1990s lies in the acknowledgement of the existence of prejudice combined with the *exemption of responsibility* for this prejudice. Because for various legal and political reasons charities cannot offer an analysis of the causes of the oppression of disabled people, their publicity images depend on an empiricist visual logic addressing a reformed viewer who can now *see* the disabled person straight and truthfully. In fact it is the whole language of 'seeing them' which is the problem precisely because the oppression and inequality of disabled people is not caused by their bodily impairments but by the social arrangements which allow those impairments to become disabilities.

Charity representation is an aspect of the process whereby, in our society, social issues are continually reduced to being about pathologies inherent in particular individuals. So instead of ensuring that all buildings are accessible for wheelchair users, or that sign language becomes integral to all television programmes, or that learning-disabled people have their needs met in an integrated fashion, millions are poured into finding a 'cure' for congenital forms of disability. The research departments of impairment charities spend a large part of their income on research to remove the source of the impairment, for example, to isolate negative genes. In fact if we look at the spending figures for charities, for many their priorities are weighted heavily toward 'cure' rather than 'care'. For example, the Muscular Dystrophy Society spends £2.3 million per year on research, £276,000 on welfare (and £286,000 on advertising); see Hevey 1992: 31.

This fantasy of eradication, a continuation from the eugenic discourse of the Social Darwinists, is based on a denial of the fact that there will always be disabled people and most of us will at some point in our lives be disabled – whether congenitally, or through old age, illness, or accident, and so on. My position is informed here by Ian Craib (1994) who argues that we need to recognize the social and psychical 'importance of disappointment'. He thinks that our culture is dangerously close to denying the inevitability and necessity of suffering and of messy or 'negative' feelings, as part of normal life.

Unless this dependency is consciously thought about as something that we have all experienced as babies and more importantly will experience again as a normal part of human life, it will continue to be parcelled off as the specialized experience of people who, by the terms of our culture, are useless and need 'special' and paternalist treatment. Dependency and suffering, painful as they are, have to be acknowledged as a part of life itself, and particular groups should not be made to carry their associations for everyone else.

Questions

1 Find a charity advertisement in the area of disability and compare it with a commercial advert for a commodity. What are the similarities and differences in terms of the conventions employed? How does each image construct what is being sold by providing a visual scenario for it, and at whom are they aimed?

2 Look at the television scheduling for a whole week's viewing. What signals are used to indicate that a programme has reference to disability or a disabled person? In what ways is that person categorized? Are we to assume that the rest of the programming is for/about non-disabled people?

3 What image of disabled people, in terms of their identity and status, is provided by events such as the Para-Olympics and by 'minority' broadcast programmes such as Radio Four's 'Does He Take Sugar'? Why do they exist, as specialist events and programmes?

Notes

1 The link between degeneracy and racial ranking has left us with one legacy – the term 'mongolism' (English word) for the chromosomal disorder of Trisomy 21. Dr Down, in the 1860s, linked 'idiocy' with the working classes and was worried about the propagation of an enfeebled race. He based his categorization of idiots on observation of their bodies, and recorded visual similarities of eyes and skin colour of Mongolian nationals and some 'idiots' – his perceptions fitted the nineteenth-century theory of 'recapitulation' which held that certain forms of idiocy were the result of arrested development at an earlier stage in the evolution of the white males. The 'idiots' of the 'race' of white males could be explained as being simply the living residues of primitive races. Dr Down's Eurocentric theories led him, therefore, to perceive certain idiots as 'mongols' – the observation of arbitrary characteristics seemed to him to be proof of his theory. Down's fallacy should serve as a warning for those who would make deductions from the observation of appearance to that of social policy. For the seminal account of Dr Down's eugenic persuasion see Gould (1983; see also Gould 1981: 134–35; Evans 1986/7, 1988).

For references to eugenics as it relates to disability see Ryan and Thomas (1987: ch. 5); for a historical survey of how mentally ill and learning-disabled people have been pictorially represented, including the Social Darwinism of photographic physiognomy see Gilman (1982); for the history of intelligence testing and ranking and the biological determinist categorization of people as feeble-minded see Gould (1981). On the Nazi 'Euthanasia' Programme see Proctor (1988) and Burleigh (1994). See Pfeiffer (1994) for material on eugenics legislation historically and today in the USA. In the UK the courts have the power to declare the lawfulness of an operation to sterilize, and there have been several compulsory sterilizations since 1989. For British debates on sterilization, abortion and the 'right to live' see Ryan and Thomas (1987: ch. 8); Morris (1991); Shearer (1981, 1984). The British Abortion Act

1967 was amended in 1990 by the Human Fertilization and Embryology Act, which has the effect of introducing a new time limit of 24 weeks for all abortions unless prenatal diagnosis indicates a serious chance of the child being disabled. Termination of pregnancy is now legal in the case of, for example, Down's Syndrome, right up to the moment of birth. There is evidence that women are pressured into 'choosing not to have a disabled child' – a 1985 study found that a majority of doctors would offer amniocentesis to women only if they agreed in advance to have a termination if the foetus was 'abnormal'. As Jenny Morris puts it, 'It is outrageous that . . . a foetus of more than 24 weeks gestation is treated as having rights as a human being but loses these rights once it is diagnosed as being disabled' (1991: 75).

2 David Hevey has argued that the purpose of charity advertising is not to appeal to a general public, for the income generated by this process is negligible compared to that of legacies and other donations. Its central purpose is to appeal to the internal army of volunteers, a kind of mission statement from the leaders (1992: 44).

There have not been many empirical investigations of actual viewer-response to disability images; however, one study in 1990 found that posters which generated feelings of guilt, pity, and sympathy were those which generated the greatest desire to donate (Eayrs and Ellis 1990; see also Doddington *et al.* 1994). My own view is that the kind of research which sets out to measure 'the public's attitudes' is problematic for three reasons: first, that it is limited to people's conscious response which may be in deep conflict with their unconscious feelings; second, that this conscious response is likely to be modified by what the interviewees think they ought to say, for many people do not want to appear to be prejudiced; and third, that it assumes a one-to-one cause–effect relationship between a single text and attitude-formation and thus neglects both the cumulative effects of certain kinds of images, and how their meaning is a consequence of their articulation with cultural values and discourses and with developments and transformations in social relations – all of which provide a structuring context for the ways in which people may think about disability, which, for example, may be closely linked to the way they think about ageing or the welfare state.

References

Barnes, C. (1992) *Disabling Imagery and the Media: An Exploration of Media Representations of Disabled People*, Belper: British Council of Organisations for Disabled People.

Barthes, R. (1973) *Mythologies*, London: Granada.

Barton, L. (ed.) (1996) *Disability and Society*, Harlow: Addison Wesley Longman.

Bogdan, R. (1988) *Freakshow: Presenting Human Oddities for Amusement and Profit*, Chicago: University of Chicago Press.

Burleigh, M. (1994) *Death and Deliverance: 'Euthanasia' in Germany 1900–45*, Cambridge: Cambridge University Press.

Craib, I. (1994) *The Importance of Disappointment*, London: Routledge.

Cumberbatch, G. and Negrine, R. (1992) *Images of Disability on Television*, London: Routledge.

Doddington, K., Jones, R.S.P. and Miller, B.Y. (1994) 'Are attitudes to people with learning disabilities negatively influenced by charity advertising? An experimental analysis', *Disability and Society* 9(2).

Donzolot, P. (1977) *The Policing of Families*, New York: Pantheon.

Douglas, M. (1966), *Purity and Danger*, Harmondsworth: Penguin.

Drake, R. (1996) 'Disability, charities, normalisation and representation', in L. Barton (ed.) *Disability and Society*, Harlow: Addison Wesley Longman.

Eayrs, C.B. and Ellis, N. (1990) 'Charity advertising: for or against people with a mental handicap?', *British Journal of Social Psychology* 29.

Evans, J. (1986/7) 'The imagined referent', *Block* 12 (Winter).

Evans, J. (1988) 'The iron cage of visibility', *Ten: 8 International Photography Magazine* 29.

Foucault, M. (1980) 'The politics of health in the eighteenth century', in C. Gordon (ed.) *Michel Foucault: Power/Knowledge*, Brighton: Harvester.

Gilman, S.L. (1982) *Seeing the Insane*, New York: Wiley.

Goffman, E. (1963) *Stigma*, Harmondsworth: Penguin.

Gould, S.J. (1981) *The Mismeasure of Man*, Harmondsworth: Penguin.

Gould, S.J. (1983) *The Panda's Thumb: More Reflections in Natural History*, Harmondsworth: Penguin.

Graham, P. and Oehlsclaeger, F. (1992) *Articulating the Elephant Man: Joseph Merrick and his Interpreters*, Baltimore, MD: Johns Hopkins University Press.

Green, D. (1984) 'Veins of resemblance', *Oxford Art Journal* 7(2).

Green, D. (1996) 'On Foucault: disciplinary power and photography', in J. Evans (ed.) *The Camerawork Essays*, London: Rivers Oram.

Haffter, C. (1968) 'The changeling: history and psychodynamics of attitudes to handicapped children in European folklore', *Journal of the History of Behavioural Studies* 4.

Hevey, D. (ed.) (1992) *The Creatures Time Forgot: Photography and Disability Imagery*, London: Routledge.

Jordanova, L. (1989) *Sexual Vision*, New York: Harvester.

Longmore, P.K. (1987) 'Screening sterotypes: images of disabled people in television and motion pictures', in A. Gartner and T. Joe (eds) *Images of the Disabled, Disabling Images*, New York: Praeger.

Morris, J. (1991) *Pride Against Prejudice: Tranforming Attitudes to Disability*, London: Women's Press.

Parkin, D. (1985) 'Entitling evil: Muslims and non-Muslims in coastal Kenya', in D. Parkin (ed.) *The Anthropology of Evil*, Oxford: Basil Blackwell.

Pfeiffer, D. (1994) 'Eugenics and disability discrimination', *Disability and Society* 9(4).

Proctor, R. (1988) *Racial Hygeine: Medicine under the Nazis*, London: Harvard University Press.

Ryan, J. and Thomas, F. (1987) *The Politics of Mental Handicap*, revised edn, London: Free Association Press.

Scott-Parker, S. (1989) *They Aren't in the Brief: Advertising People with Disabilities*, discussion paper, London: King's Fund Centre.

Shearer, A. (1981) *Helping to Live or Allowing to Die?*, London: CMH (Campaign for People with Mental Handicaps), now called VIA (Values into Action), Oxford House, Derbyshire Street, London, E2 6HG.

Shearer, A. (1984) *Everybody's Ethics: What Future for Handicapped Babies?*, London: CMH (as above).

Tagg, J. (1988) *The Burden of Representation*, London: Macmillan.

Williamson, J. (1990) 'Hell on wheels', *Guardian* 10 May.

Further reading

Barnes, C. (1992) *Disabling Imagery and the Media: An Exploration of Media Representations of Disabled People*, Belper: British Council of Organisations for Disabled People.

Barton, L. (1996) *Disability and Society*, Harlow: Addison Wesley Longman.

Cumberbatch, G. and Negrine, R. (1992) *Images of Disability on Television*, London: Routledge.

Evans, J. (1988) 'The iron cage of visibility', *Ten: 8 International Photography Magazine* 29.

Evans, J. (1992) 'Little Stephen: infantalism, projection and naturalism in the construction of mental disablement', in D. Hevey (ed.) *The Creatures Time Forgot: Photography and Disability Imagery*, London: Routledge.

Gartner, A. and Joe, T. (eds) (1987) *Images of the Disabled, Disabling Images*, New York: Praeger.

Gilman, S.L. (1982) *Seeing the Insane*, New York: Wiley.

Gilman, S.L. (1988) *Disease and Representation*, Ithaca, NY: Cornell University Press.

Gould, S.J. (1981) *The Mismeasure of Man*, Harmondsworth: Penguin.

Green, D. (1984) 'Veins of resemblance', *Oxford Art Journal* 7(2).

Hevey, D. (ed.) *The Creatures Time Forgot: Photography and Disability Imagery*, London: Routledge.

Morris, J. (1991) *Pride Against Prejudice: Tranforming Attitudes to Disability*, London: Women's Press.

Ryan, J. and Thomas, F. (1987) *The Politics of Mental Handicap*, revised edn, London: Free Association Press.

Sibley, D. (1995) *Geographies of Exclusion: Society and Difference in the West*, London: Routledge.

Tagg, J. (1988) *The Burden of Representation*, London: Macmillan.

Chapter 25

Nationality

NATIONAL IDENTITY AND THE MEDIA

ANDREW HIGSON

What is national identity?

National identity is generally understood to be the shared identity of the naturalized inhabitants of a particular political-geographical space – that is, a particular nation. But how is that identity generated? How do the members of a particular nation come to take on that identity? Is national identity something we are born with as subjects of a particular nation? Or is it something we learn?

If we were to consider national identity as in part a question of appearance, of physical attributes, then we might conclude that national identity is something we are born with. Most Italians have dark hair, most Swedes have light hair; most Zimbabweans are Black, most Britons are White. But this will clearly not do, since not all Italians have dark hair, and there are many Black Britons. Similarly, it would be difficult to distinguish between the Belgians and the Dutch on the basis of physical attributes, yet for various political and historical reasons, national boundaries have been drawn around the proximate geographical spaces we call Belgium and the Netherlands, legally dividing into two a body of people who have many shared physical attributes.

This suggests that it would be inadequate to define national identity on the basis of physical attributes. We might therefore conclude that national identity is not biological but cultural, and to that extent something that is learned, often subconsciously. The purpose of this chapter is to explore the role of the media in this process of learning. What part do the media play in promoting particular ideas of national identity? What part do they play in helping us to learn how to be British, or Australian, or American? What part do they play in developing the culture of nationality?

Although I shall be addressing general issues, most of my examples, because of my own particular interests, will be drawn from British cinema. One of your tasks will be to explore the extent to which the issues I raise are applicable to other media, and other national identities.

Imagined communities

One influential argument about the formation of nations and identities in recent years has developed out of the work of Benedict Anderson (1983). Anderson explores the historical development of the modern nation, in an effort to explain how such nations have emerged, and how they have maintained their status as nations. Comparing the modern nation to more archaic or traditional social formations, it becomes clear that the nation is far too vast an entity for all its members to know each other. Yet vital to the sense of a nation is that its members form a unified community of people with shared interests and concerns. Anderson argues that the unification of people in the modern nation is achieved not by military means (though they will often play a part) but by cultural means. In particular, Anderson looks at the role of national media and the education system in enabling a nation to imagine itself as a coherent, meaningful and homogeneous community.

This imaginative process takes place all the time, but it comes into increasingly sharp focus at times of crisis, and especially during wars which threaten the stability and sovereignty of the nation. Historians of British cinema, for instance, have demonstrated how many British films of the Second World War period, whether specifically promoted as propaganda or not, can be read as representations of a nation of people with common interests pulling together for the common good (Barr 1993; Higson 1995; Hurd 1984). Thus Charles Barr's work on Ealing Studios shows how several Ealing films of the period tell the story of how a group of relatively diverse people, thrown together by circumstance, pull together to achieve a common goal (Barr 1993). In *San Demetrio, London* (1943), for instance, the diverse members of the crew of a ship work collectively to ensure its safe arrival in a British port.

Social and cultural differences, from this point of view, seem less significant than what is shared. The common purpose pulls the individual characters of the drama together, forges them into an organic, self-functioning community, and ensures that each person has a clear role within that community. This small, self-contained functional community can then be read as standing in for the nation, which is thereby imagined as a consensual gathering together of the diverse interests and concerns of the individuals that make up that community.

Such consensual images of the nation are vital to the state machinery during times of war. So what happens in peacetime? It is of course still possible to find plenty of consensual images of communities in media texts at such times, and it is still possible to read those representations metaphorically: the tight-knit, microcosmic community stands in for the nation. The British musical comedy, *Sing As We Go* (1934), for instance, deals with representatives of different classes pulling together for the common purpose of putting a cotton mill back in business during the depression. The final scene sees Gracie Fields leading the massed ranks of the workers back into the factory, all waving Union Jack flags. In other words, the imagined community is explicitly 'nationalized' in the final scene (Higson 1995).

It is also possible to read British television soap operas like *Coronation Street* and *EastEnders* in the same way. Both series deal with relatively small, tight-knit and clearly local communities which can be read as metaphoric representations of the nation. But is the image of consensus so strong in recent media texts? Let us have a look at the film, *My Beautiful Laundrette* (1985).

Hybrid identities

My Beautiful Laundrette tells the story of Omar, a young British Asian man living in south London. He is situated as a member of the local Asian community, who provide him with work. But he is also friends with Johnny, who is white, and who spends most of his time with a street-wise gaggle of youths with racist inclinations. Omar employs Johnny to help him run a launderette which a local Asian businessman has asked him to take care of. Omar and Johnny also become lovers.

The film therefore sets out quite clearly to offer a vision of contemporary multicultural Britain. But it can also be read as suggesting that identity is always fluid, unstable, contingent upon circumstances (Corrigan 1992). There is little sense of consensus here. Allegiances are forever being made, unmade and remade; communities cannot be taken for granted: they are insecure, and often self-destructive. The tensions within the Asian community are manifold, with young and old generations pitted against each other, as well as tensions at the level of gender, sexuality, and the family, and clear differences of opinion about business ethics. The White street gang is similarly at odds with itself, especially when Johnny 'defects' to the other side, to work for the immigrant Asian community.

In this case, then, the nation is represented not simply as multicultural, but in disarray. Images of social and cultural disturbance and fragmentation are more prominent than images of consensual community. Yet this is still a representation of the nation, which raises profound and challenging questions about what it is to be British. National identity in such texts is imagined not as consensual but as hybrid, not as pure but as variegated.

What is new about such representations is the recognition of social and cultural tensions, the shift from consensus to dissent. Of course, we can go back to earlier 'national' representations and argue that the image of consensus was always precisely no more than an image, a powerful cultural myth important to the nation's sense of its own identity. The function of such texts, it might be argued, is ideological: to win the consent of the people to a shared image of the nation and identity.

We can also go back to representations of Britain in the 1930s and 1940s and argue that the image of national identity as hybrid was just as strong then as it is now. Britain has always been multicultural, even if the dominant cultural strands have changed. Films like *San Demetrio, London* always made room for cultural differences, particularly in terms of class, regional and subnational identities. And the sense of community being forged in the circumstances of the moment out of a very hybrid group of people (rather than being taken for granted as a long-standing fact) is just as strong in this film as it is in *My Beautiful Laundrette* – or at least, it is perfectly possible to read the film in this way. Perhaps the sense of a core national identity is more difficult to find in a recent non-consensual film like *My Beautiful Laundrette*. In wartime films, on the other hand, there is a much stronger sense of a core middle-class Englishness, with more peripheral identities gathered around that core. In *My Beautiful Laundrette*, all identities seem equally marginal and central.

My Beautiful Laundrette and other such films of recent times perhaps more sharply stress cultural diversity and difference, hybridity and heterogeneity. The idea that the nation – the body of people that collectively constitute the national – is not simply diverse but also inconstant, fluid, changing, is something that has been increasingly central to recent debates about the formation of contemporary Britain. As the UK becomes visibly more multicultural, so the makers of media texts have attempted to deal with plurality, to find space in representation for cultural minorities, ethnic or otherwise. In so doing, the cultural boundaries of the nation have been redefined, and a wider, more extended and hybrid national 'community' imagined.

The emergence of the new Black British cinema, from *My Beautiful Laundrette*, through *Young Soul Rebels* (1990), *Bhaji on the Beach* (1993) and beyond, is a vital sign of such shifts in the national imagination. Parallel developments can be seen on television too, with 'Black' sit-coms like *Desmond's* making the ratings charts.

Equally significant is the emergence of Channel Four, a television channel that was created in 1982 in the wake of the Annan Report (Home Office 1977) on the *Future of Broadcasting* as a means of responding more sensitively to the plurality and multiculturalism of contemporary Britain. The sensitivity was to be built into the organization of the television channel. Where existing British television companies were highly centralized institutions bringing together the functions of both programme-making and broadcasting, Channel Four was set up as a broadcaster only. It would not make its own programmes, but would draw them from diverse sources, including independent programme-makers. Its remit was to address interests not otherwise catered for on the mainstream commercial channel, ITV. Channel Four can then be seen as an attempt to encourage new representations of the nation and its place in the global village, and new representations of national identity – or rather, of the diverse identities that make up the modern UK. To some extent, this institutional experiment has been successful in this way, with British television now opened up to many more voices and images than were available in the 1970s: it has indeed been a force for plurality.

Constructing images of national identity

If representations of national identity are partly imagined in relation to some idea of a shared community, there are two other ways in which the process of constructing images of national identity should be understood. The first involves an inward-looking process, defining the nation in terms of its own internal cultural history. The second is a more outward-looking process, defining the nation in terms of its difference from others (Higson 1989).

National identity is not just about sharing in a sense of community, however contingent. National identity is about belonging – to a community, yes, but also to a place, a homeland. And it is about recognizing as familiar the established indigenous cultural traditions of that homeland and community.

Media texts can invoke indigenous traditions in various ways: they can, for instance, quite self-consciously explore national cultural traditions, or they can simply work within established traditions. What we recognize as national in any given media text is, then, in part the extent to which that text deals with cultural material which we recognize as distinctively British, or French, or American, or whatever. The Hollywood Western, for instance, is clearly working with some very specific cultural-historical reference points that are unique to the USA. And of course each successive Western further reinforces the sense of that material as indigenous and distinctive.

Representations of the nation thus work to imagine the nation as a community partly by invoking this sense of a distinctive and familiar cultural history and indigenous tradition. To this extent, then, the sense of a shared national identity is established through an inward-looking process, through conjuring up a particular vision of the internal history of the nation.

The other important way in which nationality is imagined is in terms of difference. The national identity of the subjects of a particular nation are at this level understood not in terms of their own internal history, but in terms of their difference from others, outside the national borders. Thus on the one hand, a British film seems British because it works with distinctively British material – it reproduces what we already recognize as British cultural traditions. On the other hand, a British film seems British because it is not French, or Irish, or American – that is, because it is different from films from other national cinemas. Distinctiveness in this case is forged in a system of differences. What it is to be British is thus defined partly in terms of what it is: another version of a familiar indigenous identity; and partly in terms of what it is not: it is not French, it is not German, it is not African.

Except of course that it is! If we were to proceed on these lines, and take these notions of cultural distinctiveness and national difference for granted, we would be eliding all sense of the hybridity and instability of identity (as discussed above). Culture, the nation and national identity would all appear as homogeneous and monolithic entities, when in fact this is far from the case, as we have already noted.

National identity is about belonging. It is therefore bound up in a process of inclusion and exclusion. Who is to be included as British? Who is to be excluded as not-British? The answers to such questions are historically specific. Nationality is not natural but contingent: it changes with historical circumstance. National cultural traditions too are always in flux, always subject to struggle for recognition over against other traditions.

Films like *Trainspotting* (1995), for instance, deal with quite specific cultural traditions, including working-class traditions, youth cultures and (sub)-national (in this case, Scottish) traditions, all of which can be subsumed under the umbrella term Britishness. Films like *Howards End* (1991) also deal with quite specific cultural traditions which can be subsumed as British, but which in this case are self-consciously southern English, White, upper- and middle-class traditions, and which lay claim to a notion of national heritage which is not available to many other films. Each set of traditions, as embodied by these two quite distinct sets of films, struggles for ascendancy in the national cultural formation.

Dramas of nationality

How are representations of national identity formed in a media text? In part, they are constructed in and by the text: as the narrative of the text unfolds, as characters are pitted one against another, so a sense of identity emerges. To this extent, character is not defined in advance, but forged in the heat of the text, by the conditions of the narrative (whether it is a news story in the tabloid press, television coverage of a major international sports event, or a Hollywood feature film). But there is also a historical dimension to the representation of national identity – to that extent, identity is inherited from previous representations. We know this person is English because there is a history to representations of Englishness, and we recognize what we take to be Englishness in this particular representation. Let us examine a British film in which the question of Englishness and national identity is central to the way the text unfolds.

One of the most successful British films of the 1980s was *Chariots of Fire* (1981). That seems a fairly incontrovertible statement. But what made *Chariots* a British film? Certainly, the director, producer and scriptwriter were British, as were most of the actors. But most of the money for the film was put up by Twentieth-Century Fox, the Hollywood studio, and Allied Stars, a company run by Dodi Fayed, an Egyptian. To that extent, it was a multinational project.

The distribution of films is also international, even for relatively low-budget British films, since the domestic market is not large enough to cover costs. So films have to be made with the international market in mind; this inevitably has an impact on the ways in which national identities are represented in them. Identity and character can to some extent be allowed to emerge as the text unfolds and as actions lend substance to characters. But at the same time, they will often resort to stereotyping as a means of readily establishing character and identity.

Stereotyping is in effect a form of shorthand, a way of establishing character by adopting recognizable and well-established conventions of representation. Such representations imply a sense of history, of character being established through a history of representations. Markers of identity are accrued over numerous texts. The stereotype reduces, or condenses these markers, this history, to their most basic form, and at the same time attempts to naturalize them. And the more widely recognizable those condensed signs of identity are, the more readily the film can be accepted at the international box-office. Except that if the stereotype has become so familiar that audiences recognize it immediately as a stereotype, then the effect becomes comic. If that is the intended effect, there is no problem. But if the effect is unintended, it is a clear sign that the stereotype needs to be renewed, so that it can once more function as a convenient and effective representational shorthand.

If they are to be accessible to a wide range of audiences, media texts almost demand that character be developed in part through stereotyping. The problem is that stereotyping tends to reproduce the idea of a core identity, a fixed and relatively stable centre. Yet as we have seen identity is invariably complex, impure, hybrid. No wonder then that the term stereotype is often used pejoratively: a particular characterization may be criticized for being stereotypical, meaning that it lacks a realistic dimension, it fails to match up to the reality of identity.

The theme of *Chariots of Fire* is in many ways precisely the question of national identity, of whether we can accept stereotypical representations at face value, and of whether change is possible. The narrative is organized around the stories of three great runners of the 1920s, one a Scotsman (Liddell), another an Englishman who has strong attachments to his Lithuanian Jewish family background (Abrahams), and the third a charismatic young English aristocrat (Lindsay). All must run for Great Britain in the Olympic Games. Already then, even in this pared-down version of the narrative, the question of national identity is brought to the fore. What is it to be British? What is the relationship between Scottishness, Jewishness, Englishness and Britishness? The film draws attention to the hybrid nature of national identity, and shows how it is constantly intertwined with other identities and allegiances, and particularly, in this case, ethnicity, religion, class and gender.

The key institutions in the film – and especially the Cambridge college where much of the film is set, and the British Olympic team – are run by the English aristocracy and upper classes. By contrast, Scottishness – and especially Liddell's overt religiosity and non-conformist principles – seems marginal. So equally is Abrahams's Jewishness and his decision to take on a professional trainer, flying in the face of the English upper-class tradition of amateurism. The impetus of the narrative sees this core–periphery relationship modified, as the upper classes literally stand aside in order to allow Liddell and Abrahams to run in the Olympics. This is the ascendancy of the meritocracy, the new middle class; it is the emergence of a modern national identity which rejects tradition and succeeds through individual enterprise.

As a drama of national identity, then, the film investigates nationality in part by negotiating this tension between tradition and modernity, by exploring character in relation to the internal history of the nation. It pits subnational identities against one another, forging a new vision of a modern, hybrid, even multicultural Britishness in the heat of the drama.

At the same time, Britishness is defined over against other nationalities: the British are different from the French, their hosts for the Olympic Games, and from the Americans, their major competitors. These differences are carefully stressed in the unfolding of the narrative. In these terms, national identity seems more coherent, more stable than the internal tensions between different subnational identities would suggest. The sense of national identity as complex, unstable and in flux is displaced by a sense of solidity and superiority by comparison with other national identities.

Yet we are always aware that this is a costume drama, and that identity is always therefore assumed. Identity is quite clearly a role, literally a masquerade – and it is important to bear in mind this sense of identity as performance, and as the product of particular historical circumstances, when faced with the apparent naturalness of so many images of the nation and nationality.

National identity and global culture

Chariots of Fire was a huge success at the box-office and became the standard-bearer for a rejuvenated British film production industry in the mid-1980s. The success of the film was not simply that it won audiences in the home market, but that it was a hit internationally; most important of all, it was a hit in the American market. The international circulation of 'national' media texts is a vital aspect of our contemporary global culture. Many would argue that the need for texts to succeed in many different markets brings with it an inevitable dilution of the national. At the level of production, the national must be reduced to internationally recognizable stereotypes if it is to have any currency. At the level of reception, so-called 'national' markets will often be saturated with texts produced or at the very least financed from outside the nation's borders.

Once again, British cinema provides an ideal example. Since the 1910s, the British box-office has been dominated by American films. The taste of British film audiences has thus to a large extent been organized around the pleasures of Hollywood cinema. While there have always been popular British films, and while some audiences have always preferred British films to American films, it remains the case that a large proportion of British audiences has over the years gained a great deal of pleasure from American films (Higson 1995).

For some cultural commentators, this has been a worrying sign of both the emergence of a 'mass' culture, and the dilution of the indigenous national culture. The problem is usually formulated in terms of the threat of Americanization, the fear that all things British will be replaced by all things American (Strinati 1992). What such arguments fail to recognize is, first, that the so-called indigenous national culture is always already a hybrid complex of cultural strands imported from many different sources; and second, that audiences will often embrace apparently 'alien' media texts because they enable those audiences to enlarge their otherwise limited cultural repertoire.

American films may well appeal to disenfranchised working-class audiences in a still heavily class-bound British society because they offer an image of the USA as an open, mobile society (Nowell-Smith 1985). Central both to the USA's own image of itself, and to the way it presents itself to others, is the idea of the American dream – that even those from the most humble origins can make it big in the enterprise culture that is the USA. The narrative structure of the mainstream American film is organized around precisely this dream that individuals can always fulfil their wishes. The beginning of the Hollywood film will very often introduce an individual who has a goal to achieve. The happy ending shows that goal being achieved. Combine this narrative structure with the *mise-en-scène* of the American dream and lavish production values and it is no wonder that such films appeal to audiences worldwide.

The future: the local and the global

Many would argue that there is little future for national identity. Traditionalists will always seek to preserve the most conservative version of the nation and nationality, but the nation itself will continue to be threatened by the globalization of culture, politics and the economy. The development of new technologies which enable the generation of media texts that need no passport to cross national boundaries, and which do so constantly and effortlessly, means that those boundaries will become increasingly blurred. There is likely to be no buffer zone between the global and the local. And the global – and before it, the national – can only ever be a hybrid amalgam of local identities and cultures.

The international concentration of ownership and control of the media industries, and the development of technologies that enable texts to be disseminated internationally with the greatest of ease, suggests that images of the nation and national identity will be confined to the realm of nostalgia. And there are already many texts that treat nationality in just such terms – notably the cycle of 'British' film costume dramas, the heritage films, that have appeared in the decade and a half following *Chariots of Fire* (Higson 1993).

For Britain, the other key development that will undoubtedly affect the representation of nationality in the future will be the consolidation of the European Union. There are already numerous pan-European media initiatives, and it seems likely that they will continue to develop. Whether we like it or not, this is bound to have an impact on how media texts deal with the national – and on whether the nation any longer seems a meaningful concept.

Questions

1 What is the role of the media in promoting a sense of national identity?

2 Most of the examples in this chapter have been taken from British films. To what extent do you think the arguments presented above are applicable to texts from other media and/or from other nations?

3 Choose any media text. How is national identity and/or the nation represented in that text?

References

Anderson, B. (1983) *Imagined Communities: Reflections on the Origin and Spread of Nationalism*, London: Verso.

Barr, C. (1993) *Ealing Studios*, revised edn, London: Studio Vista.

Corrigan, T. (1992) *A Cinema without Walls: Movies and Culture after Vietnam*, London: Routledge.

Higson, A. (1989) 'The idea of national cinema', *Screen* 30(4): 36–46.

Higson, A. (1993) 'Re-presenting the national past: nostalgia and pastiche in the heritage film', in L. Friedman (ed.) *British Cinema and Thatcherism*, London: UCL Press.

Higson, A. (1995) *Waving the Flag: Constructing a National Cinema in Britain*, Oxford: Clarendon Press.

Home Office (1977) *Report of the Committee on the Future of Broadcasting* (Annan Report), Cmnd 6753, London: HMSO.

Hurd, G. (ed.) (1984) *National Fictions: World War Two in British Film and Television*, London: British Film Institute.

Nowell-Smith, G. (1985) 'But do we need it?', in M. Auty and N. Roddick (eds) *British Cinema Now*, London: British Film Institute.

Strinati, D. (1992) 'The taste of America: Americanization and popular culture in Britain', in D. Strinati and S. Wagg (eds) *Come on Down? Popular Media Culture in Post-War Britain*, London: Routledge.

Further Reading

Anderson, B. (1983) *Imagined Communities: Reflections on the Origin and Spread of Nationalism*, London: Verso.

Barr, C. (1993) *Ealing Studios*, revised edn, London: Studo Vista.

Bhabha, H.K. (ed.) (1990) *Nation and Narration*, London: Routledge.

Cohen, R. (1994) *Frontiers of Identity: The British and Others*, London: Longman.

Cook, P. (1996) *Fashioning the Nation: Costume and Identity in British Cinema*, London: British Film Institute.

Corner, J. and Harvey, S. (eds) (1991) *Enterprise and Heritage: Crosscurrents of National Culture*, London: Routledge.

Cubitt, S. (ed.) (1989) *Screen* 30(4), special issue.

Gilroy, P. (1987) *There Ain't No Black in the Union Jack*, London: Hutchinson.

Hall, S. (1992) 'The Question of Cultural Identity', in S. Hall, D. Held and T. McGrew (eds) *Modernity and Its Futures*, Cambridge: Polity.

Higson, A. (1995) *Waving the Flag: Constructing a National Cinema in Britain*, Oxford: Clarendon Press.

Hurd, G. (ed.) (1984) *National Fictions: World War Two in British Film and Television*, London: British Film Institute.

Morley, D. and Robins, K. (1995) *Spaces of Identity: Global Media, Electronic Landscapes and Cultural Boundaries*, London: Routledge.

Nairn, T. (1981) *The Break-up of Britain*, London: Verso.

Schlesinger, P. (1991) *Media, State and Nation: Political Violence and Collective Identities*, London: Sage.

Chapter 26

Sport

SPORT AS REAL LIFE: MEDIA SPORT AND CULTURE

NEIL BLAIN AND RAYMOND BOYLE

This chapter concentrates on questions of representation in media sport but these need to be discussed in a wider context, because media sport – like sport itself – is a major economic phenomenon as well as a cultural and political one. The full cultural and ideological significance of sport, however, is brought into being only through its mediation on television and in the press.

Academic study of sport *as an activity in itself* has become increasingly important because of the major and growing role that sport plays around the world in most cultures and societies. But in recent years, as sport has become in the main a product that we consume through its greatly expanded presence in the mass media, there has been a rapid expansion of work on sport as a media form, and as a form which communicates to us about *culture as a whole*. This presents us, therefore, with other very important reasons for studying it academically.

This chapter deals with broadcasting and the press but sport is very significant in the field of radio competition, where in the UK independent local radio stations have been involved in an increasingly fierce war with the BBC over sports audiences, and also a minor but recurrent theme in the cinema.

As we shall see, much British sports coverage is not about sport. It is often about Britishness, or alternatively about Englishness (or Scottishness, or Yorkshireness); or class; or gender; or race and ethnicity, among other themes.

A note on the forms of sports mediation

Media sport has produced formal conventions in much the same way as newspaper editorials or TV soap operas tend to take certain conventional forms. For example, just as TV drama has traditionally used three camera positions to cover a two-person conversation, soccer coverage has its recurrent formal conventions, which vary from country to country, with regard to matters such as camera position, shot distance, ratios of shots of pitch action in relation to off-the-ball shots. Because the televising of a football match or a golf tournament is televisually so complex, there are numerous formal elements to be permutated in both visual and linguistic domains and in matters such as the selection of commentators and summarizers, or their visibility, or physical positioning (Blain *et al.* 1993: 149–53), or functioning as minor stars, such as motor racing's Murray Walker.

There are different press conventions with regard to qualities like 'literariness' both as between different sports and between different national press styles. Compare, for example, Italy's *Gazzetta dello Sport*'s Italia '90 World Cup description of the German fans during the game against Holland:

> The Germans shout 'Deutschland! Deutschland!' A powerful, dull, hollow sound . . . it bears the hereditary imprint of the roar which a thousand years ago brought fear to the hearts of Drusus and the legions when for the first time they ventured through forests without name.
>
> (*Gazzetta dello Sport* 25 June 1990, quoted in Blain *et al.* 1993: 68; see also pp. 4–6, 55–87)

with the English *Daily Star*'s 'Jubilant Jerry fans yesterday blasted a Euro 96 warning to England as their heroes marched into the Semi Finals' (24 June 1996): this is by no means an extreme example of the stylistic difference, and is made all the more significant when it is borne in mind that the Italian publication is a specialist sports paper.

Many such formal characteristics are themselves of ideological significance: for example there have been trends in the 1990s toward the inclusion of female presenters, especially on BBC sports magazine programmes, yet only in certain fields such as tennis are female commentators or expert summarizers encountered. The maleness of TV sport is still in the late 1990s very striking in the UK media, and this very much includes the press.

Television is constantly innovating in the realm of sport form. Among many developments in the 1990s, the 1992 Barcelona Olympics saw new underwater and overhead camera positions adding to the vocabulary of track, field and pool coverage while cricket has seen technological developments enabling microphones and cameras to be placed in the stumps, and several sports have seen developments in pitch-side eye-level camera work. During the Euro '96 soccer finals each match was covered by seventeen cameras, giving a rich multiplicity of viewpoints.

In a number of instances, the development of televisual sports forms such as those of darts and snooker have effectively initiated and produced these sports as mass spectator commodities. Further forms, which might be described as para-sports, are hybrids of sports broadcasting and showbusiness, ranging from TV wrestling to programmes such as ITV's *Gladiators*: television-orientated 'sports' such as synchronized swimming often have difficulty in establishing themselves as 'real' sports and satellite television has brought to the screens other quasi-sporting spectacles from truck derbies to log-rolling.

The sport–media relationship

First, sport on television, radio and the press is a particularly significant component of the activity of the mass media: competition for audiences for the media relies heavily on audiences for sport, and without success in this dimension of their activity it is very difficult for broadcasting companies or newspapers to remain economically viable.

Sport has always been important to the media. Since the nineteenth century coverage of sports such as football, cricket, racing and rugby has been used by newspapers both to publicize events and to attract readers (Holt 1990: 306–26; Mason, 1988: 46–59). Today sports coverage is central to many newspapers as they attempt to gain and hold readers in an increasingly competitive marketplace. While in the circulation battles among the popular press sport has always mattered, it has also become more important in recent times among the broadsheet press as traditionally working-class sports such as football have begun to attract an increasingly large middle-class audience.

Broadcasters in Britain have also viewed sport as a core component in their programme portfolios (Whannel 1992: 45–82). For television, sport was among the cheapest forms of programming and while at certain times (such as Cup Finals, football World Cups) it could attract large audiences, it also delivered substantial audiences outside peak-times. For example while Channel Four's viewing figures for its coverage of Italian football appear modest (between 1 million and 2.5 million), it delivers an audience (males 18–25) which advertisers are keen to reach but television finds difficult to attract, at a time in the schedules (Sunday afternoon) when not a great deal of television is traditionally watched.

For the public service BBC sport is an integral part of its programme output justifying the institution's claim to be reflecting the cultural life of the UK. Thus while audiences are important for the BBC so too is the range of domestic sports covered and national access given to international sporting events (such as the Olympics) in which there is a British interest. However, the traditional patterns of sports coverage in Britain are changing, driven in part by wider technological and policy shifts in the broadcasting environment.

Sport is also in the 1990s a major site of economic contestation between terrestrial broadcasters and satellite and cable television.

The introduction of increased competition from satellite and cable delivery systems has pushed up the price of broadcast rights to sporting events. Satellite companies such as BSkyB regard the securing of exclusive sports rights as vital in their attempt both to increase sales of dishes and, more importantly, to increase their subscriber base among viewers.

In 1992 BSkyB secured the exclusive live television rights for FA English Premiership football in the UK. The deal (worth £305 million over five years) also included the BBC having the sole broadcasting rights to television highlights. Other premium sporting events such as rugby league/

Superleague, Ryder Cup golf and overseas English test-match cricket have all found themselves being available only live on BSkyB. This means that less than 20 per cent of the television audience in the UK is able to watch these events as they happen.

In the future BSkyB, whose financial success is due largely to its ability to attract subscribers to its sports coverage, also intend to introduce specific pay-per-view charges for particular sporting events. In 1996 they made live coverage of the world heavyweight boxing fight between Frank Bruno and Mike Tyson available only on pay-per-view. In other words, in addition to a subscription to Sky Sports, viewers paid a one-off fee of £10 to watch the Bruno vs Tyson fight (and the rest of the undercard) from the USA. Over 10 million terrestrial viewers regularly watched Bruno fight when the rights were with the BBC; by contrast less than one-tenth of that audience watched on satellite. Such is the importance of football coverage to BSkyB's financial well-being, that in 1996 they paid £670 million to secure continued coverage of the FA Premiership from 1997.

However, while it is true to say that increased competition is changing the relationship between sport and television in the UK, it should also be noted that television has been instrumental in influencing sport for a number of years (Barnett 1990).

So we need to understand something about media sport to understand the political economy of broadcasting and the press as a whole. When England beat the Netherlands 4–1 in the European soccer championship on 17 June 1996, the fact that this item led news broadcasts the next day on ITN and BBC, ahead of the Manchester IRA bomb of the same week, or the EU ban on British beef, tells us about the economic calculations involved in news-ratings battles as well as about the cultural centrality of sport.

Television's influence on sport goes beyond simply broadcasting events and creating individual sporting stars and teams; it has also helped to shape what we actually understand to be the nature, structure and organization of modern sport. Snooker is an obvious example of a game which for most people is a TV spectator experience; its importance and the money it attracts are a product of its televisual nature and its stars over the years, like Steve Davis and Stephen Hendry, are television stars. But television transforms sport more actively still. The introduction of one-day cricket (including the Cricket World Cup played under floodlights) was instigated by television. In 1994, football World Cup matches were played in the searing noon heat of Orlando in the USA not for the benefit of players or fans, but for the armchair television spectator in Europe. English FA Premiership matches are frequently moved from their traditional Saturday afternoon slot to suit the needs of satellite television. Boxing title fights take place in the middle of the night in Britain to accommodate television audiences coast-to-coast in the USA. Television has also introduced shorter snooker matches, the tie-break in tennis and the advertising-friendly breaks in American football.

In addition there has emerged a triangular relationship between sport, television and sponsorship which now financially underpins most professional sport (Barnett 1990; Whannel 1992). The levels of sponsorship attracted by various sports are determined in part by the amount of television exposure a sport can secure, therefore sports are willing to introduce rule changes in order to facilitate television. It becomes clear that any investigation into contemporary sporting culture in Britain inevitably leads to an examination of the increasingly complex relationships which exist between various sports, the media in general and television in particular.

Representation and media sport

The term 'representation' needs some special attention in the context of sport. When the *Daily Mirror* newspaper runs its infamous 'ACHTUNG! SURRENDER' headline (24 June 1996) on the imminent England–Germany Euro '96 Wembley clash, this not only 'represents' the English and Germans as soccer combatants in an endless replay of the Second World War – this edition's first five pages were devoted to a lengthy collection of news and feature pieces on the forthcoming clash, making various wartime references – but also in a different fashion represents certain very important aspects of English society, culture, and media culture. There is hardly any sense in which the media merely use sport as a metaphor. The English media in particular, and most of all in the context of international football, often consign sport itself to a subordinate role, taking over the sports field to talk about national identity and other themes instead.

In a metaphor, something is suggested as the equivalent of something else. For example, German footballers are described at Euro '96, as they often have been before, using a military metaphor, as soldiers: 'The German blitzkrieg trampled through Croatia and now their stormtroopers aim to blast Terry Venables' men out of the tournament' (front page, *Daily Star*, 24 June 1996).

But strictly speaking, sport in the UK seems to be made to carry a different sort of relationship to other forms of cultural life, to belong to that class of signs (which the field of semiotics calls *indexical*) where something gets represented by something else with which it really is connected in everyday life.

In other words, a German football performance is felt to be truly an aspect of a wider German identity which has to do with organization, energy, commitment and aggression. Likewise, the failure at editorial and journalistic level to take women's soccer, cricket or rugby seriously stems from a masculine belief that women cannot be competitive at a range of traditionally male activities. Sport operates through the media within culture as a way of discussing characteristics of which it is assumed to present direct evidence. In the gender field this seems to be true of lots of countries other than the UK. In the field of national identity it seems that UK journalists and readers alike place much importance on sporting performance at international level, probably because of lacks elsewhere in UK culture.

Media sport is a field of production with which all manner of cultural, political and psychological matters – which do not in themselves have anything to do with sport – tend to become associated. So sport, especially on the media, becomes deeply incorporated into people's sense of who they are and what other people are like.

When England and Scotland, the world's first international soccer combatants in 1872, played each other 124 years later in the European Championship at Wembley on 15 June 1996, BBC2 television's flagship current affairs programme *Newsnight* ran an item the night before on the fate of British identity, interviewing Scotland and England supporters on their national allegiances. And when England trounced the Netherlands three days later, *Newsnight*'s next edition drew a comparison between the ease of England's victory over its European partner on the soccer pitch as distinct from its major difficulties with its European Union partners over the ban on British beef products, in the wake of the BSE controversy.

The way in which sport is written about or televised thereby becomes a source – and possibly a unique source – of information about our beliefs, opinions and attitudes as cultures. Important examples include the attitudes that men have toward women and sometimes vice versa; the attitudes that one ethnic group or nationality or race has toward another; the opinions or beliefs held by Europeans about Americans or the manner in which regions of a country see each other (how Milanese see Romans, or Londoners see Mancunians); the values we attach to questions of our own physical nature, including the characteristics of age (think of the wonderment at the mature appearance in the mid-1990s of Middlesbrough player, the 'white feather' Fabrizio Ravanelli, while still in his mid-twenties, or the discussions in athletics and tennis about older stars like Linford Christie or Martina Navratilova); the characteristics we find admirable or distasteful in other people in a period of shifting values.

The mediation of sport provides these very powerful insights into other aspects of our values just because these values are often expressed quite accidentally or innocently, as a half-conscious or unconscious by-product of our interest in the activity of sport itself. But this is not always so; sometimes what seems to be an article on a sporting theme – a newspaper piece, say, on Dutch or English fans, or African footballers – is either consciously or unconsciously a way of expressing views on another nationality or race, and only in form a piece about the world of sport. This means that media sport is not only very important *economically*, but also *politically* and *ideologically*: 'ideology' used here in both its senses, sometimes just neutrally as a 'view of the world', but often more negatively, as a 'distortion' of actual social or cultural life. There is a lot of such distortion in sports reporting, often apparently acceptable there where it would not be editorially possible elsewhere in a newspaper or in a broadcast.

And, since being a television or newspaper journalist or editor is a position of privilege, we should bear in mind that the ideologies the mainstream media produce or reproduce when giving us accounts of sports-related matters will tend to be those of socially dominant groups rather than those who may be disempowered: we are more likely to find out what men think about women than the other way round; more likely in Italy or France to find out what Whites think about Blacks than vice versa; more likely on British television networks to find out the English view of the next World Cup than the Welsh or Scottish expectations. Conversely, the accounts which we do *not* hear tell us a lot about the groups denied a voice on TV and radio or the press.

Many examples of sport being associated with the national dimension, to pursue that one example, are evidenced in the media each week. Even in as unlikely a context as ice-skating, pages of newspaper analysis (23 February 1994) attempted to show how English skaters Jayne Torvill and Christopher Dean were 'cheated' ('WAS IT RIGGED?' bellowed *Today*) out of a Winter Olympics gold medal by unscrupulous foreign judges from hostile lands like Russia and the Ukraine: the *Daily Express*, in a centre page analysis, noted that 'you could see the gaps in their marking as plainly as you might the geographic demarcation lines on a map of the old Soviet empire'.

Television entered the national frenzy over Euro '96 with as much enthusiasm as the press. GMTV offered on the morning of the England–Germany semi-final (26 June 1996) a bizarre pop video version of *Jerusalem* with the band shot against a Thames backdrop dissolving into misty pictures of St Paul's and intercut variously with montages of the Wembley opening ceremony featuring medieval jousting and St George and the dragon; clips from the quarter-final penalty shoot-out against Spain; and shots of the 1966 World Cup final: while over on BBC Breakfast News the BBC's political editor noted that John Major's interviews of that day had been carefully timed to milk advantage from the patriotic occasion and that 'probably Paul Gascoigne can do more for the feel-good factor than the Prime Minister or the Chancellor'. The political sensitivities involved in sports broadcasting led to Scottish Television dropping *Jerusalem* from their version of the Euro '96 title sequence and making visual changes, such as cutting the white cliffs of Dover: the semi-autonomous Scottish press (Blain and Boyle 1994: 132–4) likewise produced very different accounts of the national and European dimensions of the championship from those in the English tabloids.

These phenomena of representation in media sport are not historically constant, though they sometimes seem to be. For example, in the field of tennis, five years before the 1996 soccer Euro finals, the *Star* (8 July 1991) carried an article about the forthcoming Wimbledon final between Germans Boris Becker and Michael Stich entitled 'Stich as a parrot'. It is surrounded on all sides by the following exclamations:

All mein says Hun-known hero
Hun-believable
Stich it up your Junker
Triple champ Boris throws in ze towel
Deutschlark
Michael's the new power Kraut

This certainly sounds like the *Star*'s 'Jurg a Gonner' (on Jurgen Klinsmann's Euro '96 injury, 24 June 1996) or the *Mirror*'s 'Jur Out! and 'Herr we go: Krauts gun for Tel' (24 June 1996) of the later football campaign. (Incidentally it indicates how, even in tennis, a sport, played between individuals who are not formally representing their countries, the national dimension none the less intrudes.)

Yet there were signs of more disquiet in the UK at this degree of media chauvinism and xenophobia in 1996 than there had been in response to the earlier instances. There were, for example, sixty calls to the Press Complaints Commission protesting about aspects of tabloid coverage of Euro '96 prior to the England–Germany semi-final; Vauxhall Motors, a major sponsor of Euro '96, withdrew a proposed advert from the *Star* and the *Mirror* in protest. Again we need to look outside sport to understand this: for example, by 1996 it may be that government-legitimized xenophobia had declined since the Thatcher years (and indeed John Major criticized the *Mirror*'s wartime spoof approach in Parliament); that British fans had come to love (or at least respect) imported players like Eric Cantona and Jurgen Klinsmann; that knowledge has been starting to seep in to sections of the UK media audience about the baffled embarrassment with which the rest of Europe looks at the British tabloids. BBC Television's experts seated alongside anchorman Desmond Lynam throughout the Euro '96 Championship were the Dutchman Ruud Gullit and the Scot Alan Hansen (in addition to the often-chauvinistic Englishman Jimmy Hill), which suggested a growing desire in some quarters of the media to at least dilute jingoist elements in sports coverage.

But given the resistance to change of conceptions of national character (O'Donnell 1994) this may be over-optimistic, and such optimism would certainly be misplaced in the realm of the sports media's handling of gender. The same *Daily Star* which leads with 'Herr We Go: Krauts gun for Tel' (24 June 1996) presents its readers with a front page which is a complex amalgam of male and English chauvinism and a simultaneously xenophobic but also salacious interest in Germanness. For who should adorn the front page but German model Claudia Schiffer: in a provocative pose and wearing the skimpiest of bras and shorts, Schiffer occupies much of the left-hand side of the page. Under the heading 'Ooh, ja Claudia' the *Star* notes that 'Curvy Claudia Schiffer is one German striker we don't mind being great up front. Her wunder-bra's giving lots of support. Here's hoping that's the breast that they can do.' The right-hand side of the page has the headline printed over a photograph of Terry Venables dressed as a military recruiting officer in a Kitchener-style 'your country needs you' shot, over a subheading which reads 'Jerry Venables: The England boss will be down and Kraut if the Germans have their way on Wednesday'.

To place Germans as either sex objects or hate objects on the front of a newspaper would be objectionable but to do both at once is a sign of how sports coverage in the most down-market tabloids has become reduced in an especially crude manner to two of the chief determinants of sales in the UK tabloids, sex and national chauvinism (another comparable retreat to the crudest base elements has been exemplified by the *Sunday Sport*, a combination of soft pornography and rather less sport).

A further feature across pages 2 and 3 of the same edition couples a photograph of a semi-clad model who is the girlfriend of an England striker with subheaders such as 'Girls waiting to score with the guys who are keeping England's hopes alive' and 'It's all so sex-citing for us girls'. The transformative power of active men over passive women is emphasized by an account of England player David Platt's relationship with his wife Rachel: the star informs us that she was 'a lowly YTS trainee' when she met him but that 'thanks to his skills Rachel now drives a Mercedes and owns her own restaurant'; while goalkeeper David Seaman is 'also good at handling his girlfriend Debbie Rogers'. The same day's *Daily Mirror* runs a similar feature combining wartime references, English patriotism and sexism, referring to the wives and girlfriends who 'keep the home fires burning, share in the victory celebrations, and provide a shoulder to cry on if it all goes wrong' and recording how England star Stuart Pearce and his wife have a '25 ft flag-pole bearing the St George's cross' standing 'proudly on their lawn . . . a present from devoted Liz to her fiercely patriotic husband' ('Woman Who's Tamed Psycho', 24 June 1996).

This chapter does not have space to detail another equally important aspect of gender construction, namely reporting and feature material on women sports stars, which tends at its most contentious to subject women competitors to accounts based on masculine ideologies (see Hargreaves 1994: 174–208).

The bizarre ideological cocktail seen above, of jingoism, chauvinism and wartime nostalgia in the UK tabloids has little to do with sport. Indeed the quantity of technical coverage applied to the games themselves is limited, indeed very much so by European comparisons.

It must be concluded of the tabloids that sports coverage serves cultural and specifically ideological functions not in themselves in any important way related to the phenomenon of sport at all:

> If the *Sun* and its British rivals adopt an especially unacculturated and frequently degraded form of language in sports coverage, we need to remain aware (a) that it does so in most if not all other areas of its coverage, despite the special licence which sport seems to offer and (b) that this is a political fact and not just a linguistic or journalistic one. It is no coincidence that British tabloid newspapers are strongly conservative in terms of their support for existing relations of dominance. The maintenance

of a large unacculturated and potentially reactionary element in British society has clear political purposes. The language of the popular press, with its mockery of radical politics and its sneers at cultivation and culture is above all a political phenomenon, affecting areas such as gender and race as much as class.

(Blain and O'Donnell 1994: 247–8)

Yet the first half of the 1990s saw a more encouraging phenomenon, namely the development of a more sports-centred, technical interest in sport by the British quality press, which has increasingly inclined toward producing sports sections more easily comparable with the serious European sports publications like *L'Equipe* and *Gazzetta dello Sport*.

This is not to claim that the peculiar tendency to read sport as the essence of national character is absent in either the English or Scottish qualities: *Scotland on Sunday*, with a very high ABC1 readership, ran a leader during Euro '96 which claimed that

with Europhobia filling the political debate day after day, it is crucial that Scotland emerges from the championship without damage to its credentials for internationalism. It is better by far to lose a football match than to gain a reputation on the continent for thuggery and xenophobia. Ask England. There is little shame in a small nation losing a football match; there is in street battles and hooliganism.

(*Scotland on Sunday* 9 June 1996)

What is most important here is the assumption that football and culture are continuous and deeply interlocked. And perhaps there is a peculiar logic to this argument, because if Europeans do read anything of general significance into British sporting culture, and its media manifestations, it might well be because they are aware that they are looking at national traits whose relation to sport is indeed only that they are being *revealed* through sport.

It may be that the increasingly global nature of the media will impact on media sports culture in such a way as to dilute its national dimension, and this is part of a huge debate in sociology and media and cultural studies about local and global issues. But evidence suggests that local cultures are very resilient and alternative means of delivery such as satellite and cable tend to import roughly the same ideological patterns as terrestrial broadcasting (Blain *et al.* 1993: 18–36). There is an international dimension, whose long-term influence is still unknown, on TV channels like CNN: however, sports coverage of the most recent events, certainly in the UK, seems as nationalistic as ever. Ideologies of gender and race seem so deeply rooted, and class positions still so well entrenched that the likelihood is that, in the UK at least, sports mediation will continue to function as a producer and reproducer of relatively conservative views of the world, in very important areas of culture, indefinitely.

Questions

1   Why is sport viewed as important to both broadcasters and the press in the UK?

2   What does media coverage of sport tell us about national identity in the UK?

3   To what extent are media representations of sport influenced by the culture and politics of any particular country?

References

Barnett, S. (1990) *Games and Sets: The Changing Face of Sport on Television*, London: British Film Institute.

Blain, N. and Boyle, R. (1994) 'Battling along the boundaries: Scottish identity-marking in sports journalism', in G. Jarvie and G. Walker (eds) *Ninety Minute Patriots? Scottish Sport in the Making of the Nation*, Leicester: Leicester University Press.

Blain N. and O'Donnell, H. (1994) 'The stars and the flags: individuality, collective identities and the national dimension in Italia '90 and Wimbledon '91 and '92', in R. Giulianotti and J. Williams (eds) *Game without Frontiers: Football, Identity and Modernity*, Aldershot: Arena.

Blain, N., Boyle, R. and O'Donnell, H. (1993) *Sport and National Identity in the European Media*, Leicester: Leicester University Press.

Hargreaves, J. (1994) *Sporting Females*, London: Routledge.

Holt, R. (1990) *Sport and the British*, Oxford: Oxford University Press.

Mason, T. (1988) *Sport in Britain*, London: Faber & Faber.

O'Donnell, H. (1994) 'Mapping the mythical: a geopolitics of national sporting stereotypes', *Discourse and Society* 5 (3): 345–80.

Whannel, G. (1992) *Fields in Vision: Television Sport and Cultural Transformation*, London: Routledge.

Further reading

Cashmore, E. (1996) *Making Sense of Sport*, 2nd edn, London: Routledge.

Giulianotti, R. and Williams, J. (eds) (1994) *Game Without Frontiers: Football, Identity and Modernity*, Aldershot: Arena.

Jarvie, G. and Maguire, J. (1994) *Sport and Leisure in Social Thought*, London: Routledge.

Jarvie, G. and Walker, G. (eds) (1994) *Ninety Minute Patriots? Scottish Sport in the Making of the Nation*, Leicester: Leicester University Press.

Sugden, J. and Bairner, A. (1993) *Sport, Sectarianism and Society in a Divided Ireland*, Leicester: Leicester University Press.

Sugden, J. and Tomlinson, A. (eds) (1994) *Hosts and Champions: Soccer Cultures, National Identities and the USA World Cup*, Aldershot: Arena.

Wagg, S. (ed.) (1995) *Giving the Game Away: Football, Politics and Culture on Five Continents*, Leicester: Leicester University Press.

Chapter 27

News production

NEWS VALUES

JERRY PALMER

What is 'news'? Many answers have been given to this question. Some of the best known ones take the form of traditional aphorisms:

> 'Dog bites man' is not news, 'man bites dog' is.
> (John Bogart, editor of the *New York Sun*, quoted in Mott 1950: 376)

> [News is] anything that makes the reader say 'Gee whiz'.
> (quoted in Mott 1950: 126)

> News is what somebody wants to suppress; all the rest is advertising.
> (attributed to Lord Northcliffe in MacShane 1979: 46)

Each of these sayings tries to distinguish between the type of event that is likely to feature in news reporting and the type of event that will not. According to this approach, 'news' is a feature of events, some aspect or dimension of an event that distinguishes it from others. However, it is clear that in order to serve as the basis of distinction between events, this feature of them must be recognized as such by those who produce the reports of the events – since it is they who will make the judgement in question. Indeed, it is the ability to make this judgement – often called 'news sense' by journalists – which is the basis of professional ability in news media. 'News' is thus that set of events judged 'newsworthy'; it is probably best seen not as a feature of events but as a set of criteria used by professionals in their judgements about events, criteria which enable them to make a selection of events for the purposes of reporting. Of course, it is also the case that the public who buy news media must accept the judgements in question: if they do not, then sooner or later they will switch to another newspaper or TV or radio channel. The criteria are to that extent publicly shared ones.

The criteria of newsworthiness

Textbooks for use in journalist training provide definitions of the features of events that make them potentially suitable for news reporting; the most famous is Macdougall's 'timeliness, proximity, prominence, consequence and human interest' (quoted in Romano 1986: 59). However, such general principles are so general that without detailed discussion of examples they tell us relatively little. The earliest attempt to provide a more systematic definition is Galtung and Ruge (1970). They distinguish eleven features, or dimensions, of events which make them likely to be reported in news media:

- *frequency*: the event must be complete within the publication cycle of the news organization reporting it
- *threshold*: the event must pass a certain size threshold to qualify for sufficient importance to be newsworthy
- *clarity*: it must be relatively clear what has actually happened
- *cultural proximity*: it must be meaningful to the audience of the news organization in question
- *consonance*: the event must be in accordance with the framework of understanding which typifies the culture of the potential audience
- *unexpectedness*: within the framework of meaningfulness under cultural proximity and consonance, the event must be unexpected or rare
- *continuity*: if an event has already been in the news, there is a good chance it will stay there
- *composition*: coverage of events is partially dictated by the internal structure of news-gathering organizations
- *actions of the elite*: events involving elite people or organizations are more likely to be covered than those of unimportant people
- *personification*: events that can be seen in terms of individual people rather than abstractions
- *negativity*: bad events are more newsworthy than good ones.

These features of events, singly or in combination, increase the chance of an event being considered newsworthy. Inevitably most reported events are characterized by more than one of these features; particular combinations of them define the type of story in question, or the 'angle' of the event that is responsible for its newsworthiness.

An example of the application of these criteria

The usefulness of these analyses of news values can be shown by considering one news story which was prominent in British news media in the days after Tuesday, 27 June 1995. The English actor Hugh Grant, who had acquired rapid fame during the preceding twelve months due to his starring role in the internationally successful film *Four Weddings and a Funeral* (1994), was accused by the police in Los Angeles of 'lewd conduct' with a prostitute;

charges were brought and the police identification photograph was made available to the news media. Grant made no attempt to deny the charge.

First, the event was reported immediately after it occurred; the report was 'timely' in that sense, although it probably would have been 'timely' even if the information had been made public some time after the event, since the public availability of the information would itself still have had news value. However, this does not exhaust the question of timeliness. As Galtung and Ruge (1970) argue, it is important that the event in question should be complete within the cycle of publication of the news channel; they use the example of the construction of a dam: what is reported is the beginning of the project (funding agreement, for instance) and its completion (the opening ceremony, for instance), since the gradual construction on a day-by-day basis does not usually provide events that are significant. Thus 'construction' comes to mean – in news terms – inception and completion. Another example would be the reporting of a protracted event such as a war: what is reported on a day-to-day basis is what has happened during the past 24 hours, or what has happened since the previous report in the channel in question. If the latter is the case, some element of explanation of what has occurred in the time-lapse is necessary and this raises the further question of the time-frame that surrounds the news cycle and is implied in reports. As Schudson (1986) shows, stories often contain multiple time-frames: in his example, a report of President Reagan meeting Chinese President Li Xiannian, the time-frames are (1) Reagan's biography – he had just recovered from a cancer operation, (2) the negotiations about Chinese–American trade, (3) Li's biography – he was one of the last survivors of the Long March and (4) the anniversary of the Korean War, in other words the long and troubled history of Chinese–American relations (1986: 84). This multiple time-frame is necessary to supply a framework of significance for the story. Clearly, Hugh Grant's arrest does not have a complex time-frame like this, because of the nature of the event.

The next value to consider is 'prominence', which we can equate in this instance with Galtung and Ruge's (1970) categories of 'threshold' and 'elite': it is Grant's fame that is reponsible for the newsworthiness of the event. More exactly, it is Grant's fame in the UK and the USA that is responsible. Well known in journalism is 'McLurg's law' which establishes a ratio between the size of an event and its distance from (or relevance to) the news audience (Schlesinger 1987: 117): for example, a small motorway crash in the UK would certainly attract local news attention if someone was killed or badly injured, and quite possibly national news too; a motorway crash in France or Germany would need to be much bigger, or involve Britons, before it would be reported in British media; if the event occurred in India or China it would require a very large number of deaths to make UK news (all such thresholds could be lowered by the relative dearth of hard news on Sundays and during the 'silly season' in August). Gans's (1980) survey of those whose actions were reported in US news media shows that roughly 75–80 per cent of them were 'knowns', as he called them, and the rest 'unknowns'; the majority of the knowns were in fact a group of roughly fifty people, all 'high Federal officials' (1980: 12); this analysis is certainly affected by his sample of news media, all of which had national circulations in the USA, as opposed to regional, but the general principle is not in doubt. All the media in question were also non-tabloid, which would also have an effect in this respect (see pp. 384–6).

In discussing 'prominence' we have already opened up the topic of 'proximity', which Galtung and Ruge (1970) call both 'proximity' and 'consonance'. In the case of Grant's arrest, prominence and proximity are effectively the same: it is his fame that is responsible for both. 'Consonance' in this instance is unproblematic since the event is perfectly comprehensible in terms of the cultural norms of our society: prostitution in relation to male sexuality, the bizarre lifestyles of the rich and famous. A category of event that poses greater problems for the cultural norms of our society, and which therefore makes the theme of 'consonance' more visible, is the religious miracle. In September 1995, UK national dailies reported a miracle in which stone statues in Hindu temples appeared to drink milk. This constituted a problem for objective, factual news reporting since miraculous events are only partially consonant with the norms of modern western culture, and as a result UK newspapers were divided over whether to report this as a miracle or as a sham; the London *Evening Standard* (27 September 1995) presented a summary of press reporting focusing on this difficulty, and commented that the nature of the event posed problems for normal news procedures. Other mysterious events such as UFO (unidentified flying object) sightings pose the same problem for news media.

In the case of Grant's arrest, we can consider the questions of 'proximity' and 'consonance' also in relationship to 'consequence' and Galtung and Ruge's category of 'continuity'. Grant's arrest had consequence in relationship to his future as a star and especially the launch of his latest film: it was debated whether the scandal might fit well or badly with the public persona involved in the launch (*Guardian* G2 29 June 1995: 2–3; *Evening Standard* 29 June 1995: 13). Even more attention was paid to the potential consequences for his much-publicized relationship with Elizabeth Hurley, who was just about to be launched as the 'new face' of Estée Lauder products. As a result, follow-up stories in the UK media focused on her (since Grant managed to hide for some days) and her reaction to the news: for example, photographs of her were interpreted through captions drawing attention to the emotional significance of her expression. Here we can see a fundamental news value principle in operation: the notion of 'consequence' operates both in the sense that an event may be considered newsworthy because of its likely consequences, and may remain newsworthy over time because of the way in which news attention can focus upon the unravelling of these consequences – Galtung and Ruge's 'continuity'. In the case of Grant's arrest, even the prostitute's version of events was newsworthy: she was paid $100,000 for her story by the *News of the World* (*Guardian* G2 3 July 1995: 13).

The event was also unexpected. Inevitably the 'unexpectedness' of events conflicts with their 'consonance', in the sense that consonance indicates comprehensibility whereas unexpectedness points in the opposite direction; it is the balance between the two that is crucial, as was noted many years ago by an American commentator: '[the journalist's] commodity is not the normal; it is the standardised exceptional' (Bent 1927, quoted in Sigal 1973: 66). This event was unexpected, not of course in the sense that it is unexpected that men should consort with prostitutes, but in a much more emotionally charged sense: Grant and Hurley had become prominent public symbols of glamour, and it seemed incomprehensible that someone with that status should so dramatically be revealed to be involved in something sordid. (Although this was said in commentaries at the time, statements to this effect do not appear in news reports, which tend to avoid overt interpretation of this type. As a result, if you looked for this 'information' in news reports it would not be there even though – arguably – this was why so much attention was paid to the event. On the implications of this 'invisibility', see Palmer 1998.)

In this wider framework, it entered a long-term debate about the nature of relationships in general; as the *Guardian* columnist Suzanne Moore put it, famous stable heterosexual relationships have become a rare breed (*Guardian* G2 29 June 1995: 5). Even if we do not necessarily accept this interpretation, it seems likely from vox pop interviews (e.g. BBC1 *Nine O'Clock News*, 28 June 1995) and other journalists' interpretations, that the event caused questioning about the place of male sexual desire in a modern society where traditional forms of repression could not be invoked as an explanation. Clearly the event was also negative, highly personalized, and associated with elite people (Galtung and Ruge 1970) – here the importance of the event and the elite nature of Grant and Hurley's status are largely the same thing. Also, the 'personification' involved gave a personal identity to something that is usually publicly debated in the abstract. We could also invoke the example of the death of Leah Betts from Ecstasy poisoning in November 1995 as an example of this process: although she was not the first person to die under such circumstances (in fact she was approximately the fiftieth), the fact that she took the drug at a party at her parents' home, and that she apparently had no previous links with a drug-use subculture led to substantial news interest (during the following five months, some 800 press reports mentioned her name); no doubt her fate had 'personified' a debate about drug use, and many parents' fears about their children's behaviour, which had previously lacked an individual 'face' (Palmer 1998).

By 'composition', Galtung and Ruge (1970) mean that news organizations balance coverage of different areas of activity in the world according to the subdivision of news organizations into sections. This claim is substantiated by Sigal's (1973) analysis of one year of the front pages of the *New York Times* and the *Washington Post*: he shows that 'whatever the variation in world events and news flow . . . the front page [of these papers] had a tendency to contain an equal number of stories from the national, foreign and metropolitan desks' in the newsroom (Sigal 1973: 30–1). This balance is not the result of an average over time (which would not be surprising) but is achieved on a daily basis. Tuchman (1978: 33) observed the same process in a US regional daily. The explanation offered by all three studies is the bureaucratic nature of news organizations and the importance of giving different groups of journalists the amount of access they expect to news space. The Grant story happened to coincide with the election of the leader of the Conservative Party caused by the Prime Minister's sudden and dramatic decision to resign his position as leader and seek re-election; while it is likely that the Grant story would have been newsworthy under any circumstances, its nature made it a welcome relief on the pages of newspapers and broadcast bulletins dominated by the minutiae of political debate and produced predominantly by specialist political staff (according to the *Observer* on 2 July 1995, by the time Grant's story broke, radio stations had started to receive phone calls from listeners complaining about the amount of coverage given to the Tory leadership campaign). Whether the balance found by Sigal would obtain in tabloid or broadcast news is unclear; certainly major news stories have the effect of 'unbalancing' the front pages.

Another approach to the criteria of newsworthiness

Gans (1980: 145–80) defines newsworthiness in terms of the 'suitability' of events, of which there are three basic forms: 'substantive', 'product' and 'competition'. Substantive suitability consists of elements of story content, essentially its importance or interest; Gans's argument here is little different from Galtung and Ruge. 'Product' suitability is based in the relationship between the story and the format of the medium or channel reporting it. It may be, for example, the size of a story in relation to the audience's presumed interest in it; or it may be the availability of some particular element in the composition of the story. For example, in the case of both Hugh Grant's arrest and the death of Leah Betts, photographs of the central characters were made available to the media close to the moment the story broke, in a way that gave them a certain rarity value. In Leah Betts's case, the photograph was taken in the intensive care unit and showed her on life-support equipment; such a photograph is extremely rare, because families rarely give permission for them. In Hugh Grant's case, the police identity photograph was made available to the media by the local police – a routine occurrence – and an enterprising agency photographer, realizing its potential, re-photographed it and made it available on the Internet very promptly; the rapid availability of a photograph, which was the exact opposite of the kind of 'glamour' pose in which film stars are usually seen, was clearly part of the profile of the story (BBC2 *Decisive Moments*, 28 December 1995). In general, all other things being equal, television is more likely to give news attention to an event where film is available than one where it is not; this has led organizations that seek publicity via the news to ensure the availability of relevant, fresh video footage at times that fit with TV channels' output schedule. Well-organized video releases by Greenpeace were said to have inflected TV news coverage of the Brent Spar occupation (May–June 1995) against Shell and in favour of Greenpeace's argument. Competition suitability refers to the desire not to miss something that rival channels have got, and – if possible – to 'scoop' them with an 'exclusive'. As news appears throughout the 24-hour cycle, in the form of news agency reports (see Boyd-Barrett, Chapter 5 in this volume), radio and TV bulletins, morning and evening papers, journalists use the constantly changing flow of information to assess the likelihood of other channels paying attention to particular events, and this judgement feeds into their assessment of whether they should do the same. When all or most journalists come to the same conclusion over a number of days, an event may become 'theme of the week': at a certain point in the growth of a story, journalists will know that they cannot avoid trying to find more relevant fresh information about the event in question and will constantly seek new angles to update the story; where such information is not forthcoming, it may well be replaced by speculation about what may be happening: for instance, during the Prime Minister's re-election campaign as leader of the Conservative Party in June 1995, much political reporting was in fact speculation – based upon gossip and rumour – about who would or would not stand against him.

Categories of news

All of the above are features of events which make them potentially liable to attract reportorial attention and to be selected for inclusion in news reports. However, journalists also distinguish between different categories of news: the most commonly used categories are 'hard' news, 'soft' news, 'spot' news and 'breaking' news.

The distinction between 'hard' and 'soft' news involves various dimensions of events. Primarily, it is a question of the importance of the event: an event which is judged important as well as interesting is more likely to be considered hard news than one which is only interesting. For example, the personal relationships of figures in the entertainment world may be mentioned in a context defined by some other feature of their lives (e.g. a court appearance), but might find more difficulty in appearing in news media without such an event. In May 1996 an earlier scientific report about the presence of traces of chemicals in babies' bottled milk which might have an effect on human fertility was widely reported in the media. Although such a report might have been considered of interest at any stage of recent history, the context of the massive 'scare' about BSE in beef – which became a major phenomenon in March 1996 – ensured that this report became 'hard' news, and was prominently featured, despite the fact that it had been in the public domain for some time.

'Soft' news, on the other hand, consists of information which is considered to be relatively unimportant, or whose availability is not very directly related to the passage of time. For example, on 29 June 1996 it was reported that scientists at the European Centre for Nuclear Research (CERN) in Geneva were going to do a particular experiment the following day; this was linked to the fact that it was possible because of the completion of a very expensive piece of equipment. Neither the completion of the equipment, nor perhaps the experiment, were in themselves hard news: the combination of the two, plus a striking photograph, turned a piece of information that was not very date-specific and as a result very 'soft' into something with a harder edge.

Here there is an important reservation to be made: another fundamental distinction in journalism is between tabloid and broadsheet formats, and these two formats are associated with differences in news values; the type of event that might figure in tabloid formats would not pass the threshold criteria of broadsheet media. Again Hugh Grant's arrest is a good example: had the event consisted of somebody less authoritative than the police asserting that Grant had been guilty of the behaviour he was in fact charged with, it is possible that the allegations might have been reported in tabloid media but not in broadsheet ones (although the absence of an authoritative source would have brought the risk of a libel suit). This event in fact did figure in both types of media, because the arrest and charge made it hard news. The actress Gillian Taylforth sued the *Sun* over a report in which the newspaper claimed that she had been questioned by the police over an incident of lewd conduct with her lover. The original report in the *Sun* appeared some time after the incident in question, and was little mentioned by broadsheet media until the court action: soft news subsequently became hard news because of changed circumstances.

'Spot' news is defined by the circumstances under which it becomes available. Much news is the result of routinized interactions between news-gathering organizations and the various sites of likely interesting or important events in our society: police stations, law courts, Parliament, political parties, large commercial enterprises, medical services, entertainment organizations, and so on (Tuchman 1978); such organizations conventionally notify news media of their upcoming activities through press releases, pre-arranged press conferences, and so on. Such events are listed in the 'news diary' kept by media. However, other newsworthy events occur either at less predictable sites, or on less predictable occasions: accidents may occur anywhere (despite statistical patterns of regularity), scandals may be revealed by unpredictable mechanisms. 'Spot' news is the name for events that occur on unpredicted occasions.

'Breaking' news is the term used to refer to an event which is so incomplete that its profile is hard to summarize in an authoritative and reliable manner, but whose importance or interest is sufficiently great for a tentative report to be included in a bulletin none the less; it is more typical of broadcast than print media (due to the different role of the passage of time in the two media) and its typical form is 'According to reports coming in while we have been on air . . .'. The distinctive feature of breaking news is the relatively low degree of detail of the information, deriving from its timing. The reliability of information about events is another feature of decisions about their inclusion (or exclusion) in news reports, and thus part of news values. Reliability derives largely from the journalistic evaluation of the sources from which information is obtained; information is reliable when it comes from a reliable source (see Miller, Chapter 6 in this volume).

Objectivity

Reliability, considered as a journalistic criterion, is inseparable from a certain conception of what type of information news should consist of. As has often been pointed out, modern journalism differs from earlier forms by its rejection of overt partisanship in news reporting and its focus upon events rather than upon overtly evaluative interpretations of events by participants in them (Hallin 1986: 7; Schlesinger 1987: 15–18; Schudson 1978: 4–6, 13–25). Central to the new form was the establishment of the 'objective' method of reporting 'hard' news: such reports were supposed to answer five questions – What? Who? When? Where? How? – if possible supplemented by an answer to the question Why? (Manoff and Schudson 1986: 2–10; Sigal 1973: 66–9). Objectivity, in this analysis, consists of reporting verified facts without comment or interpretation, although most journalists recognize that the choice of which stories to cover cannot be entirely objective as it must involve elements of interpretation (Gans 1980: 182–3); as Leapman says, 'The selection of news is as much a political act as commenting on it' (1992: 254). There is clear evidence of journalists choosing what to cover or not to cover on personal evaluative grounds (Goldenberg 1975: 96). Verification means conformity to specified criteria: in the BBC, until roughly 1970, it meant being on two independent agency reports (Schlesinger 1987: 90); US journalists talk about 'triangulation' as the ideal basis of reliability, in other words confirmation from two independent sources (Tuchman 1978: 85). In the UK the journalistic rule of thumb for 'routine' reporting (as opposed to 'investigative') is whether the source is competent as a public authority on the subject in question (Murphy 1991: 12); Sigal (1986: 19) and Fishman (1980) come to a similar conclusion for US print journalism. To take again the case of Hugh Grant in Los Angeles: the fact that an official representative of the police force said that the charge had been brought was sufficient proof that it had; of course, the fact of prosecution did not in itself prove guilt, and under other circumstances the person prosecuted might deny the charge (as, obviously, in the case of O.J. Simpson's murder trial in 1994–5). But the objective method of reporting, in conjunction with news values, distinguishes between what actually happened, and what somebody newsworthy and authoritative claimed happened. The fact that a claim is made, and appears in the news, does not in itself imply that the claim is true; indeed, one academic commentator argues that news media rarely distinguish between 'accuracy' (correct reporting of what somebody claimed happened) and 'truth' (what actually did happen) (Willis 1991: 7–13). This distinction is particularly clear in political reporting, where many claims are reported simply because of the identity of the claimant. These features of journalism have led many writers to argue that objectivity in journalism has little to do with 'fact' in the scientific sense, but is instead the product of a professional routine (Gans 1980: 183; Schudson 1991: 151; Tuchman 1978). This is a key component in the professionalism of journalists, the special skill that distinguishes their work from other forms of information processing (Schlesinger 1987: 109). It has been debated whether such 'objectivity' is capable of achieving the level of independence and reliability of information that is traditionally claimed for news (Curran 1991: 98–100; Hallin 1986: 206–7; Lichtenberg 1991).

News values and the organization of news media

The preceding discussion of news values has concentrated primarily on the nature of the events – external to the media which report them – which are likely candidates for inclusion in news media reports. However, on various occasions the discussion has strayed across the boundary between the events themselves, and features of the organizations reporting them, for example, in the role of video in determining TV news interest in a story. This is because, ultimately, 'newsworthiness' is never exclusively a feature of events, but is always related to the nature of organizations as well. The quoted analyses refer in different ways to the distinction just drawn. Most of the 'news values' outlined in Galtung and Ruge (1970) refer to features of events, with the exception of 'frequency' and 'composition'; Gans's (1980) criteria refer not only to features of events ('substantive suitability'), but also to features of organizations ('product' and 'competition' suitability).

An obvious example is the amount of news space available – known in American journalists' jargon as the 'newshole'. Different newspapers print different amounts of pages, and on different sizes of paper. (UK newspapers are usually divided into the categories of 'tabloids', 'mid-markets' and 'broadsheets' according to the composition of their readerships and the paper format they use. The average daily size of the news space available in each category during the period 1988–90 was approximately as follows: tabloids 2000 column centimetres, mid-markets 2500 col. cm, broadsheets 3500 col. cm (Collins 1997). These proportions are unlikely to have changed substantially since then.) Television and radio news bulletins are also of different lengths. At the moment when decisions are taken about what to include and what to exclude, the total amount of space available is a crucial variable. The amount is ultimately determined by economic considerations, with (in most countries, including the UK) an addition of legal obligations on broadcasting organizations to provide news and current affairs as a public service.

Less obviously, what gets selected as news is determined in part by the internal structure of news organizations. First, we should recognize that news media are indeed complex organizations in their own right, in which different people play different roles determined by the nature of the organization. Although the partially unpredictable nature of external events means that journalistic work can never be routinized to the same extent as factories or – for example – insurance offices, none the less, much of the production routine of news and some aspects of reporting are indeed subject to bureaucratic organization (Gans 1980: 78–81, 109; Schlesinger 1987: 48; Sigal 1973: 4; Tunstall 1971: 24–42); the texts cited here contain extended descriptions of the results of this principle. Publication occurs at pre-scheduled intervals which are largely independent of what happens in the outside world. Production is geared to this schedule, and reporting is similarly subject to the 'deadline'. The production routine is responsible for the elements of the definition of news which derive from the passage of time. 'Up to date' means 'since last publication': the slogan 'yesterday's news is not news' derives its meaning from the fact that the fundamental news update is daily. (More exactly, newspapers publish on this schedule. Broadcast channels update at whatever frequency they feel appropriate. In national broadcast channels, the major updates are daily in the sense that content shifts more fundamentally overnight than at any other time. However, the increasingly widespread 'rolling news' format pioneered by CNN is not subject to the same temporal logic, especially if broadcast worldwide.)

Newsrooms are also subject to an internal division of labour. The most basic element of this is the vertical division of responsibility which gives power to make decisions about story content to editors, decisions which are reflected both in the assignment of reporters to seek information about specified topics and in the instructions given to production staff (especially subeditors) about the manner in which stories are to be treated; reporters may be subject specialists (usually called 'correspondents' in the UK) or assigned to the general staff of the newsroom (Tunstall 1971: 15, 28–36). In general, the nature of working practices in news organizations and the results this has upon news representations of the world have been little studied, and most systematic data-gathering on the subject is now old (Negrine 1993: 2–4); reporters have been more studied than editors and subeditors (Schudson 1991: 149). Previous analyses of the organizational aspect of journalism are divided about the importance of the division of labour for the understanding of news values. On the one hand, Gans (1980) argues that the division of labour is unimportant: 'who makes the final story decisions has little impact on what decisions are reached, for all abide by the considerations that govern news judgment' (1980: 100). In a similar vein, Tuchman (1978: 67) says that the basis of journalism as a trade is that everyone can do everyone else's job (see also Negrine 1993: 5–13). On the other hand, specialist reporters are more likely to espouse the values implicit in the activities of those whose deeds they report than are general reporters, and are likely to develop a background knowledge of the area in question which enables them to contextualize events, ask probing questions of sources, and so on (Ericson *et al.* 1989: 104–13; Gandy 1982: 104–7; Gans 1980: 89–93, 101–5; Goldenberg 1975: 66–7, 79, 104; Schlesinger and Tumber 1994: 150; Sigal 1973: 14–15, 19–21, 40–1, 47, 50–1).

News values and cultural contexts

So far this discussion of news values has been conducted entirely in media-centric terms. To go beyond this perspective we need to do two things: first, to consider the role of sources (see Miller, Chapter 6 in this volume), about which nothing more will be said here. Second, we need to consider the relationship between what is said about events, and the social and cultural contexts in which it is said; such analyses are sometimes called 'representationalist'.

Galtung and Ruge (1970) point out (under 'cultural proximity' and 'consonance') that news must indeed make sense within the context in question, but this says nothing about the extent to which there is a functional relationship between the news portrayal of events and the social context in question. Gans (1980: 39–69) addresses this question more directly than Galtung and Ruge (1970) when he shows that American news constantly affirms certain fundamental American cultural values; in other words, the way in which news presents us with an understanding of the events in question is predicated upon the basic cultural categories current in the society in which the reporting is done. However, this begs the question of the extent to which, as a result, news accounts of events reproduce the categories in which the world is understood in a society, and as a result contribute towards the maintenance of a status quo by implying that the terms of a culture are always right and adequate.

This has been the subject of considerable debate since the mid-1970s. Most influentially, Hall *et al.* (1978) proposed that the news portrayal of events is always subject to a process of 'primary definition' by that section of society which exercises most political and economic influence (the ruling class, in the traditional sense of this term); they demonstrate this thesis through a detailed analysis of the way in which a 'crime wave' was reported in UK media, which shows that the way in which it was reported acted to reinforce a conception of the world in which state repression of any activity likely to lead to opposition would seem justified.

Countervailing analysis suggests that control over the media is much more fragmentary and subject to negotiation than Hall *et al.* (1978) admit. In a series of analyses of particular sequences of events and their news reporting a group of authors who are broadly pluralist in their political orientation indicate that the power to define the meanings of events is always negotiated between members of various ruling elites and media personnel. The result of these negotiations cannot usually be predicted from the constellation of groups or individuals involved, and as a result definitional power must be seen as the result of these negotiations, not something that precedes it and is the result of occupying the position of a 'primary definer' (Deppa 1993; Miller 1993a, 1993b; Murphy 1991; Schlesinger 1989, 1990; Schlesinger and Tumber 1994).

It should be stressed that this way of understanding news is not incompatible with the way outlined earlier in this chapter. As Hartley (1982: 83) puts it: news values foreground 'conflict, violence, rivalry, disagreement', but these things are comprehensible only as such in terms of a background consensus on what constitutes the normality in terms of which they are defined as disruptive. Or as Chibnall (1977: 14) says, news and news values are both the product of a professional skill and a way of building consensus in a society.

Questions

1   Take any news story and analyse what are the news values that are responsible for its appearance in the medium or channel in question.

2   Compare the coverage of a small set of stories in broadsheet, tabloid and broadcast formats: what are the differences? What are the similarities? What can you learn about the different news values of each medium or channel?

3   Take a small set of news stories and analyse the extent to which the reporting conforms to the journalistic criteria of objective reporting.

References

Chibnall, S. (1977) *Law and Order News*, London: Tavistock.

Collins, J. (1997) 'Food scares and the news media', unpublished PhD thesis, London Guildhall University.

Curran, J. (1991) 'Mass media and democracy: a re-appraisal', in J. Curran and M. Gurevitch (eds) *Mass Media and Society*, London: Arnold.

Deppa, J. (1993) *The Media and Disasters: Pan Am 103*, London: Fulton.

Ericson, R.V., Baranek, P.M. and Chan, J. (1989) *Negotiating Control: A Study of News Sources*, Milton Keynes: Open University Press.

Fishman, M. (1980) *Manufacturing the News*, Austin, TX, and London: University of Texas Press.

Galtung, J. and Ruge, M.H. (1970) 'The structure of foreign news', in J. Tunstall (ed.) *Media Sociology*, London: Constable.

Gandy, O. (1982) *Beyond Agenda Setting*, Norwood, NJ: Ablex.

Gans, H.J. (1980) *Deciding What's News*, London: Constable.

Glasgow University Media Group (1993) *Getting the Message: News, Truth and Power*, London: Routledge.

Goldenberg, E. (1975) *Making the Papers: The Access of Resource-Poor Groups to the Metropolitan Press*, Lexington, MA: D.C. Heath.

Hall, S., Critcher, C., Jefferson, T., Clarke, J. and Roberts, B. (1978) *Policing the Crisis: Mugging, the State and Law and Order*, London: Macmillan.

Hallin, D. (1986) *The Uncensored War: The Media and Vietnam*, Oxford: Oxford University Press.

Hartley, J. (1982) *Reading Television*, London: Methuen.

Leapman, M. (1992) *Treacherous Estate*, London: Hodder & Stoughton.

Lichtenberg, J. (1991) 'In defence of objectivity', in J. Curran and M. Gurevich (eds) *Mass Media and Society*, London: Arnold.

MacShane, D. (1979) *Using the Media*, London: Pluto.

Manoff, R.K. and Schudson, M. (eds) (1986) *Reading the News*, New York: Pantheon.

Miller, D. (1993a) 'Official sources and "primary definition": the case of Northern Ireland', *Media Culture and Society* 15: 385–406.

Miller, D. (1993b) 'The Northern Ireland Information Service and the media: aims, strategy, tactics', in Glasgow University Media Group, *Getting the Message: News, Truth and Power*, London: Routledge.

Mott, F.L. (1950) *American Journalism*, London and New York: Macmillan.

Murphy, D. (1991) *The Stalker Affair*, London: Constable.

Negrine, R. (1993) 'The organisation of British journalism and specialist correspondents: a study of newspaper reporting', Leicester University Centre for Mass Communications Research Discussion Papers in Mass Communications MC93/1, Leicester: Leicester University.

Palmer, J.N.J. (forthcoming) *News Values and Source Strategies*.

Romano, C. (1986) 'The grisly truth about bare facts', in R. Manoff and M. Schudson (eds) *Reading the News*, New York: Pantheon.

Schlesinger, P. (1987) *Putting Reality Together*, 2nd edn, London: Methuen.

Schlesinger, P. (1989) 'From production to propaganda', *Media, Culture and Society* 11: 283–306.

Schlesinger, P. (1990) 'Rethinking the sociology of journalism: source strategies and the limits of media-centrism', in M. Ferguson (ed.) *Public Communications: The New Imperatives*, London: Sage.

Schlesinger, P. and Tumber, H. (1994) *Reporting Crime*, Oxford: Clarendon.

Schudson, M. (1978) *Discovering the News*, New York: Basic Books.

Schudson, M. (1986) 'Deadlines, datelines and history', in R. Manoff and M. Schudson (eds) *Reading the News*, New York: Pantheon.

Schudson, M. (1991) 'The sociology of news production revisited', in J. Curran and M. Gurevitch (eds) *Mass Media and Society*, London: Arnold.

Sigal, L.V. (1973) *Reporters and Officials*, Lexington, MA: D.C. Heath.

Sigal, L.V. (1986) 'Sources make the news', in R. Manoff and M. Schudson (eds) *Reading the News*, New York: Pantheon.

Tuchman, G. (1978) *Making News*, New York: Free Press.

Tunstall, J. (1971) *Journalists at Work*, London: Constable.

Weaver, P.H. (1994) *News and the Culture of Lying*, New York: Free Press.

Willis, J. (1991) *The Shadow World: Life between the News Media and Reality*, New York: Praeger.

Further reading

Cockerell, M., Hennessy, P. and Walker, D. (1984) *Sources Close to the Prime Minister*, London: Macmillan.

Curran, J. (1990) 'The new revisionism in mass communications research', *European Journal of Communication* 5: 135–64.

Ericson, R.V. (1991) 'Mass media, crime, law and justice: an institutional approach', *British Journal of Criminology* 31: 219–49.

Galtung, J. and Ruge, M.H. (1970) 'The structure of foreign news', in J. Tunstall (ed.) *Media Sociology*, London: Constable.

Gandy, O. (1982) *Beyond Agenda Setting*, Norwood, NJ: Ablex.

Gans, H.J. (1980) *Deciding What's News*, London: Constable.

Gieber, W. and Johnson, W. (1961) 'The city hall beat: a study of reporter and source roles', *Journalism Quarterly* 38: 289–97.

Goldenberg, E. (1975) *Making the Papers: The Access of Resource-Poor Groups to the Metropolitan Press*, Lexington, MA: D.C. Heath.

Harris, R. (1991) *Good and Faithful Servant: The Unauthorised Biography of Bernard Ingham*, London: Faber & Faber.

Ingham, B. (1991) *Kill the Messenger*, London: Fontana.

Keane, J. (1991) *The Media and Democracy*, Cambridge: Polity.

McQuail, D. (1991) 'Mass media in the public interest: towards a framework of norms for media performance', in J. Curran and M. Gurevitch (eds) *Mass Media and Society*, London: Arnold.

Manoff, R.K. and Schudson, M. (eds) (1986) *Reading the News*, New York: Pantheon.

Morrison, D. and Tumber, H. (1988) *Journalists at War*, London: Sage.

Robertson, G. and Nicol, A. (1984) *Media Law*, London: Sage.

Seymour-Ure, C. (1989) 'Prime ministers' reactions to television', *Media, Culture and Society* 11: 307–25.

Sigal, L.V. (1973) *Reporters and Officials*, Lexington, MA: D.C. Heath.

Chapter 28

Parliamentary politics

THE MEDIA AND POLITICS

IVOR GABER

This chapter takes an overview of the reporting of politics in the UK. It traces the history of parliamentary reporting, describes the different types of political reporting, analyses the development of political broadcasting, describes the current situation and addresses the hotly disputed question, who, if anyone, is playing the major role in driving the political news agenda – the press, the broadcasters or the politicians themselves?

The development of parliamentary reporting

Millbank is a busy thoroughfare situated on the north bank of the River Thames at Westminster. On one side of the road stands the Palace of Westminster – the Houses of Commons and Lords – on the other, Number 4, stands the real centre of political power. At least that is the argument of those who claim that in the UK today the discourse of politics is now the discourse of the television studio. Number 4 Millbank houses the production offices and studios of BBC Television and Radio, ITN, Independent Radio News and Sky News and, it is argued, it is in the power of these broadcasters to determine the political agenda, and to ignore what is taking place across the road in Parliament, that has transformed the face of political communication in the UK.

Yet just as Members of Parliament (MPs) complain about the extent to which political journalists, both in the electronic and print media, have apparently seized the political news agenda and now report politics in their own terms, they have also been complaining about what they perceive to be a general decline in the actual space that newspapers devote to the coverage of parliamentary debates. There is a great irony in these calls because up until the nineteenth century MPs did everything in their power to try to prevent journalists from reporting the proceedings of Parliament.

The British Parliament first began sitting in the thirteenth century, but no formal record of its deliberations was kept. The official journal of the House of Lords dates back to 1510 and that of the Commons to 1547; the Houses' decisions were recorded but not their discussions. Members risked punishment if they revealed what was actually taking place inside Parliament to anyone. This was because of fear of the monarch and/or the London mob taking exception to their deliberations. Through the next two centuries a constant battle raged between Parliament and those courageous editors and publishers who sought to report the proceedings of the Lords and Commons. This struggle climaxed in 1771 when John Wilkes, a radical journalist and MP, defied Parliament and, with the support of the London mob, began reporting its proceedings. Thus began the whole profession of parliamentary and political journalism.

In 1803 part of the Gallery of the House of Commons was set aside for the use of reporters and eighty-one years later the first reporters were allowed into the MPs' lobby to mingle with members and glean political intelligence. The Commons and Lords allowed in the radio microphones in 1978 and in 1985 the Lords allowed the television cameras to enter. Four years later the Commons followed suit, opening up not only the deliberations of the chamber, but also those of the committees.

Political journalists

The term political journalist is a broad-brush description of those whose work involves them in writing and broadcasting about Westminster. It covers a multitude of types – in the written press six different categories of journalists involved in political reporting can be identified:

- parliamentary reporters
- political correspondents
- political columnists
- sketchwriters
- Whitehall and Westminster correspondents
- specialist correspondents
- broadcast journalists

Parliamentary reporters

The original reporters to arrive on the Westminster scene were the debate reporters – Charles Dickens was one of the first practitioners of this trade. Nowadays the vast majority of this reporting is undertaken by specialist reporters working for the official publication of the House called *Hansard*. In addition the national news agency, the Press Association, has a team of gallery reporters who, unlike the *Hansard* reporters, do not transcribe every word uttered in the chamber but none the less supply the media with a substantial and rapid reporting service. The national newspapers also used to have their own gallery reporters but now only *The Times* and the *Daily Telegraph* still attempt any parliamentary reporting and precious little of that.

Jack Straw (1993), now Labour's Home Secretary, has been waging a campaign against the reduction in parliamentary reporting. As part of his campaign Straw measured the amount of press reporting of Parliament on three days in 1933, 1953, 1963, 1973, 1983, 1988 and 1992 in *The Times* and the *Guardian*. His research revealed that the space devoted to Parliament had, in the *Guardian* between 1933 and 1992, declined from an average of over 600 column inches a day to around 90, while the decline in *The Times* had been from an average of around 900 column inches a day to around 80. Straw adduces four reasons for this decline:

- the televising of Parliament, which has led to television displacing newspapers as the most immediate source of parliamentary news
- the large Conservative majorities of the 1980s which meant that the government was always assured of winning parliamentary votes
- a generational change among broadsheet editors who came to see parliamentary debates as 'boring'
- a consequential change in the behaviour of MPs who, seeing the trend, now use press releases and broadcast interviews as a more effective way of engaging in the national debate.

Political correspondents

The best known political journalists are members of the so-called 'lobby' or lobby correspondents. In the late 1990s there are around 140 reporters holding lobby cards; these cards entitle them to use the Members' lobby of the House of Commons and there to mix with MPs, to attend briefings which are given twice a day by the Prime Minister's Press Secretary and to receive copies of government and parliamentary publications, in advance of both the public and MPs.

The lobby, which first came into existence in the middle of the nineteenth century, has been subjected to a great deal of criticism in recent years, from both within and without. For several years in the 1980s *The Independent*, the *Guardian* and the *Scotsman* boycotted it, claiming that its influence had now become pernicious. This boycott was occasioned by one particular Downing Street Press Secretary – Bernard, now Sir Bernard, Ingham – who served Mrs Thatcher between 1979 and 1990 and was seen as either very good or very bad at his job, depending on one's point of view. Certainly he was ruthless in using the then unattributable nature of the briefings to denigrate politicians who were out of favour with the Prime Minister and to boost those whose star was in the ascendant; Ingham (1994) himself has admitted that great tension exists between political reporters and the government press officers. Eventually Mrs Thatcher was defeated, Bernard Ingham left and the boycotters returned to the fold but criticism of the lobby has continued. For not only was the Prime Minister's Press Secretary, until recently 'off-the-record' – everything that a journalist hears or sees in the lobby is still off-the-record. That does not mean that it cannot be reported but it does mean that the source of the information cannot be identified. Such a bizarre code of practice has serious implications for notions of freedom of information and, although the lobby has voted to continue its existing practices, the calls for reform or even abolition are certain to continue (see Winstone 1996).

Political columnists

As the reporting of Parliament's deliberations has declined so there has been a concomitant rise in the amount of space that newspapers devote to their star-name political columnists. Most columnists are former lobby correspondents and some still retain their lobby cards. However, their work differs significantly from their colleagues in the lobby because their job is not to report the day's political news or even to break 'exclusives'. Their job is to talk to politicians, observe them in action and then to make their own judgements and give their own opinions, usually in line with the political bias of the papers they are writing for. Increasingly columnists such as Hugo Young on the *Guardian*, Peter Riddell on *The Times* and Donald Macintyre on *The Independent* have seen their own column inches, influence and salaries rise. It is a trend that worries many MPs who believe that it places enormous power in the hands of a very small group of people and makes them the target of enormous amounts of behind-the-scenes flattery and pressure.

Sketchwriters

Similar to, but different from, the political columnist is the sketchwriter. Unlike the columnist, whose visits to the press gallery in the chamber, outside the twice-weekly ritual of Prime Minister's Questions, can be rare, the sketchwriter can often be found there during long and uncontroversial debates, with perhaps only a handful of backbenchers and a minister for company. But it is at such times that the sketchwriter often finds the angle, the quirky moment which providers writers such as Simon Hoggart in the *Guardian* or Matthew Parris in *The Times* with their material. Sketchwriters have to find something witty but also trenchant to say every day and, like the columnists, it is a trade that worries MPs since the main purpose of the sketchwriter, MPs argue, is to mock their behaviour. This might be bad enough in itself but given the absence of any straightforward reporting of Parliament, it becomes problematic in that theirs is now virtually the only perspective on the conduct of MPs to be found in the press.

Whitehall and Westminster correspondents

As the reporting of the deliberations of Parliament has dried up another source of news has come on stream. Known as Whitehall or Westminster correspondents the broadsheet newspapers have been increasing their coverage of what is cumbersomely known as the machinery of government. The first such reporter was Anthony Howard who in the 1960s was the *Sunday Times* Whitehall correspondent. (The then Prime Minister, Harold Wilson, unsuccessfully sought to scupper Howard's appointment by instructing his ministers to have no dealings with him: see Pimlott 1993: 443.) Today reporters such as David Hencke in the *Guardian* and Chris Blackhurst in *The Independent* seek to reveal the inner workings of the Civil Service, exposing incompetence, corruption and plain misguided policies. Much of their work revolves around the Commons' Public Accounts Committee and the agency that services it, the National Audit Office. The Committee and the Audit Office exist to undertake the same work as the journalist – the revelation of scandals and maladministration – the only difference is one of timescale. But the journalist wants to break the story before its official publication, and that means even before the advance copies of the document have been delivered to members of the lobby, while the Committee and the Audit Office want to bathe in the glory of their own publicity, undistracted by premature leaks in the press. This creates an odd sort of relationship for this breed of journalists: on the one hand they need to have good relations with members of the Public Accounts Committee and the National Audit Office for they are clearly important sources of information. However, they are also competitors because both they and the journalist want to have their versions of the story published before the other.

Specialist correspondents

The final category of journalist who can be identified as regularly involved in political reporting in the written press is the non-political specialist. Education, defence, diplomatic correspondents, for example, all spend a significant amount of their time in and around Westminster and Whitehall covering debates, press conferences and other meetings – their reporting tends to be more forensic, they know their subjects well and it is therefore that much harder for the minister, or whoever, to pull the wool over their eyes. However, paradoxically it can also be that much more difficult for them since the nature of any lobby system means that journalists require ongoing relationships with their primary sources. Any specialist correspondent seen to be 'difficult' will find his or her ability to gain access to these sources, on or off-the-record material, that much more difficult.

Broadcast journalists

In addition to the above categories, political journalists working in radio and television can be further subdivided, although more by the form rather than the content of their work: behind television and radio's ranks of political correspondents stand a veritable army of support staff. At a junior level there are researchers who undertake the basic research and 'phone bashing' which television and radio require.

There are the political producers who are responsible for assembling the material – parliamentary or other actuality material, as well as interviews and reporters' 'pieces-to-camera' – which make up the news packages that are then presented by the political correspondents. Then there are the programme presenters – political specialists themselves but whose work is confined to the television and radio studios and hence needs the support of producers and researchers. Finally there are political programme editors, who are taking editorial decisions about the content of their programmes based on the advice they are receiving from their teams of political correspondents and producers.

Thus in broadcasting much of the most significant decision-taking is undertaken by broadcast journalists who have no direct contact with the raw material – the politicians. Certainly lunches are arranged and receptions held where these behind-the-scenes broadcasters can get to know the politicians a little better but this can be no substitute for the day-to-day contact that journalists working in the lobby are able to maintain. Hence despite the great complexity of broadcast journalism, the system of restricted parliamentary access which the lobby symbolizes means that significant power still lies in the hands of the political correspondents and their unattributable sources.

Politicians and the broadcasters

The early days

Broadcasting itself formally began in the UK with the establishment of the BBC. Initially it was the British Broadcasting Company, formed by the radio set manufacturers in 1922, to provide programmes for the 'wireless'. Under the terms of its first licence it was specifically forbidden from collecting news – the newspapers and agencies were frightened of the competition – it was allowed to broadcast 'only such news as is obtained from news agencies approved by the Postmaster-General' (see Briggs 1995: 239–48 for a full discussion of the difficulties that this restriction imposed on the new BBC). There was just one bulletin at 7 p.m., after evening paper sales had finished. The BBC was also specifically forbidden, by the Postmaster-General, from broadcasting its own opinions on matter of public policy, nor was it allowed to broadcast on matters of political, industrial or religious controversy. However, the first broadcasting of politics in the UK did actually take place in 1924 when leaders of the Conservative, Labour and Liberal parties were allowed to make one radio broadcast each during the election campaign of that year.

Two years later the BBC received its royal charter, becoming in the process the British Broadcasting Corporation. Under the terms of this first charter and its accompanying licence the restrictions on its news-gathering were eased – one of its stated purposes was now specifically 'to collect news and information relating to current events in any part of the world and in any manner that may be thought fit and to establish and subscribe to news agencies'. However, despite the strenuous efforts of its first director-general John (later Lord) Reith the Corporation was still denied the right to broadcast on matters of public controversy; however, that ban was lifted in 1928.

The General Strike and the BBC

But it was in the crucible of Britain's first and only General Strike in 1926 that the BBC's relations with politicians were really forged (for two contrasting views of the role of the BBC during the General Strike, see Briggs 1995: ch. 6, sec. 3; Tracey 1977: ch. 8). The strike came about when the coal-owners sought to cut the wages of the miners. After nine months out on strike the miners were joined by the rest of the trade-union movement. This was a crucial moment for the BBC. Print workers, being highly unionized, were called out at once, but the BBC, whose staff were not organized into unions, carried on broadcasting and the BBC was to be the main source of national news throughout the nine days of the strike; Reith wrote later about this period: 'I do not say that I welcome crises, but I do welcome the opportunities which they bring'(1950: 107).

Arrangements were made for news bulletins to be broadcast at 10 a.m, 1 p.m., 4 p.m., 7 p.m. and 9.30 p.m. using agency material and official sources: at this stage the BBC had no news-gathering capability of its own. The government had the power to commandeer the BBC, granted by legislation the previous year, but both it and the BBC knew it would be far better if that did not happen. (The Cabinet was divided, however, with Winston Churchill very strongly believing that the Corporation should be taken over for the duration.) The BBC was able to maintain a measure of independence throughout the strike but only with great difficulty (in this it was much assisted by the wily Prime Minister of the day, Stanley Baldwin, who preferred to 'trust the BBC').

And he was right. Lord Reith in a memo to his staff at the end of the strike wrote: 'since the BBC was a national institution, and since in this crisis the Government was acting for the people . . . the BBC was for the Government in the crisis too' (quoted in Scannell and Cardiff 1991: 33 and castigated as a 'notorious syllogism'). Reith admitted that the BBC 'lacked complete liberty of action' during the strike but went on to write: 'We do not believe that any other government . . . would have allowed the broadcasting authority under its control greater freedom than was enjoyed by the BBC during the crisis' (Briggs 1995: 364–6). But the BBC's less than impartial coverage of the strike had not escaped the notice of the Labour Party and Trades Union Congress (TUC). They were angered by the Corporation's obvious opposition to the strike. After the strike came to an end Reith wrote, 'When it was all over I wondered if it would have been better had the BBC been commandeered. My conclusion was that it would have been better for me, worse for the BBC and for the country' (Reith 1950).

The arrival of television

Television broadcasts began in the UK in 1936 but under the terms of the BBC's charter and licence the only news that the service was permitted was the transmission of a recording of the main evening's radio bulletin which was broadcast at the end of the evening broadcasts over a picture of the BBC clock. It also transmitted two weekly film newsreels that could be seen in cinemas around the UK.

When the Second World War broke out in 1939 the television transmitters were switched off: there was a fear that they could act as beacons for enemy aircraft. This was to be very much a radio war, a war that cemented the role of the BBC as a national institution. Initially the plan was for the BBC to be placed under direct government control but it soon became apparent that the unity of purpose in the UK was so great that central direction of the national broadcaster was not necessary – the BBC spoke with the same voice as the government (and incidentally the people) out of choice, not compulsion (see Calder 1969: 412–22). Although just to make sure that no dissension was voiced on the public airwaves the Government introduced, and the BBC concurred with, the so-called fourteen-day rule which ensured that there could be no discussion on air of any matter which was due to be discussed in Parliament within the next two weeks.

Television recommenced in 1946 and the politicians were anxious to extend the fourteen-day rule to television. One of the keenest advocates of this extension was the wartime Prime Minister Winston Churchill, who declared: 'It would be shocking to have debates in this House forestalled time after time by expressions of opinions by persons who had not the status and responsibility of MPs' (quoted in Cockerell 1988: 8). However, as the era of postwar austerity faded in the 1950s a new mood of freedom was beginning to sweep the country. But the BBC, still borne down by the weight of the fourteen-day rule and the deference to politicians that this induced, remained aloof. The BBC News Division did not find this a problem; its reporting of politics remained sycophantic and unchallenging. Indeed the Corporation felt itself to be so regulated and fearful of disturbing the political class that, even as late as the 1955 General Election, it used the excuse of a very narrow interpretation of the Representation of the People Act to deny itself any substantial coverage of the election until the moment after the polls closed when it began its election results' programme.

Change in the air

At the same time there was a sense of change in the air. Postwar austerity had come to an end and the spirits, both commercial and artistic,
were breaking free. In the BBC this was manifest in the work of the more
adventurous producers in the current affairs department, who, under the
inspired leadership of Grace Wyndham-Goldie, were already starting to be
more abrasive and questioning in their political coverage. It was also evidenced in the establishment of ITV, the commercial channel, and its news
supplier ITN, which set out to provide as different a news service as was
possible. Under its first two editors, Aidan Crawley and Geoffrey Cox, ITN
sought to differentiate itself by, wherever possible, using the pictures to tell
the news stories, by making personalities out of its presenters and by ending
BBC habits of deference, particularly as it applied to political interviews
(Crawley 1988: 304–14).

In 1956, just one year after the birth of ITN, the UK underwent its
worst postwar political trauma. In the teeth of American opposition, the UK
collaborated with Israel and France in invading the Egyptian-controlled
Suez Canal. Far from the national unity which was the hallmark of the
British media during the Second World War, the Suez crisis sharply divided
the country. In the wave of anger and controversy that swept the nation, the
fourteen-day rule became an irrelevancy. In the words of ITN's then editor
Geoffrey Cox: 'Every interview we did at London airport, every report on
public reaction, every street interview was a breach of the fourteen-day rule.
The issues of Suez went too deeply into the lives of the public to be inhib-
ited by such formalities'(Cox 1995: 121). A few months later the Government declined to renew the fourteen-day rule when it came up for renewal
in Parliament.

The combination of the advent of ITN, the Suez crisis and the Russian
invasion of Hungary, also in 1956, added to the competitive transformation. The BBC was forced to take a more proactive stance in terms of its
reporting of politics, particularly in view of the fact that ITN interviewers
did not accord politicians the same deference as had the BBC. One of
ITN's most notable presenters was Robin Day, a barrister, who began to
develop a 'court-room' style of interviewing which confronted politicians
directly. In 1958, interviewing the then Prime Minister Harold Macmillan,
Day caused a national outcry by asking Macmillan whether he intended to
sack his Foreign Secretary, who had been the subject of much criticism. In
his memoirs Day has no doubts about the importance of this interview:

> The significance of my ITN interview with Macmillan is difficult to convey
> today. Here was the nation's leader, the most powerful and important
> politician of the time, coming to terms with the new medium of television.
> He was questioned on TV as vigorously as in Parliament. His TV performance
> . . . was an early recognition that television was not merely for entertainment
> or party propaganda, but was now a serious part of the democratic process.
>
> (Day 1989: 3)

Nor did Macmillan see the interview as an ordeal or an impertinence, as some of the Conservative press of the time claimed. His biographer records: 'His first breakthrough as a "television personality" had come with a full-length interview staged by a young, brash, and virtually unknown journalist called Robin Day' (Day 1989: 3).

Despite the apparent ending of deference, television still faced enormous handicaps in the reporting of the political process at its most intense, i.e. during a General Election campaign. Indeed no real reporting took place at all since the BBC believed, and ITN initially concurred, that even if the fourteen-day rule was no more, under the legislation governing the conduct of elections the broadcasting of politicians during a campaign could be challenged as illegal. However, ITN and one of the more adventurous of the regional ITV companies – Granada – determined to challenge this interpretation of the Representation of the People Act. The ideal opportunity arose with a by-election in the north-western town of Rochdale in 1958 – not only did it fall within Granada's transmission area but one of the candidates was a former ITN newscaster – the news imperatives were strong and both companies went ahead with very straightforward election coverage; the skies did not fall in, nor did anyone mount a legal challenge.

The politicians' response

At the same time as television was experimenting with its coverage of politics so politicians were also seeking to come to terms with the new medium. Harold Macmillan, Prime Minister between 1958 and 1963, was the first British politician who really understood the importance of the medium and learned how to exploit it. He recognized that television was his single most important instrument of communication with the electorate and he knew that the style of the hustings was not appropriate. 'I've never quite mastered the art of looking into the lens and treating it as one of the family', he said in a speech after his retirement thus revealing that he understood precisely how politicians should be using this new medium (Horne 1989: 149).

As television became ever more powerful – by the early 1960s the majority of people were claiming television as their principal news source (Blumler and McQuail 1968: 43) – it was noticeable for the way that much of the political debate shifted away from the floor of the House of Commons to the floor of the television studios. And political parties were now making televisual appeal an important factor in their choice of leader. Macmillan's Labour counterpart was Harold Wilson, who won elections in 1964, 1966 and twice in 1974. He realized that the secret of success on television was to appear as natural as possible, while in fact he and his team put a great deal of thought and effort into creating such a 'natural' effect. For example his staff noticed he had the habit of emphasizing a point with a clenched fist. This looked slightly threatening on television so they came up with the idea of holding a pipe in that hand. The pipe not only cured the clenched fist, but also gave him a 'man of the people look' (in private he actually smoked cigars); furthermore it enabled him to gain precious moments for thought during television interviews as he paused to light his pipe just at the moment a penetrating question was being posed.

In subsequent campaigns Wilson adopted yet new methods to be appear 'television friendly'. A make-up artist accompanied him around the UK on his election tours, a clean suit was always ready for him to change into after a day's hard campaigning and there was even a lemon and honey drink available to keep his voice in good order (this was always dispensed from a green decanter and drunk from a green glass so that no audience would think he was downing a glass of Scotch). Wilson used to time his most pungent remarks for when he knew he was going live into a news bulletin. Live audiences could be quite startled suddenly to hear Wilson stop mid-sentence and launch into a quip against the government. Although even at this early stage in the broadcasting of politics some television producers were getting nervous about the possibility that they were being manipu-lated: the BBC was reluctant to cover any of Wilson's meetings live because of what it felt to be its loss of editorial control. However, ITN, which always had a more 'showbiz' approach, relished the excitement that these live sound-bites created. Sir Geoffrey Cox described the live pictures of Harold Wilson dealing with interruptions during coverage of an election speech as 'some of the most remarkable television ever seen on a news programme' (Cox 1983: 180).

The current situation

In an important sense Macmillan and Wilson virtually bring the story up-to-date for it was under their leadership that the two main political parties came to accept the importance of television in the electoral battles. In the thirty years that divide us from them there were many significant develop-ments – not least the impact that Margaret Thatcher and her team of advisers made on the Conservative Party and the similar role played by Peter Mandelson, first as Labour's Director of Communications in the mid-1980s and then as adviser to Tony Blair. None the less the pattern had been set by the 1960s – a pattern that appears to be one of ongoing conflict and strain with the balance of power shifting between the two sides but which in fact is more accurately characterized as 'collusive conflict' (Kellner 1993). And it is a conflict in which, because of the structure and culture of broadcasting in the UK, the politicians retain ultimate power over broadcasters, achieved through both formal and informal methods of control.

Formal controls

The BBC operates under a charter and licence granted to it by Parliament, but in fact by the government of the day for a fixed term, usually ten years. Its previous charter expired in 1996 and in the period prior to renewal of the charter, as in similar times in the past, the BBC was perceived to be particularly sensitive to the political climate. For example in 1995 there was a major row, which later ended with the Corporation being defeated in court, over its decision to grant the Prime Minister, John Major, a full-length interview on Panorama – the BBC's flagship current affairs television programme – on the eve of local elections in Scotland. Nor are ITV companies immune to similar pressures; under the Broadcasting Act 1990 ITV franchises were awarded on the highest bidder principle (with some quality controls built-in) but in the past franchises have been, and probably will be again, awarded on less easily quantifiable criteria – such uncertainty creates an atmosphere in which ITV companies are also very sensitive to criticisms from both government and opposition. In 1990 it was widely believed that Mrs Thatcher had been determined to ensure that Thames Television did not win back its franchise because of her anger about its programme *Death on the Rock*, which examined allegations that the British army was operating a 'shoot-to-kill' policy against IRA suspects (see Bolton 1990).

Nor does the granting of the charter or the awarding of the franchises end the process of government oversight. The legislation under which the broadcasters operate requires them to show 'due impartiality' on matters of political controversy, a stricture which is wide enough to permit virtually any interpretation, by the politicians, should they choose to do so. And there are other means of formal control. The level of the BBC's licence fee is determined by a parliamentary vote; I was recently told by a former BBC executive of a Labour Northern Ireland Secretary who expressed his displeasure at the BBC's coverage of Ulster affairs by telling him that he would make sure that there would be no licence fee increase that year – fortunately the Home Secretary of the day did not follow his advice (private conversation with a former BBC Controller, Northern Ireland). In the past there have been similar battles over the size of the ITV levy; the 1990 Act ended the levy but did create a situation in which Parliament has to adjudicate between ITV and Channel Four as to the distribution of commercial television profits.

Broadcasting legislation comes before Parliament every five years or so; such periods are always a particularly sensitive time for broadcasters. Even in periods of relative parliamentary tranquillity they still have to keep a more than wary eye on the all-party Culture, Media and Sport Committee which monitors and comments on broadcasting affairs on a regular basis. The statutory body which monitors programme standards and acts on viewers' complaints is directly appointed by government, as are members of the BBC Board of Governors and the Independent Television Commission (ITC). In fact Mrs Thatcher made cavalier use of her powers of patronage in an unprecedented way by overturning the long-standing tradition that ensured that the BBC's chairman and deputy chairman were appointed from different ends of the political spectrum. Under Mrs Thatcher both offices were held by appointees known to be sympathetic to the Conservatives.

Informal controls

These public mechanisms are not the end of the story. Politicians from all parties have never been slow to bring direct pressure to bear on the broadcasters. In the run-up to the 1997 General Election the Conservatives announced the re-birth of their 'media monitoring unit' – a timely reminder of the attempts by Norman Tebbit, then chairman of the Conservative Party, in 1986 to increase the 'sensitivity' of the BBC to political pressure by attacking its coverage of the USA's bombing of Libya. Nor is such pressure solely a Conservative prerogative; Labour Prime Minister Harold Wilson sought to exercise control of the BBC by appointing Lord Hill, who had until his appointment been identified with ITV. That attempt was unsuccessful but was merely the precursor to a long-running and vitriolic feud between Wilson and the Corporation that outlived his premiership. There are many other examples of direct political pressure being applied to the broadcasters; Northern Ireland has been a particularly sensitive subject but there is also a long history of accusations of bias and inaccurate reporting which are constantly being levelled at the broadcasters by all the political parties. The present Labour Government's relations with the BBC have been none too smooth with the Prime Minister's Press Secretary Alistair Campbell leading the attack. This is the context in which politicians' complaints about the powers of the broadcasters have to be evaluated.

The structures of political broadcasting

Political broadcasting on British television can be seen as taking place within two main formats: first, those programmes exclusively devoted to the reporting of Parliament and politics, and second, the daily news and current affairs programmes.

Parliamentary broadcasting

The televising of Parliament is undertaken by an independent production company – CCT Productions. It supplies continuous coverage of the Commons and the Lords to all British and some foreign broadcasters. It is appointed and controlled by a joint committee of broadcasters and members of the Lords and Commons who form a majority of the supervising body and who entrust day-to-day supervision of the coverage to a parliamentary officer, the Supervisor of Broadcasting, one of whose most important jobs is ensuring that the very strict rules of coverage are observed by the broadcasters. These rules include forbidding the cameras from revealing how full (or more likely, empty) the House is; from covering any disturbance taking place in the Chamber or from framing an MP in anything more exciting than the standard medium close-up shot. Over the years CCT's coverage has nudged the guidelines along a little so that although the main rules of coverage are still abided to, some latitude has been taken (and accepted by the politicians) in the selection of camera angles, which at least provides some variation in shot for the viewer and also some occasional insight into how full, or otherwise, the chamber actually is.

Committee coverage is also undertaken by CCT; this coverage is not continuous but demand-driven. CCT establishes, a week in advance, what areas the various committees will be covering and then canvasses the broadcaster to find out how much interest there is in any of those hearings. Since broadcasters have to pay for this coverage on an *ad hoc* basis this provides a good discipline for establishing where their priorities really lie (this is in contrast to coverage of the Commons and Lords, for which the broadcaster pay an annual fee) (see Palmer, Chapter 27 in this volume).

Political programmes

Network television and radio programmes exclusively devoted to politics and Parliament are mainly to be found on the BBC. The BBC has been broadcasting the radio programme *The Week in Westminster* since 1929, *Today in Parliament* since 1945 and *Yesterday in Parliament* since 1947. But the regular broadcasting of Parliament on television did not begin until 1986 when the Lords first allowed the cameras in. In 1998, in addition to its daily and weekly radio staples, when Parliament is sitting the BBC broadcasts a late night summary of the day's events at Parliament and a thrice weekly live programme from Westminster. The BBC also transmits two weekly programmes devoted to politics, both on a Sunday – *The Frost Programme*, an interview programme based around the personality of broadcaster David Frost, and *On the Record*, which is broadcast Sunday lunchtimes and consists of a major interview as well as reporter packages.

In comparison, between ITV, Channel Four and Channel Five there are only four network programmes exclusively devoted to politics and Parliament and all are on Channel Four. Three times a week, at midday, Channel Four broadcasts *Power House*, a magazine programme that mixes parliamentary coverage with interviews and reports; it also has a weekly political current affairs programme. ITV has two political interview programmes on Sundays – one on GMTV in the early morning and a later one produced by LWT at lunchtime. The satellite channel Sky News devotes most weekday afternoons to live political coverage; it has a weekly political magazine programme on Sundays and it also shows weekly highlights of the House of

Lords' deliberations. Finally, mention should be made of the Parliamentary Channel – a cable channel operated by United Artists which is devoted to transmitting live coverage of the Commons and live and recorded coverage of the Commons committees and the Lords.

Television news and politics

Politics plays a consistently important role on British television news. There are news bulletins throughout the day on three of the five terrestrial networks (the exceptions being BBC2 and Channel Four) and round-the-clock coverage on Sky News and the BBC's News 24 Channel. However, the major network news programmes are on at breakfast time, lunchtime, the early evening and, the flagship bulletins for BBC and ITN, the *Nine O'Clock News* and *News at Ten*. However, the two programmes which probably give greatest coverage to politics occur outside of these main coverage times – *Channel Four News* at 7 p.m. and *Newsnight* on BBC2 at 10.30 p.m. While Parliament is sitting, the flagship bulletins contain an average two political stories per day on the BBC and one on ITN. In a study of the BBC and ITN news, which sought to identify the main sources of political news on television, it was revealed that the politicians themselves were the most important single source. Reports from Parliament rarely formed stories in themselves but clips from parliamentary debates or committee hearings would go to make up part of the political correspondents' packages (see Gaber 1997).

The dynamics of coverage

Political coverage in television bulletins is very much a joint enterprise between the bulletin producers based at their headquarters in the BBC, ITN and Sky and their political teams at Westminster. In planning and executing their daily political coverage the broadcasters and writing journalists follow well-established news-gathering routines. For most political reporters, and politicians for that matter, the day begins with BBC Radio Four's *Today* programme. *Today*'s political day, like that of their television counterparts *Breakfast News* on the BBC, GMTV on ITV and Sky News, in fact begins the previous evening when in discussions producers at the programme headquarters and their staff at Westminster plot the morning's coverage. Their reports are avidly watched and then reacted to by other broadcast journalists and reporters working for the evening newspapers. (Later in the day journalists working for the national newspapers, who obviously have later deadlines, also start picking-up on the broadcasters' political reports.) But just as the print journalists are working out how to cover stories that have been covered by radio and television, the broadcasters themselves have been reacting to newspaper reporting, either from the morning papers or the early editions of the evening papers. But perhaps more importantly all sides will be monitoring coverage coming from the Press Association (PA), which has a large team of parliamentary and political reporters and is viewed with credibility by both journalists and politicians. Indeed just to make sure that their own output is not missed, television and radio programmes frequently alert Press Association reporters to items that they are about to or have just broadcast. By getting summaries of their broadcast material on to the Press Association wire, they save other journalists the trouble of having to watch or listen to their programmes but they also benefit from the credibility associated with the PA which makes it more likely that the item will be noticed and even more importantly attributed to their programme.

In addition to the media's self-regarding behaviour there are times when the politicians also get a look-in. Twice a day the Prime Minister's Press Secretary gives members of that quasi-secret society, the parliamentary lobby, a briefing on the day's political events. Once a week the Prime Minister and the Leader of the Opposition cross swords on the floor of the House during Prime Minister's Questions and at numerous times during the day lobby correspondents can be seen in the Members' lobby in conversation with ministers, shadow ministers, humble backbenchers and members of the parties' media teams. These teams, the party press officers, follow a routine very similar to that of the journalist. Their day might easily have begun the previous evening with a series of negotiations with radio and television producers about who or what was going to be provided for the morning's news programmes. They might well have been 'spinning' – in other words trying to influence the day's forthcoming coverage by talking-up a particular news item or down-playing others. The daily editorial meetings, which form such an important part of the routines of news organizations, also take place within the party's media organizations. At these meetings they try and plan the day's political initiatives and seek to anticipate any problems that might arise. This level of activity used to be reserved only for election times but has now become the norm throughout the political cycle.

The spin doctors

Within the political culture in which the journalists and politicians are operating the role of what used to be known as 'press officers' and are now termed 'spin doctors' is growing enormously. Two of Labour leader Tony Blair's closest confidants are spin doctors and their influence is not just confined to issues of presentation – the role of the parties' (not to mention the government's) media operations is now a major factor in the political landscape. A few years ago it would have been inconceivable for political producers to feel that they had to make their 'bids' for political interviewees

with opposition frontbenchers to anyone other than the politicians themselves; today it is almost inconceivable that such bids would not go through
the relevant press officers. (The situation with ministers is somewhat different in that the activities of Whitehall press officers are not a new phenomenon.) This gives tremendous power to press officers to grant or deny
access depending on whether they are happy or otherwise with the coverage they are receiving from the particular outlet in question. Denial of
access, for example, as Labour did in 1995 with the *Guardian*, is a relatively
minor nuisance for a newspaper. (The *Guardian* published, on the eve of
the 1995 Trades Union Congress, a leaked internal Labour Party document,
written by an adviser to Labour leader Tony Blair and suggesting that the
party was 'unfit to govern'.) However, for a broadcaster denial of access is
disastrous, for a political report that does not contain the voice or picture
of the central characters is, to say the least, less than satisfactory.

Control of the political news agenda is now central to both parties' campaigning strategy. Andrew Lansley (1995), a former Head of Research at
Conservative Central Office, now a Conservative MP, has written: 'For a
political party the primary objective is to control the agenda, by determining the issues of political debate'. Such sentiments are echoed across the
political divide. Speaking after the 1992 election Labour's former deputy
leader Roy Hattersley said:

> The party which sets the agenda wins the election. Does anybody doubt that
> if the election had been fought around health, education or unemployment,
> the Labour Party would now be the Government? But the election was not
> fought around those issues, it was fought around the issue . . . of tax in
> particular. That agenda was set by the Conservative Party, aided and abetted
> by the newspapers, with the broadcasting media as accessories after the fact.
> (Hattersley 1993)

More recently Joy Johnson, Labour's former Director of Media, Campaigns
and Elections, wrote: 'the party that captures the news initiative will both
dominate the agenda and wrong-foot their opponents' (Driving the news',
internal Labour Party document).

The power of the press

If the politicians and their media advisers are successful at establishing their
own media agenda, over that of the broadcasters, how do they fare in their
similar battle with the press? After all, could it not be argued that in fact
it is the press which in itself determines the news priorities of both the
politicians and the broadcasters? This is a notion I reject. Whilst the press
do appear to play a vital part in defining political news agendas – and this
argument received powerful support from Martin Linton (1995) whose
research lent support to the contention that it WAS 'The Sun Wot Won
IT' for the Conservatives in 1992 – my argument is that, even if this is the

case, it in fact represents merely another version of the argument that says that it is the politicians who are driving the news agenda. This is because virtually all newspapers have a proprietorially defined political agenda – so although it might have been 'The Sun Wot Won It', they won it on behalf of the politicians whose bidding they were ultimately following. So discussing whether or not the politicians or the press control the political agenda is a technical matter, a bit like trying to argue that it is significant which leg of a body moves first.

Conclusion

At different times, and in different societies, the press, television or the politicians and their allies can be seen to have been in the ascendant, in terms of the setting of the political agenda. However, it is now apparent, at least to me, that in the UK at the end of the millennium, the combination of a highly regulated broadcasting system and an equally highly partisan press, the power to set the political agenda lies in Westminster, firmly in the hands of the politicians. And given the choice – between the press, the broadcasters and the politicians – there are those who would argue that in a democracy the politicians have as much claim, if not more, than the other two groups to such a position of pre-eminence. Equally in an ideal world such power should rest with the electorate. Such an aspiration might be unrealistic in an age of mass communications but with the development of interactivity, both on television, radio and the internet, will it always remain unattainable? But that question raises the issue of how universal will access to these technologies become? For how truly democratic is a political discourse which can only be participated in by those with a required level of economic and intellectual resources? Given that the answer to that is probably not democratic at all, then the present stand-off, with politicians still holding the ring, seems the best compromise on offer.

Questions

1 To what extent has the structure of political and parliamentary reporting been influenced by
   (a)   patterns of newspaper ownership
   (b)   the domination of broadcasting by the BBC
   (c)   the two-party system?

2 Is there something innately 'different' about politics as a news category?

3 To what extent will technological developments affect the pattern of political coverage?

References

Blumler, J. and McQuail, D. (1968) *Television in Politics: Its Uses and Influences*, London: Faber & Faber.

Bolton, R. (1990) *Death on the Rock and Other Stories*, London: W.H. Allen.

Briggs, A. (1995) *The History of Broadcasting, Vol. 1, The Birth of Broadcasting*, Oxford: Oxford University Press.

Calder, A. (1969) *The People's War: Britain 1939–42*, London: Panther.

Cockerell, M. (1988) *Live from Number 10*, London: Faber & Faber.

Cox, G. (1983) *See It Happen: The Making of ITN*, London: Bodley Head.

Cox, G. (1995) *Pioneering Television News*, London: John Libbey.

Crawley, A. (1988) *Leap Before You Look*, London: Collins.

Day, R. (1989) *Grand Inquisitor*, London: Pan.

Gaber, I. (1997) 'Television and political coverage', in C. Geraghty and D. Lusted (eds) *The Television Studies Handbook*, London: Edward Arnold.

Hattersley, R. (1993) Speech at The Westminster Consultation, unpublished transcript, Goldsmiths College, University of London.

Horne, A. (1989) *Macmillan, Vol. 2, 1956–86*, London: Macmillan.

Ingham, B. (1994) 'It's the message that matters', *British Journalism Review* 7(3): 6–10.

Kellner, P. (1993) Speech at The Westminster Consultation, unpublished transcript, Goldsmiths College, University of London.

Lansley, A. (1995) 'Politics and the media', unpublished lecture, London School of Economics.

Linton, M. (1995) 'The tabloids and the 1992 election', paper presented to the Elections, Public Opinion and Polling Conference, Political Studies Association, London, September.

Pimlott, B. (1993) *Harold Wilson*, London: HarperCollins.

Reith, J. (1950) *Into the Wind*, London: Hodder & Stoughton.

Scannell, P. and Cardiff, D. (1991) *A Social History of British Broadcasting, Vol. 1, 1922–1939*, Oxford: Blackwell.

Straw, J. (1993) 'Democracy on the spike', *British Journalism Review* 4(4): 45–54.

Tracey, M. (1977) *The Production of Political Television*, London: Routledge.

Winstone, R. (1996) 'Do we need political correspondents?', *Parliamentary Review* June: 26–7.

Further reading

Blumler, J. and Gurevitch, M. (1995) *The Crisis of Public Communication*, London: Routledge.

Cockerell, M. (1988) *Live from Number 10*, London: Faber & Faber.

Crewe, I. and Gosschalk, B. (eds) (1995) *Political Communications: The General Election Campaign of 1992*, Cambridge: Cambridge University Press.

Crewe, I. and Harrop, I. (eds) (1986) *Political Communications: The General Election Campaign of 1983*, Cambridge: Cambridge University Press.

Crewe, I. and Harrop, M. (eds) (1989) *Political Communications: The General Election Campaign of 1987*, Cambridge: Cambridge University Press.

Ferguson, M. (ed.) (1990) *Public Communication: The New Imperatives*, London: Sage.

Franklin, B. (1994a) *Packaging Politics*, London: Edward Arnold.

Franklin, B. (1994b) *Televising Democracies*, London: Routledge.

Ingham, B. (1991) *Kill the Messenger*, London: HarperCollins.

Jones, N. (1995) *Soundbites and Spin Doctors*, London: Cassell.

Kavanagh, D. (1995) *Electoral Campaigning*, Oxford: Blackwell.

McNair, B. (1995) *An Introduction to Political Communication*, London: Routledge.

Miller, W. (1987) *Media and Voters*, Oxford: Clarendon.

Negrine, R. (1994) *Politics and the Mass Media*, London: Routledge.

Rees, L. (1992) *Selling Politics*, London: BBC Books.

Scammell, M. (1995) *Designer Politics*, London: Macmillan.

Semetko, H. *et al.* (1991) *The Formation of Campaign Agendas: A Comparative Analysis*, Hillsdale, NJ: Lawrence Erlbaum.

Seymour-Ure, C. (1996) *The Political Impact of the Mass Media*, London: Constable.

Wyndham-Goldie, G. (1977) *Facing the Nation: Television and Politics 1936–1976*, London: Bodley Head.

Chapter 29

News photography

'THE DIRECT APPEAL TO THE EYE'? PHOTOGRAPHY AND THE
TWENTIETH-CENTURY PRESS

PATRICIA HOLLAND

Photographs and the press: the centrality of the image

Whether we think of the moving pictures of television or the striking photography on the pages of the daily and Sunday press, by the end of the
twentieth century the visual image has become the focus of news communication. We expect to *see* for ourselves and not simply be told. Since 1904,
when the *Daily Illustrated Mirror* became the first British paper to use photographs rather than engravings for news illustrations, the amount of space
given over to visual, mostly photographic, material in the press has increased
so that it is now the very being of many of our newspapers. The popular
tabloids have become essentially picture papers, and the 'quality' broadsheets, especially the Sundays, have accommodated more and more photographic imagery by changing their shape and form with alarming frequency.
They have sprouted tabloid sections, lifestyle supplements, separate sports
sections, glossy magazines, illustrated reviews, comics and other pull outs,
each one targeted at a special segment of the readership and providing
an outlet for a wide range of high quality photography. Photography in the
newspapers overlaps with that in the multicoloured magazines that crowd our
news-stands – those consumer-based publications that specialize in cookery,
DIY (do-it-yourself), computers, cars, soft porn and a host of other topics.
We live in a visual culture and the press plays a central role in that culture.

The phrase 'news photography' usually brings to mind dramatic images. The action pictures that win the awards show us riots, wars and disasters. These are the photographs that take the viewer into the middle
of a dramatic event and carry a sense of authenticity and conviction which
can overwhelm the verbal account. The photographs that are recalled in
the histories of news photography include Robert Capa's dying Republican
soldier in Spain in 1936; the terrified child running from a napalmed village, photographed by Nick Ut in Vietnam in 1972, and the burnt Iraqi at
the wheel of his jeep, photographed by Kenneth Jarecke during the Gulf War
in 1991. Each of these gets close to the immediate experience of war and
each has come to stand as a symbol for the war it represents. Nevertheless,

heroic photo-journalism forms only a small part of press photography; I shall be arguing that we cannot fully understand those photographs that seek to report the news if we do not see them within the context of newspaper imagery as a whole. Dramatic action pictures shock their audience and provide controversy and debate, but the richly visual context within which they are embedded is of equal importance.

Pictures in the contemporary press come from a wide range of photographic genres. They include fine art photographs and portraits, advertising photography, travel pictures, celebrity photographs, pin-ups, snapshots, photomontages, film and television publicity, sports photography and many other types. Each genre tends to have a separate place in the publication: pin-ups on Page Three, food photography in the magazine section, stylish portraits of business people on the business pages, and emotion-packed sports photography at the back. Just like the segments of the newspaper in which they appear, these different photographic genres serve different ends. Each has its own recognized 'rules' and conventions, which are understood by photographers, editors and reading public alike.

This means that photographers are expected to play a variety of different roles in relation to the subjects of their pictures and to their viewing audience. When operating as a photo-journalist, a photographer promises the viewer authenticity and veracity, playing the part of a dispassionate observer who is uninvolved with events as they unfold in front of the camera. Celebrity photographers, known as 'paparazzi' following their unscrupulous Italian prototype, are different. They must negotiate a relationship between themselves and their attention-seeking subjects which is sometimes cooperative and sometimes antagonistic. When celebrities put themselves on view, a photographer may act as a pure publicist, producing flattering and glamorous images. When the celebrity wishes to be private, the photographers become intrusive stalkers, tracking down their prey with unwelcome tenacity. Especially following the death of Princess Diana, much debate has centred on the degree of privacy due to someone in the public eye, whether royalty or politician.

All newspapers, and especially the broadsheets, need pictures of politicians in their public roles. However, 'We don't want the pictures [they] want you to take', says *Guardian* picture editor, Eamonn McCabe (1995), dismissing the ready smile and the genial handshake. A competitive relationship has evolved between the politicians' public relations agents, the 'spin doctors' who try to show their party to its best advantage, and the news photographer, who must always be on the look-out for some special quality in the image. This can to lead to disputes over accuracy (see below), when the photographer's entertainment role overlaps with their informational one. Nevertheless, there are times when both subjects and audience accept that, when the photographer is acting as an accomplished entertainer, the literal truth may give way to witty presentation.

Award-winning *Daily Mirror* photographer, Kent Gavin, has written with pride about the professionalism that allows him to move between several different roles:

> I consider my camera to be a window through which the public can look at the world. Sometimes they will be entertained, sometimes they will be horrified and provoked into action of some kind. . . . Always, I hope, they will be intrigued.
>
> (Gavin 1978: 5)

He describes the pictures of children with which he reported the war in Biafra (1967–70): 'What can possibly force home more the message that war is obscene than pictures of bewildered, broken children, trapped in a nightmare they cannot even begin to understand?' (Gavin 1978: 65). Playing a different role, he is proud of his pin-up photographs: 'If the photographer can talk her round, wind her up and verbally turn her on,' he wrote, 'the model is going to look like dynamite in the pictures, which is the entire object of the exercise' (1978: 99).

One of his favourite pictures is an exercise in visual humour, in which a little dog lifts his leg and pees on the off-stump just as the batsman strikes the ball during a cricket match. In his role as entertainer, Gavin had several goes at setting this one up, and finally got the picture with the aid of a thread tied to the leg of the dog, who had obstinately refused to pee on cue.

The photography of the contemporary press remains balanced between these diverse poles – that of the real, often horrific, world; that of humour; and that of glamour – the glamour of show business, of Princess Diana, of well-known celebrities and especially of the female body.

A further component, which has gained increasing importance since colour first came to the magazine supplements in the 1960s, is consumer photography. This is the photography that celebrates lifestyle, and it includes fashion, food, gardens, travel and the house beautiful, promoting an ever-widening range of products and their pleasurable consumption.

Lifestyle presentations can be difficult to distinguish from that other dominant visual feature, the advertisements. Amply funded, unhampered by the need to report or to represent the real world, free to indulge in emotion and fantasy, advertising has led the way in visual innovation.

Just as news has always been more than information, press photography has always been more than news, and problems arise when its different genres and uses overlap. The coming of digital technology, which has made the manipulation of images easier than ever before, has brought a renewed awareness of how important – yet how slippery – the boundaries are (Lister 1995; Wombell 1991).

Understanding press photography

To be properly understood, press photography in all its forms must be seen from several different perspectives, some historical, some which look at current practices. First, it occupies an important place in the long history of the photographic medium itself. Second, it is a neglected part of the history of the twentieth-century mass-circulation press. The convergence of these two popular media has made all the more urgent a third way of looking at press photographs, which considers their ideological role. Photographs are central to the manner in which news and views are presented to the public. Even more importantly, they have built up their own visual vocabulary, a photographic language which deploys a range of concepts which help shape the ways in which we understand the world. From this perspective, the most trivial of entertainment photographs carries messages which are as important as the most prestigious of news reporting.

The popular tradition

Photography's roles as an artform and as a medium of record are well documented. What is less often discussed is its long history as a form of entertainment (Freund 1980). During the nineteenth century, entertaining photographic images were produced and consumed in a wide variety of forms, from the purchase of mounted prints and post-cards, to those forerunners of the domestic television set, the lantern slide show and the stereoscope (Macdonald 1979). Many of the themes familiar from today's press were already in circulation. Travel pictures were among the earliest of photographic genres, as were images of the famous and the infamous. Photographic cards of royalty, seductive actresses and murderers sold in their thousands. Sentimental pictures, photographs of pets and children, as well as half-clothed women and soft porn, were all part of Victorian photographic fare. Popular photographs included records of public events – such as parades and sports meetings, and images of war – from the Crimean War in the 1850s to the Boer War in the 1890s. The photographs in the pages of twentieth-century newspapers are above all a development of that popular tradition.

The history of photography and that of the press ran together at the turn of the century when the new technology of the day made it possible, for the first time, to reproduce photographs in print as well as by chemical photographic processes. In John Tagg's words 'the era of the throwaway image had begun' (Tagg 1982: 56). From then on, each picture could be rapidly reproduced as millions of identical copies. The most familiar experience of a photograph would no longer be as a precious individual object but as an endlessly repeatable image on a printed page.

In 1904, the *Daily Illustrated Mirror* became the first British newspaper to use photographs, with pictures from the Russo-Japanese War of 1904–5. 'Our pictures do not merely accompany the printed news, they are a valuable help to the understanding of it,' declared its editorial on 28 January 1904, '. . . the direct appeal to the eye, wherever it is possible, will supplement the written word, which is designed in a more cumbrous fashion to penetrate the mind' (quoted in Wombell 1986: 76).

Newspapers such as the *Daily Mail* (launched in 1896) and the *Daily Express* (launched in 1900), as well as the *Mirror*, were aiming for the first time at a mass circulation among working-class readers. In their appeal to a wider public they became an outlet for popular taste as well as for news information. Scandal and gossip now rubbed shoulders with political and overseas reporting. Pages given over to advertisers, who paid for the space, helped to keep prices down (Curran and Seaton 1991). Paul Wombell has pointed out that the newspapers' 'direct appeal to the eye' paralleled the need of advertisers to 'catch the eye' of the reader in the expanding markets of the new century (1986: 76).

Manipulation, the juxtaposition of contrasting images and a light-hearted use of pictures were all part of the Victorian entertainment legacy. The *Daily Mirror* (it soon dropped '*Illustrated*' from its title) introduced the front-page photograph and used photography to make political points. A First World War front page of 1916 was headed 'A Contrast: British Humanity and Hun Brutality' and juxtaposed pictures of happy Germans held prisoners of war by the British, with wounded British prisoners held by the Germans (Allen and Frost 1981: 19). The paper introduced a centre-page picture-spread, which was often humorous and featured 'beautiful girls and playful animals' (Dunkin 1981: 8). In May 1910 the *Mirror* won a scoop with its centre-page spread of Edward VII as he lay dead, which it had persuaded the court photographer to hand over for its exclusive use. But the Victorian custom of photographing the dead already seemed inappropriate in such a public medium, and the combination of a fascination with morbidity and an intrusion into the private lives of royalty brought accusations of bad taste (Allen and Frost 1981: 11).

The pattern fast became established in which many different photographic genres rub shoulders on the pages of the newspapers; in which the entertainment pictures draw in readers, the news pictures aim to shock and horrify as well as to inform, and the advertising sets out to stimulate consumer desire.

Reading news photographs

Offered this richly varied fare, those who look at the photographs in the newspapers must of necessity become more than passive viewers. They also become 'readers' who interpret the image and bring different sorts of understanding to it. Sometimes this is seen as a disadvantage, leading to *mis*understanding. From the perspective of a newspaper editor, Harold Evans writes:

> The reader imposes on the photographer's work a matrix of memory, appetite, prejudice and sophistication, and when his [*sic*] emotions are strong, he can see the opposite of what was intended.
>
> (Evans 1978: ii)

An alternative view is that this ability to carry multiple, complex meanings is in the very nature of the visual, even when, as with a photograph, the image represents the real world. Roland Barthes (1977) calls this the 'polysemy' of an image. He demonstrated how a photograph is always open to a wide variety of interpretations, partly determined by the content of the picture, partly by its context, but always drawing something from the assumptions brought to it by its 'readers' (Barthes 1977).

Barthes has identified some of the 'codes' that go to construct news photographs and which can be brought into play when the decoding work done by an alert 'reader' becomes conscious and analytical instead of merely intuitive (1977: 21). Similarly, in an influential article, Stuart Hall produced a detailed analysis of the processes by which news photographs are first encoded by those who produce them, and then decoded by their readers, emphasizing the ways in which interpretations are influenced by the context of the image (Hall 1973: 176).

A recognition of the shifting meanings which characterize visual images sometimes seems to suggest that news photography is intrinsically untrustworthy. And yet, once we have understood that the 'truth' cannot be contained within the edges of the frame, the work of understanding the codes, of 'reading' the image, of exploring the context and of recognizing the history of a photograph, become central concerns, and a news photographer's commitment to truth becomes ever more important.

Photo-journalism, objectivity and partiality

The documentary style that came to characterize photo-journalism was first developed not by newspapers, but by news picture magazines.

'In the 1950s photo-journalism meant something different from news photography and nobody in Fleet Street would have made the mistake of confusing the two,' wrote the photographer, Grace Robertson, who was one of the very few women to work for the prestigious *Picture Post.* On an assignment for that magazine, 'you were very aware that you were expected to bring back a story, one with a beginning, middle and an end and not just a lot of photographically interesting images that you hoped would fit the text.' She recalled that the 'general press photographers' who used large format cameras with flash attachments and were not at all concerned about drawing attention to themselves, kidded her about the tiny 35 mm Leica with which she captured her candid shots (Robertson 1990: 4).

Picture magazines had first developed in Germany during the 1920s. As the decade progressed, many German journalists and photographers were forced to flee the Nazi regime, and the development of documentary photography was taken up elsewhere, notably by *Vu* in France (1928–38), and the first *Life* in the USA (1936–72). In the UK, *Picture Post* (1938–57) was edited by the exiled Stefan Lorant, who, as editor of the *Munchener Illustrierte,* was already celebrated as one of the founders of photo-journalism. The magazines gave priority to pictures over text and favoured a style in which unobtrusive cameras were used to observe events as they happened, paying attention to the visual detail of everyday life. *Picture Post* came to build up a documentary record of its times (Hall 1972: 71).

The observational style, in which photographers seek to 'capture' their subjects unawares at precisely that moment which conveys the essence of a scene – what its most celebrated exponent, Henri Cartier-Bresson, described as 'the decisive moment' – has come to carry an aura of objective record (Cartier-Bresson 1952). The style was at the heart of the photo-agency Magnum, founded in 1947 by a group of photographers, including Cartier-Bresson and Robert Capa, who had been through the war and were seeking to promote a style of photography which put people and human values at the centre.

Photo-journalism lays claims to neutrality and objectivity, which means that 'readers' of such pictures are justified in asking questions about photographic truth. Photo-journalists enter an unwritten contract with the public to report accurately what they see. If there is an indication that the photographer has interfered with the scene in front of the camera, its authenticity may be brought into question and the contract with the viewer may be broken. Was that starving baby separated from its mother so that it looked even more forlorn in the picture? Was that man waving a stick really shouting at the policeman or simply telling the photographer to get out of the way? Was there help at hand for those desperate people just beyond the edge of the frame?

These questions are important. However, partiality may operate in more subtle ways, not necessarily by showing untruths, but by putting one set of meanings into circulation to the exclusion of others. During the Second World War, the photo-journalism of *Picture Post* helped establish the imagery of that war for the British nation. It showed the rubble of the Blitz, the determined faces under air-raid warden helmets, the gallant boys in their flying jackets and fragile little planes, and the plump women in wrap-around aprons and turbaned scarves who were keeping the country going. Photographic imagery was deployed to report on the activities of a people at war and at the same time to enhance the national morale (Kee 1989). That imagery would be recalled at future moments of national crisis.

In a different political climate, during the strikes, demonstrations and riots which hit the front pages of the national press in the 1970s and early 1980s, critics pointed out that the view from the safer spot behind the police lines influenced the public's impression of what was going on and allowed the grievances of the demonstrators to go unshown (*Camerawork* 1977). Some independent photographers and photographic agencies set out to produce pictures from another perspective.

Although the issue of objectivity is always up for negotiation, the need for factual reporting becomes ever clearer when there are limitations on access which are formally enforced, as at time of war. 'War is an anxious time in the press' writes John Taylor. News photographers are exposed to censorship and limitations, because of a 'fear of documentary realism' on the part of the authorities, at a time when information is itself a weapon (Taylor 1991). From the First World War to the Gulf, there have been disputes over censorship, propaganda and truth (Knightly 1975; Taylor 1992; Wombell 1986). A commitment to discover and make public those perspectives that governments want to conceal is, for the news photographer, both urgent and dangerous. For the sceptical reader, even greater attention must be given to the history of each individual photograph.

History of the individual photograph

For every photograph we may ask who the photographer was, when, where and, most importantly, why the picture was taken. Paradoxically, the understanding of an image may depend on the answers to these questions rather than on anything that is visible within the frame.

Every photograph is the result of a complex of decisions taken not only by the person who pushes the button but also by a host of other individuals and institutions (Sontag 1979). The first decisions are taken long before the film is exposed, and are made by the body which commissions the work, usually a newspaper or a news agency such as Reuters or Associated Press. For Winston Churchill's funeral in 1965, the *Sunday Times* assigned twenty-one photographers to twenty-five different viewpoints to cover both the ceremonial and the personal. Every detail was planned well in advance. 'Picture editors Jack Hallam and Chris Angeloglou negotiated shooting positions from a church tower, a bank and office windows even before the death' (Evans 1978: 27).

Of course, photographers will take crucial decisions concerning both content and style while making their pictures. Their decisions inevitably draw on photographic codes which, as Roland Barthes (1977: 21) pointed out, are laden with meaning. They may choose a wide panoramic shot or select a long lens for a close up; they may go for a high angle which dwarfs their subject, or prefer a low angle which emphasizes the subject's height; they may look for dramatic shadows or choose the more sober effect of even lighting. At the same time, decisions are likely to be based on a pragmatic assessment of what it is the newspaper wants. At every level, prejudice and 'common sense' are at work and a wide range of political opinions and social expectations may well come into play, both in deciding what events to cover and which photographic techniques to use.

Anthropologist Mark Pedelty, while accompanying war correspondents and photographers during the civil war in El Salvador during the early 1990s, observed the taking of a photograph that never made the pages of a newspaper. The picture showed the bones of a child, discovered among many others in a mass grave. Despite the startling nature of the content, the photographer, who was young and ambitious, decided not to send it back to his editor in the USA. His decision followed discussions with the other North American correspondents based in San Salvador. Their view, and that of the news organizations they represented, was that the atrocity he had documented was of dubious authenticity. It was an opinion with which the photographer instinctively agreed, even though he had, unlike them, seen and photographed the actual grave (Pedelty 1995: 159).

By contrast, *Picture Post* photographer Bert Hardy told Harold Evans about his highly successful photograph of an American soldier 'sharing his last drop of water with a dying peasant' during the Korean War. It was a felicitous image that fulfilled the expectations of both news editors and viewers, but which hardly reflected the state of affairs in which it was taken. 'I had the idea and asked a GI to give the old man some water for the sake of my picture. He said he would if I was quick – and if we used my water ration' (Evans 1978: i).

Once a photograph has been sent to a paper, often via a news agency, the decision-making is taken over by the picture editor who selects from among the hundreds which arrive daily down the wire. There are many people in the decision-making chain, including those who do the layout of the paper, the art editors, section editors and the overall editor of the paper. Most of these have a view – based on their experience and often claimed to be 'instinctive' – about which photographs 'work', and about news and marketing values. Decisions are taken about the placing of a picture – whether it is of front-page quality or deserves to be relegated to an inside page – how it will be cropped and how it will be juxtaposed with captions and text.

The most remarkable photographs will be taken up by several newspapers and they may continue to be used and reused in many different contexts. A picture can take on a life of its own, well beyond the control of the original photographer. It may be cut out, montaged, recoloured or otherwise treated, gathering meanings as it continues to be circulated in what John Tagg has described as its 'currency' (Tagg 1982: 110).

One of the most reproduced photographs ever comes from the Spanish Civil War of 1936–9 and depends almost entirely on its caption. It shows a soldier falling backwards, arms flung out, a rifle falling from his right hand. The image is slightly out of focus and there is no background nor other feature in the picture. Without more information it makes little sense. We do not know who the person is or where he is; we may not recognize the uniform; we cannot make out whether he has tripped or been pushed; there is nothing to indicate the circumstances of the action. The caption in *Life Magazine* (12 July 1937) read: 'Robert Capa's camera catches a Spanish soldier the instant he is dropped by a bullet through the head in front of Cordoba'. The historian of war reporting, Phillip Knightly, points out that despite this uncertainty, and a wide belief in its lack of authenticity, the picture is widely regarded to be the best war photograph ever taken, and its circulation over the years has reinforced its status as the very image of the commitment of the anti-fascists in the Spanish war (Knightly 1975: 210). It has entered the pictorial vocabulary, becoming instantly recognizable so that the original caption is largely redundant.

Consumerism and spectacle

The 1960s saw the beginnings of two pivotal changes in twentieth-century press photography. The first was the explosion into colour of the advertising media and consumer magazines. Magazine supplements to the Sunday newspapers began to provide a consumer-led context for news images that was richly visual. The *Sunday Times* launched its supplement in 1961 and the *Observer* in 1963. They provided a new outlet for photo-journalism, which was often problematically juxtaposed with ever lusher and more expensive advertising. Advertisements for cigarettes, home photography, furniture, food, cars and all the goods which supported the postwar readjustment to a consumer economy, rubbed uneasily against the grimmer photo-stories, such as those by Don McCullin on Cyprus and Vietnam.

The second development was Rupert Murdoch's revamping of the *Sun* in 1969 as a down-market tabloid unashamedly based on hedonism and fun, in which entertainment values became more important than news information. With the transformation of the *Sun* a new popular press was launched which made use of the visual to push at the hitherto guarded limits of respectability and seriousness.

The sexualization of the popular press

The *Sun* was a reincarnation of a more sober working-class newspaper, the *Daily Herald*, which had been backed by trade unions and the Labour Party but had failed to attract sufficient advertising to survive (Curran and Seaton 1991). Like the *Daily Herald*, the *Sun* based itself on its class appeal. But by the 1970s the working-class pride in work and industry which had characterized the war years was transformed into a celebration of relaxation, gossip and scandal, celebrity watching, pictures of royalty and humour. A politics of pleasure, which reacted against moralism and the old-fashioned sense of working-class duty, underpinned the *Sun*'s approach. It revelled in its hatred of do-gooders, teachers, the Labour Party (although not any longer, see p. 204) and anyone who might order you about or tell you what to do in a convergence of political opinion and entertainment values (see Curran and Sparks 1991: 215). Above all came the invitation to bodily enjoyment and sexuality, which centred on the half-clothed image of a woman, the Page Three 'girl'.

Page Three rapidly developed its own culture. The Page Three girls, such as Linda Lusardi, became personalities in their own right and the

Sun described Page Three photographer, Beverley Goodway, as 'the most envied man in Britain'. Women readers were encouraged to pose as a Page Three girl, and their boyfriends were given advice on how to photograph them. The sexualization of newspaper imagery was launched as an gesture of defiant liberation. This is how the change was described in the *Sun*'s own version of its history,

> *The Sun* called its women's pages 'Pacesetters' and filled them with sex. They were produced by women *for* women. But they were subtitled 'The pages for women that men can't resist' acknowledging that there are plenty of topics that fascinate both men and women. Like sex.
>
> (Grose 1989: 94)

This attitude gave the *Sun* licence to exploit the Page Three principle in its approach to images of women in general. Photographers were on the look-out for the naked breast, the nipple peeping out at a party, the see-through dress. When the task force returned after the Falklands War, the *Sun* celebrated with a front-page headline, 'Lovely to see you!' above a photograph of a young woman baring her breasts (Holland 1983: 100), in contrast with the *Daily Mirror*'s emotional evocation of a reunited family, taken by George Phillips (see p. 423).

When the MP Clare Short mobilized a considerable body of feminist opinion behind her Bill to ban Page Three on the grounds that it was degrading to women, the response was a vilification campaign against Clare Short herself (Snoddy 1992: 110). In the popular tabloids, the entertainment role of press photography has come to take precedence. The visual documentation of royal marriages and marital problems, an uninhibited use of personal attack, often disguised as humour, and extensive features on sex that border on soft porn with their images of naked men and women and their frankness about sexual technique, all have become the order of the day.

The division between the popular tabloids and the 'quality' press has increased in recent years (Curran and Seaton 1991: 117), yet both in their own way continue to stage dramas around truth, reality and the visual. Across the different genres press photographs hold reportage and entertainment in tension, as each of the various sections of a newspaper exerts its influence on the others.

At the same time, the commitment to seek out and report on unwelcome truths has taken on a new urgency. As we have seen, a photograph has always been unstable as a guarantor of 'reality', but now that digital technology can make changes to an image that are impossible to trace, the role of the photographer has become, paradoxically, more important, for, very often, it is only the photographer who can vouch for the reliability of a picture. Such contemporary developments make the work of 'reading' a press photograph and of understanding the cultural, political and historical influences which shaped it, ever more important.

Daily Mirror front page, May 28, 1982 (Courtesy of Mirror Syndication)

Questions

1   On a given day, compare the photographs used in all the daily
    newspapers. Note, in particular, what front-page pictures have been
    chosen, and how the presentation differs between the papers. In
    light of the different aims and audiences of each paper, give an
    account of the differences.

2   Compare and contrast the photographic styles in the different
    sections of a given newspaper. Make reference to the concept
    of photographic genre and the activity of 'reading' a picture.

3   Discuss the representation of one particular group of people –
    examples might be: child victims of war; grieving mothers following
    a disaster; Black youth; anorexic young girls; businessmen; MPs from
    the opposition parties. Use at least six photographs from recent
    newspapers to illustrate your discussion.

References

Allen, R. and Frost, J. (1981) *Daily Mirror*, Cambridge: Patrick Stephens.

Barthes, R. (1977) 'The photographic message' and 'Rhetoric of the image',
both in his *Image-Music-Text*, London: Fontana.

Camerawork (1977) 'Lewisham: what are you taking pictures for?', London:
Half Moon Photogaphy Workshop.

Cartier-Bresson, H. (1952) *The Decisive Moment*, New York: Simon & Schuster.

Curran, J. and Seaton, J. (1991) *Power without Responsibility: The Press and
Broadcasting in Britain*, 4th edn, London: Routledge.

Curran, J. and Sparks, C. (1991) 'Press and popular culture', *Media, Culture and
Society* 13: 215–37.

Dunkin, M. (ed.) (1981) *What a Picture*, London: Weidenfeld & Nicolson.

Evans, H. (1978) *Pictures on a Page: Photo-journalism, Graphics and Picture Editing*,
London: Heinemann.

Freund, G. (1980) *Photography and Society*, London: Gordon Fraser.

Gavin, K. (1978) *Flash Bang Wallop! The Intimate Experiences of Fleet Street's Top Press
Photographer*, London: Westbridge.

Grose, R. (1989) *The Sun-sation*, London: Angus & Robertson.

Hall, S. (1972) 'The social eye of *Picture Post*', in *Working Papers in Cultural
Studies 2*, Birmingham: University of Birmingham.

Hall, S. (1973) 'The determinations of news photographs', in S. Cohen and
J. Young (eds) *The Manufacture of News: Deviance, Social Problems and the Mass
Media*, London: Constable.

Holland, P. (1983) 'The Page Three Girl speaks to women, too', *Screen* 34
(May/June): 3.

Kee, R. (1989) *The Picture Post Album*, London: Barrie & Jenkins.

Knightly, P. (1975) *The First Casualty*, London: Pan.

Lister, M. (ed.) (1995) *The Photographic Image in Digital Culture*, London: Routledge.

McCabe, E. (1995) 'Shots that hit the front page', *Guardian* 24 April.

Macdonald, G. (1979) *Camera: A Victorian Eyewitness* (based on a Granada television series), London: Batsford.

Pedelty, M. (1995) *War Stories: The Culture of Foreign Correspondents*, London: Routledge.

Robertson, G. (1990) *Portfolio Magazine* (Spring), Edinburgh: Photography Workshop.

Snoddy, R. (1992) *The Good, the Bad and the Unacceptable: The Hard News about the British Press*, London: Faber & Faber.

Sontag, S. (1979) *On Photography*, Harmondsworh: Penguin.

Tagg, J. (1982) 'The currency of the photograph', in V. Burgin (ed.) *Thinking Photography*, London: Macmillan.

Taylor, J. (1991) *War Photography: Realism in the British Press*, London: Routledge.

Taylor, P. (1992) *War and the Media: Propaganda and Persuasion in the Gulf War*, Manchester: Manchester University Press.

Wombell, P. (1986) 'Face to face with themselves: photography and the First World War', in P. Holland, J. Spence and S. Watney (eds) *Photography Politics Two*, London: Comedia.

Further reading

Becker, K. (1992) 'Photojournalism and the tabloid press', in P. Dahlgren and C. Sparks (eds) *Journalism and Popular Culture*, London: Sage.

Benthall, J. (1993) *Disasters, Relief and the Media*, London: I.B.Tauris.

Hall, S., Critcher, C., Jefferson, T., Clarke, J. and Roberts, B. (1978) *Policing the Crisis: Mugging, the State and Law and Order*, London: Macmillan.

Hartley, J. (1982) *Understanding News*, London: Methuen.

Holland, P. (1992) *What is a Child? Popular Images of Childhood*, London: Virago.

Seymore-Ure, C. (1991) *The British Press and Broadcasting since 1945*, Institute of Contemporary British History, Oxford: Blackwell.

Tagg, J. (1988) *The Burden of Representation: Essays on Photographies and Histories*, London: Macmillan.

Wombell, P. (ed.) (1991) *Photovideo: Photography in the Age of the Computer*, London: Rivers Oram.

Chapter 30

Pornography and censorship

SEX AND CENSORIOUSNESS: PORNOGRAPHY AND
CENSORSHIP IN BRITAIN

LINDA RUTH WILLIAMS

*I shall not today attempt further to define the kinds of material I understand to
be embraced within that shorthand description [hard-core pornography]. . . . But
I know it when I see it.*

> (*Justice Potter Stewart 1964, quoted in Linda Williams
> 1991: 5, 283 n. 9, my emphasis*)

*Advising a newsagent whom he had recently acquitted of video obscenity charges,
a judge in Wales offered the following advice: 'Remember, if it's dubious, it's
dirty!'*

> (*quoted in Kermode 1995: 64*)

The pornographic moving image is as old as cinema itself: as soon as moving
bodies could be filmed, they were filmed engaging in sexual activity. Pornography in the form of written text or still image has flourished in cultures
as diverse as Ancient Greece and nineteenth-century Japan; it predates the
printing press and mass media. It is present wherever cultures produce and
consume any kinds of images of human activity; it can be found at the
periphery, if not at the heart, of all 'respectable' cultures. And if pornography has readily taken up the cue offered to it by available technology,
censorship has just as quickly dogged its production and distribution. 'Censorship is probably as old as society', writes Sigrid Nielsen (1988: 19) in her
account of feminism's response to censorship practices. In his survey of one
hundred years of British film censorship, Philip French is more specific:
'Wherever films were made or shown', he writes, 'censorship boards sprang
up' (French 1995: 23). For the campaigning group Feminists Against Censorship, 'until feminism entered the debate, pornography and censoriousness were an inseparable couple' (Rodgerson and Wilson 1991: 25–6). The
dynamic between the production and the prohibition of pornography is a
complex one.

Definitions of pornography are, however, notoriously problematic, and
cultural critics are no more capable of giving clear explications than are
legislators. The differentiation between 'soft' erotica and 'harder' pornography is particularly difficult, since it generally rests on subjective judgements of personal disgust or arousal, making one person's soft another
person's hard. For Susan Griffin (1982) pornography must be distinguished
from erotica in order that the latter can be rescued from the debasing

influence of the former: eroticism encourages soulful, holistic sexuality, pornography indulges power and violence (it 'is an expression not of human erotic feeling and desire, and not of a love of the life of the body, but of a fear of bodily knowledge, and a desire to silence eros': Griffin 1982: 1). There may indeed be a firmer case for distinguishing 'soft' as legally obtainable material and 'hard' as that which cannot legitimately be seen in the UK. In his humorous survey of sex cinema Jonathan Ross (1995) differentiates 'between sex in films, and films which only exist to show sex'; he also cites a letter from HM Customs and Excise, justifying its seizure of a laserdisc copy of the 1973 film *Deep Throat* that Ross had shipped to Britain:

> the importation of indecent or obscene material is prohibited by the Customs Consolidation Act 1876. The material you attempted to import has been examined, and the laser disc titled *Deep Throat* was found to contain scenes of troilism, buggery, masturbation, ejaculation, cunnilingus, fellatio and intercourse.
>
> (Ross 1995: 18)

These may sound like an alarming litany of sins, but what makes *Deep Throat* pornographic is – according to Ross's definition – not the simple fact of the acts here listed, but the nature of their representation, for pornography is not sex itself, nor its representation in a simulated form, it is the representation of actual sex. Unlike the censorship of some scenes in horror films, which may be depicting acts that are themselves violent and illegal (murder, assault, violence to animals or children), many of these acts from *Deep Throat* are not only legal between consenting adults, but also practised by the majority of the population. Their *public* practice does of course remain illegal, yet this does not prevent mainstream cinema from representing them rather less explicitly, and in *simulated* versions. What makes *Deep Throat* pornographic is then something quite specific. Ross concludes: 'if the sex is the driving force of a picture, the only real selling point or theme, then it's a sex movie. And if what is shown is actually happening, if the actors and actresses are really doing it, then it's pornography' (Ross 1995: 3).

For feminist writer Andrea Dworkin (1981), however, this definition needs to be radically politicized. In *Pornography: Men Possessing Women*, Dworkin supports her feminist polemic with reference to the word's etymology:

> The word *pornography*, derived from the ancient Greek *pornē* and *graphos*, means 'writing about whores' . . . [it] does not mean 'writing about sex' or 'depictions of the erotic' or 'depictions of sexual acts' or 'depictions of nude bodies' or 'sexual representations' or any other such euphemism. It means the graphic description of women as vile whores.
>
> (Dworkin 1981: 199–200)

For Linda Williams in *Hard Core: Power, Pleasure and the 'Frenzy of the Visible'* (1991), pornographic films typically include certain key elements or images which produce bodily response in the audience as an effect of the spectacle of bodily response and action on-screen. Williams analyses the ambiguities and difficulties at stake in showing both the male 'money shot' and the essentially *in*visible female orgasm (which porn is nevertheless desperate to represent), and warns against simplistic generalizations about the genre, which is as complex as any other in cinema. Porn is then not just an issue around the body (and how bodies are represented), it moves the body (to arousal), just as other low cultural forms provoke tears (melodrama or romance) or screams (horror). Williams also quotes US Justice Potter Stewart's notoriously subjective explication which forms one of my epigraphs: refusing to define pornography, he nevertheless assured his court that he knew it when he saw it. As Mandy Merck (1992) has pointed out, Dawn Primarolo's Location of Pornographic Materials Bill 1989 first introduced the term 'pornography' into British legislative discourse. Primarolo's definition runs:

> 3(1)   Pornographic material means film and video and any printed matter which, for the purposes of sexual arousal or titilation, depicts women, or parts of women's bodies, as objects, things or commodities, or in sexually humiliating or degrading poses or being subject to violence.
>
> 3(2)   The reference to women in sub-section (1) above includes men.
>
> (quoted in Merck 1992: 51;
> see also Rodgerson and Wilson 1991: 27–8)

Merck does, however, go on to quote Annette Kuhn's important point that pornography is largely defined in common-sense terms 'whose reference is not specified representations, but the effects that representations may be thought, in certain circumstances, to produce' (Kuhn 1984, quoted in Merck 1992: 51). Pornography, and the presumed effects of pornography, are thus bound together in law, censorship and the polemic of opposition.

This brief discussion of censorship and pornography in the UK is not predicated on the assumption that porn is an alien, decadent or a solely modern activity, even though I shall concentrate on its production and censorship in the UK since the early 1960s. I shall not refer to materials which in their actual production break British law protecting the participants from violence, such as child or bestial pornography, which can be produced only by actually and illegally violating children or animals. Although it is true that such materials may often have been produced in countries where these acts were in fact quite legal, their prosecution in the UK is possible under a number of laws, not just the obscenity laws which generally govern the prosecution of what we might call 'mainstream' adult material. Child pornography clearly infringes laws other than the obscenity or censorship legislation with which we are concerned here. It is also not generally included in debates about 'mainstream' porn, which is mainly concerned with representations of consenting adults. Although there is much to be said about material which is entirely and unproblematically illegal, I shall concentrate on 'borderline' material, and the kind of material which the vast majority of porn consumers are interested in: images that show adults engaging in legal acts which may fall on one side of the censorable or the prosecutable divide, or the other. How the law seeks to define this borderline of the unacceptable or the illegal, and how bodies such as the British Board of Film Classification (BBFC) seek to implement that law, is my concern. I shall look at how the boundaries of what is considered 'obscene' have shifted as debate around sexual behaviour has affected what can and cannot be filmed, published or distributed in the UK. Both Christian-moral and feminist pro-censor oppositions to pornography have shaped the debate; libertarians have responded with calls for a more lenient climate in which a wider range of sexual images can be produced. British censorship legislation is the most draconian in Europe; according to Tom Dewe Matthews (1994), the UK has 'the most rigorous film censorship system in the Western World'. In his substantial diatribe against the secret, non-accountable practices of the BBFC, Dewe Matthews argues for greater awareness of the decisions made on our behalf. Censorship 'as a way of filtering culture lies at the core of English custom' (Dewe Matthews 1994: 1). British censorship legislation has radically affected and shaped the kind of pornography – written, photographed or filmed – that is available, leaving a wide range of materials which are perfectly legal in other EU countries still outside the bounds of the law.

Shifting boundaries: classification and censorship

The Obscene Publications Act (OPA) 1959, which is one of the pieces of legislation currently in place under which pornography can be prosecuted, was an attempt to clarify vague definitions of what constituted obscenity which existed in earlier law. It did, however, retain the earlier formulation that obscenity is that which has a 'tendency to deprave and corrupt', thus emphasizing the problem as that of the *effect* that material might have on those likely to come into contact with it. Top-shelf heterosexual male-orientated magazine pornography like the titles published by Paul Raymond (*Men Only, Escort, Club*) or international titles such as *Playboy* work within this definition fairly successfully, avoiding images of real sex, illegal acts or violence. (For a discussion of how magazines have negotiated the terms of the OPA, see Kermode and Petley 1990; Linda Ruth Williams 1994.) Until recently, however, correspondingly 'soft' gay porn had been the subject of stringent scrutiny, and 'harder' images, themselves deemed 'hard' often only by virtue of the fact that they show actual sex between bodies which are male as well as female, is policed even more strictly. In cinema, while naked female bodies have been seen on screen and in printed image in widespread form since the 1960s, representations of the male body, and particularly of the male organ in a state of excitement, have been the subject of the most stringent censorship in postwar Britain. The effect of this has been that the 'obscenity' definition has worked to outlaw the nude or excited man, thus reinforcing the predictable omnipresence of the heterosexually orientated naked woman.

In its role as classifiers of film and video, the BBFC is the main body which filters out the 'unacceptable' from our screens, implicitly defining and sanctioning the 'acceptable'. During the 1980s it took a more specific lead from the terms of the Williams Report (Home Office 1979) which 'argued that offensiveness ought to be the main principle of intervention, demanding an end in particular to the "unworkable" tendency-to-deprave-and-corrupt test of the Obscene Publications Act' (quoted in Brown 1982: 2, from her introduction to her interview with James Ferman). The terms of the Williams Report subsequently fed into the Local Government and Cinematographic Acts 1982, which restricted the circulation of sexual materials to private cinema clubs and, as Mandy Merck has pointed out, 'defined, for the first time in British legislation, the sex film':

> Moving pictures . . . concerned primarily with . . . (i) sexual activity; or (ii) acts of force or restraint which are associated with sexual activity; or . . . genital organs or urinary functions.
>
> (Merck 1992: 52)

The BBFC actually has no strictly enshrined legal status, in effect acting as advisers to cinemas and local councils. Regional councils take BBFC classification as their guide that a film is suitable to be shown in their area, but they can also overrule it, retaining the discretion to refuse it a local certificate, or even give it one if the BBFC have themselves denied it any classification (for example during the 'reign' of John Trevelyan in the 1960s and early 1970s, see Dewe Matthews 1994: ch. 11). However, it was only in the mid-1970s that films themselves became prosecutable under the OPA; strictly speaking they are not a publication, but were brought within the terms of this law on the recommendation of the current chief censor of the BBFC, James Ferman (see Dewe Matthews 1994: ch. 13). Two more highly significant pieces of legislation regulating moving-image pornography were passed in 1984 and 1994, with the Video Recordings Act (VRA) 1984 and the Amendment to the Criminal Justice Act 1994. I shall look at these more closely in the final section of this chapter.

We might then trace the relationship between pornography and censorship through a history of the kinds of images that have lain on either side of the censored divide. As far as the history of legitimate film pornography is concerned, we can, for instance, trace the erosion of thresholds of acceptability (beyond which we might say lies hard-core) through the gradual acceptance of certain body parts and bodily acts on-screen. Nudity was first allowed in mainstream cinema in the 1950s in pseudo-documentary films about naturism. (In 1958 John Trevelyan, the new secretary of the BBFC, deemed that 'breasts and buttocks, but not genitalia, would be accepted by the Board "provided that the setting was recognisable as a nudist camp or nature reserve"': Dewe Matthews 1994: 169.) (Here I am using 'mainstream cinema' as including all films which gained a BBFC certificate and could thus be shown at public cinemas with (from 1951 to 1982) a U, A or X certificate (AA was added in 1970), or (from 1982 onwards) the current classifications of U, PG, 15 and 18; Restricted 18 or R18 was also then invented to cover 'harder' porn films which would be able to be shown only in licensed sex cinemas, but its use has been limited.) The first mainstream screen orgasm was *heard* (but not seen) in Polanski's *Repulsion* (1965). Pubic hair was first allowed in Lindsay Anderson's *If* (1968). Former BBFC chief censor John Trevelyan, who worked there until 1971, remembers

> giving a simplified description of our policy by saying that in a 'U' film we could allow a man and a girl to be seen going together to a bedroom door; that in an 'A' film they could be seen going into the bedroom and up to the bed; and that in an 'X' film they could be seen in or on the bed engaged in what appeared to be sexual intercourse provided that there was reasonable discretion in what was shown.
>
> (Trevelyan 1973: 105)

However, it was only in the mid-1990s that erections could be seen on film in forms other than rare art-house classics such Andy Warhol's *Flesh* (1970 – the first erection shown on British screens). Even the notorious Japanese tale of strangulation and arousal, Nagisa Oshima's *Ai No Corrida* (*In the Realm of the Senses*, 1976), gained BBFC certification only in 1991, and this was largely also because of its lingering art-house status. Such films were (eventually) tolerated because they were presumed to have a self-selecting, non-damageable middle-class audience, indicating that the 'tendency to deprave and corrupt' criteria are still in operation in respect of the way in which the BBFC classifies not on pure image content but in terms of how it perceives a film's potential audience. A lingering anxiety about those who need protection from 'obscenity' – children and the non-art-house video viewer – shapes many of the BBFC's decisions. This anxiety was enshrined in the 1984 and 1994 Acts mentioned earlier.

These thresholds were crossed by a combination of the BBFC acknowledging that public opinion had changed and so liberalizing its categories, and film-makers, publishers or distributors making an argument for the artistic or scientific merit of their work. The OPA 1959 also allowed for a work to be defended on the grounds of artistic or scientific merit, and this was the defence mounted in support of D.H. Lawrence's sexually explicit novel *Lady Chatterley's Lover* during the famous 1960 trial which tested the terms of the Act. The novel was vindicated with the victory of Penguin Books, which had garnered a respectable range of expert witnesses testifying to the novel's literary merit and justifying its use of what was then deemed obscene language (see Rolph 1961). (Lawrence, whose writing and paintings were subject to stringent censorship, confiscation and burning during his lifetime (his paintings still cannot be brought back into Britain), discusses obscenity and offers his own definition of pornography in two essays, '*A Propos* of *Lady Chatterley's Lover*' (1929) and 'Pornography and Obscenity' (1929). See Lawrence 1955.)

The door was thereby opened for similar defences to be mounted in other fields. From this point onwards it became increasingly difficult for written texts to be prosecuted under the terms of the Act, and with a few notable exceptions (such as Mary Whitehouse's successful prosecution of *Gay News* for publishing a poem about Christ having a homosexual fantasy), writing is now rarely subject to legislative censure (blasphemy is perhaps rather more vulnerable than pornography; Whitehouse's victory rested on this element of the poem, not solely its sexuality). As Sigrid Nielsen writes, a 'liberal publishing climate' developed after the Chatterley trial, when 'Obscenity trials . . . became rare, while destruction orders and private prosecutions for obscenity were eventually abolished' (Nielsen 1988: 23). However, this was to be challenged with an increased intolerance to sexual material which was to take its terms from feminism in the 1970s and after.

Andrea Dworkin and pro-censorship feminism

The BBFC responded to social change and slowly liberalized its practices (though not quickly enough, argues Dewe Matthews: it may be that the British public were way ahead of the British censors in what they would accept during this period: 'John Trevelyan seemed to take on the persona of King Canute' in the early 1960s: Dewe Matthews 1994: 153). A radical shift took place on British screens in the 1960s, leading to arguably the most 'permissive' period in censorship history during the early 1970s. This was the moment when BBFC-legitimized forms of cinematic sexual violence hit the screen, with the certification of *Straw Dogs* and *A Clockwork Orange* in 1971, neither of which could be deemed pornographic, but both of which contained images of rape that would be arguably unlikely to gain certification in the 1990s. Bernardo Bertolucci's *Last Tango In Paris*, the art-house sex film that scandalized audiences in 1973, has retained its certificate and had no problem gaining a video certificate years later, although it was cut before its original cinema release and, according to Tom Dewe Matthews (1994), was the first film with a BBFC certificate to be tried under the OPA. (In January 1974 Edward Shackelton, member of the right-wing Christian group the Festival of Light, argued that 'the film was a record of obscenities practised by Marlon Brando and Maria Schneider and was not a fictional event', although the prosecution against United Artists failed when Judge Kenneth Jones threw the case out of court: Dewe Matthews 1994: 213.)

Certainly not certificated, but as central to the ethos of this permissive moment, was the 1972 release of the first widely known hard core film, *Deep Throat*, made famous after its New York trial (unlike *Chatterley*, *Deep Throat* was deemed devoid of artistic merit so the New World Theatre, where the film was being shown, was fined $3 million: Ross 1995: 16). However, as Jonathan Ross has pointed out, the film's notoriety notwithstanding, this was the moment when porn came out of the closet of the stag club and was increasingly consumed by a couples audience:

Deep Throat heralded the beginning of 'porno-chic', a short but telling phase
in the history of cinema when it actually became hip and cool and
fashionable to watch dirty movies, ideally with your partner, then talk
endlessly about them at dinner parties.

(Ross 1995: 15–16)

But it was ironically at this same moment that a counter-movement
was developing through both radical feminism and Christianity. Andrea
Dworkin's important study *Pornography: Men Possessing Women* (1981) had
such a profound influence on the women's movement that many of its
campaigning energies during the 1970s and 1980s were diverted into the
pro-censorship opposition to pornography. For Dworkin, pornography is
defined by the way a film, image or text represents women as victims of
masculinity; its 'major theme . . . as a genre is male power, its nature, its
magnitude, its use, its meaning' (Dworkin 1981: 24). This is fixed on 'the
annihilation of women's sexual integrity'; as a genre it is the textual proof
and culmination of the 'seedy pact' men have made 'with and for male
power' (Dworkin 1981: 47, 66). The book itself is largely a series of readings
of sundry sexual materials strung together by an uncompromising polemic
which defines men as objectifying sexual monsters and women as their
objectified victims, who live frightened lives 'circumscribed by the sexual
sadism of males'; 'force is intrinsic to male sexuality' (Dworkin 1981: 136,
198). In her later book *Intercourse* (Dworkin 1987) she argues that the act
of penetration itself embodies this aggressive sadism, with the penis as muti-
lating weapon. The 'hit-and-run sexuality' (Dworkin 1981: 134) of the man
is both aggressively controlling and out of control, finding the perfect trigger for release and vehicle for satisfaction in the pornographic representation of women. Written at the same time and emerging from the same
feminist moment, Susan Griffin's *Pornography and Silence* (1982) deploys a
similar argumentative armoury, although her conclusions are rather more
mystical. For Griffin, 'Not women, but feelings, are the object of sadistic
fantasy', and pornography's prime sin is the separation of 'culture from
nature. It would desacralize matter' (Griffin 1982: 55, 49). As prone to
sweeping generalizations as Dworkin, Griffin argues that,

One can look at the whole history of civilization as a struggle between the
force of eros in our lives and the mind's attempt to forget eros. We have
believed pornography to be an expression of eros. But we find that after all,
pornography exists to silence eros.

(Griffin 1982: 255)

Dworkin has no truck with Griffin's attempt to rescue the 'high' cultural
term 'erotica' from its debased sister 'pornography', arguing that sexuality
in its publicly expressed form is dominated and dictated by male power, so
any sexual materials will be infected by masculinity's contaminating influence. Thus the writings of the Marquis de Sade are placed alongside *Hustler*,
gay male pornography alongside girlie magazines, literary texts alongside
pictures, *Emmanuelle* alongside *Snuff*.

Dworkin's *Pornography* had enormous currency when it appeared in the UK in the early 1980s. Essentially, however, the text is a forceful crystallization of a number of ideas already in circulation, concerning the politics of the pleasurable image, the male gaze, the psychosexuality of sadism and masochism. An argument posited by many feminists of Dworkin's generation saw pleasure and its representations as key signs or symptoms of wider sexual politics. Laura Mulvey's agenda-setting *Screen* article of 1975, 'Visual pleasure and narrative cinema', argued that Classical Hollywood film had 'coded the erotic into the language of the dominant patriarchal order'; its pleasures were guided and guarded by male desire targeted on the fetishised female object of the gaze. Mulvey's cinematic women were intrinsically imbued with what she called '*to-be-looked-at-ness*': 'Woman displayed as sexual object is the *leitmotif* of erotic spectacle: from pin-ups to strip-tease, from Ziegfeld to Busby Berkeley, she holds the look, and plays to and signifies male desire' (Mulvey 1975). Thus the pornographic bleeds into the everyday in the way in which women's bodies are represented in accordance with the pattern of male fantasy; for Mulvey women's 'to-be-looked-at-ness' holds true whether they are posing for *Playboy* or starring in mainstream cinema. This basic argument was also posited in 1972 by John Berger in the book that accompanied his BBC series which challenged traditional readings of the history of art, *Ways of Seeing*. Here Berger read a number of images of women through an similar theory of the power of the gaze:

> To be born a woman has been to be born, within an allotted and confined space, into the keeping of men. . . . *men act* and *women appear*. Men look at women. Women watch themselves being looked at. This determines not only most relations between men and women but also the relation of women to themselves. The surveyor of woman in herself is male: the surveyed female. Thus she turns herself into an object – and most particularly an object of vision: a sight.
>
> (Berger 1972: 46–7)

It is clear then that Dworkin is drawing on a number of wider cultural readings of the sexuality of the image, even when it is not technically pornographic, in her insistence on the objectifying power of the male gaze to submit the prone female body to the model of its desire. However, two things single out her approach and influence. First, what is peculiar about Dworkin's argument is its literalness. This ranges from the notion that porn is the explicit rendering of all male desire ('Women do not believe that men believe what pornography says about women. But they do. From the worst to the best of them, they do': Dworkin 1981: 167), to the larger position that porn is not textual expression of desire but actualized performance of that desire. Even given the argument that all pornography is intrinsically the expression of a sadistic (male) sexuality, we may still wish to consider it as artefact, as cultural object, the *representation* of a set of acts rather than those acts themselves. But for Dworkin porn is not representation, it *is* act; it does not just depict violence against women, it *is* violence against women. Or, in Robin Morgan's (in)famous phrase, 'pornography is the theory, rape is the practice'.

Second, *Pornography* set the agenda for a whole programme of action as Dworkin took its conclusions into a campaigning political arena, using it as springboard into a lengthy career of anti-porn, pro-censorship work. 'We will know that we are free when the pornography no longer exists', she writes in the book's conclusion (Dworkin 1981: 224), and she went about trying to achieve this by drafting, with feminist attorney Catherine MacKinnon, an ordinance which gave women the power to take legal action on the grounds that they had been damaged by pornography (the effects argument in another guise). Backed by right-wing non-feminists who had a quite different stake in the issue, the ordinance was initially passed by the City Council in Minneapolis, Minnesota, in 1984, only to be vetoed by the Mayor, then taken up in Indiana by the Indianapolis City Council. After bitter campaigning by feminists on both sides of the censorship/libertarian divide, with the Dworkin/MacKinnon group primarily pitted against the Feminist Anti-Censorship Taskforce (FACT), the ordinance was finally overruled as unconstitutional by the Supreme Court in 1986 (this is cogently outlined in Rodgerson and Wilson 1991: introduction). Nevertheless, Dworkin and MacKinnon were not slow to elicit the support of anyone who would help promote this legislation, even if it meant hitching their wagon to Moral Majority right-wing groups who had traditionally had little sympathy for feminist causes. As Lynne Segal correctly points out,

> Anti-pornography campaigning was the single feminist issue which the Right had no wish to attack; on the contrary, they welcomed and supported it, since censorship of sexual explicitness had always been central to their moral agenda.
>
> (Segal 1994: 62)

In the UK, two groups sprang up during the 1980s, in part taking their cue from these American developments. I said earlier that in Britain soft-porn magazines such as those published by the Paul Raymond stable now operate relatively free from the risk of prosecution, but they were the target for at least one feminist group, objecting to both the location of soft porn and its invasion into, for instance, the daily tabloids. The Campaign Against Pornography developed out of Claire Short's 'Page Three Bill', which opposed the ubiquity of female flesh across the spectrum from the mass-circulation *Sun* to the top shelf of the newsagents. Another prominent British group is the Campaign Against Pornography and Censorship (CPC), which, in the words of its coordinator Catherine Itzin, militates against a pornography which 'actually censors women's rights and freedoms' (quoted by Mead-King 1990). Emulating Dworkin and MacKinnon's argument that the core issue is not censorship but civil liberties, Itzin's group have specifically claimed that theirs is not strictly a call for censorship in itself, but rather a lesser censorship pitted against the greater 'censorship' of the sex industry which in effect restricts women's behaviour. Against these arguments

Feminists Against Censorship has stressed, on the one hand, that 'Films and publications which glorify non-sexual violence probably do far more damage than "Page Three" and *Hustler*' (Rodgerson and Wilson 1991: 75) and, more positively, they urge that we do not

> close down on sex and narrow the boundaries of the permissible but . . . expand the possibilities of women's sexual pleasure. After all, part of feminism had been a flowering of books, magazines and films on feminist erotic themes, encouraging women to be sexually expressive, not repressive.
> (Rodgerson and Wilson 1991: 12)

It is this final point which I wish to expand upon in the last section of this chapter.

New pornographies and different pleasures: video, safe sex and voices from the sex industry

What might we find today in pornographic magazines or films which pushes against or beyond legal definitions of the 'acceptable'? The law has perhaps served to inspire publishers or film-makers to test its terms to the limit, encouraging inventive or risky image-making which pushes at the OPA's vague definitions to see how far they can go. Still images in magazines have always been able to represent far more than their filmic counterparts, particularly regarding images of genitals. For instance, what the magazine *Playbirds Continental* delightfully refers to as 'held wide open close-ups' can be found in more and less explicit forms in even 'soft' top-shelf magazines, yet, the all-pervasive presence of female nudity in western culture notwithstanding, the female genitals remain fairly shrouded on-screen. Sharon Stone's famous leg-crossing scene in Paul Verhoeven's *Basic Instinct* (1992) was considered a pioneering mainstream moment, but in the 'Adult' section of any local video store can be found a slightly riskier moment when a masturbating woman's labia are briefly visible in the soft-porn erotic thriller *Night Rhythms* (1992). Neither of these images comes close to what can be shown in still magazine form, however. (In 1994 a leaked BBFC report about *Satin and Lace: An Erotic History of Lingerie* (1992) gave a sense of what Tom Dewe Matthews calls 'the stringent exactness' of BBFC procedure with a definition of the absurd rule regarding female genital exposure: 'The examiners said that this type of exploitation came under the so-called ILOOLI rule which declares that "inner labia is out but outer labia can be in"': Dewe Matthews 1994: 279.)

I mentioned earlier the Video Recordings Act 1984 and the Amendment to the Criminal Justice Act 1994. The first was passed after a landslide Conservative Party victory and in response to a virulent tabloid newspaper campaign against so-called 'video nasties'. The rise of video in the late 1970s and early 1980s was so rapid (and so apparently unexpected) that distribution of unclassified and uncensored material briefly proliferated unchecked. While film was covered by a number of laws and regulated by the BBFC, and 'obscene' magazines could be prosecuted under an OPA designed primarily with the published text in mind, video was another matter – no law set out specific terms for its regulation. The VRA gave the BBFC a power in respect of videos which they already held over cinema, so that under it all video materials had to be BBFC classified prior to release with 'special regard to the likelihood of video works . . . being viewed in the home' (quoted in Kermode 1995: 64). The figure of children as vulnerable viewers seeing video materials from which they should rightly be protected has thus underpinned the BBFC's more draconian recent decisions. Since video's audience cannot be regulated as strictly as cinema's, its censorship has tended to be harsher than films' (lengthy debates over withheld video certificates for *Reservoir Dogs* (1992), *Natural Born Killers* (1994) and *The Exorcist* (1973) have highlighted this).

The Amendment to the Criminal Justice Act 1994 built upon the terms of the VRA, requiring the BBFC to pay specific attention to the possibility that children might come into contact with videos not meant for them. Coming in the wake of the James Bulger trial and tabloid tales of the role that the horror film *Child's Play 3* (1992) had in that crime, the 1994 legislation concretized a pervading fear about children as viewers of difficult material (see Cumberbatch, Chapter 19 in this volume). However, the debate has largely focused on horror films, and it might be argued that the treatment of sexual material on video, which has also had to be judged under the terms of the VRA, has been rather different. Although the child viewer, ostensibly eminently 'affectable' and, for the tabloid headline writer, vulnerable to the corruptions of celluloid, haunts our legislation and even justifies the limitation of what adults are allowed to see – Philip French (1995: 29) writes that *all* 'audiences have been treated like untrustworthy children' – the battle against the powers of the VRA has been waged on this issue of violence rather than sex. Educational sex videos promoting consensual safe sex have, for example, been allowed to push forward the boundaries of visibility in the 1990s against the grain of the trend set by the 'video nasties' scare and the passing of both of these pieces of legislation.

In fact, if anything sexual material on video has been able to become even more explicit, and the market has grown rapidly. (Jonathan Ross (1995: 19) writes that: 'In 1990 it was estimated that in the United States the sale and rental of hard-core films accounts for one-third of the video market'.) Three forces have worked to open up access to a wider range of sexual materials in the late 1980s and early 1990s: the growth of Aids and the need to distribute explicit materials advocating safe sex practices; increasingly vocal and self-motivated women from the sex industry themselves developing different images; and new voices from feminism demanding a wider range of non-sexist pornography tailored to women's desire. The first condition has had a very clear impact on what can and cannot be seen onscreen at present. I cited above different possibilities for representing the female body across the still/moving image divide. In neither the case of *Basic Instinct* nor that of *Night Rhythms* can film come near to what magazines can represent, nor even what can now be represented on screen of the *male* body. Three videos released in 1993 pushed forward what can be shown within the context of a broadly 'educational' rubric: *Well Sexy Woman: A Lesbian Guide to Sexual Health* and *Getting it Right: Safer Sex for Young Gay Men* (both produced by Pride Video in association with The Terence Higgins Trust) and *Seriously Sexy: Safer Sex for Young People* (Paradox Films in association with The Terence Higgins Trust). All were given 18 certificates. They showed erections aplenty in tandem with incessant safe sex messages, which apparently worked on the understanding that arousal offered a good medium for the absorption of advice. This is again where the terms of the OPA come into play: the messages are 'educational' (urging that one should use a condom), the images instructional (showing *how* to use a condom). Ironically this means that it is the male body which, for once, is more overtly on show, yet a residual problem remains. There is a moment in *Seriously Sexy* when a female condom is alluded to: the woman on screen holds one up and then apparently inserts it, while the camera stays resolutely fixed on her body above the waist. There are many shots of how to put a male condom on an erect penis, so why no visual help with the female version? Similarly, in *Well Sexy Woman*, there are debates about safe oral sex and even a scene within which two women seem to be practising it, but apart from a fairly nebulous image of apparent oral contact, there are no explicit demonstrations of the use of dental dams, presumably because of this continued taboo about the graphic depiction of the female genitals.

In conclusion, I should like to consider the second and third challenges to the old model of the pornographic together. If feminist debate around pornography and censorship has been at best difficult, this new turn towards interest in the sex industry itself focuses a number of issues. The 1990s have brought a shift in some women's attitudes towards the representations of pornography, with key voices calling for the gap between analysis of images and the working world of production and consumption to be bridged. Dworkin's highly public support only for prostitute groups which highlight the horrors of sex work, such as WHISPER (Women Hurt in Systems of Prostitution Engaged in Revolt), meant that there was no space within her agenda to view the sex industry at all positively, or even to appropriate its powers and position for women. We can approach this new debate by looking at two texts published in the mid-1990s, *Dirty Looks: Women, Pornography, Power* (Church Gibson and Gibson 1993) and the winter 1993 edition of *Social Text* (which includes a special section edited by Anne McClintock on the sex trade). Both books do something that 1970s and 1980s discussions didn't, looking more at what sex workers offer their clients (on film or in body), and what the clients want from the sex industry and its images. Their writers are often keen to mark the radical difference between their own positions and those of Dworkin, MacKinnon or Itzin, adding to the burgeoning corpus of challenges to the marriage of cultural feminism with right-wing pro-censors which I discussed above. Here the pleasures as well as the dangers of pornography and sex work are emphasized, looking towards, at the most extreme point represented in either collection, a women-orientated not male-dominated 'pornotopia' (Koch 1993: 42).

These writings radically depart from the positions of anti-pornography campaigners. Yet it is ironically here, through a new tone on sexual practice and sexual purchase, that the personal and the political are really being read together again, as escort workers discuss their autonomy, crossdressers articulate their femininity as clients in S/M scenarios, sociologists debate the difficulties of participant observation in the sex trade, and alternative female pornographers describe the new ways in which sex videos by and for women are being devised and made. One of the most prominent figures in this movement, ex-porn actress Candida Royalle, grasped a moment of opportunity in identifying the new niche of legitimized female desire. Royalle, the prototype 'couples' pornographer and president of Femme Production and Distribution Inc., tailors her products to (her perception of) female desire, casting herself as the capitalist feminist identifying her market while also stressing the risks of her work. As she writes in 'Porn in the U.S.A.', she is both a woman who 'dare[s] to break with a cultural taboo' and the capitalist who 'recognized and created the market' (Royalle 1993: 24, 32). She also claims that 'Now that [porn] is being taken into the bedroom where women – the wives, madonnas, and sisters – can see it, it's very threatening to the Right' (Royalle 1993: 29). As *Skin Two* photographer Grace Lau writes in her own 'Confessions of a complete scopophiliac', 'During the 1980s, female desire became a lucrative business' (Lau 1993: 205).

The excessive figure of pornographic performance artiste Annie Sprinkle also looms large in many recent discussions. Her spectacular transformations, from hooker to porn actress to film-maker to live performer blurring the boundary between sexually arousing and avant garde spectacle, challenge the traditional distinction between the 'high' concerns of live art and the 'low' concerns of porn. By highlighting the elements of performance, artifice and pastiche, Sprinkle manages to problematize models of 'natural' or 'authentic' sexual response while also evidently enjoying herself. In the process, she offers herself and her audiences, in Chris Straayer's words, 'a virtual identity orgy' (Straayer 1993: 163).

Perhaps Annie Sprinkle is important because her work exposes a wider problem about our need to explain and categorize pornography and its effects, and our ultimate failure to do so. If legal response to controversial materials shies away from trying to define the obscene and instead focuses on 'effects', recent debate has suggested that the way in which we are moved by such images is itself highly complex. New work has celebrated the possibility of enjoying and identifying across sexual divides, picking up on a long history of gay pleasure in heterosexual images (American lesbian sex campaigner Susie Bright in particular has discussed the lesbian use of male-orientated images of women in the absence of specifically tailored lesbian materials, and the male gay readership of the recent explosion of heterosexual women's porn such as magazines *For Women* or *Playgirl* is widespread). Linda Williams (1993) has revised the position upon which *Hard Core* was based – that heterosexual porn is for heterosexuals, and access to the porn of another sexuality is difficult. In 'Second thoughts on *Hard Core*: American obscenity law and the scapegoating of deviance' she writes,

> Speaking from what I now recognise to be a false sense of fixed sexual identity ... I was unable to see then that what I was learning from the book was actually how easy it was to identify with diverse subject positions and to desire diverse objects, indeed how polymorphously perverse the genre of pornography could be.
>
> (Linda Williams 1993: 56)

The debate is then muddied by the suggestion that there can be no single response to porn of any kind: however crude its images, what they do to us is complex. And just as our responses are fluid, so are the objects upon which we choose to fix pornographically. In an important essay dating from 1982, Susan Barrowclough opened up the possibility that hard-core porn, which offers images of men as well as women, might be giving the male viewer visual pleasures other than those obvious heterosexual ones which he would most readily admit to:

> Contrary to the assumption that the male uses pornography to confirm and celebrate his gender's sexual activity and dominance, is the possibility of his pleasure in identifying with a 'feminine' passivity or subordination. ... It may be that his gaze falls, not on the female genitals (which he may be accustomed to seeing elsewhere) but on the male, and that the chief part of his pleasure, which he may disown subsequently, is homoerotic rather than heterosexual. This ambiguity pornography permits.
>
> (Barrowclough 1982: 36)

There is, then, no single dominant image which is intrinsically pornographic or offers its consumer straightforward pleasure. Simple as this sounds, 'Context really does matter' (Segal 1993: 15).

> *It is never possible, whatever the image, to isolate it, to fix its meaning and predict some inevitable pattern of response, independently from assessing its wider representational context and the particular recreational, educational or social context in which it is being received.*
>
> (Segal 1993: 15, original italics)

Sexual representations, nudity, the obscene: these remain political issues. Contemporary attitudes to sexual material may be shifting again towards a more open sense that such representations should be welcomed as long as they can appeal to a wider sexual spectrum, including women and gays. But this new pornography must practise in an awareness that the sexual is never apolitical, the bedroom, and its representations, is the arena of power as well as pleasure.

It is difficult to conclude by reflecting anything other than a sense of flux. The BBFC has shifted its boundaries more rapidly in the 1990s than at any other time, with the possible exception of the early 1970s. Cinema has given way to video and home viewing as the theatre of live-action porn. But the traditional analogue moving image itself, as well as the even more arcane still photograph reproduced by the printing press, look likely to become less of a focus of moral, media and legislative anxiety than the new proliferating technologies of the Internet, virtual reality, even satellite and cable broadcasting. These are the future territories of pornography, and its censure.

Questions

1 Discuss the various arguments for and against pornography offered by feminist writers, and assess their importance in the general debate about sexual material.

2 Debate the usefulness of the 'tendency to deprave and corrupt' criteria of the Obscene Publications Act 1959 in assessing pornographic materials.

3 Is it possible to be anti-pornography and anti-censorship at the same time?

References

Barrowclough, S. (1982) 'Not a love story', *Screen* 23(5).

Berger, J. (1972) *Ways of Seeing*, Harmondsworth: Penguin.

Brown, B. (1982) 'A curious arrangement', *Screen* 23(5).

Chester, G. and Dickey, J. (eds) (1988) *Feminism and Censorship: The Current Debate*, Bridport: Prism.

Church Gibson, P. and Gibson, R. (eds) (1993) *Dirty Looks: Women, Pornography, Power*, London: British Film Institute.

Dewe Matthews, T. (1994) *Censored*, London: Chatto & Windus.

Dworkin, A. (1981) *Pornography: Men Possessing Women*, London: Women's Press.

Dworkin, A. (1987) *Intercourse*, London: Secker & Warburg.

French, P. (1995) 'No end in sight', *Index on Censorship* 6.

Griffin, S. (1982) *Pornography and Silence: Culture's Revenge Against Nature*, London: Women's Press.

Home Office (1979) *Report of the Committee on Obscenity and Film Censorship* (Williams Report), London: HMSO.

Kermode, M. (1995) 'Horror: on the edge of taste', *Index on Censorship* 6.

Kermode, M. and Petley, J. (1990) 'Members of the press', *Time Out* 1026(April).

Koch, G. (1993) 'The body's shadow realm', in P. Church Gibson and R. Gibson (eds) *Dirty Looks: Women, Pornography, Power*, London: British Film Institute.

Kuhn, A. (1984) 'Public versus private: the case of indecency and obscenity', *Leisure Studies* 3: 53–4.

Lau, G. (1993) 'Confessions of a complete scopophiliac', in P. Church Gibson and R. Gibson (eds) *Dirty Looks: Women, Pornography, Power*, London: British Film Institute.

Lawrence, D.H. (1955) *Sex, Literature and Censorship: Essays*, London: Heinemann.

McClintock, A. (ed.) (1993) *Social Text* 37 (winter): special edition on the sex trade.

Mead-King, M. (1990) 'Should pornography come off the top shelf?', *Guardian* 15 February.

Merck, M. (1992) 'From Minneapolis to Westminster', in L. Segal and M. McIntosh (eds) *Sex Exposed: Sexuality and the Pornography Debate*, London: Virago.

Mulvey, L. (1975) 'Visual pleasure and narrative cinema', *Screen* 6.

Nielsen, S. (1988) 'Books for bad women: a feminist looks at censorship', in G. Chester and J. Dickey (eds) *Feminism and Censorship: The Current Debate*, Bridport: Prism.

Rodgerson, G. and Wilson, E. (eds) (1991) *Pornography and Censorship: The Case Against Censorship, by Feminists Against Censorship*, London: Lawrence & Wishart.

Rolph, C.H. (ed.) (1961) *The Trial of Lady Chatterley: Regina v. Penguin Books Limited*, Harmondsworth: Penguin.

Ross, J. (1995) *The Incredibly Strange Film Book*, London: Simon & Schuster.

Royalle, C. (1993) 'Porn in the U.S.A.', *Social Text* 37.

Segal, L. (1993) 'Does pornography cause violence? The search for evidence', in P. Church Gibson and R. Gibson (eds) *Dirty Looks: Women, Pornography, Power*, London: British Film Institute.

Segal, L. (1994) *Straight Sex: The Politics of Pleasure*, London: Virago.

Segal, L. and McIntosh, M. (eds) (1992) *Sex Exposed: Sexuality and the Pornography Debate*, London: Virago.

Straayer, C. (1993) 'The seduction of boundaries: feminist fluidity in Annie Sprinkle's Art/Education/Sex', in P. Church Gibson and R. Gibson (eds) *Dirty Looks: Women, Pornography, Power*, London: British Film Institute.

Trevelyan, J. (1973) *What the Censor Saw*, London: Michael Joseph.

Williams, Linda (1991) *Hard Core: Power, Pleasure, and the 'Frenzy of the Visible'*, London: HarperCollins.

Williams, Linda (1993) 'Second thoughts on *Hard Core*: American obscenity and the scapegoating of deviance', in P. Church Gibson and R. Gibson (eds) *Dirty Looks: Women, Pornography, Power*, London: British Film Institute.

Williams, Linda Ruth (1994) 'The pornographic subject: feminism and censorship in the 1990s', in S. Ledger, J. McDonagh and J. Spencer (eds) *Political Gender: Texts and Contexts*, London: Harvester Wheatsheaf.

Further reading

Chester, G. and Dickey, J. (eds) (1988) *Feminism and Censorship: The Current Debate*, Bridport: Prism.

Church Gibson, P. and Gibson, R. (eds) (1993) *Dirty Looks: Women, Pornography, Power*, London: British Film Institute.

Dewe Matthews, T. (1994) *Censored*, London: Chatto & Windus.

Dworkin, A. (1981) *Pornography: Men Possessing Women*, London: Women's Press.

Rodgerson, G. and Wilson, E. (eds) (1991) *Pornography and Censorship: The Case Against Censorship, by Feminists Against Censorship*, London: Lawrence & Wishart.

Segal, L. and McIntosh, M. (eds) (1992) *Sex Exposed: Sexuality and the Pornography Debate*, London: Virago.

Williams, Linda (1991) *Hard Core: Power, Pleasure, and the 'Frenzy of the Visible'*, London: HarperCollins.

Index